D1611780

DRAMATIC LITERATURE
FOR CHILDREN:
A CENTURY IN REVIEW

Edited With Introduction

And Critical Essays

by

ROGER L. BEDARD

Anchorage Press, Inc.
Post Office Box 8067
New Orleans, La. 70182
Copyright, 1984

ISBN 0-87602-045-7
Library of Congress Number: 83-070028

i

To

Jo and Sarah

ISBN: 0-87602-045-7

Cover Design by Susan Russell

FOREWORD

In common with almost everything else in our modern world, there is no clean-cut, universally accepted opinion as to the place, the importance, and the standards of children's theatre. Some have stressed the use of classic stories and fairy tales, others have urged the use of recognizable characters and situations from everyday life. Some insist that the plots of plays for children should be simplified, and purified, and, if necessary, distorted enough to present a moral; others insist that the playwright's view of human behavior should be brutally honest, even if unpleasant. Some believe that children should be dazzled by the visual and aural aspects of a production; others have literally insisted that children's plays should be imaginatively produced on a shoestring; some have used paper bags for costumes. One thing, however, can be said about children's theatre with some degree of certainty: thousands of very intelligent, sophisticated, and public-spirited adults—amateur and professional on both sides of the iron curtain—are involved in it; tens of thousands of young people study it and/or perform in it; while hundreds of thousands, even millions, young and old, attend performances of it. In twentieth century America it has attracted the support of settlement houses, community recreation centers, educational theatres, and, more recently, professional theatres. State arts councils and foundations, including the Ford and the Rockefeller Foundations, have contributed funding to selected projects. Countless plays have been written and hundreds have been published by over twenty publishing houses.

And yet, curiously enough, until this anthology by Professor Roger L. Bedard, no one has attempted to collect and publish an anthology containing representative, influential plays for children from many publishers, in chronology of their appearance and in relation to the world theatre, providing producers, playwrights, students and readers a century's overview of the historical and literary development of the field. This is the need that Professor Bedard seeks to rectify. After examining the playwriting of the century 1880–1980, he has selected and written illuminating introductions to thirteen plays for young people, beginning with E. L. Blanchard's *Cinderella* of 1883, concluding with Aurand Harris' *The Arkansaw Bear*.

Generally speaking, the evolution found in these plays parallels that in plays for adults, although, as should be expected, there is a time lag. For example, in the adult theatre the moralistic and simplistic world of human behavior portrayed by nineteenth century melodrama was shattered around the turn of the century by writers like Ibsen, Chekhov, and Shaw, who no longer wrote about villains and heroes but about human beings, confused, lonely, frightened, funny, complicated but still recognizably human. Writers of children's plays have been influenced by such realism, but have, for obvious reasons, hesitated to examine the lives of unfortunate children with the brutal honesty characteristic of writers like Strindberg, O'Neill, and Williams. But although children's authors have avoided the more sordid and hard-hitting qualities of realism, they have found it easy to adopt or even to anticipate many characteristics of the more recent *avant garde* theatre. Although the basic philosophies underlying much of this ultra-modern theatre of despair and protest have had little appeal to writers of children's plays, they have responded easily to its external qualities, especially to the lure of being frankly theatrical, colorful, and impro-visational — even to the extent of sometimes soliciting audience par-ticipation.

In any case, children's theatre like the adult theatre, has "prog-ressed" from a nineteenth century world where almost everyone "knew" the difference between right and wrong, into a late twentieth century world where human behaviour, including the behaviour of children, baffles not only playwrights but parents, teachers, judges, psychiatrists, and philosophers.

But regardless of confusion, theories, and personal prejudices, we are indebted to Professor Bedard for this unique literary resource, the first such collection of widely performed and popular plays for children of an entire century's sweep. It is illuminating of an entire era of theatre, children, society. In children's theatre, even as in Shakespeare's theatre, "the play's the thing to catch" many insights and possibilities. This perspective implies a new seriousness in children's theatre, and that is long overdue.

—Frank M. Whiting
1982

PREFACE

American children's theatre has matured significantly since its inception in the playgrounds and professional theatres of the late nineteenth century. Playwrights, however, have not always figured prominently in this development. Throughout the century drama for children has sometimes been shaped more by the wishes of box office managers, interested in building larger audiences, and social workers, concerned with the moral development of children, than by writers offering meaningful aesthetic experiences. This, in turn, has fostered an attitude among some that drama for children need not — perhaps should not — be judged by universal standards of dramatic art.

Fortunately, from the very beginning of children's theatre activity in this country there has also been a sustained plea for a theatre where the playwright is more powerful than the box office manager, where artistry prevails over custom, and where artistic truth is more important than a familiar title. Although this plea has not always been heard, the last one hundred years have brought great changes in the literature as playwrights have begun to respond to the demands of more discerning audiences and the guidance of more rigorous criticism.

It is an exciting time for those of us who work with theatre for children. As we come to understand that the field does have a rich and interesting history, we also gain insight into the successes of the present and the challenges of the future. Perhaps we are indeed moving toward a time when the playwright as artist will prevail in American children's theatre.

The plays in this anthology were chosen to provide an overview of the growth and development of the literature throughout the last one hundred years. Each play was chosen either as a representative of a type of work popular at one time or because the play itself had an important influence on the changing repertoire. An attempt was made to include at least one play from each of the decades discussed; but, in some instances, such as with the 1920's, the absence of a play from the period reflects the lack of significant activity in the field at the time. Conversely, the several plays included that were written in the last twenty years reflect the vigorous and innovative work of contemporary writers.

Many people have contributed to the completion of this book. I would like to thank my students, who have stimulated my interest in the history of children's theatre, and my colleagues in the Theatre Arts Department at Virginia Tech, who have tolerated my preoccupation with the mounds of playscripts that inhabit every corner of my office. I would particularly like to thank David D. Mays and P. Antonie Distler for their helpful editorial suggestions.

I extend a special thanks to Anne Gowdy and Orlin Corey of Anchorage Press. Their assistance through the many phases of this project and their sound editorial advice have been invaluable.

Roger L. Bedard
July, 1982

TABLE OF CONTENTS

THE CENTURY IN REVIEW

The history of dramatic literature for children in this country is a confused and confusing trail of professional and amateur endeavors, of classroom playlets and settlement house moralities, of plays written to be performed *by* children and plays written to be performed *for* children. As a result of this confusion, few attempts have been made to chart the growth of this unique and varied theatre form. A closer look, however, reveals a rich and interesting history and a course of maturation and increased theatrical sophistication.

The creation of plays for child audiences has been inextricably tied with the economic realities of theatre production. Writers have turned their attention to this form only when there was a market for such plays. The growth periods in the development of dramatic literature for children thus correspond with those periods in our history when producing organizations, both professional and amateur, provided an audience for the plays.

The history of this genre comprises three distinct periods of development. The beginning years stretch from approximately 1880 through 1920; during this forty-year period, vigorous activity in the professional theatre helped establish children's theatre as a legitimate and popular theatre form. This activity, in turn, led to the development of a small repertoire of children's plays that was subsequently performed in amateur theatres throughout the country.

The second period, from 1920 until 1950, was a time for regrouping and redefinition. This was a period when professional children's theatre activity waned and the amateur organizations defined the nature and the scope of the literature.

The contemporary period, from 1950 to the present day, is characterized by a reawakened professional interest in children's theatre and significant influence on the form by dramatists from other countries. This period has created a repertoire of dramatic literature that is more diverse and far more theatrically sophisticated than the literature of the periods that preceded it.

1880–1920

Except for isolated examples of moralistic "plays" written to be read to or by children, there is little activity of record regarding dramatic literature for children in this country until the late nineteenth century. Prior to that time, many children were first introduced to theatre at performances of such adult plays as *Uncle Tom's Cabin* and *Rip Van Winkle*—suspenseful and action-filled dramas that, ironically, differ little from plays written specifically for child audiences in later

1

years.[1] While the popularity of these plays with children did not, by itself, cause writers to create plays for younger audiences, it did suggest to producers that there might be a market for such work.

Some historians contend that professional theatre activities had little influence on the early development of dramatic literature for children in this country. One can find support for this theory by noting that the vast majority of children's theatre productions throughout the last century have been in community, university, or civic theatres. It was the professional theatre, however, that first stimulated the development of child drama by producing theatre that appealed to child audiences.

Throughout much of the nineteenth century, adults and children alike were entertained by a new addition to the American professional theatre: adaptations of British pantomimes. Although still very popular in England today, these spectacular plays, steeped in the traditions of British popular entertainment, did not remain popular in this country much beyond the beginning of the twentieth century. Regardless of their longevity on the New York stage, these pantomimes exerted a significant influence on the early forms of dramatic literature for children, simply because they were among the first professional theatre productions in this country that acknowledged the presence of children in the audience.

The American versions of the pantomime varied in form and content in terms of their target audiences. Some tended more toward burlesque, and thus were definitely aimed at adult audiences; others, often billed as "Spectacles" or "Extravaganzas," attempted to develop an audience comprised of both young and old. Regardless of their design, virtually all of these pantomimes presented the traditional fairy tale characters and stories amid lavish visual spectacles. While adults were generally put off by the many conventions peculiar to this British form, children were awed by the spectacle and captivated by the stories.

Between 1878 and 1903 (a particularly active period in this regard) there were at least ten pantomimes produced on the New York stage.[2] These included such titles as "Cinderella" (1878), "The Crystal Slipper" (1888), "Aladdin" (1895), and "Little Red Riding Hood" (1900). A production of "Jack and the Beanstalk" (1896) was specifically described as a "nursery play" presented "in the manner of the English Christmas Pantomime."[3]

During this period professional producers also began offering more traditional children's theatre presentations. In December of 1888, a dramatization of Frances H. Burnett's *Little Lord Fauntleroy* was presented at the Broadway theatre in New York—an event that ushered in a period of active professional children's theatre activity. Counting revivals of this and other productions, there averaged at least one play for children presented in a Broadway theatre in each of the next thirty years. In some years, such as 1899, 1913, and 1918, there were as many as four different plays offered to child audiences.

Such a busy production schedule suggests that a large and diverse repertoire of children's plays existed at this time. This was not the case. The majority of plays produced in this period were dramatizations of fairy tales and popular children's stories. There were few plays available and very few playwrights working in the field. Children's theatre production at this time was strictly a pioneering venture, and adaptations of other material were far more prevalent than wholly original plays. Although the practice of adapting material to the stage grew out of the particular needs of the time, it gave strong reinforcement to a trend that became so pronounced that, for several decades after, playwrights rarely used original subjects for children's plays.

Children's book author Frances H. Burnett was perhaps the most important dramatist of this period. She adapted three of her famous children's stories for the stage, and one of them, *The Little Princess*, continues to be produced over eighty years after it was first presented. Other notable adaptations from this period include *Snow White and the Seven Dwarfs*, by Jessie Braham White; *Alice in Wonderland*, by Alice Gerstenberg; and *Treasure Island*, by Jules Eckert Goodman.

By far the most popular play to come out of this period was James M. Barrie's *Peter Pan*, which premiered in 1905 and has remained popular in revival after revival throughout the century. This British import was followed closely in popularity by *The Blue Bird*, written by Belgian-born, French playwright, Maurice Maeterlinck. Although originally written for adult audiences, this brooding allegory about the search for the "bluebird of happiness" quickly caught the imagination of child audiences in this country. (*The Blue Bird* was particularly popular during the 1920's and 1930's; its popularity has waned considerably since then.)

Plays of interest to family audiences grew out of the work of Stuart Walker and his Portmanteau Theatre Company, which was organized in 1915. Concentrating on adaptations of well-known literary works, Walker wrote such plays as *The Birthday of the Infanta*, *Six Who Pass While the Lentils Boil*, and *Jonathan Makes a Wish*.

The robust professional activity at the turn of the century was coupled with the growing interest in children's theatre in community centers in large cities throughout the country. The most noteworthy of the theatres spawned by these groups was the Children's Educational Theatre, founded in New York City, in 1903, by Alice Minnie Herts. Such organizations were significant in bringing theatre to the children of this country, but they did little to spur the development of new dramatic literature. These groups traditionally presented either plays that had been successful in the professional theatre or informal dramatizations of popular fairy tales.

Although children's theatre production increased significantly during the years following the introduction of the pantomime to the New York stage, it did not retain its foothold in the professional theatre. By 1920 professional children's theatre activity had virtually ceased; and, for several decades after, the only professional productions presented—and these were very few—consisted primarily of revivals of *Peter Pan*, *The Blue Bird*, and *The Little Princess*. Not one of the playwrights active during these early years contributed anything of note to the field after that time; in fact, none of these writers considered themselves primarily children's playwrights. Barrie went on to write many successful adult plays; Maeterlinck concentrated on experiments with symbolist drama; and Burnett pursued her career as an author of children's books.

As the professional market for children's plays dwindled, the growth in the repertoire of dramatic literature for children slowed accordingly. By 1920 this first period in the development of dramatic literature for children ended quite abruptly, having spawned only a handful of worthwhile plays.

The decline in professional children's theatre activity was caused, in part, because the professional producers exhausted the economic potential of the small body of available children's plays. An additional factor was the concurrent growth in educational and recreational dramatics that began around the turn of the century. By 1910 child drama activities were being included in community center programs, recreational settings, and in classrooms throughout the country. The commercial children's theatre market was thus diffused by the increase in theatre activity elsewhere. As children's theatre appeared under all manner of umbrella organizations, child drama began to include plays written to be performed *by* children, as well as plays written to be performed *for* children. Because each type of play had distinctly different requirements, the literature of the field began to change rapidly. Unfortunately, it was the dramatic literature for children that suffered most.

Constance D'Arcy Mackay, who promoted amateur theatre production, underscored the use of drama as recreation in her book, *How to Produce Children's Plays*, which was published in 1915.[4] She also compiled four volumes of her own dramatizations of legends and folk tales for use by amateur theatre groups: *House of the Heart and Other Plays*, *Silver Thread and Other Plays*, *Patriotic Plays and Pageants for Young People*, and *Forest Princess and Other Masques*.[5]

A similar perspective of children's theatre was offered at this time by the Drama League of America. In a bibliography of children's plays published by this group in 1915, the focus is clearly on plays that reflect children's theatre as a "popular branch of recreation" and an "important branch of education."[6]

4

Although few writers had shown an interest in writing plays for the professional children's theatre of the time, the new recreational emphasis spurred the creation of scores of new plays. Many of these new writers, however, had little interest in the theatre and much interest in playground activities; and the field soon became saturated with plays designed more for "play-time" situations than for theatre performances. Anthologies from the period with such titles as *Child's Book of Holiday Plays*, *Household Plays for Young People*, *Industrial Plays for Young People*, and *Red Letter Day Plays* accurately reflect this trend in child drama.[7] These plays, most of which were written by teachers or social workers, typically present highly moralistic stories that sacrifice character and plot development to the need for casts of characters that could be enacted by children.

The majority of the plays from this period are distinguished more for their position in the history of the literature, than for any values inherent in the works themselves. Because of their status as pioneering works, these plays virtually defined the parameters of theatre for children in this country in its beginning stages. The repertoire in 1920 was narrow in focus and limited in subject matter, to the extent that many theatre professionals hardly considered the field worthy of a second notice. With the naive dramatizations of fairy tales and sentimental stories, writers generated an image that suggested that children's theatre was more appropriate for the playground than for the stage.

During this first period in the development of the genre, the child had been recognized as a potential audience member, and a small body of plays for children had been written. As the commercial producers abandoned the field and as the primary arena for child drama shifted into recreational and educational settings, progress in the development of plays for children came to a standstill. For the next few years, the children's theatre community strove to sustain itself on the limited repertoire of fairy tale plays and story dramatizations that grew out of this brief — but important — flurry of professional children's theatre productions.

1920–1950

Montrose Moses, editor of three anthologies of children's plays, described the status of the development of dramatic literature for children in the early 1920's in this manner:

> The paucity of children's plays continues: yet the schoolroom, the club, the recreation groups still make their insistent demands. And where there is the demand, there is the supply. . . . Teachers are frantically teaching educational dramatics. Little bodies are being swathed in Dennison paper, little arms are being stretched in Dalcroze eurythmics, little minds are being crammed with innocuous

dialogue. Wrong kinds of books are being written, demonstrating easy methods of play production, by Professors of Athletics, who know nothing whatsoever about the theatre, and recommend rules for acting that are totally absurd. Those who write children's plays have in mind all the limitations of a child's ability. . . .

These educational requirements are having a devastating effect on the dramatic output, and the editor has oftentimes been discouraged by the seeming indifference on the part of the writers of children's plays to attempt anything of an artistic nature.[8]

Fortunately, not all amateur children's theatre producers were caught up in the recreational theatre movement, as the most significant influence on children's theatre production in this country during the 1920's was the rapidly growing, community-based, Little Theatre movement. Beginning with three theatres established in 1911-1912, this movement grew so that by 1917 there were over fifty such organizations spread throughout the country. Although these theatres came to offer widely diverse programming, they all shared a non-commercial orientation, and, more importantly, many included theatre for children in their production programs. In a survey taken in 1928, it was found that over half of the "outstanding" community-based theatres in this country produced theatre for child audiences.[9]

Those producers who chose plays for aesthetic rather than recreational values were, however, severely restricted by the small number of appropriate plays available. Since these amateur groups had neither the status nor the money to attract professional writers to create new children's plays, they relied primarily on the successes of the professional theatres from the previous decade for their production seasons. Particular favorites during this time were Burnett's *The Little Princess*, and White's *Snow White and the Seven Dwarfs*.

A notable exception to these revivals were the new plays of English novelist A.A. Milne. Milne, the author of the popular Pooh books, supplied two plays during this period that have become popular with American child audiences: *Make Believe* and *Toad of Toad Hall*.

The most significant professional organization of this time was the Clare Tree Major Children's Theatre, begun in 1924. This organization lasted almost thirty years and through an intricate network of touring companies ultimately reached tens of thousands of children throughout the country. Unfortunately, the work of this group did little to expand the child drama repertoire. Major herself wrote over fifty-seven plays, but these works—which are dramatizations of fairy tales and popular children's stories—were not produced widely by other organizations.[10]

During the 1920's, the fairy tale plays were repeated over and over again, as the community theatre producers, like the professional children's theatre producers who preceded them, quickly recognized the profits to be made from these familiar titles. As a consequence, the development of the literature became stalled between the economic considerations, which discouraged the professionals and greatly inhibited the amateurs, and the recreational considerations, which spawned a new and different body of literature. It was not until 1928, when playwright Charlotte B. Chorpenning began to write children's plays, that American children's theatre slowly began to break from this lethargic state.

Chorpenning, who had experience as a teacher, social worker, and professional playwright — albeit for adults — almost single-handedly charted a new course for the development of dramatic literature for children. While serving as director of children's theatre at the Goodman Theatre of the Chicago Art Institute (1932–1952), Chorpenning wrote over forty children's plays and collaborated on several others. In addition, she taught playwriting, conducted workshops, and advised scores of fledgling playwrights.[11] Under Chorpenning's leadership a renaissance occurred in writing plays for child audiences, and before long such playwrights as Madge Miller, Nora MacAlvay, Martha B. King, Geraldine B. Siks, and Rosemary Musil were making significant contributions to a growing repertoire.

Once Chorpenning's work was discovered, it influenced the field in a way that was both invigorating and delimiting. Producers looked to Chorpenning's plays to bolster their predictable production seasons; playwrights looked to these plays for standards and even formulas that they might apply to their own writing.

Although not all of the playwrights of this time were Chorpenning's students, most of their plays strongly echoed her techniques. Chorpenning wrote plays and taught playwriting very much in the style she was taught by George Pierce Baker in 1913. Emphasizing formal structure and clearly defined characters and action, she created melodramatic, well-made plays *(pièces bien faites)*, with a strong moralistic perspective. Most of Chorpenning's plays are dramatizations of well-known fairy and folk tales, designed to be presented in a realistic manner. Among her more popular works at that time were: *The Emperor's New Clothes, Rumpelstiltskin, The Sleeping Beauty, Jack and the Beanstalk,* and *Hansel and Gretel.*

During the 1930's and 1940's the children's theatre field was taken from the playground and returned to the stage. A new generation of playwrights did little to expand the subject matter boundaries of children's plays, but these writers did introduce a sophistication of structure and technique that sharply differentiated their plays from the recreational drama of the 1920's. The prolific output of these writers also provided material for an expanding amateur children's theatre network.

A significant, but often over-looked, factor in the development of dramatic literature for children was the publication of these plays. Although throughout this century several book publishing firms have published children's plays, the major forces in the distribution of these works have been the theatrical publishing houses. In 1900, two such organizations, Samuel French, Inc. and Dramatic Publishing Co. offered the majority of the few children's plays published at that time.

Samuel French, Inc., the largest of the theatrical publishing houses, began offering children's plays in the late nineteenth century, but only on a very limited scale. *Peter Pan*, *The Little Princess*, and *Snow White and the Seven Dwarfs* owe much of their success throughout the first half of the century to the fact that they were marketed by this agency. During the 1920's, this organization placed more emphasis on plays for children by gradually increasing the number of such works among its publications. In 1932, Samuel French offered the first of Chorpenning's published plays, *The Emperor's New Clothes*.

The majority of Chorpenning's plays were published by the Children's Theatre Press, which was established in 1935. This organization (since 1962, called Anchorage Press) is devoted entirely to publishing plays for children, and, in its first twenty years of operation it published over fifty new works.

During the 1930's, the Association of Junior Leagues of America also assumed a role somewhat like that of a publisher, when it began encouraging local league chapters to produce plays for child audiences. When confronted with the small number of plays available, the Association developed a manuscript play library and encouraged writers to create plays suitable for production by its chapters. Although the Association was primarily interested in "trouping" plays, and thus encouraged playwrights to create works that could be toured easily, the manuscript library proved to be very successful. For the first time, playwrights were encouraged in their work by being given the opportunity to have their work read by scores of would-be producers.

From the publication of a small number of children's plays by two agencies at the beginning of the century, the field expanded to the extent that by mid-century there were several theatrical publishing companies offering plays for children. This both reflected the increased activity in the field and contributed to it. The quantitative contributions of these organizations to the development of the literature are readily apparent, but what is less discernible is the degree to which the publishers defined the shape and scope of the literature. Since the children's theatre field of this period was not led by professional theatre artists, amateur producers could only look to the publishing houses as a source of new material. Therefore, what they published essentially constituted the repertoire. This situation accommodated little experimentation and reinforced the use of the fairy tales, the well-made play structure, and the sentimental stories.

The decade of the 1930's also saw the development of two important professional children's theatre organizations. Although both of these groups were short-lived and had little immediate impact on the development of the literature, their work pointed toward a future diversification and maturation in children's drama.

The first of these was Junior Programs, begun by Dorothy McFadden in 1936. For almost a decade this group produced and toured highly original forms of children's theatre entertainment, including plays, operas, musical dramas, and ballets, all based on a wide variety of subject matter. It is significant that McFadden strove to find new works, rather than to rely upon new productions of old plays. Although no particular plays or playwrights gained prominence through this organization, Junior Programs did much to break the hold that the fairy tale had on children's drama.

The second professional organization, part of the Federal Theatre Project, existed for only five years, but was more influential than Junior Programs. Organized as a part of the Works Progress Administration in 1935, the Federal Theatre Project was designed to provide employment for theatre artists. During its brief existence, the Federal Theatre Project produced over fifty plays for child audiences, more than half of which were new plays created specifically for this group. All manner of subjects were addressed in these new plays, from adaptations of fairy tales such as "Alice in Wonderland," to the controversial allegory, "Revolt of the Beavers." Many of these works also imaginatively incorporated acrobats, vaudevillians, and other entertainers. It was an ambitious experiment that not only expanded the horizons of child drama in this country, but also rekindled an interest in children's theatre among professional actors, directors, and writers. It would be some years before the professional theatre would once again turn its attention to child drama, but the Federal Theatre Project proved that a market for such work still existed.[12]

In 1949, the Children's Scripts Evaluation Committee of The American Educational Theatre Association compiled a list of sixty-one "recommended," full-length plays for children.[13] This list, divided among "Fairy Tale Plays," "Favorite Story Plays," and "Historical Plays," reflects both the quantitative growth in the field to that time as well as the very narrow view of children's plays that had been perpetuated. As the three groupings indicate, the dramatists of the day had yet to venture successfully into wholly original material.

Some of the more popular of the "recommended" plays include

Aladdin and the Wonderful Lamp (Norris), *The Elves and the Shoemaker* (MacAlvay), *The Emperor's New Clothes* (Chorpenning), *Jack and the Beanstalk* (Chorpenning), *The Land of the Dragon* (Miller), *Marco Polo* (Siks), *Peter, Peter, Pumpkin Eater* (King), and *Rumpelstiltskin* (Chorpenning). This list also includes the ever-present successes from the professional theatre: *Snow White and the Seven Dwarfs* (White), *Peter Pan* (Barrie) and *The Little Princess* (Burnett).

The years between 1920 and 1950 saw important changes in dramatic literature for children. Although the growth in the field was initially stalled, if not confused, by the preoccupation with recreational drama, the children's theatre activity in civic and community theatres gradually filled the void left by the professional theatre; and by 1940 many new plays had been added to the repertoire. Unfortunately, as Chorpenning and others articulated philosophies of writing children's plays, some would-be playwrights turned these ideas into formulas and eagerly churned out their own versions of the fairy tales. Before long virtually all of the most familiar tales were dramatized, and producers became content to repeat the most popular of these every few years to a new generation of children. It was a system that perpetuated most of the restrictive and stereotypical facets of the field and offered little stimulus for growth or change.

In the context of the modern literature, the majority of these plays appear dated and lifeless, more like historical artifacts than entertaining dramas. However, even if these plays have little meaning to modern audiences, the spirit with which they were created was still an important factor in the development of the literature. For the first time in the history of the genre, people were attempting to teach the skills necessary for writing children's plays and to outline what they considered to be appropriate formalistic elements of such plays. While these teachings were delimiting, they also reinforced a seriousness of purpose that ultimately led to greater expansion in the literature.

1950–1980

The most visible change in the field after mid-century was a slow but steady increase in professional children's theatre production. This movement began with a very small number of groups formed in New York during the 1950's; by 1970 there were professional children's theatre companies in most of the major cities in this country, as well as touring groups operating in the smaller towns and communities.

This professional theatre activity was very different in its approach from that attempted at the turn of the century. The earlier work was organized on a production-to-production basis dependent upon the interest of a single producer. In contrast, these new professional productions were presented by companies organized to offer entire seasons of children's plays. This innovation required a long-term commitment to children's theatre that often provided the spark for experiments in style of presentation and the creation of entirely new dramatic works.

Initially, these companies gingerly tested their audiences with plays that had been popular during the preceding decades. The Children's World Theatre, for example, produced four Chorpenning plays for its first season in 1947. Serving as a model for similar theatre companies, this group moved from its permanent setting in New York and developed several touring companies that traveled widely throughout the eastern United States. Although these early groups did not generally perform original works, they did constitute a new market for dramatic literature for children—a market that was ultimately far more successful than the amateur theatre in attracting new writers to the field.

As the professional network expanded, the pressure for change in the literature began to be felt. For every new professional theatre company content to perform *Rumpelstiltskin* or *Jack and the Beanstalk*, there appeared others who were intent on developing new plays. Some companies worked with resident playwrights, while others used improvisation and group effort to develop scripts. Such efforts were not always successful, but a number of excellent performing groups—The Paper Bag Players, The Improvisational Theatre Project of The Mark Taper Forum. The Performing Arts Repertory Company, The Little Theatre of the Deaf, to name but a few — came onto the scene with highly imaginative theatre fare. These groups were composed primarily of professional theatre artists rather than teachers or recreation leaders, and they often began their projects with a conscious effort to break away from the themes, subjects, and styles traditionally associated with children's theatre.

From such companies came vaudeville revues, dramas based on current events, story theatre, comedy sketches, dramas improvised from suggestions from the audience, dramatized profiles of historical figures, musical dramas, and other "plays" that have little in common except their deliberate deviation from traditional fairy tale material. Although the scripts were often less important to these groups than the overall shape and style of the performance itself, these works were produced with a level of artistry not often found in the amateur children's theatre of the preceding decades.

These scripts were developed in terms of the goals of each company, the needs and expectations of their respective audiences, and from the skills and special talents of the company members. Although few of these works have been produced by other organizations, and fewer still have been published, these groups exerted a significant influence on the development of the literature by the example they set in imaginatively and artistically addressing the aesthetic needs of modern audiences.

During the 1960's professional children's theatre productions could also be found in a growing network of regional children's theatres. Like their counterparts in theatre for adult audiences, these regional theatres were dedicated both to the preservation of the "classics" in the child drama repertoire and to the creation of new plays. Within these organizations, playwrights have been able to experiment within well-equipped facilities, utilizing generous production budgets and working with teams of professional designers, directors, and actors. The non-touring emphasis of these groups has also nurtured the development of new plays that utilize the most sophisticated theatre production techniques.

A prominent example of a regional children's theatre is the Children's Theatre Company of Minneapolis. Since its inception in 1961, this group has created such innovative productions as *Sleeping Beauty* in the Kabuki style, *Treasure Island* complete with a fully-rigged ship on the stage, and a version of *A Christmas Carol* presented as in a British Music Hall. Along with these uniquely staged classics, this group has also created several original works including *Hang On To Your Head* and *Good Morning, Mr. Tillie.*

As American professional theatre artists challenged the stereotypes of child drama and experimented with new styles of presentation, children's plays from other countries began to exert a significant influence on the American repertoire. In the first half of the century, these imports consisted primarily of traditional plays by British writers; but by 1950 this situation was beginning to change. At that time, the number of foreign plays performed in this country increased significantly. More importantly, many of these plays were very different from those of American playwrights.

Initially, the plays of British playwrights Nicholas Stuart Gray, Alan Cullen, and Alan Broadhurst represented a major portion of these imported works. Gray, the most traditional of the three, offered such plays as *Beauty and the Beast* and *The Princess and the Swineherd.* In contrast, the works of Cullen and Broadhurst rely less on well-known tales and present more unique characters and situations. Broadhurst is noted particularly for *The Great Cross Country Race*, a dramatization of "The Tortoise and the Hare" story. Cullen deviated even further from familiar subjects with *The Beeple*, within which he created an entire world of "bee-people" in a fantasy setting.

These plays appear very traditional in contrast to the more innovative works of the British playwright Mary Melwood. Utilizing techniques similar to those used by the Absurdists in adult theatre, Melwood has been successful in creating challenging and entertaining plays that include provocative ambiguities of character and story. Two of her plays, *The Tingalary Bird* and *Five Minutes to Morning* (both published during the 1960's), introduced American audiences and writers

12

to a new and different style of drama.

The most influential of these imported plays has been *Reynard the Fox*, by a Belgian playwright, Arthur Fauquez. First produced in this country in 1960, *Reynard the Fox* boldly challenged many conventions of American child drama by presenting human-like animal characters, whose clever, cynical, and self-serving behavior obscures the traditional "good guy" versus "bad guy" conflict. Reynard is a prototype rogue hero, who repeatedly defies the moral and social codes of his world and outwits his adversaries by capitalizing on their own greed and stupidity.

A very different type of children's play, participation drama, also became popular at this time. Participation plays, made popular through the work of British playwright Brian Way, invite audience members to physically and vocally "participate" in the action of the play itself. In one of Way's most popular works, *The Mirrorman*, actions and sounds supplied by the audience thwart the antagonist, Witch, in her attempt to capture the character, Beauty. Way's *On Trial* places the audience in in the role of a trial jury. At the beginning of the play the audience is asked to watch the replaying of a story so that they might ultimately judge whether a character should be punished for certain actions. While *On Trial* allows a small portion of the audience to improvise roles in the play, it is primarily oriented toward creating discussion around moral issues in the story.

Participation plays directly address questions of style in terms of the audience/actor relationship. Throughout the history of dramatic literature for children in this country, the emphasis has been on representational styles presented in a realistic manner. By the 1960's, when participation plays began to catch the attention of producers in this country, American playwrights were experimenting freely with presentational styles. But participation plays represented a radical style of production for most American playwrights; one which helped some writers pull away from the rigidly representational styles and caused others to cling to them.

Some American writers have worked with participation drama, but not all of this work has been completely successful. While playwrights and directors have easily found excuses to ask the audience members to "participate" in their plays (by chanting, pointing, or whatever), only a few have integrated participation into their works without greatly diminishing the plays themselves.

An important synthesis of American theories of participation drama came with *Participation Theatre for Young People*, edited by Pat Hale.[14] American writers who have written participation plays of note include Moses Goldberg with *Aladdin* and *Hansel and Gretel* and Bernice Bronson with *Most Powerful Jujus* and *In the Beginning*.

13

The most important theme in plays written after 1950 is the presentation of children in contemporary situations, grappling with contemporary problems. Such plays have only begun to rival the escapist, fantasy literature; but, in the last three decades they have appeared with increasing frequency in children's theatre in many countries.

The repertory of Berlin's Grips Theatre illustrates the political use that some countries make of this contemporary child drama. The Grips Theatre presents plays that explore the child's role in the family and in society — a role that is viewed through a socialistic perspective. Three of these plays were translated and published in the United States in 1967 by Jack Zipes, in *Political Plays for Children*.[15]

Regardless of the activity elsewhere, the traditional fairy tale and story dramatizations continued to occupy a dominant place in American Children's Theatre even after mid-century. While only a few of Chorpenning's plays (*Jack and the Beanstalk, Rumpelstiltskin* and *The Emperor's New Clothes*, in particular) remained popular into the modern era, traditional adaptations were still being added to the repertoire. The decade of 1950's alone saw the creation of dozens of such plays including Kristin Sergel's *Winnie-the-Pooh*, Madge Miller's *Hansel and Gretel*, Margery Evernden's *King Arthur's Sword*, and Martha Bennett King's *The Snow Queen and the Goblin*.

By the 1960's, however, even this traditional strain in the development of the literature was beginning to change, as playwrights gave more attention to original stories, characters with real dimensions, and styles that reflect a freer and more artistic use of the medium. The rapid expansion in professional children's theatre after mid-century created a gap between the plays available and the expectations of the modern audiences. A new generation of playwrights worked to fill this gap.

Influenced by foreign writers, challenged by the "educational" thrust of children's television, and goaded by the call for relevance in children's entertainment, contemporary playwrights have been exploring subjects ranging from the problems of the handicapped to racial problems in the cities. These subjects have been written into plays that run a gamut of styles, from representational to presentational, from story theatre to participation theatre. Like the drama created by social workers seventy years ago, some of these works are more appropriate for the classroom or playground than for the theatre; however, amid these thematic and stylistic wanderings several important plays and playwrights have emerged in this country in the last two decades.

The most prolific and successful of the modern playwrights is Aurand Harris. With over thirty children's plays written since 1945, Harris's work stands as an important bridge between the more traditional dramatizations and the styles of the modern era. Harris has adapted material for the stage, such as *Just So Stories*, and he has written original plays, such as *Yankee Doodle*. He has presented themes and subjects ranging from the seemingly frivolous *Once Upon a Clothesline* to the serious treatment of death in *The Arkansaw Bear*. His *Androcles and the Lion*, one of the most popular plays of the last twenty years, is a dramatization of the old Italian tale in the flamboyant and theatrical style of *Commedia dell' arte*. The wide range of styles, themes, and subjects in Harris's plays stands as a good example of the growth and development in the field over the last thirty years and of a growing diversity in the contemporary repertoire.[16]

Consistent with the worldwide trend toward more "meaningful" drama, playwright Joanna Kraus has created several plays that explore serious subjects, seriously. *The Ice Wolf*, first produced in 1967, presents the relevant theme of prejudice, set in the world of the Eskimo culture. *Circus Home* tells of a young boy who, labeled a "freak" because of his size, wants only to belong. Kraus's *Mean to be Free* relates the story of two black children, who travel north to freedom on the Underground Railway.

Suzan Zeder's *Step on a Crack* is a more recent example of an important contemporary theme dramatized in an entertaining manner. Centered on a young girl's relationship with her father and her new step-mother, this play reflects the spontaneity and theatricality of the most modern professional work in the field.

The contemporary repertoire includes a great variety of themes, subjects, and styles, some of which are reflected in the following plays: *Special Class*, by Brian Kral — an insightful portrait of children, some of whom have developmental handicaps; *The Men's Cottage*, by Moses Goldberg — a meaningful story of tribal rites of passage; *The Marvelous Adventures of Tyl*, by Jonathon Levy—a fluid, fast-paced ensemble play, wherein a small group of actors play a variety of roles; *Golliwhoppers*, by Flora Atkin — a story theatre version of American tall tales; *The Hide and Seek Odyssey of Madeline Gimple*, by Frank Gagliano — a humorous and fantastic game-like world; *The Odyssey* by Greg Falls and Kurt Beattie — a dramatization of Homer's epic of Odysseus; *Jim Thorpe, All-American*, by Saul Levitt — a musical play that moves quickly and simply, through many times and places, telling the story of Jim Thorpe; *Story Theatre*, by Paul Sills — the original collection of stories that gave its name to this staging technique; and *The Little Princess, Sara Crewe*, by Nancy Seale — a new musical version of this classic melodrama.

While the previous periods in the development of the literature are readily definable in terms of dominant trends or styles, the modern era is characterized by its diversity. The repertoire now includes traditional fairy tale plays, operas, musical drama, farce, history, story theatre, participation drama, improvisational drama, and serious contemporary plays.

The modern era began in the midst of preoccupation with the traditional fairy tale dramatization. Although now dated, these plays have provided a perspective, a history — one generation's definition of theatre for children — which contemporary writers have been able to attack, praise, imitate, denigrate, and, paradoxically, *build upon.*

Led by professional theatre artists and influenced by plays from other countries, playwrights have subsequently found new approaches, new subjects, a more imaginative use of the theatre medium, and an increased sensitivity to the needs and capabilities of contemporary children. Some of the plays in the modern repertoire are much like the naive adaptations from the turn of the century; still others continue in the tradition of the well-made fairy tale plays from the 1930's and 1940's. But more than at any other time in the history of the field, the repertoire is expanding, changing, and growing.

The development of dramatic literature for children has progressed markedly over the last one hundred years. Beginning when children were given only passing notice as audience members viewing adult plays, the repertoire has expanded to the extent that there now are several hundred published plays for child audiences. Where there were initially only two agencies publishing children's plays, there are now over twenty such companies offering a diverse selection of dramatic literature for children. Where once the field was comprised almost entirely of dramatizations of fairy tales and popular children's stories, the repertoire now includes the traditional adaptations, plus original plays, operas, musical comedies, improvisational dramas, and participatory plays.

The field has endured an inconsistent relationship with the professional theatre, the manipulation of social workers and educators, the biases of parents, and the sometimes strangling hold of the fairy tale. The literature has met these challenges, and it has gained maturity with each complication.

The development of the literature has lagged behing the stylistic, formalistic, and thematic innovations of the American theatre as a whole; but the last thirty years in particular have seen the introduction of new perspectives that hold promise for future growth in the field. The repertoire of plays has grown larger; the stylistic and thematic parameters have widened; and the market for new plays continues to expand. Quantitative growth is still more apparent than qualitative growth, but significant progress has been made toward plays for children that, in the words of Montrose Moses, "are written as all good plays written—according to laws that make of drama an art."[17]

NOTES

1. Publication information for all plays discussed in this book can be found in Appendix B.

2. Production statistics and information about individual productions taken from theatre reviews printed in *The New York Times* during the period under discussion.

3. Edward a Dithmar, "Jack and the Beanstalk," *The New York Times,* 8 November 1896, II, p. 11, col. 1.

4. (New York: Holt, 1915).

5. These volumes were published by Holt Co., New York, in 1909, 1910, 1911, and 1916, respectively.

6. Kate Oglebay, ed., *Plays for Children* (New York: The Drama League, 1915), p. 3.

7. Kate Oglebay and Marjorie Seligman, eds., *Plays for Children: A Selected List,* 3rd. ed. (New York: Wilson, 1920), pp. 10-21.

8. Montrose Moses, ed., *Another Treasury of Plays for Children* (Boston: Little Brown & Co., 1926), pp. 604-605. Other anthologies edited by Moses include *A Treasury of Plays for Children* (Boston: Little Brown & Co., 1926) and *Ring Up the Curtain* (Boston: Little Brown & Co., 1932).

9. Kenneth Macgowan, *Footlights Across America* (1929; rpt. New York: Kraus, 1969), pp. 359-365.

10. Michael W. Gamble, "Clare Tree Major: Children's Theatre, 1923–1954," Diss. New York University 1976.

11. Roger L. Bedard, "The Life and Work of Charlotte B. Chorpenning," Diss. Kansas 1978.

12. For a detailed account of this activity see Jane Dehart Mathews, *The Federal Theatre 1935–1939 Plays, Relief, and Politics* (Princeton: Princeton Univ. Press, 1967).

13. Louise C. Horton, ed., *Handbook for Children's Theatre Directors* (Cincinnati: National Thespian Society, 1949), pp. 22–23.

14. (New York: New Plays for Children, 1972).

15. (St. Louis: Telos Press, 1967).

16. Coleman Jennings, ed., *Six Plays for Children by Aurand Harris* (Austin: University of Texas Press, 1977).

17. Montrose Moses, *Another Treasury of Plays for Children* (Boston: Little Brown & Co., 1926), p. 608.

PLAYS FROM THE PERIOD

BOOK OF THE WORDS

of

CINDERELLA

THE DRURY LANE PANTOMIME,

1883 - 4.

BY

E. L. BLANCHARD

MUSIC

BY

OSCAR BARRETT

––––––––––

ORIGINALLY PUBLISHED BY

ALFRED GIBBONS, 172, STRAND

21

CINDERELLA:

THE DRURY LANE PANTOMIME,

1883-1884

Pantomimes were not originally produced for child audiences, but as these zany extravaganzas began to include fairy tale stories and characters, slapstick humor, and large doses of exuberant fun, they gradually became popular with children and adults alike. By the end of the nineteenth century the pantomime had become the center of British popular entertainment, and children looked with anticipation toward the annual productions that were presented for family audiences.

The British pantomime has a long and complex history. Early versions of this theatre form consisted of short plays which presented the ever-popular characters Harlequin, Columbine, Clown and Pantaloon. These works generally opened with the abduction of Columbine from Pantaloon's house, which was followed by a series of comic confrontations as Pantaloon attempted to rescue his daughter from the amorous advances of Harlequin. Clown served as Harlequin's assistant, and it was his job to deceive and beguile Pantaloon while Harlequin was courting Columbine. This simple scenario was played with stock business, the highlights of which were the complications caused by Harlequin's use of his magic wand. Since this Harlequinade, as it came to be called, was not considered substantial enough to stand alone, it was attached to a more serious "opening." The combination of the two constituted the early form of the pantomime, which was used as an after-piece in an evening of adult theatre entertainment.

Initially these "openings" consisted of disjointed dramatic fare wherein an "immortal" bestowed Harlequin with his magic wand in preparation for the antics of the harlequinade. Striving to outdo one another, producers expanded the openings by incorporating elaborately staged songs and dances, lavish visual spectacle, and characters and stories from fairy tales. These openings thus became the most popular part of the pantomime, and the harlequinade was reduced to a single scene at the end. By the end of the nineteenth century it had become customary to stage these pantomimes in conjunction with the Christmas holiday season — a practice which further guaranteed their popularity with audiences of all ages.

The pantomime was a British creation, and it has become a British institution as even today pantomimes are presented in England during the holiday season. However, the influence of these works has not been confined to that country. With the appearance of adaptations of the British pantomime on the New York stage during the nineteenth century, this theatre form also influenced the development of dramatic literature for children in this country.

Cinderella, the Drury Lane pantomime of 1883–1884, is a typical example of the pantomimes of this period and is quite similar to many works that were presented in this country. E.L. Blanchard, the acknowledged master of this form, spared no tricks in introducing spectacle, pageantry, song, and dance into the Cinderella story.

Because these extravaganzas relied heavily on staging techniques, the scripts themselves offer only the barest suggestion of what the pantomime was actually like. As explained by the Fairy in Scene XI: "From Cinderella's story — often told, here we have sought fresh beauties to unfold." Consistent with this statement, Blanchard focuses more on the externals of the production than on either character or plot development.

Blanchard does, however, remain true to the basic Cinderella story. The step sisters are appropriately harsh, ill-tempered, and ugly, while Cinderella is gentle, naive, and totally admirable. It is apparent from the beginning of the play that Blanchard is interested only in character types — indeed, almost caricatures — rather than in detailed characterizations. Although the Cinderella story is fundamentally melodramatic, Blanchard does little to reinforce these values; the play does not linger on the oppression of Cinderella, nor does it include prolonged suspense with the Prince's search for his bride. Instead, Blanchard provides a framework of eleven scenes that relate the basic elements of the popular story, within which every excuse is used to introduce songs, dances, and spectacle.

The script contains very little actual dialogue, and the characters' action and the many songs convey the major portions of the story. Blanchard adds to the spectacle by introducing extras into each scene to serve as chorus and as dancers. A high point in the action comes when Cinderella, spectacularly dressed, arrives in her coach at the ball. As typical of the pantomime, Blanchard embellishes this scene with a procession that includes over 100 characters representing 36 separate fairy and nursery stories. By the time the play progresses to the grand transformation scene, the traditional high point of the action, there is little that can be done to further increase the surprise and amazement of the audience.

The satirical look at people and customs of the time is an important aspect of many pantomimes. In *Cinderella*, Blanchard pokes fun at the fops and dandies of the period by picturing them as affected and mindless companions of the king. This topical allusion was probably beyond the grasp of most of the children in the audience, but it was most certainly a source of delight for the middle class audience that flocked to these entertainments.

Although it has been criticized as being superficial and vacuous, the pantomime occupies an important place in the development of dramatic literature for children. The pantomime was the first commercial theatre activity that addressed itself, in part, to children; and the success of these grand spectacles contributed significantly to the establishment of the fairy tale as a practical and popular subject for children's plays.

The influence of the pantomime, however, extended beyond just the subject matter that it dramatized. Utilizing all the techniques of theatrical wizardry, the pantomime capitalizes on the immediacy of the theatrical event by incorporating an exuberant style, irreverent topics, and visual spectacle to sweep the audience up in the occasion of the performance itself.

There is no contemporary children's theatre activity that compares *directly* with the pantomime; but the subjects, techniques, and style of this theatre form have always been an important part of the literature. From the spectacle-laden fairy tale dramas of mid-century, to the to the contemporary spoofs such as *Aesop's Falables* and *The Near-Sighted Knight and the Far-Sighted Dragon*, the spirit of the pantomime can be clearly seen. The pantomime championed the idea of drama for children as pure, escapist entertainment through the use of spectacle as a major part of the message of the play. Such a perspective has continued to exert an influence on much of the dramatic literature for children in this country.

EDWARD LITT LAMAN BLANCHARD (1820–1889) wrote his first pantomime for an amateur organization in 1839. Under the pseudonyms Francisco Frost and the Brothers Grinn, as well as under his own name, Blanchard wrote dramas, farces and burlesques. He is most noted for the fact that between the years 1852 and 1888 he supplied every pantomime produced by the Drury Lane Theatre. Blanchard was also a frequent contributor to literary journals, as well as serving as theatre critic for such papers as the *Sunday Times*, the *Weekly Dispatch*, and the *Daily Telegraph*. Blanchard is said to have written over one hundred plays, and, although very few of these works have been published, he was one of the most popular writers of his time.

Prominent Characters

BARON FILLETTOVILLE

HOBBEDYHOY (His Page)

GENERAL SHARPWITZ (Commdr.-in-Chief)

PRINCE PASTORELLE

POUSSETTE (His Attendant)

KING GALLOPADE (The Grand)

BARONESS FILLETTOVILLE

BLONDINA

BRUNETTA   (Her Daughters)

TORTOISESHELL TOM

CINDERELLA (The Baron's Daughter)

FAIRY QUEEN

ELECTRA (Spirit of Light)

IGNORAMUS (Spirit of Darkness)

CLOWN

FAIRIES, MASHERS, &c.,&c.

THE MUSIC COMPOSED AND ARRANGED
BY OSCAR BARRETT

BEAUTIFUL SCENERY BY W. BEVERLEY,
W. TELBIN, W. PERKINS,
T. W. GREIVE, AND HENRY EMDEN

PROPERTIES BY LABHART   MACHINERY BY WHITE
ARMOUR BY KENNEDY & PHILLIPS

BALLET ARRANGED BY MADAME KATTI LANNER

DRESSES by AUGUSTE ET CIE, MISS FISHER,
Mons. and Mdmes. ALIAS, Messrs. HARRISON, and
Miss YATES, from Designs by A. CHASEMORE

The whole produced by
AUGUSTUS HARRIS
Assisted by CHARLES HARRIS

This information is reproduced from the original English publication

26

Synopsis of Scenery and Incidents

SCENE 1—Court of the Baron's Manor House.
THE WEDDING FESTIVAL AND HONEYMOON DANCE

SCENE 2—Interior of the Old Manor House.
CINDERELLA AND THE CRUEL SISTERS
FAMILY JARS

SCENE 3—The Moonlight Glen.
GATHERING OF THE FOREST FAIRIES
SUN-RISE. THE ROYAL HUNT
MEETING OF THE PRINCE AND CINDERELLA—
LOVE AT FIRST SIGHT

SCENE 4—Interior of the Junior Masher's Club.
THE MASHERS AT HOME

SCENE 5—The Baronial Kitchen.
Invitation to the Ball. Cinderella's Dream
The Magic Change. The Toughened Glass Slipper brought by Electra
CINDERELLA GOES TO THE BALL IN HER FAIRY CARRIAGE

SCENE 6—Panorama.
ON THE WAY TO THE PALACE

SCENE 7—The Prince's Palace.
GRAND PROCESSION OF FAIRY TALES
Arrival of Cinderella in Her Golden Carriage

SCENE 8—The Conservatory.
TWELVE O'CLOCK. MISCHIEF TRIUMPHANT

SCENE 9—On the Road Home.
THE ROYAL PROCLAMATION
The Slipper a Perfect Fit
THE BETROTHAL OF THE PRINCE AND CINDERELLA

SCENE 10—The Black Castle.
THE FLYING DANCER AND THE PHANTOM FIGHT
The Cats' Catdrille, by the Rosa Troupe

SCENE 11—Transformation.
THE HOME OF LIGHT AND LOVE

SCENE I

Court Yard of the BARON'S MANOR HOUSE.—*Lively Music as Curtain rises.—Rapid entrance of* PRETTY PASTRYCOOKS *and* ATTENDANTS, *bearing Refreshments for the Wedding Guests: Rounds of Beef, Fowls and Ham, Trays of Custards and Jellies. Large Basket labelled "The Wedding Cake." Hampers of Wine, Etc.*

HOBBEDYHOY, *the* BARON'S PAGE, *enters from* MANOR HOUSE. *Tastes the various Viands, signifies approval, and quickens the progress of the* PASTRYCOOKS *into* MANOR HOUSE *after usual pantomime fashion.*

PAGE.	On cakes and custards I could feed incessantly.
	Oh! won't I polish the whole lot off presently.
	[While PAGE *is dancing about the Stage, enter* GENERAL SHARPWITZ, *hurriedly. They have a collision.*
GENERAL.	Zounds! Guns and gunpowder! What's this I hear!
	Why don't the Bride and Bridegroom both appear?
PAGE.	They have been and gone—
GENERAL.	And done it?—And not tarried?—
	I was invited here to see them married!
	A big affair—and Sharpwitz should be in it;—
	We great folks can't be punctual to a minute.
PAGE.	Of course not.
GENERAL.	I'm for Etiquette a stickler;
	Pop, bang!—a General can't be too partick-ler.
	But what's the lady like?

AIR: *"She's Fair, Fat and Forty!"*

PAGE.	*(Singing)*
	Oh, she's fair, fat and forty.
	Rather haughty—haughty—haughty.
	Golden hair, right down to there;
	It is not all her own;
	But she has hooked Baron-Filley—Silley, Filley-Filley,
	Though he, I think, was old enough to leave the girls alone.
	[Wedding bells heard in distance
PAGE.	Hark! Wedding Bells are ringing!

GENERAL.	That's a knack with them.

PAGE.　　　　　　And see, our happy villagers come back with them!
　　　　　　　　　　　　　　　[Wedding peal heard louder.

Enter Village Lads *and* Lasses, *gaily attired with Wedding Favours.*

　　MUSIC and CHORUS: *"Ting, ting, that's how the Bell goes."*

　　　　　　　　Ting, ting! that's how the bells go,
　　　　　　　　Ting, ting! that's how they ring.
　　　　　　　　A husband and wife
　　　　　　　　Made happy for life;
　　　　　　　　And that's why the bells ring out—
　　　　　　　　　　Ting! ting! ting!

Enter BARON, *and* BARONESS.—*They come up Stage between Rows of Children.*

　　　　　　　　DUET: BARON *and* BARONESS.

　　　　　　　　"Lots of Love for Breakfast."

BARON.　　　　Now we are married let's all be gay,
　　　　　　　　　For this is my darling wife;
　　　　　　　　How happy was I when the parson did say
　　　　　　　　　That we were united for life!

BARONESS.　　Yes, now we are tied in a true lover's knot,
　　　　　　　　　And I feel as shy as a dove.
　　　　　　　　Of money my hubby has got such a lot,
　　　　　　　　　We are sure to have lots of love.

　　　　　　　　　Chorus—

BARON.　　　　We'll have lots of love for breakfast.

BARONESS.　　Lots of love for tea.

BARON.　　　　And lots of love for supper;

BARONESS.　　Yes, on that we may agree.
Together.　　Our lives will be so happy, for we've plenty £ s.d.;

　　　　　　　　And we're going to live on love from night till morning.
　　　　　　　　[Chorus to be repeated by the whole of the Children,
　　　　　　　　　and to be followed by "Ting, ting, ting."

　　　　　　　　　　[BARON introduces BARONESS *to* GENERAL
　　　　　　　　　　　with great ceremony.

29

BARON.	Behold the Baroness!—whom I adore! The Baroness, General! *[Mutual exchange of courtesies.*
GENERAL.	Most proud, I'm sure! *[GENERAL advances toward BARONESS, who* *receives his salute with great diffidence.*
BARONESS.	Oh, spare my blushes!
BARON.	It stands not to reason We will spare nothing, that may be in season. Spread everywhere the news we beef bestow— Spread tablecloths—spread everything you know; And when you've feasted all from door to door, And nothing's left, spread *that* among the poor.
BARONESS.	My generous husband! How can I repay you?
BARON.	*(To General.)* Of course you'll take pot-lock with us?
BARONESS.	What say you?
GENERAL.	For wedding breakfasts I have quite a zest.
BARONESS.	*(Coaxingly.)* You'll come?
GENERAL.	I will, fair lady, as your guest.
BARON.	Now, as your landlord never knew a better day, Let this be marked a General Red Letter Day. Our happy married life, then, here commences— Drink, dance, make merry, we'll pay all expenses. *[Rustic dance led off by BARON and BARONESS.*

Chorus:	On Monday, we'll go to the Zoo—the Zoo!
	  On Tuesday we'll go to the Park.
	On Wednesday we'll go to the Aquarium,
	  And have such a jolly good lark;
	On Thursday we'll go out to tea—to tea!
	  On Friday we'll travel by train,
	Old *Blue Beard* to see at the Crystal C.P.
	  And on Saturday go to the Lane.

ENSEMBLE

"Honeymoon Dance." "There's nae Luck about the House."
"Blue Bells of Scotland."

Now let's all gang unto the house,
  And let's be merry a'.
Yes, let's all gang unto the house,
  Yes, let's all gang awa'.

And—

    'Tis there, yes 'tis there we should go this wedding morn.

                           [Scene closes.

SCENE II

Interior of old MANOR HOUSE.—*Rapid music.*—SERVANTS *cross stage with remains of Wedding Breakfast.*—*Usual extra* WAITER *with viands concealed in his Umbrella.*—*Bustle and exit.*

                  Enter BARON *and* BARONESS.

BARON.	All bottles emptied, joints reduced to bone— Our guests have gone, at length we are alone.
BARONESS.	Yes, quite alone! How beautiful all this is.
BARON.	And what an opportunity for kisses. *[They spoon.*
BARONESS.	But I've a secret which I ought to tell.
BARON.	You haven't— —
BARONESS.	Yes, I have!
BARON.	Go on—'tis well! If you had loved another, off I'd carried him.
BARONESS.	Once, only once, and then I went and married him.
BARON.	A widow!
BARONESS.	Yes; I know men are afraid of them, But men remember first a widow made of them.
BARON.	Aha! Is 't so?
BARONESS.	It is!
BARON.	Enough, 'tis well! I also have a secret got to tell.
BARONESS.	O, dreadful thought! Reveal it, I implore. You are not already married?
BARON.	Once before A beauteous bride I to the altar led.
BARONESS.	Who was—?

BARON.	Divorced and with another fled.
BARONESS.	Oh! the brute! [*Smacks face.*
BARON.	And now we have each made conscience right, And told each other everything.
BARONESS.	Not quite. I had— —
BARON.	A child?
BARONESS.	A daughter!
BARON.	That will do.
BARONESS.	It would have done, but fortune gave me two.
BARON.	*Two* daughters!
BARONESS.	Each a pretty little dear, The very sight of them you heart will cheer.
BARON.	I'm not so sure we shall agree on that, For I've a daughter too.
BARONESS.	Two?
BARON.	One.
BARONESS.	The brat! She'll put my daughters' nose out of joint.
BARON.	An observation hardly to the point, [*Slaps his face. They wrangle and fight.*
BARON.	Oh, faints, please; how very hard you strike. Be quiet and I'll do anything you like.
BARONESS.	Banish your daughter and take mine instead.
BARON.	(*Aside.*) I rather wish that I had not been wed. (*Aloud.*) I'll buy new toys for them and sugar candy.
BARONESS.	I'll take you to my cherubs, they're close handy.
BARON.	Before we go, I hope you have forgiven me?
BARONESS.	Oh, yes.
BARON.	Then, just one little kiss.
BARONESS.	Only one then, just like this.

DUET.—*"Kissy, Kissy."*

Together   Kissy-kissy! kissy-kissy! kissing is so nice.
      How to kiss—how to kiss, I'll show you in a trice.

BARON.   See, put your little hand in mine (BARONESS) so.
      Now lift your little head and smile,
      So; yes, that will do.
      And say you love me true.

BARONESS.   How sweet it is to have a row,
      And make it up like this.
      So, hubby darling give me now
       A cuddle and a kiss.

   [They both dance off. Recitative. Business, and Chorus.

Knock at door. Enter the PAGE, HOBBEDYHOY. *Crosses Stage with Boxes labelled, "Mdlle. Fillettoville. Carriage Paid."—Business.*

Enter CINDERELLA *with Battledore and Shuttlecock, as if fresh from School, singing—*

      Papa, papa,
      I'm my papa's darling.
      Home from School now I have come
       My own papa to see.
      Papa, papa,
      I'm my papa's darling.
      Schooldays now are over,
       And I've just come home to tea.

CINDERELLA. Well, here I am. I really feel quite dreamy,
      But fancy someone will be glad to see me.
      I am pleased, I know, when school at length is
       ended,
      With holidays to six long weeks extended.
      But where's Papa? Pa always wrote to say,
      Home he would bring me in his one horse chay.

PAGE.   Ah, Miss! an older girl your love will smother;
      You have been and gone and got another mother.
      This day the wedding— —

CIND.   Don't, say "ceremonial."

PAGE.   I do—took place.

CIND.   Oh, misery! matrimonial.
      Oh, la! and must our loves divided be.
      Large was my share!

PAGE.   So was *his share! Ah, me!*
             [Exit Page.

CIND.	Oh, pa, why didn't you ask your daughter Whether a mother she ever desired? Just at the end of my dancing quarter, Not a step-farther I ever required.

SONG: CINDERELLA.

"I am a giddy and a wilful little School-girl."

[*Dance.*

During end of Dance, enter BLONDINA *and* BRUNETTA. *They look on in astonishment as* CINDERELLA *dances off. They quarrel and display temper.*

DUET: BLONDINA *and* BRUNETTA.

"I Beg Your Pardon!"

Enter the BARONESS *and* BARON, *the latter with his arms laden with Toys.*

BARON.	Hollo! My toys won't do for girls like these?
BARONESS.	(*Introducing.*) The Baron!
BLON. N BRUN.	Give us something, dad,
BARON.	Say please. And then I will. But each of these, my dear, <div align="right">[*To Baroness.*</div>Are much too big for dolls like these, I fear. [*Business. Girls playfully chase* BARON *round Stage,* *and play tricks with him.* BARONESS *interposes.*

Enter rapidly CINDERELLA.

CIND.	Oh, dear papa! <div align="right">[*Rushes to embrace him—is repulsed.*</div>
BARON.	Hush child, don't make a row. Learn, you have got another mother now; With two more sisters, as they say in trade, Both stout commodities, and ready made.
CIND.	Are these my sisters?
BRUNETTA.	Yes, we'll let you know it.
BLONDINA.	And every night and morning mean to show it.
BRUNETTA.	You'll have to wait on us,
BLONDINA.	And dress our hair,

34

BRUNETTA.   And in the kitchen all our meals prepare.

BLONDINA.   On errands go, in every direction,

BRUNETTA.   With other signs of sisterly affection.

CIND.   Can this be home?

BARON.   It's Home, sweet Home! Bewitchen!

BARONESS
and the two }   Now go and get some firewood for the kitchen.
Daughters.

Enter PAGE *and* SERVANTS *to take off Boxes.*

AIR: *"I'll Meet Her When the Sun goes Down."*

CINDERELLA.   Must I go from my home to the lonely wood?

BLONDINA.   Yes, at once, Miss, without a word or frown!

BRUNETTA.   You must learn to behave as a servant should,

BARONESS.   And get back before the sun goes down!

BARON.   Yes, my dear, you must go to the lonely wood,

BARONESS.   'Tis not more than a mile or so from town;

BLONDINA.   And be sure you are back ere we go to bed,

BRUNETTA.   For you'll have to let my back-hair down!

CINDERELLA.   And it's oh!—I must go—
                    Wood I must be fetching,
                    For the fire that's in the kitchen.
                 And it's oh!—I must go—
                    And be back before the sun goes down.

                      [*Repeat altogether, and all dance off.*

35

SCENE III

"The Moonlight Glen."

Fairy music heard off stage.—Appearance of SCINTILLA, *the* FAIRY QUEEN, *and attended by* FAIRIES.

SCENA: *"Here in Mossy Woodland Glade."*

CHORUS OF ELVES.

Here in mossy woodland glade,
In the moonlight in the shade,
We fays our revels hold.

F. QUEEN.   Attend my call!

CHORUS.   We come!
We dance to yonder rippling stream.
Its music sweeter far doth seem
Than any voice in fairy dream,
Or note of dulcet lute.

F. QUEEN.   While silver moonbeams play o'er the brook,
And all the flowers in dell and nook
Combine to fill with sweet perfume
The glade that Luna doth illume,
We sing our Fairy lay.

SCINTILLA.   My faithful elves who haunt this moonlit wood,
Whose duty 'tis to guard the true and good,
Here at the summons of your Fairy Queen,
This only being the time you can be seen,
You know a charming child.

OMNES.   We do! we do!

SCINTILLA.   Over whose infancy

OMNES.   You watched, quite true.

SCINTILLA.   Whose future happiness we held most dear,
Being worthy of our guardianship.

OMNES.   Hear, hear!

SCINTILLA.   Whose pretty name I hardly need to tell a
Meeting like this was—

OMNES.   *We* know, Cinderella!

SCINTILLA.   The same! Well, Cinderella had a father,
A circumstance you may have heard of?

36

OMNES.	Rather!
SCINTILLA.	Who now a second marriage has completed, And Cinderella is being most illtreated.
OMNES.	Rush to the resue!
SCINTILLA.	Stay! That Prince means much Whose heart no female beauty yet could touch. With joy his subjects would be overladen, If that young Prince could marry this young maiden.
OMNES.	He shall! He shall!

[IGNORAMUS, *the Demon of Mischief, appears up trap.*

IGNO.	He shall not!
SCINTILLA.	Who are you?
IGNO.	I am a demon from a darksome realm, With ignorance the world I overwhelm. Against all goodness I have often fought; And, now, you fairies I will try to thwart.
SCINTILLA.	Down, vampire, down! your tricks are all accurst, We'll shield the maiden, though you do your worst.

[*Exit* IGNORAMUS *down trap.*

Then please observe that what I moved, that end meant,
Our Resolutions carried—no Amendment.
And, now, this most important business done,
I think it time we had some fairy fun.

BALLET.

*Early Morning—Hunter's Horn heard—*FAIRIES *disappear with the Dawn.*

CHORUS

F. QUEEN.	(*Recit.*) The hunter's horn draws near; Away!—Away!
CHORUS.	Lightly, lightly trip away, Here we must no longer stay. Lightly, lightly trip away, For the dawn is breaking. Sweet, good night, fare thee well, Good night!

37

Hunting Music—PRINCE *and* HUNTSMEN *enter.*

HUNTING CHORUS: *"John Peel."*

[*Huntsmen go off in pursuit of Game, leaving*
PRINCE *and* POUSSETTE *on Stage.*

POUSSETTE. Your Highness—hark! the fox is well away.

PRINCE. Nay, mind me not; I shall not hunt to-day.
[*Exit* POUSSETTE.
How strange I feel! Whatever is the matter?
To-day I cannot stand their idle chatter.
My heart throbs loud—I feel it faster beat;
Perchance, this morn, my fate I have to meet!
No woman yet has ever turned my head;—
Pooh! nonsense! I'm resolved I'll never wed.
[*Heard off Stage.*

MUSIC: *"Through the Wood."*

PRINCE. What voice is that?
[CINDRELLA, *with a few withered branches
in her hand, is seen crossing Bridge.*

CINDERELLA—Air: *"Through the Wood."*

Through the wood—through the wood,
    Here may they find me
Searching each hollow in dingle and dell,
    I don't think I've left many branches behind me.
And those here before me will do very well.
[*Gathering sticks.*
PRINCE *goes on to Bridge, and stops.*

[CINDERELLA *turns. Sees* PRINCE.

DUET.—AIR: *Old Song.*

PRINCE. Where are you going to, my pretty maid?
Where are you going to, my pretty maid?

CINDERELLA. Going to pass you, Sir,

PRINCE. *(Delightedly.)*
She said, *Sir*, she said, *Sir*, she said—

CINDERELLA. Oh please, let me pass you, Sir,

PRINCE. She said.
Shall I go with you, my Pretty Maid?
Shall I go with you, my Pretty Maid?

38

CINDERELLA. No, if you please, kind Sir, instead—Sir, instead—
   Sir, instead—
  I'll go home by myself, as I'm hurri-*ed*.
     [CINDERELLA *is running off when*
      the PRINCE *detains her.*

PRINCE. Before you leave me thus, o, tell me pray,
  By what sweet name I may recall this day?

CINDERELLA. My name! Ah, no! there is a sadness in it,
  I cannot give it you.   [*Going.*

PRINCE. Stay one more minute.
    [*Picks flowers and offers it to her.*
  Take this small offering before we part,
  'Tis but a pansy; but it holds my heart.

  DUET.—AIR: " *'Tis but a Pansy Blossom.*"

PRINCE. 'Tis only a pansy blossom,
   Only a little flower,
  Yet to me far dearer
   Than all in Earth's fair bower;
  Bearing to you a message,
   A message fond and true,
  The flower may fade, but, ah! never
   The heart I give to you.
CINDERELLA. Ah! from this pansy blossom
   Often a face will start—
  A face that will say the flower
   Carries my true love's heart.

Together. 'Tis only a pansy blossom, &c.
    [CINDRELLA *exit across Bridge, while*
     PRINCE, *entranced by her grace*
     and beauty, advances to front.

PRINCE. What means this sudden warmth thro' all my
   frame?
  'Tis love! Till now I never knew the name.
    [*Horn heard.* HUNTERS *return.*

  HUNTING CHORUS:—

  (La Chasee de Jeune Henri.)
  Tallo ho!—Tally ho!—Tally ho!
   The fox has had his run;
  Tally ho!—Tally ho!
   Here is the brush!—the hunt is done.

SCENE IV

Interior of the "Junior JOHNNIE'S Club."

Enter MASHERS *severally.*

CHORUS.—AIR: *"Toujours le Méme."*

MASHERS.	Chappies are we! Chappies are we! Say! shall we split, boys, A Soda and B?
WAITERS.	Say, sirs, shall we— Say sirs, shall we Give you some ice with Your Soda and B?
MASHERS.	Yes, James pray see— Yes, James, pray see That we've some ice with Our Soda and B.

Enter GENERAL SHARPWITZ *and* POUSSETTE.

[*They go to tables and play Baccarat.*

Enter the KING, *greatly concerned about his son.*

KING.	We must do something to improve his looks. Let's see now what great names are on my books.
OMNES.	Let's have the list.
KING.	(*Turning over Portrait Album.*) Kamschatka's Queen.
GENERAL.	The ugliest woman that was ever seen.
KING.	Her Majesty, the Snow Queen.
POUSSETTE.	He won't *choose her*.
KING.	Empress of China.
POUSSETTE.	Sure he will refuse her!
KING.	Princess of Persia!
POUSSETTE.	Oh! he hates a Persian!
KING.	Queen of the Cannibal Islands.
POUSSETTE.	*His* aversion.

40

KING.	What shall we do? It's getting very serious.
GENERAL.	Guns and gunpowder, it is most mysterious!
KING.	I've an idea!
MASHERS.	Hurrah! that is a wonder.
KING.	Dear boys, I wish you'd keep your feelings under.
	To find this lady, who is so divine,
	Is no small task, but yet it shall be mine.
	This is my happy thought—I'll give a ball.
OMNES.	A ball! A ball!
KING.	And I'll invite you all!
	Yes, all my subjects shall have invitations;
	Let everybody come with their relations.
	Yes, every woman in the world invite,
	We're certain then to get the one that's right.
	We'll have a royal rout; oh, won't I go it!
	Can't I just dance? and don't I mean to show it.

Enter PRINCE, *over-dressed as a* MASHER—*very high Collar, &c.*

PRINCE.	Dear chappies all, I give you greeting.
KING.	My son, this is a most peculiar meeting.
	What means this strange attire?
PRINCE.	I'm happy
	To tell you now that I've become a Chappy.
	Isn't this right, Poussette?
POUSSETTE.	Oh, yes, that's the form.

DUET: *"You're Bound to Do the Same."*

If you a Johnnie want to be,
    I'll tell you what to do;
You've only got to follow me,
    For I'm a Johnnie true.
To be a swell I always aim,
    Although I have no cash,
And you are bound to do the same,
    If you the girls would mash.

Chorus:	You must learn to say, "By Jove, Dear Boy!"
	You must shoot your cuff—just so,
	You must have your collars cut too high,
	Your waistcoat cut too low;
	Of each lady in the ballet,
	You must know the Christian name,

41

For all the Johnnies do it,
    And you're bound to do the same.

Of course you'll read the *Sporting Times,*
    And understand its chaff;
The *Referee,* its pars. and rhymes,
    Will often make you laugh;
To supper at Romano's, you
    Must take your latest flame,
For this is what the Johnnies do,
    And you must do the same.

    Chorus: You must learn, &c.

Just find a snip to give you tick,
    And always be in debt,
You must sport a silver-mounted stick,
    And smoke a cigarette.
With lemon squash and S. and B.
    Support your manly frame.
I do, and if you'd be like me,
    You'll have to do the same.

    Chorus: You must learn, &c.

        [*The* KING *determines to give a ball.*

GENERAL.   Powder and balls! before the night is past
This General may a conquest make at last.
        [MASHERS *grow excited. One says—*
            "I'll Write to Ada," &c.
Boys, this won't do, don't thus forget your duty,
Fall in, attention, charge for home and beauty.

    CHORUS: *"Charlestown Blues."*

        [*All march off.*

SCENE V

"The Baronial Kitchen," *and* End View *of* Staircase.

CINDERELLA *discovered Sitting, at the* Kitchen Fire, *and polishing a* Large Fire Shovel.

CINDERELLA.   It isn't lively sitting here alone,
With not one act of kindness ever shown!
I drudge all day.—Hard work I shouldn't mind;
But from my kin, I've words much less than kind!

A nice life's mine!—I'm pushed all ways about,—
A maid-of-all-work, with no Sunday out!
Whatever sought is, I am ever fetchin' it;
And in my *kitchen*, I am always *ketchin' it!*
Abuse from every one!—No thanks, no cash;
And when I cook, I only make a *hash!*
To polish pokers, tho' there's no disgrace in it,
Shovel so bright, that I can see my face in it!
Altho' my sisters do not seem to pity one,
That face reflected, really looks a pretty one!
                    [*Bells ring, and voices call* CINDERELLA.

BRUNETTA *and* BLONDINA.

BLONDINA.	Now, Cinderella!
BRUNETTA.	Lazy, idle thing!
BLONDINA.	Why didn't you answer me?
BRUNETTA.	You heard me ring.
CINDERELLA.	Oh, sisters! why so cruel? Don't be wroth, I am sure I do my best, to please you both.
BRUNETTA.	You saucy minx!
BLONDINA.	The good-for-nothing jade To wait upon her betters must be made.

Enter the Page, HOBBEDYHOY, *with large Letter—Letter inscribed, "Baron Fillettoville, Grand Chateau."*

PAGE.	This letter for the Baron—such a whopper!
BRUNETTA.	And so am I—that language is improper. [*Cuffs him off.*
BRUNETTA.	The envelope is long.
BLONDINA.	And also wide.
BRUNETTA.	I'd like to find out what is said inside. [*Opens Letter.* Good gracious! It's a ticket for us all This night to go to our young Prince's Ball.

Enter BARON *and* BARONESS.

BARON.	What means this family disturbance now?
BARONESS.	In plainer language—Hullo! what's the row?

BLONDINA.	Our Prince to-night invites us to a ball.
	[*Shows large Card.*

CINDERELLA *comes up.*

BARONESS.	What do you want?
CINDERELLA.	I want to go—that's all.
BLONDINA.	Enough for you to do what mother wishes,
BRUNETTA.	You're only fit to wash up plates and dishes.
BARONESS.	The Prince's ball, and this his invitation,
	Oh, how it spurs your Ma's imagination.
BARON.	Some noble lord, possessed of wealth and lands,
	May marry each, and take both off my hands.
	Now, to send answer, bring me pens and paper,
	A stick of sealing-wax, and light the taper.
	Get all in order, and mind what you do;
	For if you don't, you'll get some *whacks* on you.
	[PAGE *brings Pens and Paper, Candle, and Gigantic*
	Stick of Sealing-wax. Comic Business.
	[*Exit* PAGE *with Letter.*

DUET: BLONDINA *and* BRUNETTA.

Air: "I'll tell them my Father's a Marquis."

BRUNETTA.	Oh, I reckon we know how to do it,
	And I think we shall captivate all,
	By our manners so aristocratic
	To-night at His Majesty's Ball.
BLONDINA.	Won't it be awfully jolly
	Through all the great Palace to roam,
	While we'll leave you, my dear Cinderella,
	To look after matters at home.
Together.	We'll tell them our mother's a Duchess;
	But wouldn't His Majesty frown
	If he knew that she once kept a second-hand shop
	In a little street down Somer's Town.
	We'll tell them she rides in her brougham—
	A beauty she is of the day.
	If a Prince we should marry instead of a "Arry,"
	I wonder whatever they'd say.
BARON.	Now, quick, my girls, it's late! your dress prepare.
	Soap well your face, and well pomade your hair.

44

BARONESS.   Lace tight your stays, but let's have no delay,
                   And mind you're decked out in your best array.
                   Where's Cinderella? I will make the jade
                   Come and assist you as your waiting-maid.

[*The two* Ugly Sisters *go into room on one side.* BARON
              and BARONESS *into room on other.* CINDERELLA
                   is constantly summoned from each side.
                        Things are called for by Telephone.

CONCERTED PIECE.—AIR: "*'Arry.*"

BARONESS.   (*Popping out her head.*)
                   Where is my cap and where is my dress?
                      Now, then, hurry!

BARON.   (*Ditto.*)
                   Things are in a horrible mess!
                      Now, then, hurry!

CINDERELLA.   It's hurry here and hurry there—
                      Hurry near and far!
                   It's hurry—hurry everywhere,
                      Oh, what a plague you are!

BLONDINA.   (*Popping out her head.*)
                   Now hurry!—then hurry!
                      We are in a hurry!

BRUNETTA.   (*Do.*)
                   Now girl—hurry!
                      Wherever has she gone?

BARONESS.   (*Do.*)
                   Oh, hurry!

BARON.   (*Do.*)
                      Come hurry!

BLONDINA.   (*Do.*)
                   Paint and powder—hurry!

BRUNETTA.   (*Do.*)
                   Bring all our clothes, and we will start,
                   When we have got 'em on!

[Full Chorus, *to be repeated by all.*
[BARON *and* BARONESS, BLONDINA *and* BRUNETTA,
                        return to their Rooms.

45

CINDERELLA.—*Alone.*—*Sings.*

Air: *"My Home!"*

And this is home—and this is home!
Never from these walls am I allowed to roam.
And this is home—and this is home!
More dreary than a prison is my home!

BARON, BARONESS *and* SISTERS, *make their Re-appearance, ready to start, all dressed most outrageously.*

Ensemble.

We are going to the ball this evening;
Yes, this evening. Oh! what an evening.
We are going to the ball this evening;
Yes, this evening. Tra-la-la!

AIR: *"Cenerentola," Rossini.*

BARONESS.   Now we're ready—now we are dressed,
Let us be starting for the ball.

BLONDINA.   Paint and powder all of the best,
We shall attract the gaze of all.

BARON.   Mount the donkeys, order the cab.
Come, let us show them how to dance.

BRUNETTA.   You stay here, you kitchen drab.

CINDERELLA (*aside*) Would that I could have their chance.

CHORUS.   Come along then; let's be going.
Tra la la la la!
How to dance we will be showing.
Tra la la la la!

[*Exeunt* BARON, BARONESS, BRUNETTA,
and BLONDINA.

CINDERELLA *resumes her place mournfully by* Fireside.

CINDERELLA.   They have gone, and here must Cinderella stay,
Passing long hours wearily away.
Kept thus below, no wonder I feel lonely;
Here if I stir, it's with the poker only.
The one sweet thought I cherish in my bosom,
Springs from my little withered pansy blossom.
[*Takes flower from her breast and sinks to sleep
to music, " 'Tis but a Pansy Blossom."*

46

CINDERELLA

DANCE OF KITCHEN INSECTS.

Vision of CINDERELLA'S *Marriage with the* PRINCE.

[*As vision fades away,* CINDERELLA
awakes with a start.

CINDERELLA.   Oh, what a dream in fancy I pursue!
                   FAIRY QUEEN *appears.*

F. QUEEN.   A dream, my little lady, I'll make true,

CINDERELLA.   You are—

FAIRY.   I am. The Fairy Queen I am styled,
                   Conferring gifts on each deserving child.
                   I know your wishes, and can grant them all.

CINDERELLA.   Oh, please then, might I go and see—

F. QUEEN.   The Ball.
                   Of course, you shall, and be arrayed with splendour,
                   Tradesmen from Fairy Land your service render.

Successive Appearance of Little Dressmakers, Haberdashers, Florists,
    Glovers, Jewellers, &c. *They crowd around* CINDERELLA, *and she
    is borne off by them to be dressed.*

F. QUEEN.   (*Pointing to them leaving* Stage.) So vanity, sweet
                       Love, for ever chases,
                   And pleasure often beams on mere Dream Faces.

                   SONG: *"Dream Faces."*

F. QUEEN.   This comes of being good, and kind, and dutiful.

CINDERELLA.   I hardly know myself, I look so beautiful.

F. QUEEN.   Dear me! That Fairies should their memory lose,
                   I had quite forgotten all about the shoes.

CINDERELLA.   My shoes— —

F. QUEEN.   Of course, you cannot go in those.
                   Electra! quick! your magic powder disclose!

(*Flight of* ELECTRA *to earth with slippers.*)

CINDERELLA.   What beauteous slippers!—yet I cannot take them;
                   For should I dance in them, I am sure to break
                       them.

F. QUEEN.   Fear not, sweet maid, whate'er may come to pass;
                   These cannot break—they're made of toughened
                       glass.

47

CINDERELLA.   And all this kindness—how can I repay?

F. QUEEN.   By paying attention now to what I say—
                        While these you wear, whatever may be wanted
                     Has only to be wished for to be granted.
                     One stipulation only do I make
                     And mind you keep it for your true love's sake—
                     Be home by twelve!

CINDERELLA.   I will; but how to go?

F. QUEEN.   That your attendant, newly dressed, will show.

The PAGE HOBBEDYHOY *enters, grandly attired, and much bewildered.*

F. QUEEN.   First for your coach, from yonder wall behind,
                     Bring me the largest pumpkin you can find.
                                             [*Pumpkin brought.*
                     So, place it there. I see a trap with mice,
                     These we will turn to ponies in a trice.
                                             [*Trap with white mice brought.*
                     A whiskered coachman, now, is indispensable,
                     That rat will do, he's steady, and looks sensible.
                                             [*Rat-trap brought.*
                     For Footmen a few lizards just arrange.
                                             [*Lizards brought in flower-pot.*
                     And now observe me closely. Presto! Change!
                                             [*Transformation takes place*—Carriage,
                                                 Coachman, Footmen, &c.
                                             [CINDERELLA *is assisted into* Carriage *by the*
                                                 PAGE. *As she is getting in, the* FAIRY
                                                 QUEEN *gives her last instructions.*

F. QUEEN.   Till twelve they're yours; if past that hour you stay,
                     Coach, coachman, footmen, all will run away.
                                             [CINDERELLA *starts. Coach traverses*
                                                 Stage and passes off.
                                             [*Scene changes.*

SCENE VI

"Panorama of the Route."

Enter BLONDINA *and* BRUNETTA.

DUET:

BLONDINA *and* BRUNETTA.

"THE HAPPY LAND."

48

*[BRUNETTA and BLONDINA pass across Stage,
attended with numerous Mishaps.*

*Enter BARON and BARONESS in a Cab. Pantomime Business
as they cross Stage.*

SCENE VII

"The Prince's Fancy Ball."

*The Palace Gardens Illuminated. Panorama passes off and leaves
BARON and BARONESS on Scene.*

Enter KING preceded by Heralds and followed by Guests.

KING.   Well, things, so far, are going very pleasantly;
        I think I'll dance a little hornpipe presently.
        But as the children soon to be must go,
        I think they first should have a dance you know.

DANCE OF CHILDREN, *followed by the*

GRAND PROCESSION

*Of all the Illustrious Personages invited to the Fancy Ball. Heroes of
Nursery Rhymes and Fairy Stories. And ending with Ali Baba
and the Forty Thieves.*

*[CINDERELLA'S Carriage dashes in amidst great excitement.
Scene closes.*

SCENE VIII

"The Conservatory."

An Illuminated Clock indicates quarter to Twelve.

Enter IGNORAMUS.

IGNO.   Ah! ah! oh! oh! not late then after all;
        I've come in time to have my game at Ball.
        Quarter to twelve, no quarter will I show;
        I'll try it now—old Time, pray backward go.
        But let that clock deceive her by a minute,
        She'll find she's danced to put her foot well in it.
           [Puts Clock back five minutes. Exit

49

[*Enter* GUESTS, BLONDINA *and* BRUNETTA *make up to the* GENERAL.

GENERAL. Dances and Dynamite! This ball is glorious.
Over a hundred hearts I reign victorious.

Enter PRINCE *and* POUSSETTE, *accompanied by* Pages.

[PRINCE *looks in vain among* Guests *for Cinderella.*

PRINCE. Vainly I seek that face among them all,
Whose matchless beauty caused this Fancy Ball.

POUSSETTE. The Prince is searching for his pretty pet;
Her charms it seems he never will forget.

DUET AND CHORUS: *"The Reign of the Roses."*

PRINCE. 'Twas in the forest, she and I
Awoke love's spell to weave
The love that with the morning came.
Was but a dream at eve.

POUSSETTE. 'Twas out in the forest they met, and they parted.
The love of a day, and the love of a life;
But watching and waiting, we've seen through the
seasons,
The turn of the tide o'er the ocean of strife.

CHORUS. Ah, Love it is for ever!
Love, why should they sever!
Oh, lovely beauty!
Come back once more!

Enter CINDERELLA.

PRINCE. (*Aside.*) What! Eh! that face, those eyes! that wink!
'tis she.
A great Princess! I'm sure that she must be.
[*Goes to* CINDERELLA, *and takes her hand.*

PRINCE. At last, the object of my adoration!
A great Princess, no less can be your station!

CINDERELLA. Your Royal Highness honours me too much.
I a Princess, I must behave as such.

SONG: *"Ducky Darling."*

PRINCE. At last we have met, my own little pet,
For you we have given the ball.
We now have a chance for a chat and a dance,
For you I love better than all.

50

CINDERELLA.   Oh, Prince! I'm afraid, too long I have stayed,
                       And soon I must hurry away;
                       But still there is time, before the clock's chime,
                       To hear you once lovingly say—

                                 Little darling, I love you, &c.

Enter BARON *and* BARONESS *and* TWO SISTERS.

BARON.   Well, here we are at last.

BARONESS.   Girls seize your chances,
                       He'll be a Duke at least, who with you dances.

BRUNETTA.   Oh! mayn't I have a Marquis if I see one?

BLONDINA.   Of course not; I'm his partner should there be one.
                                   [*Pushes him back.*

Enter KING *and* Guests, *including* MASHERS *and* BARON, BARONESS, BLONDINA, BRUNETTA, GENERAL SHARPWITZ, *the* Page, HOBBEDY-HOY, *who is taken to be a Foreigner of distinction. Refreshments are handed round. Business.*

                           [BARON *and* BARONESS *advance.*

BARON.   What a remarkable—now, did you ever?

BARONESS.   Likeness to Cinderella! Well, I never— —

BRUNETTA.   Why I could swear——

BLONDINA.   You could, I oft have heard you.

BRUNETTA.   That here is Cin——

BLONDINA.   —Derella. Too absurd you.
                           [*Retire up Stage disputing.*
PRINCE.   On me your hand as partner be bestowing;
                       This dance is short.

CINDERELLA.   How quick the time is going.
                       I must be home by twelve——

PRINCE.   That can be done,
                       But please remember here you have struck one.
                                   [*All dance.*

     [*At end of Dance,* Clock *outside strikes Twelve, while the* Illuminated Clock *shows only Five minutes to Twelve.* PAGE *rushes across in rags.*

Enter IGNORAMUS.

IGNO.   Ah! ah! 'tis done! This mischief's to my liking.

Enter FAIRY QUEEN.

F. QUEEN.　　　　He's stopped the Clock, and Twelve o'clock is
　　　　　　　　　　striking.

　　　　　　　　　　　　　　　　　[*General Consternation.*

Rats, Mice, Lizards, and Pumpkin rapidly cross Stage. CINDERELLA'S
　　Dress changes. CINDERELLA *rushes off. One of the Mashers picks
　　up the dropped Glass Slipper, and brings it to the* PRINCE.

PRINCE.　　　　　Where has she gone to? Left us in the lurch!
　　　　　　　　　　Bring lanterns! Find her! Everybody search.

　　　　　　　　　　　　　　　　　[*They get lanterns.*

CHORUS.—AIR: *"I kissed her under the Parlour Stairs."*

　　　　　　　　We'll look for her under the damson tree,
　　　　　　　　　　We'll look for her under the rose,
　　　　　　　　We'll look for her under the balcony—
　　　　　　　　　　Be sure and follow your nose.
　　　　　　　　We'll look for her over the garden wall,
　　　　　　　　　　And under all the chairs;
　　　　　　　　But let us look for her first of all,
　　　　　　　　　　Under the parlour stairs.

SCENE IX.

"On the Road Home."

Enter BARON, BARONESS *and* Two Ugly Sisters.

BARON.　　　　　All our conveyances have broken down.
　　　　　　　　　　I'm bumps and bruises from my foot to crown.

BARONESS.　　　　If this is going to a Prince's ball,
　　　　　　　　　　I wish he'd never given one—that's all!

BRUNETTA.　　　　You brazen hussy! How you have been going it.

BLONDINA.　　　　Don't lose your temper, dear; you are always
　　　　　　　　　　showing it.

　　　　　　　　　　　　　　　　　[*They quarrel.*

BARON.　　　　　Peace, children; leave off quarrelling and jangling.
　　　　　　　　　　Your mother's quite enough for one night's
　　　　　　　　　　wrangling.

BRUNETTA.　　[*Together*]　Papa! (*Expostulating.*)

BLONDINA.　　　　　　　　Mama! (*Entreating.*)

52

BARONESS.	Be thankful! I've no umbrella.
	Let's all go home, and give it Cinderella.

QUARTET.—AIRS: *"Oh! Clara, Clara!"*

"Mathilda's up to Snuff!"

[*Family tranquility restored with this peaceful compromise, and all trip gaily home.*

Enter CINDERELLA *and* HOBBEDYHOY, *the* PAGE, *in their changed Apparel, both weary and deplorable.*

CINDERELLA.—SONG.—AIR: *"The Broken Pitcher."*

Trip, trip, homeward I go,
Merrily went the hours, you know;
And that is the reason I'm in woe,
    All on a Summer morning.

The slipper is lost I wore last night.
Alas! I am now in a dreadful plight.
To stay so late was, of course, not right,
    And forget the Fairy's warning.

Oh, dear! what have I done?
Ah, me! where shall I run?
My slipper's gone, I have but one,
    What will the Fairy say?

CINDERELLA.	Exactly as the Fairy said it *would* be,
	If we were not at home the hour we should be.
	How fast the time did fly.
PAGE.	So I should think.
	I didn't get the time to eat and drink.
CINDERELLA.	And I so tired am getting! Why, what's this?
	One of my crystal slippers here I miss!

Enter PRINCE, KING, *the* GENERAL, *and the* MASHERS.

PRINCE.	Vainly you urge, no other bride will do
	But one whose foot has graced that crystal shoe.
KING.	The Prince is right, the slipper left behind her,
	Should somehow, somewhere, help someone to find her.
GENERAL.	Brides, Boots, and Blunderbusses! show expedition.
	Every foot regiment put into commission.
PRINCE.	Throughout our kingdom be the notice seen,
	Who owns that slipper is the future queen.

Enter BARON, BARONESS, BRUNETTA, BLONDINA, CINDERELLA, *and*
Village Lads and Lasses.

Enter Heralds.

[Heralds *show Proclamation.*
Whereas some lady at the Prince's Ball,
Dropped a Glass Slipper, very neat and small.
Whoever will the foot to match it bring,
The Prince will marry. (OMNES.) So long live the
King!

Enter POUSSETTE, *carrying Glass Slipper on a Crimson Cushion.*

CHORUS.—AIR: *"The Masher and the Maid."*

Chorus:	Come now and show your feet. Oh! la! la!
	Ankles so small and neat. Oh! la! la!
	This slipper shall decide. Oh! la! la!
	Who shall be the Prince's bride. Oh! la! la!
BARONESS.	Come, girls! on you he may his hand bestow,
	One's sure to put his foot in it, I know.
BARON.	Here's the proud moment I foresaw long since
	When I should have for son-in-law a Prince
BARONESS.	Squeeze yourself in if you're for life a crawler.
BRUNETTA.	Oh, Ma! why wasn't I born a trifle smaller?
BLONDINA.	Why did you let me thus go on expanding,
	And tell me to enlarge my understanding?

*The action from this point to the end of the Scene takes place through
the following* Concerted Piece:—

[BLONDINA *struggles with the Slipper.*

DUET.—AIR: *"Pardonnez Moi?"*

BRUNETTA.	Pardonnez moi, pardonnez moi,
	Pardonnez moi, ma soeur;
BLONDINA.	Excuse me, sister if you please;
BRUNETTA.	Oh, lor! just look at her.
BLONDINA.	I really should be much obliged
	If you would hold your jaw;
	I do declare I've got 'em on,

BRUNETTA.   My dear—pardonnez moi?

> [BRUNETTA *turns out* BLONDINA, *and proceeds to try on the slipper.*

AIR: *"Oh, What a Mug!"*

BRUNETTA.   Of slippers I have tried a few on.

CHORUS.   Oh! what a mug!

BRUNETTA.   Has anybody got a shoehorn?

CHORUS.   Oh! what a mug!

BLONDINA.   Her foot's too long by eighteen inches
               Never mind, you envious wenches.

BRUNETTA.   Lor, good gracious, how it pinches?

CHORUS.   Oh! what a mug!

> [She gives it up. CINDERELLA *comes forward, and is recognized by the* PRINCE.

AIR: *"You are, You know; You know You are!"*

PRINCE.   Why, who is this? I do declare
               I've seen that face before.
               It is—it is, I'm sure it is
               The girl that I adore.

CINDERELLA.   There's some mistake about it, sir,
               Too humble I'm by far.

PRINCE.   Oh, no, you are the Princess
               Of the ball last night—you are!

CHORUS.   You are, you know, you know you are!
               We have no cause to doubt it.
               You are, you know, you know you are,
               There's no mistake about it.
               > [PRINCE *conducts her to seat to try on Slipper.*

AIR: *"Milly's Cigar Divan."*

PRINCE.   Now sit down, dear, and try it,
               It's a natty little shoe;
               But though the size is rather small
               I'm sure it will fit you.
               'Tis clear you are my darling
               Of the forest and the ball.
               So prove it, Cinderella love,
               Before the gaze of all.

CHORUS.   Such a nice little slipper, come try my plan,
               See now if get it right on you can,
               If you are but true, and your duty will do,
               You can get on the slipper, you can, you can.
                              [CINDERELLA *puts on Slipper*.

          AIR: *"Tut, tut! Who'd have Thought it."*

CHORUS.   Tut, tut, tut, tut, who'd have thought it!
                   Tut, tut, tut, you don't say so!
               Oh, I never, who'd have thought it!
                   Goodness me! oh, here's a go!

                       [PRINCE *leads* CINDERELLA *to centre of Stage*.

          DUET.—AIR: *"My Sweeter Self."*

PRINCE.   Mine, mine for ever!
               Love shall endeavour
               Fitly to frame, Love
               For thee a Nave, Love.
               Light of love's passion
               My heart would fashion
               Some new name for thee,
               For my sweeter self thou art!

CHORUS.   Cinderella, thy troubles are over!
               From thy side, Prince, no more she's a rover!
               And together you both are in clover!

CINDERELLA.   My Life!

PRINCE.   My Love!

TOGETHER.   My sweeter self thou shall be.

CHORUS.   Poor in expression,
               Rich in possession,
               Day unto day, Love,
               Two lovers shall say, "Love."
               Each dawn the dearer,
               Each night the nearer,
               My heart of hearts, Love,
               And my sweeter Self thou shall be.
               Oh, Cinderella! as good as she's fair,
               Oh, happy Prince! with a bride for thy care,
               Oh, love! oh, life! oh, happy pair!

                              [Waltz, *and Scene closes*.

SCENE X.

THE GRAND TRANSFORMATION.

Part I.—*The Black Castle. The Home of Malice and Darkness.*

IGNORAMUS, The Demon, *enters.*

IGNO.   Foiled after all; but mortals never mind,
       Some other means of mischief I must find.

Enter all Principals *and* FAIRY QUEEN.

PRINCE.   To hunt out mischief from the realms of mirth,
       And banish Ignorance from off the Earth,
       Is now our mission; Spirit of Light appear.
       And overcome Dark Ignoramus here.
         [ELECTRA *appears—The Fight—Ignoramus*
                is vanquished.

Part II.—*The Home of Love and Light.*

FAIRY.   From Cinderella's story—often told,
       Here have we sought fresh beauties to unfold;
       For good old Fairy Tales must ever please
       The Young—when followed by Old Friends like
         these.
         [Pantomime Characters *appear.*

HARLEQUINADE.

SCENE I.—AN UNKNOWN STREET.

SCENE II.—COVENT GARDEN MARKET.

SCENE III.—SHADOWS OF THE WALL.

THE CAT'S CATDRILLE.

RULE BRITANNIA AND SAILOR'S HORNPIPE BY THE ENTIRE CORPS

DE BALLET AND THE CHILDREN OF THE NATIONAL

SCHOOL OF DANCING.

PREMIERE DANSEUSE—MDDLE. ROSA.

THE LITTLE PRINCESS

*A PLAY FOR CHILDREN AND GROWN-UP CHILDREN
IN THREE ACTS*

BY

MRS. FRANCES HODGSON BURNETT

THE LITTLE PRINCESS

By Frances H. Burnett

THE LITTLE PRINCESS

The story of the little princess is one of the most popular children's stories of all time, and it has been no less popular in its dramatized form. Burnett's story of Sara Crewe first appeared in *St. Nicholas* magazine in the late 1880's. In 1905 the story was published in a single edition entitled *A Little Princess*. In the interim Burnett wrote a dramatized version which was ultimately published as *The Little Princess*. The play was presented several times in England before it opened in New York in 1903. It has subsequently been produced by both amateur and professional groups.

The strong appeal of this play can be traced to Burnett's skill at creating simple melodrama that is reflected consistently in plot, characters, and theme. The play presents the story of Sara Crewe, a very romantic thirteen-year-old who, through no fault of her own, suffers a dramatic reversal of fortunes, only to be rescued in the end. Burnett created one-dimensional characters, a transparent and predictable plot structure, and unabashedly sentimental situations.

If there is an overriding theme or message to this play, it too is the message of melodrama — namely, that good *will* triumph over evil. From the very beginning of the play Sara is shown as a kind and gentle character, and she retains these qualities even when badly mistreated. Sara has faith in the goodness of the people around her, and Burnett is very clear to show that such optimism and strength of character will be rewarded.

The Little Princess follows a typical melodrama plot structure that is designed to elicit a strong emotional response from an audience involved in Sara's struggles. Act One shows Sara in a pleasant situation that changes quickly when the greedy school mistress, Miss Minchin, discovers that Sara's family fortune has been lost. The second act reveals Sara's unfortunate new role as an abused servant in the household. The conflict between Sara and Miss Minchin is sharpened, and with each new confrontation Sara's circumstances become increasingly dismal. Act Three appropriately presents a series of amazing coincidences that cause Sara to be reunited with a family friend, who assures her that her family fortune is intact. Miss Minchin is then rebuked for her behavior, and it is apparent that Sara will live "happily ever after."

By today's standards, *The Little Princess* appears crudely constructed, trite, and overly sentimental, but the play is little different in that regard than most of the popular adult theatre of that time. The commercial theatre in this country at the turn of the century had not yet been influenced by the brooding naturalism or the new staging styles growing out of the experimental theatres of Europe. The adult theatre-goers of 1903 were primarily interested in *entertainment*, which they translated into a desire for musical plays and sentimental melodrama. Given the interest in such works among adults, it follows that these same adults would find the melodramatic tale of Sara Crewe appropriate for their children.

This play had several things to recommend it to both the adults and the children of the time. First, the production of this play followed the very successful production of Burnett's *Little Lord Fauntleroy*, which premiered in 1888 and was revived in 1889. By 1903 Burnett had established a reputation as a writer, and even the story of Sara Crewe had, through magazine serialization, become known throughout the country. But even more important is the fact that *The Little Princess* offered the turn-of-the-century audiences a Victorian version of the Cinderella story. That the evil stepmother is, in this play, a greedy school mistress, or that the Prince is a friendly neighbor, probably mattered little to the children in the audience, who were compensated by the delight of seeing this familiar story played out with realistic characters in a realistic setting. And for the parents — if not the children — Burnett offers very proper Victorian attitudes about children and childhood: attitudes that are made explicit in Sarah's unquestioning obedience.

Sara Crewe was one of the first in a long line of popular protagonists in dramatic literature for children, and she is one of the very few created at that time who are not fairy tale characters. She is a totally romantic child with neither the mythic proportions of a character like Anatou in *The Ice Wolf*, nor the life-like qualities of a character like Ellie in *Step on a Crack*. But, unlike Anatou, Sara is not used as a vehicle for philosophical discussions; unlike Ellie, Sara's struggle is against a well-defined external force rather than very personal fears and insecurities. Burnett's emphasis is on the precise demands of the structure of melodrama as a means of expression, rather than on ideas or character.

Sara is a very endearing character who laughs, cries, and charms her way through her many misfortunes. At the point in the play where her predicament is the most critical, she discovers a note from a friendly neighbor. She then declares aloud to the spirit of her father: "Papa, I have a friend, I have a friend!" It is the key to the success of the play that by this time she has also made friends with every member of the audience.

Burnett creates this audience empathy more with a skillful use of exaggerated sentimentality than with realistic detail. To the audience of 1903, Sara was a recognizable character, who was neither distanced by the trappings of a fairy tale nor diminished by the spectacle of a pantomime. But what the audience saw was a romanticized portrait of a young girl, behaving more like the audience of the time thought she should behave than a young girl of the time might actually behave. And although the work as a whole has a realistic veneer, the improbable action, the machinations of plot structure, and the generalized view of the Victorian world make the play more akin to a fairy tale than to a modern problem play.

The popularity of this play in 1903 did much to stimulate other children's theatre production, but it did not inspire direct imitation. Throughout the history of dramatic literature for children in this country the characters, theme, and structure of melodrama have been used often, particularly in the dramatizations of fairy tale stories, but few plays have captured the essence of this popular theatre form as successfully as *The Little Princess*. Burnett was a master at melodrama, and although *The Little Princess* was shaped by critical perspectives much different than those of the modern theatre, it has been one of the most popular plays of this century.

FRANCES HODGSON BURNETT (1849-1924) emigrated from England to the United States in 1865, and shortly thereafter she began her formal writing career. In 1873 Hodgson married S.M. Burnett, a physician who also gained considerable prominence in his field.

Burnett's first literary success, "That Lass o' Lowries," was printed as a serial in *Scribner's Monthly* from August 1876 through May 1877, and issued as a volume in 1879. By 1886, with the publication of the very popular *Little Lord Fauntleroy*, Burnett had built for herself a very large critical and popular following.

Throughout her career Burnett wrote over forty novels and several plays. The plays, dramatizations of her own writings and original dramatizations, have included works for children and adults. *Little Lord Fauntleroy, Rackety Packety House,* and *The Little Princess* have been particular favorites with child audiences.

THE LITTLE PRINCESS

Characters

SARA.

MISS MINCHIN.

BECKY.

LOTTIE.

LAVINIA.

JANET.

NORA.

JESSIE.

MAZIE.

LILLY.

DONALD.

ERMENGARDE.

AMELIA.

MRS. CARMICHAEL.

RAM DASS.

BARROW.

CARRISFORD.

JAMES. [*Servant*].

EMMA.

BLANCHE.

NED.

THE LITTLE PRINCESS

ACT I

SCENE. *A large schoolroom at Miss Minchin's boarding school. Central window with view of snow street. Fireplace with fire lighted. On the walls four bracket-lamps and four maps. A green carpet. In front window a platform on which there is a blackboard easel. The room contains a large table, a sofa above fireplace, a piano with bench behind it, and several chairs. Lace curtains behind central window curtains for Ermengarde.*

At the rise of curtain: Jessie at piano; extra Children, Lilly and others in ring. Lavinia and one of the girls sitting. Amelia up stage. Jessie plays a waltz. Children dance, singing, "One, Two, Three, Four."

CHILDREN *(singing).*
> One, two, three, four.
> [*All around the other way. Change dance.*
> One, two, three, four.
> [*Repeat.*

AMELIA *(breaking in upon the noise).* Stop, stop, children; do stop. I only wanted to try the music before the company came. *(Children stop and get into lines)* Let me look at you all. *(Lavinia crossing)* Don't poke your head forward. Please turn out your toes. *(Lilly has crossed to right)* Lilly, your sash is untied. Let me tie it for you. *(Does so)* You know Miss Minchin ——

LAVINIA. Huh! Huh!

AMELIA. I will be very angry if there is any rude or unladylike conduct this afternoon. The lady and gentleman who live across the street in number 46 are coming in to see you. They have a very large family — nearly all old enough to go to a genteel school. That's why dear Sara is giving you this party.

LAVINIA. Dear Sara . . . huh! ——

AMELIA. Now, Lavinia, what do you mean by that?

LAVINIA. Oh, nothing, Miss Amelia.

ERMENGARDE. Oh, she did it because she's jealous of Sara.

LAVINIA. I didn't.

ERMENGARDE. You did.

LAVINIA. I didn't.

ERMENGARDE. Did——

LAVINIA. Didn't!
[*This ad lib. three times.*

ERMENGARDE. Did.

AMELIA *(coming between them).* Stop. I never saw such rude conduct. *(Lavinia laughs)* You are a spiteful child, Lavinia. I believe you *are* jealous. It's very nice indeed of Sara to give you all this party on her birthday. It's not every child who cares about her school-fellows. And she has not looked at one of her beautiful presents yet because she wanted you to have the pleasure of seeing them unpacked.
[*Children crowd around her.*

CHILDREN. Ah . . . ! [*Dance around her.*

ERMENGARDE. Are they going to be unpacked here?

CHILDREN. Yes, yes, yes!

LAVINIA *(sarcastically).* Did her papa send them all from India, Miss Amelia?

LILLY. Did he?

AMELIA *(grandly).* Most of them came from Paris.

CHILDREN. Oh . . . ! Paris.

AMELIA. There is a doll that was ordered months ago.

CHILDREN. Oh, a doll!

AMELIA. And a whole trunk full of things like a real young lady.

LOTTIE *(jumping up and down).* Are we going to see them right this minute?

AMELIA. Miss Minchin said they might be brought in after you had tried the new waltz.

LOTTIE. Tra-la-la! [*Dancing.*

AMELIA. I am going to tell her you have finished. *(Laughter)* Now *do* be nice and quiet when I leave you. *(Ermengarde swings Lottie around)* Lottie, don't rumple your new sash. One of you big girls look after her. *(Lottie picks up pillow from sofa, ready to throw at Lavinia)* Now do *(at door)* be quiet.
[*Exit. As Amelia exits, Ermengarde runs up to door. Children, except Lavinia, form picture on platform.*

ERMENGARDE. It's all right girls. She's gone.
[*Lottie throws pillow at Lavinia and runs, with Lavinia in pursuit. Ermengarde runs to Lottie's rescue.*

LOTTIE (*as Lavinia catches her and drags her*). Ermy, Ermy. Oh! Oh!
[*Ermengarde catches Lottie's other hand and drags her away from Lavinia; other Children watch.*

CHILDREN. Now.
[*Jessie playing piano, Children begin to do "ring around" again, laughing and chattering the while.*

LAVINIA. I wish you children wouldn't make so much noise. Jessie, stop playing that silly polka.

CHILDREN. No, no, go on, Jessie, go on. [*Lottie runs over and pushes Lavinia twice; falls the second time — hurts her knee.*

LOTTIE. Oh! Ah! Oh!

LAVINIA. I never saw such rough things. I wish Miss Minchin would come in and catch you.

LOTTIE. I guess it's all right.

BLANCHE. You girls think you are so big. You always try to stop the fun. Jessie, go on. (*Piano begins again*). We're not going to stop, just because you want to talk.

ERMENGARDE. I'm going to be the leader.
[*Jessie stops playing suddenly.*

CHILDREN. What's the matter?

JESSIE. Oh girls! Ermengarde has thrown all the music into the piano.
[*Girls crowd around her, and take music out of piano. Ermengarde laughing.*

LAVINIA. You'd stop fast enough if it was the Princess Sara talking.

ERMENGARDE. Oh, we all *like* Sara. *We're* not jealous of her.

CHILDREN. [*Exclamations of assent; playing "London Bridge."*

LAVINIA. Oh, of course you like Sara, just because she's the rich girl of the school and the show pupil. There's nothing so very grand in having a father who lives in India, even if he *is* in the army.
[*Jessie plays.*

LOTTIE. At any rate he's killed *tigers*, and he sends Sara the most beautiful presents! [*Pulls Lavinia's hair.*

LILLY. And he's told Miss Minchin that she can have *anything* she wants.

ERMENGARDE. She's cleverer than any of us. My father says he'd give thousands of pounds if I were as clever as she is. She actually *likes* to read books. I can't bear them.

THE LITTLE PRINCESS

LAVINIA *(contemptuously)*.   We all know that.

ERMENGARDE.   Well, if I am the stupidest girl in the school, Sara's the
nicest. You don't see Sara walking with her friends and saying
spiteful things.
[*Bell rings off. Children run into straight lines. Ermengarde to
blackboard and draws a cat. Lavinia up stage.*

CHILDREN.   Miss Minchin's coming, Miss Minchin's coming!

LAVINIA.   Yes, and leading Sara by the hand as if she were a "Little
Princess."

ERMENGARDE *(pointing to board)*. That old cat, Miss Minchin [*Children
laugh. Enter Miss Minchin, leading Sara, followed by James, William, Emma, and Becky. Servants carry presents.*

MISS MINCHIN *(sweeping grandly down)*. Silence, young ladies . . .
James, place the box *(doll)* on the table and remove the lid. Wil-
liam, place yours there. *(Trunk)* Emma, put yours on the table.
(Nine books) Becky, put yours on the floor. *(Becky looks at the
Children)* Becky, it is not your place to look at the young ladies.
You forget yourself. *(Waving servants off)* Now you may leave us.
[*Exeunt servants. Becky starts to follow them. Sara stops her.*

SARA.   Ah, please, Miss Minchin, mayn't Becky stay?

MISS MINCHIN.   Becky — my dearest Sara —

SARA.   I want her because I'm sure she would so like to see the doll.
She's a little girl, you know.

MISS MINCHIN *(amazed)*.   My dear Sara — Becky is the scullery-maid.
Scullery-maids are not little girls — at least they ought not to be.

SARA.   But Becky *is*, you know.

MISS MINCHIN.   I'm sorry to hear it.

SARA.   But I don't believe she can help it. And I know she would enjoy herself so. *(Crosses to Miss Minchin)* Please let her stay — because it's my birthday. [*Becky backs into the corner in mingled
terror and delight.*

MISS MINCHIN *(dignified)*. Well, as you ask it as a birthday favour —
she may stay.

SARA.   Thank you.

MISS MINCHIN.   Rebecca, thank Miss Sara for her great kindness.

BECKY *(comes forward, making little charity curtseys, words tumbling
over each other)*. Oh, if you please, Miss — thank you, Miss. I

am that grateful, Miss. I did want to see the doll, Miss — that — that bad. I thank you, Miss. *(Sara nods happily to Becky, who bobs to Miss Minchin)* And thank you, Ma'am, for letting me take the liberty.

MISS MINCHIN. Go stand over there. *(Pointing grandly to corner)* Not too near the young ladies. *(Becky backs into corner, rolls down sleeves, etc.)* Now, young ladies, I have a few words to say to you. *(Sweeping grandly up to platform)* You are aware, young ladies, that dear Sara is thirteen years old to-day.

CHILDREN. Yes, Miss Minchin.

MISS MINCHIN. There are a few of you here who have also been thirteen years old, but Sara's birthdays are different from most little girls' birthdays.

CHILDREN. Yes, Miss Minchin.

MISS MINCHIN. When she is older she will be heiress to a large fortune which it will be her duty to spend in a meritorious manner.

ERMENGARDE. No, Miss Minchin — I mean yes, Miss Minchin.

MISS MINCHIN. When her papa, Captain Crewe, brought her from India and gave her into my care, he said to me, in a jesting manner, "I'm afraid she will be very rich, Miss Minchin."

CHILDREN. Oh! — Ah! — Oh!

MISS MINCHIN. My reply was, "Her education at my seminary, Captain Crewe, shall be such as will fit her to adorn the largest fortune." *(Lottie sniffs loudly)* Lottie, do not sniff. Use your pockethandkerchief. *(Ermengarde wipes Lottie's nose. Lottie sniffs again. Miss Minchin coughs Lottie down)* Sara has become my most accomplished pupil. Her French and her dancing are a credit to the seminary. Her manners — which have caused you all to call her Princess Sara — are perfect. Her amiability she exhibits by giving you this party. I hope you appreciate her generosity. I wish you to express your appreciation by saying aloud, all together, "Thank you, Sara."

ALL. Thank you, Sara.

ERMENGARDE *(alone)*. Thank you, Sara.

BECKY. I thank you, Miss.

SARA. I thank *you* for coming to my party. And you [*Retires.*

MISS MINCHIN. Very pretty indeed, Sara. That is what a real princess does when the populace applauds. I have one thing more to say.

The visitors coming are the father and mother of a large family. I wish you to conduct yourselves in such a manner as will cause them to observe that elegance of deportment can be acquired at Miss Minchin's seminary. *(Ermengarde poses in corner)* I will now go back to the drawing-room until they arrive. Sara, you may show your presents. [*Exits. Ermengarde imitates her walk.*

ERMENGARDE. Sara, you may show your presents!

AMELIA *(coming out from behind)*. Ermengarde ——

ERMENGARDE. Oh! Miss —— *(Amelia crosses to door)* Amelia, please forgive me — I did — didn't ——

[*Exit Amelia. Children laugh and flock around the boxes on table, etc.*

SARA *(getting chair from piano)*. She caught you that time, Ermy. *(Getting on chair behind table)* Which shall we look at first? *(Picking up books)* These are books, I know. [*Trying to untie them.*

CHILDREN. Oh — books ——Oh! [*Disgusted.*

ERMENGARDE. *(aghast)*. Does your papa send you *books* for a birthday present? He's as bad as mine. Don't open them, Sara.

SARA *(laughing)*. But I like them the best — never mind though. This is the doll. *(Uncovering long wooden box)* I'll open that first. [*Stands doll upon its feet. Doll is on a metal stand.*

CHILDREN. Oh! — Ah! — Oh!

LILLY. Isn't she a beauty? [*Becky gets stool from above door and stands on it to see doll.*

JESSIE. She's almost as big as Lottie.

LOTTIE *(dancing down)*. Tra-la-la.

LILLY. She's dressed for the theater. See her magnificent opera-cloak. [*Lavinia does not get on floor.*

ERMENGARDE. She has an opera-glass in her hand.

SARA. So she has. *(Getting down)* Here's her trunk. Let us open that and looks at her things; Ermy, you open the other. *(Takes trunk with Jessie down stage; opens it. Ermy takes other one with help of Jessie and opens it too. Children crowd around trunks, sit on floor, looking at the clothes. Becky looks on from behind)* Here is the key.

CHILDREN. Oh!

SARA.   This is full of lace collars and silk stockings and handkerchiefs. Here's a jewel-case with a necklace and a tiara of diamonds. Put them on her, Lilly. All of her underclothes. Ah, look. [*Showing.*

ERMENGARDE.   Here's a velvet coat trimmed with chinchilla, and one lined with ermine, and muffs. Oh, what darling dresses! A pale cloth, trimmed with sable, and a long coat. *(Lottie takes coat and puts it on)* A pink, covered with white little buttons, and a white tulle dress, and dresses, dresses, dresses!

SARA.   And here are hats, and hats, and hats. Becky, can you see? [*Rises.*

BECKY.   Oh, yes, Miss, and it's like 'eaven. [*Falls off stool backwards.*

SARA *(rises)*.   She is a lovely doll. *(Looking at doll)* Suppose she understands human talk, and feels proud of being admired.

LAVINIA.   You are always *supposing* things, Sara.

SARA.   I know I am — I like it. There's nothing so nice as supposing. It's almost like being a fairy. If you suppose anything hard enough, it seems as if it were real. Have you never done it?

LAVINIA *(contemptuously)*.   No — of course not — it's ridiculous.

SARA.   Is it? Well, it makes you happy at any rate. *(Lavinia turns away; changing her tone)* Suppose we finish looking at the doll's things when we have more time. Becky will put them back in the trunk. [*Lottie goes up to doll, to see tiara.*

BECKY *(comes forward quickly — shyly)*.   Me, Miss? Yes, Miss. Thank you, Miss, for letting me touch them. *(Down on knees, wiping hands)* Oh — my — they are beautiful.

LAVINIA *(at table, catching Lottie touching doll)*   Get down this minute. That's not for babies to touch. [*Takes her.*

LOTTIE *(crying)*.   I'm not a baby — I'm not — Sar-a, Sar-a — oh!

JESSIE.   There now, you've made her cry — the spoiled thing.

SARA *(runs to Lottie; kneeling)*.   Now, Lottie. *(Puts her on side)* Lottie, dear, you mustn't cry.

LOTTIE *(howling)*.   I don't want to stay in a nasty school with nasty girls.

SARA *(to Lavinia and Jessie)*.   You ought not to have scolded her. She's such a little thing. And you know she's only at boarding-school because she hasn't any mother. [*Children sympathetically. Jessie to door.*

LOTTIE *(wailing)*.   I haven't any mamma.

JESSIE.   If she doesn't stop, Miss Minchin will hear her. [*Ermengarde gets tiara from doll.*

LILLY.   And she'll be so cross that she may stop the party. Do stop, Lottie darling. I'll give you a penny.

LOTTIE.   Don't want your old penny.

ERMENGARDE.   Yes, do stop, and I'll give you anything. [*Offering box.*

LOTTIE.   She called me a baby. [*Crying.*

SARA *(petting her).*   But you will be a baby if you cry, Lottie, pet. There, there.

LOTTIE.   I haven't any mamma.

SARA *(cheerfully).*   Yes, you have, darling. Don't you know we said Sara'd be your mamma. Don't you want Sara to be your mamma? *(Lottie stops crying)* See. *(Rising and giving doll to Lottie)* I'll lend you my doll to hold while I tell you that story I promised you.

LILLY.   Oh, do tell us a story, Sara. [*Puts doll on chair.*

JESSIE.   Oh, yes, do.

CHILDREN.   Oh!

SARA.   I may not have time to finish it before the company comes — but I'll tell you the end some other time. [*Lottie takes doll to chair.*

LAVINIA.   That's always the way, Princess Sara. *(Passionately)* Nasty little spoilt beast. I should like to *slap* her.

SARA *(firing up).*   I should like to slap you too. But I don't want to slap you — at least I both *want* to slap you and should *like* to slap you.

CHILDREN *(in group, interested in fight).*   Oh, Oh!

SARA.   We are not little gutter children. We are old enough to know better.

LAVINIA.   Oh, we are *princesses*, I believe — or at least one of us is — Jessie told me you often pretended to yourself that you were a princess.

SARA *(getting control of herself).*   It's true. Sometimes I do pretend I'm a princess. I pretend I am a princess so that I can try to behave like one.

CHILDREN.   Ah!

ERMENGARDE.   You *are* queer, Sara, but you're nice. [*Hugs her.*

73

SARA. I know I'm queer, and I try to be nice. Shall I begin the story?

CHILDREN (ad lib.). Story. Oh, oh! Yes, yes, begin, Sara, do.

SARA. I'm going to turn all the lights out. It's always so much nicer to tell a story by firelight.
[*Turns out brackets with switch above fireplace; gets on sofa for story. All the children sit, except Lavinia, who stands near the piano. Children on the floor in front of the sofa. Ermengarde goes up to the window and pulls curtains apart and makes up in them for ghost.*

LILLY. It's such fun to sit in the dark.

SARA. Once upon a time ——

ERMENGARDE (*from behind curtain*). Woo-o-oo ——

JESSIE. What's that?

SARA. It's nothing but the wind. Once upon a time ——

ERMENGARDE (*coming down in curtains*). Whoo-oo-oo-oopee ———
[*Frightens Children. Sara turns on lights. Children scream and get up; fall on Ermengarde and take curtain off her. Laugh.*

CHILDREN. Oh, it's Ermengarde.

LILLY. Begin again, Sara. [*Sara turns out lights.*

ALL. Yes.

SARA (*all seated as before, — Sara on sofa*). Once upon a time —long ago — there lived on the edge of a deep, deep forest a little girl and her grandmother.

LILLY. Was she pretty?

SARA. She was so fair and sweet that people called her Snowflower. She had no relations in the world but her old grandmother, Dame Frostyface.

JESSIE. Was she a nice old woman?

SARA. She was always nice to Snowflower. They lived together in a little cottage thatched with reeds. Tall trees sheltered it, daisies grew thick about the door, and swallows built in the eaves.

CHILDREN. Oh, Lottie!

LILLY. What a nice place!

SARA. One sunny morning Dame Frostyface said, "My child, I am going on a long journey, and I cannot take you with me, and I will tell you what to do when you feel lonely. You know that carved oak chair I sit in by the fire. Well, lay your head on the velvet cushions and say, 'Chair of my grandmother, tell me a story,' and it will tell you one."

CHILDREN. Oh!

SARA. "And if you want to travel anywhere, just seat yourself in it, and say, 'Chair of my grandmother, take me where I want to go.' "

ERMENGARDE. Oh, I wish I had a chair like that.

LOTTIE. Oh, go on, Sara.

CHILDREN. Do go on.

ERMENGARDE. And so ——

LOTTIE. And so ——

SARA. And so Dame Frostyface went away. And every day Snowflower baked herself a barleycake, *and every night the chair told her a beautiful new story.*

ERMENGARDE. If it had been my chair, I should have told it to take me to the King's Palace.

SARA. That is what happened — but listen. The time passed on, but Dame Frostyface did not come back for such a long time that Snowflower thought she would go and find her.

LOTTIE. Did she find her?

SARA. Wait and listen. One day she jumped into the chair and said, "Chair of my grandmother, take me the way she went." And the chair gave a creak and began to move out of the cottage and into the forest where all the birds were singing.

ERMENGARDE. How I *wish* I could have gone with her.

SARA. And the chair went on, and on, and on — like a coach and six.

LOTTIE. How far did it go?

SARA. It traveled through the forest and through the ferns, and over the velvet moss — it traveled one day, and two days, and three days — and on the fourth day ——

LILLY. What did it do?

SARA. (slowly). It came to an open place in the forest where a hundred workmen were felling trees and a hundred wagons were carrying them away to the King's Palace.

ERMENGARDE. Was the King giving a ball?

SARA. He was giving seven of them. Seven days' feasting to celebrate the birthday of his daughter, the Princess Greedalend.

LOTTIE. Did he invite Snowflower?

SARA. Listen. The chair marched up to the palace, and all the people ran after it. And the King heard of it, and the lords and ladies crowded to see it, and when the Princess heard it was a chair that could tell stories she cried until the King sent an order to the little girl to come and make it tell her one.

LOTTIE. Did she go in?

LILLY. Oh, how lovely.

SARA. The chair marched in a grave and courtly manner up the grand staircase and into the palace hall. The King sat on an ivory throne in a robe of purple velvet, stiff with flowers of gold. The Queen sat on his right hand in a mantle clasped with pearls, and the Princess wore a robe of gold sewn with diamonds.

LILLY. Oh, what splendid clothes!

SARA. But Snowflower had little bare feet, and nothing but a clean, coarse linen dress. She got off the chair and made a curtsey to the grand company. Then she laid her head on the cushion, and said, "Chair of my grandmother, tell me a story," and a clear, silvery voice came out from the old velvet cushion, and said, "Listen to the story of the Christmas Cuckoo." [*Door-bell peals.*

ALL (*jumping up from floor and sofa, forming two lines, in readiness for the visitors*). Miss Minchin is coming — Miss Minchin is coming.
[*Enter Miss Minchin, followed by Amelia. Becky under table.*

MISS MINCHIN. What are you naughty children doing in the dark? Amelia, turn up the lights immediately. (*She does so with switch above fireplace*) How dare you?

SARA. I beg pardon, Miss Minchin. It was all my fault. I was telling them a story, and I like to tell them in the firelight.

MISS MINCHIN (*changing*). Oh, it was you, Sara. That is a different matter. I can always trust you.

LAVINIA (*aside*). Yes, of course, if it's the Princess Sara, it's a different matter.

MISS MINCHIN (*speaking off to Mrs. Carmichael*). Won't you come in, Mrs. Carmichael?
[*Enter Mrs. Carmichael, followed by Donald, Mazie, Nora, and Janet in a line. Donald has mother's skirt in his hand, playing*

*horse; three children are dressed for the street. They follow their
mother to a sofa and sit down.*

MISS MINCHIN.   She is *(referring to Sara)* such a clever child. Such an
imagination. She amuses the children by the hour with her wonderful story-telling.

MRS. CARMICHAEL.   She has a clever little face. [*Ermengarde offers to
make friends with Donald, who fights her into her corner.*

MISS MINCHIN.   Won't you sit here, Mrs. Carmichael? [*Indicating
sofa.*

MRS. CARMICHAEL.   I hope I won't disturb the dancing if I am obliged
to leave you suddenly.

MISS MINCHIN.   You will not disturb us, although we shall, of course,
be very sorry.

MRS. CARMICHAEL.   Mr. Carmichael has just had bad news from an
important client in India. The poor man has suddenly lost all his
money and is on his way to England, very ill indeed.

MISS MINCHIN.   How distressing!

MRS. CARMICHAEL.   Mr. Carmichael may be called away at any
moment. He said he would send a servant for me if he received a
summons to go. If it comes I shall be obliged to run away at once.
The children wanted so much to see the dancing that I did not like
to disappoint them.

MISS MINCHIN.   Sara, my dear, come here. *(Aside to Mrs. Carmichael)* Her mother died when she was born. Her father is a most
distinguished young officer — very rich, fortunately. *(To Sara)*
Shake hands with Mrs. Carmichael. *(Sara does so. To Mrs. Carmichael)* Sara is thirteen years old to-day, Mrs. Carmichael, and is
giving a party to her schoolfellows. She is always doing things to
give her friends pleasure.

MRS. CARMICHAEL *(motherly woman, pats Sara's hand).*   She looks like
a kind little girl. *(Lottie brings doll over to sofa and shows it to
the Carmichael children)* I'm sure my children would like to hear
her tell stories. They love stories, and some day you must come
and tell them one. *(Turns and sees doll)* Oh, what a splendid doll!
Is it yours?

MISS MINCHIN *(grandly).*   Her papa ordered it in Paris. Its wardrobe was made by a fashionable dressmaker. Nothing is too superb
for the child.

LOTTIE *(to Sara).*   Sara, may that little boy hold your doll?

SARA. Yes, dear. [*Lottie takes doll to Donald, who boxes it away from him, boy fashion.*

LOTTIE (*taking doll out of harm's way*). He's one of the large family across the street — the ones you make up stories about.

MRS. CARMICHAEL (*good-naturedly*). Do you make up stories about *us*?

SARA. I hope you won't mind. I can see your house out of my window, and there are so many of you, and you all look so happy together, that I like to pretend I know you all. I *suppose* things about you.

LILLY (*the Children have been standing in two lines listening to all this*). She has made up names for all of you.

MRS. CARMICHAEL. Has she? What are they?

SARA. They are only pretended names — perhaps you'll think they're silly.

MRS. CARMICHAEL. No, I shall not. What do you call us?

LOTTIE (*solemnly*). You are Mrs. and Mister Mont-mor-ency.

MRS. CARMICHAEL. (*laughing*). What a grand name! And what do you call the children?

SARA (*shyly but smiling*). The little boy in the lace cap is Ethelbert Beaucham Montmorency — and the *second* baby is Violette Cholmondeley Montmorency, and the little boy with the fat brown legs and socks is Sidney Cecil Vivienne Montmorency.

LOTTIE (*interrupting and dancing*). Then there's Lillian Evangeline — and Guy Clarence — and Maude — Marion — and Veronia Eustacia — and Claude Audrey Harold Hector. [*Laughs and goes into corner.*

MRS. CARMICHAEL. You romantic little thing!

SARA (*apologetically*). I shouldn't have *supposed* so much about you if you hadn't all looked so happy together. *My* papa is a soldier in India, you know, and my mamma died when I was a baby. So I like to look at children who have mammas and papas.

MRS. CARMICHAEL (*kissing Sara*). You poor little dear, — Miss Minchin *must* let you come and have tea with us.

MISS MINCHIN. Certainly, certainly. Sara will be delighted. Now, young ladies, you may begin the entertainment Sara has prepared for Mrs. Carmichael.
[*Enter Maid.*

MAID. A gentleman would like to see you, Ma'm. He says he comes from Messrs. Barrow & Skipworth.

MISS MINCHIN. The lawyers? *(Annoyed)* What can he want? I cannot be disturbed at present. Ask him to wait.

MAID. And if you please, Ma'm, a note for Mrs. Carmichael. [*Delivers same to Mrs. Carmichael, who rises to receive it, and goes down stage. Exit Maid.*

MRS. CARMICHAEL. A note for me? [*Takes it. Opens note.*

MISS MINCHIN. Not bad news, I hope?

MRS. CARMICHAEL. Very bad, I am afraid. My husband's client, poor Mr. Carrisford, has just landed, dangerously ill. Much worse. Mr. Carmichael wants me to go and see him at once. I am sorry to run away like this. It has all been charming. Thank you for asking us. Come, children. Say good afternoon. Papa needs us. *(Shaking hands with Miss Minchin)* Your school is delightful.
[*Exit Mrs. Carmichael and Children in same order as entrance, Donald driving his mother as before.*

DONALD. Geddap — whoa — go along.

ALL. Good-bye. Good afternoon, etc.

MISS AMELIA. What a pity she was obliged to leave so soon.

MISS MINCHIN. She was evidently very much pleased.

MAID *(entering)*. Will you see the gentleman from Messrs. Barrow & Skipworth, Ma'am?

MISS AMELIA *(meekly)*. The children's refreshments are laid in your parlour, sister. Could you see him in here while the children have their cake and sherry and negus?

MISS MINCHIN. Yes. *(To Children)* Now, young ladies, you must go and enjoy the nice things Sara has provided for you. [*Children all troop out.*

CHILDREN. Cake and sherry and negus.

MISS MINCHIN *(to servant)*. Bring the gentleman in here.
[*Exit Servant. Enter Barrow, ushered on by Servant. Barrow is a middle-aged, high-class lawyer, well dressed.*

MAID. Mr. Barrow, Ma'am. [*Exit Maid.*

MISS MINCHIN. Good evening, sir. Be seated. *(Indicating sofa)* Of the legal firm of Barrow & Skipworth, I believe?

BARROW.   Yes, Barrow, representing the late Captain Crewe, of the
——

MISS MINCHIN *(startled)*.   The late Captain Crewe? You don't mean
to say that Captain Crewe is ——

BARROW *(sits on sofa)*.   Dead, Madam, dead of jungle fever.

MISS MINCHIN *(shocked)*.   It seems impossible. How shocking! How
sudden!

BARROW.   It was sudden. The firm thought that you should be told
at once, as his child is in your care.

MISS MINCHIN.   Very right and proper. Poor Captain Crewe! Poor
little orphaned Sara. *(Handkerchief to her eyes)* She will need
my care more than ever.

BARROW.   She will indeed, Madam.

MISS MINCHIN.   What do you mean?

BARROW.   That, as she has apparently no relations to take charge of
her, she is fortunate in having such a friend as yourself.

MISS MINCHIN.   Most certainly. An heiress to so large a fortune — for
I believe it is a very large fortune? *(Barrow clears throat signifi-
cantly. Miss Minchin takes him up sharply)* What do you mean?
You certainly mean something. What is it?

BARROW.   She has *no* fortune, Madam, large or small. She is left without a penny.

MISS MINCHIN.   Without a penny! It's impossible. Captain Crewe was
a rich man.

BARROW.   Ah! *Was*, — that's it, Madam, he *was*.

MISS MINCHIN *(leaning forward excitedly)*.   You don't mean he has
lost his money? Lost it?

BARROW.   Every penny of it. That young man had too much money.
He didn't know what to do with it, so he let a speculating friend —
a very dear friend — *(sarcastically)* play ducks and drakes with it.
The friend was mad on the subject of a high diamond mine — put
all his own money into it —all of Captain Crewe's — the mine
proved a failure — the dear friend — the very dear friend — ran
away. Captain Crewe was already stricken with fever when the
news came — the shock was too much for him. He died delirious.
(Rises) Ruined.

MISS MINCHIN.   Do you mean to tell me that he has left *nothing?* that
Sara will have no fortune — that the child is a *beggar* — that she's

left on my hands a little pauper instead of an heiress?

BARROW. She is certainly left a beggar — and she is certainly left on your hands, Ma'am.

MISS MINCHIN *(rising)*. It's monstrous. She's in my drawing-room, at this moment, dressed in a pink silk gown and lace petticoats, giving a party at my expense.

BARROW. She's certainly giving it at your expense, Ma'am, if she's giving it. Barrow & Skipworth are not responsible for anything. Captain Crewe died without paying our last bill, and it was a considerable one.

MISS MINCHIN. That is what happened to me. I was always so sure of his payments that I have been to all sorts of expenses since his last check came. I actually paid the bill for that ridiculous doll and all its ridiculous fantastic wardrobe. The child was to have *anything* she wanted. She has a carriage and a pony and a maid, and I've paid for all of them.

BARROW. You hadn't better pay for anything more unless you want to make presents to the young lady. She has *not a brass farthing to call her own.*

MISS MINCHIN. But what am I to do?

BARROW. There isn't anything to do, Ma'am. Captain Crewe is dead. The child is left a pauper. Nobody is responsible for her but you.

MISS MINCHIN. I'm not responsible for her. I refuse to be made responsible for her.

BARROW. I have nothing to do with that, Ma'am. I only know that Barrow & Skipworth are not responsible. [*Bows and turns to go.*

MISS MINCHIN. But you cannot go like that and leave her on my hands, — I won't have it. I have been cheated; I have been swindled; I'll turn her out into the streets.

BARROW. *(impersonally)*. I wouldn't, Madam, if I were you; you can if you like, but I wouldn't. Bad for the school — ugly story to get about. Pay you better to keep her as a sort of charity pupil.

MISS MINCHIN. This is infamous. I'll do nothing of the sort.

BARROW. She might teach the little ones, run errands, and that sort of thing.

MISS MINCHIN. Ah, you want to foist her off on me. I won't have her foisted off on me.

BARROW. Just as you please, Madam. The matter is entirely in your hands. Good evening. Very sorry the thing has happened, of course. Unpleasant for all parties. Good evening.
[*Exit. Children off stage singing.*

CHILDREN (*singing*). "Here we go round the mulberry bush, the mulberry bush, the mulberry bush, — here we go round the mulberry bush, so early in the morning." [*Miss Minchin stands a moment glaring after Barrow. Then she starts toward door. Stops as Amelia enters.*

AMELIA. What's the matter, sister?

MISS MINCHIN (*fiercely and hoarsely*). Where is Sara Crewe?

AMELIA (*astonished*). Sara? Why, she's with the children in your room.

MISS MINCHIN. Has she a black frock in her sumptuous wardrobe?

AMELIA (*stammering*). Why — what — she has only an old black velvet one that is much too small for her — it is too short for her to wear.

MISS MINCHIN. Go tell her to take off that preposterous pink silk gown, and put the black one on, whether it is too short or not. She is done with finery.

AMELIA. Sister, what can have happened?

MISS MINCHIN. Captain Crewe is dead.

AMELIA. Oh!

MISS MINCHIN. He died without a penny.

AMELIA. Oh!

MISS MINCHIN. That spoilt, pampered, fanciful child is left a pauper on my hands.

AMELIA. Oh! Oh!

MISS MINCHIN. Hundreds of pounds have I spent on nonsense for her — hundreds of pounds — I shall never see a penny of it.

CHILDREN (*outside*). Ha, ha, ha! [*Applause.*

MISS MINCHIN. Go, put a stop to that ridiculous party of hers. Go and make her change her frock.

AMELIA (*gapes and stares*). M-must I go and tell her now?

MISS MINCHIN (*fiercely*). This moment. Don't stand there staring like a goose. Go.
[*Exit Amelia.*

CHILDREN *(singing)*. "Here we go round the mulberry bush."

MISS MINCHIN.   Hundreds of pounds! I never hesitated at the cost of anything. Princess Sara, indeed! The child has been pampered as if she had been a queen. *(Loud sniffles from Becky under table)* What's that?

BECKY *(coming from under table)*. If you please, Ma'am. *(Sobs)* It's me, Ma'am. I hadn't ought to, but I hid under the table when you came in, and I heard.

MISS MINCHIN.   You impudent child!

BECKY *(sobs frequently)*. Oh, please 'm, I daresay you'll give we warnin', but I'm sorry for poor Miss Sara — she is such a kind young lady, Ma'am.

MISS MINCHIN.   Leave the room.

BECKY.   Yes, 'm, I will, 'm, but I just wanted to arst you — Miss Sara's been such a rich young lady — 'm — she's been waited on and — poor — and what'll she do, Ma'am, without no maid? If — if — oh, please, would you let me wait on her after I'm done my pots and kettles? I'd do them so quick — if you'd let me wait on her — now she's so poor — or — poor little Miss Sara — Ma'am — that was called a princess.

MISS MINCHIN.   No, certainly not. She'll wait on herself and on other people too. *(Stamping foot)* Leave the room this instant — or you — leave this place.

BECKY *(at door, turns)*. Wouldn't you?

MISS MINCHIN *(in pantomime, says "Go." Exit Becky. Fiercely)*. Wait on her! No, she will not be waited on. *(Enter Sara, with doll in arms, in black dress)* Come here. *(Sara advances a little)* Put down that doll. You will have no time for dolls in the future.

SARA.   She was the last thing my papa gave me before he died.

MISS MINCHIN.   He did not pay for her, at any rate. I paid for her.

SARA *(crossing to chair and putting doll on it)*. Then she is your doll, not mine.

MISS MINCHIN.   Of course she is my doll. *(Crossing to table)* Everything that you have is mine. For a whole year I've been spending money on all sorts of ridiculously extravagant things for you, and I shall never be paid for one of them. I've been robbed, robbed, robbed!

SARA *(turning from doll, suddenly and strongly)*.   My papa did not mean to rob you — he did not — he did not!

MISS MINCHIN. Whether he meant to do it or not, he did it — and here I am left with you on my hands. Do you understand?

SARA. Yes, I understand, — Miss Amelia told me. *(Kneels, covering face with arms, in doll's lap, and bursting into tears)* My papa is dead — my papa is dead!

MISS MINCHIN. Stop crying. I sent for you to talk to you, and I have no time to waste. (Sara sobs) Stop crying, do you hear? *(Pause until Sara rises and faces Miss Minchin)* You are not a princess any longer. Remember that. You have no friends. You have no money. You have no one to take care of you. Your pony and carriage will be sold at once. Your maid will be sent away. You'll wear your plainest and oldest frocks. Your extravagant ones are no longer suited for your station. You're like Becky — you will have to work for your living.

SARA. If you tell me what to do, I'll do it.

MISS MINCHIN. You will be obliged to do it whether you like it or not. If I do not choose to keep you out of charity, you have no home but the street.

SARA *(sobbing)*. I know that.

MISS MINCHIN. Then listen to what I say. If you work hard, and try to make yourself useful, I may let you stay here. You are a sharp child, and pick up things readily. You speak French very well, and you can help with the younger children.

SARA. Yes, I can help with the little ones. I like them and they like me.

MISS MINCHIN. Don't talk nonsense about people liking you. You will have more to do than to teach the little ones. You will run errands and help in the kitchen as well as in the schoolroom. If you don't please me you will be sent away. Now go. *(Sara crosses to door to go)* Stop, don't you intend to thank me?

SARA. What for?

MISS MINCHIN. For my kindness to you — for my kindness in giving you a home.

SARA *(wildly)*. You're *not* kind, you are *not* kind!

MISS MINCHIN. Leave the room instantly. *(Sara starts to go)* Stop. *(Sara stops)* You are not to go to the bedroom you used to sleep in.

SARA. Where must I go?

Miss Minchin.   In future you will occupy the garret next to Becky's — under the roof.

Sara.   The garret, next to Becky's, where the rats are?

Miss Minchin.   Rubbish! There are no rats there. [*Crossing to door.*

Sara (*following to chair*).   There are. Oh, Miss Minchin, there are! Sometimes Becky can hardly sleep at all. She says that in the garret next to hers they run about all night.

Miss Minchin.   Whether there are rats or not, you will sleep there. Leave the room.
[*Exit Miss Minchin. Door opens.*

Lottie (*outside*).   Sara. (*Enters*) Sara! (*Embraces Sara who is on her knees*) The big girls say your papa is dead, like my mamma; they say you haven't any papa. Haven't you any papa?

Sara.   No, I haven't, Lottie; no, I haven't.

Lottie.   You said you'd be my mamma. I'll be your papa, Sara. Let Lottie be your papa.

Sara.   Oh, Lottie, love me; please, Lottie, love me — love me ——

CURTAIN

———

ACT II

Scene.   *A garret under the roof at Miss Minchin's; rake roof with garret window, outside of which are showing housetops with snow on them. There are rat holes around. A bed, covered with old blanket, sheet, and old coverlet, badly torn. A table with bench behind it. Chairs, an armchair, and a four-legged stool above fireplace. A washstand with pitcher, bowl, soap-dish, and mug. An old trunk. A candle in stick unlighted.*

At the rise of curtain: Wind off stage; window opens and snow flutters through. Stage in semi-darkness. Broken pane in window.

Ram Dass appears on platform back of window, with dark lantern. He raises window, examines room from platform with light, then beckons Guest to follow him. Enter Guest on platform, also carrying lantern.

GUEST *(kneeling beside Ram Dass).*   You saw the child go out?

RAM DASS.   Yes, Sahib. *(Guest lets himself down by table through window)* She has been sent out upon an errand.

GUEST.   And no one ever enters here, but herself? You are sure?

RAM DASS.   Sure, Sahib.

GUEST.   Then we are safe for a few moments. We must look about and plan quickly. You have sharp ears; stand near the door. If you hear a sound on the stairs, we must bolt through the window.

RAM DASS *(going to door).*   Yes, Sahib. [*Stands listening.*

GUEST.   What a place to keep a child in! *(Going to fire)* No fire — no sign of one. *(Crosses to bed)* Blanket thin, sheet miserable. We must alter this.

RAM DASS *(at door).*   When first my master thought of this plan, it made him smile, and he has not smiled for many days. He said: "The poor child will think a magician has worked a spell."

GUEST *(back of table, making notes).*   She will indeed. It's a curious plan, but the Sahib is a sick man and lonely. Now listen, Ram Dass. You lascars can be as silent as ghosts. Can you, with the other three to help you, steal in through that window, and do what your master wishes, and make no sound?

RAM DASS.   Yes, Sahib, Ram Dass can do it. He knows well how to make no sound at all.

GUEST.   Will it be safer to do it while she is out upon some errand, or at night when she is asleep?

RAM DASS.   At night when she sleeps. Children sleep soundly, even the unhappy ones.

GUEST.   As Mr. Carrisford's house is next door, you and I can bring the things across the roof together. Yes, yes, the window is wide enough to allow them to pass through.

RAM DASS.   Shall it be done tonight?

GUEST.   Yes. Everything is ready, — the measurements are correct. What's that?

RAM DASS *(at door).*   On the staircase two flights below. It is the child herself returning.

GUEST.   Here — through here, quickly.
[*Exit through window.*

RAM DASS *(in window).*   Yes, Ram Dass will do this thing tonight.

[*Exit. Enter Sara, shabbily dressed, wet, and tired; she closes door and stands a second leaning against it; looks about the room, out of breath and exhausted with climbing up stairs.*

SARA. I thought I should never get back, never, never. (*To table. Lights candle*) How miserable it looks and how tired I am. (*Takes hat and shawl and puts them on chair*) They are wet as though they'd fallen in a pond. (*Coming down to armchair; sits in same*) I've been sent out on errands ten times since breakfast. I'm cold — I'm wet — I'm as hungry as a wolf. (*Wind. Rats squeak. Sara has dropped head in lap on square stool. Hears rats, looks up. Wind howls during this pause*) What a noise my rats are making; they must have heard me come in. (*1st rat runs on*) Oh, there's Melchisedek. Poor thing, he's come to ask for crumbs. (*Puts hand into pocket to hunt for crumbs and turns it out*) Are you hungry too, poor Melchisedek. I'm sorry, I haven't one crumb left. Go home, Melchisedek, and tell your wife that there was nothing in my pocket. She's not as hungry as I am. (*1st rat off under bed*) Good night. Poor thing. (*Crosses back to armchair, drops into chair, and takes Emily in her arms*) Do you hear, Emily, why don't you say something? Sometimes I'm sure you could, if you tried. You are the only relation I have in the world. Why don't you try? Do you hear? I've walked a thousand miles to-day, — errands and errands, and errands and errands. Errands for the cook, errands for Miss Amelia — and for Miss Minchin — and even for the girls — I had to go for pencils for Lavinia. (*Outburst*) Everybody sends me errands. And because I came in late they wouldn't give me any supper. I'm so hungry I could almost eat you. (*Wind, Passionately*) Do you hear? (*Pause, and breaks out again*) You are nothing but a doll, doll, doll — you are stuffed with sawdust — you never had a heart. (*Throws Emily on stool and cries. Picks her up; sets her in chair, sits on stool, elbows on knees, and gazes at her relentingly*) You can't help being a doll, I suppose, any more than good-natured Ermengarde can help being stupid. I oughtn't have slapped you. You were *born* a doll — perhaps you do your sawdust best. (*Knock on door*) I wonder who it is. (*Rises hesitating*) Lottie is in bed and poor Becky was crying when I came through the kitchen. The cook was in a passion and she couldn't get away. (*Opens door, sees Lottie alarmed, surprised. Enter Lottie in nightgown, hugging a birthday doll. Wind*) Oh, Lottie, you oughtn't to come here so late. Miss Minchin would be so cross if she caught you. What do you want, darling?

LOTTIE (*who has run to Sara and is clinging to her*). I want you, mamma, Sara. Oh, I had such an ugly dream, and I got frightened ——

SARA (*leads her to armchair, and takes her up in lap*). I'll hug you a minute, Lottie, but you mustn't stay, — it's too cold.

87

LOTTIE.   Hug me and kiss me like a real mamma — Sara, it was such an ugly dream ——

SARA *(hugs her).*   Are you better now darling?

LOTTIE.   Yes. You are such a comfty hugger, Sara — *(Sits up cheerfully, and sees doll on ottoman)* There's Emily. She's not so pretty as Arabella, is she?

SARA.   No, but she's the only relation I've got in the world. My papa gave her to me when he brought me to Miss Minchin's, six years ago.

LOTTIE *(putting her doll beside Emily).* There, Emily, Lady Arabella has come to see you. *(To Sara)* Have you seen your rat lately, mamma Sara?

SARA.   Yes — poor Melchisedek — he came out to-night to beg for crumbs, and I hadn't any for him. But there, Lottie dear, you must not stay in the cold. *(Coaxing her)* You won't have any more ugly dreams — for Sara will keep thinking good dreams for you after you've gone back to bye-lows, — you must run back now, like a sweet Lottie ——

LOTTIE.   Oh, but Sara, I like to stay with you. I like your old garret and Emily and the rat. [*Wind and snow.*

SARA.   But listen to the wind. See the snow coming through the broken window. You mustn't stay here in your little nightie. I'll take you to the top of the stairs and you must go back to bed.

LOTTIE.   But mayn't I say my seven times to you before I go? I have to say it to Miss Amelia in the morning. May I sit here on your bed — *(does so)* and say it?

SARA *(kneeling in front of Lottie).*   Well, you can say it to me once.

LOTTIE *(singsong).*
>   Seven times one are seven —
>   Seven times two are fourteen —
>   Seven times three are twenty-one —
>   Seven times four are forty-eight —

SARA *(caressingly).*   Oh, no, Lottie, not forty-eight.

LOTTIE *(anxiously).*   Not forty-eight ——

SARA *(suggestively).*   Not forty-eight ——

LOTTIE *(catching at straws).*   Not forty-eight — then — it's sume-ty other eight ——

SARA *(encouragingly).*
>   Seven times one are seven —
>   Seven times two are fourteen —

LOTTIE *(drawing hope)*. Seven times three are twenty-one — *(Excited haste)* Seven times four are twenty-eight ——

SARA *(hugs and kisses her)*. Yes, that's it — go on.

LOTTIE *(much cheered — singsong)*.
>Seven times five are thirty-five,
>Seven times six are forty-two,
>Seven times seven are forty-nine —
>Seven times eight are fifty-six —

(Slowing up) Seven times — nine — seven times — seven times ni — nine — seven times nine are — *(Despairingly)* Oh, Sara, seven times nine is such a hard one.

SARA. *(slow, suggestively)*.
>Seven times nine — are — si — si —
>Seven times nine are six —

LOTTIE *(catching her up with a shout of glee)*. Sixty-three — seven times nine are sixty-three — *(Rattles off with triumphant glee and ease)*
>Seven times ten are seventy —
>Seven times eleven are seventy-seven and
>Seven times twelve are eighty-four.

SARA *(hugs her)*. That's beautiful — all you have to remember is seven fours are twenty-eight and seven nines are sixty-three. Now we must go, pet. [*Sets Lottie down, giving her doll — leads her out of room door. Garret left empty for few minutes, then cautious knock — outside. Door is opened by Ermengarde who at first looks around edge cautiously and enters. Wind. Ermengarde has pile of books under arm, is dressed in nightgown, with bare feet, and has hair done in curl papers.*

ERMENGARDE. I wonder where she's gone. *(Rats squeak. Ermengarde screams, runs and jumps on bed)* Oh, these rats — oh — *(ad lib. — Rat comes out from behind wash-stand, stops. Ermengarde drops slipper)* Oh, Melchy — *(to rat)* please go way — oh, do go way — and let me get my slipper, — there's a good Melchy — *(As rat moves)* I'll give you a bun to-morrow. *(Rat runs off. Ermengarde, out of bed, hops across floor to get her slipper, and sinks in chair, sighing. She puts on slipper)* I wonder where she's gone. I wonder if that nasty cook has sent her out in all the snow and slush. *(Rises and sees hat and shawl on chair)* No, she's not gone out — there are her hat and shawl, — they are dripping wet. It's a shame. *(Puts books on table)* These came to-day from my papa. He wants me to read *every* one of them, and he'll ask me questions about them when he sees me. It's awful. *(Impatiently)* I'm not clever like Sara. I'd as soon take castor-oil as read them, and if I did read them, I couldn't remember what's in them. *(Drops books on floor)* I was born stupid. *(Wind. Rises from chair)* I wish Sara would come. *(Goes to bed)* What a horrible little bed. She must nearly freeze to death on these cold nights. Oh, it is a shame. She's treated worse than poor little Becky, the scullerymaid. *(Rat heard squeaking. Ermengarde screams again, runs to chair, and hides feet under her in terror)* I wish she'd come. *(Enter Sara)* Sara!

SARA. I didn't know you were coming here to-night, Ermengarde.

ERMENGARDE. I crept out of my room after the other girls were asleep. Papa has sent me some more books, Sara. *(Dejectedly pointing to table and books on floor)* There they are.

SARA *(delightedly).* Oh, has he? *(Runs to books, and sits on floor. Looks at titles on books, opens them)* How beautiful. Carlyle's "French Revolution." I have *so* wanted to read that!

ERMENGARDE. I haven't. And papa will be so cross if I don't. He'll want me to know all about it when I go home for the holidays. What shall I do?

SARA *(excited).* Look here, Ermengarde. If you'll lend me these books, I'll read them, and tell you everything that's in them afterwards, and I'll tell it so that you'll remember it too.

ERMENGARDE. Oh, Sara, Sara, do you think you could?

SARA. I know I can. The little A, B, C children always remember what I tell them.

ERMENGARDE *(pause).* Sara, if you'll do that, and make me *remember*, I'll — I'll give you some of my pocket-money.

SARA. I don't want your money, Ermy, I want your books. *(Holds them tight in arms)* I want them!

ERMENGARDE. Take them then, — you're welcome. I wish I wanted them.

SARA *(cheerfully).* Well, that's all right. I'm so glad. *(Puts books on floor beside her)* Now let's tell each other things. How are you getting on with your French lessons?

ERMENGARDE. Ever so much better since I began to come up into your garret, and you began to teach me.

SARA. I am glad. *(Looks around room)* The garret would be rather nice if it wasn't so very dreadful. *(Laughs)* It's a good place to pretend in.

ERMENGARDE *(eagerly).* What do you pretend, Sara?

SARA. Well, generally I pretend it is the Bastille, and I'm kept a prisoner here like Doctor Manette in "A Tale of Two Cities."

ERMENGARDE (*interested*). And what else?

SARA. I pretend I have been here for years — and years and years — and years — and everyone has forgotten all about me, and Miss Minchin is the jailer. And I pretend that there's another prisoner in the next cell, — that's Becky, you know, — I've told her about it — and I knock on the wall to make her hear, and she knocks like this, — you know. (*Knocks three times on wall; listens a moment*) She's not there; if she were she'd knock back. Ah!

ERMENGARDE. Ah, it's just like a story.

SARA. It is a story; everything is a story — you're a story, I'm a story, Miss Minchin's a story. [*Rats squeak.*

ERMENGARDE (*gets on stool and screams*). Ah, there are the rats again. Are you never afraid of the rats, Sara?

SARA (*on floor*). Not now. I was at first, but now they're a part of the story. There were always rats in prisons, and the prisoners tamed them with crumbs. That is how I tamed Melchisedek and his wife. (*Calls rats*) Come on, Melchy dear, come, nice Melchy.

ERMENGARDE (*stumbles*). Oh, don't call them out; come back, Sara. Tell me some more stories — they are so nice. [*They resume former positions.*

SARA. Well, I tell myself stories about the people who live in the other houses in the square. The *large* family, you know.

ERMENGARDE (*seated on stool*). Did Miss Minchin ever let you go there to tea?

SARA (*shakes head*). No, she said visits were not suited to my station.

ERMENGARDE. Old — cat ——

SARA. But I watch them out of the garret window there. When I stand on the table under it, I can see all up and down the street. That's how I got to know the lascar and the monkey.

ERMENGARDE. What lascar and what monkey?

SARA. The lascar is the Indian gentleman's servant, and the monkey is the Indian gentleman's monkey.

ERMENGARDE. Where do they live?

SARA. They live next door. He is the rich gentleman who is always ill — (*Stops and listens*) Didn't you hear something at the window?

ERMENGARDE *(frightened).* Yes.

SARA *(gets up and goes to window).* There's nothing there. *(Laughs)* Perhaps Melchisedek and his wife are having a party under the roof. The lascar lives in the next garret, and the monkey lives with him — one day the monkey ran away and came in through my window, and the lascar had to come after him.

ERMENGARDE. What, that black Indian man in the white turban, Sara? Did he really come in here?

SARA. Yes, and he took the monkey back. I like him and he likes me. I remember enough Hindustani to talk to him a little, — so now he salaams to me when he sees me. Like this —— *(Salaams, Stops, and listens again)* I'm sure there's something at the window; it sounds like a cat trying to get in. *(Goes to window. Ermengarde stumbles. Turns from window, pleased)* Suppose it was the monkey who had got away again. Oh, suppose it was —— *(Tiptoes to window, lifts it and looks out)* It is the monkey.

ERMENGARDE *(crossing to end of table).* He lost his way and saw the light. Are you going to let him in, Sara?

SARA *(on table).* Yes, it's too cold for monkeys to be out — they are delicate. I'll coax him in. He's quite close; how he shivers. He's so cold — he's quite *tame. (Coaxingly)* Come along, monkey darling, I won't hurt you. [*Takes monkey through window — jumps down.*

ERMENGARDE *(Sara crosses to end of table, and sits. Ermengarde back of table).* Oh, Sara, how funny he is — aren't you afraid he'll bite you?

SARA. Oh, no — nice monkey, nice monkey —— Oh, I do *love* little animal things —— Oh, you queer little darling.

ERMENGARDE *(sits to right of table).* He looks like a very ugly baby.

SARA. I'm glad he's not a baby. His mother couldn't be proud of him — and no one would *dare* to say he was like any of his relations. I do like you — perhaps he's sorry he's so ugly and it's always on his mind. I wonder if he has a mind?

ERMENGARDE. What are you going to do with him?

SARA. I must take him back to the Indian gentleman. But I am sorry —— Oh, the company *you would* be to a person in a garret!

ERMENGARDE. Shall we take him back to-night?

SARA. It is too late to-night. I must keep you here, monkey my love, but I'll be kind to you.

ERMENGARDE. Where will he sleep?

SARA *(looks around).* Oh, I know — that cupboard —— *(Gets up, crosses to cupboard, and opens door)* See, I can make a bed for him here. I'll give him one of my pillows to lie on, and cover him with my blanket. [*Crosses to bed.*

ERMENGARDE. But you'll be so cold.

SARA. But I'm used to being cold and he isn't. I wasn't born in a tropical forest. Let's make his bed now and see if he likes it.

(Takes pillow from bed) You bring the blanket. *(Ermengarde takes blanket)* Yes, monkey, pet lamb, you shall have nice bye-lows and go rock-a-bye baby.

ERMENGARDE. What?

SARA. I mean rock-a-bye monkey —— *(Makes bed in closet)* And Sara will take you back home to your family. [*Noise outside, of Becky coming upstairs.*

ERMENGARDE *(frightened).* What's that?

SARA. It's only Becky coming up to bed.

MISS MINCHIN *(outside door).* Rebecca, Rebecca!

SARA. What, — Miss Minchin, — she might come up. [*Ermengarde, looking wildly about the room, suddenly tucks nightgown around her and rolls under bed. Sara hurriedly shuts monkey up in cupboard.*

MISS MINCHIN *(outside).* Remember, Rebecca, you get up at five in the morning.

BECKY *(outside).* Yes, mum, thank 'e, mum ——
[*Miss Minchin heard outside, descending steps. Sara to bed and lifts cover so Ermengarde can get out from under it.*

SARA. Come out. — it's all right. She's gone to bed herself.

ERMENGARDE *(sees she's gone —crawling out).* What if she caught us —— [*Three knocks heard from Becky.*

SARA *(disappointedly).* Oh, that means — "the cook would not give me the cold potatoes."

ERMENGARDE. Cold potatoes — were they to feed the rats with?

SARA. They were to feed me with. *(Little laugh. Ermengarde amazed)* You know how nice cold potatoes are — if you pretend they are something quite different — and put salt on — that is — if you are hungry.

ERMENGARDE *(aghast).* Sara — Sara — are you ever hungry enough for cold potatoes?

SARA. Yes, I am. I am so hungry now that I could eat — I could eat Miss Minchin if she were different — but she'd have to be very different.

ERMENGARDE. She wouldn't be different enough if you'd put pepper on her as well as salt — Sara — *(suddenly)* I've just thought of something splendid. *(Inspirited)* I've just thought of something splendid!

SARA. What is it?

ERMENGARDE *(excited hurry).* This very afternoon, I had a box full of good things sent me. My aunt sent it. I haven't touched it. It's got cakes in it — and little meat pies and jam tarts and buns and red currant wine, and figs and raisins and chocolates. I'll creep back to my room and get it this minute. And we'll eat it now.

SARA *(clutches Ermengarde's arm).* Oh, it makes me faint to hear it. You are good, Ermy. *(Hug)* Do you think you *could?*

ERMENGARDE. I know I could.

SARA. Don't make a noise.

ERMENGARDE *(runs to door, peeps out, then back to Sara).* The lights are out. Miss Minchin turned out the gas when she went down. I can creep and creep, and no one will hear me. [*Dance.*

SARA. Ermy, let's pretend — let's pretend it's a party — and oh, *won't* you invite the prisoner in the next cell?

ERMENGARDE *(delighted).* Yes, yes, let's knock on the wall now, — the jailer won't hear.

SARA *(goes to wall and knocks once).* That means "Prisoner, the jailer has made his last rounds and we can talk." *(They both listen until two knocks are heard in response)* That means "Are you sure it is safe?" *(Knocks three times herself)* That means "Quite sure, I heard the iron gates clang and the key turn in the lock." *(Becky knocks four times)* That means "Is it safe for me to come to you through the secret passage we have dug under the wall?" *(Knocks smartly one knock — and then two — separated by pause)* That means — "Quite safe — come." *(Knock at door is heard)* Here she comes. *(Opens door. Becky enters. She starts at sight of Ermengarde)* Don't be frightened, Becky. *(Catching Becky, who tries to run off)* Miss Ermengarde is our friend; she asked you to come in here, because she's going to bring a box of good things up here.

BECKY. To eat, Miss —— *(Bursting in)* Things that's good to eat?

SARA. Yes, and we're going to pretend a party.

ERMENGARDE. And you shall have all you want to eat ——[*All dance and exclaim. Becky stops them by* ——

BECKY. Sh — [*Points down.*

ERMENGARDE. Oh, that old cat, Miss Minchin — but there's Magus and Brazil nuts and lots of good things ——

BECKY. Ow 'ev'nly. [*Ermengarde drops shawl.*

SARA. Ermy, you go for the box and we will set the table. [*Puts Ermengarde out of the door.*

BECKY. Oh, Miss — oh, Miss, I know it's you that asked her to let me come. It makes me cry to think of it.

SARA (*cheerfully, embracing her*) No, no, you mustn't cry. We must make haste and set the table. What can we put on it? (*Sees red shawl*) Here's her shawl — I know she won't mind. It will make such a nice red table-cloth. (*Picks it up and spreads it on table with Becky's help*) What next? Oh! (*Clasps hands delightedly*) I know, I'll look for something in my old trunk, that I used to have when I was a princess. (*Runs to trunk, opens it and rummages in it. Stops and sees Becky*) Becky, do you know what a banquet is?

BECKY. No, Miss, is it something to be 'et, or something to be wore?

SARA (*sitting by trunk*). It's a magnificent feast. Kings have them, and Queens, and Lord Mayors. We are going to have one. Now begin to pretend just as hard as ever you can — and straighten the richly embroidered table-cloth. [*Sara turns to trunk again, as Becky straightens table-cloth. Becky then stands, squeezing her eyes tight shut, clenching her hands and holding her breath. Sara takes package of handkerchiefs from trunk, rises to go to table, sees Becky and laughs.*

SARA. What are you doing, Becky?

BECKY (*opening her eyes and catching her breath*). I was pretending, Miss. It takes a good bit of strength.

SARA. Yes, it does — just at first. But it doesn't take so much when you get used to it. I'm used to it. Now what do you suppose these are?

BECKY (*delighted*). They looks like 'ankerchiefs, Miss, but I know they ain't ——

SARA. No, they are not. They are plates and napkins. Gold and silver plates and richly embroidered napkins — to match the table-cloth. These are the plates and these are the napkins. *(Giving each bundle to Becky separately)* You must not take the napkins for the plates, or the plates for the napkins, Becky.

BECKY. Lor', no, Miss. They ain't nothin' like each other.

SARA. No, they're not. If you pretend hard enough. *(Steps back)* Don't they look nice?

BECKY. Jest lovely, Miss. Particular them gold and silver plates.

SARA. Yes, but the embroidery on the napkins is beautiful; nuns did it in a convent in Spain. *(Suddenly)* Oh, Becky, I forgot to tell you. This isn't the Bastille now.

BECKY *(eagerly)*. Ain't it, Miss? Lor' now, what has it turned into?

SARA *(grandly)*. It's a marble hall.

BECKY. A marble hall? I say ——

SARA. Yes, it's a marble hall in a palace — it's a banquet hall.

BECKY *(looking around room, opening eyes wide)*. A banket hall!

SARA. No. — a banquet hall — that window opens into the vast conservatory where the tropical plants grow — *(Suddenly)* Oh, that reminds me of flowers. We ought to have some flowers.

BECKY. Oh, yes, Miss, we ought to have some flowers.

SARA. Where can we get flowers from? Oh, the trunk again — *(Runs to trunk, tumbles out the contents. Drags out old summer hat with flowers on it)* Here they are —— *(Tears flowers off hat)* What shall we put them in? *(Looks about and sees wash-stand)* Becky, there's something that looks like a toothbrush mug — but it isn't. It's a crystal flagon — bring it here. [*Becky brings it — Sara arranges flowers in it.*

BECKY. There you are, Miss, a Christmas Dragon. There's something else there, Miss, that looks like a soap dish — but it ain't. Shall I get it?

SARA *(nods "Yes")*. Yes. [*Becky brings it.*

SARA *(takes it from Becky)*. It's a gold epergne encrusted with gems. *(Wreathes flowers about it)* Oh, Becky, Becky ——
(They both gaze with delight. Becky clutches her lips with one hand and lifts them up and down) Now if we had something for bonbon dishes — there, I remember — I saw something this minute. The darling old trunk —— *(Crosses to it)* It's like a fairy. [*Takes out bundle of wool, wrapped in scarlet and white tissue-*

THE LITTLE PRINCESS

paper. Goes back of table, tears off paper and twists into shapes of little dishes.

BECKY.   Ah, Miss Sara, this 'ere Blanket Hall — I mean Banket 'all, and all them golden gems — ain't them beautiful? [*Sara puts candle on table from mantel shelf. Enter Ermengarde with hamper of goodies. She starts back with exclamations of joy.*

ERMENGARDE.   Oh, Sara, you are the cleverest girl I ever saw.

SARA.   Isn't it nice? They are things out of my old trunk.

ERMENGARDE.   And here's the hamper —— *(Sets it on chair)* You take the things out, Sara. You'll make them look nice.

BECKY.   Yes, Miss, you take them out — I don't dast trust myself.

SARA.   Thank you —— *(Looks in box)* What a lovely cake. *(Takes out same and puts it on table)* And mince pie — a chicken patty — and grapes — and oranges — and plum buns with sugar on — and crystallized fruit in an angel box and chocolate caramels.

BECKY.   Chocolate camels —— [*Arranging the goodies, etc., until table is quite decorated.*

SARA.   There.

ERMENGARDE.   It's like a real party.

BECKY.   It's like a Queen's table.

ERMENGARDE *(sudden thought)*.   Sara, do you ever pretend you are a princess now? [*Becky puts basket on bed, and chairs at table.*

SARA.   Oh, yes, I have to pretend it all the time. It helps me to be polite to people when they are rude to me. I'm a princess in rags and tatters, but I'm a princess inside.

ERMENGARDE *(suddenly)*.   I'll tell you what, Sara. Pretend you are a princess now, and that you are giving a banquet.

SARA.   But it is your banquet — you must be the Princess, Ermy. We'll be your maids of honour.

ERMENGARDE.   Oh, I can't — I'm too stupid — and I don't know how — *you* be her.

BECKY.   Yes, Miss — go on, you be her.

SARA.   Well, if you want me to —— *(Pause, — then suddenly)* But I've thought of something else —— *(Goes to fireplace)* Yes, there is a lot of paper and rubbish left in here. If we light it, it will blaze up for a few minutes, and we can pretend it's a real fire. If we only had more paper.

ERMENGARDE *(with sudden inspiration, running to books).* I know — books ——

SARA. No, no, don't tear the books, Ermy.

ERMENGARDE *(pause, then quickly).* The curl papers then. *(Runs to Sara, kneels before fire. Sara pulls papers off Ermy's head)* Oh, oh, they hurt.

SARA. By the time it stops blazing we shall forget it's not being real. *(Strikes light on box, starts fire. The three girls before it)* Doesn't it look real? Now we will begin the party —— *(From behind table)* Oh, girls — this — *(paper off a cake)* shall be my crown, and this my sceptre. *(Making spill of paper)* Advance, fair damsels, and be seated at the banquet table —— *(Sara sings)* Tra-la-la — tra-la-la —— *(Beats time with paper)* Take each other's hand and advance —— *(Becky not knowing how)* No, no; Ermy, show Becky how, you know —show Becky. *(Sings again)* Tra-la-la —— *(Becky and Ermengarde join hands and dance to music. Becky falls over books. Finally at end of strain both are in chairs, — all sit together)* My noble father, the King, who is absent on a long journey, has commanded me to feast you. *(Addressing air)* What ho, there —— *(Looking into mid-air. Ermy and Becky look puzzled, not understanding)* Minstrels, strike up with your viols and your bassoons. *(Ermengarde and Becky look puzzled. Sara explains to them, resuming her natural manner)* Princes always have minstrels at the feast. Pretend there's a minstrel gallery up there. *(Points up toward audience)* What ho there — strike —— *(Ermengarde and Becky stare at her in rapture, then jump to feet. Imitate trombone, humming "Johnny, get your hair cut." At end of song they sit)* Now we will begin.

THE LITTLE PRINCESS

Close your eyes tight now and fancy
    How Grandmother looked when a girl,
With soft dimpled cheek and manners so sweet,
    With her powder, patches and curl.
Suppose I pretend I am like her
    With her quaint, dainty ways, at a ball,—
See the dance she is in — 'tis about to begin;
    Can you fancy scene, costumes and all?

Suppose you were all at this old-fashioned ball,
    Suppose, suppose, suppose ——
Here's what you would see if you could be
    Her guest at a dance of '73.

Suppose in a far-off country,
    In the days of long ago,
You've entered the gate at the time of a fête
    In a garden of Tokio.
Can you see the Japanese maidens
    With their dainty figures so small,
See the dance they are in — it's about to begin.
    Can you fancy scene, flowers and all?

Suppose you are hid in Snowflower's chair,
    Suppose, suppose, suppose,
See their black heads bow low as they dance to and fro?
    These quaint little geishas of Tokio?

Suppose in the fairies' country,
    Where the moss makes a carpet green
Out under the trees with their rustling leaves
    At the Court of the Elfin Queen,
You could hide yourself in a tree-top
    And peep into Hazel Brush Hall,
See the dance they are in — 'tis about to begin.
    See the Brownies, moonbeams and all?

Suppose you are there, unseen to the stare,
    Suppose, suppose, suppose,
Here's what you would see if you could be
    A visiting sprite in the top of a tree.

[*Door is thrown violently open. Enter Miss Minchin. Ermy dives under table. Becky cowers with cake in hand; afterwards puts cake back on table. Sara stands behind table with crown on.*

MISS MINCHIN. What does this mean?

ERMENGARDE (*under table*). It's a party.

MISS MINCHIN (*to Becky*). You audacious creature. You leave the house in the morning.

BECKY. Yes, mum.

ERMENGARDE. Don't send her away, please. My aunt sent me a box full of good things ——

BECKY. Yes, mum — an' we're only just 'avin' a party.

MISS MINCHIN (*witheringly*). So I see, with the Princess Sara at the the head of the table. (*Turns on Sara*) This is your doing, I know — Ermengarde would have never thought of such a thing. You

99

decorated the table, I suppose, with this rubbish. *(To Becky)* Go back to your garret. *[Becky crosses, steals off, face in apron.*

MISS MINCHIN *(to Ermengarde).* Ermengarde, put those things in the hamper. *(To Sara)* As for you, I will attend to you to-morrow. You shall have neither breakfast, dinner nor supper!

SARA. I've neither dinner nor supper to-day, Miss Minchin.

MISS MINCHIN. Then all the better. You will have something to remember. Don't look at me like that. *(Sara has not taken her eyes from Miss Minchin. To Ermengarde, after seeing her books on floor — Sara front of table)* Ermengarde, you have brought your beautiful new books into this dirty garret; pick them up and go back to bed. You will stay there all to-morrow, and I shall write to your papa. What would he say, if he knew where you are to-night?

ERMENGARDE. I don't know, Miss Minchin.

MISS MINCHIN. Take that hamper.

ERMENGARDE. Yes, Miss Minchin. *(Does so. Exits, turning at door)* Cat ——
[Noise heard of her falling down stairs.

MISS MINCHIN *(turning on Sara fiercely).* What are you thinking of — why do you stare at me in that fashion?

SARA *(quietly).* I was wondering.

MISS MINCHIN. What?

SARA *(not pertly but sadly and quietly).* I was wondering what *my* papa would say if he knew where I am to-night.

MISS MINCHIN *(threateningly).* You insolent minx, how dare you! I will leave you to wonder. Go to bed at once. *[Exits.*

SARA *(left alone, takes up Emily, sits on ottoman).* There isn't any party left, Emily — there isn't any princess — there's nothing left but the prisoner in the Bastille. *(Head down and cries softly)* I won't cry. *(To table with Emily)* I'll go to bed and sleep. I can't pretend any more to-night. *(Blows out candle)* I wish I could. *(Going to bed)* I'll go to sleep and perhaps a dream will come to pretend for me —*(Takes off shoes —in bed)* I'll suppose a little to make it easier. Suppose there was a bright fire in that grate — with lots of little dancing flames — suppose there was a soft rug on the floor and that was a comfortable chair — and suppose the attic was furnished in lovely colours —— *(Voice becomes dreamy)* And suppose there was a little table by the fire with a little hot supper on it — and suppose this was a beautiful soft bed with

100

white sheets and fleecy blankets and large downy pillows — suppose — sup-p-ose — sup-po-se —— [*Falls asleep.*

[*Ram Dass appears at window with three lascars. He carries one dark lantern. Surveys the room, sees Sara asleep, raises window, enters with others, and without noise makes the trick change, bringing everything through window. First, three men help Ram Dass to clear away the old furniture. After furniture is cleared, Indian stuff is brought on and placed. At end of change three lamps are brought on. Ram Dass lays fire in grate and, before lighting same, stands with lighted taper in front of grate which is signal for other lascars to light their lamps. Discovered, three lascars standing by their respective lamps with folded arms. Ram Dass then takes books from tray on table, puts them on cushions, and exits through window.*

[*Sara wakes slowly, sees the wonderful change and is bewildered.*

SARA.   What a nice dream. I feel quite warm. (*Stretches out arms, feels blanket dreamily*) I don't want to wake up — (*Trying to sleep*) Oh, I am awakening. (*Opens eyes, sees everything — thinks she is dreaming*) I have not wakened. I'm dreaming yet. (*Looks around smiling, bewildered but waking*) It does not melt away, — it stays. I never had such a dream before. (*Pushes bedclothes aside, puts feet on floor, smiling*) I am dreaming, I'm getting out of bed. (*Closes eyes as she gets out, as if to prolong dream; then opens eyes*) I'm dreaming, it stays real — I'm dreaming, it feels real. (*Moves forward, staring about her*) It's bewitched, or I'm bewitched. (*Words hurrying themselves*) I only think I see it all. But if I can only keep on thinking it, I don't care, I don't care. (*Sudden outburst of emotion. Sees fire and runs to it*) A fire, a little supper. (*Kneels at fire — hands before it*) A fire I only dreamed wouldn't be hot. (*Jumping up, sees dressing-gown and slippers*) A dressing-gown! (*Holding it to face, then putting it on*) It is real — it is, it must be. It's warm, it's soft. (*Puts feet in slippers, cries out*) Slippers — they are real too. They are real, it's all real. I am not — I am not dreaming. (*Sees books on cushions. Runs to them*) Books, books —— (*Opens one, turns over leaves rapidly*) Some one has written something. Oh, what is it? (*Runs to lamp. Reads aloud*) "To the little girl in the garret from a friend." (*Clasping book to her breast, grabs up Emily and hugs her*) Oh Emily, oh papa —— (*Kneels*) Papa, I have a friend, I have a friend!

CURTAIN

ACT III

SCENE. *Mr. Carrisford's study in house next door to Miss Min-chin's seminary for young ladies. Room handsomely furnished. Window looks out on winter street. Chairs, bric-à-brac cabinet, curtains, with soft cushions on window seat, lady's writing-desk, fireplace and fire-dogs. A table with books on it, and a big armchair nearby. Oriental rugs on floor with a tiger's head rug for Donald. Large sofa beside baby grand piano. Noah's ark with animals in it.*

At the rise of curtain: Door opens. Enter Ram Dass, followed by Donald, Mazie, Nora, and Janet Carmichael. Ram Dass stands up stage. Donald with a whoop sits on tiger's head. Mazie and Nora to piano, to play with toys in ark.

JANET. Please tell Mr. Carrisford we can wait as long as he likes. We'll go away if he doesn't want us. We're only come to cheer him up a little.

RAM DASS. The Sahib will be glad. I go. [*Exits.*

DONALD. I'll sit here on the tiger's head. Gee up — gee up — gee up! I'm on the tiger's head.

JANET. Now, Donald, you must *remember*. Mr. Carrisford has been very ill, and when you come to cheer up a person who is ill you don't cheer him up at the top of your voice.

DONALD (*riding tiger's head*). Well, I can cheer him up better when I'm sitting on the tiger's head than I can on a chair. Gee up —— [*Falls off.*

JANET. You can sit there, if you'll be quiet. (*Crosses and sits in chair*) Mr. Carrisford is very anxious to-day. He is waiting for papa to come back from Paris. Mamma said we might help pass the time for him — because he likes us when we're quiet. (*At piano with animals*) I'm going to be quiet.

MAZIE (*with her*). So am I.

DONALD (*riding tiger boisterously*). We'll all be as quiet as mice.

JANET (*to him*). Mice don't make a noise like that.

DONALD. A whole lot of mice might. A thousand mice might.

JANET (*severely*). I don't believe fifty thousand mice might. And we have to be as quiet as one mouse. I'm the oldest and I'm responsible. [*Mazie gets down from the piano, and pushes Donald off tiger's head on the floor. He retaliates by pushing her off on the floor.*

102

MAZIE. Oh, Donald, you are rough!

DONALD. You pushed me off, I pushed you off. [*Sits on tiger again.*

JANET (*arranges pillows*). Now, that will be ready for him when Ram Dass brings him in, poor thing. *(Leans head on hands on table)* Oh dear, I wish papa would come. I do hope he will say he has found the lost little girl.

DONALD. Yes.

NORA. Perhaps he will bring her back from Paris.

DONALD. I wish he would. She could tell us about when her papa shot this tiger in India. Mr. Carrisford said Captain Crewe shot it.

MAZIE. I want her to be found because I want to play with her.

NORA. I want her to be found because I'm sorry for her.

JANET. I'm sorry for her. Perhaps she's a poor little beggar in the streets. She has no father and no mother, and Mr. Carrisford does not know where she is. He only thinks she was sent to a boarding-school in Paris. [*Donald throws animals into ark.*

CHILDREN. Oh, ah, Donald!

NORA. Papa has been to ever so many schools to look for her.

MAZIE. But he could never find her.

JANET. But he went to Paris on Thursday because he heard of a school where there was a little girl whose papa died in India. If he doesn't find her this time, he says he shall not know what to do.

[*Donald bangs the piano.*

JANET AND MAZIE. Oh, Donald, Donald!

NORA. Oh, I wish it was time for him to come. *(To window)* Perhaps she is cold and miserable somewhere. And all the while, Mr. Carrisford wants her so much.

MAZIE (*tearfully*). Perhaps she's out in the wet in bare feet and torn frock. It makes me want to cry.

DONALD (*taking stage manfully*). I say, if papa doesn't bring her back from Paris, let's all go and look for her, — every one of us. Let's go to the park and stand at the gate, and every time we see a little girl let's ask her what her name is.

JANET (*desperately*). We can't let her stay lost and be poor always when she ought to be so rich and live in such a beautiful house. I can't bear it.

103

[*Door opens. Enter Carrisford and Ram Dass. They cross to arm-chair.*

CHILDREN *(when they see him).* Oh, Mr. Carrisford, there you are! Oh, how do you do. [*Running to him and leading him down.*

CARRISFORD. How do you do, my dears; it's very good of you to come and see me.

CHILDREN. Oh, no!

NORA. We like to come.

JANET *(who has fixed pillows for Carrisford).* Mamma said we might come and see you on our way from the party.

MAZIE. We wanted to show you our party frocks.

DONALD. We're not going to make a noise. [*Blows whistle.*

CARRISFORD. Oh, dear me, let me see — how smart you all are. Let me look at you. [*Donald struts, showing coat and pants.*

DONALD. Would you like to see the back? [*Showing it.*

NORA. Mamma lent me her locket.

MAZIE *(showing frock).* Mine is quite a new frock.

DONALD. I have four pockets. *(Showing them)* One, two three —— *(Loses fourth; suddenly finds it)* Ah, four.

CARRISFORD. I have only two.

DONALD. Oh, ho, he has only two!

JANET. Do you think you are any better, Mr. Carrisford?

CARRISFORD. I'm afraid not, Janet. I'm anxious and it isn't good for me. I shall be better if your papa brings me good news. Ram Dass, you may go. [*Exit Ram Dass.*

NORA. He won't be long now. When he comes from Paris, he always comes in the afternoon.

DONALD. I say, I'll go to the window and watch for the cab. Mazie, you come and watch too.

JANET. Mr. Carrisford, do you think he will come back and say he found the lost little girl?

CARRISFORD. I hope so, Janet, I hope so. I shall be very unhappy if he does not.

NORA. Do you think that perhaps she is so poor that she is begging

104

in the streets this very minute — while we are waiting for her to be found?

CARRISFORD *(startled and miserable).* I hope not — I hope not — Heaven knows what she may be doing. That is what makes me so miserable.

DONALD *(shouts from window).* Here's a cab, here's a cab ——

ALL. Oh ——

DONALD. I believe it's going to stop here. *(Carrisford rises, partly turns up stage. Nora and Janet rise)* Oh, no, it isn't and there's only a fat old lady in it with a blue bonnet on. [*Carrisford sinks back into chair.*

JANET. Oh, Donald, you must be careful.

DONALD. I was careful. It was a cab. The cabman looked at this house when the umbrella was poked out.

CARRISFORD *(pats Janet's hand).* You are a nice little girl, Janet. Thank you.

JANET *(kneels beside him).* I wish I could cheer you up until papa does come — but when anyone feels ill perhaps cheering up is too loud.

CARRISFORD. Oh, no, no ——

JANET. May we talk about the little girl?

CARRISFORD. I don't think I can talk about anything else just now.

NORA. We like her very much. We call her the little lost Princess.

CARRISFORD. Do you, — why?

JANET. Because she will be so rich when she is found that she will be quite like a little princess. Is it true that her papa gave all of his money to one of his friends to spend in a mine that had diamonds in it — and then his friend thought he had lost all and ran away because he felt as if he was a robber?

NORA. But he wasn't really, you know!

CARRISFORD. No, he wasn't really. The mine turned out well after all. But it was too late. Captain Crewe was dead. If he had lived he and his little girl would have been very rich indeed.

JANET. I'm sorry for the friend.

CARRISFORD. Are you?

JANET. I can't help it.

CARRISFORD. I am sorry for him too. *I* am the friend, Janet.

JANET. Oh, de-ar —— *Poor* Mr. Carrisford.

NORA. Oh, papa must find her!

JANET. Yes, he must find her!

DONALD *(from window, dancing up and down in seat with Mazie)*. Here he is, here he is.

ALL. Oh, ah ——

CARRISFORD *(trying to rise)*. I wish I could get up, but it's no use, I cannot, I cannot —— [*Nora and Janet to window.*

JANET *(coming down)* But there isn't any little girl. [*Enter Ram Dass.*

RAM DASS. Sahib, Mr. Carmichael is at the door.

ALL. May we go?

CARRISFORD. Yes, yes, go, go —— [*Children exeunt running, followed by Ram Dass.*

CARMICHAEL *(outside)* No, no, children. Not now ——

CHILDREN. Daddy, daddy ——

CARMICHAEL. Not now, — you can come in after I have talked with Mr. Carrisford. Go away and play with Ram Dass.

CHILDREN. All right. [*Enter Carmichael.*

CARRISFORD *(shaking hands)*. I am glad to see you — very glad. Pray sit down. What news do you bring?

CARMICHAEL *(sits)*. No good news, I am sorry to say. I went to the school in Paris and saw the little girl. But she is not the child you are searching for.

CARRISFORD. Then the search must begin all over again.

CARMICHAEL. I'm afraid so.

CARRISFORD. Have you any new suggestions to make?

CARMICHAEL. Well, perhaps. Are you quite sure the child was put in school in Paris?

CARRISFORD. My dear fellow, I am sure of *nothing*.

CARMICHAEL. But you thought the school was in Paris?

CARRISFORD. Because her mother was a French woman, and had wished that the child should be educated in Paris. It seemed only likely that she should be there.

CARMICHAEL. I assure you I have searched the schools in Paris thoroughly. The journey I have just returned from was really my last hope.

CARRISFORD. Carmichael, I must find her, — I shall never get well until I do find her and give her the fortune the mine has made. It is hers, and she, poor child, may be begging in the streets. Poor Crewe put into the scheme every penny he owned, and he died thinking I had ruined him.

CARMICHAEL. You were not yourself at the time. You were stricken with brain fever two days after you left the place — remember that.

CARRISFORD. Yes, and when I returned to consciousness, poor Crewe was dead.

CARMICHAEL. You did not remember the child; you did not speak of her for months.

CARRISFORD. No, I had forgotten, and now I shall never remember.

CARMICHAEL. Come, come. We shall find her yet. [*Rises.*

CARRISFORD. We will find her if we search every city in Europe. Help me to find her. [*Shake hands.*

CARMICHAEL. We *will* find her. As you say — if she is alive she is *somewhere*. We have searched the schools in Paris. Let us try London.

CARRISFORD. There are schools enough in London. By the way, there is one next door.

CARMICHAEL. Then we will begin there. We cannot begin nearer than next door.

CARRISFORD. There's a child there who interests me. But she is not a pupil. (*Enter Ram Dass*) She is a little forlorn creature as unlike poor Crewe as a child could be. Well, Ram Dass? ——

RAM DASS. Sahib, the child, she herself has come — the child the Sahib felt pity for. She brings back the monkey who had again run away to her garret. I have asked that she remain. It was my thought that it would please the Sahib to see and speak with her.

CARMICHAEL. Who is she?

CARRISFORD. God knows. She is the child I spoke of. (*To Ram Dass*) Yes, yes, I should like to see her. [*Children enter, except Donald, crying and dancing with joy.*

107

JANET. Mr. Carrisford, Mr. Carrisford, papa, papa, the little girl, she's the little girl we saw at the school ——

CARMICHAEL AND CARRISFORD. At the school?

NORA. She was quite a rich little girl in a beautiful frock.

MAZIE. And now she's poor and thin and ragged — at least almost ragged.
[*Enter Mrs. Carmichael.*

MRS. CARMICHAEL. My dears, my dears, what are you talking about — all at once?

JANET. It's the little girl who made up names about us — and now she's quite poor and shabby.

MAZIE. She brought the monkey back.

DONALD (*runs on — joining clamour*). I say, I say, she won't come in, she won't come in, — I want her to come in! She talked Indian to Ram Dass, but she won't come in. [*During this he jumps behind Mr. Carrisford, pulls his bath robe — is taken away by his father.*

CARRISFORD (*to Ram Dass*). She spoke Hindustani?

RAM DASS. Yes, Sahib, a few words.

CARRISFORD. Ask her to come here. [*Exit Ram Dass.*

CARMICHAEL (*to Carrisford*). You must compose yourself. Remember your weakness. The fact that the child knows a little Hindustani may mean nothing. Don't prepare yourself for another disappointment.

CARRISFORD. No, no.

CARMICHAEL (*to Donald*). Here, you young rascal.

[*Spanking. Enter Sara with monkey in arm.*

MRS. CARMICHAEL. I believe it is the same child, but I should not have known her.

SARA. Your monkey got away again. He came to my garret window and I took him in last night. I would have brought him back if it had not been so late. I knew you were ill and might not like to be disturbed.

CARRISFORD. That was very thoughtful of you.

SARA. Shall I give him to the lascar?

CARRISFORD. How do you know he is a lascar?

SARA. Oh, I know lascars. I was born in India.

CARRISFORD (excited). Were you? (Holds out his hand) Come here. (To Ram Dass) Ram Dass, take the monkey away. (Exit Ram Dass with monkey. To Sara) Come, you live next door, do you not?

SARA. Yes, sir, I live at Miss Minchin's.

CARRISFORD. She keeps a boarding-school. But you are not a pupil, are you?

SARA. I don't know what I am.

CARRISFORD. Why not?

SARA. At first I was a pupil and a parlour-boarder, but now ——

CARRISFORD. What now?

SARA. I sleep in the garret next to the scullery-maid. I run errands for the cook and I teach the little ones their lessons.

MRS. CARMICHAEL (to Mr. Carmichael). Poor little thing.

CARRISFORD (gestures to Carmichael as if agitation was too much for him). Question her, Carmichael,— I cannot.

CARMICHAEL. What do you mean by "at first," my child?

SARA (turning to him). When I was first taken there by papa.

CARMICHAEL. Where is your father?

SARA. My papa died. He lost all his money, and there was none left for me, and so ——

CARRISFORD. Carmichael!

CARMICHAEL (pantomime with wife). And so — you were sent up into the garret and made a little drudge? That's about it, isn't it?

SARA. There was no one to take care of me. I belong to nobody.

CARRISFORD (breaking in). How — how — did your father lose his money?

SARA. He didn't lose it himself. He had a friend he was very fond of — he was very fond of him — it was his friend who took his money. I don't know how. (To Carmichael) I don't understand. (To Carrisford) He trusted his friend too much.

CARRISFORD (agitated). But the friend might not have meant to do harm. It might have happened through a mistake.

SARA. But the suffering was just as bad for my papa. It killed him——

109

CARRISFORD (*faints*). Carmichael!
[*Confusion. Carmichael goes to Carrisford. Sara stands before them, bewildered; she picks up shawl and starts to go.*

SARA. I think I had better go.

CARRISFORD (*recovering*). Stay. What was your father's name?

SARA. His name was Ralph Crewe ——

CARRISFORD. Oh ——

SARA. Captain Crewe — perhaps you knew him. He died in India.

CARRISFORD. Yes, yes, yes — Carmichael, it is the child!

SARA (*looking from Carrisford to Carmichael, trembling*). What does he mean? What child am I?

CARRISFORD. I was your father's friend — he loved me — he trusted me — if he had lived he would have known — but now ——
[*Sinks back.*

MRS. CARMICHAEL (*to Sara*). My dear little girl. My poor little girl!
[*Children start to go to Sara; Janet stops them.*

SARA. Did he know my papa? Was *he* the wicked friend? Oh, do tell me!

MRS. CARMICHAEL. He was not wicked, my dear; he did not really lose your papa's money — he only thought he had lost it — he was ill — and when he got well — your poor papa was dead, and he didn't know where to find you.

SARA. And I was at Miss Minchin's all the time.

MRS. CARMICHAEL. Yes, he saw you pass by, and he was *sorry* for you, and he told Ram Dass to climb through your attic window and try to make you comfortable ——

SARA (*joyfully*). Did Ram Dass bring the things, — did he tell Ram Dass to do it? Did he make the dream that came true?

MRS. CARMICHAEL. Yes —yes — my dear — he did. He is kind and good, and was sorry for you.

SARA (*going to Carrisford*). You sent the things to me — the beautiful things — the beautiful, beautiful things — you sent them?

CARRISFORD. Yes — poor dear child — I did.

SARA. Then it is you who are *my friend*. [*Kneels to Carrisford.*

SERVANT (*outside*). Pardon me, Madam, but Mr. Carrisford is not well enough to see visitors.

MISS MINCHIN *(partly off stage)*. I am sorry *(enters door)* to disturb Mr. Carrisford, but I must see him at once. I have explanations to make. *(Meeting Carmichael)* I am Miss Minchin, the proprietress of *"The Young Ladies' Seminary"* next door.

CARMICHAEL. So you are Miss Minchin?

MISS MINCHIN. I am, sir.

CARMICHAEL. In that case you have arrived at the right time.

MISS MINCHIN. I have come to explain that an insolent charity pupil of mine has intruded here without my knowledge. [*Sees Sara.*

CARRISFORD *(to Sara)*. There, there, it's all right.

MISS MINCHIN. You are here still — the forwardness of such conduct — *(indignantly)* go home at once — you shall be severely punished! Go home at once, at once!

[*Sara rises and starts to go.*

JANET. Oh, please don't let her go.

ALL CHILDREN *(going to Mr. Carrisford)*. Oh, please don't let her go!

CARRISFORD. No, no — she is not going.

ALL CHILDREN. Ah ——

[*Children back to sofa.*

MISS MINCHIN. Not going ——

CARRISFORD. No, Miss Minchin. She is not going *home* — if you give your house that name. Her home for the future will be with me.

MISS MINCHIN. With *you*, with *you*, — what does this mean?

CARRISFORD. That she is done with you, Madam, — with you and her misery and her garret.

MISS MINCHIN. I am dumbfounded. Such insults. *(To Sara)* This is your doing — come back to the school at once. [*Starts forward as though to take her.*

CARMICHAEL *(coming down)*. That will do, Miss Minchin.

MISS MINCHIN *(violently)* Not do? How dare you interfere! *(To Carrisford)* How dare *you*? She shall go back if I have to call in the police.

CARRISFORD. The lady is too violent for me, Carmichael, — please explain to her.

CARMICHAEL. I am Mr. Carrisford's lawyer, Madam. Mr. Carrisford was an intimate friend of the late Captain Crewe — the fortune which Captain Crewe supposed he had lost is in the hands of Mr. Carrisford.

MISS MINCHIN (*startled*). The fortune — Sara's fortune? [*Turns, and stares aghast at Sara.*

CARMICHAEL. It will be Sara's fortune — it is Sara's fortune now.

MISS MINCHIN (*to Carmichael*). Captain Crewe left her in my charge. She must return to it until she is of age. The law will interfere in my behalf.

CARMICHAEL. No, the law will not, Miss Minchin. Captain Crewe constituted Mr. Carrisford her guardian long ago. If Sara herself wishes to return to you, I dare say he would not refuse her. But that rests with Sara.

MISS MINCHIN. Then I appeal to Sara. (To Sara) I have not spoiled you, perhaps, but I have always been very fond of you.

SARA. Have you, Miss Minchin? I did not know that——

MISS MINCHIN. Yes. Will you not do your duty to your poor papa and come home with me?

SARA (*steps forward*). No, I will not. *You* know why I will not go home with you, Miss Minchin, you know —— [*This spoken quietly, steadily, and politely, looking squarely at her.*

MISS MINCHIN (*spitefully*). Then you will never see your little companions again, — Ermengarde and Lottie.

CARMICHAEL. Oh, yes, she will, she will see any one she wishes in her guardian's house.

[*Miss Minchin goes wrathfully to Carmichael.*

CARRISFORD. Ram Dass — show this lady out. (*Miss Minchin makes for Carrisford*) That is all, Miss Minchin — your bill will be paid.

[*Miss Minchin looks around and, putting shawl over head, exits. Donald whistles.*

CHILDREN (*delightedly*). Good-bye.
[*Ram Dass follows her off.*

SARA (*goes toward Carrisford, drawing in breath; shuts eyes and then opens them wide with wondering expression, like waking from dream of night before*). I — I — did not wake up from the other — last — night — that was real. I shall not wake up from *this*, shall I?

CARRISFORD.   No, no, you shall never wake up again to anything that is not happiness.

SARA.   But there was another little girl — she was as lonely and cold and hungry as I was — *could* you save her too?

CARRISFORD.   Yes, indeed.   Who was she?

SARA.   Her name is Becky — she is the scullery-maid. She has no one but me, and she will miss me so. She was the prisoner in the next cell.

CARRISFORD.   You shall take care of her — Carmichael — *(who turns)* will bring back to us the prisoner in the next cell.

CHILDREN *(rushing around her)*.   You're found — you're found, — we are so glad you're found! [*All joyfully.*

SARA.   I didn't know I was lost, and now I'm found I can't quite believe it.

MRS. CARMICHAEL.   What shall we do to make her feel that her troubles are over and that she may be happy as she used to be?

DONALD.   I say, you said you would tell us a story. Tell us one now.

SARA.   Shall I?

ALL.   Yes, oh, yes, a story.

SARA.   Just as I used to ——?

CHILDREN.   Just as you used to.

SARA.   Well, — once upon a time, long, long ago — there lived a little Princess ——

CURTAIN

114

THE BIRTHDAY OF THE INFANTA

BASED ON A STORY BY OSCAR WILDE

By

STUART WALKER

THE BIRTHDAY OF THE INFANTA

By

STUART WALKER

Reprinted by permission of Hawthorn Properties (Elsevier-Dutton Publishing Co., Inc.) from the book *Portmanteau Adaptations* by Stuart Walker.

THE BIRTHDAY OF THE INFANTA

The Birthday of the Infanta was first produced in Binghamton, New York, on 4 November 1916. It was subsequently performed in New York City on 11 December of the same year.

By 1916 the number of professional children's theatre productions had begun to diminish markedly, both because of the lack of suitable plays to produce and because of the corresponding increase in children's theatre production in settlement house theatres and recreation centers. By that time numerous children's plays had been presented successfully in Broadway theatres, the most notable of which were Burnett's *The Little Princess*, James M. Barrie's *Peter Pan*, Alice Gerstenberg's *Alice in Wonderland*, and Jessie Braham White's *Snow White and the Seven Dwarfs*. There was still a market for professional children's theatre productions, but there were very few new playwrights working in the field. Stuart Walker was an important exception.

Walker functioned as producer, director, and playwright for his Portmanteau Theatre company, and he was thus in an excellent position to implement his goal of bringing quality theatre to *family* audiences. Such plays were a rarity at that time because, with the exception of the pantomime entertainment, the professional theatre productions generally reflected a sharp delineation between plays for children and plays for adults. Walker's Portmanteau Theatre productions provided an interesting bridge between the two by combining the simplicity usually found in plays for children with the more sophisticated characters and themes often associated with adult drama.

The Birthday of the Infanta, based on a story by Oscar Wilde, is the most famous of the plays produced by this group. It is a haunting work that is much different than the plays for children that preceded it. In the description of the setting offered at the beginning of the play, Walker describes a "grim stone arch" framing a "brilliant sky." Therein he subtly embodies the entire world of the play — a world of harsh contrasts. As the play opens we quickly discover that *The Birthday of the Infanta* is more a play of character than of action. Walker does not create a suspenseful plot structure, nor does he clearly articulate a conflict *between* characters. Instead, he effectively depicts complex characters in conflict with the contrasts within themselves.

The first major character that we meet is the Infanta, the young daughter of the King of Spain. Because of the rules of royalty this child is forced to act as an adult. The Infanta struggles with this situation, wanting both to be free to experience her childhood and to have the power and control she enjoys in her adult world. By the end of the play we see the resolution of this conflict in her simplistic, but very cynical, perspective of life. This is particularly apparent in the last scene, when, upon hearing that the Fantastic has died of a broken heart, she scornfully declares: "For the future let those who come to play with me have no hearts."

The Fantastic is the major focus of the play, and internal conflicts such as those briefly sketched in the Infanta are drawn in vivid detail in his interesting and pathetic character. His gnarled body creates a repulsive and, to some people, laughable image, yet his external features are in marked contrast to the gentle, naive, and romantic personality of the child inside. The play focuses first on the Fantastic's discovery of this duality and, second, on his complete inability to reconcile the two. The Infanta is able to find a precarious balance in her two personalities from which to manage her world; the Fantastic cannot. The reality of his physical being, coupled with the knowledge of just why he is a source of laughter, completely overpowers his gentle soul.

The play is not without its overly-sentimental moments, but Walker makes effective use of dialogue to evoke vivid images, particularly with the Fantastic's gradual and moving death. That this death corresponds directly with the Fantastic's increase in self-knowledge adds to the irony of the situation.

The Birthday of the Infanta is a study on the subject of death. During the course of the play we hear of the King who is in mourning for his dead wife. The Infanta talks of her uncle who "wishes" she "were dead." The Chamberlain reminisces about his dead son. Even the passing of the Infanta's childhood is made complete in her final, bitter tirade against the Fantastic who dared to die.

Before Walker established the Portmanteau Theatre he had studied at the American Academy of Dramatic Art and had worked for several years as an actor, play reader, and stage manager for David Belasco. He was thus well-trained in both the practical and commercial aspects of the business. But Walker elected not to mimic the naturalistic styles favored by Belasco, and chose instead to place more emphasis on the plays presented than on the details of physical production. The work of the Portmanteau Theatre Company was based on Walker's belief that a theatre experience should be centered on plays of high literary quality. He believed that audiences did not have to be dazzled by spectacle or be caught up in suspenseful plot structures. More importantly, he believed that even young people could understand and be entertained by serious dramatic literature.

The importance of *The Birthday of the Infanta* rests both in the play itself and in the spirit with which it was presented. It is a serious play, dealing with a serious subject, and although the story is distanced in time and place from a contemporary audience, it is told in an honest and forthright manner. It is a simple, evocative drama that offers

118

a poignant view of two tormented children. The characters are romanticized, but the play does not present a romantic view of the world. Unlike the happy-ever-after ending of *The Little Princess*, the Fantastic dies at the end of this play as a direct result of the cruelty of the Infanta. It is harsh material, unaltered for the child audience.

The Portmanteau Theatre Company operated for less than two years, and, coincidentally, its productions were among the last professional children's theatre productions presented during that era. By 1920 professional children's theatre activity had virtually ceased, and amateur groups struggled to continue the tradition.

The Birthday of the Infanta is an anomaly in the history of dramatic literature for children in this country. In the years after the demise of the Portmanteau Theatre, the children's theatre field was dominated by melodramatic dramatizations of fairy and folk tales. Although *The Birthday of the Infanta* is very different from these plays, it did not die with the Portmanteau Theatre operation. It has, in fact, been produced many times, by many different organizations, in the years since it was written. There have been very few plays like it in the history of the genre; however, as a testimony to a small but constant interest in serious plays for children, it has endured.

In the last twenty years the literature has become more diverse as several playwrights have included serious themes and subjects in plays for children. Such modern plays as Kraus's *The Ice Wolf* and *Circus Home*, Harris's *The Arkansaw Bear*, Kral's *Special Class*, Kesselman's "Maggie Magalita" and Zeder's *Step on a Crack* present life-like protagonists struggling with very real personal problems. Although these plays are all very different from one another, they are alike in that they directly address serious and, in some instances, controversial subjects. When compared with such works, *The Birthday of the Infanta* creaks with age, appearing more as a detached period piece than a serious statement about life. But as quaint as *The Birthday of the Infanta* may seem from that perspective, when one considers the nature of the dramatic literature for children in 1916 the significance of this play becomes clear. Children's theatre of that era was comprised primarily of settlement house recreational dramas, more formal theatre productions of plays like *Peter Pan* and *The Little Princess*, and a host of fairy tale dramas. These plays reinforced the idea that evil in the world is always punished and that all conflicts have happy endings. *The Birthday of the Infanta* presented that audience with a different perspective contained in a well-written and provocative drama.

STUART ARMSTRONG WALKER (1880–1941) was born at Augusta, Kentucky, and educated at University of Cincinnati (B.S. 1903) and The American Academy of Dramatic Art. After working as an actor and stage manager for David Belasco, Walker established his own Portmanteau Theatre Company in 1915. This group played at two theatres in New York then toured throughout the midwestern United States.

Walker abandoned this project in 1917 and went on to other theatre-related positions. He was director of the Indianapolis Repertory Company (1917–1923) and the Cincinnati Repertory Company (1923–1931). Walker then pursued a career as a film director, for which he is best known as the director of *Great Expectations* for Universal Pictures. Other plays of note written by Walker and performed by the Portmanteau Theatre Company include *Six Who Pass While the Lentils Boil*, *Jonathan Makes a Wish*, and *Seventeen.*

THE BIRTHDAY OF THE INFANTA

(Founded on Oscar Wilde's Story)

Characters

THE INFANTA OF SPAIN.

THE DUCHESS OF ALBUQUERQUE.

THE COUNT OF TIERRA-NUEVA.

THE CHAMBERLAIN.

THE FANTASTIC.

A MOORISH PAGE.

ANOTHER PAGE.

The scene is the royal balcony overlooking a garden.
The time is the sixteenth century.

THE BIRTHDAY OF THE INFANTA

The opening of the curtains discloses a balcony overlooking a garden. The grim stone arch frames a brilliant sky. Gay flowers and a few white roses cover the railing. A bit of gaudy awning which can be lowered over the arch flutters in the breeze. At the right is a large mirror so draped that the dull, black hangings can be lowered to cover the mirror entirely. The hangings are of velvet, powdered with suns and stars. At the left similar hangings adorn a doorway. There are rich floor coverings and several formal chairs.

A Moorish attendant in black and yellow livery enters and arranges the chairs, and stands at attention.

The Infanta enters, followed by the Duchess of Albuquerque. The Infanta is dressed in gray brocade, very, very stiff and stately. She is small, with reddish hair and a settled air of self-possession and formality. Occasionally her eyes twinkle and her feet suggest her childishness; but she soon recovers herself under the watchful eye of the Camerera, and she never really forgets that she is the Infanta of Spain.

The Infanta bows, if the slight inclination of her head can be called bowing, to the Moorish attendant. The Duchess also inclines her head and stands in the doorway.

INFANTA.   I would be alone.

DUCHESS.   Your Highness —

INFANTA.   I would be alone.
    [*The Duchess turns in the doorway and speaks to those behind her.*

DUCHESS.   Her highness would be alone. (*Then to the Infanta*) This is unheard of.

INFANTA.   My birthday is rare enough to be almost unheard of, your Grace of Albuquerque. I would be alone on my birthday — and I'm going to be alone! (*Then to the attendant*) You may go! . . . But wait. . . . (*She stands admiringly before the mirror*) Hold back the curtain. (*The attendant lifts the curtain. She preens herself*) Why do I not look so well in my own suite? See how wonderful this is here. Look at the gold in my hair.

DUCHESS.   That is vanity, your Highness.

INFANTA.   Can I not admire myself on my birthday? Have I so many birthdays that I must live them as I live every other day?

DUCHESS.   What is wickedness on other days is also wickedness on your birthday.

INFANTA. *(taking a white rose from the balustrade and trying it in her hair and at her waist).* See — see — I like it here.

[*The Duchess, outraged, speaks to the attendant.*

DUCHESS. You may go.

INFANTA. No, no — stay — draw the curtains across the mirror!

DUCHESS. What will your father say?

[*The Infanta is quite beside her little self.*

INFANTA. Draw the curtains across the mirror and hide me from myself as those curtains hide my dead mother's room!

DUCHESS. Please —

INFANTA. I have spoken, your Grace. The curtains are to be drawn. We shall have no mirror to-day.

[*The attendant closes the curtain.*

INFANTA. You may go!

[*The attendant exits.*

The Infanta goes to the balustrade and looks into the gardens below.

The Duchess, quite at a loss what to do, finally crosses to the Infanta.

DUCHESS. Your Highness, I am compelled to remonstrate with you. What will his Majesty, your father, say?

INFANTA. My father will say nothing. He does not seem to care.

DUCHESS. Oh — Oh — Oh —

INFANTA. And my uncle wishes that I were dead. . . . No one cares. I have to be a queen all the time, and I can never be a little girl like the little girl I saw in Valladolid. She just played . . . and no one corrected her every moment.

DUCHESS. You play with the finest dolls in the world.

INFANTA. I do not have mud like hers!

DUCHESS. Mud!

INFANTA. I'd like to smear my face!

DUCHESS. Oh!

INFANTA. And I'd like to climb a tree!

DUCHESS. Oh, your Highness, you fill me with horror! You forget that you are the daughter of a king!

INFANTA. Well, it's my birthday — and I'm tired of being a wooden body.

[*She seats herself most unmajestically on the footstool.*

DUCHESS. Such wickedness! I shall have to call the Grand Inquisitor. There is a devil in you!

INFANTA. Call him! I'll rumple my hair at him.

DUCHESS. He'll forbid you to enjoy your birthday.

INFANTA. What is it for my birthday — the same old story.

DUCHESS (*mysteriously*). Who knows?

INFANTA (*not so surely*). When I was ten, they had dancing in the garden, but I could not go amongst the little girls. They played and I looked on.

DUCHESS. An Infanta of the house of Aragon must not play with children.

INFANTA. And when I was eleven they had dancing in the garden and a shaggy bear and some Barbary apes; but I could only sit here. I couldn't touch the bear, even when he smiled at me. And when one of the apes climbed to this balustrade, you drew me away.

DUCHESS. Such animals are very dangerous, your Highness.

INFANTA. I do not care. I do not want to be an Infanta.

DUCHESS. You are the daughter of Ferdinand, by grace of God, King of Spain!

INFANTA. Will my father come to me to-day? And will he smile?

DUCHESS. This is all for you alone.

INFANTA. Will not my sad father then come to me to-day? And will he not smile?

DUCHESS. He will see you after the surprise.

INFANTA. A surprise?

DUCHESS. Yes, your Highness.

INFANTA. What is it?

DUCHESS. I cannot tell.

INFANTA.   If I guess?

DUCHESS.   Perhaps.

INFANTA.   It's hobby-horses!

DUCHESS.   No.
   [*They almost forget their royalty.*

INFANTA.   It's an African juggler with two green and gold snakes in a red basket.

DUCHESS.   No.

INFANTA.   In a blue basket?

DUCHESS.   No.

INFANTA *(ecstatically).*   Three snakes?

DUCHESS.   Not at all.

INFANTA *(dully).*   Is it a sermon by the Grand Inquisitor?

DUCHESS.   No.

INFANTA *(with new hope).*   Is it a troupe of Egyptians with tambourines and zithers?

DUCHESS.   No.

INFANTA.   Is it something I've never seen before?

DUCHESS.   Never in the palace.

INFANTA *(screaming).*   It's a fantastic!

DUCHESS.   Who knows?

INFANTA.   Oh, it's a fantastic. It's a fantastic!
   [*She dances about.*

DUCHESS.   Your Highness forgets herself.

INFANTA.   It's a fantastic! It's a fantastic! *(She suddenly regains her poise)* Where is my cousin, the Count of Tierra-Nueva? I shall tell him that I am to be entertained on my birthday by a fantastic. And I shall let him come here to see it.
   [*The Moorish attendant steps inside the door and holds the curtain aside.*

INFANTA.   Your Grace, inform the Chamberlain that I shall have the fantastic dance for me in my balcony. The sun in the garden hurts my eyes. Besides, I want to touch his back.
   [*She goes out, every inch a queen.*

DUCHESS.   She has guessed. Tell the Chamberlain to send the fantastic here.

ATTENDANT.   The fantastic is waiting in the ante-chamber, your Grace.

[*The Duchess exits after the Infanta.*

The Attendant crosses to ante-chamber.

ATTENDANT.   Her Grace, the Duchess of Albuquerque, bids you enter. Inform the Chamberlain that her Highness, the Infanta, is ready for the dance.

[*The Fantastic and an Attendant enter. The Fantastic is a hunchback, with a huge mane of black hair and a bright face that shows no trace of beauty, but great light and wonder.*

The Fantastic looks about the balcony. It is all so strange to him. As he goes about touching the things in the place the Attendant follows him closely, watching him with eagle eyes. As the boy nears the mirror and lays his hand upon the black velvet hangings the Attendant steps in front of him and prevents his opening the curtains. The little boy then sits — a very small, misshapen little creature — on the steps of the balcony. The Chamberlain enters. He is a middle-aged man, with some tenderness left in his somewhat immobile face, and when he addresses the little boy there is a note of pathos that is almost indefinable.

CHAMBERLAIN.   Little grotesque, you are to see the King's daughter!

FANTASTIC (*almost overcome*).   Where is she?

CHAMBERLAIN.   Come now, you must not be afraid.

FANTASTIC.   I have never seen a king's daughter.

CHAMBERLAIN.   You must smile.

FANTASTIC.   Is she very big — and all bright and shiny?

CHAMBERLAIN.   Smile! You did not have such a long face yesterday. That is why we bought you.

FANTASTIC.   Will she smile upon me?

CHAMBERLAIN.   You must make her smile.

FANTASTIC.   Will she beat me if I do not make her smile?

CHAMBERLAIN.   You shall be beaten if you displease her. This is her Highness's birthday. And you are to dance for her to make her happy.

FANTASTIC.   I have never danced for a king's daughter before.

CHAMBERLAIN. You must dance bravely before her as you danced when we found you in the woods yesterday.

FANTASTIC. I am afraid of the King's daughter.

CHAMBERLAIN. We cannot have fear on the Infanta's birthday. We must have happiness.

FANTASTIC. I wish my father had not sold me.

CHAMBERLAIN. Your father was very poor, and he wanted you to make the Infanta happy.

FANTASTIC. My father did not care for me.

CHAMBERLAIN. You shall make the Infanta happy.

FANTASTIC. If you had a son would you sell him?

CHAMBERLAIN. You were sold to the Infanta.

FANTASTIC. Have you a son?

CHAMBERLAIN. No.

FANTASTIC. My father had seven sons.

CHAMBERLAIN. I had a little boy once.

FANTASTIC. And did you sell him?

CHAMBERLAIN. No. He went away. . . . He died.

FANTASTIC. Could he make the Infanta smile?

CHAMBERLAIN. I think he could.

FANTASTIC. Did he dance for her?

CHAMBERLAIN. No, he rode a hobby-horse in the mock bull fight.

FANTASTIC. What is a hobby-horse?

CHAMBERLAIN. A hobby-horse is a make-believe horse — like the stick that you ride through the woods.

FANTASTIC. Oh, can't I ride a hobby-horse in a bull fight?

CHAMBERLAIN. Some time. . . . If you make the Infanta happy on her birthday I'll give you a hobby-horse.

FANTASTIC. Can I ride it to-day — for her?

CHAMBERLAIN. No. You'll have to dance for her.

FANTASTIC. Is she terrible?

CHAMBERLAIN. Not if you are good.

FANTASTIC.   I think — I'm afraid.

CHAMBERLAIN.   Afraid? You were not afraid of the woods.

FANTASTIC.   They would not hurt me. I did not have to make them smile.

CHAMBERLAIN.   What will you do when you see the Infanta?

FANTASTIC.   I don't know. That man who dressed me up said I must smile and bow. My smile was very funny, he said, and my bow was funnier. I didn't try to be funny.

CHAMBERLAIN.   Some boys are funny even when they don't try to be.

FANTASTIC.   I don't feel funny. I just feel happy, and when I am happy people laugh. . . . Did she smile upon your son when he rode the hobby-horse?

CHAMBERLAIN.   She threw a rose to him.

FANTASTIC.   Do you think she'll throw a rose to me? I like roses. . . . Am I like your son?

CHAMBERLAIN.   My son was tall.

FANTASTIC.   I would be tall and strong, too; but I broke my back, and my brothers say I am very crooked. . . . I do not know. . . . I am not as strong as they are, but I can dance and sometimes I sing, too. . . . I make up my songs as I go along. And they are good songs, too, I know, because I've heard them.

CHAMBERLAIN.   How did you hear them, Señor Merry-Face?

FANTASTIC.   Some one sang them back to me.

CHAMBERLAIN.   A little girl, perhaps?

FANTASTIC.   Some one. . . . When I sang in the valley she would mock me.

CHAMBERLAIN.   Who was it? . . . Tell me.

FANTASTIC.   It was Echo.

CHAMBERLAIN.   Echo? And does she live near your house?

FANTASTIC.   She lives in the hills — and sometimes she used to come into the woods when it was very still.

CHAMBERLAIN.   Did you ever see Echo?

FANTASTIC.   No. You can't see her. . . . You can only hear her.

CHAMBERLAIN.   Would you like to see her?

128

FANTASTIC. I always wonder if Echo might not mock my face as she mocks my voice?

CHAMBERLAIN. Who knows?

FANTASTIC. I go into the hills and I sing a song and then Echo sings back to me — just as I sing. . . . But when I go into the woods Echo doesn't stand in front of me — just as I look.

CHAMBERLAIN. Haven't you ever seen yourself?

FANTASTIC. No, but I would like to. I always make people happy when they look at me. They always laugh. Would I laugh if Echo mocked my face?

CHAMBERLAIN. I do not know.

FANTASTIC. Am I really happy looking?

CHAMBERLAIN. You are a fantastic.

FANTASTIC. That sounds happy.

CHAMBERLAIN. I hope it always will be.

FANTASTIC. Have you ever seen yourself?

CHAMBERLAIN. Yes.

FANTASTIC. Did your son see himself?

CHAMBERLAIN. Yes.

FANTASTIC. Where?

CHAMBERLAIN. In a mirror.

FANTASTIC. Is that Echo's other name?

CHAMBERLAIN. Yes.

FANTASTIC. Can I see myself sometime?

CHAMBERLAIN. Yes.

FANTASTIC. I'll sing, too.
      [*The Attendant enters.*

ATTENDANT. Her Royal Majesty, the Infanta of Spain!
      [*The Fantastic is very much frightened.*

CHAMBERLAIN. Go behind the door there. . . . Wait. . . . Be brave. . . . Smile. . . . And do not speak until you are asked to.
      [*The Infanta enters sedately, followed by the Duchess and the Count of Tierra-Nueva, an unpleasant-looking boy of sixteen.*

The Chamberlain bows very low and kisses the Infanta's stiffly proffered hand.

INFANTA *(regally)*. My lord Chamberlain, this is our royal birthday, and in accord with the wish of our father, the King of Spain, we are to be entertained with some mirthful sport *(suddenly a little girl)* — and I know what it is. It's a fantastic.

CHAMBERLAIN. Your Highness, it is the pleasure of the Chamberlain to His Majesty, your father, the King of Spain, to offer my felicitations this day on which God has deigned to send happiness and good fortune to Spain in your royal person. His Majesty the King through me desired to surprise you with mirth this day.

INFANTA. Is our royal father well? And does he smile to-day?

CHAMBERLAIN. His Majesty does not smile, your Highness. He cannot smile in his great grief.

INFANTA. Let the surprise be brought to us. But I guessed what it was! . . . It must be very ugly and very crooked and very, very funny to look at — or we shall be highly displeased.

[*She settles into her royal place and takes on a manner.*

The Fantastic, having been summoned by the page, barely enters the door.

The Infanta, looking royally straight before her, does not turn her head.

After a moment.

INFANTA. Well?

CHAMBERLAIN. Here is the surprise, your Highness.

[*The Fantastic is the picture of grotesque misery. He looks first at the Chamberlain and then at the Infanta. Finally she turns to him, and he tries a timid smile and an awkward bow.*

The Infanta claps her little hands and laughs in sheer delight.

The Fantastic looks desperately at the Chamberlain.

INFANTA. Go on. . . . Isn't he funny!

CHAMBERLAIN *(to Fantastic)*. Bow again and then begin to dance.

FANTASTIC *(joyfully)*. She is only a little girl, and I've made her happy!

CHAMBERLAIN. What will you dance, Señor Merry-Face?

FANTASTIC. I'll dance the one I made up and no one ever saw or heard it except Echo. It's the dance of the autumn leaf. I'll show you what the autumn leaves do and I'll tell you what they say.

130

INFANTA. How do you know, you comic little beast?

FANTASTIC. I know because I live in the woods, up in the hills, and I dance with the leaves — and I have two pet woodpigeons.

INFANTA. Where is the music?

FANTASTIC. I sing — it's happier that way.

INFANTA. Dance! Dance!

[*The Fantastic bows in an absurdly grotesque way — his idea of stateliness and grace.*

INFANTA. I've never seen such a monstrous fantastic.

COUNT. We must touch his back before he goes — for good luck.

[*The Fantastic begins to sing and dance The Song of the Autumn Leaf.*

FANTASTIC (*singing*).
>All summer long
>I cling to the tree,
>Merrily, merrily!
>The winds play and play,
>But I cling to the tree,
>Merrily, merrily!
>The summer sun
>Is hot and gold.
>Cheerily, cheerily.
>But I hang on
>In the August heat,
>Wearily, wearily!
>I am not free,
>For I have to hang
>Wearily, wearily!
>Until autumn frosts
>Release my grasp,
>Cheerily, cheerily!
>Then I'm free,
>All crumpled and brown
>Merrily, merrily!
>I roll and I blow
>Up and around,
>Merrily, merrily!
>All crumpled and brown
>In my autumn coat,
>I dance in the wind,
>I hide in the rain,
>Dancing and blowing

And waiting for winter,
Cheerily, cheerily,
Merrily, merrily,
Wearily, wearily.

[*He falls like a dead leaf on to the floor.*
The Infanta is delighted.

INFANTA.   I'm going to throw him a rose!

DUCHESS.   Your Highness!

INFANTA.   See — like the Court ladies to Caffarelli, the treble.
[*The Fantastic has risen and bowed in his grotesque way.*
The Infanta tosses the rose to him.
He takes it up and, bowing absurdly, presses it to his lips.

DUCHESS (*who has never smiled*).   Your Highness, you must prepare
for your birthday feast.

INFANTA.   Oh, let him dance again! The same dance!

DUCHESS.   Think of the birthday feast, your Highness. Your father,
the King of Spain; your uncle, the Grand Inquisitor; the noble
children.

INFANTA.   Once more!

DUCHESS.   Your Highness, you must see the huge birthday cake with
your initials on it in painted sugar — and a silver flag. . . .

INFANTA.   Very well. He can dance again after my siesta. . . . My
cousin, I trust that you will see the next dance.

COUNT.   I'll ride a hobby-horse and he'll be the bull. It will be very
funny with such a funny bull.
[*He kisses her hand and exits the opposite way.*
*The Infanta, followed by the Duchess, exits, and as she goes she
looks once more at the Fantastic and breaks into a laugh.*
The Fantastic is delighted and stands looking after her.

CHAMBERLAIN.   Come!

FANTASTIC (*putting out his hand*).   I think she liked me.

CHAMBERLAIN.   The Infanta of Spain is the daughter of the King of
Spain. You have made her smile. Come!
[*They go out.*

*The Attendant crosses and closes the awning. He draws the cur-
tains from the mirror and preens himself a bit, looking now and
then until he disappears.*

A sunbeam coming through the fluttering awning, strikes the mirror, and reflects on to the tessellated floor.

There is a short intermezzo. Far-a-way harps and violins echo the Fantastic's little song.

The Fantastic enters furtively, looking about. He takes the rose from his bosom.

FANTASTIC. I think I'll ask her to come away with me when I've finished my dance.

[*He crosses to her door and listens. Then smiles and skips a step or two. He sees the sunbeam through the awning and goes to it. He again takes the rose from his coat and holds it in the sunlight. Again he dances to the door and listens, then turns facing the mirror for the first time. He breaks into a smile, but first hides the rose hastily. He waves his hand.*

FANTASTIC. Good morrow!...You are very funny!... You are very crooked!... Don't look that way!... Why do you frown at me? ... Can't you talk?... You only move your lips.... Oh, you funny little boy!

[*He puts his hands on his sides and breaks into a great laugh*

FANTASTIC. If you could see yourself, you'd laugh still more.

[*He makes a mocking bow and breaks into shouts. He plays before the mirror. The mockery is too clever.*

FANTASTIC. You mock me, you little beast!... Stop it! Speak to me. ... You make me afraid.... Like night in the forest.

[*He has never known anything like this. He is in turn enraged, terrified.*

He runs forward and puts out his hand. He rubs his hand over the face of the mirror and the cold, hard surface mystifies him. He brushes the hair from his eyes. He makes faces. He retreats. He looks about the room. He sees everything repeated in the mirror — the awning, the chairs, the sunbeam on the floor.

FANTASTIC *(calling)*. Echo!

[*He strains for an answer. He hides behind a chair. He makes a plan.*

FANTASTIC. I know, miserable little monster. You shan't mock me.

[*He takes the rose from his coat.*

FANTASTIC. She gave me this rose. It is the only one in the world. ... She gave it to me — to me.

[*He emerges from behind the chair and holds out the rose. With a dry sob he shrinks away and, fascinated, stares at the mirror. He compares the rose, petal by petal, terror and rage rising in*

*him. He kisses it and presses it to his heart. Suddenly he rushes
to the mirror with a cry. He touches the glass again, then with a
cry of despair he hurls himself sobbing on the floor. Once more
he looks upon the picture and then, covering his face with his
hands, he crawls away like a wounded animal, lies moaning in the
shadows and beating the ground with his impotent hands.*

*The Infanta enters, followed by the Count. At the sight of the
Fantastic the Infanta stops and breaks into a laugh.*

INFANTA. His dancing was funny, but his acting is funnier still. Indeed he is almost as good as the puppets.

[*His sobs grow fainter and fainter. He drags himself toward the
door, trying to hide his face. Then with a sudden gasp he clutches
his side and falls back across the step and lies quite still.*

The Infanta waits a moment.

INFANTA. That is capital; it would make even my father, the King
of Spain, smile. . . . But now you must dance for me:
Cheerily, cheerily!
Merrily, merrily!
Wearily, wearily!

COUNT. Yes, you must get up and dance and then we'll have a bull
fight and I'll kill you.

[*The Fantastic does not answer.*

INFANTA (*stamping her foot*). My funny little fantastic is sulking.
You must wake him up and tell him to dance for me.

COUNT. You must dance, little monster, you must dance. The Infanta
of Spain and the Indies wishes to be amused (*Then to a page*)
A whipping master should be sent for.

[*The page goes out.*

COUNT. Let's touch his back (*as the children touch his hump*) and
make a wish.

INFANTA. I *wish* he would dance.

[*Enter the Chamberlain and the Duchess.*

DUCHESS. Your Highness!

INFANTA. Make him dance or I shall have him flogged.

[*The Chamberlain rushes to the body. He kneels. Feels the heart
— sees the sunbeam and the exposed mirror — shrugs his shoulders — rises.*

CHAMBERLAIN. Mi bella Princess, your funny little fantastic will
never dance again.

134

INFANTA *(laughing).* But why will he not dance again?

CHAMBERLAIN. Because his heart is broken.

INFANTA *(thinks a moment, then frowns).* For the future let those who come to play with me have no hearts.

[*She passes out, not deigning to look back, every inch the queen — the disappointed, lonely, shut-in little queen.*

The others follow her properly according to rank; but the Chamberlain, remembering a little boy who would ride hobby-horses no more in mock bull fights, returns and throws the Infanta's mantilla over the little warped body. It is a moment of glory. The Chamberlain again starts to follow his Mistress; but memory is stronger than etiquette. He goes to the Fantastic and takes up the little hand which clutches something precious. He opens the fingers and finds the rose. He holds it out and lets the petals flutter to the floor. That is all.

THE CURTAINS CLOSE

THE EMPEROR'S NEW CLOTHES

A PLAY FOR CHILDREN IN THREE ACTS

By

CHARLOTTE CHORPENNING

THE EMPEROR'S NEW CLOTHES

By

CHARLOTTE B. CHORPENNING

THE EMPEROR'S NEW CLOTHES

The 1920's saw little significant growth in the repertoire of dramatic literature for children. With the almost complete cessation of professional children's theatre production at this time, very few writers were working in the field, and amateur theatre companies were forced to rely primarily on repeated revivals of the few plays that grew out of the professional work of the previous decades. Even the increase in children's theatre activity in community centers did little to offset this problem, because there the focus was more on plays to be performed *by* children than on plays to be performed *for* children.

While the development of dramatic literature for children was stalled, adult theatre in this country was thriving. For the first time the American theatre was gaining international recognition as groups such as the Theatre Guild and the Provincetown Players were actively encouraging new writers, directors, and designers. At the center of this surge of activity was a group of theatre artists that had, at one time or another, studied with the noted George Pierce Baker. These included Eugene O'Neill, S.N. Behrman, Sidney Howard, Robert Edmond Jones, Lee Simonson, Donald Oenslager, Philip Barry, and Samuel Hume.

It would be many years before the professional theatre community would once again turn its attention to theatre for children, or before children's theatre would enjoy as great a renaissance as that of the adult theatre of the 1920's, but by 1935 there was renewed activity in the field as several writers began making significant contributions to the repertoire of dramatic literature for children. Prominent among them was still another former student of George Pierce Baker, Charlotte B. Chorpenning.

Chorpenning worked in the amateur theatre, a theatre that did not promote experimental or innovative styles. Amateur groups were interested in producing children's plays with recognizable titles and with subjects that would not be controversial to the parents who brought their children to the theatre. Chorpenning and the other playwrights of this time wrote plays to meet this demand.

Chorpenning began writing plays for children at a time when there were few such plays available, and she subsequently became the most prolific and influential playwright for children of her time. Although *The Emperor's New Clothes*, first produced in 1931, was one of her earliest attempts at writing children's plays, it eventually became one of her most popular works. An analysis of this play reveals some of Chorpenning's techniques as a playwright, and some of the specific ways in which she influenced the literature for many years after this play was written.

Like the majority of Chorpenning's plays, this work is based on a well known story. But Chorpenning was herself a trained and practiced playwright, and she was seldom content merely to adapt such stories to the stage. *The Emperor's New Clothes* retains the basic idea of the Hans Christian Andersen tale, but Chorpenning altered the conflict and added characters and situations to the extent that the play is much different from the original story.

The Anderson tale depicts two rogues who dupe a vain Emperor by pretending to weave his gold thread and jewels into magnificent garments. The rogues tell everyone that the garments will be invisible to those who are unfit for the office they hold or those who are simpleminded. All of the people are foolish enough to fall for this clever trick, and the rogues disappear with the Emperor's riches.

In the Chorpenning play the action is still centered on the weaving of imaginary clothes, but the basic conflict is between a group of weavers and Han, the Minister of Royal Robes. Han convinces the Emperor that the weavers are hoarding the Emperor's fine thread and jewels and using inferior materials to weave the Emperor's clothes. Meanwhile, Han steals the valuable materials for himself.

The rogue characters, Zar and Zan, join the struggle on the side of the weavers and develop the charade of weaving imaginary clothes in order to expose the greedy Han. This scheme also provides the means whereby a whole range of foolish characters, both sympathetic and unsympathetic, are revealed.

Zar and Zan function more as facilitators of the action of the play than as antagonists or protagonists in the conflict. Through their conversations with each other they explain motives and relationships of other characters, reveal important expository information, and establish an emotional tone for each of the scenes. Because their relationship with the audience is more intellectual than emotional, it is important that they direct the audience sympathies to other characters in the play. As each character is presented with the test of the imaginary clothes, the two adventurers manipulate the results of the test and thus the audience's perspective of the characters involved. For example, although Zar and Zan use the test as a trap for Han, they patiently coach the Empress so that she might "see" the imaginary clothes.

Chorpenning relies heavily upon spectacle to underscore the basic ideas in this play. The formal elements of the oriental society, as seen in the costumes and in the scenery, are often in marked contrast to the frenzied action. These same elements contrast the social classes within this world and illustrate the riches that bring out the greed of some of the characters. Of particular note are the two parades wherein Han, and then the Emperor, pass among the people in the royal city.

In each of these instances, the sights and sounds of the entourages sharply delineate royalty from their subjects.

Chorpenning thus made major changes in the epigrammatic tale to develop a drama very much in the tradition of the well-made play *(piece bien faite)*. The play includes characters with very little depth and a predictable plot structure wherein first the situation is clearly revealed, the action built to a crisis and a climax, and then the conflict is resolved. It is a design used often in the history of the theatre, primarily because it entertains while making few demands upon an audience.

By restructuring the story, Chorpenning also placed more emphasis on the moralistic elements of the tale. In this play, as in all of her plays, Chorpenning clearly delineates between "good" characters and "bad" characters. In the tradition of such melodramas as *The Little Princess*, Chorpenning changed the ending of the story so that the "bad" character, Han, is punished for his deeds. It is a very clear cause-to-effect relationship that is not a part of the original story.

Chorpenning also incorporated a series of actions that make the villain appear increasingly foolish as the play progresses. Of particular note is the scene where Zar and Zan accuse Han of standing on the imaginary garments. This, in turn, causes Han to jump frantically (and comically) around the room in an attempt to avoid standing on the Emperor's clothes. He is expertly manipulated by the adventurers in the story, and this decreases his threat in the eyes of the audience.

The resolution of this conflict between the "good" and the "bad" is handled differently than in a more melodramatic play. In *The Little Princess* Sara prevails not so much through her own wits, but because of the intervention of another character — and then only after the intervention is forestalled until maximum suspense has been created. In *The Emperor's New Clothes*, Zar and Zan are quickly identified with the "good"; and they then proceed to defeat the "bad" entirely through their own actions. Suspense is thus minimized, but the action of the play is made more complex as it becomes necessary to *show how* the "good" characters outwit the "bad" characters. In contrast, a more melodramatic play would simply focus on the oppression of the protagonist until a character or incident was introduced causing a startling reversal and resolving the conflict.

The moral or theme of *The Emperor's New Clothes* is stated explicitly in the dialogue. Zar and Zan note that it is "easy to make foolish people do what you want them to do," and they then proceed to demonstrate this, repeatedly.

The Emperor's New Clothes is representative of the over thirty plays that Chorpenning added to the repertoire of dramatic literature for children in this country. It is a moralistic version of a well-known story, dramatized in a predictable manner. To modern audiences many of Chorpenning's plays seem verbose, didactic, and very much constrained by the well-made play form. But Chorpenning approached her work with a seriousness of purpose and a skill at writing that brought the level of dramatic literature for children high above the standards of the then-prevalent, recreation-oriented, children's theatre. Through her writing and teaching Chorpenning was instrumental in increasing the interest in the production of theatre *for* children and in developing an entire generation of new playwrights for the field. As Chorpenning's plays became a model for other playwrights to follow, some of these same playwrights, in turn, translated Chorpenning's ideas into formulas for writing plays for children. The result was that, in the ensuing years, there were many plays written in the Chorpenning style, but few of these reflected Chorpenning's skill as a playwright.

The Emperor's New Clothes is not as timely and as theatrically sophisticated as much of the modern literature in the field, but it is one of the better examples of what was once a very popular form. If one looks beyond the dated language and the self-conscious style, one finds a play that is soundly constructed, humorous, and entertaining.

CHARLOTTE BARROWS CHORPENNING (1872–1955) first worked as a high school English teacher in Columbus, Ohio (1895). She subsequently taught at Wolfe Hall in Denver, Colorado (1901–1904) and at Winona Normal School in Winona, Minnesota (1904–1921). In 1913 Chorpenning took a leave of absence from her teaching to study with George Pierce Baker at Radcliffe College in Cambridge, Massachusetts. Chorpenning returned to Winona in 1915, but she was then intent upon making a career as a professional playwright. When she was not immediately successful in that regard she turned her attention to community drama, becoming a noted authority on the subject.

Beginning in 1921, Chorpenning worked at the Recreation Training School in Chicago, which led to a position in the School of Speech at Northwestern University in 1927. At that time Chorpenning began writing plays for children, and, in 1932, she became director of children's theatre at the Goodman Theatre of the Chicago Art Institute. She held that position until her retirement in 1952. During her lifetime she wrote more than fifty plays for children, over thirty of which have been published. Among the most popular have been *Jack and the Beanstalk, Rumpelstiltskin, Cinderella* and *The Sleeping Beauty*.

THE EMPEROR'S NEW CLOTHES

Cast of Characters

ZAR

ZAN

TSEIN

LING

MONG

FAH

THE GONG BOY

HAN

THE GENERAL

THE EMPEROR

THE EMPRESS

A CHILD

WEAVERS OF THE ROYAL STUFFS

CITIZENS

TIME: Long ago.

PLACE: A country much like China.

ACT I: *The Street of the Royal Weavers. The middle of the morning.*

ACT II: *A room in Han's quarters, in the palace. Noon, the next day.*

ACT. III: *Same as* ACT I. *Afternoon of the same day.*

THE EMPEROR'S NEW CLOTHES

ACT I

The Street of the Royal Weavers, in the EMPEROR'S *city. It should suggest China but need not be too literal. High on one of the buildings is the sign: The Street of the Royal Weavers.*

Enter ZAR *and* ZAN, *looking eagerly about. The important thing about them is that they are full of the zest for life, and are tingling for adventure. They belong to no particular country.*

ZAR. Everything is so quiet.

ZAN. This is the emperor's own city. It ought to be a good place for things to happen.

ZAR. (*Reading the sign.*) The Street of the Royal Weavers.

ZAN. This ought to be a good street for adventures. The Royal Weavers have gold, and jewels to work with.

ZAR. And bright threads! Green, like jade. And scarlet. And the color of the sky.

ZAN. And they think up strange things to weave!

ZAR. Trees that nobody ever saw! And white birds, like the ones you see in the clouds!

ZAN. And dragons!

ZAR. Oh, strange things could happen here!

ZAN. We have come to a fine place!

ZAR. But why is it so quiet?

ZAN. They can't be asleep. It's the middle of the morning.

ZAR. (*Pointing to the houses.*) I feel as if something exciting were happening in there.

ZAN. Listen, and find out. (*They run to put an ear to the door of one of the houses, but just as they do so a great gong sounds, off, making them leap high in the air with fright. A* GONG BOY *enters [or it could be a group of Chinese court maidens, if desired to use more girls] followed by* HAN, *the minister of the* EMPEROR'S *robes.* HAN *stalks by, ferocious, proud, looking neither to the right nor left, the gong being struck at every second or third step. The rogues leap to hide at first sight of them, peering from behind some corner.* HAN *crosses the stage and exits. The rogues steal out to gaze after him.*) What do you suppose that means?

144

ZAR. It makes me shiver.

ZAN. I don't like that man.

ZAR. I don't like his face.

ZAN. I don't like the way he walks.

ZAR. He wants people to be afraid of him.

(Again the gong sounds, and sends them scurrying to hide. The GONG BOY *[or the maidens] returns, halts center, and strikes the gong with a flourish.)*

GONG BOY. *(Chanting.)*
Weavers of cunning silks!
Bring out your wares!
Han passes by! *(Flourish on the gong.)*
Great Han passes by! *(Flourish.)*
He buys stuff for the emperor's new clothes!
One hundred and one robes the emperor needs
Before the April moon is old!
Bring out your wares!
Great Han will choose!
Bring out your shining silks!
(Flourish and exit.)

ZAN. The man's name is Han.

ZAR. He's coming here again!

ZAN. To buy cloth for the emperor's robes!

ZAR. How can he choose for the emperor's robes? He doesn't know what is beautiful!

ZAN. He doesn't care whether things are beautiful or not!

ZAR. He'll cheat the weavers!

ZAN. If he tries to cheat the weavers, we'll take their part!

ZAR. This will be the best adventure we've ever had!

ZAN. I wonder why the weavers don't bring out their stuff?

ZAR. I wonder if they heard the call. *(He crosses to listen at a door.)* Someone's crying.

ZAN. *(At another door.)* Some one's crying here. *(The doors are suddenly pushed open, sending the rogues tumbling across the stage.* TSEIN *and* MONG *enter.)*

TSEIN. Aha! I heard you at my door!

MONG.   That wicked Han sent you!

ROGUES.   *(Together.)*   Nobody sent us!

TSEIN.   What were you doing at my door?

BOTH.   We were looking for an adventure.

MONG.   I'll give you an adventure! *(She runs about, beating on the doors.)* Ling! Fah! all of you! A spy! Another spy!

TSEIN. *(As crowd enters.)*   They were listening at our doors!

CROWD.   A spy! Han's men! Han sent them! *(Etc.)*

LING.   Beat the coats off their backs!

CROWD.   Beat them!

LING.   The way Han's servants beat me, when I stuck to my price!

MONG.   Starve them! The way Han is starving our children!

FAH.   Bring some cord! Tie them up! Bring me a lash!

ZAN.   We aren't Han's men!

ZAR.   We don't like Han!

ZAN.   We want to take your part against him!

TSEIN.   What has he done to you?

ZAN.   He hasn't done anything to us.

ZAR.   We never heard of him till he went past just now.

FAH.   Don't believe them! Everyone knows Han!

MONG.   Every one knows how he robs the people!

CROWD.   Beat them! Lash them!

   (They raise their lashes, etc., but the OLD WOMAN *checks them.)*

OLD WOMAN.   Wait!—Why do you take our part against him if he has done nothing to you?

ZAR.   We don't like his face.

ZAN.   We don't like the way he walks.

FAH.   Those are not reasons.

ZAN.   Yes they are. We don't like people who do those things.

ZAR.   That's why we want to take your part.

OLD WOMAN.   Come here. *(They approach her fearfully. She fixes her piercing eye on their faces, probing their eyes.)* What they say is true. Untie their hands.

FAH.   Put away the lash.

TSEIN.   Who are you?

ZAN.   His name is Zar.

ZAR.   His name is Zan.

FAH.   Where do you come from?

ZAR.   From wherever we've had an adventure.

MONG.   Where have you had adventures?

ZAN.   In towered cities, and green fields.

ZAR.   Beyond the mountains and across the seas.

TSEIN.   What is your trade?

ZAR.   Whatever we need to make things happen right.

MONG.   There isn't any sense to that.

ZAN.   Once we were sailors, because our plan needed ships.

ZAR.   Once we carried a beggar's bowl because we needed to watch the faces of many men.

FAH.   What will you do in our city?

ZAN.   We don't know yet.

ZAR.   Our plan hasn't come.

TSEIN.   How can you take our part against Han?

ZAN.   We don't know that yet, either.

MONG.   You talk foolish talk.

ZAR.   Do you know what flowers and dragons and birds you will weave into your next piece of cloth?

MONG.   Of course not. Not till we start.

TSEIN.   They are waiting in our fingers and our hearts.

ZAR.   Our next adventure is waiting in us like that.

ZAN.   Just trust us and we will take your part against Han!

LING.   Aren't you afraid? Han is the richest man in the kingdom.

FAH.   And the most powerful.

147

MONG.   Even the emperor does what Han says. He thinks of nothing but his new clothes and believes whatever Han tells him.

TSEIN.   It is a great risk to go against Han. He has spies everywhere.

LING.   You see it is dangerous to take our part.

ZAR.   If it were safe it wouldn't be an adventure!

ZAN.   Have you any plan against Han now?

MANY.   Yes.

TSEIN.   We were praying to our ancestors for courage to carry it out.

ZAN.   Tell us your plan.

(The gong sounds off. Every one starts in terror.)

TSEIN.   He is coming! Listen, and you will hear our plan. *(The rogues run to hide. The weavers gather together, like a herd in danger.)* Who will speak for us?

FAH.   I will speak!

MONG.   No! You will be too angry. Han will have us all killed for what you say!

TSEIN.   Let Ling speak. His tongue runs smooth.
(Enter HAN, preceded by the GONG BOY, who stops with a flourish.)

HAN.   What is this? Did you not hear the boy, who told you I was coming?

FAH.   We heard!!
(LING, putting FAH aside and trying to smooth over his violence.)

LING.   We heard, great Han.

HAN.   Then why is not your cloth spread out for me to see?

LING.   You are very great, O Han. But it is in our minds to return to the way of our fathers.

HAN.   Your fathers were weavers like yourselves.

LING.   That is true, great Han. But our fathers, and their fathers before them, showed the stuff they wove to the emperor himself. From the emperor's hand they received the price of their work.

HAN.   This is insolence! Bring out your cloth!

LING.   When the emperor comes, O great and mighty Han.

HAN.   The emperor has no time to be picking and choosing from many pieces of cloth! He must be dressed in splendor, and every

148

hour in a new robe. Bring out your goods that I may choose for him before he comes! *(No one moves.)* How! *(The weavers crowd closer together, trembling but doggedly silent.)* My word is the same as the emperor's word! I can cast those who disobey me into a dungeon! I can have their heads struck off! Fetch it out! What are you waiting for?

LING. We wish to show it only to the emperor, Oh just and merciful Han.

HAN. The emperor will see what I show him, and nothing more!

FAH. *(Breaking out of the crowd.)* And you will show him only what we pay you to show him! And when we have put our price in gold into your hand, you will find fault with our weaving, and keep the best for yourself, pretending it is unfit! *(The weavers try to restrain him, but he breaks from them, shaking his fist in* HAN's *face.)* You are a thief and a liar! You keep the costly gold the emperor sends for our weaving and give us make-believe gold! You keep the rare jewels and send us glass in their place! We will not pay you a penny! Our stuff is safe locked up in our houses! The price of it shall never touch your fingers!

(The weavers try to hush him, more and more terrified as HAN's *anger mounts. Finally they hold him quiet.)*

HAN. *(Quiet but fierce.)* The emperor shall never see one thread of your work.

LING. When the emperor comes, Great Han ——

HAN. I will tell him that not a piece of it is fit for his eyes to rest on. You shall not sell the emperor one yard this whole year.
(Murmurs from the crowd.)

A BYSTANDER *(Above it.)* How shall we live?

HAN. After the emperor has gone, I will send my servants into your houses to find out your stuff and tear it into tatters and cast it into the mud of the streets.

TSEIN. *(On her knees.)* No, no, Great Han! This time I have woven the most beautiful thing of my life. Do not destroy it!

HAN. Let me see it.
(TSEIN struggles with herself. The weavers hang on her decision, anxious lest she give up.)

TSEIN. *(Lifting her head resolutely.)* I am a weaver. Ling spoke for us all.

HAN. The emperor is on his way to your street, with his empress. I will go to prepare his mind. Be ready for his wrath.

(Exit HAN, *preceded by the* GONG BOY. *Weeping and despair among the weavers.)*

LING.   Tsein! Bring out the most beautiful thing of your life. If it is here, the emperor's eyes may rest on it.

TSEIN.   If he sees it he never can destroy it!

MONG.   We will all bring out our work!

(They run into the houses. ZAR *and* ZAN, *who have been huddled together, attentive, come out of the corner.)*

ZAN *(Very anxiously.)*   What is your plan?

ZAR.   It hasn't come yet.

ZAN.   Do you remember, once, how an old, old woman pulled yards and yards of shining stuff out of a nutshell?

ZAR.   It was like a ribbon of spider web with the dew on it in the moonlight.

ZAN.   I wish we had it here. We could sell it and give the gold to the weavers.

ZAR.   A wish isn't a plan.

ZAN.   We must think!

(They shut their eyes and twist their bodies and screw up their faces.)

ZAR. *(His eyes tight closed.)*   I can see shining stuffs, all green and coral and turquoise. And petals of roses blowing over it. And gold, like ripening rice fields in the sun. And purple, like far hills at sunset time. If I could only weave, I could make the most wonderful cloth in the world.

ZAN.   That isn't a plan, either.

ZAR.   No. The plan hasn't come yet.

(They think harder than ever.)

ZAN. *(With a great leap.)*   I have thought something!

ZAR.   What?

ZAN.   It is easy to make foolish people do what you want them to do!

ZAR.   That is true! You have only to call out what is most foolish in them, and you can make them do anything you wish!

ZAN.   Is there anything foolish in Han?

ZAR. Han is too wicked to be foolish.

ZAN. *(Cautiously.)* Is there anything foolish in the emperor?
(They think hard.)

ZAR. *(With secrecy.)* I have thought of something foolish in the emperor.

ZAN. Tell it to me.

ZAR. He cares about nothing but clothes.

ZAN. We must think about that!
(They almost have convulsions with the intensity of their thought. The EMPEROR'S music is heard, distant, approaching. The weavers enter in haste, and kneel, putting their bundles of weaving beside them, ready to kowtow to the EMPEROR as soon as he appears. The EMPEROR enters, preceded by the GONG BOY and HAN. After kowtowing three times, the weavers lift their stuffs, holding them out to the EMPEROR, beseechingly. The EMPRESS walks with the EMPEROR. She is entranced with the stuffs. She is very young and very pretty.)

HAN. Put up your stuffs. They are not fit for the eyes of the emperor to rest on.

WEAVERS *(Supplicating.)* Let us show you our work. See! Look at the beauty of it. Etc.

EMPEROR. Tell them to be silent.

HAN. Silence!

EMPEROR. Tell them my will.

HAN. Bow to the ground before your emperor. Hear his august word. *(They prostrate themselves.)* You have become a shame to your trade! You have left the patterns of your fathers for new and easy ones! You have used glass for jewels!
EMPRESS. *(Eagerly.)* Those jewels are not glass.

HAN. *(To the EMPEROR.)* You see? It is as I have told you. The empress is too stupid to know real jewels from false.

EMPEROR. *(Uneasy.)* The empress should not be stupid.

HAN. If it is the will of the emperor, I will instruct the empress for an hour every morning and an hour every evening. Then she may learn to tell pure jewels. She will no longer be stupid. The emperor will not need to send her away.
(The EMPRESS gasps and shrinks, wide-eyed with terror at the thought, but murmurs under her breath.)

EMPRESS. I do not want to be with Han. I do not like him.

EMPEROR. I should not like to send her away.

HAN. A stupid person is not fit to be empress.

EMPEROR. You shall instruct the empress.

(*Weavers who have looked up during this, reach their goods to the* EMPRESS, *murmuring.*)

WEAVERS. Your eyes are true. You are right. The jewels are pure, Etc.

(HAN *gives a signal to the gong, which is sounded and they prostrate themselves again.*)

HAN. You have tried to deceive the empress, because she is stupid. For this your looms shall be broken and your weaving destroyed. You shall bear this unfit stuff before me to my rooms in the palace, that I may see it cut to pieces and utterly destroyed.

FAH. (*Above cries of grief and rage from the weavers.*) You will sell it! You will make yourself rich on it! (*To the* EMPEROR.) He is robbing us, because we refuse to give him half the price.

CROWD. (*Wildly.*) He's a cheat! He takes our money! The empress is right! He starves us! He's grinding us down! Etc.

(*Great pounding on the gong. The* EMPRESS *struggles between her desire to defend her judgment and her fear of* HAN, *but the fear is greater and keeps her silent. The* EMPEROR *lifts a hand, his eyes flashing. There is sudden and absolute silence.*)

EMPEROR. Han is my minister. His word is my word. (ZAR *and* ZAN *think, desperately.*)

HAN. From this day you are no longer the royal weavers. I will find others to live in these houses and weave the patterns that have been used in this street from early times.

TSEIN. Great emperor, our fathers have taught us. There are in the whole land no others who know the secret ways to weave for the emperor.

HAN. If there are none in this land I will fetch them from other lands.

ZAR. (*Softly to* ZAN) It has come. (*He crosses to the* EMPEROR, *and kowtows.* ZAN *follows, at his heels.*) Great emperor, we are weavers from a far-away land. We can weave you a stuff that is like no other stuff in the world. We can weave a power into it, that no one else under the sun or moon can weave into cloth.

EMPEROR. What power is that?

ZAR. Our stuff has this wonderful quality. It cannot be seen by any one who is stupid, or unfit for the position he holds.

(HAN *turns away, startled.* EMPRESS *frightened. Weavers, amazed, eager.*)

EMPEROR. That is capital stuff! If I had a robe of that, I could tell what people about me are not fit to hold the positions they have!

ZAR. (*Cutting off* HAN *who is about to protest.*) That is true, great emperor! If you had a minister of your robes, who was dishonest, or not fit to be your minister, he would be afraid to have you order the stuff, even! He would say it could not be true. But Great Han has no fear.

ZAN. See how eager he is to have you order the stuff!

ZAR. You can tell by that, that Han is honest and fit for the position he holds.

HAN. Uh—yes, your majesty. You must order the stuff woven at once.

EMPEROR. What price do you ask for this wonderful stuff?

ZAR. We ask nothing at all. Our pay is our joy in what we do.

ZAN. We need only twenty chests of the purest gold, and twenty jars of the costliest jewels and we can begin at once.

ZAR. That is all we ask.

ZAN. Only bid Han give us a room in the palace where we may set up our loom, and the stuff shall be woven by this time to-morrow, and the garments cut and sewed by noon.

EMPEROR. I can hardly wait until to-morrow! In the afternoon I will walk through all the streets of the city, to show the people my wonderful new clothes! Fetch your loom at once! I will send gold and silk and jewels for your weaving from the royal stores! As for these bad weavers, Han shall deal with them as he will.

(*He moves out, to his music, leading the* EMPRESS. HAN *motions to the weavers, after the* EMPEROR'S *exit.*)

HAN. Lift up your bundles. Bear them before me to the palace. You shall leave them there. To-morrow, I will make way with them. When they are destroyed, you shall be driven out of the city.

(*The weavers lift their bundles and stumble out, bowed with grief. The* GONG BOY *crosses to* HAN, *strokes his gong, and they exit as they entered.* ZAR *and* ZAN *leap out, and hug each other with joy.*)

ZAN. We are going to the emperor's palace!

ZAR.   He will send us silk and gold and jewels!

ZAN.   We will give them to the weavers!

ZAR.   It will be enough to make them rich for a year!

ZAN.   We must find a strange loom.

ZAR.   We must find out what people do when they weave!

ZAN.   I will go among the people and find out how to weave!

ZAR.   I will go and search out a strange loom!

BOTH.   This will be the best adventure we ever had!

(Exit, laughing and leaping.)

CURTAIN

ACT II

A room in HAN'S *quarters, in the palace. A decorated panel with jewels on it, one great ruby especially brilliant. It should be as big as a pigeon's egg. Chest, bags of gold, and box of silk thread. Chest not too large to be handled easily by one, and hidden in the cupboard — about the size of a large shoe box, but carven and glittering with jewels and gold.*

ZAR is alone, examining the loom. He does not understand at all, how cloth could be made on it, and is very anxious. A great gong, different from that of the GONG BOY, *is struck, off, and* ZAR *jumps and runs about in fright. He gets himself together and stands by the loom.*

ZAN leaps in. ZAR *runs to seize him.*

ZAR. Zan! I heard the gong! I thought Han was coming!

ZAN. The gong is the signal to open the gate! It always sounds, when any one is coming, no matter who it is. It has a very different sound from Han's gong.

ZAR. I am glad you are here.

ZAN. You act frightened.

ZAR. Han sent word he is coming to see the stuff! He will expect us to weave. Have you found out how?

ZAN. I found an old man to teach me. I practiced all night long.

ZAR. Show me! Quick!

ZAN. Oh! This is a fine loom you found!

ZAR. I can think of fine stuff when I look at it. But I couldn't find out how to weave.

ZAN. *(Illustrating with his hands.)*   There are a thousand threads, running from top to bottom, like strings on a lyre.

ZAR. *(Shutting his eyes and having a good time.)*   I see them! Bright threads! They make a rainbow on the loom.

ZAN. In the shuttle are more threads.

ZAR. I can't see the shuttle. (Opening his eyes.) I don't know what it is.

ZAN. It is this shape. In it, there is a long spool. On it, is wound a long, long thread.

ZAR. *(Shutting his eyes.)*   I see it! Gold thread! Shining! Fine as a spider weaves!

155

ZAN. *(Illustrating.)* You pass the shuttle under the threads on the loom, then under, then over, then under—if you keep on long enough, it's cloth!

ZAR. *(His eyes screwed up in his ecstasy.)* I see it! With patterns in it! Like the shadow of many leaves! And stars, in a pool!

ZAN. Come and practice.

ZAR. We'll pretend to put the bobbin through.
(They sit, one on each side of the loom, on their heels, and go through the motions of throwing the shuttle back and forth.)

ZAN. Under. Over. Under. Over. Under! Over! Faster! Faster! Faster yet!
(They work so fast that they break down, laughing. ZAR stops suddenly, pointing to the chest and bags.)

ZAR. Oh, We must hide the gold and jewels and silk the emperor sent us to weave our stuff of! If Han sees them he will know we haven't woven them up!

ZAN. We must put them out of sight, and pretend we have woven them into wonderful thread that no one can see.

ZAR. Where shall we put them? *(They run about, looking.)* There is no place in this room to hide anything.

ZAN. That is strange.

ZAR. I don't like this room. I feel as if sly things went on here. I think Han has secrets here.

ZAN. He couldn't have things to hide. There are no chests to hide them in.

ZAR. Han wouldn't have chests. He has dark ways of doing things.

ZAN. It is a very fine room. Look at that great jewel, in the panel, there.

ZAR. I don't like that ruby. It makes me creepy. I feel as if there were blood on it. And tears.

ZAN. It is large as a pigeon's egg.

ZAR. I think it is larger.

ZAN. *(Feeling it.)* No, it isn't.

ZAR. *(Feeling it.)* It spreads my fingertips more than a pigeon's egg does. Oh!!! It has come off!

ZAN. Hide it. Quick! Before Han comes!

ZAR. Han would miss it. There is a hole where it was.

ZAN. I feel my head coming off this very minute! Put it back! Put it back!

ZAR. It won't go!

ZAN. Twist it! Press hard!
(ZAR does. The panel parts silently, one side moving right, the other left. It reveals shelves piled with treasure, chests of gold, jars of jewels, and much glittering stuff. Conspicuous is the piece TSEIN held up, which the EMPRESS noticed. ZAR and ZAN are so startled that they leap backward, colliding and falling over each other. They get untangled and approach the outlay in awe.)

ZAR. Look! There is the most beautiful thing of Tsein's life.

ZAN. And there is the stuff Fah was carrying.

ZAR. This is all the stuff he has stolen from the weavers! And bags of gold! And jars of jewels! Look! Look!
(The great gong is struck.)

ZAN. The great gates are opening!

ZAR. Han is coming!

ZAN. We must shut these doors!

ZAR. Wait! Wait! We must hide these jewels the emperor sent us! In here!

ZAN. Put them behind the others so Han can't see them if he opens his doors.

ZAR. You push that door.

ZAN. You push that.
(They close the doors and leap to the loom, but as soon as they take their hands off, the doors open again, silently. They close them again, and again they open as soon as they are not held. This happens three times.)

ZAR. We must think about this!

ZAN. *(Running around.)* I can't think with Han out there, on his way to come in!

ZAR. You must think! Stop running around! *(They think, with terrific concentration.)*

ZAN. *(Leaping.)* I have thought something!

ZAR. What?

ZAN. It is the ruby! We must put it back!

ZAR. It was on a secret spring!
(They rush to shut the doors and screw the ruby in but are too excited to be accurate. It drops.)

ZAN. Let me!

ZAR. Let me!

ZAN. Let me!! It is in! It stays!
(They fall back with sighs of relief, but the door opens as before. ZAN seizes the ruby and runs about with it.)

ZAR. *(Clasping his head.)* I've thought something, without even trying!

ZAN. What?! What?!!

ZAR. We must put it in before we shut the doors!
(They twist the ruby frantically, seizing it from each other, dropping it, running after it wilder and wilder.)

ZAN. Hurry! Han is near!

ZAR. *(Stopping short.)* We are acting like sheep when a wolf is near. We must act like men! Stand still! What is the first thing to do?

ZAN. You stand still, too.

ZAR. I am. What next?

ZAN. Hold the ruby firmly so it won't drop.

ZAR. What next?

ZAN. Look at the hole to see how it fits.

ZAR. I see. What next?

ZAN. Put it where it fits.
(ZAR makes one direct movement and it stays.)

ZAR. It is in!

ZAN. *(Running to help.)* Now shut the doors.
(The doors stay closed. They take their hands from them cautiously, and start back several times, but they do not open again. They rush to the loom, ready to pretend to weave.)

ZAR. When Han comes, I'll feel afraid.

ZAN. Han will not know there is nothing on the loom. He'll think it is because he has told lies to the emperor and robbed the weavers that he sees nothing on the loom.

ZAR. He'll pretend that he sees the stuff!

ZAN. We must pretend that he does, too!

ZAR. We must describe the stuff to him so that he will know what to say!

ZAN. You do that. You see things that aren't there so much better than I do.

ZAR. Oh, I'll make up fine things! Colors! And patterns! —— *(As some one is heard at the door.)* Weave!

ZAN. *(In swift whisper.)* Don't look up till he speaks. By that time he won't show how he feels when he can't see the stuff.

ZAR. This is exciting!
(They weave rapidly, not looking up. The door is thrown open and the GENERAL enters, marked by the flags worn on his back. He is smiling complacently, having no fear that he will not see the stuff. He is about to speak, when he sees the empty loom. He can hardly believe his eyes. It had never occurred to him to fear the test. He gulps, and looks away and back again. He is overwhelmed, and struggles for composure. The rogues weave away, apparently unconscious of his presence. GENERAL poses himself carefully before he speaks.)

GENERAL. *(Swallowing hard).* Uh—that is very wonderful stuff.
(The two leap to their feet, whirling around to face the GENERAL.)

ZAR. We thought great Han was coming.

GENERAL. I am a general in the emperor's army. Han sent me ahead. He wished me to report to him on the stuff.

ZAR. Look, then. Is it not lovely?

GENERAL. It is enchanting.

ZAN. I am sure you never saw anything like it before.

GENERAL. No. No, I never saw anything quite like it before.

ZAR. That is not strange. There is nothing like it in the whole world.

ZAN. Do you like the colors?

GENERAL. They are — uh — most unusual. *(Making a great bluff.)* I would not know how to name that color, right there.

ZAR. That is red.

GENERAL. Oh, yes, yes. Yes. Red. Of course. I—I meant —— What shade of red would you call it?

159

ZAR. That is coral.

GENERAL. Coral. Yes. Coral.

ZAR. I like best the green and turquoise and amethyst, all shining together.

GENERAL. Ah, the green—— it is superb. And the — the ——

ZAR. Turquoise.

GENERAL. Yes, the turquoise. I must tell Han about — *(fixing them
in his mind)* the green and the turquoise.

ZAR. And the amethyst.

GENERAL. Oh, Oh, yes. The amethyst.

ZAR. And see the gold, like the sun on ripening rice fields.

GENERAL. *(His courage growing).* Ah, Han will like the gold. Yes,
it is like the sun on a yellowing field of rice.

ZAN. What else do you like?

GENERAL. *(Wiping his brow.)* Uh — I like it all.

ZAR. I like this purple, with the look of far hills at twilight time.

GENERAL. Yes, that is one of the finest things of all. *(Memorizing.)*
Green, and gold and purple and coral and turquoise ——

ZAN. Touch it. It is so light and airy, you would think there was
nothing there at all.

GENERAL. *(Swallowing..)* My fingers are too clumsy to touch such a
fine-spun web. I — I will go at once and tell Han how beautiful
it is.

*(He goes in almost indecent haste. ZAR and ZAN seize each other in
spasms of laughter.)*

ZAN. It is a fine plan you thought of!

ZAR. The general is a strong man, yet he was afraid to tell the truth.

ZAN. He is foolish.

ZAR. Every one is a little foolish. Every one will be afraid to tell the
truth!

ZAN. Han was afraid to come, even! He sent the general ahead to
find out for him!

*(The great gong sounds, and then HAN's gong sounds off, ap-
proaching.)*

160

ZAR. Weave!

(They spring to the loom and make-believe to weave swiftly. The GENERAL *reenters, followed by* HAN. *The* GONG BOY *stops at the door.* HAN *casts a swift desperate look at the loom as he enters, then makes elaborate pretense of not having looked.)*

GENERAL. *(Bowing low.)* Great Han, here is the wonderful stuff.

HAN. *(Carefully turning his back to the loom.)* I shall have to look for myself, before I can believe the extravagant things you say.

GENERAL. *(Purple with anger.)* What reason have you to doubt the things I say?

HAN. They sound like things one imagines. Purple, and gold, and coral ——

GENERAL. I am a general in the emperor's army. I command a hundred thousand men for every flag I wear on my back. Is that not proof that I speak the truth?

HAN. High position is not proof of a man's word.

ZAN. That is true, high Han.

GENERAL. *(Puffing.)* I have heard the only proof you will accept is gold in your hand!

HAN. The proof I will accept is what my own eyes tell me! If you have lied to me about the splendor of this stuff, I shall have you punished, in spite of your flags!

GENERAL. You are nothing but a buyer of cloth! You cannot punish a general in the emperor's army!

HAN. I am the minister of the emperor's robes! One new dress is more to the emperor than his whole army! I can punish any man I please! Stand aside. I will see the stuff these men have made. *(He turns elaborately to the loom, and makes an exaggerated gesture of surprise and delight.)* Ah-h-h-! You did not say half enough! Ah, that green! That turquoise! And the gold! It reminds me of a rice field I saw once, at harvest time!

ZAR. With the low sun slanting over it.

HAN. Yes! It is like the sun on a harvest field of rice! The emperor must see this at once.

ZAN. We are ready to fit the garments on him.

HAN. *(Cautiously.)* Are all the garments made of the same cloth?

BOTH. *(With a bow.)* All the same.

161

HAN. They all have green and coral and purple and gold?

BOTH. All.

ZAN. But every one has a different pattern in the middle of the back.

HAN. Oh. A different pattern. Uh —— What is the pattern in the middle of the great train?

ZAR. That is like the shadow of many leaves. And below, stars in a pool. And the border is purple, like far-away hills at twilight time.

HAN. Hm-m. Shadow of many leaves. Stars in a pool. That sounds a little dull.

ZAN. With a jewel in each star.

HAN. Ah. A jewel in each star. That ought to please the emperor. Yes. And the border, like ripening rice fields, did you say?

GENERAL. *(Who has been moving his lips to form each word.)* Oh, no, no, no, no, — The border is like far-away hills at twilight time.

HAN. Yes, of course. Purple. I am glad of that. I should not have liked gold in the border. And what shall you make of the piece on the loom?

ZAR. That is for the undermost garment of all.

HAN. Oh. The undermost garment of all.

ZAR. The great train is woven and sewed, and the splendid outer garment, and the long tunic under that, and the short tunic under that, and the beautiful long trousers, and the glittering shoes. But the straight little shirt that goes next to the sacred body of the emperor, is not yet cut or sewed. It lacks one inch of the weaving.

ZAN. It will be done by the time you fetch the emperor.

HAN. Are not coral and turquoise and gold too beautiful for the undermost garment of all?

ZAR. Nothing is too beautiful to touch the sacred body of the emperor!

HAN. That is true. The emperor is waiting outside the gates, under the pomegranate trees. I will fetch him at once. *(On his way out he stops to examine the ruby in the panel. The rogues stiffen with terror and move together.)* The servants have left finger marks on my great ruby. I will have them lashed a thousand times!
(Exit HAN and the GENERAL.)

ZAN. I have thought a fine thing!

162

ZAR.   What?

ZAN.   Han will bring the emperor. If we let the emperor know that Han sees nothing on the loom, he will not trust Han any more!

ZAR.   He will take his position away from him!

ZAN.   Then he cannot beat and rob the weavers!

ZAR.   The emperor must know!

ZAN.   We must let the emperor catch Han in his lies!

ZAR.   But Han must not catch the emperor!

ZAN.   What is your plan?

ZAR.   It hasn't come yet.
    (*A knock, from a different side than the door is on.*)

ZAN.   What was that?

ZAR.   Somebody knocked.

ZAN.   (*At the door.*)   There is nobody here. (*Another knock.*)

ZAR.   It came from there.

ZAN.   That couldn't be. There is no door.
    (*As they stare at the place, a panel slides back, and an arm comes through, holding a great fan. They step back in awe. The arm belongs to the* EMPRESS, *who enters, holding her great fan in front of her face, her other hand groping before her.*)

EMPRESS.   (*To herself, frightened.*)   I wonder which way the loom is.

ZAN.   It is here.

EMPRESS.   Oh-h-h — who is that?

ZAN.   We are the weavers from a far-away land.

EMPRESS.   (*In great agitation.*)   Why did you not answer when I knocked?

ZAR.   We could not find the door.

EMPRESS.   (*More and more terrified.*)   There is no door. It is a secret passage of the emperor. You should have called out. Then I would have gone away.
    (*She sways and slips down in a faint. They run to her.*)

ZAR. (*In terror.*)   She has gone to her ancestors!

ZAN.   She has a crown on her head!

ZAR. It is the empress. (ZAN *kowtows, madly.*) Get up! Get up! She can't see what you are doing.

ZAN. What if Han finds her here!

ZAR. (*Peering gently under the fan.*) How beautiful she is.

ZAN. How still.

ZAR. I feel a soft breath on my hand!

ZAN. She is not with her ancestors!

ZAR. Her spirit is only a little way off!

ZAN. (*Fanning furiously with the first thing to come to hand.*) Bring it back!

ZAR. (*Also fanning wildly.*) Quick! Before Han comes with the emperor!

ZAN. Fan hard!
(*The* EMPRESS *sits up slowly. They stop fanning to watch her.*)

EMPRESS. You are blowing my hair about.

ZAR. We are blowing your spirit back to your body.

EMPRESS. It is back.

ZAN. Why did it go away?

EMPRESS. I was afraid. Oh-h-h! I am afraid again! (*She faints again and they call to her frantically.*)

BOTH. No, no, no! Do not be afraid. — Do not be afraid!

ZAR. We must be more gentle.

BOTH. (*Very gentle.*) Do not be afraid.
(*She sits up again, her fan still held in front of her face.*)

ZAN. Why are you afraid?

EMPRESS. I was afraid you would tell the emperor that I came here. Oh-h-h-h ——
(*She swoons more deeply.*)

ZAN. (*Into her ear.*) Come back. We will not tell.

ZAR. She is too far away. She cannot hear.

ZAN. (*Louder.*) We will not tell!

ZAR. She is still too far away.
(*They lift her between them, one at each ear.*)

BOTH *(Shouting.)* We will not tell!!

EMPRESS *(Looking about dazedly.)* Did you say something?

ZAN. We said that we would not tell the emperor that you came here.

EMPRESS *(Getting to her feet in haste.)* If you should tell the emperor, he would believe what Han says.

ZAR. We heard what Han said.

ZAN. He says you are stupid.

ZAR. He says you are not fit to be empress.

EMPRESS. Yes. So the emperor wants to know whether I see the stuff. He wants to watch me look at it, the first time. He ordered me to stay in my inner room, and speak to no one who had seen the stuff. He is going to send for me to come and see it when he is here. I cannot bear to be watched when I look. That is why I came in secret.

ZAN. Look, then.

EMPRESS. I am afraid to look.

ZAR. Do not be afraid.

EMPRESS. If I cannot see the stuff, the emperor will send me away. I cried real tears, from the evening star to the morning star, for fear I could not see it.

ZAR. You cannot be unfit to be empress. You are beautiful. *(This comforts the* EMPRESS.*)* You are wise. *(This fills her with doubt).* You are good. *(This makes her widen her eyes and pucker her face.)*

EMPRESS. *(Courageously.)* I will look! *(She makes a little run to loom, and lowers her fan a little, but jerks it up again in a panic before she can see the loom.)* Turn your backs. You must not watch me look. I could not bear it to be watched.

(They turn their backs, but twist their heads around to watch her. They are so alert that though she turns suddenly once or twice, she does not catch them. She makes several attempts to screw up her courage sufficiently to face the test, but can never quite bring herself to do it.)

ZAN. You have looked?

EMPRESS. I can't get my fan down enough.

ZAN. I will put your fan down for you.

165

EMPRESS *(Waving him back desperately).* Oh, no, no, no, no, Look the other way. *(At last she gets her fan below her eyes, and peers over it at the empty loom. She lowers it slowly, staring, aghast. Her face quivers and she bursts into tears. ZAR and ZAN are aghast that she is about to acknowledge she sees nothing. They seize each other, and think wildly.)* I can't —— *(Sobs.)* I can't —— *(Sobs.)* I can't ——*(More sobs.)*

ZAR. *(Running to her.)* You cannot keep the sacred water drops from your eyes. Zan! The beauty of our stuff moves the empress to tears!

(The EMPRESS lifts her head and checks her sobs.)

ZAN. The empress' tears are the highest praise our stuff could have.

ZAR. *(Clearly, with intention.)* The green, and the turquoise, and the gold like the sun slanting over the ripening field of rice, and the purple like far hills at twilight time, make even the empress weep with joy.

(The EMPRESS turns her head to them and follows the above closely, a little ghost of a nod marking her fixing of each word.)

ZAN. Ah, yes. When I look long at it, I weep too.

ZAR. And the pattern, like the shadow of many leaves, is like sad memories of beautiful things that are gone.

ZAN. It is not strange that her eyes brim over.

ZAR. She would not be fit to be empress if our stuff did not hurt her heart with its beauty.

EMPRESS. *(To herself.)* It would be terrible not to be empress.

ZAR. I am glad the empress came to look in secret. She might have wept before all the people tomorrow, when she saw the emperor in his wonderful new clothes.

ZAN. The people might not understand.

ZAR. Han would never understand.

ZAN. Even the emperor might not understand that the empress wept because the beauty of our stuff moved her to tears.

ZAR. When she talks to the emperor about the wonderful colors, he will see that she is not stupid.

EMPRESS. *(Softly, to herself.)* The green, and the turquoise, and the gold, and the purple ——

ZAN. Like far-away hills at twilight time.

ZAR. And the pattern, like the shadow of many leaves.

EMPRESS. Like sweet memories. — Like sad memories — of beautiful things that are gone.

(The gong sounds, and the EMPEROR'S *music, approaching, immediately after.)*

ROGUES. The emperor!

EMPRESS. He will send for me! *(She runs to the panel through which she entered.* ZAN *shuts it after her. As the two leap to the loom, she sticks her head in again.)* You will not tell the emperor?

ZAN. *(Urging her out again.)* No, no!

EMPRESS *(Sticking her head in.)* When I come in you must act as if you had never seen me.

ZAN. Yes, yes, yes!

EMPRESS. *(Head in again.)* Don't let him send for me right away. I must wash the tears from my face.

ZAN. *(Desperately hurrying her.)* He is almost here!

EMPRESS. I will go.

*(*ZAN *shuts the panel after her, and leaps back to the loom. The* EMPEROR'S *music is very near by now.)*

ZAR. We must pretend the stuff is done.

ZAN. We have taken it from the loom.

ZAR. The finished garments are folded, and piled over there.

EMPRESS *(Head in, breathless with haste.)* Give me plenty of time to wash the tears from my face.

ZAN. The sooner you go the more time you will have.

EMPRESS. *(Head in just as* ZAN *gets in position by the loom.)* I have gone.

ZAR. We must pretend to be making the undermost garment of all.

ZAN. I will be cutting it.

ZAR. I will be threading the needle. So.

ZAN. What shape is the undermost garment of all?

ZAR. *(Drawing a picture in the air.)* Like this.

ZAN. How are you going to let the emperor catch Han in his lies?

ZAR. The plan hasn't come yet.

(They cut and sew intently as the EMPEROR enters, ushered in by HAN.)

EMPEROR. *(Turning back to GENERAL at the door.)* Fetch the empress at once.

ROGUES *(Whirling to kowtow.)* The emperor!

(The EMPEROR blinks at the loom, shuts his eyes, blinks again. He draws a sharp breath of terror which he converts into a cough. He looks suddenly at HAN, and catches him leering as he watches him intently.)

EMPEROR *(In a fury.)* Why do you grin?

HAN. I am not grinning.

EMPEROR. You watched my face as a yellow cat watches a hole where a mouse may come out! What thought was stealing around in your mind when your eyes went sliding up and down my face?

HAN. I — uh — wished to rejoice my eyes in your delight when you saw the stuff.

EMPEROR. It is death to ferret for thoughts in your emperor's face. To your knees! *(HAN kowtows, like the rogues who are still prone. The EMPEROR steals in swift strides to the loom, gathering up his skirts to step over ZAN, who is in his path. The others lift their heads, like turtles, to watch as the EMPEROR stares at the loom, bends to touch the empty air. Feeling nothing he shrinks back in terror. He clutches his crown. Finally he returns to his original position, and takes up an imperial pose.)* Rise.

ZAR. Alas! The emperor is angry. We should have left the cloth on the loom till he came.

ZAN. We ask pardon that we took the stuff from the loom, to make it up into garments.

(EMPEROR's face is by now wreathed in smiles, as he realizes the cloth was not on the loom.)

EMPEROR. Ah! Where have you put the garments?

ZAN. If the emperor will look behind him, he will see the garments folded and piled high.

ZAR *(Pretending to hold up the shirt.)* All except this undermost garment of all, which I have cut and am about to sew.

(Both HAN and the EMPEROR look dazedly at the empty chair.)

HAN. *(Clearing his throat.)* Will the emperor be pleased to look at the great train these men have woven for you? Coral, and green, and purple, and gold, with a pattern like the shadow of many leaves in the middle of the back?

EMPEROR. They may show me their work.

ZAN. If great Han will turn the other way, I can fasten the train onto his shoulders that the emperor may see the colors shine as it sweeps the floor.

(HAN *turns, and* ZAN *makes-believe to shake out a train.*)

ZAR. I will help you spread it out.

ZAN. *(Whispering.)* Go and make up a plan.

ZAR. *(Also whispering.)* The plan won't come!

ZAN. *(Waving him away.)* Think!

(ZAR *returns to his pretense of sewing, but soon sits motionless, with his head clasped in his hands, his body screwed up.*)

HAN. *(Jumping as* ZAN *pretends to pin the train to his shoulder.)* Ouch! You have put your pin through my coat!

ZAN. Forgive the pin, great Han. Walk, that the emperor may see the shimmer as you move. (HAN *walks, looking uneasily over his shoulder.* ZAN *makes-believe to carry the train and lay it in a sweeping curve.*) Do not the folds make you think of a rainbow?

EMPEROR. Those are colors such as I have never seen before.

ZAN. They are very rare colors. *(Lifting one after another imaginary garment.)* See the petals of roses blown across this splendid outer garment! And the border the color of a turquoise, at the bottom of this long tunic. If the emperor will remove his outer coat, I will slip this tunic over his head to make sure that it fits as it should.

EMPEROR *(Dazedly.)* You may remove my coat.

(ZAN *removes the outer coat and throws it over the loom. He almost forgets* HAN's *imaginary train, and but for a swift signal from* ZAR *would have stepped where it is supposed to be.*)

ZAN. *(Going through the motions of pulling a tunic over the* EM-PEROR's *head.)* If the emperor will lower his head. . . . Wait! Wait! It is caught. (*The* EMPEROR *ducks and twists, as* ZAN *indicates, trying hard to seem to know what it is all about.* ZAN, *stepping back.)* Marvelous! The tunic has the lines of a red lily, on the edge of a stream! The emperor has the look of a god! He is a pattern of beauty in this tunic. What will he be when all the new clothes are on!

(EMPEROR *bridles and preens himself, almost forgetting his plight in his satisfaction in the praise. The gong is struck without.*)

EMPEROR.   The empress! Let no one speak till she has seen the stuff. Han, stand there, where the great train is plain from the door. I will stand here, where the tunic will greet her eyes as she enters.

(Enter the GENERAL, *followed by the* EMPRESS. *She looks around nervously, her breath coming faster with every pair of eyes she finds fastened on her in the silence.)*

EMPRESS.   Look the other way. I cannot bear your eyes.

HAN. *(Maliciously.)*   Why does the empress fear our eyes? *(She looks toward the loom, and seeing the* EMPEROR'S *coat on it, breaks into a triumphant little laugh. HAN, spitefully.)*   Why does the empress laugh when he sees the emperor's* old *coat?

(She stops short in her laugh, trembling. ZAN makes-believe to spread the train more widely. Her face is working piteously.)

ZAN.   If great Han will turn a little more, the empress can better see the pattern, in the middle of the back of the stuff which I have pinned to his shoulders.

(HAN turns, still watching the EMPRESS *over his shoulder. The* EMPRESS *stares at the supposed train, and bursts into tears.)*

HAN *(Triumphant.)*   Why does the empress weep?

ZAN *(Quickly and pointedly.)*   It is the pattern, in the middle of the back. The beauty of it moves her to tears!

EMPRESS. *(Choking back her sobs.)*   The pattern—like the shadow of many leaves, is like sweet memories — sad memories — of beautiful things that are gone.

EMPEROR *(Delighted.)*   Ah-h-!

HAN.   But why did she laugh when she first came in?

ZAN.   The colors of the tunic I put on the emperor when I removed the old coat make her laugh with joy.

EMPRESS *(Looking at the* EMPEROR, *and tumbling the words out.)* The green, and the coral, and the turquoise, and the gold. It is like sunlight, dancing on a ripening field of rice.

ZAR.   It makes her spirit dance too.

ZAN.   She would not be fit to be empress if she was too stupid to feel the beauty of our stuff!

EMPEROR. *(Joyfully.)*   Ah-h-h! Han! You are wrong! The empress is not stupid!

170

(She laughs and flutters over to the EMPEROR, *smiling up at him. There is a commotion at the door as* FAH *breaks past the* GENERAL.)*

FAH *(Flinging himself at* HAN's *feet.)* Great Han!

HAN. This is the most insolent of the weavers! Take him away!

FAH. I am not insolent now, great Han. See! I kneel! I knock my head against the floor! All the weavers pray by my voice! Hear me!

HAN. Why are you not outside the gates now?

FAH. Do not drive us from the city! We cannot leave the shrines of our ancestors! Our fathers worshipped there before us, and their fathers before them! Our hearts will wither and die where they are not.

HAN. In an hour the emperor will pass through the streets in his new clothes. When he comes to yours, let the houses be empty and the doors shut!

FAH. We will serve you! We will give you gold! Only let us stay where our fathers have been!

HAN. If any of you is still in your street when the emperor comes, he shall die!

FAH. *(Turning to kowtow to the* EMPEROR, *and in so doing resting his foot on the* EMPEROR's *coat on the loom.)* Emperor!

HAN *(Seizing him and flinging him to the* GENERAL.)* You have set foot on the emperor's coat! Take this man and have him lashed till his coat is in tatters and his knees will bear him up no more! Then thrust him into the street! Make haste to your fellows, weaver! If any are not gone when the emperor comes, they shall feel my wrath before they die!
(The GENERAL *leads* FAH *off.* ZAN *pounds on* ZAR's *head in desperation.)*

ZAN *(Whispering but intense.)* What is your plan?

ZAR *(Rising, softly.)* It has come! *(He points to* HAN's *feet, and gives a terrible cry.)* The train! The emperor's train! Your feet are on it! It will tear!

ZAN. Get off! Get off! Get off!
(HAN steps aside, bewildered, in haste. The rogues redouble their cries. HAN *jumps and stumbles around.)*

ZAR and ZAN. No, no! Not there! No! Get off the train!! Not there! Oh, no! no! No, no, no!!! Get off! Get off! Off! Off! Off!!!

171

(HAN *finally leaps clear across the stage in one terrified bound. The rogues cry out more wildly than before.*)

ZAR *(Screaming.)* Your foot is on the undermost garment of all!

ZAN. *(Kneeling to lift it.)* Take your foot off!

BOTH *(Kneeling one on either side and lifting first one foot and then the other.)* Lift your foot! Not that one! No!! The other! The other! The other! Oh-h-h! You have torn it to rags!

ZAR. *(Pretending to hold it up.)* Look, your majesty! He has ruined the undermost garment of all!

ZAN. When the emperor walks the streets this afternoon, he will have to wear one *not* of our weaving!

EMPEROR. I will have your head struck off for this!

HAN *(On his knees.)* No, no! Mercy! Mercy! I did not mean to do it!

EMPEROR *(To the GENERAL.)* Cast him into a dungeon till I decide how he shall be punished.

HAN. No! No! It was not my fault!

ZAR. Any one might step on it once!

ZAN. But why did you dance and stamp on it?

EMPEROR. It is death to stamp on the Emperor's robes!

HAN. I did not mean to stamp on it! I could not see the stu ——(*He catches himself, clapping his hand over his mouth.*)
(*The* EMPRESS *breaks the silence by laughing softly.* ZAR *and* ZAN *rejoice secretly. The* EMPEROR *stares in amazement, the significance of* HAN'S *slip dawning on him slowly.*)

EMPEROR. How? — Han is not fit to be my minister? — This is truly wonderful stuff, to find a man's thoughts. *(To* ZAR *and* ZAN.*)* You have done me a great service. Ask what reward you will.

ZAR. As a keepsake of this room, the ruby, in the panel there, would be dear to us.

HAN. The great ruby! In my panel?

EMPEROR. Why do you stare? It is easily replaced.

HAN. The stone is dear to me. Give them some other.

EMPEROR. They shall have what they ask. They could have asked much more.

HAN. *(To* ZAR.*)* I will give you a topaz twice the size of that.

172

ZAR. The topaz would be too large, great Han.

ZAN. The ruby is just large enough.

HAN. I will give you thrice its worth in gold.

ZAN. That would be a great sum.

HAN. I will give you its worth ten times over, if you will take another stone and go your way.

EMPEROR. You set a great price upon it.

EMPRESS. *(Examining it.)* It is a very pure jewel.

ZAR. If the empress would give us the jewel with her own sacred hands, it would be worth all the other jewels in the world.

EMPRESS *(Flattered.)* I do not know how to get it off.

ZAN. If the empress twists a little, perhaps ——

ZAR. And presses as she twists.

EMPRESS. So?

ZAR. Push on it.

EMPRESS. So?

ZAN. A little more ——
  (The door opens. Everyone cries out except HAN, the rogues most of all.)

EMPEROR. How?!

HAN *(Quick-witted.)* It is the bad work I took from the weavers. There has not been time to cut it to pieces!

EMPEROR. Is that all that there is in the hiding place?

HAN. That is all.

EMPEROR. There is nothing there but bad weaving and false jewels?

HAN. There is nothing else.

EMPEROR *(To GENERAL.)* Bind him, and lock him safe. I myself will set out all this treasure to prove his words.
  (Exit GENERAL and HAN. EMPEROR turns to the treasure.)

ZAR. Uh — uh — have a care! The tunic! It is thin as air! It is fragile as butterfly's wings. Something may catch it.

EMPEROR *(Looking in surprise at his stiff embroidered tunic.)* Fragile? *(Then he remembers.)* Oh! Oh, yes. Remove the tunic.

ZAN. Oh! The great train! Han has worn it away!

EMPEROR. Remove the train!
  (ZAN dashes off, and returns, as if carrying a folded garment. ZAR makes-believe to take the tunic from the EMPEROR.)

ZAR. The hour for the procession through the streets is almost here. If the new clothes should feel strange to the Emperor he would not walk with the grace which makes the people praise him.

ZAN. They feel strange. They are as light as a moonbeam that falls across the arm.

ZAR. They have no more weight than a dream.

ZAN. Would it be well for the Emperor to walk about in them before he goes among the people?

ZAR. Then he would not feel strange in them when he walks through the streets.

EMPEROR. You have made a good plan. First, I will bathe in the pool under the pomegranate trees.

ZAN. If it is the will of the emperor, we will set out this stuff, while he is made ready for his wonderful new clothes.

ZAR. Then his eyes can judge of great Han's guilt.

ZAN. And his sacred hands will not be soiled.

EMPEROR. You may set out the stuffs.

ZAR. Is it the emperor's wish that we help him put on the garments we have made?

ZAN. They are sheer as the wings of a dragonfly, and soft as the silk of milkweed pod. They must be handled by one who knows.

EMPEROR. You shall array me with your own hands. When I am dressed, you shall carry the great train before the people. You shall wear rich garments, and chains of gold about your necks, and be called the imperial court weavers. *(To the EMPRESS.)* At last, I know you are not stupid. You shall return with me to judge this stuff. *(He leads her out, to his music.)*

ZAR. Quick! We must get the stuff out of here!

ZAN. We will take it to the weavers!

ZAR. We will tell them Han has fallen, and they need not leave the city

ZAN. We must run fast! Fah will hurry them away!

ZAR *(Stops short, as they start to run, their arms full of the gold, etc.)* Oh!

ZAN What?

ZAR. Do you know the way to the street?

ZAN. NO! Do you?

ZAR. No!

ZAN. We must ask the first man we meet. *(They start to run again.*

ZAN *stops short.)* OH-h!

ZAR. What?

ZAN. Do you know the name of the street?

ZAR. No. Do you?

ZAN. No.

ZAR. Then how can we ask the first man we meet the way?

ZAN. We must run through all the streets till we find it.

ZAR. There are many streets!

ZAN. Then we must run fast!

ZAR. Yes! Or the weavers will be gone!

ZAN. And the emperor will send for us to put on his clothes!

ZAR. And if we are not there, off with our heads!

BOTH. Oh-h! *(Exit, running very fast.)*

CURTAIN

ACT III

The street of the royal weavers. The weavers sit in doorways and and on steps, silent, bowed with anxiety. TSEIN is in front with her child beside her. The OLD WOMAN is watching the entrance of the street, her eyes shaded by her hand, for better seeing.

CHILD.   Mother, I am hungry.

TSEIN.   You must be patient, child of a weaver.

CHILD.   I want a bowl of rice.

TSEIN.   There is no more rice.

CHILD.   But mother, I am hungry.

TSEIN.   I have nothing to give you, little jade drop.

CHILD.   Let us go in and pray to our ancestor-gods for food.

TSEIN.   I have prayed *long.*

CHILD.   Do not the gods hear, mother?

TSEIN.   Sh-h-h ——

OLD WOMAN.   Fah is coming.
        (The people rise, tense, waiting.)

CHILD.   Where has Fah been, mother?

TSEIN.   He has been to Han.

CHILD.   Why did Fah go to Han, mother?

TSEIN.   To beg him to let us stay in the homes of our fathers.

CHILD.   Fah doesn't beg for what he wants. He speaks loud.

TSEIN. *(Deeply.)*   Fah has begged Han for mercy.

OLD WOMAN.   Fah walks wearily.
        (A wave of uneasiness sweeps over the group.)

CHILD.   Why does Fah walk wearily, mother?

TSEIN.   His news is heavy in his feet.

OLD WOMAN.   Fah's coat is in tatters.
        (Weavers show anger and despair.)

CHILD.   Why is Fah's coat in tatters, mother? — Mother! Do you know why Fah's coat is in tatters?

TSEIN.   They have used the lash on him.

OLD WOMAN. Fah is here.
(They all turn, silently, toward the end of the street. FAH enters, weak, in tatters. He shows his tatters. There is dead silence and stillness. He wavers and is about to fall. Some of them catch him and support him.)

FAH. Give me to drink.
(Some one swiftly puts a cup to his lips. He gathers strength and speaks.)

CHILD. *(Before he speaks, in the deep silence.)* Why are you so still, mother?

TSEIN. Sh-h-h-h.

FAH. We are to leave the gods of our ancestors in the shrines our fathers have built and go forth.

OLD WOMAN. What is to happen will happen.

FAH. The emperor walks through the streets this afternoon, to show the people his wonderful new clothes. At every street he will stop, to let the people look their fill. When he comes here, the doors must be shut and the houses empty. If any is still here, he will die.

OLD WOMAN. Let us go in. Be swift to gather up what you will carry from the city.

FAH. Be swift. My knees would not bear me up and I was long in coming. By now, the emperor will be upon his way.
(They go into houses. ZAR and ZAN enter, running. ZAR stops so suddenly they collide.)

ZAN. Why did you stop?

ZAR. I felt as if this were the street.

ZAN. Why did you feel like that?

ZAR. I don't know.

ZAN. You must know.

ZAR. I think it is the street. I haven't any reason.

ZAN. You can't think a thing is true without a reason.

ZAR. It is often done.

ZAN. That is true. But then, people make up reasons.

ZAR. I don't like made up reasons.

ZAN. It must be the way it makes you feel.

ZAR. That is it!

ZAN. How does it make you feel?

ZAR. I don't know. I feel things, but I don't know what they are.

ZAN. You can't feel things without knowing what they are!

ZAR. I do it all the time!

ZAN. I remember something!

ZAR. What?

ZAN. There was a sign!

ZAR. It said, the street of — of ——

ZAN. The street of — of ——

ZAR. It won't come!

ZAN. I know how to make it come.

ZAR. How?

ZAN. Stop trying. Then it will pop into your head all of a sudden.

ZAR. What if it pops too late?

ZAN. It is almost too late, now.

ZAR. I feel as if the weavers were getting ready to leave this minute!

ZAN. Something has popped into my head!

ZAR. What?

ZAN. If this is the street, the sign will be *here.*

ZAR. Maybe we will remember what it is if we see it!

ZAN. Look for a sign! *(They look everywhere except in the right place. Finally they stand under the sign, discouraged.)* There is no sign.

ZAR. We have looked everywhere.

ZAN. This is not the street.

ZAR. We must run to the next street.

ZAN. There is not time. The emperor will be calling for us.

ZAR. If we go back now, the weavers will go out of the city! They will weep about it. They will never be happy again.

178

Zan. *(With a sign of beheading.)*   If we don't go back now, we'll wake up to-morrow without any heads!

Zar.   We must run!
(They start, but Zan *stops short.)*

Zan.   We can't take these chests and bags of gold back to the palace!

Zar.   Let us hide them here!

Zan.   *(Pointing to a balcony, at the top of some steps.)*   There is a good place.

Zar.   We can come back and get them after the emperor has showed the people his new clothes.

Zan.   We will be late! Run! Run!
(They run off. One of the weavers peers out of the door. Ling *follows.)*

Ling.   I thought I heard some one.

Mong.   *(Following.)*   There is no one here.

Tsein.   Is it safe to come out?

Fah *(As the rest peer out, and enter cautiously.)*   We must set off at once.
(They gather, sobbing, their bundles on backs and shoulders.)

Old Woman.   Kneel. We must take leave of our ancestors.

All *(Chanting,* as they kneel.)*   We must take leave of our ancestors.

Fah. *(Chanting.)*   Shrines where our fathers have knelt ——

Another.   And their fathers before them ——

Others.   And their fathers before *them* ——

More.   And their fathers before *them* ——

Fah. *(Or any with a good voice.)*   And their fathers' fathers till the stars were young ——

One.   Farewell ——

Others.   Forever ——

All.   Forever, farewell — farewell. Forever. Forever. Forever.
(The chant trails away into a long held chord dying imperceptibly into silence. Faint and far, the Emperor's *music is heard against it. The weavers look up as it grows a little.)*

* Music for this chant is available, or it can be intoned by the cast.

179

MONG. *(In a terrified whisper.)* The emperor's music! — Come ——

FAH. It is too late. We shall all die.
(They all get to their feet.)

OLD WOMAN. Go inside. Shut the doors.

LING. Han may think that we are gone.

FAH. Let no one look out!

OLD WOMAN. Let no one answer, if any calls!
(They go swiftly and silently off. The music grows. CITIZENS enter, aflutter with excitement from many directions.)

FIRST CITIZEN. *(Meeting others.)* Have you seen the wonderful new clothes?

OTHERS. *(Cautious.)* No. No.

ANOTHER. My neighbor says that his wife says that her friend says that they are brighter than a rainbow!

ANOTHER. And shot with colors, and gold like the sun on a ripening field of rice!

ANOTHER. They say they are set with jewels, like stars in a pool!

FIRST. Everyone is talking about it!

OTHERS. We mustn't miss it!

SECOND. People are quite carried away with the beauty of them!

ANOTHER. They say the emperor walks like a God!

SEVERAL. *(As the music increases.)* He is coming!
(They run to look off, and kneel to kowtow, as the EMPEROR enters, walking with majestic grace, bowing and posing, clad only in his crown and a scrap of an undershirt. The CITIZENS rise, at his word, shoot frightened glances from him to each other, and burst into a chorus of Ohs and Ahs, intermingled with "green," "coral," etc., a little belated, and much overdone.)

EMPEROR. Rise.
(As the chorus increases the EMPEROR, smiling fatuously at their enthusiasm, switches and poses, believing he is showing off his clothes. He smiles graciously at the EMPRESS and the GENERAL who preceded him, bowing and walking backward, and at ZAN and ZAR who, gorgeously dressed, make-believe to carry the train.)

ZAR. If the emperor will walk in a circle, the people can see the folds shimmer, as they fall in a crescent, like the little new moon.

180

EMPEROR. I will walk. (*He moves to music around the stage, pausing to pose and indulging in the airs and graces which he believes show off his garments. The people applaud more and more wildly at every pause, as he looks at them expectantly. [If the* EMPEROR *has the ability, the lines can be changed to suggest that the* EMPEROR *dances before the people. In that case, the rogues should move the people back to clear more room for the dance. Chinese dancing is highly stylized posturing and walking and is delightful when used here.]*)

ZAN (*At an opportune pause, in a whisper to* ZAR.) Something has popped into my head!

ZAR. What?

ZAN. The Street of the Royal Weavers!

ZAR (*At another pause.*) Something has hopped into mine!

ZAN. What?

ZAR. It was over a gate!
(*They both look at the gate and see the sign. As they come to the doors of the houses, as the* EMPEROR *walks, and ends his display they listen at a door.*

ZAN. Some one is crying.

ZAR. A plan has come! (*He leaps to the* EMPEROR *and kowtows.* ZAN *follows.*) Great and most beautiful emperor, this is the street of your royal weavers. No one in all the city is so worthy to see the emperor's glory as they.

GENERAL. They have left the city.

ZAN. I hear weeping within.

GENERAL. Han ordered them to be gone when the emperor came.

ZAR. Will the emperor order the doors to be open and his faithful weavers called out?

EMPEROR. Beat on the doors. Call to any who are there to come out.

GENERAL (*Beating on the doors.*) Come out!

ZAN *and* ZAR. (*At the doors.*) The emperor calls you to come out!
(*The weavers enter, frightened, despairing, expecting death. They are slow to see the* EMPEROR'S *nakedness. When they do, they look at each other, humbled. Some cover their faces; some kneel. One or two murmur.*)

WEAVERS. We are not fit.

EMPEROR. How is this? *(The weavers remember to kowtow at his voice.)*

ZAR. Great emperor, they are the true children of the loom. Their hearts melt at the wonder of your new clothes.

ZAN. They do not feel themselves fit to gaze on your splendor.

EMPEROR *(Pleased.)* They have a nice feeling. *(To the* GENERAL.*)* Fetch Han, from the guard. *(Exit* GENERAL.*)* Tell them to rise.

ZAR *and* ZAN. The emperor bids you rise.
(The weavers rise, and stand dumb, eyes downcast, awaiting doom. The GENERAL *enters, with* HAN. HAN'S *hands are bound. There is a murmur of surprise from the citizens, then from the weavers who look up at the sound.)*

EMPEROR. Han! Look upon my new clothes! Tell the people what you see!

HAN *(Abject, bully that he is.)* I see nothing at all. It is to me as if the emperor wore only his undermost garment of all.
(An excited buzz from the crowd, hatred and triumph. Some self-conscious at being in the same boat with HAN. *Many too rejoiced at his disgrace to remember their own plight.)*

EMPEROR. Tell the people what you have done, that you are unfit to be my minister, and blind to my wonderful stuff.

HAN. I have robbed and beaten and starved the weavers. I have made myself rich on the emperor's robes.

EMPEROR. For long I have trusted this man! I put the fate of my faithful weavers in his hands. Now I trust them! The empress, whom Han tried to make me believe a stupid person for his own ends, has seen the stuff they wove. She says the jewels are pure and the patterns the royal patterns from the days of their fathers. I now put the fate of Han in their hands. *(To weavers.)* Judge this man. How shall he be punished?

FAH. Put him to death!
(A great supporting outcry from the weavers. HAN *sinks to his knees, his hands in supplication.)*

OLD WOMAN. Death is soon over. Drive him from the city.

WEAVERS. Send him away!

EMPEROR. *(To* GENERAL.*)* Thrust him out of the city gates!

GENERAL. To your feet!
(HAN stumbles out with the GENERAL, *the weavers menacing and muttering as he goes.)*

EMPEROR.   Take up the train. There are many streets where the wonderful stuff has not been seen.

ZAR. *(Kowtowing.)*   I have thought a great thought.

EMPEROR.   Tell your thought.

ZAR.   If we stayed here, with your weavers, we could teach them our secrets while the sight of your robes is fresh in their eyes.

EMPEROR.   That is a good thought.

ZAR *(To bystanders.)*   A great honor has come to you. And you. You shall carry the emperor's train.

BYSTANDER *(Terrified.)*   I never carried an emperor's train in my life.

ZAN.   We will show you.

ZAR *(The two illustrating.)*   You lift the train, so, together, and spread it, so, that the pattern of many leaves may be plain to see. And swing it together a little, so, as you walk, that the green and coral and purple may shine in the sun.

ZAN.   Stand here.

ZAR *(To the other.)*   You, here.

ZAN.   Hold out your hand.

ZAR.   The cloth is very fragile. You must handle it like thistle-down.
(They pretend to put the corners of the train into the bystander's hands. Their victims watch them and each other out of the corner of their eyes, uncertain, then cautiously close their fingers.)

ZAN.   Not too tight! You will crush the folds! *(Bystanders jump and fix their fingers.)*

ZAR.   They are ready, your majesty.

ZAN.   If the emperor will walk a few paces, that these lucky ones may follow the grace of his moving.

EMPEROR *(Flattered.)*   I will walk a few paces. *(He moves airly across and around.)*
ZAR and ZAN *move with the bystanders, moving their arms in the right rhythm, and showing them how to imitate the* EMPEROR'S *walk as they pretend to swing the train. Gradually the bystanders, paralyzed with embarrassment at first, gain courage.)*

ZAR.   Ah-h! That is right! Now it shines and shimmers! See the colors!
(The EMPEROR *looks around at the citizens and there is a last chorus of praise.* TSEIN *breaks through the crowd, just before the* EMPEROR *reaches exit.)*

TSEIN. Merciful emperor! Your weavers pray to you!

EMPEROR. What is your prayer?

TSEIN. Only let us remain in the houses, and weave on the looms of our ancestors.

EMPEROR. Remain in the houses and worship at the shrines of your ancestors. These men shall teach you their secrets. You and your children shall weave for the emperor in his city, forever. (*The weavers cry out in joy, some sobbing, some throwing up their hands.*) I know you are fit to be the royal weavers. If you were not, you would not have seen the beauty of my robes.

(*The weavers fall silent, suddenly. TSEIN springs after the EMPEROR as he turns to go. Confession is on her lip. ZAN leaps to cover her mouth with his hand, drawing her back. The EMPEROR passes on, not having seen the pantomime.*)

ZAN. Sh-h-h-h!

(*At the same moment the CHILD runs out from her doorway and rushes to TSEIN. She stops, gaping at the sight of the EMPEROR, and points speechlessly at him as he goes off. Her voice comes just as he disappears.*)

CHILD. Mother! The emperor has nothing on but a shirt!

(*ZAR puts a hand over her mouth and draws her into the crowd. The CHILD still points, unable to speak. The EMPEROR's music is dying away. The weavers look at each other.*)

LING (*To MONG.*) Did you see anything?

MONG (*Looking at the CHILD.*) No ——

TSEIN (*Overwhelmed.*) There was nothing.

ROGUES. Sh-h-h-h-h-h- ——
(*Rogues, fingers on lips, looking after the EMPEROR's procession. As the music dies quite away, they begin to laugh, secretly, softly. The weavers slowly take in the joke, one at a time. They join the laughter. It grows ad grows till the stage rocks with it.*)

ZAN (*Above the laughter.*) Oh-h-h! This was a glorious adventure!

ZAR. But it is over! When the emperor finds out! (*Sign of beheading.*)

ZAN. Zar! We must get far from this place!

ZAR. Zan! We must never stop running till the milky way is winking at us through the dark!

ZAN (*Leaping up to where they hid the treasure.*) Who wants gold and jewels?

ZAR. Gold for the emperor's new clothes!

ZAN *(Flinging them about.)* Jewels for the emperor's tunics! Rubies! Emeralds!

ZAR. *(Also flinging them.)* Turquoise! Opals! Jade!

BOTH. Hold out your hands!

ZAN. *(Stripping off his rich coat.)* Who wants rich robes?

ZAR. Who wants glittering shoes?!

BOTH *(Flinging fine garments and shoes.)* Catch! Catch!

ZAN *(Leaping to exit, at the top of the steps.)* We are off!

ZAR *(Following.)* We will go somewhere high up, and look down on many cities!

ZAN. We will choose the one where people are most foolish!

ZAR. There we will have our next adventure!

BOTH. *(As they leap out of sight.)* Ah-h-h-ha!

CURTAIN

Copies of this play, in individual paper covered acting editions, are available from Samuel French, Inc., 25 W. 45th St., New York, N.Y. 10036 or 7623 Sunset Blvd., Hollywood, Calif. 90046 or in Canada Samuel French (Canada) Ltd., 80 Richmond St. East, Toronto M5C 1P1, Canada.

THE GHOST OF MR. PENNY

By

ROSEMARY MUSIL

The premiere production of this play was given in March, 1939, by the Children's Theatre of Evanston, Illinois, under the direction of Miss Winifred Ward.

THE GHOST OF MR. PENNY

By

Rosemary Musil

THE GHOST OF MR. PENNY

Although the fairy tale plays written by Chorpenning, her students, and her imitators dominated theatre for children through the 1930's and 1940's, a few playwrights continued to create plays with contemporary characters and settings. The most important of these was Rosemary Musil. Musil was not as prolific as Chorpenning; nor have her plays been as popular as some of Chorpenning's writings, but she championed an approach to writing for child audiences quite different from the prevailing style.

Throughout the years, the most popular of Musil's plays has been *The Ghost of Mr. Penny*. The play is not exciting and suspenseful, as is *The Little Princess*, nor immediate and moving, as is *Step on a Crack*, but it is an important member of that family of plays that present children in life-like situations. Though each of these three plays is similar in this perspective, each is as different as the times within which they were written. What is remarkable about *The Ghost of Mr. Penny* is that it exists at all, if one considers the virtual monopoly that the fairy and folk tale had on the children's theatre of the time. This play is produced only rarely today, but its importance does not rest with its ability to live beyond the period in which it was written. *The Ghost of Mr. Penny* is representative of a small body of literature that served as a bridge between the realistic, sentimental, melodrama of the beginning of the century and the modern problem plays. With a style entirely her own, Musil borrows from melodrama and from the well-made play and adds liberal doses of sentiment and comedy to portray life-like children placed in a recognizable world.

The Ghost of Mr. Penny is the story of a young girl, Sally, who is about to be sent to an "orphan asylum" because her guardian has become ill. While playing in an abandoned coach house, Sally and her friends stumble upon Bill, a good-natured drifter, who, like Zar and Zan, facilitates the action for the "good guys" in the play. The action begins with the discovery of a picture which suggests that Sally might be the heir of the Penny fortune, and would thus not have to go to an orphanage. Meanwhile, a distant relative of Mr. Penny, Mr. Jenkins, appears on the scene to claim the estate.

Much of the story is based on events that happen prior to the beginning of the play. This, and the many characters that figure prominently in the action, necessitates an unwieldy amount of exposition in Act One. Musil delivers this exposition through lengthy conversations between the characters, so that the entire act takes on the qualities of a radio drama where the story is *told* more than it is *presented*.

The elaborate exposition provides some justification for the odd assortment of characters that are thrown together in Act Two. The setting is the Penny mansion, which is supposedly haunted. Musil makes effective use of this environment by setting up a series of situations where these characters frighten one another, and then come to suspect that there might really be a ghost in the house.

Although the action in the mansion has little to do with Sally's situation, it is the high point of the play. The children go to the house to search for a treasure they believe might be hidden there. They fully expect to be frightened by the ghost, and they are not disappointed. Musil lets the audience in on the joke that the chaos is not caused by a ghost but by the threat of such a creature, and, as a result, audience members are invited to delight in the antics rather than to fear for the well-being of the characters. This is illustrated well in the climactic scene in Act Two where Bill, who has concealed himself under a sheet covering a chair in the mansion, wraps his sheet-covered arms around Phineas, an already very frightened visitor in the house. Phineas' hasty departure is almost guaranteed to evoke laughter from the audience.

During this action Sally inadvertently finds her birth certificate (although she does not know what it is) and uses it to fill a hole in her shoe. This business is important to the resolution of the story, but only a minor incident amid many humorous and interesting complications in this act.

The third act of the play returns to the setting and style of Act One, and here Musil resorts to some of the more obvious techniques of melodrama. The suspense rises as Bill does not know how to help Sally. Only at the last minute, when Mr. Jenkins is about to prevail, does Bill find the birth certificate, recognize its significance, and use it to prove Sally's case. Mr. Jenkins is then hustled off to jail, and the play ends with the implication that Sally will live happily ever after.

The basic story of the play, which can be reduced to the question of whether Sally must go to the orphanage, is decidedly sentimental. But Musil does not over-emphasize either the sentimentality or the melodrama in the work. In contrast to Sara Crewe, who is badly mistreated by Miss Minchin, nothing bad happens to Sally. In addition, Musil avoids placing Sally in direct conflict with an evil villain. Mr. Jenkins wants the same thing as Sally, and if he prevails Sally will go to the orphanage. Mr. Jenkins never threatens Sally with harm, he only attempts to hide some important facts in the case so that he can claim the estate. He seems far more inept than mean, and the audience is left to feel that, particularly with kind people like Bill around, Sally will never suffer unjustly. The emotional involvement is usually great with characters in melodrama because they are pictured in (and rescued from) a very bad situation. Sally is only rescued from the *threat* of a bad situation.

Unlike a traditional melodrama, which often offers a startling reversal of the action, this play offers few surprises. Musil provides many clues about Sally's identity throughout the course of the play and, in the end, the audience is not surprised by the revelation of Sally's true identity, as much as interested in the means and manner in which this revelation might finally take place.

With *The Ghost of Mr. Penny*, Musil offered audiences of the time a look at contemporary characters in a contemporary setting. The characterizations are limited, and tend more toward types than individuals, but the characters are rambunctious, inquisitive, and even a little mischievous. They question Bill's veracity, and they also challenge adult authority by sneaking into the haunted house. In a manner reminiscent of detective/mystery stories long popular in children's literature, the children in this story become actively involved in an adventure. Although Musil found it necessary to let an adult finally unravel this mystery, she at least places the children in the center of the action.

The Ghost of Mr. Penny is a naive and simplistic work: the play is loosely structured, the through-line of action is unclear, the situation is implausible, and the donouncement is contrived. But it is important to note that this play is no less artistic than much of the drama written at that time, and regardless of its technical deficiencies, this play offered audiences of the time a theatre experience much different than that offered by the fairy and folk tale dramas. The story of *The Ghost of Mr. Penny* is unbelievable, but it appears much less so when compared with the far-fetched stories of plays like *The Emperor's New Clothes* or with plays that include fantasy characters like Rumpelstiltskin or Snow White.

At the turn of the century, writers like Burnett, operating under the guise of contemporary realism, pictured children as doll-like characters with little identity and less individuality. Musil's work, represented here by *The Ghost of Mr. Penny*, brought the literature a step away from that view by presenting children who are more recognizable as real people. *The Ghost of Mr. Penny* presents more external complications than nuances of character development or maturation, but the children are pictured as having feelings and ideas of their own.

It is much too simplistic to trace a direct lineage between Sally and Ellie Murphy (*Step on a Crack*), because many influences have intervened over the years to cause changes in the literature. *The Ghost of Mr. Penny* is an important example of a specific perspective about contemporary realistic drama, growing out of a particular time. It falls well short of the truth and sincerity offered in *Step on a Crack*, but it was the most popular drama of its kind during the 1940's and 1950's, and it thus stands as an important evolutionary step toward the contemporary realistic plays of the modern era.

ROSEMARY MUSIL was born in Dearborn, Missouri, in 1903. She received a degree in Fine Arts at Horner Institute in Kansas City, and also studied at the State University of Central Missouri.

Musil subsequently moved to Chicago, Illinois, where she became acquainted with Winifred Ward. With Ward's encouragement, Musil wrote more than seventeen plays, most of which were performed at Ward's Children's Theatre of Evanston.

Musil was instrumental in organizing a children's theatre organization in Elmhurst, Illinois, and served as its director for twenty-six years. Her writings over the years have included T.V. scripts, pageants and traditional children's plays — four of which have been published by Anchorage Press. In 1975 Musil was awarded the Chorpenning Cup by The Children's Theatre Association of America for her achievements in writing plays for children.

In addition to *The Ghost of Mr. Penny*, Musil's published plays include *Seven Little Rebels, Five Little Peppers, and Mystery at the Old Fort.*

THE GHOST OF MR. PENNY

By

Rosemary Musil

Cast

BILL, a tramp, good-natured, easy-going, lovable.

LEWIS, twelve years old, whose ambition is to be a "tough guy."

TOMMY, his friend and pupil.

SALLY, their playmate, a gallant and spirited girl.

ELLEN, another playmate, rather prim and cautious.

PHINEAS, an awkward boy of eighteen or so.

MR. JENKINS, a fussy little middle-aged man.

MR. SIMMONS, Ellen's father, and the neighborhood policeman.

SCENES

ACT ONE:
  SCENE: The abandoned coach-house of the old Penny estate, late one afternoon in autumn.

ACT TWO:
  SCENE: The living room of the old Penny house, after dark, that evening.

ACT THREE:
  SCENE: The coach-house, the next morning.

To
SKIPPY
and his pals

THE GHOST OF MR. PENNY

By

ROSEMARY MUSIL

ACT ONE

Scene: The abandoned coach-house of an old estate.

There are three openings in the set — the outside door up right center, the wooden casement window up left center, and a door down left which leads into the harness room. There is a manger filled with straw at right.

The room looks dusty and neglected. Just below the window is a gas plate with boxes piled high upon it, and the plate itself protected by an oil-cloth. A rickety old table occupies the center of the stage, and there are two matching chairs piled up against the door, which is locked and barred. An old rusty lantern hangs over the manger.

At the rise of the curtain, the stage is empty, but outside the window, someone can be heard approaching. The window swings open, revealing a man with a battered felt hat set on the back of his head.

Bill is evidently a sailor of sorts, for he wears part of a sailor costume. He is big and athletic-looking, though lazy, and in his prime of life. He may be thirty-five or forty-five. It is hard to tell, for he enjoys life, and his sense of humor and kindliness have kept him young. He is neat, in spite of the battered felt hat, and a two-days' growth of beard. He opens the window cautiously, looks inside, and expresses his delight in a long, low whistle.

He throws a leg over the sill, steps onto the boxes, and into the room. He is carrying some provisions tied up in a bandana handkerchief. He pushes the window to, and looks about him with pleasure, giving out a big sigh of contentment. Then he begins a more detailed examination of the premises.

He peeps into the harness-room, finding everything to his taste. Then he crosses to center, and tries the table for dust, testing it with a gingerly finger. He brushes his hands off with elaborate care, then spotting the manger at right, he crosses and punches the straw to test it for bedding.

It all suits him down to a T, and he begins to make preparations for a formal supper. Taking a handful of straw, he dusts the table efficiently, then unstacks the two chairs, and dusts them, arranging them at the table, as for a banquet. Then, spying the oil-cloth, he pulls it out and spreads it over the table, straightening it daintily. He puts his bandana on the table and opens it up, taking out spoon, knife, and fork. Placing these carefully, he casts a critical eye over the whole, and decides something is missing. Then he snaps his fingers and springs out the window, returning almost instantly with a handful of golden-rod, which he crams down into the neck of an old bottle which is found among the boxes and debris.

Surveying his handiwork with pride, Bill beams happily, and draws a can from his bandana. Then he pulls a can-opener from his pocket, and starts to tackle the can. The can-opener offers difficulties, and Bill is still trying to make it work, when a voice is heard outside calling, and he stops to listen attentively.

TOMMY *(outside)*: Lewis! Hey Lewie! I shot you. You're dead! Leeeewie!
(The voice grows fainter, but a scuffling at the window warns Bill, who hastily puts the can-opener in his pocket, gathers up his things, and piles into the manger. The window opens as he does so, and Lewis, a little boy about twelve, climbs in, carrying a home-made shotgun. He squats down beside the table, waiting. The voice of his pursuer comes closer.) Lewie! . . . Leewwie! Quit your hidin' and come on back here! You're dead! . . . Lew . . . I bet I know where you're hidin' at! *(Tommy climbs up on a box from outside, opens the window and crawls in. He is about the same age and size of Lewis, and carries a toy pistol.)*

LEWIS: Bang! Bang! . . . I got ya!
(He runs out from behind the table.)

TOMMY: Ah, you did not. I got you outside by the house. You were dead before you came in here!

LEWIS: I was not. You just got me in the shoulder.
(Sally "yoo-hoo's" from back in the deep yard surrounding the coach house.)

SALLY *(offstage)*: Leeeewis! . . . Tommieeee! Hey, Tommy, I want to play too!

LEWIS: It's Sally! Quick, shut the window! We don't want any ole girl playing in here. *(The boys slam the window shut, and pull the bar across it.)*

SALLY *(at the window)*: Tommy Tommy Higgins! . . . I saw you slam this window. Open it up. I want to play in the coach house too.

TOMMY: Ah, go away.

LEWIS: We're playin' G-Men. Girls can't be G-men.

SALLY: I'll be a G-woman then.
(The boys think this remark terribly funny. They go off into gales of derisive laughter.)

BOYS: Ha, ha, ha! She'll be a G-woman. Silly old girls think they can be G-women.

SALLY *(outside)*:   I've got as much right in there as you have.

TOMMY: Ah, go cook a radish!
(Overcome with this brilliant retort, the boys howl with laughter and slap each other on the back.)

SALLY: You open this window! The coach house doesn't belong to you.

LEWIS: It doesn't belong to you either.

SALLY: Well, anyway, you let me in!

TOMMY *(whispering)*:   Don't answer, and maybe she'll go away.

SALLY: You let me in, or I'll—I'll bust the door down!

TOMMY: She'll bust the door down! Ha! Ha! That's good!

TOMMY: Ho! Ha! Ole door's got about a million bolts in it, I reckon, but she's gonta bust it in! That's good!

SALLY: All right. I'll show you.
(Sally throws her weight against the door. The boys are surprised at her attempt.)

TOMMY: She's tryin' it!

LEWIS: Of all the silly . . .
(The rusty old door, weak in the hinges, suddenly gives way, and Sally falls headlong upon it, into the coach house. For a moment, no one can speak, so surprised are they. Then Sally gets up slowly, rubbing certain parts.)

SALLY: Gee, I did it!

TOMMY: Gosh!

LEWIS: She busted the door in!

SALLY: I told you I would.
(The boys examine the door. Sally smoothes her dress and hair.)

TOMMY: Look, the hinges were rusty and they busted right off!

LEWIS: Yeah . . . Hey, hadn't we better set up the door.
(Sally has taken off her shoe and is hopping about trying to find the paper she lost out of it.)

TOMMY: I say we had. What if somebody saw it busted in! Come on, Sally, help us put the door back.

SALLY: Wait a minute, I've got to find the paper out of my shoe.

LEWIS: Paper out of your shoe?

SALLY: Yes, there's a hole in the sole, and I'll ruin my stocking if I don't keep a paper in it.

LEWIS *(picking up folded paper)*:   This it?

SALLY: Yes ... Thanks *(She sits on chair and puts paper back in shoe.)* Now! ... Do you think we can pick it up?

TOMMY: Grab hold of here and shove it as you raise it; *(The children set the door up, and wonder of wonders, it jams into the doorway and stands by itself.)* Gee! It sticks by itself!

SALLY: Careful, it might fall down!
(The children hold their hands out for a minute, then breathe easier as they see it is going to stand.)

LEWIS: Nope, she really sticks ... Can't even tell it was knocked down!

SALLY: We'd better get away, in case the wind blows it over, or something! *(They back off and turn to the table, leaning on it, and Sally sits in one of the chairs.)*

TOMMY *(examining the table suddenly)*:   Hey look!

SALLY: What?

TOMMY: There's oil cloth on the table!

LEWIS: Gee, yes, and the chairs are drawn up too, just like somebody had put them there! I never noticed that before!

SALLY: Do you suppose somebody's been here besides us?

LEWIS: Who could have?

TOMMY: Maybe it was the ghost!

SALLY: The ghost!

LEWIS *(derisively)*:   What ghost?

TOMMY *(lowering his voice and looking about him)*: The ghost of Mr. Penny!

SALLY: Of all the silly things! There isn't any such thing as ghosts!

LEWIS: I don't know. They say the big house is haunted.

TOMMY: Yeah, and old Mr. Penny's ghost walks up and down the steps at night, looking for his little boy that shot himself accidentally with a gun!

SALLY: Oh, that's too silly for words! Mr. Penny isn't even dead!

TOMMY: No? Then where is he?

SALLY: Nobody knows. After his little boy shot himself, Mrs. Penny died from shock, and Mr. Penny just wandered away and went to sea.

TOMMY: Well, people have seen his ghost wandering about the big house at night, so he must be dead!

SALLY: The idea! If there'd been a ghost wandering around old Mr. Herman would have seen him, wouldn't he? And Mr. Herman says Mr. Penny isn't dead and that he's coming back some day. That's the reason he stays on there in the big house, waiting for Mr. Penny to come back!

LEWIS: If Mr. Herman saw that ole ghost wanderin' around, he'd have him arrested fer trespassin'!

SALLY: Shh! Somebody's calling!
(Children listen.)

ELLEN *(outside window)*: Sally, are you in there?

SALLY: It's Ellen! *(Opens window.)* Hello, Ellen, come on in!

ELLEN *(standing at the window)*: I don't want to climb in the window. I'll get my dress dirty *(superiorly.)*

LEWIS *(mischievously)*: Then why don't you come in by the door?

ELLEN: Is the door open?

LEWIS: Sure it is! Sally came in that way!

ELLEN: Well for pity sakes, why didn't you say so, Sally?

SALLY: Oh, but Ellen you—
(Ellen starts to turn toward the door, and Lewis puts his hand over Sally's mouth to keep her from telling.)

LEWIS: Just push against the door real hard!

SALLY *(jerking free from Lewis)*: Don't you do it, Ellen!
(Lewis grabs her again and keeps her from talking.)

ELLEN: Well, I guess I can do it if you did, Sally Andrews!
(Ellen pushes, the door falls in, and the boys howl with laughter.

Ellen is mad as a wet pussy cat, and Sally runs to her solicitiously to help her up.)

ELLEN: You think you are funny, don't you, Lewis Bleck?

LEWIS *(laughing)*: No! I think you are!

SALLY: I tried to tell you, Ellen!

ELLEN: Well, I came over here to tell you something exciting, but if you're going to act mean— *(She starts out the door, but Sally brings her back.)*

SALLY: Oh, don't pay any attention to the old boys, Ellen!

LEWIS *(helping Tommy lift the door back into place)*: Sure, we're sorry. What's doing?

TOMMY: Did your father capture a bandit or somethin'?

ELLEN: No. Mr. Herman's dead!

CHILDREN: Mr. Herman!

SALLY: Oh, when did it happen?

ELLEN: Sometime yesterday, I guess. My mamma went over to the big house at supper time to take him some hot soup, and he was lying on the table. He'd had a heart attack. He'd been writing, the papers were scattered all over.... Mamma went over and swept them up in the fireplace!

SALLY: For goodness sake!

TOMMY: Gee!

LEWIS: Poor old Mr. Herman can't have us arrested for trespassin' now, I reckon!

ELLEN: And that isn't the worst of it!

SALLY: No?

ELLEN: My mother went back over there late last night, intending to burn the papers she'd swept up in the fireplace ... and she ... *(her voice breaks with the weight of her horrible tale)* she took my father's flashlight and went into the old house, and right away ... right away ... *(her voice breaks again.)*

TOMMY: Yeah, go on!

ELLEN: She saw it!

SALLY: What?

ELLEN: The ghost, of course!

SALLY: Ah, that's silly!

ELLEN: Yes? Well, maybe you think my mamma would tell a story. Maybe you think . . .

TOMMY: Gosh, Ellen, what was it like?

ELLEN: It was a kind of head hanging in space, and pink cheeks, and purple . . .

LEWIS: Whiskers!

ELLEN: Whiskers . . . er . . . *(The spell is broken, the children laugh at Ellen's story.)* It did not! It had whiskers, though . . . and a purple tie!

LEWIS: A pink ghost with purple whiskers! Ha, ha!
(Children laugh at her, and Ellen is angry.)

ELLEN: All right, smarties, laugh all you please, but I guess my mamma knows what she saw. She was too scared to even burn the papers!

SALLY: Poor Mr. Herman. All these years, he's kept that house open, waiting for Mr. Penny to come back. And now—he's dead.

LEWIS: Gosh, it gives me the creeps.

TOMMY: Let's don't think about it. Let's play G-men. You girls go away now. We want to play G-men.

SALLY: We'll be G-women, and play too.

LEWIS: Of all the silly—there isn't any such thing as G-women! *(Disgustedly)* G-women!

TOMMY: Why don't we play Secret Service? They got girls in that.

SALLY: Sure! Let's do!

LEWIS: Ah, we don't want to play with girls! *(He throws his gun down on the table, and looks disgusted.)*

ELLEN: You'd better treat Sally nice, 'cause she's got to go to the orphan's asylum tomorrow, and you won't get a chance to play with her any more.
(The children all look at Sally pityingly. Sally is serious, too.)

LEWIS: Gee, Sally, do you haff to go tomorrow?

SALLY: I—I reckon so.

TOMMY: Gee, Sally, I'm sure sorry.

SALLY (*rallying and attempting to make light of it*): Oh, it's . . . it's just a temporary arrangement, Uncle Jim says . . . I'm just going to stay long enough for Uncle Jim to get well, then he's going to get me back again. Besides, it really isn't an orphan asylum, Ellen . . . It's a boarding house for children, and it's got swings and slides, and everything.

(The children are sad, they love Sally.)

TOMMY (*impulsively*): Here, you can have my gun, Sally.

LEWIS: Mine too.

SALLY (*lighthearted once more, for she has learned to take her troubles a step at a time*): Thanks . . . but what will Ellen do?

ELLEN (*airily*): Oh, I could have a real gun if I wanted it!

TOMMY: Gee, Ellen, you mean your father's policeman's gun?

SALLY: Ellen, you wouldn't!

ELLEN: I could if I wanted to. I saw where he keeps it, last night!

LEWIS: Gosh, is it loaded?

ELLEN: Of course. Policemen always keep their guns loaded.

TOMMY: Gee! Go get it, Ellen!

ELLEN: All right, wait here a minute!

(She turns and goes to the window to climb out of it, but the tramp can not stand by now. He hurries out of the stall, crosses quickly to the window, shuts it and bars the way.)

BILL: Oh, no! No, no, Princess! Don't do it! *(The children scream, and scramble together in a heap downstage at left.)* Guns is bad medicine fer children . . . er anybody fer that matter!

ELLEN: Who—who are you?

TOMMY: You'd better let us out of here!

LEWIS: Yeah, her father's a policeman.

ELLEN: And he'll arrest you for trespassing!

BILL: Aw, shucks! Don't be afraid of me . . . I wouldn't hurt no one, and I like kids! I wouldn't 'a let you know I was here, but shucks, I couldn't stand by and let the Princess here get her pappy's loaded gun. . . . Why, you kids might of shot each other! That would have been awful!

ELLEN: You were hiding in there! *(pointing to the stall)*

BILL: Aw, now!

TOMMY: Yes, and you'd better get out of here!

BILL: Aw, shucks, I'm not a goin' to hurt nothin' er nobody; I wasn't goin' t' stay long nowhow. I'll go now if you say so. But, listen, kids, about guns—guns don't do nobody any good ever! Not even grown up people, let alone kids!

LEWIS: Yeah? Well, I'll bet they do G-men some good!

BILL: G-men? Why, they don't even use 'em most of the time!

TOMMY: Aw, like fun they don't!

(The boys have forgotten to be afraid, and come out and speak boldly with the gentle Bill.)

BILL: Naw, they don't. They use their brains to catch crooks! Take this here feller at the head of the G-men . . . you know what he says?

LEWIS: What?

(The children relax perfectly now, grouping themselves about Bill who is at the table.)

BILL: Well, he says only cowards use guns . . . you know, people who are afraid! And he never uses a gun 'ceptin' in self-defense, 'cause he's seen so many cowardly people dependin' on guns to make 'em brave, that he's downright ashamed t' have a gun!

LEWIS: Honest?

BILL: Sure, that's what he says . . . and me, I never like guns! I don't even like to see kids play with toy guns, 'cause I've seen too much grief they've cause in the world.

TOMMY: You mean like in wars?

BILL: Sure, and in peace times too. So don't ever fool with your pappy's loaded gun, Princess. Why, didn't that poor little Penny boy get killed playin' with his pappy's gun? Just like you were goin' t' do!

(Sally looks at him and catches her breath in sudden excitement. Maybe this tramp is Mr. Penny come back!)

SALLY: Why! How did you know that?

BILL *(unconsciously contributing to her thought)*:   Oh, I know a lot of things that would surprise you!

ELLEN: You're just a tramp, that's all, and you can't boss us around! I'll tell my father . . . he's a policeman, and he'll have you—

BILL (*patiently*): Yeah, I know...arrested fer trespassin'...but first we got to sort of figure out which one of us is trespassin', ain't we?

ELLEN: Which one of us? Why, you are, of course!

BILL: Well, that depends. Now this here coach house don't belong to you kids, does it?

ELLEN: It doesn't belong to you either! It belongs to Mr. Penny, only he's dead!

SALLY (*quickly*): No, he isn't dead, either!

BILL (*amused*): Now, you see there? You don't know much about it after all, do you? Why, for all you know, maybe I own the place!

SALLY: Oh! Oh, are you...

ELLEN: Own the place! Why, you're just a tramp!

TOMMY: Are you?

BILL: Am I what?

TOMMY: Just a tramp like Ellen says?

BILL: Me a tramp? Shucks, Matey, I'm a sailor!

TOMMY: A sailor?

SALLY (*suddenly sure of herself*): Of course he is!
        (*Bill looks at her surprised.*)

ELLEN: Oh, what do you know about it? If you aren't a tramp, why were you hidin' over there in the manger?

BILL: I just stopped in the manger there to take a little seesta!

LEWIS: A what?

BILL: Seesta! You know...a beauty nap. I was kinda tired when I got off the train this morning, so...

ELLEN: I knew it! You're just a tramp that comes off of freight trains. My papa's arrested them plenty of times. He'll arrest you, too!

BILL: Aw now, Princess!

SALLY: Her name's Ellen.

BILL: Is it now? She's the very spittin' image of a Princess I onct knowed in the South Sea islands, time I got wrecked off the coast of Singapore.

TOMMY: Gee, are you a sailor sure enough?

BILL: Me a sailor? Why shucks, Matey, look here!
(He rolls up his sleeve, and the children crowd about him, even Ellen.)

TOMMY: Gee! Look at the tattoos!

BILL: Look at this here one.
(He doubles up his fist and the lady on his arm dances.)

LEWIS: Look! The lady's dancin'!

TOMMY: Yes, sir! Boy, look at her go!

BILL: And look at this here one!
(Rolls up other sleeve and displays arm.)

TOMMY: Gee, look at the swell snake.

LEWIS: Have you really been shipwrecked?

BILL: Shipwrecked? He asks me have I been shipwrecked! Why Matey, I've been shipwrecked more times than you got fingers er toes! Why, man and boy I sailed the six seas fer . . .

ELLEN *(triumphantly)*: I knew you weren't a sailor?

BILL: Huh?

ELLEN: You said you'd sailed the six seas . . . they're seven! I learned that in geography!

BILL: Yeah, but hadn't you heard? One of 'em died.

ELLEN: Which one?

BILL: Ain't you never heard of the dead sea?
(Rest of children laugh at Ellen's angry face.)

TOMMY: Ha, ha! . . . I get it. They're seven seas, but one of 'em is the dead sea . . . so that leaves six!

ELLEN: I don't think it's funny at all. I don't believe you ever saw the sea!

BILL: What? Me not saw the sea? Why Princess!

SALLY *(slyly looking at Bill as she tries out this next remark on him)*: Mr. Penny was a sailor! Did you know him?

BILL: Sure, I know all about him. His little boy got shot, and his wife died, and he went away and never came back . . . at least not up to now.

(Bill loves children, and he plays their game, talking seriously to them, and giving them the courtesy of answering all their questions in detail. But this answer to Sally is just about perfect to confirm her suspicions that Bill is Mr. Penny himself.)

SALLY: I knew you'd know?
(She smiles knowingly at Bill, who looks at her a little puzzled.)

ELLEN: I'll bet when my father sees you, you'll get out of here mighty quick!

BILL: Aw now Princess, you wouldn't give me away, would you? I haven't hurt nothin' . . .

ELLEN: You're a trespasser and—

SALLY: He is not!

ELLEN: He is too! Anybody that is on property that don't belong to them is a tres—

SALLY: Well, this property belongs to him!
(She tosses her head triumphantly. The children and Bill look at her in amazement.)

ELLEN: Have you gone crazy?

SALLY: Certainly not. This man you've been calling a tramp is just Mr. Penny come back, that's all! *(Airily)*

LEWIS and TOMMY: Mr. Penny come back??

SALLY: Of course he is! Don't you see? He's a sailor, isn't he? Well, Mr. Penny was a sailor, too, after he ran away! Mr. Herman said so!

LEWIS: Gee!

SALLY: And he knows all about the little boy shooting himself with a gun.

TOMMY: Gosh!
(The boys look at the dazed Bill in awe. Bill looks a little uncomfortable. He doesn't want to sail under false colors, but he doesn't want to let Sally down. He finally decides she is just tormenting Ellen, and so he backs her up as best he can without deliberately committing himself.)

ELLEN: Well, that's just about the silliest thing you ever made up, Sally Andrews! He looks like Mr. Penny, doesn't he? Sneaking around the coach house and hidin' in the hay!

TOMMY: Yes, if he's Mr. Penny, why didn't he go right to the big

206

house, and walk in the front door?

SALLY: How you talk? Suppose your wife and little boy had died in that house years ago, and you had gone away trying to forget your troubles. And then you came back, after years of wandering, and found that your faithful old servant had just died there too. Would you feel like bouncing right up to the front door, and walkin' in just like a—a heathen?

TOMMY: Well—maybe not. But—

SALLY: Think of it! *(She uncorks her fertile imagination, and fairly revels in her fanciful tale of the heart-broken Mr. Penny. The boys are immensely impressed. Bill has to put his hands over his mouth, to keep from laughing. Ellen is about to explode with growing indignation.)* Poor Mr. Penny! Too grief-stricken with memories, he hides out here in the coach house, unable to go back and return to the—*(She reaches for the proper expression, then comes through with a flourish.)* the scene of his former triumph!

ELLEN *(snorting in her disgust)*: If that isn't about the . . . You got that out of one of your Uncle Jim's books, Sally Andrews! *(She takes Bill in her confidence, so disgusted is she that she forgets he is an enemy.)* She's always making things like that up! Her uncle writes stories and she's got too big an imagination!

SALLY: I have not!

ELLEN: You have so! I guess even my mother said so! Talking about going to a boarding school for children . . . when everybody knows it's just a plain old orphan asylum!

SALLY *(yelling)*: It is too a boarding house for children!

ELLEN: It is not! My mamma said so!
(Sally begins to cry, and Bill takes a hand.)

BILL: Here, here. *(He soothes Sally.)* Of course it's a—boarding house. *(He puts his arms about her protectingly and she sobs against him.)*

SALLY: It's got swings and slides and little tents!

BILL: Of course it has, and anybody says it hasn't is crazy! Don't you pay any attention to the Princess here. She just wound up her tongue and let it fly!

ELLEN: I did not! I'm telling the truth. . . . She even makes it up when she says Mr. Andrews is her Uncle Jim. He's not really her Uncle!

SALLY: He is too my Uncle Jim!

ELLEN: He is not! He found you on his doorstep when you were a little baby. He's no relation of yours at all! *(To Bill)* And now he's sick and has to go to a sanitorium and Sally has to go to a—

BILL *(glaring)*: WHERE?

ELLEN *(backing away frightened)*: To a—a boarding house!

BILL: That's better!

SALLY: It's only for a short time, Mr. Penny, and when Uncle Jim is well again he'll write more stories and—

BILL: And he'll make so much money that you'll have a big red automobile and silk dresses and servants and—

SALLY *(happy right away when someone can play her own game)*: And ice cream every day!

BILL: You bet! With chocolate sauce!

SALLY: And nuts!

ELLEN *(under her breath)*: Nuts is right!

SALLY: But you're rich already, aren't you, Mr. Penny?

BILL: Who? Me?

ELLEN: He looks it!

SALLY: Of course! You've got the big house and all the furniture, and the land is VERY valuable!

BILL: You don't say!

LEWIS: Yeah, and I heard you had money hid in the big house too, Mr. Penny.

TOMMY: Yeah, everybody talks about that. Did you hide some money in the big house, Mr. Penny?

BILL: Why, I—er . . . *(He looks at Sally for a cue, but she seems just as interested as the boys, and Bill hesitates about lying.)*

MR. JENKINS *(outside with Phineas)*: Now stand back, Phineas, my boy, while I try to open the door. These keys may not work in this rusty lock without a great deal of pushing and pulling.

(The children and Bill get to their feet, electrified motionless for a second. Then they all scamper with one accord to safety.)

TOMMY: Gosh, somebody's coming!

SALLY: They'll find we busted the door down!

LEWIS: Hide in the harness room, quick!

(The children hide in the harness room, and Bill scoots back into his stall.)

PHINEAS *(outside)*: Maybe I'd better haul off and give it a kind of running push when you put the key in the lock.

MR. JENKINS: Yes, yes, Phineas, that's a good idea!

(Phineas makes a flying tackle against the door, and comes down with it to the floor with a bang. Shocked and surprised, he stares up at Mr. Jenkins with mouth wide open.)

PHINEAS: The door fell down;

MR. JENKINS *(sarcastically)*: Do tell!

PHINEAS: Guess I don't know my own strength! *(Gets up stiffly and sets the door against the wall.)* I'm awfully sorry, Mr. Jenkins . . . I didn't go to do it!

MR. JENKINS: Well, no matter now! We haven't time for apologies!

(Mr. Jenkins is a fussy, prissy little nervous man, never smiling and easily annoyed. Phineas is a tall, overgrown boy of eighteen who takes himself quite seriously, though he is not very bright. He is quite important to himself, but good-natured too.)

Hummmm! *(He inspects the table.)* This place looks as if it had been occupied recently.

PHINEAS *(knowingly)*: It's those kids. They play in here lots of times. They come in at the window.

MR. JENKINS: Dear, dear. Something will have to be done about that. I can't have children running all over my property!

PHINEAS: Is the property all yours now, Jenkins?

MR. JENKINS *(inspecting the gas plate)*: Oh yes. I am the closest of kin, and the property will all come to me. My, my! Such gross negligence! The gas is still turned on.

PHINEAS: What kin are you?

(Mr. Jenkins is peering into the manger. He starts, draws back, thinks he saw something. He looks again, then decides he is mistaken.)

MR. JENKINS: Eh—eh—what's that?

PHINEAS: I said—what kin are you?

MR. JENKINS: Oh! Mr. Penny was my brother-in-law.

PHINEAS: Brother-in-law, eh?

MR. JENKINS: That's right!

(Mr. Jenkins is prissing around, examining chairs, tables, and peering into corners. Phineas, with his hat pushed back on his head, is lounging against the wall, conversationally inclined.)

PHINEAS: If you're Mr. Penny's brother-in-law, why didn't you turn up here a long time ago, when he first disappeared?

MR. JENKINS: I live a good piece away from this town, Phineas, and I did not keep in touch with the Pennys, and until last night, nobody ever troubled to inform me that the Penny family was all dead.

PHINEAS: Well, they do say that Mr. Penny himself ain't dead.

MR. JENKINS: Nonsense!

PHINEAS: Old Mr. Herman always thought Mr. Penny would come back.

MR. JENKINS: That's ridiculous. It's been established by law that he died at sea in a shipwreck. What's in here, Phineas?

(He has his hand on the knob of the harness-room door.)

PHINEAS: There's an old carriage and some harness. That's all.

(There is a loud scuffling sound, as the children scurry about to find a better hiding place.)

MR. JENKINS *(terrified)*:   I heard a noise in there!

PHINEAS *(listens, then nods his head knowingly)*:   Yeah—rats. There's lots of 'em out here in the coach house.

MR. JENKINS: Oh my! Oh my! How terribly embarrassing! I have a phobia about rats.

PHINEAS: A what?

MR. JENKINS: A phobia.

PHINEAS: Oh, a fobula. Is it a kind of trap?

MR. JENKINS: Is what a kind of trap?

PHINEAS: That fobula thing you said you had fer rats.

MR. JENKINS: Certainly not! A phobia is a—well, it's a fear! I'm afraid of rats, if you want to know. Well—*(looking about)* I don't see anything more here—

PHINEAS: Say, Jenkins, if you're Mr. Penny's brother-in-law, why, I reckon you might want to keep this. It's a picture I found this

210

morning up at the big house, when I was goin' around with them lawyer fellers.

MR. JENKINS: A picture?

PHINEAS: Yep. It was throwed away, in the old fireplace, in the living room. I thought nobody'd want it, and the lady was kinda purty—

MR. JENKINS: Why, this is a picture of my brother-in-law and his family. There's Penny with his little boy, just as I knew him. And there's his wife and—why, whose baby is this in the picture?

PHINEAS: I wouldn't know. I didn't even know who the lady was, but she looked so purty. But then you bein' a relation, I reckon it's only right you should have it.

MR. JENKINS (*thinking aloud, and suddenly very much upset*): He didn't have another child. He just had a little boy. The one that shot himself with the gun. (*Sharply:*) Phineas!

PHINEAS (*jumps*): Uh huh?

MR. JENKINS: Phineas, did anyone ever say my brother-in-law had another baby?

PHINEAS: Heck, nobody round here even knew Mr. Penny 'ceptin' maybe Jim Andrews.

MR. JENKINS: Jim Andrews?

PHINEAS: Yeah, he lives back in the woods, and when Mr. Penny built his house Jim was the only one lived hereabouts. It was the Andrews that found the baby on their doorstep, you know, just 'bout the time Mr. Penny left.

MR. JENKINS (*angrily, and with great suspicion that all is not well*): Confound it, Phineas, I don't know anything about this neighborhood. I told you I haven't heard of my brother-in-law these past fifteen years . . . Now out with it . . . what about this baby left on a doorstep? When did it happen?

PHINEAS: About ten years ago, I reckon; Sally's ten years old now.

MR. JENKINS: Sally? You mean this baby that was found on the doorstep is still around here?

PHINEAS: Yep. Sure, she's Sally . . . Sally Andrews, they call her . . . Only she won't be around here long. She's going to an orphan asylum tomorrow.

MR. JENKINS (*relieved*): She is? Then this Andrews fellow must be dead.

PHINEAS: Nope, but he's sick, and Sally ain't got nobody to stay with 'cause Jim has to go to the sanitarium.

MR. JENKINS (to himself): What luck!

PHINEAS: Yeah. Bad luck, ain't it?

MR. JENKINS: Eh? Oh, yes, yes, of course. Very sad.

PHINEAS: Yep, you bet. Everybody likes little Sally. (There is a loud scuffling noise here. Mr. Jenkins is petrified with fear. Uttering a little scream he drops the picture in his hand, and flees. Phineas looks at him in astonishment, and goes after him, talking reassuringly. As Phineas stands in the doorway, his back to the audience, an arm reaches out of the manger, and picks up the picture Mr. Jenkins has just dropped.) Hey, Jenkins. It's just rats.

MR. JENKINS (from outside, peering in gingerly): Are—are they gone?

PHINEAS: Well, not very far, I reckon. But rats won't hurt you. Rats is fun.

MR. JENKINS (shuddering): Fun? Ugh! Phineas, I dropped that picture over there somewhere. You bring it along, and let's get out of here.

PHINEAS (looking around): Where'd you drop it?

MR. JENKINS: Why, I don't know. Isn't it there?

PHINEAS: Don't see it anywhere.

MR. JENKINS: I was standing right there by the manger. It couldn't have gone far.

PHINEAS: Well, don't that beat all! Reckon the rats could have got it?

MR. JENKINS: Phineas! Don't mention it!

PHINEAS: I've known 'em to get away with bigger things than that. If you say so, I'll look for their nest, and find it.

MR. JENKINS: No, no! Let them have the picture! So long as it's out of the way, I don't care what happens to it.

PHINEAS: It's kind of a shame. The lady was so purty.

MR. JENKINS: Phineas, there wasn't anything else in that fireplace, was there?

PHINEAS: There's lots of papers and things stuck back in there.

MR. JENKINS: Papers! We'll have to get them out of there!

PHINEAS: Oh, no sir! Them lawyers said absolutely nothing was to be taken off the place.

MR. JENKINS: But the place is mine, Phineas. I've got a right to dispose of my own property.

PHINEAS: Yes, sir. But I got instructions to keep everything just like it is, till the lawyers are through with it.

MR. JENKINS: But those old papers, Phineas. It's dangerous to keep things like that around. Why, anything might happen!

PHINEAS: Anything! 'Tain't likely, is it?

MR. JENKINS: Why, with those old papers scattered around in the fireplace, mice or rats might get in, and somehow start a fire. And that old house would go up, just like that.

PHINEAS: Gee, I never thought of that! They've hired me to keep watch there tonight, and I wouldn't like to get burned up!

MR. JENKINS: Phineas, you take my advice, and burn those papers, before they catch fire.

PHINEAS: Oh, I'd be scared to, Jenkins. Them lawyers said—

MR. JENKINS: Phineas, you burn those papers, and I'll give you five dollars.

PHINEAS: But them lawyers said—five dollars!

MR. JENKINS: That's what I said.

PHINEAS: What fer?

MR. JENKINS: Why, for burning the papers.

PHINEAS: Five dollars fer burnin' some papers?

MR. JENKINS: Yes. It's worth that much to me to see the property protected.

PHINEAS: But what if those lawyer fellers finds out?

MR. JENKINS: Don't worry. They won't find out. I won't tell them. And I'm sure you won't.

PHINEAS: Jenkins, tell you what. I couldn't take the responsibility of burning them papers myself. But—fer five dollars I'll let you into the house tonight, since it's your own property, and you can burn them yourself.

MR. JENKINS: That's a very good idea, Phineas.

PHINEAS (*putting out his hand, importantly*): It's a deal!

MR. JENKINS (*looking down at his hand in astonishment*):   A what?

PHINEAS: A deal. Put her there, Jenkins!

MR. JENKINS: Oh! Yes, indeed.
(*Phineas pumps his hand down with a bang, and Mr. Jenkins groans.*)

PHINEAS: Yes, sir. It's a deal.

MR. JENKINS: Let's get away from here. Do you think you can set up that door, Phineas, till it can be fixed?

PHINEAS: Yep, sure. You go on out. I'll take it like this, and—
(*He turns about with the door, pulling it up to the opening with him outside. As he tries to put it in place, his long foot gets caught in it. He picks it up again, and comes back into the coach house with it. This time, his hands get caught, as he tries to fix it up into the frame. Finally, he succeeds in propping it upright, but then finds himself inside the coach house, instead of outside. He gives up, and climbs out the window. When he is safely gone Bill climbs out of the manger, looks through the crack in the door, then takes the picture downstage, to examine it with great eagerness. He looks from it to the harness room, where Sally is. The door of the harness room opens cautiously, and Tommy peeps out.*)

TOMMY: They gone?

BILL (*startled, hastily puts the picture in an inner pocket*):   Huh? Oh, sure. Sure they've gone. You can come out now.

TOMMY (*to Lewis, behind him*):   They've gone. Tell the girls.

LEWIS: Hey, you all can come out now.
(*The four children appear, somewhat the worse for hay, cobwebs, etc.*)

SALLY: Whew! That was a close call. It's a good thing he was afraid of rats.

LEWIS: Rats nothin'! That was Tommy rollin' all over the bottom of the carriage.

TOMMY: Yeah, you'd have wriggled too, if somebody's foot had been in your mouth.

ELLEN: Now I know you're not Mr. Penny, or you wouldn't have run and hid.

TOMMY: Yeah, that was strange!

SALLY: Why so? You don't think he wants to meet people around here yet, do you?

ELLEN: Of course not. They'd arrest him for trespassing.

SALLY: Trespassing? When he owns all this property, and has all that money?

ELLEN (*scornfully*): What money?

SALLY: The money that's hidden in the big house.

ELLEN: Well, if he's got money there, why don't he go and get it, 'stead of hiding out here in a barn? I don't think there's any money hidden in the house at all. And you're not Mr. Penny either. You're just a tramp!

SALLY: He is too Mr. Penny! Aren't you, Mr. Penny?

BILL (*uncomfortable*): Well, you see, I—
(He hardly knows what to say.)

ELLEN: If you're Mr. Penny, where's your key to the big house?

BILL: The key?

ELLEN: Certainly. If you own the house, you must have a key to it, haven't you?

(Bill looks at Sally blankly, but she only encourages him to produce.)

SALLY: Go on, Mr. Penny. Show her the key.

BILL: Well, now, you know—a key's a mighty easy thing to lose.

ELLEN (*triumphantly*): Aha!

SALLY: Oh, but you wouldn't lose that key, Mr. Penny. I bet it's right in your pocket. (*She plunges her hand into his coat pocket, and brings out the can opener.*) There! Now what do you say!

(The children cluster around to look at it closely.)

ELLEN (*skeptically*): It's a very funny key.

SALLY: Well, it's a very funny door!

BILL (*weak with relief*): My, my! I don't see how you do it, lassie.

TOMMY: Gosh! The key to the big house! Will it really open the big house, Mr. Penny?

BILL (*broadly*): Why, sure!

ELLEN: Like fun it will! Come on up to the big house, and let's see you try it!

SALLY: Ellen, don't you have any feelings at all? If you don't, I do. Mr. Penny, I'm so sorry about all the troubles you've had, and I know you haven't got the heart to go near the big house yet, or meet any people. But you'll feel better in a little while. And in the meantime, you can just stay right here in the quiet, and we won't breathe a word.

LEWIS: Sure you can. And if Ellen looks like she's going to tell her father, I'll bop her one.

TOMMY: And if you want anything, why just tell us. We'll fix you up.

BILL: Well, now, that's real thoughtful of you.

SALLY: Is there anything you want, Mr. Penny?

BILL (*fingering the picture, and looking furtively from it to Sally*) Well,—yes. There is something I want. But it's up at the big house and I don't much like—

SALLY: Is it something we can get for you, Mr. Penny?

BILL: Well—yes. I reckon you could. But—

TOMMY: I bet I know what it is! The hidden money!

SALLY: The treasure? Oh, Mr. Penny, is it? How wonderful!

LEWIS: Sure, we can get that for you, Mr. Penny—if you'll just tell us where it is.

BILL: Now here, hold on. I didn't say I wanted any hidden money, did I?

TOMMY: No, but you do, don't you?

BILL: I didn't even say there was any hidden money there, did I?

SALLY: No. But there is, isn't there?

BILL: Lassie, there may be. And there may not be. I didn't put any there myself, but it's quite likely Mr. Herman did. And as far as I'm concerned, you're perfectly welcome to look for it.

LEWIS: Let's do!

SALLY: All right, we will! We'll go tonight!

BILL: Listen lassie. You be careful. There'll be a night watchman there tonight. Named Phineas.

ELLEN: Yes. My father is hiring Phineas to guard the place.

TOMMY: Oh pooh! Who's afraid of Phineas? Anybody could get by Phineas.

BILL: Anybody?

LEWIS: Yeah. Anybody. Why, you could get by Phineas yourself, if you wanted to.

BILL: You think I could?

TOMMY: Why, sure. Phineas is scared of his own shadow.

LEWIS: If he saw you coming, he'd hide.

SALLY: Well, just the same—we won't risk it. We'll go early, before Phineas gets there.

ELLEN: We'll have to go before eight o'clock then. Phineas gets there at eight.

SALLY: Oh, Ellen, you do believe he is Mr. Penny now, don't you?

ELLEN: I didn't say so.

SALLY: But you're going!

LEWIS: Sure, she's afraid she'll miss out on something.

BILL: How'll you get in?

SALLY (*holding up the can opener*): We've got your key!

BILL (*uneasily*): Ellen here says it won't work.

ELLEN: I just said *maybe* it wouldn't work.

SALLY: Well, it will work!

TOMMY: Even if it won't—there's the pantry window!

BILL: What about the pantry window?

LEWIS: The catch is broken. We'll get in, all right.

BILL: Well—yes. It looks like there's a way to get in, all right.

SALLY: And when we do, Mr. Penny, what is it you want us to get for you?

BILL: Oh, never mind, Sally girl. It—it's not important.

SALLY: Are you sure? We'd be glad to get it for you.

BILL: No, don't bother. Just forget it.

SALLY: Oh. Well, I wish we could do something for you, Mr. Penny.

BILL: Aw, don't worry about me. I'll be all right.

PHINEAS (*outside the window*): Hey, you kids in there? You gotta get out. Open the window.

217

SALLY: It's Phineas!

BILL (*making for the manger*): Don't tell on me, will you?

LEWIS: Of course not.

SALLY: Let's tell Phineas about the ghost!

TOMMY: Let's do! He'll be scared polka-dotted.

PHINEAS (*outside*): I know you're in there now. Open up this window, or I'll get old man Simmons.

LEWIS: Aw, keep your shirt on, Sill. We're a'comin'.

(*Waiting till Bill is well concealed, he opens the window.*)

PHINEAS: Well, it's about time. You kids can't play in here any more. I made a deal with old man Jenkins to keep you out of here.

LEWIS: Say, Phineas, did you see the ghost when you were in the big house this afternoon?

PHINEAS: Now come on, you kids, 'cause I ... huh! Ghost?

LEWIS: Sure ... The Ghost of old Mr. Penny.

TOMMY: Yeah, it's got pink cheeks and purple whiskers.

(*Boys snicker.*)

PHINEAS: Aw, you're just tryin' t' scare me.

ELLEN: I guess my mamma wouldn't tell a story!

PHINEAS: Who? Old lady Simmons? Did she see it?

ELLEN: She certainly did! She went in there to burn the papers in the fireplace, and—

PHINEAS: Yeah, I know!

ELLEN: Well, she saw it. It was a kind of pink face with white whiskers and a purple tie!

PHINEAS (*impressively*): Gosh!

SALLY: If I were you, Phineas, I sure wouldn't sleep in that old house tonight.

PHINEAS (*impressed*): Gosh, no. You're right. I'll ... say! (*suddenly catching on*) How'd you know I was goin' t' sleep there t'night? (*Sally puts her hands over her mouth realizing she's made a slip.*) Huh, I see now! You kids were tryin' t' scare me so's you could play 'round there and nobody 'ud bother you! Well, you can't now, see? Now come on and git outta here ... come on!

TOMMY: Put us out!

LEWIS: Yeah!

PHINEAS: Don't you think I can't!

TOMMY: You got to catch us first!
(Round and round the table they go, the boys laughing. Phineas muttering. The door falls down. Phineas trips over it and falls flat. The boys laugh and run out. Phineas gets up grumbling, shakes his fist after the kids, rubs his hips, and sets the door back up as before.)

PHINEAS: Those crazy kids, tryin' t' scare a feller outta a deal just when he's gettin' in the money.... Hope ole man Jenkins don't go charging me fer the door! I didn't go to do it! I'm jest too strong!

CURTAIN

ACT TWO

Scene: The living room of the old Penny house.

The room is long and narrow, and furnished in late Victorian gingerbread fashion. Downstage right is the front door of the house, leading out of doors. Up left is the first flight of a stairway leading to the upper regions of the house, and down left is the fireplace, containing the fateful scraps of paper. Equally spaced across the back are two high old-fashioned windows, hung with faded draperies. Between them a Victorian sofa sits against the wall and directly over it hangs an old chromo of a man with a white beard and pink cheeks. Down right from the sofa is a table with a comfortable chair beside it, and there is another chair near the fireplace. All the furniture is covered with big white sheets for protection, which gives a rather ghostly effect. Two old swords are crossed over the fireplace, and the andirons, fire-screen, poker and broom are on the hearth.

The stage is quiet for a moment, then the children's voices are heard approaching.

TOMMY *(outside)*: Hey, Sally, have you got the key?

SALLY *(outside)*: I don't need it. Look, the door's not locked!
(She opens the door wide, and the four children are seen standing together on the threshold, all peering into the room.)

TOMMY: Gee, I wonder if old Phineas is here already.

LEWIS: It isn't eight yet.

ELLEN: Go see, Sally.

SALLY: Well, don't push me! *(Sally enters on tip-toe, flashing her light about cautiously. The white sheets over the furniture, and the ghostly moonlight through the back windows, give all the children a thrill.)* No, he's not here. Come on in.
(The children enter, almost holding their breath. Their lights are directed straight ahead at first, and the light all goes one way.)

TOMMY: Gee, look!

ELLEN: I—I think I'm going home!

SALLY: Oh Ellen, they're just white sheets.

ELLEN: But the ghost!

SALLY: Now in the first place there aren't any ghosts, and if they were, you said yourself, they don't come out till midnight . . . and it's only eight o'clock!

TOMMY: Just the same, I'm a-gonta go kinda slow!
(The children are in the room well up front now, flashing their lights about. Suddenly Ellen's light falls on the picture of the old man hanging above the sofa. She utters a shriek and dashes for the door. The boys hear and dash with her. In the doorway they fight to get through all at once, and are stuck tightly.) Let me outta here!

ELLEN: Oh! Oh!

LEWIS: Get outta my way!

SALLY: Stop it! What's the matter?

ELLEN: The ghost! I saw the ghost!

SALLY: Where?

ELLEN: Up there!

SALLY: On the wall? *(She flashes her light on the picture.)* You mean that thing?

ELLEN *(reassured)*:   Oh!

SALLY: It's just a picture of an old man!

ELLEN: But it had pink cheeks and a purple tie, and . . .

SALLY: Yes, and that's what your mother saw when she came in here the other night, too. There aren't any such things as ghosts!

TOMMY: Of all the silly fraid-cats!

LEWIS: Yeah, you did your share of runnin', boy!

TOMMY: Aw, she hollered so loud she scared me!

SALLY: Look, there's the fireplace!

LEWIS: Gee, and look at the old swords, would you!
(Their lights on the fireplace reveal the trash within, and the crossed swords above the mantel. Lewis quickly sets his light upon the mantel and pulls up a chair, climbs up and gets the swords down.)

TOMMY: Are they swell, though! Real swords!

SALLY: You haven't any right to take them down, Lewis. Leave them alone.

LEWIS: Aw, we just want to see what they're like. Here, Tommy!

TOMMY: Yeah, we won't hurt 'em. I'm Robin Hood! Look!
(He brandishes his sword.)

LEWIS: Robin Hood nothin'.... He had a bow. *(He jumps down and assumes a ferocious pose.)* Out of me way, you landlubbers ... Captain John Silver speaks!

TOMMY: Yeah! Treasure Island! *(He begins to stomp about the room, brandishing his sword and chanting in rhythm with his step):* Fifteen men on a dead man's chest! Yo-ho-ho and a bottle of rum!

(Lewis runs to him, puts his hand on his shoulder and joins the chanting and stomping.)

BOYS: Drink and the devil have done for the rest! Yo-ho-ho and a bottle of rum!

(Sally is delighted.)

SALLY: Oh, come on, Ellen! We're all pirates hunting buried treasure!

(They line up with hands on each other's shoulders and in big hoarse voices stomp about the room and repeat the chant.)

ALL: Fifteen men on a dead man's chest! Yo-ho-ho and a bottle of rum! Drink and the devil have done for the rest! Yo-ho-ho and a bottle of rum!

ELLEN: But where's the treasure?

SALLY: Yes, we'd better hurry and find it before old Phineas gets here. Put the swords up, boys, and let's go get it.

LEWIS: Where?

SALLY: Where what?

LEWIS: Where'll we go to find it?

TOMMY: Where do you hide money in houses, Sally?

SALLY: In books, there's usually a map to guide you.

ELLEN *(sarcastically)*: Now wouldn't you just imagine Mr. Herman would have made a map and left it around?

TOMMY: Aw, he might, to show Mr. Penny where to look.

SALLY: Oh, the fireplace! They nearly always hide things in fireplaces.

(The children turn to the littered fireplace.)

TOMMY: There's enough junk here! What's this thing? *(He picks up a piece of paper and reads):* "To whom it may concern ..."

ELLEN: Oh, I know what that is! *(She takes it from Tommy, casually looks at it, then tosses it aside.)* It's a reference. We had them in grammar and they always start out, "To whom it may concern . . ."

SALLY: Look, could this be a map?
(She has a rectangular piece of crumpled paper. The children all inspect it).

LEWIS: Oh, that's the thing they have in hospitals where babies are born. My mom has one in my baby book. Those are the baby's footprints, and see, there's the baby's name and the doctor and nurse and—

ELLEN: Well, for goodness sakes, did we come here to read or find money? We've got to hurry! *(She takes it and tosses it aside.)*

SALLY: Wait a minute. *(She stops, picks up the paper and folds it.)* I've got to have some more paper for my shoe. *(She sticks the paper in, tries the shoe, finds it's too thin, and picks up the letter also which had been tossed aside. All this time Tommy has been poring over a blueprint he has found.)*

TOMMY: Hey, is this thing a map? Look, it's got drawings of floors and things.

LEWIS: Naw, that's a blueprint to a house!

ELLEN: Oh, there's nothing but trash here, let's look somewhere else!

TOMMY: Look, here's something on the back! *(Children crowd around.)* It's a drawing of some stairs, with a little arrow leading up it . . .

SALLY: Do you suppose that means to go up the stairs? Maybe it is a map!

LEWIS: Yeah, and see that little box like thing at the head of those three flights of stairs? Know what that is?

TOMMY: Sure, that's the little cupola up on top of the house!

SALLY: Oh, do you suppose the money's hid up there?

ELLEN: Why not? That would be the best place for it.

TOMMY: Come on, let's get goin'! Up the stairs, me hearties! *(He still has his sword, which he brandishes.)*

SALLY *(catching the spirit of the thing)*: Men—up yon hill, a treasure awaits us. Fall in!

ALL: Fifteen men on a dead man's chest,
　　　　Yo-ho-ho, and a bottle of rum!
　　　Drink and the devil have done for the rest,
　　　　Yo-ho-ho, and a bottle of rum!

(They line up as before, and start up the stairs, chanting and stomping. As they disappear from view, another light wavers across the stage, and Bill comes in cautiously, carrying the old lantern that he found in the stable. He goes quickly to the fireplace and begins searching. Suddenly he hears two people approaching the house. He gathers up the trash on the hearth quickly and stuffs it down his shirt, then hides behind the chair at the fireplace.

Enter: Phineas and Officer Simmons. The policeman is carrying a lantern type flashlight. Mr. Simmons' entrance is brisk and cheerful, but Phineas takes one look at the ghostly place and his knees begin to tremble.)

SIMMONS: Well, here you are, Phineas. . . . See, there's a soft sofa you can sleep on if you want to. The lawyers won't care. They just want somebody in the place until they . . . hey, what's the matter with you?

PHINEAS: Th-hose white things! ! ! !

SIMMONS: You mean these sheets? *(He picks one off the chair and puts it back again.)* Don't be silly. They're just to cover the furniture to keep it from getting dirty. Mrs. Simmons put them on when she cleaned up yesterday.

PHINEAS: They sure look like ghosts or something.

SIMMONS: Well, they're not. They're just sheets! Well, Phineas, as I said, make yourself comfortable, I've got a beat to patrol, so I'll be going. Good night!

PHINEAS: Hey, Mr. Simmons!

SIMMONS: Yes?

PHINEAS: Did—did you . . . er . . . did you ever hear of ghosts with pink whiskers?

SIMMONS: Ghosts with pink whiskers? Ha, ha! That's good, yes sir! Well, good night, Phineas!

(He leaves and Phineas stares dumbly for a minute, then streaks after him.)

PHINEAS: But Mr. Simmons, Mr. Simmons! *(He realizes the policeman is gone.)* Gosh!

(Phineas stands uncertain for a moment, then takes the lantern off the mantel where the policeman has placed it, and walking on tip-toe, as if he were treading egg-shells, he looks under every sheet. His method of doing this is to give a quick look behind him just as he takes the sheet in hand, then to stoop and glance quickly

224

with the lantern. He looks under everything, coming to Bill's chair last of all. He is startled for a moment, as he seems to see something. His knees tremble, then cautiously and very slowly he starts around the chair. As he comes, Bill slides around it behind him. Phineas makes a complete circle around the chair, without catching sight of Bill, and while he stops to scratch his head, Bill seizes the opportunity to glide behind the fire screen. Phineas reverses direction and goes around the chair again. Then, greatly relieved, he mops his perspiring brow.) Whew! For a moment there, I thought I saw sumepun!

(He takes the lantern now, and inspects the sofa.)

Well, the bed's soft. That's somepun'!

(He puts the lantern on the table near the sofa, unlaces his shoes and drops them to the floor with a thump. While he is absorbed in this task, Bill picks up the fire screen, and holding it for a shield, glides up towards the back window. Phineas does not notice at first, but when he does, his hair simply stands on end. He makes a dive for the table, and waits for the roof to fall. Bill peeps out above the fire screen, but ducks back as Phineas peeps out above the table. Finally Phineas emerges, quaking. The fire screen is quietly behaving itself by the window. Phineas looks it over from a safe distance.)

Funny! I thought that thing was over in front of the fireplace.

(He starts to lie down again on the sofa, but then decides to make provision for easy escape, if necessary. He makes sure the outside door is unlocked, places the table right nearby the sofa, and pantomimes his intention to dive under the sheet-covered table, scoot it over to the door, and crawl out, in case of trouble. As he starts to lie down again, the searchlight in his hand flashes on the awful picture! With a yell, he makes for the table, bumps his head, and sits on the floor moaning. Then he sees it is just a picture, and is disgusted with himself.)

Dern them kids! Tellin' me about ghosts.

(He puts the light on the table and lies down determinedly on the sofa again. But he is no sooner settled than there is a loud thump above him, and the picture falls down on the couch, right on Phineas' feet. He jumps up, yells, dives under the table, then sees it is only the picture. He climbs out sheepishly.)

Doggone the doggone old picture. The wire's busted! *(He throws it onto the floor by the door)* Stay there on the floor, you crazy old mutt. They oughtta have things like that in the museum—or the zoo.—He looks like an old walrus, with that—

(He freezes upright on the sofa in a listening position. The children are heard descending the stairs, chanting their pirate tune in deep, awful tones. Phineas is too paralyzed to move. Slowly, and with quaking knees, he makes for the table, and gets under it.)

It's them! It's the ghosts! They've come to get me! Oh! Oh!

(With trembling fingers, he puts up a hand, and draws the flashlight under the table with him. Then he walks the table toward the outer door, but bumps into the chair at right. Confused, he turns the table around, and starts the other way. He stops right in the children's line of march, and as the children enter the room, he can go no further. Bill arranges his fire screen to look as innocent as possible.)

CHILDREN *(entering)*: Fifteen men on a dead man's chest,
    Yo-ho-ho, and a bottle of rum!
   Drink and the devil have done for the rest,
    Yo-ho-ho, and a bottle of rum!

(Tommy, leading the march, and coming up to the table, pretends it is an enemy blocking their path. He draws his sword and cries out in a hoarse voice.)

TOMMY: So, ye traitorous dog! Ye will seek to block me path, eh? Take that, and that—*(hitting his sword on the table as if he were cutting his enemy)* and . . .

(He stops and the children stare in horror. The table is walking! Phineas walks it over to the doorway, sneaks out from underneath and runs outside . . . but the children, naturally, do not see his escape. They think it must be the work of the ghost! They scream and bunch together downstage at left.)

ELLEN: It's the ghost!

SALLY: The table's walkin'!

TOMMY: Oh! Oh!

LEWIS: Help!

ELLEN: I wish I was home!

TOMMY: Me—me too!

SALLY: We've got to get out of here!

LEWIS: We can't! It's in the way.

ELLEN: Isn't there a back door?

TOMMY: It'ud be locked.

ELLEN: Oh dear!

SALLY: Maybe there wasn't anybody under the table! Maybe the table just scooted when Tommy hit it.

LEWIS: Is—is somebody under there?
(Pause while children listen breakthlessly for an answer.)

SALLY: That's what it was! The table just slid when Tommy kinda pushed it with his sword. We—we're sillies to be so scared!

(She isn't as brave as she sounds. She's trying to bolster up their courage.)

TOMMY: Yeah . . . I'll bet you're afraid to look.

ELLEN: Oh, don't! It might be something awwwwwful!

LEWIS: Go on, Sally, you're not afraid!

SALLY: Of course I'm not! *(She is, though; her knees are shaking.)*

TOMMY: Let's see you do it then.

SALLY: All right! *(But she makes no move, just stares fascinated at the table. Tommy gives her a shove toward it. She draws back.)*

Don't! Stop shoving me! I'm going! *(Cautiously, she slides a step at a time nearer to the table . . . then with lightning speed, she snatches the cloth off and runs back with it to the group. Once there, she stoops, looks under the table and is reassured.)* There! I told you there was no one there! *(She takes the sheet back and puts it on the table with assurance. The children look, and are reassured. Tommy swaggers about.)*

TOMMY: Shucks, I knew it all the time! I was just trying to scare' the rest of you!

LEWIS: Oh yeah? Boy, you're sure a good actor!

ELLEN: Yes, but what was it doing in the middle of the floor?

SALLY: What was it doing? Why, what does any table . . . *(She stops, remembering the table wasn't there at first.)*

LEWIS: It wasn't there when we came in! Somebody's been here!

SALLY: Yes it was! *(Affirming it to make it so, but as she looks at the others, she's not sure either.)* Or wasn't it?

ELLEN: It was not!

TOMMY: Are you s-s-s-s-sure?

ELLEN: Of course I'm sure!

227

(She flashes her light to the picture, and sees it is gone from the wall.)

It—it's gone!

LEWIS: What's gone?

ELLEN: Him! The ghost! . . . I'm getting out of here!

TOMMY: Me too!

SALLY: But we haven't found the treasure yet.

TOMMY: You can have the whole blame treasure, for all I care.

ELLEN: There isn't any treasure, Sally Andrews. And Mr. Penny is dead! And that man in the coach house is just a tramp! And I'm going to tell my father about him the first thing in the morning. *(At this, the fire-screen topples slightly, then falls over with a crash. The children all scream at once, and Ellen and Tommy fly out the door. Lewis follows close behind, and Sally after him. Bill, looking quite lost without his screen, slips behind the drapery at the window. Sally on her way to the door, stumbles into the picture.)*

SALLY: Lewis! Lewis, come back here. Look what I found.

LEWIS *(poking a wary head in)*: What?

SALLY: Remember when you and Tommy fell up there on the floor, when you were in that bedroom upstairs?

LEWIS: Yeah.

SALLY: Well, your fall jarred this old picture, and broke the wire. See, here it is. There aren't any such things as ghosts, honest there aren't. Uncle Jim says there's a reason for everything.

LEWIS: Yeah—but what about that table?

SALLY: Oh, that was nothing. It was—

LEWIS: Oh yeah? And what about that noise

SALLY *(suddenly terrified)*: Lewis! Lewis, look!

LEWIS: What is it?

SALLY *(pointing to Phineas' shoes, peeping out from under the sheeted couch)*: There's a man under there! *(Lewis just gives one big gulp, and starts for the door. Sally grabs him.)* Lewis, don't you dare go and leave me!

LEWIS: Hang on, then.

SALLY: Lewis, let's capture him! We're two to one.

228

LEWIS: We haven't any weapons.

SALLY: Here's your sword. And I'll hit him with the picture. *(They stand quaking, but armed, and challenge the invisible figure.)* Come on out of there, you!

LEWIS: We g-got you c-c-covered!
(Nothing happens. The feet do not move. Sally and Lewis look at each other.)

SALLY *(suddenly, in a terrified whisper)*: Lewis! Maybe it's a dead man! *(Lewis yells, drops the sword instantly, and breaks away. The sword, in falling, strikes one of the shoes, knocking it over, and Sally calls Lewis back.)* Lewis, it's only a pair of shoes!

LEWIS: Shoes? Whose shoes?

BOTH CHILDREN *(suddenly remembering)*: Phineas! It's Phineas' shoes!

SALLY: Of course! Lewis, you know what?

LEWIS: What?

SALLY: I'll bet—*(she giggles)* I'll bet old Phineas was down here when we were upstairs!

LEWIS: Golly! I'll bet he was! . . . Oh! and it was him under the table!

SALLY: Yes. Remember how we came down yelling about "dead men"? I'll bet old Phineas thought we were ghosts!

LEWIS: Yeah, and when Tommy hit the table with his sword . . .

SALLY *(she is giggling fit to kill)*: He ran! Ha, ha, ha!

LEWIS *(laughing)*: Boy, that's it! Ha, ha! I'll bet old Phineas thought a herd of elephants were after him! Gee, we were silly to get so scared.

SALLY: Uncle Jim says there's nothing to ever be scared of!

LEWIS: I wish he was here. I'll bet he could think of places to look for the treasure. Where do they hide treasure in your Uncle Jim's books?

SALLY: Oh, in fireplaces and . . .

LEWIS: We looked there.

SALLY: And in hollow panels . . . Oh, we could do that!

LEWIS: What?

SALLY: Knock on the walls with something to see if any of them are hollow. Come on, we'll try it. Here's the poker, and I'll take this thing . . .

(She hands Lewis the poker and she takes a little broom used to sweep the fireplace.)

LEWIS: How do you do it?

SALLY: You just knock . . . like this *(she knocks)* . . . and listen to see if it's hollow. It'll kinda echo if it's a hollow panel.

LEWIS: We ought to do it all over . . . upstairs too.

SALLY: All right . . . come on, we'll start upstairs, then try down here next.

(Sally and Lewis go up the stairs, knocking on the walls as they go. As the sound gets fainter and fainter, Bill creeps out from behind the draperies, and comes down to the table. He pulls the papers out of his shirt, and starts to look through them, but he hears someone coming. He scoops up the papers, and starts to dodge behind the chair. A voice calls softly outside the door.)

MR. JENKINS *(outside)*: Phineas! Phineas, my boy—are you in there? *(Bill recognizes the voice, and suddenly decides to hide in the chair. He climbs under the sheet, and covers himself and the chair completely. Mr. Jenkins enters cautiously, flashing his light about.)* Phineas! I say, Phineas, where are you? *(He looks all about, but the only trace he finds of Phineas is the shoes, which he picks up and puts on the table.)* That's strange!

(He picks up the fallen portrait, and props it against the chair where Bill is hidden. Then he crosses directly to the fireplace. Just as he stoops to look for the papers there, Bill knocks over the picture with a crash. Mr. Jenkins straightens up, frozen with fright. When he finally nerves himself to look around, and sees only the fallen picture, he is vastly relieved, and puts his hand over his heart, to stop its racing. Then he bends to the fireplace again. Suddenly, from upstairs, is heard a dull, rhythmic pounding. Mr. Jenkins raises his head and listens, stricken dumb with fright. Then he rises silently, and with a minimum of wasted effort, makes his way toward the door. When he gets as far as Bill's chair, the pounding suddenly stops, and Mr. Jenkins, holding his heart again, sinks into the chair with relief. Immediately, Bill folds his sheeted arms about him gently. Mr. Jenkins looks at the arms about him, and begins to tremble. His eyes pop out, his mouth hangs open, and slowly he slides off onto the floor. Quickly picking himself up, he scurries out, squeaking like a frightened mouse. Bill follows, waving his sheet about like a ghost. Then, sure that Jenkins is gone, he takes the sheet off, and laughs to himself.)

230

BILL: Nice work, Bill, me jolly old ghost. *(He starts to spread the sheet back on the chair, but stops when he hears more voices coming.)* Oh! Oh! *(Again he sits in the chair, and pulls the sheet over it. Mr. Simmons appears at the door, followed somewhat shakily by Phineas.)*

SIMMONS: Fine night watchman you are! The next time I get you a job, you'll know it! Seeing ghosts! Why, Phineas, I'm ashamed of you! *(Phineas comes in cautiously, peering about.)* Well, now that we're here, where's the ghost?

PHINEAS *(doggedly)*: They come down the stairs, and they had clubs and things. . . . First they tried to bean me with the picture, and then they ganged up on me. . . I hit 'em this way and that way *(he shadow boxes)* but they was too many fer me!

SIMMONS: Oh yeah? Well, there's not even a mouse in here now! How do you account for that? Now, what am I going to do with you? I promised the lawyers this place would be protected tonight.

PHINEAS: Maybe you'd like to do it, Mr. Simmons. *(Hopefully):* The bed's nice and soft!

SIMMONS: Just like your head! The idea of a grown man seeing ghosts!

PHINEAS: I didn't see 'em . . . I heard 'em!

SIMMONS: Now if you had been a woman . . . my wife, for instance . . . I'd understand this silliness . . . but a grown man!

PHINEAS: I tell you they come down the stairs . . . they had clubs . . .

SIMMONS: Yes, and just now you said you didn't even see them. Now Phineas, you just had a nightmare, that's all. You go on back there and forget all about it. *(He waves his hand toward the sofa. Phineas is almost convinced. He goes over to the sofa and sits on it, looking up at Mr. Simmons, almost persuaded.)*

PHINEAS: You think I could a' dreamed it?

SIMMONS: Of course you did!

PHINEAS *(laughing shakily)*: Well—m-maybe I did.

SIMMONS: Now you just lie back down there and stop having nightmares. I've got a beat to patrol tonight, boy. I can't play nursemaid to an eighteen-year-old fraid-cat.

PHINEAS: Sure, sure, I know. I'm sorry, Simmons. Them crazy kids just got me jittery, I reckon. And then the picture dropping off the wall and—

SIMMONS: Of course! You just heard the wind. See the table's right where you left it. The sheet's on it, and everything.

PHINEAS (*grinning sheepishly*): Sure, sure.

SIMMONS: All right now. Go to sleep and forget it. So long! (*He goes out.*)

PHINEAS (*waving his hand airily*): So long, Simmons . . . Gosh, I sure am ashamed of myself, I am. (*All at once, he looks under the couch and notices his shoes are missing.*) Where's my shoes? My shoes! Hey Simmons! Simm—(*But on his way to the door, he finds his shoes sitting peacefully on the table. His new confidence is decidedly shaken by his discovery.*) I don't care what Simmons says, I ain't a-goin' to sleep again. I'll set right down in this chair, where I can see if any gho—(*He sits on Bill, and at once realizes something is wrong. He lets a feeble ejaculation escape from him, but he cannot move.*) Whoa-ho-ho—

BILL (*putting his arms about Phineas*): Comfortable, dearie?

PHINEAS (*galvanized*): Wahoo! Let me outta here! Simmons! Hey, Simmons!

SIMMONS (*answering outside*): Now what?

PHINEAS (*outside*): They're back!

SIMMONS: Who's back?

PHINEAS: The ghosts! Inside! (*Sally and Lewis are heard continuing their rhythmic pounding as they come down the steps. Bill, stranded center stage, realizes there is only one thing to do, to escape discovery. Throwing the sheet over the chair, he springs quickly to the window up left, throws it open, and vanishes. The pounding grows louder—and nearer—as Simmons rushes inside, with Phineas in his wake.*) Look! The window! (*Mr. Simmons rushes to the window, and looks out.*) Listen!

(*Mr. Simmons whirls around from the window, and listens intently to the pounding. Phineas, shaking and trembling, slides over to the door, takes one quick look behind him, and runs for all he's worth. Mr. Simmons locks the window quickly, draws his gun, and slips behind the chair, where he can command the stairway. The knocks come closer and closer, as Sally and Lewis come down the steps. Finally, the pounding ceases, and they come into the room. With a shock Mr. Simmons recognizes the ghosts.*)

SALLY: It's no use, I reckon, Lewis. We've tapped all over.

LEWIS: I guess we might as well give up.

(Mr. Simmons rises up behind the chair, and both children shriek, and cling together.)

SIMMONS: Sally! What are you and Lewis doing here?

SALLY: Gee, Mr. Simmons, you scared us!

LEWIS: Boy! I never did think I'd be so glad to see a policeman!

SIMMONS: What are you two doing in this old house? Don't you know you could be arrested for prowling around in old houses like this? How did you get in?

LEWIS: Oh, we had a key.

SIMMONS: A key? Let's see it.

SALLY: Here it is. Only we didn't have to use it, because the door was already open.
(Simmons looks at the can opener, and grins, spreading his feet wide apart. He looks down at Sally, amused in spite of himself.)

SIMMONS: Sally, you're some girl!

SALLY: Am I, Mr. Simmons?

SIMMONS: Yeah, but you be careful, or that imagination of yours will get you into trouble.

SALLY: But that is the key, isn't it? Of course the door was open, but—

SIMMONS: Yes, I left the door open—for Phineas. . . . This is a can opener!

LEWIS: A can opener! *(He looks at Sally.)* And you said that guy was Mr. Penny, eh?

SALLY: Oh, Lewis, really and truly—he is!

SIMMONS: Now, Lewis, you ought to know better than to believe Sally's stories. You know she's always making up things.

SALLY: But Mr. Simmons, really and truly—

SIMMONS *(laughing)*:   Now, now, now! Don't go tryin' any of your stories on me! You've scared the liver out of Poor Phineas. Now I don't have any night watchman for this house. Come on, get out of here. You two got to go to bed! *(He shoos them out the door, inserts the key in the lock, then turns and flashes his light all about the place.)* Well, ghostie, if you're in here—you'll stay in! *(The key is heard turning in the lock as—*

CURTAIN

ACT THREE

Setting: The old coach house, same as Act One.

There is a faint snoring at the rise of the curtain, to indicate that Bill is asleep in the manger. Outside Sally is calling.

SALLY: Mr. Penny! Mr. Penny! *(Snoring stops.)* Mr. Penny! It's Sally! Please let me in. I have something to tell you!

BILL: Eh? What's that? Who is it? Sally?

SALLY: Yes, open the window, please, Mr. Penny. I've got something to tell you. It's important.

BILL: Sure ... sure, just a minute ... *(He hurries out of the stall, suspenders dangling about his hips, his shoes and shirt off. He is so sleepy that at first he doesn't realize he's not presentable. He hurries across the stage, then remembers as he looks at his dangling suspenders.)* Oh! *(To Sally):* Hey, Princess, wait just a minute, won't you? I got to perform my morning ablutions.

SALLY: You got to do what?

BILL: Got to get dressed.... Won't take but a minute, though. Can you wait?

SALLY: Oh! Yes, I'll wait but hurry, won't you?

BILL: Sure ... sure ... *(He slips on his shirt, pulls his middy tie over his head already knotted, then puts on his shoes.)* Won't take but just a minute! Almost through now! *(He knots his other shoe.)* There! Now I'm ready! *(He crosses the floor, opens the window, and just as Sally gets up to come through, thinks of something else and closes it again quickly.)* Oh! 'Scuse me, I forgot something! Just a minute! Just a minute! *(He dances on tiptoe hurrying over to the gas plate where he has a can of water and an old plate. He pours some water out in the pan, dips in fingertips cautiously, makes a circle about both his eyes, and his mouth ... puts his fingers in and shakes them ... then dries it all on a bandana out of his pocket. Then he takes out a mirror and pocket comb from his pocket and combs the straw out of his hair.)*

SALLY: Are you hurrying, Mr. Penny?

BILL: Sure, sure! I'm almost through ... There! *(He puts mirror and comb back in his pocket, turns to the window, opens it with a great flourish.)* Good mornin' to you, Princess. You're an early riser!

SALLY: Oh, Mr. Penny, I had to come early because there's not much

234

time! *(She climbs in over the window sill. She is still carrying the blueprint they found the night before.)* Uncle Jim and I are going away this morning.

BILL: Gee, Princess, I'm awful sorry.

SALLY: I wanted to show you this. Is this a map?

BILL: This?
(He takes the blue print, and looks at it.)

SALLY: I thought maybe that was a map pointing to the treasure that Mr. Herman hid for you. But we looked all over the house, Mr. Penny, and we didn't find it.

BILL: Yeah. I know.

SALLY: You know?

BILL: Yeah. I—I went in too.

SALLY: Oh, did you, Mr. Penny?

BILL *(very uncomfortable)*:   Sally.

SALLY: Yes, Mr. Penny?

BILL: Don't call me Mr. Penny.

SALLY: But why not, Mr. Penny?

BILL *(worried)*:   Sally . . . you—you didn't really think I was Mr. Penny, did you?

SALLY *(horrified)*:   Think you were Mr. Penny?

BILL: Naw. You were just foolin' that little smarty Ellen, weren't you?

SALLY: But you said you were Mr. Penny. And you gave us the key—

BILL: Now, now, now!

SALLY *(she knows what he means)*:   Yes, but you—well, anyhow, when I said you were Mr. Penny, you let me think it.

BILL: Listen here, Sally. Yesterday when you kids were here, I thought you were just—well, kinda stringin' that Ellen along by makin' out I was the Mr. Penny feller. Remember, I never said I was him. Not once. I don't tell lies. But you got such a big imagination—and you seemed to like to pretend so well—that I didn't think it'd do no harm to help you put one over on the kids.

SALLY: But if you're not Mr. Penny, who are you?

235

BILL: Aw, Sally, I'm just an old sailor, like I said. I'm on my way to the East coast to catch a ship. I don't amount to much, but I'm not a bad feller. Looky here, Sally, I got something to show you.

SALLY: What?

BILL *(taking out the picture)*: See this here picture?

SALLY: Why, it's a picture of a man and his wife and little boy and baby, isn't it?

BILL: That man is Mr. Penny. And that lady is his wife. And that's his little boy and girl baby.

SALLY: But Mr. Penny didn't have a girl baby did he?

BILL: Yes, Sally. I think maybe he did.

SALLY *(puzzled)*: But—

BILL: Look at that lady in the picture, Sally.

SALLY: She's pretty. She has an awful sweet smile. She looks kind of like somebody I've seen somewhere.

BILL: I reckon she does. She's the very spittin' image of you!

SALLY: Me?

BILL: Here, hold this. *(He hands her his pocket mirror.)* Now look, when I pile your hair up on your head like this—see?

SALLY: I do look like her!

BILL: Sure you do. And Sally, I got a big imagination too, and—you know what I think?

SALLY: What?

BILL: I think the baby in this picture is you!

SALLY: Me?

BILL: Um hum.

SALLY: You mean—I'm Mr. Penny's little girl, and the lady is—

BILL: I think so.

SALLY: Oh, that would be wonderful!

BILL: And I'll tell you something else. Listen. That brother-in-law of Mr. Penny's—this Jenkins guy—he thinks you're the little Penny girl too. And he is afraid all this property would go to you instead of him. So last night, he fixed it all up with Phineas to burn any possible proof that this baby was ever born.

236

SALLY: Why, the meany!

BILL: But I went up to the big house last night to try to get those papers before he did.

SALLY: Did you find them?

BILL: I got all the papers there were, Sally—but no proofs. And with out proofs—we can't do a thing.

SALLY: Oh!

BILL: I'm awful sorry, honey.

SALLY (*trying not to show her disappointment*): Oh, that's all right. Thank you for trying, Mr.—Mr.—

BILL: Just call me Bill, Sally.

SALLY: Mr. Bill.

BILL: Even if you're not the little Penny girl, you're my idea of one swell girl!

SALLY (*through her tears*): Thank you, Mr. Bill.

BILL (*to keep from crying himself*): Sally girl, I gotta be goin'. First thing you know, they'll be lockin' me up for trespassin', and if I don't get that train outta here this afternoon, I'll miss my boat.

(*While he is talking, he is putting things back where he found them—shoving the table back, covering up the gas plate, getting his bundle out of the manger. Sally watches him dolefully.*)

SALLY: I wish you were going to stay here, Mr. Bill.

BILL: Me, with my disposition? Don't try to fool me. Well . . . (*He looks about him.*) I guess things are just like I found 'em so I better be sayin' good bye. It sure was nice knowin' you, Sally.

(*He stands there a little awkwardly, his whole heart aching for her disappointment.*)

SALLY: Yes, it's been nice knowing you too, Mr. Pen—Mr. Bill.

BILL: Gosh, honey, I wish I had some money. Do you have to go to that—er—boarding house?

SALLY: I'm afraid so, Mr. Bill. They're coming for Uncle Jim and me this morning.

BILL: Gosh! (*He gets out his handkerchief and blows his nose lustily. Then realizing there is nothing more he can do for her, he squares his shoulders and starts for the window.*) Well, good bye, honey. Keep your chin up.

237

SALLY: Good bye, Mr. Bill. *(Bill swings his foot over the window ledge, but he stops and looks back. The pause is fatal. Sally flings herself at him, sobbing wildly.)* Oh, Mr. Bill, don't go! Don't go!

BILL *(holding her close)*: Now, now, Sally girl.

SALLY: It's not a boarding house, Mr. Bill. It's an orphan asylum. And I'm so scared Uncle Jim won't get well.

BILL: Aw now, honey . . . Gosh! Look what you got me doing.

SALLY: What?

BILL: Bawlin' like a big overgrown calf after his mammy, that's what!

SALLY: You mean crying? I guess maybe it was my fault. I guess I just sort of hated to see you go, I guess.

BILL: Sure, that's what's the matter with me too, I guess. Here. Blow.

(He holds his handkerchief to her nose. Sally blows her nose hard.)

Now. The storm's all over, isn't it? *(Sally nods.)* All right, let's see the sunshine come out. *(Sally smiles.)* There now, that's more like it. That's fine!

(Sally steps back, and as she does so, she reaches for her offending shoe.)

SALLY *(taking the shoe off)*: Oh!

BILL: What's the matter now?

SALLY: My other shoe's got a hole in it now, and I haven't any paper to put in it.

BILL: Say, I can fix shoes!

SALLY: Doesn't it cost a lot of money?

BILL: Doesn't cost a cent. Here, give 'em to me. I can make some soles to fit inside 'em, out of tree bark.

SALLY *(taking them off and handing them to him)*: But have you got time?

BILL: Sure, and I'll take time, by golly. I wish my knife was sharper.

SALLY: There's a grind stone out there, around the corner of the coach house.

BILL: Is there now? Well, whaddya know? Here, hold my bag, and I'll just find me some soft tree bark, and—

(He is out of the window, and Sally climbs up after him.)

SALLY *(calling after him)*: There's an old mallet there, too, you can use for a hammer. I'll show you.

BILL *(from outside)*: No, you just stay there, lassie. You'll catch cold without your shoes. I'll find it.

SALLY: It's around the corner, by the rain barrel. *(Sally sits in the window ledge, cheerfully humming a tune. All at once, she stiffens in alarm, as she sees the enemy approaching. She tries to warn Bill.)* Mr. Bill! Mr. Bill! *(But Bill is out of sight, and out of earshot. Sally wrings her hands helplessly.)*

MR. JENKINS *(at a distance)*: I see you! I see you, you little scamp! *(Sally leaps inside the room, and bars the window. She stands there uncertainly for a moment, then notices Bill's bandana in her hand, and shoves it down her dress. It bulges out ludicrously, and she tries to pat it down, but failing to conceal it, she sits up close to the table, so it will not show. She shuts her eyes tightly and prays):* Please don't let him find Mr. Bill! Please don't let him find Mr. Bill! *(Meanwhile, Mr. Jenkins has reached the door of the coach house. He speaks to the policeman outside.)* I saw one of those children climb in here, officer. It's trespassing, that's what it is! Tres—

(The door suddenly falls down, and Mr. Jenkins with it.)

SIMMONS *(helping him up)*: Don't be in surch a hurry, Jenkins.

MR. JENKINS: Confound that door! There! *(He points to Sally dramatically.)* There she is!

SIMMONS: Yes, I see her. Well, Sally, I seem to find you in all sorts of unexpected places, lately.

MR. JENKINS: Well, ask her where that tramp is.

SIMMONS: Where is he, Sally?

SALLY: Where is who?

MR. JENKINS: You know who we mean!

SIMMONS: Ellen told us about him, Sally. That fellow who went around here yesterday calling himself Mr. Penny. Has he gone?

SALLY: Oh! Yes, he—he's not here any more.

MR. JENKINS: I don't believe her. He's hiding in there! *(He crosses swiftly to the harness room, and throws open the door.)* Come out of there, you! *(Nothing happens.)* He isn't there . . . I know! The manager! That's where I heard that noise yesterday when— *(He darts over to the manger, and grabs up the hay.)* I've found you! I've got you! I've—he's not there!

SALLY: I told you he wasn't here.

MR. JENKINS (*pointing to Sally*): She knows where he is! Arrest her!

SIMMONS: Now, Jenkins, keep your shirt on. Sally, this property belongs to Mr. Jenkins here now, and you'll have to stay out of it, understand?

SALLY: Y-yes sir.

SIMMONS: All right now, Sally. Come on and clear out.

MR. JENKINS: She ought to be arrested, and put under lock and key.

SIMMONS: Never mind, Jenkins. You won't have to worry about Sally any more. She's going away today. Come on, Sally.

MR. JENKINS: I'll board this place up. That's what I'll do.

SIMMONS (*as Sally sits still*): Sally, didn't you hear me? I said come on.

SALLY: I—I can't.

SIMMONS: You can't? Why not?

SALLY: I—I haven't got any shoes on.

SIMMONS: Where are they?

SALLY: They—they got mud on 'em, and Phineas took 'em off to clean 'em.

(*Mr. Simmons stares at her in amazement. Outside, Bill begins to hammer. The two men look at each other, and Jenkins rushes toward the harness room.*)

MR. JENKINS: He's in here. (*But he looks in and sees nothing. To Simmons*): Didn't you hear that, too? (*Sally is kicking the table.*)

SALLY: You mean this? Like I was swinging my feet?

MR. JENKINS (*annoyed*): Oh! Then don't do it!

SIMMONS: How long is Phineas going to be, Sally?

SALLYS Oh, he'll be back in a minute. You don't have to wait, Mr. Simmons, I'll leave here just as soon as I get my shoes.

SIMMONS (*suddenly suspicious of Sally*): I think maybe I'd better wait.

(*Bill starts working the grindstone industriously outside, and the noise penetrates the room. The men are alert, and instantly Sally begins a buzzing noise with her teeth.*)

SALLY: Bzzz! I'm a bee! Bzzz! Bzzz! *(The men say nothing, but look at each other understandingly, and rush into the harness room together. Sally springs up and runs to the window, calling softly.)* Mr. Bill! Mr. Bill! *(The two men rush out, and she jumps away from the window, guiltily.)*

MR. JENKINS: That tramp's still around here, and she knows where he is!

SIMMONS: Sally, you mustn't protect this tramp. If you know where he is, say so.

MR. JENKINS: What's that inside her dress? What's that inside her—

SIMMONS *(disgustedly)*: The tramp, no doubt! Sally, honey, what's this all about? What have you there?

SALLY: It's—it's just some old things we—we—

(At this moment, Bill lets out a wild war whoop, and comes bounding through the window, everything else temporarily forgotten. Mr. Jenkins grabs him by the collar, but Bill doesn't even see him. He shakes him off as he would a flea, and Jenkins staggers back, protesting.)

BILL: Sally! Sally honey! I've found a real treasure! Look what I found in your shoes!

SALLY: Oh, Mr. Bill, why didn't you stay hidden?

BILL: Look, Sally, you're rich!

MR. JENKIINS: It's the tramp, and he's gone crazy. *(To Simmons):* Do something quick!

SIMMONS *(collaring Bill)*: Come on, you. We've been looking for you.

BILL: Hey, hold on a minute. Listen, Officer, that feller's a crook!

MR. JENKINS: Why, you—you—how dare you call me names, you—

BILL: Because I got the goods on you, that's why.

MR. JENKINS: Officer, lock him up. He's a tramp, and a dangerous character.

SIMMONS: Yeah? *(To Bill):* And what's your side of the story?

BILL: Listen, Officer. Yesterday I came in here to rest a bit before I continued my journey, and—

MR. JENKINS: See, he admits it. He's been trespassing on my property. Why do you stand there—

SIMMONS: Just a minute, Jenkins. *(To Bill):* Go on.

BILL: Well, this feller came in here with a guy named Phineas, and Phineas had this here picture. It's a picture of Mr. Penny and his wife and little boy—and baby.

SIMMONS: Baby? I didn't know he had a baby.

BILL: Neither did anybody else, it seems like. But there it is.

SIMMONS: But then, in that case—

MR. JENKINS (*indignantly*): He didn't have a baby! That picture is a forgery! Officer, would you take the word of a tramp against mine?

BILL: You don't have to take my word. Those papers there prove it, in black and white!

MR. JENKINS: Those papers? You stole them out of the house, you rascal! (*He makes a lunge toward Sally, to seize the papers, but Mr. Simmons intercepts and takes the papers himself.*)

SIMMONS: Now hold on here, Jenkins. These papers came out of the big house, you say?

BILL: Yes, they did! This here's the footprints and birth notice of a baby girl born the time of Sally here, and read this!

SIMMONS (*looking at it*): It's a letter written by—written by Mr. Herman, Penny's old servant that just died.

BILL: And this Jenkins offered Phineas five dollars to let him into the house last night, so that he could burn those papers. Because they prove that Sally there is heir to the whole Penny estate!

MR. JENKINS: That's not true! I'm the heir to this estate. He's made this all up. Give me those papers!
(*He grabs the papers out of Mr. Simmons' hand, and tears them. Bill makes a dive for him, brings him to the ground, wrenches the papers away and gives them to Mr. Simmons. Then he sits on Mr. Jenkins.*)

BILL: Here now, read it.

MR. JENKINS: Get off of me! You're killing me!

BILL: Well, I ain't yet, but if you don't keep still—
(*He swings his fist. Mr. Jenkins subsides, and Mr. Simmons sits at the table and reads the letter, with Sally at his side.*)

SIMMONS (*reading*): "To whom it may concern: Feeling at last that my master will never return home, and afraid this heart attack will be my last . . ." He was having a heart attack when he wrote this letter! He died of a heart attack!

242

BILL: Go on.

SIMMONS (*reading*): "... will be my last, I am writing this letter to tell the real story of this tragic household." (*Simmons reads slowly, and with many significant pauses, as if this revelation were too much for him to digest in a hurry.*) "This picture, taken after the birth of the baby girl, shows the baby of whom I alone know the fate. Her name is Nancy Bell Penny, and she has been raised by a neighbor, Jim Andrews, and is now called Sally Andrews"... Sally!

BILL: Sure. Sure, I told you; This Herman feller put her on Mr. Andrews' doorstep when Mr. Penny left, because her mother was dead, and he didn't know what to do with her. It tells it there in the letter. And that other thing is her birth cerificate and everything to prove it.

MR. JENKINS: It's not so! It's a frame-up! Let me up from here!

SIMMONS (*eyeing Mr. Jenkins coldly*): If it's not so, then why did you try to destroy these papers?

MR. JENKINS: It's a frame-up, I tell you! Let me up, you ruffian! You're stuffing the breath out of me! You're going to kill me!

BILL (*spitting on his fist significantly*): That's not a bad idea!

SIMMONS: Sally, the little Penny girl! I can't get over it! It—it's fantastic!

SALLY: Mr. Simmons, does it mean that—that I own the house and property?

SIMMONS: Well, I just guess you do, honey! Why, Sally—er—Nancy, maybe I should say—you're rich! Do you realize that? Rich!

SALLY: And then I won't have to go to the orphan asylum?

SIMMONS (*laughing*): Ohphan asylum? I should say not! Why, you can build one, if you like.

SALLY: But will Uncle Jim have to go away?

SIMMONS: You just bet he won't! We'll go tell him about it right away. You can have doctors and nurses, and get him well in no time!

SALLY: Oh, Mr. Bill!
(*She throws herself down on Bill's lap, sobbing in her happiness. Mr. Jenkins gives a grunt, and cries out at the extra weight.*)

MR. JENKINS (*panting*): Officer, you get me up from here before they kill me. I demand my rights!

SIMMONS (*squinting down at him significantly*):   Oh, yes, your rights! Well, you let him up, Bill—and give him his rights!

BILL (*understanding*):   Sure, if you say so, Officer. Jump up, honey. I gotta give him his rights.

(As Jenkins rises to his feet, Bill plants a good solid kick in his pants. Mr. Jenkins squeals.)

SIMMONS: Now, that's your first right. And when I get you down at the police station, and tell the Chief about you, you crooked swindler, you're going to get some more rights that belong to you. Come along now, march outta here.

(He takes him out by the collar, Mr. Jenkins protesting feebly all the while. Sally throws herself into Bill's arms.)

SALLY: Mr. Bill! Oh, Mr. Bill!

BILL: Shhh!

(He pushes her away gently, then putting his finger to his lips for silence, tip-toes over to the door, and looks anxiously after the departing men.)

SALLY (*whispering*):   What is it?

BILL (*whispering back*):   They forgot to arrest me!

SALLY: Oh!

BILL (*wiping his forehead with relief, and sitting weakly at the table*):   They forgot me! Whew! I just have to make that boat this week.

SALLY (*sitting on his knee*):   But Mr. Bill, you don't now.

BILL: No?

SALLY: Of course not! I'm rich now and I got all this big house and everything, and you can stay with uncle Jim and me!

BILL: And what 'ud I be doin' t' pass the time away?

SALLY: Oh! (*thinking*) Well, you could fix my shoes!

BILL: No, Sally girl, it wouldn't work! I gotta get back t' a ship! I been sailin' too long t' sprout land legs at my age! (*Gets up and gets his bandana.*)

SALLY: But you will come back, won't you?

BILL: Well, I tell you, Princess, I never like t' make promises like that! A seaman's life is kinda at the mercy of a ship, you know, an' . . .

SALLY: Oh, but you got to come back!

244

BILL: Well, sir, I tell you what! Remember that story about Cinderella and how the prince got back t' Cinderella?

SALLY: Of course; he kept her slipper and ... *Oh! (She grabs up her shoes off the table where Bill laid them and shoves them in his hand.)* Take both of them, Mr. Bill, and then you'll be sure to come back!

BILL: You bet I will! I reckon I can't fail now! *(Sticks them in his pocket.)* It's all set then! I'll come back soon as my ship gets in ... long about next Christmas time, I reckon. *(Moves toward door.)*

SALLY: That will be wonderful! I'll hang up a stocking for you!

BILL: All right now ... Don't say goodbye then ... cause goodbye means forever!

SALLY: What'll I say, then, Mr. Bill?

BILL: They's a French name fer saying goodbye fer just a short time. You say "Over the river," see? *(Stoops and kisses her on the cheek. She hugs him tightly.)* Well, "Over the river." *(With a wave of his hand, he's gone out the door. Sally runs to the door and stands there waving.)*

SALLY: Over the river, Mr. Bill ... Over the river till next Christmas!

CURTAIN

THE LAND OF THE DRAGON

A CHINESE FANTASY

By

Madge Miller

This play was given its premiere production in 1945, by the Children's Theatre of Pittsburgh, under the direction of Miss Grace Price.

THE LAND OF THE DRAGON

By Madge Miller

THE LAND OF THE DRAGON

The period between 1930 and 1950 was one of steady growth in the repertoire of dramatic literature for children. But this growth was generally more quantitative than qualitative as the majority of plays written at this time were uninspired dramatizations of fairy and folk tales. It was an era shaped by Chorpenning's prolific output and the work of the many writers who imitated her style. Unfortunately, many of the writers who modeled their work after Chorpenning's very successful plays had neither the training nor the talent to create original works. This resulted in the creation of a large body of dramatizations that look very much like Chorpenning's plays, but that reflects neither the technical skill or artistic talent that she brought to her writing. It was as if a formula had been developed, and writers had only to create a new setting and new names for the characters and add these to the well-made play structure, to write an acceptable children's play.

The Land of the Dragon, first produced in 1945, is an important example of a play that reflects little of that formula approach. It is a refreshingly original play, that seems even more so when one considers the nature of the plays popular at that time. The play reflects a sense of style that foreshadowed the writers of the modern period, and as a result, is as vital and entertaining today as it was almost forty years ago. It is built around a simple story, complicated by a series of funny incidents that create one comic climax after another.

The formal tone of the play is created initially by the Stage Manager, who addresses the audience directly and describes each scene in the play. This character is paired with the mute Property Master who, shuffling lethargically in and out of the action, supplies the properties necessary to play the story on the bare stage. Miller further underscores this frankly presentational style by having all of the major characters, upon their entrance, walk to center stage and introduce themselves to the audience. This technique allows each character to establish an appropriate relationship with the audience while delivering necessary expository information.

The story focuses on Jade Pure, who must marry by the time she is eighteen years old to inherit the throne. Miller introduces two groups of antagonists that struggle against Jade Pure—and each other—for this right to the throne. A triangular structure is thus created whereby the action slowly builds from successive confrontations between the individual factions, to a riotous ending where all the characters are thrown together to settle the dispute. There is never much doubt that Jade Pure will triumph in the end, but this novel treatment of the story is interesting and fun.

249

The characters in the play are colorful, flamboyant, and one-dimensional. When they introduce themselves they state in simple terms both who they are and what they want, and even their names reinforce their simple lines of action. Jade Pure is sweet, innocent, and beautiful. Covet Spring is devious and culpably greedy. This lack of depth suggests a naivete in the work as a whole, but the purposefulness with which it is revealed lends the work a charming simplicity.

The six scenes in the story are played with increasingly farcical action. The ostensible climax occurs in Scene Five, where a group of Jade Pure's adversaries, having disguised themselves as a dragon, come face-to-face with a "real" dragon. For this confrontation Miller uses simple sight gags that escalate to an outrageous, free-for-all chase scene. Miller then artfully and humorously forestalls the imminent climax of the story for yet another scene, and employs a series of theatrical gimmicks to create heightened and prolonged suspense prior to the resolution.

The play ends with the heroine defeating her adversaries, marrying the young man, and inheriting the throne. But this play offers far more than a re-telling of this story. It is a complex play that presents a world of humorous contrasts: elaborate costumes against a bare stage, soft-spoken and polite characters who engage in outrageous activity, and a simple story that is told with myriad complications. It is a deceptively difficult play that, when produced well, offers hilarious action with a charming style that belies its stereotypical elements.

The Land of the Dragon has probably had little *direct* influence on the development of dramatic literature for children. But this play is, and has been, a very popular work; although it has not spawned imitation in kind, it has been important as an example of well-written and unpretentious drama for children. When the play was first introduced, it was not considered shockingly new and different; in many ways, Miller wrote the play in the language of a fairy or folk tale: the characters are types rather than multi-dimensional individuals; the story is set in a far off land of kings, princesses, and villains; the conflict is clearly defined; and the "good" characters ultimately triumph over the "bad."

But this play *is* very different from other plays of that time. First, it is based on an original story; that factor alone provides a freshness and unpredictability seldom found in the formula-based fairy tale dramas. Second, Miller let the story she was dramatizing dictate the shape of the play rather than attempting to confine the story to the well-made play form. Finally, Miller enlivened her story with a skillful use of the theatre medium. The play is a well-constructed farce that places as much importance on style as it does on theme or story.

It is because of this theatrical sophistication that the play stands out in the history of dramatic literature for children. *The Land of the*

Dragon represents well an important transition in the field that did not begin in earnest until after 1950. At that time writers slowly began to discover the importance of imaginative insight over polished, formula writing, and audiences began to favor plays that were first and foremost good theatre, rather than just dramatized moral lessons. Although this play, by itself, did not precipitate great changes in the field, it was at the forefront of this movement toward more sophisticated drama for children.

With such contemporary works as *Androcles and the Lion*, farce has proven itself to be a form particularly suitable for child audiences. It was, however, in *The Land of the Dragon* that the field was first introduced both to a consistent and effective use of broad physical humor and to conventions used to poke gentle fun at the characters and the world of the play. Miller introduced a serious world, but she did not take this world seriously. Such a perspective helped to minimize the tendency toward moralizing in children's plays, and paved the way for a future generation of far more outrageous works.

The Land of the Dragon is considered by many to be one of the classics from the history of dramatic literature for children. This work has achieved this status not just because of its possible influence on the modern repertoire, but also because it is still popular today. It is a tribute to Miller's skill as a playwright that while many plays of this period are of interest only to historians in the field, *The Land of the Dragon* continues to be a source of delight for child audiences across the land.

MADGE MILLER (Mrs. Howard Eulenstein) was born in Pittsburgh, Pennsylvania, on May 31, 1918. After attending Catham College (B.A. 1939) and Case Western Reserve (A.M. 1940), Miller worked in several different careers. These included serving as a teacher in the Pittsburgh Public Schools, playwright for the Pittsburgh Children's Theatre, and director-playwright for the Knickerty-Knockerty Players of Pittsburgh. Miller has written over forty plays for child audiences. In 1970 she was the recipient of the Chorpenning Cup, an award presented by the Children's Theatre Association of America to recognize excellence in writing children's plays. Miller's newest play, "OPQRS," is scheduled to be published by Anchorage Press. Other successful works by Miller include *The Princess and the Swineherd*, *Hansel and Gretel*, *Robinson Crusoe* and *The Emperor's Nightingale*.

THE LAND OF THE DRAGON

Cast

JADE PURE, Princess of the Southern Kingdom

PRECIOUS HARP, Aunt to Jade Pure

TWENTY-FIRST COUSIN
TWENTY-SECOND COUSIN   } Maids to Jade Pure
TWENTY-THIRD COUSIN

ROAD WANDERER, A Student

COVET SPRING, Chancellor of the Southern Kingdom

TWENTY-FOURTH COUSIN, A Farmer

SMALL ONE, A Dragon

THE STAGE MANAGER

THE PROPERTY MANAGER (non-speaking)

NOTE: If a larger cast is desired, townspeople, etc., indicated as voices offstage may be played on-stage by additional actors.

TIME: In those days

PLACE: The Land of the Dragon

Synopsis

PART ONE

    Scene 1.   Jade Pure's apartment.

    Scene 2.   A distant field.

    Scene 3.   Royal garden, outside the Princess' window.

    Scene 4.   A grassy meadow.

    Scene 5.   A city street.

    Scene 6.   Jade Pure's apartment.

    Scene 7.   Royal Garden.

INTERMISSION

PART TWO

    Scene 1.   A lonely field.

    Scene 2.   Before the palace wall.

    Scene 3.   A dungeon

    Scene 4.   Jade Pure's apartment.

    Scene 5.   The royal throne-room.

    Scene 6.   A lonely field.

THE LAND OF THE DRAGON

PART ONE

(The curtains remain open throughout. The stage is completely empty. A handsome curtain, black with a red-and-gold dragon painted on it, is hung without folds across the back.

Chinese music — recorded — is played for several minutes before the lights come up on stage, indicating the beginning of the play. The Stage Manager enters right. He is gorgeously dressed, carries an ornamental fan which he uses gracefully, and hops, rather than walks, with short bobbing steps.)

SCENE ONE

STAGE MANAGER. *(bowing).* Greetings, Exalted Audience. You are most welcome. May the humble efforts of our actors to please you meet with flowery success. I am the Stage Manager, here to introduce to you each scene as it unfolds. You must pay no attention to me, for to a POLITE audience I am invisible!

(The Property Man has entered with a small black bench which he places center stage. He — or she — is dressed entirely in black, including black gloves. He shuffles with maddening slowness; his face is vacant and sleepy-looking.)

This lazy fellow is our Property Man. He, too should be invisible as he prepares the stage. The first scene takes place in the apartment of the lovely and gracious Jade Pure, Princess of the Southern Kingdom. There is the door, as you can plainly see . . .

(The Property Man opens an imaginary door, steps through it, and closes the door after him.)

And there the window . . .
(The Property Man opens an imaginary window, thrusts his head out and in again, then closes the window and shuffles offstage.)

But our play begins. Approaching us is the Princess Jade Pure herself. I bow to you, and respectfully withdraw.

(He bows and steps to the extreme downstage right of the stage, where he stands throughout the play. Jade Pure, charmingly but simply dressed in lavender and silver, enters, crosses to center stage, turns to face the audience.)

JADE PURE. I am Jade Pure, Princess of the Southern Kingdom. The death of my father, the Emperor, some years ago, left me an orphan, and alone. Sorrowfully I seat myself to await the coming of my cousins and the start of another day.

254

(As she is seating herself, the three Cousins enter right, one following another, the tallest first. They come down center stage, turn to face the audience in the same movement, hiding the Princess from view in their speeches. They are richly dressed; Twenty-First Cousin's costume is predominantly green, Twenty-Second Cousin's, blue; Twenty-Third Cousin's, orange.)

COUSINS *(in unison).* We are . . .

TWENTY-FIRST *(bowing).* Twenty-First Cousin . . .

TWENTY-SECOND *(bowing).* Twenty-Second Cousin . . .

TWENTY-THIRD *(bowing).* Twenty-Third Cousin . . .

COUSINS. Honorable Ladies in the service of Her Highness, the Princess Jade Pure.

(leaning forward, fingers to lips) What we really think of her, you will learn most promptly.

(Twenty-First Cousin and Twenty-Second Cousin step to the left, Twenty-Third Cousin to the right, and bow to the Princess. They remain bent over until she speaks to them. Their attitude toward her is one of thinly-veiled insolence).

Good morning, Your Most Gracious Augustness . . .

TWENTY-FIRST. Daughter to the Sun . . .

TWENTY-SECOND. Sister to the Moon . . .

TWENTY-THIRD. Cousin to each dazzling star!

JADE PURE *(stretching out her hands).* Good morning, dear cousins.

TWENTY-FIRST *(circling to her left to stand behind the bench).* Will this unworthy one be granted the inestimable privilege of arranging Her Highness' hair?

TWENTY-SECOND *(taking Jade's left hand).* And I, the care of the nails on this, the Princess' left hand?

TWENTY-THIRD *(taking her right hand).* And I, the five remaining here?

JADE PURE. Yes, yes, yes. Begin, I beg of you. And cheer my heart with some gay tale, for I am bitterly unhappy.

(The Cousins arrange her hair, buff her nails with imaginary equipment, as they speak).

TWENTY-FIRST *(pretending astonishment).* Unhappy? You, the Princess of the Southern Kingdom?

TWENTY-SECOND. How can this be so?

TWENTY-THIRD (with a titter). And why?

JADE. You know as well as I!

FIRST (nodding wisely). Ah, yes, to be sure.

SECOND. In just one week you celebrate your eighteenth birthday.

FIRST. If you are not wed, when the clock strikes noon that day, you shall lose all claim to the throne.

THIRD. And Lady Precious Harp, sister to your father, shall ascend it.

JADE (sighing deeply). Yes.

SECOND. Empress you cannot be unless you first become a wife.

THIRD. But no man yet has sought your hand, because . . . (pausing deliberately).

JADE. Because?

FIRST. You ask?

SECOND (maliciously). All know the reason why.

THIRD. Does not the Princess?

JADE. Yes, yes. Because my face is ugly. Do not hesitate to say it.

COUSINS (scornfully). Ugly, ugly, ugly!

JADE (springing up). Cruel, hateful word!

COUSINS (drawing back). We have offended you?

JADE (her hands over face). You have! You have!

FIRST (haughtily). You have offended us, Your Highness!

SECOND. First you bid us speak —

THIRD. And then you storm!

(With quick mincing steps they have lined up, facing rigidly front).

JADE. Ah . . . pardon, cousins.

COUSINS (turning with one motion to the door, starting forward). We go!

JADE (placing herself between them and the exit). Oh, do not! I have no one else to talk to. Well I know you speak the truth. My aunt, Lady Precious Harp, and Covet Spring, the Chancellor, say it too.

They and you say that I am ugly, and I see no one else. And yet
. . . come near, dear cousin.

*(She takes Twenty-First Cousin's hand and draws her close; with
the other hand she touches lightly the girl's eyelids and eyebrows,
and then her own).*

You have eyes set so . . . and brows above them. So do I!

FIRST *(pulling away quickly).*   But they are not the same!

JADE *(turning to Twenty-Second Cousin).*   And see . . . your nose is
fashioned so . . . and mine feels very like.

SECOND.   Oh, nothing like!

JADE *(following the same procedure with Twenty-Third).*   Mouths cannot be so very different, when their sizes are so nearly one. And
what else is there? Skin . . . but mine is soft; my fingers tell me.
Hair . . . you dress it well.

FIRST *(her back to the Princess.)*   Extremely well!

JADE *(going to her).*   Then let me see for myself! Bring me a mirror,
cousins . . .

(to Twenty-First, who, back turned, shakes her head vigorously)

. . . *(to Twenty-Second, who duplicates her sister's action)* . . .
dear cousin

(to Twenty-Third, who does likewise).

It is my coiffure I wish to see . . . truly that is all!

COUSINS *(turning to face her, arms folded primly, in unison).*   No, no,
no! "By order of the Lady Precious Harp, Her Highness Princess
Jade Pure shall not be permitted —"

JADE.   I know. "Shall not be permitted to possess a mirror." But, I
beg you, cousins, tell me why.

FIRST.   We have told you, many times.

SECOND.   It is for your sake alone.

THIRD *(Mockingly).*   You are much too ugly!

JADE.   Shall I never marry then?

SECOND.   You have had no suitors.

FIRST.   None could ever love you.

JADE *(moving restlessly to the imaginary window).*   Shall I stay in here forever, with no mirror and no suitors, never to go outside to the garden I see from my window?

THIRD *(with a derisive titter).* No doubt!

JADE. But then I am a prisoner, no better off than my tiny caged bird here!

(The Property Man has shuffled on with a gilded cut-out bird-cage which he holds aloft; Jade touches it lightly as she speaks to the imaginary bird inside).

Do you hate it too, poor thing? Why, where are your seeds! Almost gone? And very little water! Cousins, you have not been kind to him;

(They ignore her).

I shall go to bring fresh water and seeds myself.

(She exits left).

FIRST *(flouncing down on the bench).* Let her then!

(She extends her hands to her sisters standing at either end of the bench; they buff her nails just as they have done Jade Pure's).

SECOND. How restless she becomes!

THIRD. There is no chance of her escaping?

FIRST. None. A guard stays at the door.

SECOND. The window is too high.

THIRD. And she has no friends to help.

FIRST. Our vigil will be ended soon. In just a week Lady Precious Harp becomes Empress. Ouch!

(She pulls her hand away from Twenty-Third Cousin, glaring at her and then at her fingers. The Property Man who, listing to the right, is about to doze off, pulls himself upright with a start).

SECOND. Will she reward us as she promised?

THIRD. Can we trust her? She is crafty.

FIRST. We can be as sly as she. But truly, she is clever. Who else would have thought of such a scheme?

SECOND. To spread word throughout the kingdom that Jade Pure is very ugly . . .

THIRD. So that she will not be wed before her eighteenth birthday . . .

258

FIRST.   And so that Precious Harp herself can claim the throne as next in line! A clever woman!

SECOND.   What if someone learns of the Princess' beauty?

FIRST.   Stupid! How? There is no way.

THIRD.   What if Jade Pure learns of it herself?

FIRST.   She never can, with no one near to tell her, and no mirror. Ouch!

(She pulls her hand away from Twenty-Second Cousin, regards her nails tenderly. The Property Man, who has listed to the left, again jerks upright, awakened by her shriek).

That is why she cannot go outside into the garden. There are pools and streams of water there.

SECOND.   She might see her face in one of them.

THIRD.   Or see a gardener.

FIRST.   Exactly. *(rising quickly)* Hush . . . someone is coming.

SECOND *(looking off right)*.   Lady Precious Harp . . .

THIRD.   And Covet Spring.

(They enter right. Lady Precious Harp, a coldly handsome woman in her thirties, is exquisitely costumed in royal yellow, bright with gold and jewels. Covet Spring, a corpulent wheezing ancient, wears red, and carries a huge fan which he flutters affectedly. The Property Man sighs deeply, and rests the bird-cage on his hip, assuming a comfortable position).

COUSINS *(bowing)*.   Most hearty greetings to Her Exalted Ladyship.

PRECIOUS HARP *(arrogantly)*.   I, Lady Precious Harp, sister to the departed Emperor, graciously accept your unworthy greetings.

COUSINS *(bowing)*.   We bow in welcome to His Mighty Excellency.

COVET SPRING *(also arrogantly)*.   I, Covet Spring, Chancellor of the Southern Kingdom, nod in reply.

PRECIOUS HARP *(after glancing about, in sudden alarm)*.   Where is the Princess, my niece? Where is she? Speak!

COVET SPRING.   She has not escaped?

FIRST.   No. She has gone to fetch water for that wretched bird.

PRECIOUS HARP.   Do not leave her unattended for a moment!

(to Twenty-third Cousin, who exits)

259

You — run quickly to watch her. "A single false move loses the game."

COVET SPRING. She might find a pane of glass in which to see her face, or a polished kettle.

(fanning himself violently) That would be a tragedy!

PRECIOUS HARP. It would indeed. For, knowing her own beauty, she might prove troublesome. I should much regret using violence until after I am Empress.

FIRST. Have no fear. We shall watch her diligently, mindful of the generous reward you have promised my sisters and me.

SECOND *(pointedly)*. The most generous reward!

PRECIOUS HARP. *(coldly)*. Reward . . . ah, yes.

FIRST. You had not forgotten?

PRECIOUS HARP. Indeed not. Faithful servants should be fittingly repaid, and so you will be — most fittingly, when I ascend the throne.

FIRST. *(boldly)*. And not a moment later!

(aside to her sister) I mistrust her tone of voice.

PRECIOUS HARP *(aside to Covet Spring)*. Fittingly repaid indeed! They know too much!

COVET SPRING *(to her, his fan vibrating vigorously)*. Impertinent maids!

PRECIOUS HARP *(ducking, touching her hair disturbed by the breeze)*. Only take care that your tongue not wag too saucily, girl, when speaking to your betters.

FIRST *(aside)*. Old witch!

SECOND *(aside)*. Fat rogue!

COVET SPRING. Here is the Princess.

(He and Precious Harp bow slightly as Jade re-enters with imaginary cups of water and seeds; Twenty-Third Cousin follows).

JADE. Welcome, worthy aunt and noble Chancellor.

PRECIOUS HARP. *(falsely sweet)*. Sweet child, good-day. How is my niece?

JADE *(busying herself at the cage which the Property Man quickly holds up in position again)*. In good health, thank you. And you?

PRECIOUS HARP.   Well enough, well enough. But my thoughts are sorrowful when they dwell on you. Dear child, your eighteenth birthday draws near.

COVET SPRING.   And still no husband! Not one suitor even! What a pity!

PRECIOUS HARP.   My poor ugly pet, I grieve for you. The throne is yours if you but marry. Think—if this birthday comes, and you remain unwed, I must be Empress! I who dislike intensely any pomp and show. I who loathe power, and have no wish to rule the land!

COVET SPRING.   She who is but a simple soul content to paint on silk, and stroll the garden paths!

(Jade has turned from the cage to them; the Property Man exits with it, yawning).

JADE.   I should be glad to change the name of Princess then for yours, to be allowed to go outdoors. May I slip out for just an hour or two? There is no one near to be frightened by my ugliness. Please . . . just an hour.

PRECIOUS HARP *(coldly).*   My sweet niece, no.

COVET SPRING.   Be guided by your aunt, your father's sister, in whose charge he placed you.

PRECIOUS HARP. *(as Jade Pure turns sorrowfully away, placing a hand gingerly on her shoulder).*   There! I shall be generous. Come with us as we leave, and you may glance just once out of the door. For just a moment it will be held open, for your single look. Come, child.

JADE *(following her as she exits).*   Oh, thank you, thank you!

COVET SPRING *(as she exits).*   Lady Precious Harp is ever gracious!

(The Cousins, who have bowed as the others exited, now straighten and look at each other).

THIRD.   Ugh! What a dreadful pair!

SECOND.   Such arrogance!

FIRST *(furious).*   Servants! We are of the royal blood as well as she!

SECOND.   But only distantly related.

THIRD.   Do you know, I almost wish a suitor might arrive in time to wed the princess.

(giggling) Then old Princess Harp would howl!

FIRST. Why should she have the throne?

SECOND. How can we stop her?

FIRST (*suddenly*). Sisters, I have a plan of plans! A suitor shall arrive!

SECOND. But who?

FIRST. Our brother, Twenty-Fourth Cousin!

THIRD. Our Farmer-brother?

SECOND. That simple-minded lout?

THIRD (*with a titter*). Without two coins in his ragged smock!

SECOND (*also tittering*). A suitor to the Princess?

FIRST (*sharply*). Be still and listen. True, he is nothing as he is, but what is to prevent our buying splendid robes, and teaching him court manners?

THIRD (*giggling*). But a suitor to Jade Pure!

FIRST (*clutching her arm*). Think! Is there any other who seeks her hand? Where are his rivals?

SECOND (*slowly*). Why . . . why, there is not a one!

FIRST. Exactly! Since there is no other, he will be crowned Emperor.

THIRD. But what of us?

FIRST. We shall rule through him, the poor weak thing. He has no mind or spirit of his own!

SECOND. But do you think it will succeed? She might refuse him!

FIRST. What? Refuse a foreign prince bedecked in jewels, dazzling as a peacock, bringing costly gifts? Come, we must send for Twenty-Fourth Cousin.

SECOND. Dear brother!

THIRD. Dear, dear brother!

(*They exit right, hastily, in great excitement*).

JADE (*entering right, looking back*). Where do my cousins go so hastily? Just see, they walk out through the door as if it were a simple thing. But I, Princess, may not leave!

(*at the window*) They cross the garden when they please, but I remain shut up day after day.

(*A bird trill is sounded from offstage; the Property Man runs tardily in with the cage, to which Jade goes*).

262

Will you sing in your cage, little bird? I cannot sing in mine.

(suddenly) But there is something I can do; I can set you free, poor prisoner. Here, perch upon my finger . . .

(The Property Man shuffles off with the cage) . . .

carefully now . . . I shall bring you to the open window. There . . . slip between the bars . . . go free!

(a second trill from offstage)

I must remain!

(She exits left, hands to face. The Property Man enters to carry off the bench; the Stage Manager steps forward, bows, and speaks).

SCENE TWO

STAGE MANAGER. For the next scene of our illustrious play, we are transported to this distant field. The sun shines hot upon the earth; the farmer with his plow draws near.

(He steps back, as Twenty-Fourth Cousin enters right, plowing his field with an imaginary handplow. He is a meek little man, guileless and cheerful in appearance; his costume is a drab brown and gray, and quite shabby; a large hat rests on the back of his head. When he reaches center stage he stops, straightens, draws a hand across his forehead, removes his hat, and holding it in front of him, turns to the audience).

TWENTY-FOURTH. I am, as you see, a simple farmer, yet Twenty-Fourth Cousin to the ugly Princess Jade Pure, whom my sisters serve. They are fashionable ladies accustomed to court life, but I have no desire to go to the City. I am a farmer. Now you see me plowing my field.

(And he begins again, taking no notice of happy whistling offstage. Road Wanderer enters right; he is a sturdy handsome young man, carelessly dressed in bright if tattered clothes: patches of all colors are splashed over them).

ROAD WANDERER *(to the audience, modestly).* I am Road Wanderer, the humble hero of this play. You will learn more of me as I talk with the good farmer.

TWENTY-FOURTH *(who has straightened, and is watching him).* Good-day, sir.

ROAD WANDERER. Good-day to you, sir.

(calling offstage) Go back, Small One, and wait. Mrograff . . . uzcark!

TWENTY-FOURTH *(his eyes wide, but politely).* You are with a friend?

ROAD WANDERER. Why, yes. My — my watch dog.

TWENTY-FOURTH *(eagerly).* I have a great fondness for dogs, sir. May I perhaps see this one of yours?

ROAD WANDERER *(doubtfully).* He is . . . of an unusual type: Tell me, friend, how do you call yourself?

TWENTY-FOURTH. Twenty-fourth Cousin . . . that is, twenty-four times removed from the royal family. I am a farmer, as you see.

ROAD WANDERER *(sitting down, pretending to lean against a tree).* I do. Is this your tree that I sit down beneath, and lean my back against?

(The Property Man has shuffled in with a tree branch, stylized, which he waves languidly over Road Wanderer's head).

TWENTY-FOURTH. It is. *(proudly)* All this is mine, *(pointing)* and that small cottage . . . O, it is little enough. My sisters say that it is nothing. They are elegant ladies who serve the ugly Princess Jade Pure in the palace.

ROAD WANDERER. Indeed! What would they say of me who has no more than Small One, and my health?

TWENTY-FOURTH. You have no house?

ROAD WANDERER. I want no house. I am a student who wanders here and there, to and fro.

TWENTY-FOURTH. See here, how do you live? What do you eat?

ROAD WANDERER. That is simple, very simple. I have many friends.

TWENTY-FOURTH. Oh?

ROAD WANDERER. They bring me the ripest fruits from the top-most branches, the tenderest roots from below the ground, the sweetest honey, the choicest nuts.

TWENTY-FOURTH *(pushing his hat back on his head).* What are these friends of yours? Magicians?

ROAD WANDERER. No. They are the birds, the insects, the creatures that climb and dig and swim . . . in short, all animals know me.

TWENTY-FOURTH. They are all your friends? But why? How?

ROAD WANDERER. I know a secret. I am one who can speak and understand their many languages.

264

TWENTY-FOURTH *(scratching his head in bewilderment).* My ancestors! Whose languages?

ROAD WANDERER. Why, the language of my friends, the animals. The speech of every smallest one of them is known to me.

TWENTY-FOURTH. Ho! That I cannot believe. You are joking with me.

ROAD WANDERER *(sitting up).* I swear it is the truth. I learned it in my wanderings. Show me the creature I cannot converse with.

TWENTY-FOURTH. *(looking about.* But . . . there is no creature here. Ah, wait . . . I have it! Your pet — your dog! Call him here!

ROAD WANDERER *(rising hastily).* No, no . . . not Small One.

TWENTY-FOURTH. A-ha! You dare not try!

ROAD WANDERER. It is for your sake that I —

TWENTY-FOURTH. You shall prove what you say!

(calling offstage) Here, Small One, Come, boy come!

ROAD WANDERER. Wait! It is no dog!

TWENTY-FOURTH. Good Dog! Come here!

(his voice raising to a shriek of terror) Oh . . . oh . . . oh!

(Small One, a medium-sized highly-colored dragon, enters with a bound and a roar)

A dragon! Help! A dragon! Save me!

(For a moment there is a lively chase: Twenty-Fourth Cousin finally collapses on his knees, clinging to Road Wanderer).

ROAD WANDERER. There! Do you see? Small one, araf . . . err-gad.

TWENTY-FOURTH *(moaning).* Oh . . . oh . . . oh . . .

ROAD WANDERER *(good-humoredly).* Cease wailing, man; Do you not see that he is harmless if you are my friend?

(stroking the dragon) Yes, this is Small One, my fond watch-dog.

TWENTY-FOURTH *(fearfully, getting to his feet).* Dog, indeed! Who would have guessed a dragon was your pet? Is he—are you certain he is tame, kind sir?

ROAD WANDERER. He will obey me. You need have no fear. Mowta . . . kagota . . . harsk.

TWENTY-FOURTH. What? What do you say!

(as dragon starts for him) He comes!

ROAD WANDERER.   Wait! Wait! I have told him to approach, and bow to you.

TWENTY-FOURTH.   *(staring, open-mouthed, as the dragon attempts a bow)*   You spoke to him?

ROAD WANDERER.   Have I not told you that I can? Will you see further proof?

(indicating the hat) There is your hat, dropped as you ran. Small One shall be told to take it to you. Quirtech . . . mowta harrad.

(Small One goes obediently to the hat; Twenty-Fourth Cousin finally nerves himself to accept it from the dragon).

TWENTY-FOURTH.   But he obeys! My head is spinning!

(The dragon turns to Road Wanderer, growling gutturally. Road Wanderer throws back his head and laughs heartily).

ROAD WANDERER.   Small One, that is not polite.

TWENTY-FOURTH *(approaching cautiously).*   See . . . you laugh. What has he said?

ROAD WANDERER.   Eh? Nothing.

TWENTY-FOURTH.   Nothing?

(The dragon mutters again).

ROAD WANDERER *(laughing as he strokes its head).*   Aggaruk . . . murraf.

TWENTY-FOURTH.   I will believe it, truly, that you talk together if you tell me what the monster said. Was it about me?

ROAD WANDERER.   Well, . . . yes. He merely asked me . . .

TWENTY-FOURTH *(still closer).*   What?

ROAD WANDERER.   Who the foolish-looking dunce was I was speaking to, and remarked —

TWENTY-FOURTH.   Oh, he did, did he? What else?

ROAD WANDERER.   That you might serve as dinner for him, but appeared too lean and stringy!

TWENTY-FOURTH *(leaping away in fright as Small One snaps playfully at his ankles).*   Aaaahhh!

ROAD WANDERER.   Come back! He meant no harm. But do you now believe my power with animals?

TWENTY-FOURTH.   Oh, yes! Indeed I do! You will forgive this humble toiler for his doubts? Such knowledge is beyond belief; that is, it seemed —

(A bird trill sounds from offstage).

ROAD WANDERER. Hush! Listen!

TWENTY-FOURTH. What do you hear?

ROAD WANDERER *(indicating the branch which the Property Man holds).* That small bird in the tree. She tells of a prisoner . . . I will call her closer.

(He trills, holding up a finger as if inviting a bird to alight upon it; the Property Man exits, yawning, with the tree-branch).

TWENTY-FOURTH. Why, she comes to sit upon your finger!

(a trill from offstage)

Listen to her song!

ROAD WANDERER *(listening).* Hush . . . she tells me of a girl . . . a lovely maiden . . . shut up in a tower . . .

TWENTY-FOURTH. But how does she know this

ROAD WANDERER *(after listening to another trill.)* She was a caged bird in the prisoner's room . . . until her young mistress set her free.

TWENTY-FOURTH. And the girl?

ROAD WANDERER. Is a prisoner still. She longs to run about the garden in the sun, and through the meadows . . . but is not permitted.

TWENTY-FOURTH. What a cruel fate!

ROAD WANDERER *(after another trill from offstage).* Ah . . . the little bird asks me to free her mistress . . . help her escape from the tower.

TWENTY-FOURTH. Good! "To help another helps yourself."

ROAD WANDERER. But it is no concern of mine. I want no gratitude, no gifts, no one to care for and look after.

TWENTY-FOURTH *(as a particularly loud twittering sounds).* How the bird does chirp!

ROAD WANDERER. She scolds me for my words . . . and doubtless she she is right. Well, then, I shall go to see this prisoner, to learn if she is worthy. Then, perhaps . . . Good-bye, friend Cousin; may we meet again!

TWENTY-FOURTH.   I wish the same.

> *(wistfully)* A lovely prisoner . . . oh, but I must stay here with my farm. How will you find her?

ROAD WANDERER.   On the back of Small One, who can fly — like all dragons, I shall follow this small bird.

> *(He tosses his hand into the air, as if to send off an imaginary bird, and trills once more; there is an answer from offstage.)*

Now she will lead us there. Farewell!

> *(Small One has already waddled off; Road Wanderer follows. Twenty-Fourth Cousin pushes his hat back and gazes up, waving a hand forlornly).*

TWENTY-FOURTH.   Farewell! May your shadow not grow less!

> *(awed)*   Why, there my friend goes, on the dragon's back!

> *(wistfully)*   Such a life of high adventure, while to this poor wretch no moment of excitement comes. Alas, I still must plow . . .

> *(gazing off-stage in the opposite direction)*   But look! Drawing near my cottage door . . . a messenger, in handsome dress. From whom? What message does he bring?

> *(calling)*   I come — I come!

> *(hurrying off)*   Perhaps adventure knocks with him!

SCENE THREE

(The Property Man enters with a high box, painted gray and black to simulate a section of stone wall, which he places right center).

STAGE MANAGER *(stepping forward)*.   Our scene has changed now to the royal garden outside Princess Jade Pure's window. Here in this stone tower she stays a prisoner, looking down from her high window.

> *(He steps back as Jade Pure enters; the Property Man assists her to mount the box, after which he exits. The Princess is dressed as before, but now wears a silver headdress with flowing drapery which may be brought forward to serve as a veil. She places her hands on either side of an imaginary window-frame).*

JADE.   Alas, I am forlorn! Not even my sweet caged bird to cheer my loneliness! While there below me stretch the beauties of the country-side, which I shall never know. Why am I so ugly? Why? If it were not so, I should marry and escape this hateful prison.

(Road Wanderer enters cautiously left, followed by Small One, who puffs and sighs from his recent exertions).

What was that? I see nothing. No . . . it was the sighing of my heart . . . no more.

ROAD WANDERER.   Softly, Small One, softly. That must be her window there.

(Jade sighs)   Ah, now I hear a voice.

JADE.   On the road which leads to the City I see people . . . many people, but they cannot see me. There is no one who can help me.

ROAD WANDERER *(coming closer).*   What a lovely voice. But I cannot see her face.

JADE *(drawing back).*   Who is there? Is there someone there below my window?

ROAD WANDERER.   I am here . . . he who is called Road Wanderer.

JADE *(frightened).*   Why have you come, Road Wanderer?

ROAD WANDERER.   To set you free. Will you climb down now?

JADE.   Free? You will help me to escape?

(aside)   Oh, no, for he might see my face!

ROAD WANDERER.   What are you saying? You do not want to come outside?

JADE.   Oh, yes! I think of nothing else!

ROAD WANDERER.   So your small bird told me.

JADE.   My Bird?

ROAD WANDERER.   The bird you freed. I understood her song.

JADE.   But what a mighty gift! To understand the speech of birds!

ROAD WANDERER.   Of all animals! I shall tell you more when you descend. But come, a guard may pass by soon.

JADE.   Yes, yes, I shall try to climb down if you will help me, but . . . wait . . .

ROAD WANDERER.   For what?

JADE. *(aside, adjusting her veil).*   My veil . . . I first must veil my face, so that he will not be frightened.

ROAD WANDERER.   What? I cannot hear you.

JADE. Now . . . now I am ready.

(thrusting a foot forward timidly, drawing it back) But afraid!

ROAD WANDERER. Have no fear. Just give your hand, and I will catch you . . . so!

JADE *(in delight).* Oh . . . oh, I am free, and here, outside!

ROAD WANDERER. Remove your veil so that you may better see the world.

JADE. No, no, I cannot! Do not ask me —

(Small One makes a friendly bounce toward her; she screams and rushes to Road Wanderer).

Oohh!

ROAD WANDERER. Hush! Will you call the guards?

JADE. Behind you——

ROAD WANDERER *(laughing).* That is only Small One, my dragon. He is gentle, and a friend.

JADE *(as Small One, making friendly noises, rubs his head against her skirt, timidly touching his head).*
Why, yes, he is! I am not afraid of him. I am not afraid of anything!

ROAD WANDERER. Come along. I know a nearby field if it is flowers you want to see —

JADE. And trees . . . and streams of clear, calm water!

ROAD WANDERER. All that. Take my hand and come!

JADE *(taking his hand and going off with him).* Yes, Yes!

(The dragon skips about playfully for a moment, then realizing he has been left behind, dashes off with a howl. The Property Man enters to remove the box, returns at once with a roll of blue cloth).

SCENE FOUR

STAGE MANAGER. And so our hero and our heroine run off to find a grassy meadow.

(with a sweeping gesture) This is it. Here is a tree . . . and there, flowers . . . here a pool of fresh spring water.

(He indicates the blue cloth which the Property Man unrolls and places on the stage down right; the Property Man shuffles off as

Jade Pure and Road Wanderer re-enter still hand in hand. She breaks and runs about like a child in her joy).

JADE. It is more beautiful than I dreamed! I want to see and hear and touch everything at once!

(stooping to pluck an imaginary flower, then whirling about) What a lovely flower! Just see that small white cloud shaped like a fish!

(embracing an imaginary tree) And this slim tree whose fragrant blossoms — oh! You are laughing at me!

ROAD WANDERER *(gently).* I am laughing with you, because you are so happy. See, even Small One laughs!

(The dragon capers about, roaring happily).

JADE *(stopping, suddenly serious).* Happy . . . that is so. I am happy! I have never been happy before.

ROAD WANDERER *(stretching out his hand).* Take off your veil now.

JADE *(covering her face with her hand).* No, no!

ROAD WANDERER. Why . . . what have I said to grieve you?

JADE. Nothing. You are kind. I shall be ever grateful. Look — is that a pool of water?

ROAD WANDERER. Yes. As clear as crystal. Drink from it if you like.

JADE *(softly).* A pool that is very like a mirror . . . I may see my face.

(to him) Please, will you be so kind as to stand over there?

ROAD WANDERER. There? Why should I?

JADE. I—I cannot tell you yet. But please, stand there . . . away from me, and do not look in this direction.

ROAD WANDERER *(puzzled).* If you wish it.

JADE *(kneeling beside the imaginary pool stage right).* Now . . . I shall remove my veil and look! Oh, no . . . I am afraid! . . . But I have said I was afraid of nothing. This must be the test.

(slowly) And so—I lift my veil.

(She stares for a moment into the water, speechless).

Why . . . why, can my eyes be trusted? I am — I am —

(calling) Road Wanderer! Road Wanderer!

ROAD WANDERER *(hurrying to her, raising her to her feet).* What is it? What have you found?

271

JADE. I have found myself! Tell me, is my face displeasing to you?

ROAD WANDERER (*dazed*). Why . . . you are beautiful! More beautiful than any maiden I have ever looked upon!

JADE. Oh, thank you!

ROAD WANDERER. I am speechless . . . I can find no words; forgive me.

JADE. I am in your debt forever. You have given me this new face!

ROAD WANDERER. I?

JADE. How am I to repay you? Anything you ask—

(*Bells are rung excitedly offstage*)

Those bells! What can have happened?

ROAD WANDERER. Does it matter? They are ringing in the City.

JADE. But you do not understand! They ring only when some disaster befalls the royal family!

ROAD WANDERER. And I still ask you, does it matter now?

JADE. It does to me! What can it be? We must go back at once!

ROAD WANDERER. To the City?

JADE. Yes!

(*running off*)

Please hurry!

ROAD WANDERER. But I—

JADE (*imperiously*). Come!

(*Road Wanderer, with a shrug, takes one of Small One's forepaws, and they hurry off after her. The Property Man enters, rolls up the blue cloth, tucks it under his arm, and exits*).

SCENE FIVE

STAGE MANAGER (*stepping forward*). Our scene is changing once again. I stand now on a city street. But where are the illustrious citizens?

(*looking off*) Oh, there they are, crowding around that city official who is about to read a Royal Proclamation.

(*He steps back. The bells ring again; there is the sound of many*

272

voices offstage. Twenty-Fourth Cousin backs on right, on the fringe of an imaginary crowd. He continues to look offstage).

TWENTY-FOURTH.   Here! Cease shoving! And back and back they push me, to the edge of the crowd! This city life does not agree with me! Why have my sisters sent such an urgent message bidding me to come? There is something queer about all this. But before I go to the palace, I shall learn why the bells ring, and what that city official has to say.

JADE *(entering right, running).*   What is is? Have you shouted it yet? Oh, good sir, can you tell us?

TWENTY-FOURTH.   I? I do not —

(noticing Road Wanderer, who has also entered) — why, it is my friend, Road Wanderer!

ROAD WANDERER *(still concerned about Jade's conduct).*   My respects to you.

TWENTY-FOURTH.   Many thanks! And this . . . this must be the lovely prisoner.

JADE *(who has been peering offstage).*   Why were the bells rung? Why?

VOICE OFFSTAGE.   Royal Proclamation —

JADE *(as Twenty-Fourth Cousin opens his mouth to reply).*   Listen, listen!

VOICE OFFSTAGE.   "Know, subjects of the Southern Kingdom, that your princess, Her Highness, Jade Pure, has mysteriously vanished away, no doubt carried off by the evil demons."

(There are murmurs and exclamations of surprise from offstage).

JADE *(angrily).*   Demons!

TWENTY-FOURTH.   Think of that!

VOICE.   Silence! "Her Aunt, the Lady Precious Harp, sister of the late Emperor, has therefore graciously consented to ascend the throne and to assume the title of Empress."

(There are feeble cheers, boos, offstage).

JADE *(stamping her foot).*   No! No, no, no!

ROAD WANDERER.   What is wrong?

JADE.   She shall do no such thing! I, Princess Jade Pure, am very much alive!

TWENTY-FOURTH.   Princess Jade Pure!

ROAD WANDERER.   You — a princess?

TWENTY-FOURTH.   But you are . . . you are —

JADE.   Yes! Beautiful!

> (looking offstage)   Subjects, my aunt would have you believe that I am ugly. Now you see for yourselves.

VOICE OFFSTAGE.   Is she really the Princess?

JADE (holding her hand out imperiously).   See — the royal ring upon my hand. Can you doubt it? Bow before your Princess!

> (Twenty-Fourth Cousin bows low; Road Wanderer, completely ignored by Jade Pure, whose back is to him, stands straight and stiff).

VOICE OFFSTAGE.   But how beautiful she is!

SECOND VOICE.   There is none more beautiful!

THIRD VOICE.   I shall court her!

FIRST VOICE.   And I!

JADE.   Ring the bells joyously to announce my return! Let Lady Precious Harp know that her plot has failed.

> (To Twenty-Fourth Cousin)   For I am beautiful, am I not?

TWENTY-FOURTH (overcome).   Yes, indeed, Your Highness . . . yes!

JADE (to Wanderer).   Am I not beautiful?

ROAD WANDERER (coldly).   Yes, Your Highness.

JADE (whirling about, enchanted with her triumph).   Thank you, my good fellow! My very good fellow!

> (Road Wanderer turns away with an exclamation of anger.)

Why — where are you going?

ROAD WANDERER.   To resume my wandering. I have already stayed too long here.

JADE.   But I thought . . . that is ——

ROAD WANDERER (bitterly).   A Princess! More than that, a thoughtless and ungrateful minx!

JADE.   How dare you!

ROAD WANDERER.   You seek new admirers and forget me!

JADE.   Oh!

TWENTY-FOURTH.   My friend ——

ROAD WANDERER.   Eternal gratitude! Your beauty and your throne are all that interest you! You shall not make sport of me a second time.

(He stalks off angrily; Twenty-Fourth Cousin is aghast; Jade Pure becomes aware of her feelings toward him).

JADE *(calling off).*   Wait, please! Do come back!

VOICE *(offstage).*   How beautiful she is!

SECOND VOICE *(offstage).*   When angry!

THIRD VOICE *(offstage).*   When sad!

JADE.   What does it matter now! I have lost Road Wanderer!

(The Property Man enters with two elaborate handkerchiefs, one in each hand. Jade Pure takes one from him, bursts into tears, and exits drying her eyes. Twenty-Fourth Cousin, shaking his head sorrowfully, goes off right).

STAGE MANAGER *(stepping forward).*   Yes, it is indeed an unhappy moment for the beauteous Jade Pure.

(He takes the second handkerchief from the Property Man who continues to stand motionless with face blank and expressionless, gracefully touches his eyes, and hands it back to the Property Man, who exits).

But do not weep too hard, Kind Audience, for our play has a joyful ending. Others are unhappy in the Royal Palace too. Here in this room, we find the three deceitful Cousins.

(He steps back. Twenty-First, Twenty-Second, and Twenty-Third Cousins sail in, wringing their hands in despair).

TWENTY-FIRST.   What a dreadful calamity!

TWENTY-SECOND.   All is lost!

TWENTY-THIRD.   O unhappy day!

FIRST.   We should have watched her every minute!

SECOND.   Now all know of Jade Pure's beauty!

THIRD.   Suitors are arriving by the dozens! She can marry if she likes this very day!

FIRST.   And Twenty-Fourth Cousin . . . no, there is no hope.

SECOND.   Shall he not still be a suitor?

FIRST (*pacing back and forth*). Have you seen those who have come? Kings, princes, nobles of every rank and degree! With unbelievable wealth! Handsome and young and elegant! And our brother —pah!

THIRD. Alas!

SECOND. But you have sent him, and he will come.

FIRST. Then he must go away again.

(*Twenty-Fourth Cousin, who has entered timidly, tries to nerve himself to rap at an imaginary door*).

SECOND. Do not be hasty, sister.

(*The knock is sounded offstage*).

FIRST. Hear! A knock—it must be he. Let him in, quickly.

THIRD (*opening an imaginary door*). Come in.

(*As Twenty-Fourth Cousin, clutching his hat, hesitates and clears his throat*). Come in, quickly.

TWENTY-FOURTH (*whom she has pulled inside by the sleeve*). Thank you, gracious lady. I — am looking for my —

FIRST. Brother, can you fail to know us?

FOURTH. What! Those robes, this splendor — are you my three sisters?

FIRST. Of course. Do not speak so loudly.

SECOND. You have had your trip in vain, it seems.

FOURTH. Oh? How is that? Why did you send for me?

THIRD. You were to marry the Princess!

FOURTH. I — what?

FIRST. When it was thought that she was ugly, there were no suitors for her hand. You, brother, as the only prince to ask her hand, would win it.

FOURTH (*his eyes wider than ever*). A prince! But I am not a prince!

SECOND. With handsome robes and borrowed jewels you might have posed —

FIRST (*impatiently*). Enough! Her suitors throng the halls. Such a one as you can stand no chance.
(*pushing him one way*) Just see his shape! It is not regal!

276

THIRD (*pulling him another*).   And the nose — in profile very bad!

SECOND (*pulling his queue*).   That queue! It is too short. Not nearly twenty inches!

FIRST.   Such feet! So large and flat! The feet of a prince are dainty.

SECOND (*taking one and holding it up*).   The hands show callouses and stains, the marks of work!

FOURTH (*feebly*).   I am a farmer, sisters!

THIRD (*just realizing it*).   Without a fan he comes here to the palace!

SECOND.   Yes, without a fan!

FIRST (*turning her back on him and folding her arms*).   Begone! We have no use for you.

SECOND (*doing the same*).   Begone!

THIRD (*doing the same*).   Begone!

FOURTH.   Sisters, I — I —

COUSINS (*wheeling about in the same motion, each extending an arm stiffly toward the door*).   Begone!

FOURTH (*gulping, bowing and shaking hands solemnly with himself*). I take my leave; good day, my sisters.

(*He exits, after closing the imaginary door behind him. Lady Precious Harp and Covet Spring enter from the other side, behind the Cousins*).

PRECIOUS HARP.   Aha!

(*the Cousins, startled, turn quickly, their hand to their mouths, then bow*).

So there you are! Stupid creatures! Have you left the Princess unattended again?

FIRST.   Only for one small moment. Your Ladyship.

SECOND.   But not alone. She was occupied in interviewing suitors.

THIRD (*maliciously*).   Some of the many who came.

PRECIOUS (*sourly*).   Ah, yes.

FIRST (*sweetly*).   Her ladyship is doubtless overjoyed at the numbers of young men who have proposed.

SECOND.   The Princess soon will marry.

THIRD. And dear Lady Precious Harp need not assume the cares of state!

PRECIOUS. Silence!

COVET SPRING. Impudent servants! Begone at once!

PRECIOUS. Attend your mistress!

COVET. Leave us!

COUSINS *(bowing and exiting quickly).* Yes, Your Ladyship . . . Your Excellency.

(Precious Harp and Covet Spring, left alone, begin to pace from opposite sides of the stage, passing and repassing each other center stage).

COVET. So! All is lost! Spilt water cannot be gathered up.

PRECIOUS. Those simpering bunglers shall pay dear for the failure of our plan. If Jade Pure had been guarded every moment — ah!

COVET. Alas! All know her beauty now. And she will marry. You have lost the throne!

PRECIOUS *(stopping suddenly).* Not yet! Her birthday comes within the week.

COVET *(also stopping).* That is so. This is quite so.

PRECIOUS. The stroke of noon that marks her eighteenth birthday still may find her single. No suitor seems to please her.

COVET *(beginning to pace again).* But she will wed, if just to spite you. Mark my words!

PRECIOUS. I am not beaten! Come!

(Covet Spring does not heed her; she catches his arm, pulling him off-balance).

Come I say. We shall lay new and better plans!

(They exit. The Stage Manager steps forward.)

SCENE SEVEN

STAGE MANAGER. Again we change our scene, this time going outside the Royal Garden. The day is warm and clear. Butterflies come to light upon fragrant lilies. Everything about us is bright and beautiful. But the fair Princess who approaches has no welcoming smile.

(He steps back; Jade Pure enters, protesting to someone offstage).

278

JADE. No, no. Leave me, I beg of you. Guards, hold them back!

(walking slowly across the stage) I am weary of suitors, and would be alone to rest and think. Let me wander through the garden paths . . .

(The Property Man hastily brings the bench out to place directly behind her).

perhaps to sit a moment on this bench. Strange . . . Strange . . . I am still lonely. Beauty is not happiness. What good are suitors if Road Wanderer is not among them?

(voices offstage)

Voices — who has followed me here? Ah, the Cousins . . . whom I can no longer trust.

TWENTY-FIRST *(entering, bowing).* My Princess, fairer than a day in spring —

TWENTY-SECOND *(entering, bowing).* More lovely than fragile flowers.

TWENTY-THIRD *(entering, bowing).* Whose voice is sweeter yet than the nightingale's song —

JADE. Stop! I have heard enough! What do you want of me?

FIRST. Nothing but to serve you, regal cousin.

SECOND. Who are the most beloved of Princesses.

THIRD. Whose suitors number in the thousands.

FIRST. Who is now the happiest of mortals.

JADE. Ah!

FIRST. What? She sighs?

SECOND. She comes to sit alone.

THIRD. Do not her suitors please her?

JADE. No! I have dismissed them, everyone who came today.

FIRST. But your marriage —

JADE. It shall not take place, unless the right one comes.

SECOND *(aside to the others).* Good! She has chosen no one yet.

THIRD. Perhaps our brother should return!

FIRST. Wait . . . I shall question her about the man of her choice. Now mark down what she answers.

(to Jade Pure) Sweet Princess, tell us of the man you wait for. First, of what height should he be?

JADE *(remembering).* Why, half a head as tall as I.

(The Property Man has shuffled in to hand a parchment and a brush to Twenty-Second Cousin, exiting immediately).

SECOND *(marking with the brush on the parchment, which rests on her sister's back).* Our brother must wear thick-soled shoes!

THIRD *(bent double, serving as a desk).* Or walk on stilts!

FIRST. His hair next — of what color should it be?

JADE. Black as a raven's wing, and long.

THIRD. Very long and black!

FIRST. And features?

JADE. Great dark eyes, a fine straight nose —

SECOND. Alas, his nose! What can be done with it?

JADE. Delightful smile, and such a voice!

THIRD. Aha! Our brother has a voice!

SECOND *(despairingly).* But such a voice!

FIRST. What else? What qualities of mind?

JADE. Why, he must know how to be gay . . .

SECOND. Brother shall laugh ho-ho at all he hears.

JADE. And must love nature and all animals . . .

THIRD. Ah, Good! A farmer can do that!

JADE *(dreamingly).* All animals, and dragons too . . . such a sweet small dragon he had!

FIRST *(misunderstanding).* What? He must have a dragon?

SECOND. Impossible!

THIRD *(straightening abruptly).* That cannot be!

JADE. But I once knew —

FIRST. You'll have no suitors left if this is known!

SECOND. What man can bring a dragon to you?

JADE *(thoughtfully).* What man indeed!

THIRD. Ridiculous!

FIRST *(conferring with them)*. Why, sisters . . .

JADE *(rising, delighted)*. Of course, Possession of a dragon! Who but my dear Road Wanderer can meet such a requirement. I must send decrees throughout the kingdom.

FIRST *(to her again)*. Surely Your Highness cannot mean —

SECOND. A dragon!

JADE. I do indeed.

THIRD. Dragons! Pah!

PRECIOUS HARP *(entering with Covet Spring)*. What is this? What do I hear?

COVET SPRING. Dragons? Dragons? W-where?

FIRST. Incredible!

JADE *(gaily)*. My respects to Her Ladyship and His Excellency.

PRECIOUS. Do not stand on ceremony, niece, but tell us: what has caused this uproar?

JADE. Most venerable aunt, I have come to a decision about my marriage.

PRECIOUS *(caught off guard)*. Oh, no!

JADE. Let a proclamation be cried throughout the land.

COVET. Too late, too late!

JADE. And this is my royal decision: the suitor who wins my hand must possess a dragon.

PRECIOUS. Why —

COVET. Why —

JADE. That is my only condition. The dragon must, of course, be brought before me by its owner.

PRECIOUS. But this will simply mean —

COVET. Do I understand —

FIRST. How can a —

JADE. Just one thing more! If two dragon-owners should appear, it shall be my privilege to select whichever dragon pleases me most.

COVET.   Why, I cannot believe —

PRECIOUS.   She is mad! How fortunate for us!

JADE *(aside).*   Surely Road Wonderer will hear of my decision and come back to me!

PRECIOUS *(slyly).*   But, see here, niece, what if no dragon-owner appears?

JADE *(calmly).*   Then I shall marry no one.

PRECIOUS.   Splendid! Er — that is —

JADE.   But have no fear upon that score.

(reseating herself) At least one dragon will be entered.

(The two groups, one on either side of her, talk among themselves. All carry fans. Each group, on finishing its line of dialogue, freezes in conference behind its fans, while the other group says its sequence. This continues to the end of the scene).

FIRST *(to her sisters).*   How can she be so certain?

COVET *(to Precious).*   This is perfect! She will never marry with such a requirement.

PRECIOUS.   I wonder.

SECOND.   Does our brother own a dragon, do you think?

FIRST.   Nonsense!

THIRD.   There will be no suitors left once this decree is read.

COVET.   We need only wait until her birthday comes and goes.

PRECIOUS.   But see how she smiles . . . she does not fear the outcome. Why not? Does she know of a dragon?

FIRST.   There must be a dragon somewhere. If our brother could present it —

SECOND.   See how the Princess smiles. She knows . . .

THIRD.   Knows what?

COVET.   She must know something. If there is a dragon, we have lost again. "Out of the wolf's den into the tiger's mouth!"

PRECIOUS.   Listen to me. Our course is plain. We must enter a dragon, too!

FIRST.   Yes, there can be no other way. We must discover a dragon at once!

SECOND. But where?

THIRD. They are surely all dead!

PRECIOUS. Do you know where to find such a thing?

COVET. Ah, that is the problem. A live dragon . . .

PRECIOUS. Do you suppose — ah, but it might not work . . .

FIRST. A live dragon! It is true we may not find . . . I wonder!

SECOND. What?

THIRD. Have you a plan?

COVET. What thought has come to you?

PRECIOUS. Need it be a live dragon?

COVET. But — I see! I see!

FIRST. Why not a make-believe dragon?

SECOND. Oh!

THIRD. Of course! Of course!

PRECIOUS. A cleverly contrived disguise would do. We must find someone whom we can trust to wear a dragon costume.

COVET. Good!

FIRST. A costume made with skill and care —

SECOND. But who would put it on?

THIRD. Whom can we trust in such a risky business?

PRECIOUS. Who shall it be?

COVET. But, more important, who shall be the suitor who presents it?

PRECIOUS. Why, I overlooked that point.

COVET *(smugly).* But I have not!

FIRST. Our brother!

SECOND. Yes!

THIRD. But wait—he cannot be both suitor and dragon!

PRECIOUS. Well then?

COVET. I shall seek the Princess' hand!

PRECIOUS. You?

COVET. Of course! And you shall play the dragon!

FIRST. I have it!

(indicating both of them)

You shall play the dragon!

PRECIOUS. Preposterous!

SECOND. Not I, sister!

THIRD. Nor I!

COVET. But think, Your Ladyship! The plot is dangerous at best; we two must work it out alone.

FIRST. You must! We have no choice!

SECOND. But why not you?

FIRST. I must coach our brother, and prepare his speeches for him.

PRECIOUS. But I — a dragon!

COVET. There is much to gain: a throne!

PRECIOUS. Then if you win Jade Pure, she must be done away with.

COVET. Agreed! And you shall be my Empress.

(aside). And the next to die.

PRECIOUS *(aside).* He shall not live long after.

FIRST. Come, let us go to find a costume that you two may don.

SECOND. But the Princess?

FIRST. She is dreaming, and will take no notice.

PRECIOUS. Ugh! A dragon! But it must be so. Come now, a costume must be made at once.

COVET. The Princess?

PRECIOUS. Leave her to her dreams. We go to find a dragon!

(And they exit).

THIRD *(who has tiptoed up to the princess to look).* Yes, her thoughts are far away.

FIRST. Twenty-Fourth Cousin must be sent for too. But first, we go to find a dragon!

284

(And they exit off the opposite side of the stage. Jade Pure, who has been oblivious to the hushed conversation, now stirs and sighs happily).

JADE. Of course! The dragon was the answer. Who but the Road Wanderer can bring one to me?

(rising) Yes, he will return . . . I feel it . . . and my happiness with him. I go now to fold my hands and wait . . . for the coming of my dragon!

(she exits happily. The Property Man enters to remove the bench. The Stage Manager steps forward).

STAGE MANAGER. Thus ends the first act of our worthy play, most gracious Audience. The noble actors will now rest a moment, sip their tea, and don new costumes. But have patience; they will soon return. And that your wait may be more pleasant,

(clapping his hands) Music shall be played.

(He bows and exits. Chinese music — recorded — is played softly throughout the intermission).

PART TWO

SCENE ONE

(The Stage Manager enters, bows, and speaks).

STAGE MANAGER. Again, our greetings, O-most-gracious Audience! We thank you for your kind attention thus far, and promise you much laughter and excitement in what follows. The stage is now a lonely field far from the palace.

(looking offstage) But the worthy actors are approaching; I once more become invisible.

(He bows again, and withdraws to his corner of the stage. Covet Spring tiptoes cautiously in, looks back offstage, and beckons).

COVET SPRING. Hsst! We are alone, Your Ladyship.

PRECIOUS HARP *(entering in dragon costume, puffing and groaning).* Alas! O woe! That I should come to this! Ancestors, have mercy!

COVET. Yes, this is a place where none will spy us out. And you, Your Ladyship, may practice both your walk and roar.

PRECIOUS *(straightening up).* No, no, Covet Spring! This is too much! my senses must have left me when I gave consent!

COVET. But, my dear Precious Harp, how else can we obtain the throne? It is a prize worth any risk!

PRECIOUS. But oh, the shame — the gross indignity of Precious Harp impersonating a dragon!

COVET *(smoothly)*. Her Ladyship cannot appreciate the beauty of the costume and the brilliance of her own portrayal half so well as I. You are a dragon beyond all others, I assure you! Come now, roar again, and let me see that graceful walk.

PRECIOUS *(croaching on all fours)*. Alas! But if it must be so, it must. *(She attempts a feeble roar)*.

COVET. A-ha! Good, good! But if Her Ladyship could roar somewhat more loudly —

(He roars vigorously, frightens her).

PRECIOUS *(leaping away in fright)*. Covet Spring! How dare you? But it was a most impressive roar . . . I shall try one . . . now then . . . *(and she roars)*

COVET. Ah, good! Better! Yes, much better! Now, the walk; I lead you — so, with this gold chain, and we approach Jade Pure.

(They circle the stage rather rapidly, Precious Harp grunting and gasping, resembling an unwilling dog at the end of a leash).

PRECIOUS. Ugh! Stay . . . you move too swiftly . . . stop, I say!

COVET *(stopping)*. A thousand pardons! You are right; a stately pace will give us dignity. As we walk, a roar or two might add —

PRECIOUS. A roar! Ugh . . . oh . . . my breath is all but stopped!

COVET. And when we reach the throne, we both shall bow, and I shall make my speech.

PRECIOUS *(as he begins to pull her along)*. Wait! Let us practice singly, you your speech, and I my roars. Ah, what a sorry business!

COVET. Very well, I shall go over here.

(They stand on opposite sides of the stage).

Princess Jade Pure *(a roar from Precious Harp)*, I come before you *(roar)*

not as your Chancellor today, *(roar, Covet Spring grimaces)* but as a suitor with a dragon

(another roar; Covet Spring glares; suddenly Precious Harp begins to cough and choke).

PRECIOUS. Eh . . . oh! I shall choke! Covet Spring —

COVET *(trying helplessly to thump the dragon on the back).* What is it? How am I to —

PRECIOUS. Oh, my throat! It is dry as dust, and rough with roaring! *(straightening)* I can stand no more!

COVET *(taking her arm).* Let us find a brook where we may quench our thirst. There will be time to practice later.

PRECIOUS. Yes, yes! I shall lose this hateful dragon's head with pleasure!

(They exit, Lady Precious Harp beginning to tug at her head. Almost immediately Twenty-First and Twenty-Fourth Cousins enter. The latter is now costumed in gorgeous robes of a variety of colors, and carries an enormous fan; he looks, and is, extremely uncomfortable).

TWENTY-FIRST. Yes, this field will do quite well. We shall have space to practice. Our two sisters are now putting on the costume.

TWENTY-FOURTH *(jerking at his robes and headdress).* But — but, I tell you, I protest again — all this is not what I should like to —

FIRST. Oh, be still! And do not twitch about so. Hold your fan like this.

FOURTH. But I never wanted to hold a fan at all! I want to get back to my farm. Why have you brought me here?

FIRST *(forcibly readjusting his robe).* You know why, stupid one!

FOURTH *(as she jams his headdress down at a slightly different angle).* Ouch! Be merciful, sister!

FIRST. What shall I do with you? Nothing is right — nothing! Turn your toes out . . . out, I say!

(Pushing him, as he teeters, toes turned out) Let me see you walk. No. No! Not huge, long strides, but dainty steps! Like this . . .

FOURTH *(starting off).* No, sister, I regretfully refuse —

FIRST *(seizing him by the shoulder, turning him, and hissing in his ear).* You will do as I say, little brother! Now, walk! Walk, do you hear?

(He walks, watching his feet) Your head erect.

(pulling his queue from behind) erect! Nose pointed to the sky! But now you have forgotten the fan — flutter it! Flutter it gracefully! Watch . . . toes out, small steps . . .

FOURTH (*thoroughly bewildered*). I cannot . . . remember . . . so many things at one time . . .

FIRST. You must! Now bow before the Princess.

FOURTH (*becoming himself again*). The Princess? Where?

FIRST. Not here, idiot of idiots! Bow as you will bow that day before her.

FOURTH. Oh! A bow, you say . . . I am not sure how . . . does it go like this?

(*He bows awkwardly, glancing anxiously toward Twenty-First Cousin. A dragon's head is seen moving on stage on the same level as Twenty-Fourth Cousin's head*).

FOURTH (*turning his head, gazing into the dragon's eyes*). What do I do then —

(*terrified, dashing across to his sister*) A d-dragon! Look out! Let us flee! Come quickly!

FIRST. Be still

(*A large, awkward-looking dragon, occupied by the two sisters, enters and advances on Twenty-Fourth Cousin, roaring fiercely*).

TWENTY-SECOND (*gruffly*). We have come, little brother —

TWENTY-THIRD. To eat you!

FOURTH (*starting off again*). Farewell!

FIRST. Come back! These are your sisters in their dragon costume.

FOURTH. My sisters?

FIRST (*as the dragon preens itself*). Is it not a splendid disguise? So realistic!

FOURTH (*shuddering*). Yes!

FIRST. Come, sisters, walk about a little.

SECOND (*starting off in one direction*). Very well.

THIRD (*moving in the other*). I shall be happy — eh!

FIRST. What has gone wrong now?

SECOND. Sister, move with me in this direction!

THIRD (*turning*). But I cannot see! How can I tell which way to go?
(*The dragon begins to turn in circles, faster and faster, both girls exclaiming in dismay*).

FIRST. No, no! You are moving in a circle!

FOURTH. All this will never work! Never! I want no part of it!

SECOND. Ah, sister, stop! My head is spinning!

THIRD. I am giddy too! Oh! Oh!

(Both ends of the dragon sit down abruptly with wails and groans).

FIRST *(attempting to get the front end of the dragon on its feet).* See here, get on your feet again . . . heavy creature! Brother . . . help your other sister! We must try again — a thousand times if need be! A throne depends on it!

SECOND. No more of this, I beg you!

THIRD. My bones are surely broken, every one!

FIRST *(when both are standing again).* Enough! Now, brother, stand away. And dragon, listen to me carefully. I am here, holding your shoulder, younger sister . . .

SECOND *(the front half).* Yes, elder sister.

FIRST. You will move as I command you. Younger sister, you also will follow my voice.

THIRD *(unhappily).* Yes, eldest sister.

FIRST. Now, brother! Take hold of the silken cord about the dragon's neck.

(He does so).

We are ready at last. March forward . . . left foot, right foot, left foot . . . brother! This one is your left! . . . left and right — roar now, sisters . . .

(they roar feebly) . . . louder . . . left foot, right foot, left foot — roar now! Brother, head back . . . hold the fan high, and flutter it in time to left and right and —

(They have circled the stage and now march off, the dragon roaring, Twenty-First Cousin still counting. As if in answer to a particular loud roar from their side of the wings, a shrill roar comes from the other side of the stage. There is a moment of dead silence).

FOURTH *(offstage, quavering).* Sister, what was that?

FIRST *(offstage).* Yes, I heard it too.

COVET *(backing on).* What can it be?

FOURTH (*backing on opposite side of the stage, whispering*). It sounded very like a . . . like a dragon!

FIRST (*backing on with the dragon, whispering*). A dragon? Nonsense!

COVET (*whispering*). Such a fearful sound!

PRECIOUS (*backing on*). We must not be discovered!

FIRST. I see no one!

FOURTH (*somewhat louder*). Let us go away!

COVET. Hark! Voices!

FIRST. Hush! A voice!

PRECIOUS (*continuing to back*). Come! Let us slip away!

FIRST. You may be right . . . it does seem best to leave! But silently . . .

COVET. But quietly . . . ssshhh!

FOURTH. Ssshhh!

(*The two groups, backing slowly and elaborately on tiptoe, meet center stage: Twenty-Fourth Cousin and Covet Spring collide, as do the two dragons. There is general panic, and the stage is cleared in a moment*).

COUSINS (*dashing off*). Dragon! Dragon!

PRECIOUS AND COVET (*dashing off*). Dragon! Dragon!

(*There is silence. Then Twenty-First Cousin peeps in, comes cautiously on, pulling her extremely reluctant brother by the sleeve*).

FIRST. O, come along! There is no one about. I want to see —

FOURTH. But I — I do not want to see! Ah, what an ill-fated wretch am I, doomed to —

FIRST. Silence! There was something strange about the dragon, I tell you. And I heard a woman's scream, of that I am certain. Here, hold aside these bushes.

(*The Property Man has shuffled on, and holds up two cut-out branches, crossed. Twenty-Fourth Cousin spreads them apart for Twenty-First Cousin.*)

Ah-a

FOURTH (*Jumping*). Eh? What do you see?

FIRST. Just as I suspected! That dragon was no dragon at all!

FOURTH. Not a dragon?

FIRST. I see Precious Harp, Her August Ladyship, even now stepping out of the disguise.

FOURTH *(still dazed)*. Disguise?

FIRST *(turning on him angrily)*. Where have your wits fled? Precious Harp and Covet Spring have done the same as we. They will enter a fraudulent dragon, too.

(The Property Man exits with the branches).

FOURTH *(brightening)*. Ah, well, then ours can never win. I shall go back home.

FIRST *(pulling him back)*. You will do nothing of the sort! We shall win! Ours is far larger and handsomer than theirs.

FOURTH. Alas!

FIRST. And if by further trickery our dragon is not chosen, we can denounce their creature as a fraud and them as traitors. What a stroke of luck!

(exiting with him)

Our sisters must be told of it!

(They exit. Lady Precious Harp peeps in cautiously, then enters; Covet Spring follows, staggering under the weight of the dragon costume).

PRECIOUS. No, there is no sight of anything . . . nor sound.

COVET. My ears still ring with the roaring of the beast!

PRECIOUS. But did you mark its size? Far larger than our dragon, and more handsome.

COVET. And more real. How can a costume dragon triumph now?

PRECIOUS. That miserable treacherous girl, Twenty-First Cousin! Where could she have found such a thing?

COVET. Who can tell? I know only that our plot has failed. "Spilt water cannot be gathered up."

PRECIOUS. What if we should steal it?

COVET. What?

PRECIOUS. Their dragon!

COVET. No, not I. I would not go near it!

PRECIOUS (*pacing*). No, it will be hidden well, there are too many caves to search. Tomorrow is the day . . .

(*throwing back her head, her fist pressed against her forehead*) tomorrow . . .

(*suddenly*) Covet Spring!

COVET. Yes? Yes?

PRECIOUS. Look up! What is that — in the sky? Do I dream?

COVET (*also staring up*). I see it too . . . a large bird, flying now above the city . . . growing larger as it comes toward us . . .

PRECIOUS. Bird — it is too large! A dragon, Covet Spring! I know it is a dragon!

COVET. Flying . . . but then, it is a real one!

PRECIOUS. Yes! An authentic live dragon! Keep your eyes upon it! We must catch it at all costs!

COVET. But look! Upon its back — a man! I see him clearly!

PRECIOUS. They are heading for the palace! Come!

(*They circle the stage, running, several times. The Property Man enters with a rod around which is wrapped gray cloth or canvas*).

SCENE TWO

STAGE MANAGER (*stepping forward*). The Lady Precious Harp and Covet Spring run rapidly, and soon draw near the palace walls. (*indicating the Property Man*). That lazy fellow is to represent the wall, if he can but stay awake!

(*The Property Man has seated himself crosslegged on the stage, holding the rod at arm's length above his head, and now permits the canvas to unroll to the floor, hiding him from view*).

COVET SPRING (*winded*). Oh . . . oh . . . I can go no further.

PRECIOUS HARP. Faster! It is flying low! The palace walls are just ahead!

COVET. But the man . . . its master . . .

PRECIOUS. Shall be done away with!

(*approaching the "wall," looking over it offstage*) See — the thing is circling, coming back to alight inside the walls!

292

(She seizes a whistle suspended from her sash by a gold cord, and blows several shrill blasts).

Guards! Guards! Capture that creature and its master!

COVET *(also peering over the "wall").* We shall remain outside!

(roars and shouts come from offstage. Covet Spring leans heavily on the rod; the wall sags but straightens quickly as the Property Man makes an effort to hold it upright).

PRECIOUS. How it struggles! Watch it's scales, and do not scratch them!

COVET. Not a large dragon, though. Rather a small one.

PRECIOUS. But real — that is the thing! Aha! They have it now.

COVET. And the young man too.

PRECIOUS. Guards! Take the dragon to the stable in the south field, and secure it there.

VOICE *(offstage).* It shall be done, Your Ladyship.

PRECIOUS. See that it has food and water in abundance, and the softest straw to lie upon.

VOICE *(offstage).* We run to do your bidding.

COVET. What of the young man?

PRECIOUS. Ho, guards; Fling that young man, its master, into the darkest dungeon to await execution!

VOICE *(offstage).* All shall be carried out, Your Gracious Ladyship.

PRECIOUS. He is a traitor dangerous to the safety —

COVET. Hsst! Lady Precious Harp, someone approaches!

PRECIOUS. Go, guards, quickly, with your prisoners. Your silence shall be handsomely rewarded.

COVET. A lady comes.

(The Property Man lowers the wall to rest his arms).

PRECIOUS. Why, Covet Spring, it is my niece, Jade Pure.

COVET. The Princess!

JADE *(who has entered, throwing back her veil).* Greetings, noble aunt and august chancellor. What do you do here outside the palace walls?

(She looks pointedly at the Property Man, who raises the wall to its proper position again).

PRECIOUS.   My child, where have you been?

COVET.   Alone and unattended?

PRECIOUS.   A Princess — walking the highway?

COVET.   Such a shocking breach of court decorum! Why, —

PRECIOUS.   Exactly! Jade Pure, how do you explain —

JADE.   One moment! How can I explain if you refuse to listen? Now then, I have been to the City; I went alone because I could not find my three Cousins. But no one could recognize me in my heavy veil, and thus no harm was done!

PRECIOUS.   Perhaps not, but for what purpose did you go!

JADE.   Why, to hear news of Road — that is, to learn if any have come with dragons to enter in the contest for my hand.

COVET.   Ah! And have any such come — with dragons?

JADE.   Not a one. All my former suitors, being dragonless, have returned to their homes. The townspeople question my decision openly, saying that no dragons still exist! But I am not convinced.

PRECIOUS.   Nor I!

COVET.   Nor I!

PRECIOUS.   Rest assured that you shall have at least one dragon!

COVET *(muttering).*   Very likely two.

JADE.   You know this? You are certain? But how?

PRECIOUS.   Be patient till tomorrow. Covet Spring, accompany me; there are matters to take up.

COVET *(as they exit).*   Good-day, your Highness.

JADE.   Farewell, both.

(after they have gone)   My mind starts up in fear again! Tomorrow is to be my marriage day, and if a dragon is presented to me, I must wed its owner. Ah, Road Wanderer, why have you not yet come?

(She exits in great agitation. The Property Man rises, rolls up the wall, and tucks it under his arm, exiting yawning).

SCENE THREE

STAGE MANAGER *(stepping forward).* Alas, kind listeners, our next scene is a dungeon.

(The Property Man re-enters with a bench which he places center stage).

Light can enter through the bars of that strong door . . .

(glaring at the Property Man who has sunk down on the bench) which all of you can see quite clearly.

(He claps his hands impatiently, and the Property Man stands, goes to stage left, sketches a door in pantomime, and takes hold of the imaginary bars and shakes them. He then opens the door, steps out, locks it carefully, and exits).

Who is the prisoner here? If you cannot guess it, wait with patience, for the dismal noise of chains will soon announce his coming.

(The clank of chains begins offstage. Road Wanderer enters, an imaginary ball-and-chain hindering his walking; the chains clank in accompaniment to his steps. He seats himself on the bench).

ROAD WANDERER. A prisoner! And in chains! Is this the order of the the Princess? Who wants my death? And where is my dragon, Small One?

(Footsteps sound offstage; Road Wanderer springs up and looks through the imaginary bars of the imaginary cell door).

Guard! Guard! Where is Small One?

GUARD *(offstage).* Small One?

ROAD WANDERER. My dragon. What have you done with him?

GUARD *(offstage).* The dragon? It is being fed and washed and polished. They tell me that tomorrow it is to be entered in the contest for the hand of the Princess, Jade Pure.

ROAD WANDERER. But — but that cannot be! The dragon is mine! I planned to enter it.

GUARD *(offstage).* Ah, but you will not be its owner long. The headman's knife will see to that!

ROAD WANDERER. Does the Princess Jade Pure know that I am here?

GUARD. That I cannot say. But my duties call me elsewhere. Farewell.

ROAD WANDERER. Wait! Will you carry a message to the Princess for me?

GUARD. What? Not I?

ROAD WANDERER. But she knows me. She will see to my release!

GUARD. I will carry no messages from one condemned by Lady Precious Harp. I value my own neck too highly. Your misfortune is not mine, poor fellow. Farewell!

ROAD WANDERER. Guard! He is gone, and in a few short hours they will behead me. But what of Jade Pure? She will wait for me, not knowing. I must find some way to tell her. I must send a message somehow. Why, of course . . . an animal can be my messenger! I who speak their language must find some tiny creature nearby who will serve me. True, the Princess cannot understand its speech, but still may guess that it has come from me.

(Striding about the cell, he examines walls and floor and ceiling). Friends . . . friends . . . hear me. It is I, Road Wanderer! Who will go fetch the Princess? . . . Not a sound. I hear no creature stirring. Have they too deserted me?

(whirling about) What was — ah! A mouse! A tiny mouse here in my cell.

(stopping to pick up an imaginary mouse) Come, small friend. We shall talk together, you and I; then out between the bars you go to take my message to the Princess!

(He walks off, stroking the mouse; the clanking of chains accompanies his exit. The Property Man enters to remove the bench).

SCENE FOUR

STAGE MANAGER *(stepping forward).* You will come away with me most gladly, I am certain, to a room more pleasant. Look about you — do you recognize once again the elegant apartment of the soon-to-be wedded Princess Jade Pure?

(He steps back. Jade Pure dashes in; she wears an elegant costume of cloth-of-gold. Twenty-First Cousin, running after her, rearranges her robe and headdress. The Princess continues to walk quickly to and fro, the maid following).

JADE. Look graciously upon me, august ancestors! For this must be my wedding day! What shall I find when I descend to the throne room? Many suitors with dragons, or none?

TWENTY-FIRST. There will be one . . . or two, I think.

JADE. Hurry, dear cousin . . . make haste! I cannot wait to know much longer!

FIRST. But if Her Highness would remain still just one moment, I could —

JADE. All is ready for the ceremony: The temple attendants await my coming. It will take but a few short moments. Make your fingers fly more swiftly! Where are your sisters who should help you?

FIRST. My sisters? A strange sickness has come over them most suddenly. Indeed, they are so changed that Your Highness would not recognize —

(catching sight of something on the floor) Eeeeee!

JADE. What is it?

(looking in the direction of Twenty-First Cousin's pointing finger)

Ohh! A mouse!

FIRST. A mouse! It runs toward you!

JADE *(in horror)*. No. no! A bench . . . a chair . . . oh, quickly! *(The Property Man shuffles in with a bench; both girls make a leap for it almost before he sets it down; he exits yawning).*

FIRST. It comes closer!

JADE. Hurry! Hurry!

(as they leap up) Ah . . . we have escaped!

(The mouse's squeaking sounds from offstage).

FIRST. But look! It will not leave!

(hands to her ears) That horrid squeaking!

JADE. Back and forth . . . and back and forth again it runs below us!

FIRST. Hateful creature!

JADE *(thoughtfully)*. Looking up, as if at me!

FIRST *(Striking out with her fan)*. Go! Run away! Be silent!

JADE. Listen, cousin! How it squeaks . . . as if it tries to tell us something.

FIRST. It can tell me nothing!

JADE. Look! It runs now to the door . . . now back to me . . .

FIRST.   And to the door once more. The thing is mad!

JADE.   Or else it tries to tell me to come also. But I wonder why —

(clapping her hands)   Road Wanderer! He has come back, and sends it as a joke! Perhaps he waits for me already in the throne room!

(leaping down)   Come!

FIRST *(as Jade Pure runs out).*   No, no! Do not leave me here; I dare not set foot down! Cursed day! This is an omen surely . . . a bad omen!

(The Property Man has shuffled in to remove the bench).

No! I will not leave this bench! I — no, no! Ohhhhhhh!

(As he stolidly takes hold of either end of the bench, tipping it forward slightly, she squeals, gathers up her skirts, and makes a dash for the door. The Property Man calmly removes the bench and brings in a gilded chair which he places center stage, exiting immediately after).

SCENE FIVE

STAGE MANAGER *(who has stepped forward).*   Our slothful servant is placing there the gilded chair in which the Princess Jade Pure sits in state. For this is now the exalted Royal Throne Room, and the ruler of this great kingdom approaches, in considerable haste.
(He steps back, as Jade Pure runs in, stops short).

JADE.   No one! But Road Wanderer must be here! He has sent the mouse — I know it!

(after a moment)   Oh — perhaps he hides, and waits for me to find him! I shall search each room!

(She runs off the opposite side of the stage. A roar or two is heard from offstage; Lady Precious Harp and Covet Spring back on, both tugging at ropes tied around the kidnapped dragon's neck. Small One emerges reluctantly; they leap back as he snaps at their ankles).

COVET SPRING *(in what he hopes is a soothing tone).*   Now then, take care! We are loving friends!

PRECIOUS HARP.   Ugly vicious brute! How dare it snap at me?

COVET.   It can be disposed of once Jade Pure is won. But its young master, this . . . Road Wanderer —
(at the mention of the name the dragon roars and lunges. They tug frantically at the ropes).

298

PRECIOUS *(after they have somewhat subdued Small One)*.   Fool! See that you do not name his name aloud again! The beast must know it. There is no young man, and never was.

COVET.   Oh, no!

PRECIOUS *(prompting him)*.   The dragon's master is, without a doubt—?

COVET.   Why, of course. I am its master.

PRECIOUS.   So!

(whispering)   The — person whom you spoke of I shall cause to lose his head just after the marriage ceremony.

COVET *(loud)*.   Good!

(then whispering)   But why not sooner? If he should escape, the head that falls will not be his!

PRECIOUS.   Escape? I do not think it possible. Still, it might be best to post a second line of guards.

(handing him her end of the rope)   Take care that Small One does not run away.

COVET *(as she exits)*.   You leave me with this — Precious Harp. I cannot —!

(gazing at the dragon)   O, unhappy fate! And I, afraid of house cats!

FIRST *(entering from the other side)*.   Through this arch, now. Guide the beast with care, brother!

(Twenty-Fourth Cousin enters unhappily, leading their dragon, which swishes about coquettishly).

FOURTH.   Yes, I come, I come.

(sighing deeply)   But with a heavy heart, and still no liking for this —

FIRST.   Hush!

(indicating Covet Spring whose hands are full keeping his dragon under control)   Old Covet Spring is here!

(with a titter behind her fan, indicating Small One, who looks to be asleep)   And there is Precious Harp!

(This dragon prances near to get a better look, then darts back, giggling in a most un-dragonlike manner. Twenty-Fourth Cousin

does not laugh, but stares fixedly at the dragon entered by the opposition).

FOURTH *(suddenly).* But that is —

FIRST *(tapping their dragon smartly with her fan).* Sisters, you forget yourselves! A dragon must not laugh.

SECOND. But Precious Harp —

THIRD. In that!

(All three girls giggle; Twenty-First Cousin quickly becomes business-like again).

FIRST. Enough! Forget that you are girls now. If you must speak, roar!

SECOND and THIRD. Yes, sister.

(They roar obediently. Small One lifts his head and looks at them. Covet Spring starts, gazing in mingled scorn and alarm at the rival dragon, takes a firmer hold on Small One's leash, and turns his back haughtily on the others).

FIRST *(jovially).* You are solemn, brother. Is it that you do not find her laughable, the haughty Precious Harp, inside a dragon's costume?

FOURTH. That dragon — I have seen it once before!

FIRST. Of course.

FOURTH. No, not then in the field, but at my farm.

(going closer to the dragon, then to her again) Yes! That is Small One!

FIRST *(dreamily).* Much smaller than our dragon, I agree! And not one-tenth so handsome or so real!

FOURTH *(following, pulling her sleeve).* You do not understand!

(The Cousin's dragon has edged playfully closer and closer to Small One, who watches warily; Covet Spring also watches nervously, the cord in his hand twitching violently; suddenly the Cousin's dragon makes a rush at Small One, roaring, then skips away; Small One crouches, roars in reply).

FIRST *(surprised).* Why, what a splendid roar she has! I should not have thought —

FOURTH *(in desperation).* That is not Precious Harp, I tell you, but Small One! A dragon! A live dragon!

FIRST. Nonsense!

(Growing still bolder, the Cousin's dragon darts up, stamps on Small One's toes, puffs derisively in his face, and leaps away. But Small One, angered, gives chase, pulling the frightened Covet Spring along after him. Twenty-Fourth groans, covers his eyes with his hand. Only the Cousins inside the dragon, and Twenty-First Cousin fail to take the case seriously).

COVET. Oh — oh — oh! Stop! Stop! I beg you!

FIRST *(laughing)*. Lady Precious Harp, who scrambles on the floor — my eyes stream tears of laughter!

FOURTH *(going to her again.)* No, not Precious Harp! That is not Precious Harp inside!

FIRST. But I have seen her! Seeing is believing, foolish one!

FOURTH *(suddenly pointing to the far door)*. Then look!

(Lady Precious Harp stands there, gazing at the scene in consternation).

FIRST *(aghast)*. Precious Harp!

PRECIOUS. Covet Spring! Take care! Our dragon — bring him here!

SECOND and THIRD *(stopping short)*. Lady Precious Harp?

FIRST. It is a dragon! A live dragon!

(With screams of fright, the Cousin's dragon begins to run in earnest, unfortunately, they dash in opposite directions so determinedly that the dragon costume divides. The two sections run wildly about, then discover that they are separated, and try to fit themselves together, Twenty-First Cousin assisting. Lady Precious Harp goes to the aid of Covet Spring, and helps him to pull Small One back to a neutral corner. In the excitement no one immediately notices Jade Pure who enters quietly, looking worried; what she sees both astonishes and amuses her, but she does not yet become aware of Small One).

SECOND. Save me!

THIRD. Save yourself! I cannot!

PRECIOUS *(to Covet Spring)*. Hold him back!

COVET. Do I not struggle?

FOURTH. We are doomed! Alas!

FIRST *(chasing first one half, then the other)*. Sisters! Sister, come back!

PRECIOUS.   What? Does their dragon divide itself?

COVET.   Why, it is not a dragon after all!

PRECIOUS.   Ho! Treason!

FOURTH.   O woe!

SECOND.   Look! The Princess!

PRECIOUS and COVET (*bowing*).   The Princess . . .

ALL COUSINS (*bowing even lower*).   The Princess . . .

> (*There is silence as Jade Pure crosses slowly to the gilded chair and sits down; all hold their bent-over poses, motionless*).

JADE.   I thank you for your salutations. Do not stand on ceremony, but look up now.

PRECIOUS (*stepping forward*).   Your Radiant Highness, I would bring a charge against —

COVET (*breaking in excitedly*).   There stand the traitors!

FIRST (*falling to her knees*).   Mercy! Spare us, O Most-Gracious Sovereign!

SECOND and THIRD (*also kneeling awkwardly*).   Mercy! Mercy!

JADE (*smothering a smile*).   What are those creatures?

PRECIOUS.   A bogus dragon, brought to trick Your Highness.

COVET.   Inside are the wretch's sisters!

PRECIOUS.   I demand that they be put in dungeons, charged with treason.

COVET.   Yes, and that false prince who is their brother.

FOURTH (*removing his headdress and robe*).   Then if I must die, I die the simple farmer that I am.

JADE.   Why, now I know you! You are his friend — the friend of my Road Wanderer!

> (*The dragon, with a happy roar, pulls away from his captors and rushes to her, resting its head on her knee*).

And — yes, it is Small One, his dragon!

> (*stroking the dragon's head*)   I had feared that we should never meet again!

PRECIOUS.   The dragon pleases you?

302

JADE *(delighted).* He does! Indeed he does! I have decided, this is my choice, and I shall wed his master. Bring him now before me.

COVET *(stepping forward).* I am he, Your Highness, the fortunate owner of this worthy beast.

JADE. You? Oh, no!

FOURTH. Indeed, no!

JADE. You are not he, for I know him well!

COVET *(turning to Precious Harp, in confusion).* Your Ladyship —

PRECIOUS *(smoothly).* Ah, but Your Highness, Covet Spring is surely the present owner. That young man you speak of willingly parted with the dragon for a sum of gold, saying that he had no wish to marry.

JADE. He sold Small One?

COVET *(picking up his cue).* Er — yes, to me! Then since this dragon is your choice, I shall become your husband.

PRECIOUS. Exactly! You have pledged your royal word.

JADE. But — Covet Spring!

(low, sinking back) It is not he I love!

COVET. Your word is law. I go at once to prepare for the happy ceremony.

JADE. No! No, I will not marry him! That hateful sly old man!

PRECIOUS *(triumphantly).* You have made your choice, niece.

(To Covet) Let us see to that beheading now.

COVET. I agree, I agree. Delay may still prove dangerous. Your Highness, we beg leave to withdraw.

(Jade gestures permission).

We leave you to judge these unworthy traitors.

(They exit).

COUSINS *(timidly).* Your Highness ...

JADE. Go. Later I shall judge you. Please go and leave me.

FIRST *(scrambling to her feet and backing out, bowing).* Yes, great and glorious Princess.

SECOND *(following suit).* We thank you.

THIRD (*following suit*).   We most gratefully thank you.

(*Twenty-Fourth Cousin remains, fidgeting nervously, gathering courage to speak.*

JADE.   So, Small One, he has left you too! And now, deserted, I must marry Covet Spring.

FOURTH.   Ahem!

JADE.   Still here? Why have you waited?

FOURTH.   Why to tell you —

JADE.   Speak!

FOURTH.   That I do not believe it!

JADE.   What?

FOURTH.   I still do not believe that Small One's master sold him to these villians! Nor do I believe he willingly has stayed away.

JADE.   But then, where is he?

FOURTH.   Something is afoot, I fear. If Small One there could talk, we should know what it is.

JADE.   Oh, Small One, try to tell us! Where is he? Where is Road Wanderer?

(*The dragon roars, dashes toward the door, then returns, pointing off with a paw, pulling Jade by the skirt*).

FOURTH.   He knows the name!

JADE.   He means that we should follow!

(*To Twenty-Fourth Cousin*)   Come with me! Now, lead us, Small One, to Road Wanderer!

(*They exit, following Small One. The Property Man enters, removes the gilded chair, then brings on a small wooden block which he puts downstage, left, exiting*).

SCENE SIX

STAGE MANAGER (*who has stepped forward*).   And none too soon they go forward to find Road Wanderer, for in a lonely field not far from the palace, a dreadful deed will soon be done, unless The Princess comes in time. For is that not a headman's block? And is that not Road Wanderer who comes to kneel before it? Ah, alas!

304

(He steps back, as Precious Harp and Covet Spring enter stealthily, in haste).

PRECIOUS HARP.   There is no time to spare. This spot will do as well as any.

COVET SPRING.   Yes, My mind will not rest while he is alive. Jade Pure might learn of it.

PRECIOUS *(calling offstage).*   Ho, guards! Send forth the prisoner.

VOICE *(offstage).*   Prisoner, go forward.

ROAD WANDERER *(entering).*   Are you the Lady Precious Harp who has imprisoned me?

PRECIOUS.   That is my name.

ROAD WANDERER.   Of what crime am I guilty? Can you tell me that?

COVET.   She cannot!

(confused) Er, that is —

PRECIOUS *(smoothly).*   It is enough that I condemn you. Go to kneel before that block.

COVET.   Yes, go!

ROAD WANDERER.   Does Jade Pure know of this? Does she too wish my death?

PRECIOUS *(quickly).*   She knows of it, certainly, and she approves.

COVET *(prompted by a poke).*   Why, yes . . . approves most heartily!

ROAD WANDERER *(bitterly).*   She knows! Then her ingratitude is now complete. I go to kneel before the headman's block with bitter pleasure!

(He goes to the block, kneels before it, facing the audience, and places his head on it).

COVET.   Good!

PRECIOUS *(stretching out her hand imperiously).*   Bring me the great beheading sword.

(The Property Man shuffles in with a large curved sword; she takes it, seemingly unaware of his presence; he exits).

COVET.   What a fine broad blade! Is it quite sharp?

PRECIOUS.   We soon shall see. First, I pluck a hair from your gray beard —

(plucking an imaginary hair) — so!

COVET *(clutching at his beard).* Ouch! Ouch!

PRECIOUS. And next, test the edge against it.

(She holds up the hair, brings the blade against it).

Ah! I have dropped the hair. Another one will do as well.

COVET *(as she plucks another).* Ouch! Ouch!

ROAD WANDERER. Why do you mock my misery with these delays?
Dispatch me quickly.

PRECIOUS. He is right. We must make haste.

COVET *(rubbing his chin).* Then give the sword to me.

PRECIOUS. To you? What do you want with it?

COVET *(taking it from her).* I myself shall deliver the fatal blow.

PRECIOUS *(taking it back).* Ah, no! That privilege is mine.

COVET *(snatching it away).* You are a woman!

PRECIOUS *(snatching it back).* But my right arm has more strength
than yours!

COVET *(struggling for possession of it).* That is not so!

ROAD WANDERER. The death blow! Come!

COVET *(as she wrests it away).* Well then, I give it up to you.

(slyly as she takes a few practice swings) What a pity! That is
such a lovely robe!

PRECIOUS *(stopping abruptly).* My robe? Why do you speak of it?

COVET *(shrugging).* His blood will stain it, doubtless. But no matter.
(moving away) I shall stand here and watch.

PRECIOUS. My silken gown stained with his . . . no!
(going after him) Covet Spring, I yield the right to you.

COVET *(refusing the sword).* I should not dream of so depriving you!
No, no . . .

PRECIOUS *(shaking her head vigorously).* No. You may strike.
(with a wave of her hand) His neck awaits you!

PRECIOUS. Covet Spring, I must insist that you perform the deed!

ROAD WANDERER *(raising his head and looking at them).* Good Covet
Spring, I beg you, end my heart-ache!

Covet *(smugly).* Then, since you both insist, I shall make ready.

(He tucks his robe up higher under his sash, pulls his headdress down more firmly about his ears, painstakingly rolls his sleeves to his elbows. Precious Harp taps her feet impatiently; Road Wanderer sits back on his heels and views the proceedings gloomily).

Precious *(impatiently).* Do you intend to strike or not? Someone may come.

Road Wanderer. Have mercy, and act swiftly!

Precious. Or I may yet forget my gown!

Covet. I am ready now. Give me the sword.

(He stands by Road Wanderer, who obligingly places his head on the block again, rests the blade lightly on his neck, then raises it for a mighty swing).

Road Wanderer. Good-bye, false Princess!

Covet. Now!

Precious *(catching his arm as it descends).* Stop! You are holding the blade upside-down! The sharp edge faces the sky!

Covet. So it does, so it does!

(changing its position to the correct one and swinging it aloft)

This time I shall not fail!

Road Wanderer. Let nothing stop you.

Covet. Nothing! Prepare to meet your doom!

(Jade Pure, Twenty-Fourth Cousin, and Small One run in left, in that order).

Jade *(horrified).* No. no!

Twenty-Fourth. Stop!

Jade. Put down that sword!

Precious. Strike quickly!

Covet *(dropping his sword as Small One makes a rush at him).* Save me, save me!

(The dragon, roaring fiercely, backs Precious Harp and Covet Spring off into a corner; Jade Pure and Twenty-Fourth Cousin go to Road Wanderer, remove the imaginary bonds that secure his hands behind his back, help him to rise).

ROAD WANDERER. Jade Pure!

FOURTH. My friend!

JADE *(tenderly)*. My poor Road Wanderer.

PRECIOUS. Guards! Guards!

FOURTH. They all ran off when the dragon approached.

COVET *(his teeth chattering)*. M-miserable cowards!

JADE. What a near escape from death!

ROAD WANDERER. Then you did not order my beheading?

JADE. I? Never! It was all her doing!

COVET. We are lost!

JADE *(severely)*. You are lost indeed! Your plot has failed. Road Wanderer, the true owner of this dragon, shall become my husband and be the Emperor.

(The first of a series of slow chimes sounds from offstage).

PRECIOUS. Listen! The great clock in the square is striking noon! At the twentieth stroke you will reach your eighteenth year, and I shall claim the throne.

(jubilantly) We have won, Covet Spring, we have won!

COVET. At last!

PRECIOUS *(to him)*. Come to the square with me! Let us stand beneath the clock and at its final stroke you shall proclaim me Empress!

(They hurry out left).

FOURTH. Alas! Three . . . four . . .

JADE *(despairingly)*. What can we do now? Five . . . six . . . I am not yet married!

ROAD WANDERER. There may be a way!

(He faces offstage and gives two shrill whistles, fingers between his teeth).

FOURTH. What now? Have his senses left him?

JADE *(wringing her hands)*. Listen! Eight . . . nine . . .

FOURTH. But the strokes are slower!

(Road Wanderer gives several short whistles).

JADE and FOURTH.   Ten . . . . . eleven . . . . .

JADE.   But the twelfth — it does not strike!

FOURTH.   What can have happened. I shall run to see!

> *(He runs off left).*

JADE.   Road Wanderer, have you done this?

ROAD WANDERER.   Not I, but the dragon-flies which come at my call. They are clinging by the thousands to the hammer of the great clock so that it may not strike twelve!

JADE *(clapping her hands).*   Oh, wonderful! Then you have saved the kingdom!

ROAD WANDERER.   But you are not wed! Where is a temple and a holy man to marry us?

JADE.   All is ready.

ROAD WANDERER.   Let us run swiftly!

FOURTH *(reentering).*   O sorry day!

> *(as he looks at them)*   Where are you going?

JADE.   To be married so that I may claim the throne.

FOURTH.   Too late! Precious Harp and Covet Spring are coming with my sisters! They are riding horses, and will overtake you!

JADE *(anxiously).*   Road Wanderer —

ROAD WANDERER.   Riding horses, are they? But all animals obey me! Shall I teach you what to say to stop their horses?

FOURTH.   Well . . .

JADE.   Oh, yes!

ROAD WANDERER.   Then listen; meh-neh cho-po tee-ka.

FOURTH.   Many choppy — what?

ROAD WANDERER.   No, no! Listen, man, once more; meh-neh cho-po tee-ka.

FOURTH.   I do not know . . .

ROAD WANDERER.   They will run in a circle till I bid the dragonflies to let the clock strike twelve.

JADE *(looking offstage).*   Road Wanderer! I see them! We must hurry to the temple!

FOURTH. But the words . . . If I cannot remember . . .

ROAD WANDERER. You must remember. Meh-neh cho-po tee-ka!

FOURTH. Meh-neh cho-po tee-ka. Of course! I have it now!

(horses' hoofbeats sound faintly offstage left).

Hoofbeats! They are coming! But the horses cannot hear me from this distance. I shall wait. Meh-eh po-co . . . these are not the right words! What are they? Ma-ny tea-cups . . . I forget! I do not know them!

(hoofbeats louder)

They are nearer! I must try!

(running to look offstage left and shouting) Chop-sticks! Ma-ny chop-stocks!

(running back) But they do not stop!

(from center stage, shouting above the hoofbeats) Teacups! Choppy teacups! Many choppy teacups! and still they come!

(thumping his forehead) The words, the words!

(Precious Harp, Covet Spring, and the three Cousins gallop in on imaginary horses. Twenty-Fourth Cousin makes a last desperate effort, almost backed offstage right)

Meh-neh cho-po tee-ka! Meh-neh cho-po tee-ka!

(The "horses" rear and begin galloping in a circle, their riders hanging on frantically, slapping the reins, and attempting to stop them).

PRECIOUS *(to her "horse")*. No, no! That way!

COVET. What affects the horses?

FIRST. Mine must be bewitched!

SECOND. Mine will not turn!

THIRD. Mine runs away! Oh, oh!

FOURTH *(jubilantly)*. I have remembered! And the horses heard me! See them trotting in a circle!

(beginning to chuckle) See my sisters . . .

(laughing harder as he watches) . . . Lady Precious Harp . . . and Covet Spring! Go faster, horses, horses, faster!

(repeating rapidly) Meh-neh cho-po tee-ka!

PRECIOUS *(jolted)*. He — gallops — faster!

COVET. But — I cannot — stay astride —

FIRST. Brother — what have — you said to them?

SECOND. Have mercy, brother!

THIRD. Make them — stop, I beg — of you!

FOURTH. I cannot, for I do not know the words!

> *(laughing)* Oh, what a most delightful sight! My haughty sisters . . . wicked Lady Precious Harp . . .

COVET. You must ride until the twelfth stroke sounds. And then . . . *(scratching his head)* I cannot say!

PRECIOUS *(hope stirring)*. The — twelfth stroke?

> *(Two shrill whistles sound from offstage; there is a pause, then the clock strikes once).*

FOURTH *(anxiously)*. It is noon!

PRECIOUS *(suddenly)*. My horse . . . he throws me off!

COVET. And mine!

FIRST. And mine!

> *(with wails of despair each "rider" is bucked off in turn, around the circle; they sprawl in grotesque positions).*

PRECIOUS *(dazed but determined)*. But it is noon; then I must be the Empress!

> *(Bells peal joyfully from offstage).*

FOURTH *(who has run to look offstage, jubilantly.)*. Not so! Listen to the joyful bells! Listen, and bow down to the Emperor and Empress, newly crowned, of the mighty Southern Kingdom!

> *(Stately Chinese music is played as background from here to the end. To its strains Jade Pure and Road Wanderer reenter; he is now dressed in a gorgeous robe slipped over his original costume; both wear elaborate crowns. Small One follows on his hind legs, strutting importantly; he wears a small crown cocked rakishly over one eye. The five conspirators scramble to their feet, the three Cousins to the royal couple's right, Precious Harp and Covet Spring to their left; Twenty-Fourth Cousin stands with the last-named pair. Twenty-First and Twenty-Third, Precious Harp and Twenty-Fourth bow simultaneously; then Twenty-Second and Covet Spring. The alternate bowing continues to the end).*

311

JADE.   I, Empress Jade Pure, salute my worthy —

(then with a frown at the conspirators nearest her; who clasp their hands over their heads in supplication)

and my unworthy subjects!

ALL.   Long live our glorious Empress Jade Pure!

ROAD WANDERER.   I, Emperor Road Wanderer, salute my royal —
(with a frown at the conspirators nearest him, who also clasp their hands over their heads)

and my soon-to-be-imprisoned subjects!

ALL.   Long live our matchless Emperor Road Wanderer!

(All turn simultaneously to face the audience; there is a peal of bells. The Stage Manager and the Property Man take their places between Jade Pure and Road Wanderer).

STAGE MANAGER.   These, the illustrious actors of our play, and this modest helper salute each most polite and generous spectator!

ALL *(except the Property Man, who appears to be asleep).*   Long live this gracious and exalted Audience! The End!

(The curtain falls slowly as the music plays, the bells ring out again, and those on stage bob merrily up and down. If several curtain calls are taken, the Property Man may slump lower with each, until at last, he is seated cross-legged on the floor, snoring).

FINIS

REYNARD THE FOX

Adapted from *Gestes de Renart le Goupil*

By

ARTHUR FAUQUEZ

Translation by Marie-Louise Roelants

*With Costume-Make-Up Designs by
IRENE COREY

*Introduction by
MOUZON LAW

*Included in the separate play-book only.

REYNARD THE FOX

By

ARTHUR FAUQUEZ

translated by Marie-Louise Roelants

REYNARD THE FOX

After mid-century the children's theatre field slowly began to respond to the needs and interests of an increasingly sophisticated audience. The Chorpenning-style fairy tale dramas still comprised the bulk of the repertoire, but the maturation of a new generation of playwrights, and a renewed interest in professional children's theatre production combined to stimulate further development in the literature.

Change was not immediate, but slowly — very slowly — new types of plays were introduced into the repertoire. Plays written by foreign writers were an important source of the new literature. Because British writers (from the authors of Pantomimes to Barrie, Milne, Cullen, and Broadhurst) have always been well-represented among plays produced in this country — primarily because their plays tend to be similar to American plays of corresponding periods — the search was expanded beyond English-speaking countries. Producers and publishing houses have discovered many important plays from abroad, but by far the most important of the plays imported at that time was *Reynard the Fox*, by Arthur Fauquez. Although this was not the first play originally written in a foreign language to become popular in American children's theatre — recall, for example, Maeterlinck's *The Blue Bird* — the publication of this play is considered by many authorities to mark a significant turning point in the development of dramatic literature for children in this country.

Reynard the Fox is, ostensibly, an anecdotal story of a group of animals in a forest — which suggests that the work is no more innovative than the popular fairy tale dramatizations that abound in the literature. In this play, however, Fauquez uses a well-conceived view of the animal world to create a sophisticated satire on human greed and hypocrisy — a satire that is still one of the best of its kind in the modern repertoire. The play offers an interesting story, unique characters, an unpredictable plot structure, and a delightfully provocative look at human foibles and weaknesses.

The major character in this animal world is the cunning, mischievous, yet loveable, Reynard, whose unscrupulous pranks have the animal kingdom in a constant uproar. Reynard's sometimes vicious trickery, which causes successive conflicts between himself and the other characters of the forest society, defines the basic through-line of the play; but the ramifications of this action, made very real through the detailed characterizations, extend far beyond the resolution of these conflicts.

In the story, Reynard repeatedly harasses the other animals until, totally exasperated, they band together to plot his downfall. When Reynard is finally caught in the act of one of his pranks, Noble the

Lion, king of the forest, decrees that if Reynard commits more than 24 pranks during the next year he will be hanged. There then occur a series of episodes where Reynard, seemingly oblivious to his own fate, tricks first one character and then another by appealing to their own less-than-upright behavior. The animals become increasingly frustrated with Reynard, and they eagerly await the punishment he earns by committing prank number 25. But Reynard has a different idea. By resorting to his unscrupulous ways, he tricks his way out of even this seemingly hopeless situation.

The characters in the play are as cleverly drawn as any found in dramatic literature for children. The fact that they are depicted as animals suggests a superficial approach, but Fauquez effectively embodies each animal type while at the same time creating analogs to the human world. Their very human behavior reveals a whole chorus of human frailties: there is Brun, the greedy Bear, who is easily compromised by the promise of fresh honey; there is Noble the Lion, whose vanity makes him an easy target for Reynard's manipulation; and there is Tiecelin the Crow, whose shrill impudence raises the ire of all the other animals in the forest.

Fauquez uses these characters to create a world without clear-cut heroes and villains. Each character is revealed, in turn, to have both moral strengths and moral weaknesses, and it is particularly revealing that in most instances the inclination of each character is toward selfish or anti-social behavior when it serves his or her own needs. This world is made even more complex by the fact that although Reynard is nominally the protagonist in the play (the story centers around his actions), he is also the antagonist in the action. It is his practical jokes that keep the world of the play in constant turmoil. In addition, although Reynard is the object of derision by the other animals, this is often motivated by jealousy of Reynard's cunning wit. He repeatedly tricks the other animals; but these tricks succeed in part because of the foolishness of the victims.

In a more typical play for children, the audience is given one, and sometimes two, completely good protagonists with whom to identify. *Reynard the Fox* does not offer this clear moral choice. Audience sympathies are initially extended to the victimized animals, but as these characters reveal themselves as less than admirable, these sympathies wander from character to character, only to return to Reynard in the end. Reynard is a true rogue hero who operates on the fringes of accepted moral standards, but his sense of exuberance, his cleverness, and his insights into human behavior transcend his lack of scruples. When the other animals fail to capture Reynard in the end, the audience is happy to cheer his escape, but reticent to argue in his defense.

When this play was first introduced, the concept of the rogue hero

316

was not new to dramatic literature for children. Such characters as Huck Finn, Zar and Zan, and Tyl Eulenspiegel had cleared the way for this clever rascal, Reynard. But the sheer harshness of Reynard's pranks separates this character from the others. Reynard is sometimes cynical, sometimes untruthful, and sometimes mean, but he is always very lifelike. And unlike the rogue characters who preceded him there is little justification presented in the play for his behavior. It is not an idealized world, but it is a very real world.

At one point in the play Tiecelin the Crow comments on a plan to gain revenge against Reynard by noting: "As far as being fair, certainly not. Honest — even less so. But as for being smart — ha ha!" With this statement Fauquez is not suggesting that "smart" behavior should be favored over "honest" behavior. He is, instead, leaving such provocative questions to the audience. There is little or no moralizing in this work; instead, the moral questions that are raised in the play are left for the audience to answer.

These thematic elements are supported by a plot structure that deviates markedly from the well-made play form. Fauquez opens the play with a clear statement of impending action, but rather than build the action suspensefully from complication to complication, Fauquez focuses more on the individual episodes, with each standing as a microcosm of the play as a whole. And in the end, just as the "good" and the "bad" are confused in the play as a whole, so too is the traditional punishment of the defeated villain left unresolved. The audience is left to decide who wins, and if that victory is, by any standards, just.

Perhaps the most important influence that this play has had on the American repertoire is that it is a play of ideas. There are very few plays written before this time that offer anything more than heavily moralistic stories wherein "right" is clearly defined, and wherein "right" proudly prevails. Such an idealized picture of the world is the only picture that was, for many years, considered appropriate for child audiences. This play was thus somewhat shocking to the children's theatre practitioners in this country who were schooled in the techniques of the moralistic, action-oriented, fairy tale dramas. But these same people were slowly convinced by plays such as this that American children could be captivated and challenged by a play that offers none of these characteristics.

Reynard the Fox is a skillful dramatization of a clever story. Although this play alone could not turn the attention of the American children's theatre away from the formula versions of the tired tales, it pointed the field in a new direction, a direction that greatly expanded the themes, styles, and techniques of dramatic literature for children.

ARTHUR FAUQUEZ was born in Antwerp, Belgium, in 1912. Before his retirement he worked for many years as a businessman in Brussels. Fauquez currently resides in France with his wife, Elizabeth.

Fauquez, working closely with his wife, has written over seventy plays. These include twenty-five children's plays, two plays for adults, thirty-four puppet plays, two radio serials, and nine short television plays.

Three of Fauquez's plays have been translated and published in the United States: *Reynard the Fox, Don Quixote of La Mancha* and *The Man Who Killed Time.*

REYNARD THE FOX

By

ARTHUR FAUQUEZ

Translation by Marie-Louise Roelants

CHARACTERS

TIECELIN, *the Crow*

REVEREND EPINARD, *the Hedgehog*

BRUN, *the Bear*

NOBLE, *the Lion*

YSENGRIN, *the Wolf*

REYNARD, *the Fox*

LENDORE, *the Marmot*

SYNOPSIS

The entire play takes place in the heart of the forest.

Prologue

Epilogue

319

REYNARD THE FOX

By

Arthur Fauquez

PROLOGUE

(Tiecelin, perched in the crotch of a tree, practicing.)

TIECELIN: Caw! *(Higher)* Caw! *(Higher)* Caw!

(Brun enters, patch over one eye, his arm in a sling.)

BRUN: Stop that infernal racket!

TIECELIN: Caw! *(Higher)* Caw!

BRUN: Stop!

TIECELIN: You are interrupting my practice, Seigneur Brun. Caw!

BRUN: Stop this instant, and summon the King!

TIECELIN: *(notices him.)* The King? Good heavens, what has happened to you? Have you been caught in a bramble bush? Ha, ha, ha!

BRUN: Enough of your insolence! Call the King at once!

TIECELIN: Lord Bear, I am the King's Registrar. If you wish an audience with the King, you must state your reason to me.

BRUN: I have been beaten, do you hear? Look at me!

TIECELIN: Ha, ha, ha!

BRUN: I have been beaten, and it is all the fault of Reynard the Fox!

TIECELIN: Reynard did this to the mighty Bear?

BRUN: He tricked me. I want the King to punish him.

TIECELIN: Oh, if it was only one of Reynard's tricks —

BRUN: But look at me!

TIECELIN: I am. Ha, ha, ha!

(Ysengrin limps in, on a crutch, his head bandaged.)

YSENGRIN: Sound the trumpets!

TIECELIN: Baron Ysengrin!

BRUN: You, too?

320

TIECELIN: What a pair! Ha, ha, ha!

YSENGRIN: One more caw from you, Crow, and I'll wring your
scrawny neck. Summon the King!

TIECELEIN: The king is not to be called just because you stubbed your
toe.

YSENGRIN: Stubbed my toe? I have been attacked by dogs. Look at
me!

TIECELIN: Yes, I see. Ha, ha, ha!

BRUN: Who has done this to you?

YSENGRIN: It is all the doing of Reynard the Fox!

BRUN: Gr-r-r-r!

TIECELIN: Reynard did this to the powerful Wolf?

YSENGRIN: He tricked me.

BRUN: Me, too.

BOTH: Summon the King!

TIECELIN: *(climbs down.)*   Gentlemen, if I were to summon the King
every time Reynard played a trick, he would soon appoint a new
Registrar.

YSENGRIN: But this is not to be borne!

BRUN: I intend to accuse Reynard in court.

YSENGRIN: Yes. We'll bring him to trial.

BRUN: And we shall demand his punishment.

YSENGRIN: I shall demand his hanging.

TIECELIN: Hanging?

BRUN: Yes! We have had enough of his tricks.

YSENGRIN: We are going to get rid of the Fox!

TIECELIN: If you have been unable to get rid of him in the field,
how do you expect to get rid of him in Court?

BRUN: The King will do us justice.

YSENGRIN: Bring us to the King!

TIECELIN: Gentlemen, I am a man of law, and I will give you my
best legal advice. Go home and lick your wounds. Reynard will

321

trick you in Court, just as he has tricked you in the field. You have no evidence.

BRUN: Evidence? What of my black eye? And my arm?

YSENGRIN: Look at my lame leg. And my head!

TIECELIN: Yes, ha, ha, ha! What a picture! Now you will excuse me. I must return to my practicing.

(He climbs up.)

BRUN: You miserable Crow! The King shall hear of your insolence!

YSENGRIN: If you had a little more meat on your bones, I should have a nice fat crow's wing for my supper!

TIECELIN: Caw!

BRUN: Save us from that deafening noise!

(Exit, holding his ears.)

TIECELIN: Caw!

YSENGRIN: Take care, Crow, that the Fox does not trick you.

(Exit, limping. Reynard enters, unseen by Tiecelin.)

TIECELIN: Ho, ho, ho! The Fox trick me? What a joke! I am too smart for that. Caw! Caw! Caw!

REYNARD: *(groaning with pain)* Oh-h-h-h-h!

TIECELIN: Can I never practice in peace? Caw-w-w-w — Good Heavens, it is the Fox himself!

REYNARD: *(weakly)* Tiecelin, my friend — Oh-h-h-h!

TIECELIN: What is your tale of woe? Do you wish to summon the King too?

REYNARD: No. I wish only to die in peace.

TIECELIN: To die?

REYNARD: Tiecelin, I have been poisoned.

TIECELIN: Poisoned?

REYNARD: Oh-h-h-h! It was an oyster I found. Sing me one of your sweetest songs, so that I may die with your music in my ears.

TIECELIN: You are not serious?

REYNARD: Sing, my good fellow.

TIECELIN: Like this? Caw-w-w-w-!

REYNARD: Thanks, old friend.

(He gasps, then falls quiet.)

TIECELIN: Reynard? Reynard! Don't act the sleeping beauty. I know you. You are only faking. Oh, very well. I will rouse you. Caw! Caw! Caw! Not a wince. Not a quiver. He is very smart. Reynard? Is he really faking?

(He climbs down to look.)

My word, he sleeps like the dead. I can't even see him breathe. Good Heavens, he isn't breathing! Could he really be dead! What a release, Lord, if this is so!

(He moves Reynard's tail, which drops back, limp.)

But how could he be dead? This is too much to hope. He said an oyster. It is possible.

(He pokes the Fox with a long stick. Reynard rolls over, a dead weight.)

It's true! Brun! Ysengrin! No, I am the one who found him. It will win me the gratitude of the whole kingdom if I hint that I am a tiny bit responsible for this — oh, just a very tiny bit — just enough to make them think I am the one who liberated the world from this rascal. I should be hailed as a hero. I shall have my portrait painted in triumphant attire, crushing my vanquished enemy, and I shall sell his skin for a fur.

(He rests his foot upon Reynard, in a conqueror's pose.)

REYNARD: *(grasping his ankle)* Dear Tiecelin!

TIECELIN: Help! Help! He is not dead!

REYNARD: You had better learn, dear friend, never to sell Reynard's skin before you have killed him.

TIECELIN: What I said about it was only in fun. I — I only wanted to give you a laugh.

REYNARD: Well, you see, you succeeded. I am laughing. I am laughing with all my teeth, which in a few moments are going to gobble you up.

TIECELIN: You are not going to kill me like a simple chicken?

REYNARD: Why not?

TIECELIN: I am the Royal Registrar. And besides I am your friend.

REYNARD: Yes?

TIECELIN: Only a minute ago, I saved you from a Court trial.

REYNARD: I am very grateful, believe me. And because of that I'll swallow you in one gulp, without chewing.

TIECELIN: Let me go!

REYNARD: (plucking a feather from Tiecelin's tail) And moreover, I'll keep this to remember you by.

TIECELIN: Aie! You have ruined my beautiful tail!

REYNARD: Never mind, Tiecelin. You will not be needing it any more.

TIECELIN: Oh-h-h, you monster! I am going to be eaten, and I can see no escape.

REYNARD: None whatever.

TIECELIN: Then at least grant my last wish. If I have to be eaten, don't just gobble me down like a piece of cheese. Treat me as a delicacy, and prepare your stomach for this feast.

REYNARD: My stomach is always prepared.

TIECELIN: Oh, no. To enjoy a dainty morsel fully, it is necessary to warm your stomach and your head — like this.

(He rubs his stomach and his head.)

REYNARD: Why your head?

TIECELIN: To eat intelligently.

REYNARD: And why your stomach?

TIECELIN: To warm your appetite.

REYNARD: It is an odd method.

TIECELIN: But it works, I assure you.

REYNARD: Like this?

(He lets go of Tiecelin, to rub head and stomach.)

TIECELIN: Oh, harder than that.

REYNARD: It certainly does warm me up.

TIECELIN: (clambering up to his perch) The best way to digest well is to eat nothing.

REYNARD: Why, Tiecelin!

324

TIECELIN: You savage! Did you think I was going to let you eat me for lunch?

REYNARD: Eat you for lunch? I would have to be starving.

TIECELIN: I am going to denounce you to the King.

REYNARD: *(laughing)* Oh, Tiecelin, you take yourself so seriously.

TIECELIN: The King also will take me seriously. Trumpets!
   (Trumpets.)

REYNARD: Caw! Caw! Caw! *(Mimicking)* Oh, Tiecelin, sing me one last song before I die.

   (Exit, laughing. Returns immediately.)

   By the way, keep this to remember me by.

   (Tosses feather. Exit.)

TIECELIN: My feather! Monster! Thief! Cannibal!

   (He climbs down to retrieve the feather.)

   My beautiful feather! But this is evidence. Now we have him! Brun! Ysengrin! Bring the fox to trial! I have the evidence! Trumpets!

   (Trumpets. Epinard enters quietly.)

EPINARD: My dear fellow, what are the trumpets all about?

TIECELIN: Reverend Epinard. Stand there. I am about to make a proclamation. Trumpets!

   (Trumpets.)

   We, Tiecelin, the Crow, Royal Registrar, announce a great Court of Justice meeting, to put on trial the most infamous of all criminals, His Majesty's Own Knight —

   (Drum roll.) Reynard the Fox!

EPINARD: Reynard, on trial? But will you explain —

TIECELIN: One moment. Whoever wishes to accuse the Fox is requested to give his name to the Registrar. I am the Registrar. Trumpets!

   (Trumpets.)

EPINARD: What is this all about?

TIECELIN: It means, Reverend, that we are at last going to put Reynard on trial, and punish him for his misdeeds. Don't you yourself have some complaint to make against the Fox?

EPINARD: I?

TIECELIN: Yes, you. Has your religious robe protected you from his tricks?

EPINARD: Oh, no. Only last week, he got a duck-egg away from me.

TIECELIN: Well, then. You will lodge a charge against him?

EPINARD: Ahem! I should not wish it made public how I — ah — came by the duck-egg.

TIECELIN: As you wish. Sit over there. Here come two who will testify.

(Epinard sits and reads in his Bible. Brun and Ysengrin enter.)

YSENGRIN: You are bringing him to trial?

TIECELIN: I have the evidence.

BRUN: Where is the King?

(Noble the Lion enters, majestically, theatrically.)

NOBLE: Since when do the trumpets not greet my arrival?

TIECELIN: *(bowing)*   Sire — your Majesty — I think — I thought — Trum — Trumpets!

(Trumpets.)

NOBLE: Let my arrival be announced to the Court.

TIECELIN: Yes, Sire. Trumpets!

(Trumpets.) Gentlemen, the King!

(All bow, as Noble seats himself.)

NOBLE: I declare the Court of Justice open. Now, Tiecelin, why have you assembled us all in Court?

TIECELIN: To hear charges against your Majesty's Knight, Sir Reynard the Fox.

NOBLE: Reynard? What charges?

YSENGRIN: I have been attacked!

BRUN: I have been beaten!

TIECELIN: My very life has been threatened!

NOBLE: Brun! Ysengrin! Where have you received these terrible injuries? Have you been fighting again?

326

BRUN: Sire, it is Reynard!

YSENGRIN: We are the victims of Reynard's trickery!

TIECELIN: This is Reynard's doing!

NOBLE: If this is true, Reynard is a dangerous criminal indeed. Bring him in.

TIECELIN: But your Majesty —

BRUN: We do not require his presence to recite his crimes.

YSENGRIN: We can tell you —

NOBLE: Where is Reynard?

TIECELIN: Knight Reynard thinks — he does not know — actually, I think he thinks —

NOBLE: Enough thinking. Where is Reynard?

TIECELIN: He th — I mean, he believes — your Majesty, I will have him brought before you.

NOBLE: Let this insolent character be called at once.

TIECELIN: Y-y-yes, Sire. S-s-s-sir Reynard the Fox! Trumpets!

(Trumpets, resembling a hunter's call, ending with a drum roll. During this fanfare, each animal makes his own preparation for Reynard's entrance, reflecting his attitude toward this dangerous criminal.)

YSENGRIN: Here comes the villain!

(Reynard enters, smiling, confident. Bows to the King.)

NOBLE: I greet you, Knight Reynard.

REYNARD: Good evening, Sire.

NOBLE: Just answer our questions.

REYNARD: Allow me, Sire, to wish that this day may not go by without being the best one of your life.

NOBLE: Quiet. We have assembled the High Court of Justice, for the express purpose of putting you on trial.

REYNARD: On trial? Me? The most devoted and faithful of all your subjects? But why, Sire? What have I done to be tried for?

NOBLE: You shall know this very minute. Tiecelin, announce the first accuser.

TIECELIN: Master Ysengrin the Wolf.

NOBLE: We are listening, Ysengrin.

YSENGRIN: I accuse —

REYNARD: Cousin Ysengrin, you, my accuser?

YSENGRIN: I accuse! Do you deny that you led me into a farm-yard under the pretext of showing me a flock of nice, plump ducks?

REYNARD: Not at all. I did show you a flock of nice, plump ducks, Cousin. Is that a crime?

YSENGRIN: And do you deny that you fastened me in, and roused the dogs, so that I was so cruelly bitten, I barely escaped alive?

REYNARD: Oh, my dear Cousin, is that how you suffered those grievous wounds? Those dreadful dogs!

NOBLE: So you admit luring him into a trap where he almost lost his life?

REYNARD: Oh, no. Excuse me, Sire. I only took him to the farm-yard to show him nice, plump ducks, as he says. But when he saw them, he began to drool and slobber and lick his lips at the sight, and even started to chase them. I could not stay for this. I fled, and cried out for help. Was it my fault if the gate shut behind me, and locked Ysengrin in with the dogs?

NOBLE: If the story is as you tell it —

YSENGRIN: Allow me —

NOBLE: And I am inclined to believe you — the Marshal Ysengrin is as guilty as you are, and by the same token, deserves the same punishment. It is up to you, Lord Wolf, to fix Reynard's fate, since the fate shall be yours also. What punishment would you suggest?

YSENGRIN: Ah — uh — in that case — yes, in that case, I think it is better — and wiser — not to punish Reynard.

REYNARD: Thanks, dear Cousin, for your generous intervention.

NOBLE: This case is settled. Who is next, Tiecelin?

TIECELIN: Seigneur Brun.

BRUN: I accuse!

REYNARD: You, my Uncle?

BRUN: Be quiet!

NOBLE: We are listening, Seigneur Brun.

BRUN: Your Majesty, I was taking a peaceful nap under an apple tree, when this creature —

REYNARD: Uncle.

BRUN: This mongrel —

REYNARD: Uncle.

BRUN: This rascal —

REYNARD: Uncle!

BRUN: For Heaven's sake, will you let me speak?

NOBLE: Proceed, Seigneur Brun.

BRUN: I was only sleeping, your Majesty, doing no harm to anyone—

REYNARD: He means, Sire, he was resting, after a large lunch. He had just stripped the apple tree, bare.

BRUN: It is not true! But this scoundrel found me there, and screamed for the farmer. Can you deny it?

REYNARD: No, not at all. I thought he was stricken. Sire. His belly was swollen till it looked like a barrel. I cried out in my grief. Could I help it if the farmer heard me? Uncle Brun heard me too, and tried to run away, but he was so full of apples, he couldn't even get to his feet.

BRUN: This is slander! He yelped for the farmer, your Majesty, and the farmer attacked me with a pitchfork. Before I could move from the spot, he gave me a black eye and four loose teeth, not to mention the hair and skin I lost in the fray.

NOBLE: If you had stolen his apples, Brun, it seems to me the punishment you received was justified. What do you think?

BRUN: I think — I think it was a very high price to pay for a few apples.

NOBLE: Forget it. Next one.

TIECELIN: The next one is myself: Master Tiecelin the Crow, Man of Law, and Royal Registrar.

NOBLE: What is your complaint against Reynard?

TIECELIN: I accuse!

REYNARD: Come, now.

TIECELIN: Yes! I accuse Reynard of trying, just a minute ago, to twist my neck and gobble me up, as simply as if I had been a chicken.

329

NOBLE: This is more serious. What nave you to reply, Master Reynard?

REYNARD: One thing only. Look at this piteous carcass, and judge for yourself, Sire. Who would wish to gobble him up, skinny and emaciated as he is? And even if I did, am I any more guilty in this matter than my Cousin Ysengrin?

YSENGRIN: I protest!

REYNARD: Or my Uncle Brun?

BRUN: I deny it!

REYNARD: Or the cat, the dog, the sparrow, the vulture — or you yourself, Sire Lion, our very beloved King, as well?

(Laughter.)

NOBLE: Silence!

(Nobody laughs any more.)

Tiecelin, you over-estimate yourself. None of us wishes to eat crow.

TIECELIN: Reynard did. And here is the evidence. He pulled out one of my tail-feathers — this very feather.

REYNARD: Pouf! The wind plucks your feathers all the time.

TIECELIN: The wind!

(General laughter.)

NOBLE: Let's file this ridiculous case. Has anybody else any complaints against Reynard?

TIECELIN: Yes! The Reverend Epinard!
(He prods Epinard, who has appeared immersed in the Bible.)

EPINARD: Uh? Yes?

NOBLE: We are listening, Reverend Epinard?

EPINARD: You are listening to me? This doesn't happen every day.

(He opens his Bible, and prepares to preach.)

NOBLE: What charge do you wish to lodge against the red-haired Fox?

EPINARD: I?

TIECELIN: Remember — that duck-egg.

EPINARD: Duck-eggs?

NOBLE: Look now, Reverend, has the Fox ever tried to harm you?

EPINARD: He wouldn't dare, Sire. My quills, you see.

NOBLE: If you have nothing to say, sit down. Is there any other accuser?

TIECELIN: Yes, Sire. There are countless ones. But they are not present.

NOBLE: Where are they?

TIECELIN: They are dead, Sire.

NOBLE: Dead?

TIECELIN: Yes, Sire. The rooster Chanticler, and his four hens. The drake, Halbran-des-Mares, and his three ducks. The guinea-fowl, Hupette. The turkey, Gloussard. And thousands of other winged creatures. All have met death and burial in the stomach of Reynard the Fox. Let's hang him, Sire.

YSENGRIN: Let's hang him upside down!

BRUN: Yes, he must hang!

NOBLE: This is a harsh judgement. Knight Reynard, can you think of any reason against it?

REYNARD: As many reasons as you have subjects, Sire. Doesn't my cousin Ysengrin himself devour innocent lambs and peaceful sheep? Doesn't my Uncle Brun treat himself to the honey he robs from the bees? Doesn't the Registrar Tiecelin eat the wheat and the grapes he steals from men? And you yourself, Sire, didn't you only yesterday have a gentle kid and half a deer for your supper!

YSENGRIN: We must hang him!

BRUN: Hang him!

TIECELIN: Hang him at once!

NOBLE: Do you hear?

REYNARD: I hear, Sire, and I don't worry too much, because I know there is more wisdom under a great King's crown than in the little brains of his courtiers. A very great King can forgive when need be.

NOBLE: A very great King can forgive when need be.

REYNARD: Mighty and gallant Majesty, I trust my fate to your hands.

NOBLE: I am a very great King, Reynard.

REYNARD: Without question, Sire.

NOBLE: You shall not hang.

REYNARD: Thank you, Sire.

TIECELIN: This is insane!

NOBLE: Who said that?

YSENGRIN: Sire, it is a mistake.

NOBLE: I pray you —

BRUN: If you will allow me, Sire —

NOBLE: I allow nothing! Silence, everybody, and let me render my sentence. You will not hang, Master Reynard. I grant you mercy for one more year.

TIECELIN: Mercy for one more year?

NOBLE: But this will be your last chance. In that year a record will be kept of your every crime.

BRUN: Of what use is a record, if he is left free to continue his crimes?

NOBLE: Twenty-four crimes we shall forgive you, without punishment.

YSENGRIN: Twenty-four crimes?

TIECELIN: Sire, this is preposterous!

NOBLE: Silence! We are all sinners, and hope for forgiveness. We shall forgive you twenty-four times.

REYNARD: You are a gracious King, Sire.

NOBLE: But take care. One crime more than twenty-four, and you shall be punished without mercy.

REYNARD: I understand, Sire.

NOBLE: One year from now, we shall hold court on this case again, and examine your record. Now you are free. Remember under what conditions.

REYNARD: Sire, you shall hear no further complaints from your humblest, most respectful servant, Reynard.

NOBLE: All right. Go.

REYNARD: I leave, Sire, broken-hearted to have earned the displeasure of so many esteemed friends.

(Exit.)

TIECELIN: Your Majesty, how can you —

YSENGRIN: Sire, this is madness!

BRUN: You have turned loose the greatest scoundrel in the kingdom!

TIECELIN: Who can keep track of all his crimes?

NOBLE: You will.

TIECELIN: I?

NOBLE: Yes. You are the Royal Registrar. I appoint you to keep a record book, and enter into it any crimes committed by Reynard.

TIECELIN: Thank you, your Majesty. It will give me pleasure.

NOBLE: I am very pleased with my judgement — stern, fair, but still merciful. Now, let each of you go peacefully back home, and recall my great justice.

TIECELIN: Trumpets!

(Trumpets.)

YSENGRIN: Hail to thee, Sire, Lion.

(Aside) What folly to let Reynard go free!

(Exit.)

BRUN: Hail, Sire.

(Aside) How foolish to forgive that redhair!

(Exit.)

NOBLE: You see, everybody is satisfied with my judgement. I am well satisfied myself. Good night, Tiecelin.

(Exit.)

TIECELIN: Good night, Sire.

(Aside) What a blunder, to leave that rascal at large!

(He goes to pinch Epinard's arm.)

EPINARD: Eh? Yes?

TIECELIN: It is all over, Reverend.

EPINARD: Yes, yes, I see. Moreover, it was very interesting. Very interesting indeed.

TIECELIN: I must say, you showed little interest in the cause of justice.

EPINARD: The cause of justice?

TIECELIN: Yes. Why didn't you tell the King about that duck-egg?

EPINARD: My dear fellow, I should not wish to earn Reynard's ill-will. The time might come when I should need Reynard on my side. Good night.

(Exit.)

TIECELIN: Good night, good night? How can I ever have another good night, after this? Reynard will make short work of me, if I give him the chance. My feathers rise with fear at the very thought.

(Lendore enters, half-asleep, pillow under her arm, bumps into Tiecelin, who freezes with terror.)

He has got me, already! Reynard?

LENDORE: What do you say?

TIECELIN: What? It is you? Lendore?

LENDORE: It's me.

TIECELIN: Why didn't you say something?

LENDORE: You didn't ask me anything?

TIECELIN: The Marmot. And I thought you were Reynard.

LENDORE: You didn't look at me very well.

TIECELIN: Where are you going?

LENDORE: To Reynard's trial. Is it here?

TIECELIN: The trial is over.

LENDORE: Already? I must have fallen asleep on my way.

TIECELIN: As usual.

LENDORE: How did it go?

TIECELIN: That rascal Reynard went scot-free, for a year!

LENDORE: Good!

TIECELIN: What is more, he is allowed to commit twenty-four crimes, without punishment.

LENDORE: Twenty-four? That will not take him long.

TIECELIN: But one crime more than twenty-four, and he shall hang! And I am appointed to keep the record.

LENDORE: The record?

TIECELIN: Yes. I am not the Royal Registrar for nothing. The King has appointed me to keep account of all his crimes. I shall make a book of them.

LENDORE: It's amazing how sleepy I still feel.

TIECELIN: Go to sleep, then. I intend to keep my eyes open, for the whole year.

LENDORE: *(settles to sleep, against a tree.)* Good night.

TIECELIN: It will be easy to accumulate twenty-five counts against him in a year. Ha, ha! I'll put an end to him, with my record-book.

End of Prologue

Scene One — Springtime

(Lendore enters, yawning. Reynard bounds in.)

REYNARD: Ah, Lendore! You have come out of your shelter. Spring is truly here.

LENDORE: Is it?

REYNARD: Melted is the cold snow that kept my feet wet all winter.

LENDORE: So it is.

REYNARD: Gone is the bitter frost that kept the burrows closed.

LENDORE: Ah, yes.

REYNARD: Quiet is the freezing wind that pinched my nose.

LENDORE: Excuse me. I don't hear any quiet.

REYNARD: Welcome, Spring — welcome to you, who brings back the innocent young rabbit, and the tender birdies, not to mention the dainty little chickens.

LENDORE: Go somewhere else to sing your Spring Song, Reynard. I need a nap.

(Sleeps. Ysengrin enters, quietly.)

REYNARD: *(at the overlook.)* Ah, look, Lendore. See the fine rooster in the farm-yard over there. I see you, Seigneur Coincoin. I have given you all winter to get fat, and now I am saving a place for you in my bag.

YSENGRIN: So! You are up to your old tricks, Reynard.

REYNARD: Cousin Ysengrin! You always tip-toe.

YSENGRIN: Naturally.

REYNARD: I was just — ah — admiring the spring.

YSENGRIN: You were just plotting to gobble up that rooster. I heard you.

REYNARD: I have always admired your ears Ysengrin.

YSENGRIN: Just dare to attack that rooster. The King shall hear of it.

REYNARD: Very well, Cousin. I leave Seigneur Coincoin to you. Happy hunting!

(Exit.)

336

YSENGRIN: Happy hunting, indeed. That wily Fox would beat me to the farm-yard, if I let him.

(Lendore stirs.)

Ah! Perhaps I won't have to go as far as the farm-yard.

(Drooling, he quietly creeps up on her, with obvious intentions. Reynard returns.)

REYNARD: Ah, Cousin, you have found what you want without hunting?

YSENGRIN: What brings you back here?

REYNARD: To do you a good turn, Cousin. I have found you a hunting companion. Here comes our Noble King.

(Noble enters, with zest and majesty.)

Your servant, Sire.

YSENGRIN: The Marmot, Sire. The Marmot. She sleeps.

NOBLE: Lendore, indeed. She has come out of her shelter. This is the herald of spring.

YSENGRIN: As you say, your Majesty.

NOBLE: Ysengrin, we have had to keep under cover all winter. Now I feel like hunting. Come and join me.

YSENGRIN: I am honored, Sire. And — ah — Reynard?

NOBLE: Reynard has given up hunting for a year. Let's go.

(Exit.)

YSENGRIN: I am coming, Sire.

(To Reynard) You — you schemer!

(To Noble, off) I come!

(Exit.)

REYNARD: *(laughs)* Happy hunting, Cousin.

(To Lendore) Lendore, Lendore, wake up.

LENDORE: Eh? What? What do you say?

REYNARD: Wake up. It is not wise to sleep when the hunting season is open.

LENDORE: I am a Marmot. It is the nature of a Marmot to sleep, any time.

337

REYNARD: Find yourself a private spot, then. And don't trust Ysengrin.

LENDORE: I don't trust anybody, Reynard — not even you.

REYNARD: Lendore.

LENDORE: All the same — I like you.

REYNARD: Thanks, old friend.

LENDORE: By the way, don't sit there. It is a bumble-bee nest.

(Exit.)

REYNARD: A bumble-bee nest? Fortunately she warns me. Ah, and here comes my Uncle Brun. What a heaven-sent opportunity to play a joke on him! But if the King should find out, there would be one of my twenty-four chances gone. Shall I do it? Yes! It is too good a chance to miss.

(Brun enters, out of sorts.)

Good morning, Uncle. Still grumbling?

BRUN: Leave me in peace.

REYNARD: That is just what I offer you. Let's make peace, and forget our little misunderstandings. As a token of good faith, I offer you some fair honey-cakes left by the bees. What do you think of that?

BRUN: I think it is another of your fabrications.

REYNARD: How unfortunate I am! My uncle himself doubts my sincerity.

BRUN: I don't believe a word. Where are those honey-cakes?

REYNARD: Why show them to you, since you don't believe there are any?

BRUN: And why, if they exist, don't you eat them yourself?

REYNARD: I am on probation for a year, Brun. It would count against me if I should rob the bees. Heigh-ho! Since you don't care for it, the honey will be lost to everyone.

(He makes a subtle move toward the bumble-bee nest.)

BRUN: *(to himself)* So there they are.

REYNARD: It's a shame.

BRUN: Yes. Too bad, isn't it? Well, I am off.

REYNARD: So am I. Good bye, Uncle.

338

BRUN: Good bye.

(Neither makes a move to go.)

Aren't you leaving?

REYNARD: Oh, certainly. And you?

BRUN: Me, too. So good bye.

(He pretends to leave.)

REYNARD: *(Pretending to leave also.)* Good bye.

BRUN: *(Comes back and finds himself in front of Reynard.)* I have lost something.

REYNARD: Can I help you look for it?

BRUN: Stupid of me. I left it at home. Good bye.

(Exit.)

REYNARD: Good bye, Uncle.

(Exit, but hides himself. Brun comes back.)

BRUN: *(Rushes to bumble-bee nest.)* Honey! That fool thought I was going to leave honey here to spoil!

(He puts his paw in the nest, withdraws it quickly.)

Bumble bees! The traitor!

(Bumble-bees come out in swarms and pursue him. Music. The flight of the bumble-bees can be suggested by light spots.)

Ah! Go away! My nose! Leave me alone! Ouch! My tail! A-h-h! it stings! My ears! Oh! Ah! It stings! Help, Help!

(Tiecelin enters.)

TIECELIN: Seigneur Brun! What is the matter?

BRUN: Out of my way, Crow! Ouch! My neck!

TIECELIN: Are you hurt?

BRUN: Am I hurt? I am eaten up! Aie! My leg! Stop blocking me! Oh, it stings! It stings!

(He runs off, followed by the bumble-bees. Tiecelin, pushed about, and stricken by fear, takes refuge on a tree. Reynard is convulsed.)

TIECELIN: Has he lost his mind?

REYNARD: Oh, no. He always acts that way, when the bees are after him.

339

TIECELIN: Well, he needn't be so rude about it. He nearly made me crush my camembert.

REYNARD: *(nostrils wide open.)* Camembert? Ah, Master Crow, that cheese looks delicious. Will you give me a taste?

TIECELIN: No. I went to too much trouble to get it.

REYNARD: But cheese is bad for your voice. A singer should never eat cheese.

TIECELIN: Nonsense. It has never harmed me in the least.

REYNARD: Nevertheless, a fine voice should not be abused. If you were unable to sing anymore, the animal kingdom would lose its best tenor.

TIECELIN: Do you think so?

(Crows.)

Do you really think so?

REYNARD: Sing, Tiecelin. Sing, and listen yourself.

(Tiecelin crows awfully.)

Ah! Very good, though a little low. I thought you could sing higher than that.

(Tiecelin croaks more shrilly.)

Better. One note higher . . . Ah! . . . More . . . Louder . . . Higher . . . Splendid! . . . Go on! . . . Higher! . . . You are almost there! Keep on! . . . More! . . . Now you have it!

(Tiecelin drops his cheese.)

And I have it too!

TIECELIN: My cheese!

REYNARD: Don't worry. It is in good hands.

TIECELIN: Give it back to me.

REYNARD: Come and get it.

TIECELIN: I know you.

REYNARD: We will share the cheese like brothers.

TIECELIN: If I come down, you will gobble me up first, and you will eat the cheese for dessert.

REYNARD: No, no. Come.

TIECELIN: Cheese robber!

REYNARD: What a wonderful aroma!

TIECELIN: Rob — you like the smell?

REYNARD: Heavenly!

TIECELIN: When you close your eyes, you find the smell even better.

REYNARD: What's that?

TIECELIN: To get the full, rich, luscious flavour of a camembert cheese, it is necessary to shut out all other senses, and enjoy it with your nose alone. Your nostrils are much more sensitive when your eyes are closed.

REYNARD: Is this possible?

(He closes his eyes and sniffs.)

You are right. It is unbelievably richer.

TIECELIN: *(Taking advantage of the chance to climb down.)* Cheese robber!

REYNARD: Tiecelin —

TIECELIN: This will go into my book!

REYNARD: Your book? What book?

TIECELIN: Aha! The King has appointed me to keep a record of all your doings in a book. This will make a fine beginning.

REYNARD: Indeed.

TIECELIN: Keep on, Master Fox. The book will soon be full. Crime Number One! Reynard stole my cheese! Cheese robber! Cheese robber! Cheese robber!

(Exit.)

REYNARD: So, he is keeping a book! And on the very first day of spring, I have managed to spend one of my twenty-four chances, and get it recorded in the book. Oh, what a stupid, bungling Fox I am! That tattle-tale will cry the news aloud, all through the forest. I'd better get rid of the evidence.

(He hides cheese, as Noble enters, followed by Ysengrin.)

NORLE: Did you see a pheasant fly over?

REYNARD: No Sire, but I can guide your Majesty toward some very attractive turkeys.

341

YSENGRIN: Oh, no. You are out of this hunt, remember.

REYNARD: I am talking about big, fat turkeys.

NOBLE: We can hardly afford to let such a chance go by, Ysengrin.

YSENGRIN: But Sire, Reynard has given up hunting for a year. You said so yourself.

NOBLE: I think — ahem — we may make an exception this time.

REYNARD: This way, Sire.

> *(Bows low. Noble and Ysengrin exeunt.)*

Let's hope that Tiecelin will not find his cheese until I get back.

> *(Exit. Music. Ballet-mime for the hunt. Noble, Ysengrin, and Reynard chasing a turkey around the stage and off. Noble in the lead, graceful but heavy; Ysengrin lumbering along behind, eager but clumsy; Reynard nimbly outstripping both. The chase carries them offstage. Lendore enters.)*

LENDORE: *(Crossing, pillow under her arm.)*   Impossible to sleep with this infernal music.

> *(Exit. The ballet ends with the entrance of Reynard, who carries a turkey with head hanging limp. Noble and Ysengrin follow.)*

NOBLE: Bravo!

YSENGRIN: You caught it right under my nose!

REYNARD: It is a matter of skill, Cousin.

NOBLE: Anyhow, now we must share.

REYNARD: *(Throwing the turkey at Noble's feet.)* Let's share, by all means.

NOBLE: You, my dear Ysengrin, may decide about each one's share.

YSENGRIN: In my opinion, it is fitting, first of all, to set aside the claim of this redhair, who had no right to be hunting anyway. The head, the neck, and one wing will be enough for me — and one leg. It is only right that you, being the King, should take all the other pieces.

NOBLE: *(Boxing his ears.)*   You don't have the first instinct of a sportsman.

> *(To Reynard.)* And you, how would you divide it?

REYNARD: It is easy. Take first what pleases you, Sire — the body and legs, for instance. Her Majesty Lioness the Queen, shall have the wings and the head. Your son, the Cub, will gladly practice on the neck, I'm sure. Ysengrin seems to have too much trouble with his teeth to eat anything. And when it comes to me, I don't really feel hungry.

NOBLE: This is what I should call a fine division. Who taught you to divide so fairly?

REYNARD: My Fox's wisdom, Sire — and most of all, the sight of your royal fist on Ysengrin's ears.

NOBLE: I congratulate you. As for you, Seigneur Wolf, take a lesson from Reynard. Well, good bye, my friends. Thank you for your company in the hunt.

(Exit, taking turkey.)

YSENGRIN: Take a lesson — take a lesson from Reynard! Ah-h-h-h! I don't know what keeps me from giving you the beating of your life, you scheming, mealy-mouthed rascal!

REYNARD: Is that not better than to have your jaw crushed under the Lion's paw?

YSENGRIN: I am mad. Oh, I am good and mad!

REYNARD: Cheer up. We don't lose much in this settlement. The turkey was so old that the King, the Queen, and the Cub face the risk of breaking their teeth on it. Anyway, I see a much better dinner coming than the King's.

YSENGRIN: Epinard?

REYNARD: Yes, the Reverend, carrying a wonderful ham! It will be ours.

YSENGRIN: Beware the quills.

REYNARD: Don't worry about the quills. Hide there, and be on the watch. I'll get Epinard to lay the ham down near your hiding place. You pick it up and wait for me. Afterward we shall divide it.

YSENGRIN: Agreed.

(He hides.)

REYNARD: *(Waiting for Epinard's entrance.)* Now is the moment. Oh, miserable fox that I am!

(Epinard enters, carrying ham.)

Shall I never be able to do anything but bad deeds? With the help of Heaven, let me find a holy man to hear my confession, and absolve me of my sins!

EPINARD: My son.

REYNARD: Reverend. Did you hear me?

EPINARD: Yes, my son.

REYNARD: I will go to Hades, won't I?

EPINARD: The one who repents will not go to Hades.

REYNARD: Ah, but I repent. I repent.

EPINARD: Very well, my son.

REYNARD: Heavens, what do I see?

EPINARD: What do you see?

REYNARD: It has gotten me again.

EPINARD: What has gotten you again?

REYNARD: My terrible sin of greediness. Ah, how wretched am I!
The very sight of your ham makes me forget my pledge.

EPINARD: Be calm, my son. Be calm.

REYNARD: It is impossible, Reverend, as long as that splendid ham
remains before my eyes. I shall be unable not to covet it.

EPINARD: My goodness! Have some will power.

REYNARD: It is Satan. It is Satan who tempts me. "Get thee behind
me, Satan." Take that ham away from my sight, Reverend, and
pray for me.

(Epinard puts his ham down.)

Take it away from my nostrils — farther — still farther, so that
its wonderful aroma will not tempt my nose any more.

EPINARD: *(Puts the ham down near Ysengrin's hiding place.)* Kneel,
my son, my dear Reynard. Kneel. I will pray for you.

*(Ysengrin seizes the ham, takes a bite, makes his escape. Reynard,
seeing this, cries out involuntarily.)*

REYNARD: Aie! Wait for me, you thief!

(Recovers himself.)

Excuse me, Reverend. Save the prayer for another time. Right
now I have — ah — other business.

(Exit hurriedly, in pursuit of Ysengrin.)

EPINARD: *(Discovering his loss.)*   Pig! Rascal! Robber! My ham! My
ham!

*(Exit. In the distance are heard the joined cries of Tiecelin —
"Cheese Robber!" — and of Epinard — "My ham!" — Noble
enters.)*

NOBLE: This morning the forest is full of strange sounds. Don't I
hear someone claiming a ham? And somewhere, this side, someone else shouting "Cheese Robber"? That joker Reynard must not
be far away. Ham? Cheese? It is strange, but I fancy my royal
nose thrills under the odor of a very near camembert.

(He searches, and discovers the cheese.)

Ha! But I am not mistaken. By jove, my royal nose is still in its
prime. Ah, this suits me admirably. It makes up for that skimpy
breakfast I had, eating that tough old turkey.

(He eats the cheese.)

It is truly fit for a King.

TIECELIN: *(Offstage, drawing nearer.)* Cheese robber! Cheese robber!

*(Noble gulps down the last of the cheese hurriedly. Tiecelin
enters.)*

Sire, my cheese.

NOBLE: What cheese?

TIECELIN: My camembert.

NOBLE: So it was your cheese that — ah — which is missing?

(Brun enters, shaking off Reynard behind him.)

BRUIN: Don't give me any of your sweet talk. I am stung all over.

TIECELIN: He stole it!

NOBLE: Who? Brun?

TIECELIN: No, Sire, Reynard.

NOBLE: Reynard, did you steal his wheeze?

REYNARD: Wheeze, Sire? No, Sire, I did not wheeze.

TIECELIN: Cheese robber! Cheese robber!

REYNARD: I did not wheeze. Nor did I hear anyone else wheeze, nor
sneeze, nor queaze, nor —

TIECELIN: Cheese robber!

REYNARD: Oh, cheese? Tiecelin has lost a cheese?

TIECELIN: Your Majesty will do me justice. He has stolen my camembert.

REYNARD: Oh, what slander!

TIECELIN: Punish that thief.

REYNARD: Your Majesty, this Crow is insane. Had I stolen his cheese, I should have eaten it at once, and you would be able to smell it. Uncle Brun, be good enough to smell my moustache.

BRUN: You stay away from me.

REYNARD: But smell, and tell us all. Do you detect the very strong odor of a camembert cheese?

BRUN: *(Sniffing)* I wouldn't put it past you, you honey-fibber — but to tell the truth, I smell nothing at all on your breath.

TIECELIN: You have taken it away from me!

REYNARD: After all, the simplest way would be to ask everyone to submit to the test, would it not!

NOBLE: Do you think this necessary?

TIECELIN: I insist! I insist!

BRUN: It seems logical to me. So smell.

TIECELIN: *(Smelling Brun's breath.)* You smell more like a honey-robber.

BRUN: It is my natural fragrance.

REYNARD: You, Sire?

NOBLE: Although my royal eminence places me above all suspicion, I submit to your insulting request.

TIECELIN: *(Smelling Noble's breath.)* Sire! Sire! One would almost think —

NOBLE: What would one think?

TIECELIN: If I weren't afraid of hurting your Majesty's feelings, I should say — it's funny, but it smells more or less like —

NOBLE: More or less like what?

TIECELIN: Like camembert.

NOBLE: This exceeds the limits. Get out of here, and go fast. Let me not set eyes on you any more today, or it might be costly for you.

TIECELIN: But —

346

NOBLE: Get out, I say!

TIECELIN: Very well, then.

   (Exit).

BRUN: What a fool!

TIECELINS *(Offstage.)*   Cheese robber! Cheese robber!

REYNARD: He has a one-track mind.

BRUN: How absurd to think that your Majesty's moustache might smell like cheese!

NOBLE: Sniff yourself, Seigneur Brun, and give us your opinion, sincerely and honestly.

BRUN: *(Sniffing.)*   Uh — ah —

NOBLE: Well?

BRUN: I don't believe I am mistaken, Sire, when I say that your moustache does have an odor —

NOBLE: What odor, I pray you?

BRUN: A very delicate perfume — ah — yes, very similar to the roses.

NOBLE: So that is your honesty! Lies and hypocrisy! Out of my sight. Bear without conscience!

BRUN: Well, then —

   (Exit hastily.)

NOBLE: It is your turn, Reynard. What do you smell?

REYNARD: To tell the truth, Sire, I don't smell anything today. I have a cold in my head.

NOBLE: This is a cold that comes at a convenient time for you, doesn't it?

REYNARD: Yes, Sire.

EPINARD: *(In the distance.)*   My ham! I claim my ham!

REYNARD: Sire, allow me to retire, and nurse my cold.

TIECELIN: *(In the distance, on the other side.)*   Cheese robber! Cheese robber!

NOBLE: You are quite right. Let's both retire and nurse our colds.

   (Exeunt. Epinard enters.)

EPINARD: My ham!

(Tiecelin enters.)

TIECELIN: My cheese!

(Brun enters.)

BRUN: I am stung all over!

(Ysengrin enters.)

YSENGRIN: I am in the King's bad graces!

BRUN: So am I!

TIECELIN: So am I!

YSENGRIN: Whose fault is it?

TIECELIN: It is Reynard!

EPINARD: Reynard!

BRUN: Reynard!

TIECELIN: It is all the fault of that rascal Reynard!

EPINARD: Tiecelin, put all this down in your book against him.

TIECELIN: Don't worry. It shall go into my book, all right. H'm, h'm! We can almost be glad. This will make three crimes on the very first day. Ha, ha!

End of Scene One

348

Scene Two — Summer

(Appropriate music. Reynard is hidden behind a tree. Lendore and Epinard enter from opposite sides, both very thirsty, both looking for the spring. They collide.)

LENDORE: Oh, it's you?

EPINARD: As you see. Don't you think it's terribly hot?

LENDORE: Yes. Are you looking for the spring?

EPINARD: Where is it?

LENDORE: The hole is there, but the water doesn't flow any more. The brook has disappeared in the sand, the pond is dried up, and the fish, turned upside down, die in the sun.

EPINARD: May Heaven save us, dear Lendore! It is a dreadful summer.

(Ysengrin enters, brushes them aside.)

YSENGRIN: Out of the way, both of you!

(Epinard bristles. Lendore puts pillow on her head.)

Where is the spring? Who emptied the spring? You?

LENDORE: Certainly not. It is the sun.

YSENGRIN: I want a drink. Where is the water?

EPINARD: In the ground.

YSENGRIN: It must come out. I want it to gush, as it did before. Come out of your hole, water. I want a drink.

EPINARD: Don't shout so. Water doesn't hear. Each of us must be patient under our sufferings.

YSENGRIN: Don't preach your sermons to me. Go somewhere else.

(He pushes Epinard, stings himself.)

Thunderation!

EPINARD: As you wish.

(Exits calmly.)

LENDORE: He who plays with needles gets stung.

YSENGRIN: You think this is funny.
(Ysengrin strikes at Lendore, who pushes her pillow into his

muzzle, and hurries off. Ysengrin fights alone with the pillow, as Brun enters, carrying a wooden bucket. He sets the bucket down, to watch Ysengrin in astonishment.)

BRUN: Here, don't upset my bucket!

YSENGRIN: What bucket?

(He throws the pillow down, and rushes to the bucket, kneeling in front of it.)

BRUN: *(Tumbles him down with a push.)* Don't touch!

YSENGRIN: Just a gulp.

BRUN: No.

YSENGRIN: I am thirsty.

BRUN: So am I.

YSENGRIN: I beg you.

BRUN: No.

YSENGRIN: One drop.

BRUN: No.

YSENGRIN: Only let me dip the tip of my tongue.

BRUN: No!

(He pushes Ysengrin back violently. Ysengrin tumbles down and rolls close to a tree, behind which Reynard is hidden. Brun drinks noisily. Reynard whispers a few secret words to Ysengrin, who then gets up and pretends to depart.)

Good bye, my nephew.

YSENGRIN: Good bye.

(He stops and pretends to gather honey, which he eats with delight.)

BRUN: *(Stops drinking to watch Ysengrin, then puts his bucket down and draws near.)* Is it honey?

(Reynard picks up the bucket and disappears.)

It is most probably honey?

YSENGRIN: No. I was just licking the wind.

(Exit, in pursuit of Reynard. Brun rushes for honey, finds none.)

BRUN: He *was* just licking the wind.

(Looks for his bucket.)

Ysengrin! Robber! Ysengrin! My bucket!

(Exit in pursuit. Reynard returns, drains the bucket, puts it back in place, then leaves. Ysengrin re-enters, rushes to the bucket, finds it empty.)

YSENGRIN: Scoundrel!

(Brun rushes in.)

BRUN: Give me that!

YSENGRIN: It is empty.

BRUN: *(Beating him.)*   I'll teach you to rob your Uncle.

YSENGRIN: Uncle! Ouch! . . . Ouch! . . . I haven't — it isn't — oh, it is —

BRUN: Don't cross my path again, or you'll get twice as much.

(Exit. Reynard returns.)

REYNARD: Well? Do you have colic from drinking too much?

YSENGRIN: I have been beaten — through your fault. I am going to give you your share.

REYNARD: You are mistaken.

YSENGRIN: You have emptied the bucket, to the last drop.

REYNARD: Ah no! Is it my fault if there is a hole in the bucket?

YSENGRIN: Where?

REYNARD: Look!

(He puts the bucket on Ysengrin's head.)

YSENGRIN: Remove the bucket! I am smothering! Reynard, where are you?

REYNARD: I am here.

YSENGRIN: Get me out of this bucket at once!

REYNARD: Eat your way out. Remember, you ate Epinard's ham, all by yourself.

(Exit quietly)

YSENGRIN: I'll strangle you! I'll pull out every hair of your moustache! I'll report this to Tiecelin to put in his book!

(Noble and Brun enter.)

BRUN: You see, Sire, the spring is dry.

351

NOBLE: Ah-h-h, yes.

BRUN: But I had the foresight to have back a bucket of water.

NOBLE: *(Panting.)* Where is it?

BRUN: That is what I am trying to tell you, Sire. I was tricked out of it.

NOBLE: Bah! Brun, I'm so thirsty I could drink the ocean.

BRUN: Drink the ocean?

NOBLE: I'd be willing to wager I could drink the ocean to the last drop.

YSENGRIN: *(Grapples with the King.)* Ah, villain, there you are!

NOBLE: *(Throwing him back so hard, it shakes the bucket.)* This will teach you to respect your King!

YSENGRIN: King? Oh, forgive me, Sire. I cannot see your Majesty.

NOBLE: Even if invisible, our Majesty is to be respected.

YSENGRIN: Take this bucket off my head, and I'll explain.

NOBLE: Quite unnecessary, I understand.
(Exit.)

YSENGRIN: Sire, I didn't rob Seigneur Brun. He jabbers a great deal lately.

BRUN: I, jabber?
(Gives him a mighty blow, and exits.)

YSENGRIN: Sire — your Majesty — will nobody help me?
(Lendore enters to pick up her pillow, notices Wolf. She knocks at the bucket discreetly.)

Who is there?

LENDORE: It's me, Lendore the Marmot, sir. And you, under the bucket, who are you?

YSENGRIN: I am the poor Ysengrin. For Heaven's sake, liberate me.

LENDORE: Promise first not to try to gobble me up again?

YSENGRIN: I promise anything, my sweet Lendore. I swear it a hundred times, a thousand times, if you wish. But remove this bucket. It is smothering me.

LENDORE: Don't move.

(She pulls the bucket.)

YSENGRIN: You are pulling my ears off!

LENDORE: I have to.

YSENGRIN: *(Free, at last.)*   You did hurt me!

LENDORE: It was unavoidable.

YSENGRIN: You deserve a thrashing.

LENDORE: Don't forget you swore —

YSENGRIN: Away with promises! Here is your reward.

> *(Trying to kick her, he misses, kicks the bucket instead. Lendore runs away. Ysengrin, in pain, hops on one foot. Tiecelin enters.)*

Oh I am in a rage — a rage — a rage!

TIECELIN: What is the matter with you? Have you lost one leg?

YSENGRIN: It is all the fault of that bounder Reynard!

TIECELINS *(Eager, pencil poised.)*   Reynard? What did he do? Tell me at once. I will put it in my book.

YSENGRIN: Your book? Your book? That for your book!

> *(He strikes the book from Tiecelin's hand.)*

TIECELIN: *(Retrieving his book.)*   Here, have a care!

YSENGRIN: Of what use is your everlasting book?

TIECELIN: It is a record of all his crimes, to bring against him at the trial.

YSENGRIN: Winter will be over before the trial. Are we to put up with his trickery till then!

TIECELIN: It is the King's judgement.

YSENGRIN: I want to deal with him now — right now!

TIECELIN: I, too. But how?

YSENGRIN: O, leave me in peace. I am lame for life!

TIECELIN: All the same, you needn't treat my book so lightly. This is legal evidence, sanctioned by the King. And it is getting full. He hasn't many chances left. If all else fails, this will bring him to account in the end.

> *(Exit.)*

YSENGRIN: Prattling Crow!

> *(Reynard enters, but finding Ysengrin alone, conceals himself.)*

It all goes back to the King's judgment. Leaving that Fox free for a year, to commit twenty-four crimes without punishment.

(Enter Brun.)

Uncle Brun!

BRUN: Don't speak to me, you water-thief!

YSENGRIN: But I beg you, listen to me. It was not I who emptied your bucket.

BRUN: Not you? Who, then?

YSENGRIN: It was Reynard.

BRUN: Reynard?

YSENGRIN: I swear it.

BRUN: Reynard, who drained my bucket dry?

YSENGRIN: And then stuck it on my head, and caused me to get a beating.

BRUN: The King shall hear of this!

YSENGRIN: Of what use is that! It was the King who set him free for a year, to perpetrate such tricks.

BRUN: And the year is not half over.

YSENGRIN: Exactly.

BRUN: It is not to be borne! We must put an end to this Fox.

YSENGRIN: If we are to get rid of the Fox, we must first get the King out of the way.

BRUN: The King is a fool. If I were King, now —

YSENGRIN: Or I —

BRUN: Why not?

YSENGRIN: Eh?

BRUN: Why should the Lion be King?

YSENGRIN: He always has been.

BRUN: Do you know any document that gives the title of King of the animals to the Lion?

YSENGRIN: All the school books say so.

BRUN: I know a way to topple him off his throne.

YSENGRIN: What way?

BRUN: Listen. This afternoon, His Majesty declared several times that he could drink the entire ocean, to the last drop.

YSENGRIN: That was only to express how thirsty he was.

BRUN: Of course. But what would happen if we should challenge him?

YSENGRIN: He would naturally be most embarrassed. I don't see how he could very well drink the ocean dry.

BRUN: Well, then! Do you think the animal kingdom will accept a King who is unable to keep his word?

YSENGRIN: No!

BRUN: No! Certainly not! We shall demand his abdication.

YSENGRIN: And take the throne ourselves!

BRUN: Tonight, my friend, we shall be Kings.

YSENGRIN: And we shall make an end of that rascal Reynard. Go and get him. I will gather the Court.

BRUN: Reynard has played his last trick.

(Exit.)

YSENGRIN: And that for you, Master Reynard. Trumpets!

(Trumpets. Reynard appears in the open, pretending to answer the trumpet call.)

REYNARD: Cousin, what is going on?

YSENGRIN: You'll see. Trumpets!

(Trumpets. Tiecelin enters.)

TIECELIN: Why are you calling a meeting when it is so hot? It must be most important.

(Trumpets. Enter Lendore.)

YSENGRIN: It certainly is. Trumpets!

LENDORE: There, there. Everybody has heard you. What is the matter now?

YSENGRIN: The King has made a very audacious boast, and he wants everybody present to see how he keeps it.

(Noble sweeps in, escorted by Brun.)

355

NOBLE: What is all this congregation for?

TIECELIN: The trumpets have called us to Assembly. I, as Royal Registrar, demand to know the business before the Court.

BRUN: You shall know it now. Sire, the animal kingdom, whose beloved sovereign you are, wishes to know if it possible for your Majesty to keep a promise made by you this afternoon.

NOBLE: Why, certainly.

BRUN: Would you be willing to put your throne at stake?

NOBLE: Of course I would. I always keep my promises. What did I promise?

BRUN: To drink the ocean, Sire.

NOBLE: Ha, ha! It is true I made that statement, I was so thirsty.

YSENGRIN: The achievement you are going to perform thrills all your people, Sire.

NOBLE: You didn't take me seriously, I hope?

BRUN: We know your Majesty is capable of accomplishing the greatest feats.

NOBLE: But you know very well —

YSENGRIN: Your people are looking forward to it, Sire.

BRUN: Gentlemen, your highly esteemed sovereign will, in a moment, lead you to the beach, and show you how, when one is a very great King, one can achieve things that would be impossible for his subjects.

YSENGRIN: His Majesty is going to drink the ocean.

BRUN: You will see how the strength of your sovereign, his bravery, his keen intelligence, his wit, and his determination will give him the power to drink the whole ocean. Our great King, gentlemen, is about to swallow the ocean. Sire, the ocean is waiting.

NOBLE: Did I actually say that I would drink the ocean?

BRUN: Indeed you did, Sire — to the last drop.

NOBLE: Did I say that?

BRUN: Those were your very words, Sire.

NOBLE: But — but I shall drown!

BRUN: Does your Majesty mean you cannot keep your promise?

356

NOBLE: I — ah —

YSENGRIN: A King always keeps his promises.

NOBLE: But it was only in jest —

REYNARD: Ah — your Majesty. Gentlemen.

YSENGRIN: You stay out of this.

REYNARD: Did the King also say that he would drink the water of all the rivers that flow into the ocean?

BRUN: Is this any business of yours?

NOBLE: No. I did not.

REYNARD: In that case, my dear Brun, will you stop all the rivers of the world, dam their flow, and prevent them from pouring their waters into his Majesty's soup? After you have done this, I'm sure his Majesty will gladly drink what is left.

BRUN: Stop up all the rivers of the world?

NOBLE: Exactly.

BRUN: How can anyone do that?

NOBLE: When you are able to do that, I will drink up all the waters of the ocean, to the last drop.

(General laughter.)

REYNARD: Bravo, Sire. It is easy to see that we have a wise King. Don't you agree, Cousin Ysengrin?

YSENGRIN: It is easy to see that the King has a clever counsellor.

BRUN: Counsellor? This redhair? Your Majesty, this is an outrage, that you should be taken in by this rogue!

NOBLE: Rogue? Are you referring to my trusted knight, Sir Reynard the Fox? Guard your tongue, Seigneur Bear.

BRUN: Only today he tricked me out of a bucket of water.

(Tiecelin writes busily.)

YSENGRIN: And then he inverted the bucket on my head, and caused me to get a beating.

(Tiecelin writes this down too.)

NOBLE: *(To Brun.)*   You dare to complain to me, when you have just tried to cheat me out of my throne?

(To Ysengrin.)   And you, who just this afternoon, without provo-

357

cation, assaulted your King? Let me not hear another word from either one of you. Come, Reynard. A rain is coming up. Let us seek shelter.

(Epinard rushes in.)

EPINARD: Sire! I beg — a matter of utmost importance!

BRUN: Save your important matters for the pulpit, Reverend.

EPINARD: Sire, give me leave to —

NOBLE: In good time, Reverend.

EPINARD: Your Majesty, it cannot wait. Does no one realize that a very serious danger threatens us all?

NOBLE: What danger can be greater than this wicked plot to overthrow my throne?

EPINARD: Men, Sire.

LENDORE: Men?

(The very word draws them together, in a tight little knot, glancing fearfully toward the overlook.)

EPINARD: Sire, I have just come from the farm. The farmer has his hunting dogs out on a leash, training them to pick up our scent.

NOBLE: How do you know this?

EPINARD: He led the dogs first to the hen-yard, where Reynard was careless enough to leave some tracks. Then he took them to the marshes where I — ahem! — paid a brief call on some ducks recently. When I left, he was heading toward the pig-pen, where the dogs will easily pick up the trail of Seigneur Brun.

BRUN: The dickens!

EPINARD: From there, he will take them to the sheep-fold, where the smell of Wolf is very strong.

YSENGRIN: Oh, no!

EPINARD: Next they will go to the wheat field, where the Crow dropped a feather on his last visit.

TIECELIN: Aie!

EPINARD: And finally they will make for the pasture, where the Lion has left his traces.

NOBLE: Is this true?

EPINARD: Send Tiecelin to see.

NOBLE: Tiecelin, to the farm!

TIECELIN: A-a-a-alone, Sire?

NOBLE: Have we anybody else with wings?

TIECELIN: Y-y-yes, Sire. I mean — no, Sire.

NOBLE: Quickly!

TIECELIN: I — I'm going, Sire.

(Exit slowly, with obvious reluctance.)

EPINARD: Your Majesty, this is no time for nonsense. I know those farmers down there. They are all united in plotting our destruction. They want our bodies; the pelt of Seigneur Brun; Reynard's fur; Tiecelin's feathers; Ysengrin's skin and teeth; yours, Sire; my quills — and Heaven knows what else. Fall is coming, when all men go hunting for game. The dogs have our scent. Men are polishing up their weapons, oiling their rifles, filling their cartridges, sharpening their knives. It will be a fearful period for those of our kind. I make it my duty, Sire, to warn you that if we wish to survive, we must all band together against the common enemy — Man.

REYNARD: That, Reverend, is one of your very best sermons.

NOBLE: You agree, then?

REYNARD: Oh, unquestionably, your Majesty. Alone, we are each of us weak and vulnerable. United, we could resist the hunters and their dogs.

NOBLE: But how can we unite?

REYNARD: Ah! That, Sire, is the question.

NOBLE: It is always the question. I am going to require each of you to take an oath.

EPINARD: Excellent, Sire.

NOBLE: And I will expect you to be bound by this oath, no matter what the emergency.

YSENGRIN: Never fear, Sire. You can depend on us.

NOBLE: Hold out your right hands. Now, repeat after me. All for one. One for all.

ALL: All for one. One for all.

(Low, distant rumble of thunder. All are frozen.)

YSENGRIN: Listen!

(Tiecelin, flies in, terrified.)

TIECELIN: Did you hear that?

YSENGRIN: It's gunfire.

BRUN: The hunters! The hunters are after us!

LENDORE: Merciful heavens! Already?

TIECELIN: Hunters? That is cannon!

YSENGRIN: They've brought in the Army!

BRUN: The Army? Soldiers?

TIECELIN: The soldiers are coming!

LENDORE: E-e-e-ek!

REYNARD: It is only thunder, Sire.

BRUN: Thunder?

(Violent cracks, as the storm breaks.)

Sire, this redhair doesn't know the difference between gunfire and thunder.

YSENGRIN: It is the hunters!

TIECELIN: It is the soldiers!

REYNARD: Gentlemen, calm yourselves. It is simply thunder.

NOBLE: Hunters, soldiers, or thunder — I am taking no chances. Excuse me, gentlemen.

(Exit, hurriedly.)

TIECELIN: Your Majesty! Wait for me!

(Tiecelin, Brun, and Ysengrin collide in their scramble to run for safety.)

BRUN: Out of my way, Crow!

(Tiecelin exits in a panic.)

YSENGRIN: No you don't. Me first!

(Exit.)

LENDORE: Where is everybody going?

BRUN: It is the hunters! Save yourself!

(Exit, on the run.)

360

LENDORE: The hunters? Oh, help me!

(Clings fearfully to Epinard as he rushes past, on his way to the overlook.)

EPINARD: Help you? Each one help himself!

LENDORE: But we just promised — All for one. One for all.

REYNARD: Only when convenient, Lendore.

EPINARD: Ah! You were right, Reynard. It was only thunder, after all. And here comes the rain.

LENDORE: Rain?

REYNARD: Yes, Lendore. Use your pillow for an umbrella.

EPINARD: These thunder-showers bring out the snails. You understand? I must be on the watch for them.

(Exit hastily.)

REYNARD: Of course, Reverend.

LENDORE: But the Reverend is the one who said we must unite.

REYNARD: Ah, yes, Lendore. And yet, you see, at the first thunderstroke, he goes off in his own interest, like everybody else.

LENDORE: But suppose it *had* been the hunters?

REYNARD: You and I would have been left to meet them, alone.

LENDORE: *(Hastening out)*   Heavens! Not me!

(Exit.)

REYNARD: Then it is Reynard alone against the hunters. Let them come! Even the rain is on my side. It will wash away my tracks, so the dogs can no longer pick up my trail. Let it rain! Ha, ha! It is a good joke on Man!

End of Scene Two

(Music. Sounds of gaiety and merriment from the distant vineyard. Epinard stands at the overlook, peering off toward the farm. Lendore enters cautiously, carrying a basket.)

LENDORE: Greetings, Reverend. Is it safe to gather my supplies here?

EPINARD: For the present. Men are still busy celebrating.

LENDORE: Blessed be God who created the autumn.

EPINARD: It is the harvest season, my dear Lendore. You can see the wine-growers' dance from here. Men are full of joy, for the grapes are ripe.

LENDORE: So are the pears and apples, and the nuts and acorns. They will make a good crop to fill my attic.

EPINARD: As long as men are dancing, we are safe. But as soon as the harvest is over, they will take down their guns, call their dogs, and sound the horn. Then our only salvation will be to flee into the heart of the forest, and hide. May Heaven help us when they blow the horn!

LENDORE: Yes. Well, meanwhile, give me a hand in gathering my provisions.

(They start out, but encounter Brun coming in.)

BRUN: Do you have to take up the whole path?

LENDORE: No, but I wish you would watch where you step. You just crushed a chestnut.

(Exit.)

BRUN: You and your chestnuts! I have an appointment with the Royal Registrar.

EPINARD: Don't venture out into the open. Men are about.

BRUN: Men?

EPINARD: You can see them from there.

(Exit. Brun goes to the overlook. Tiecelin enters.)

TIECELIN: The Royal Register is not accustomed to be kept waiting, Master Brun.

BRUN: Look — Men!

TIECELIN: *(Looking.)*   It is the wine-growers' dance.

BRUN: Don't let them see you.

TIECELIN: Do you take me for a dunce?

(Ysengrin enters.)

YSENGRIN: Brun! Tiecelin! I have been looking for you.

TIECELIN: Men are dancing, Ysengrin.

YSENGRIN: Men?

BRUN: They are celebrating the harvest.

TIECELIN: Don't show yourself. From now on, we shall have to stay under cover.

YSENGRIN: I will not be hedged into this forest all winter with that rascally Fox!

BRUN: Nor I!

TIECELIN: Gentlemen, take heart. Do you know how many counts I have accumulated against him in my book? Twenty-two!

YSENGRIN: But the year is only half over!

BRUN: Are we to suffer through the fall and winter, without any respite from his tricks?

TIECELIN: Do you have anything else to suggest?

YSENGRIN: Yes!

BRUN: Eh?

YSENGRIN: I have a new plan to dispose of the Fox!

BRUN: Now?

YSENGRIN: Now!

BRUN: Without waiting for Tiecelin's book to fill up?

YSENGRIN: Without waiting one more day.

BRUN and TIECELIN: We are listening.

YSENGRIN: Suppose I should convince the King that the lower classes — the pheasants, the ducks, geese, turkeys, chickens, rabbits, pigeons and mice — have chosen me as their defender, and have charged me to challenge Reynard to a duel.

BRUN: Yes?

YSENGRIN: If you two should back me up, with all the prestige of your position, the King would not be in position to refuse the fight, and I should make a quick end to the redhair. You know me.

BRUN: Good! Eh, Tiecelin?

TIECELIN: Why didn't you think of this sooner? You could have saved me a lot of trouble.

BRUN: We'll help you. But if you give that Fox half a chance, he will turn the tables. I want all the chances to be on your side.

YSENGRIN: The chances *are* on my side. I am the best swordsman in the kingdom.

BRUN: Nevertheless, I shall provide the swords. Reynard's will be so skillfully made, that it will break at the first stroke.

YSENGRIN: I can win without such trickery.

BRUN: Some caution is necessary, my dear nephew. Follow my advice, and Reynard will be out of our way soon. I will go to fix the swords. You inform the King.
(Exit.)

YSENGRIN: Do I need this treachery? Am I not stronger and braver than Reynard?

TIECELIN: You are, and without flattery, Siegneur Wolf. But nobody is as tricky as he is.

YSENGRIN: Tiecelin, you are a man of law. Give me your advice. Do you think it is honest and fair to allot him a faked weapon?

TIECELIN: As for being fair, certainly not. Honest — even less so. But as for being smart — ha, ha!

YSENGRIN: Do you think so?

TIECELIN: A trick is just what that Fox deserves!

YSENGRIN: But this one will cost him his skin.

TIECELIN: Isn't that what you wish? Besides, so do I.

YSENGRIN: Then consider it done. You may throw away your book, Tiecelin.

TIECELIN: Throw away my book? This book is going into history! Throw away my book, indeed!

YSENGRIN: As you wish. But we shall make an end of Reynard without it. I am going to arrange this matter with the King. As for you, not a word about this.
(Exit.)

TIECELIN: Count on me, Seigneur. This time Reynard shall definitely be punished.

(Epinard enters.)

EPINARD: Who is going to punish Reynard? You?

TIECELIN: That, Reverend, is a secret. I promised —

EPINARD: Oh, very well. I don't insist.

(Goes to the overlook to watch the wine-growers' dance.)

TIECELIN: Reverend —

EPINARD: Still dancing. Did you call me?

TIECELIN: If I told you that secret —

EPINARD: That wouldn't be very proper, would it? . . . I am listening.

TIECELIN: Ysengrin is going to challenge Reynard to a duel.

EPINARD: Is that a secret?

TIECELIN: No, but what is one — and it is this I beg you to keep secret — is that Reynard's sword will be faked.

EPINARD: Faked?

TIECELIN: It will break in two, at the first stroke.

EPINARD: That is certainly not fair, but it is fitting.

TIECELIN: Do you think so, too?

EPINARD: That scamp has tricked me out of a ham, and a duck-egg. He doesn't deserve any better.

TIECELIN: I couldn't agree with you more.

(Trumpet off.)

The King is calling me.

(He starts out.)

Not a word. It is a secret.

(Exit.)

EPINARD: *(Alone.)* It was bound to turn out this way. Reynard has so often fooled the rest of us. Now it is his turn to be fooled.

(Enter Lendore.)

LENDORE: See how much I have gathered?

EPINARD: We gather what we sow, and I pity — yes, I deeply pity the one who has sown bad seed.

LENDORE: Who has sown bad seed?

EPINARD: Reynard.

LENDORE: Has Reynard been planting seeds?

EPINARD: He has spread the spirit of trickery among the animals, and he will be destroyed by trickery.

LENDORE: Is someone going to destroy Reynard?

EPINARD: Ysengrin is calling for a duel with him.

LENDORE: The Wolf is strong, of course, but Reynard is shrewd.

EPINARD: He cannot escape this time. In fact, my dear Lendore, I will tell you — but for Goodness' sake, don't repeat it to anyone. Reynard will soon meet his end, for his sword will be faked. It will break in two at the first stroke.

LENDORE: Oh, no!

EPINARD: It is a secret, Lendore. Don't tell anybody.

   (Exit.)

LENDORE: It is wrong just the same. Oh! They all agreed we should unite against Men — and that was right. But we should also unite against those who fake swords.

   (Enter Reynard.)

REYNARD: Who fakes swords?

LENDORE: Reynard, I will tell you, because foul play is wrong.

REYNARD: Foul play?

LENDORE: Ysengrin is going to challenge you to a duel.

REYNARD: Ho! I am equal to that kind of trap.

LENDORE: That is not all. They will provide you with a faked sword. It will break in two at the first stroke. Ysengrin will kill you.

REYNARD: That remains to be seen.

TIECELIN: *(Offstage.)*   Reynard! Reynard the Redhair! Where are you?

REYNARD: Here comes the messenger of death. Leave me, Lendore — and thanks, old friend.

LENDORE: Don't forget. It is a secret.

   (Exit.)

TIECELIN *(Offstage.)*   Reynard the Redhead!

REYNARD: What do you want with me?

(Tiecelin enters.)

TIECELIN: Stay where you are. Trumpets!

(Trumpets.)

Royal message! By order of the King — stay there! His Majesty Noble the Lion — don't move! We, Tiecelin the Crow, Royal Registrar — stop — request the Knight Reynard to hold himself at the disposal of the King, in order to meet in a duel the accuser, Ysengrin the Wolf, Marshall of the Court, and defender of the lower class. Let it be known! Signed, Noble the Lion, King of the animals. Trumpets!

(Trumpets.)

REYNARD: Is that all? Pouf, it is not much. Tell your master that Reynard is ready.

(Noble enters.)

NOBLE: Come, Tiecelin, if we have to have this duel, let's get it over. Sound the call.

TIECELIN: Yes, Sire. Trumpets!

(Trumpets. The offstage festival gaiety dies away.)

REYNARD: Hail, oh Noble Sire Lion, the wisest and bravest among us all.

NOBLE: Greetings, Knight Reynard. You already know the reason for my royal call.

REYNARD: I know, Sire.

(Ysengrin enters.)

YSENGRIN: I humbly greet your Royal Majesty.

NOBLE: Greetings, Seigneur Ysengrin.

(Epinard enters.)

EPINARD: God keep you, gentlemen.

NOBLE: Knight Reynard, Marshall Ysengrin has been chosen the champion of the lower class, and I am compelled — against my will, believe me — to grant him the duel he calls for. As weapon, your Cousin has chosen the sword.

(Enter Brun, with two swords.)

BRUN: Here are the weapons, Sire.

NOBLE: You have the choice, Ysengrin.

(Brun openly hands Ysengrin the sword prepared for him.)

YSENGRIN: *(Pretending to select.)*   I'll take this one, the shorter.

BRUN: Here is yours, Reynard.

REYNARD: *(Takes the sword without looking at it.)*   Your Majesty, I cannot accept this weapon.

BRUN: Why not?

YSENGRIN: What does this mean?

NOBLE: Do you refuse to fight?

REYNARD: I am not a champion, your Majesty. I am unworthy to fight Ysengrin with a sword.

(He breaks the sword across his knee.)

NOBLE: What do you mean?

REYNARD: Sire, Ysengrin represents the lower classes, and fights as their champion. I am defending nobody but myself, a poor Fox. I will be satisfied with a Fox's weapon. Attendant!

(Lendore enters, carrying a stick.)

Here, Sire, is my weapon.

NOBLE: This is not customary, but I don't think the Marshall will object?

YSENGRIN: I agree. But under the circumstances, I require the use of a shield.

NOBLE: Granted.

(Brun brings a heavy iron shield.)

REYNARD: My shield!

(Lendore hands him her pillow.)

NOBLE: Do you expect to fight in this attire?

REYNARD: It is good enough for me, Sire.

NOBLE: As you wish, though I think this whole thing is absurd. Gentlemen, take your places. The fight will start when I give the signal, after three trumpet calls. It is strictly forbidden for anyone to interfere in the fight. On guard, Knights, and let the noblest be victorious!

ALL: Let the noblest be victorious!

TIECELIN: Trumpets!

   (Trumpets. The opponents eye each other.)

   Trumpets!

   (Trumpets. Each one raises his shield and gets ready.)

   Trumpets!

   (Trumpets.)

NOBLE: Go!

   (Music. Ballet-mime. Long duel, during which Reynard's cunning is matched against Ysengrin's strength. Reynard uses the pillow as much as the stick. Ysengrin gets nervous and loses his balance. Any impulse on the part of spectators to take Ysengrin's side is sternly frowned down by the King. After several phases, Reynard, with a masterful pillow blow, tumbles Ysengrin to the ground. Immediately he puts his foot on Ysengrin's shield, as a token of victory, and greets the King with his stick. Ysengrin, taking advantage of this moment of inattention, lifts his shield violently, throwing Reynard down, and making him drop his stick and pillow. Ysengrin leaps up and puts his foot on Reynard's chest, threatening him with his sword.)

BRUN: *(Quickly.)*   Ysengrin is the winner!

NOBLE: But only a moment ago —

EPINARD: Heaven has judged.

TIECELIN: His Majesty will declare Ysengrin the winner!

NOBLE: *(Reluctantly.)*   Seigneur Ysengrin, I proclaim you Reynard's conqueror. His life belongs to you.

YSENGRIN: I want him to hang. But first of all, I want him humiliated in front of all — to beg forgiveness for his crimes. After that, he shall die.

REYNARD: Oh, Ysengrin, you are truly generous, to give me the opportunity to confess my sins, and beg forgiveness. Let me confess privately to each of you, and ask your blessing.

NOBLE: Granted, my poor Reynard. Come, gentlemen, let us make it possible for Reynard to unburden his conscience.

BRUN: That Fox will find a way to escape, if we give him such a chance.

NOBLE: If you are afraid of that, Seigneur Brun, you may keep watch on the east side, and Ysengrin will guard the west. I myself will take care of the north.

369

EPINARD: *(Indicating the auditorium.)* Do you wish me to watch the south?

NOBLE: It is not necessary, Reverend. The forest is impenetrable, this side. Who will be the first to hear your confession?

REYNARD: Lendore, if you will allow it.

NOBLE: Granted. Let's go, gentlemen. And keep watch.

(All leave, except Lendore and Reynard.)

LENDORE: My poor Reynard.

REYNARD: *(On his knees.)* Draw nearer, Lendore, and receive my confession.

(Whispers.) Look as stern as you can, and open your ears.

LENDORE: *(Loudly.)* Go on, wretched scoundrel. Unload your conscience, and don't dally.

REYNARD: *(Whispering.)* You must get me out of this fix.

LENDORE: All the roads of escape are guarded.

REYNARD: If I cannot run away, we must make *them* do it. Go out and find a loud instrument somewhere, to make a big noise. Imitate the barking of dogs. Make a monstrous uproar. If you can make them think the hunters are here, they will run away? Do you understand?

LENDORE: You can count on me.

REYNARD: Give me your blessing, good and loud, for their benefit. Thanks, old friend, and don't fall asleep on your way. Hurry back!

LENDORE: One for all, all for one.

(Exit.)

REYNARD: Next, Ysengrin.

(Ysengrin approaches.)

YSENGRIN: Well, Master Joker. Are you expecting to receive our pardon?

REYNARD: Ysengrin, I acknowledge that I fully deserve the fate that lies in store for me.

YSENGRIN: Oh, yes?

REYNARD: Yes. And besides, if I had to lose, I'm glad to lose to so brave an adversary.

YSENGRIN: Enough hypocrisy!

REYNARD: I don't want to leave this world without proving that I hold no grudge against you for your victory. A short while ago, I spotted an easy and very appetizing prey. How would you like to benefit from it, since I shall not be here any more?

YSENGRIN: Is this your confession?

REYNARD: How would you feel about a plump hen?

YSENGRIN: Easy to catch?

REYNARD: Child's play. Every night she takes a walk right here, looking for her rooster. Just hide over there when twilight comes, imitate the rooster's cry, and the hen will come to you trustingly. You can make short work of her, if you strike her down with a heavy stick. Hit well and hit hard, for she is tough to kill, they say. That hen, Cousin, ought to be worth your benediction.

YSENGRIN: Yes. Pax vobiscum.
(Exit.)

REYNARD: Next, Uncle Brun.
(Enter Brun.)

BRUN: Not hanged yet?

REYNARD: In good time, Uncle.

BRUN: I shall not be sorry for it.

REYNARD: I will not beg your pardon, for I have done you too much wrong, but let me be remembered for one last good turn. Would you like a good meal?

BRUN: Is it another bumble-bee's nest?

REYNARD: Don't talk so loudly. It is a wonderful rooster. Each night, he strolls right here, looking for his hen. Just hide over there, and imitate her cackling to lure the rooster. It will be child's play for you to strike him down with a heavy stick. Hit well and hit hard, for he is tough to kill, they say.

BRUN: Is this not a new trap?

REYNARD: Uncle! How can you think I would play you a trick at the moment I am going to die? No. I wish you good appetite, and ask your blessing.

BRUN: Go in peace. And may the rope be quickly ready, so you may go soon.
(Exit.)

REYNARD: Thank you, Uncle. Don't forget. Over there, when twilight comes.

(To himself.) What the dickens can be keeping Lendore?

(Aloud.) Next, Sire.

(Noble enters.)

NOBLE: Reynard, I was maneuvered into this, and now I am powerless to help you.

REYNARD: Rest easy, Sire. I attach no blame to you. Let me only take this last chance to thank you, Sire, for your many kindnesses —

NOBLE: Oh, Reynard, how am I to do without you?

REYNARD: I am only a wicked Fox, Sire.

NOBLE: You are the only honest rogue among us. Why did you let yourself in for this? Don't you know they will not rest until they have your life? See, here is Brun, with the rope.

(Brun enters, with tying-rope.)

BRUN: Sire, the time has come to tie him up.

REYNARD: (To himself.) And still Lendore has not come back.

(The company re-gathers on stage. Brun ties Reynard's hands.)

YSENGRIN: (Brings hanging-rope, flings it over tree-limb.) Next. You, Reynard.

REYNARD: (Tied.) Here I am. May God have mercy on me, a miserable Fox, who was led by demons to the most dreadful crimes.

BRUN: Hang him quick, and let us forget about it.

REYNARD: But where is Lendore?

BRUN: She is gone.

REYNARD: I would like to hug her one more time.

YSENGRIN: Don't let us wait any longer, Sire.

REYNARD: May I not see her once more?

BRUN: Can't you see he is only trying to gain time?

REYNARD: She was my true friend.

BRUN: Ah, well, let's put an end to this.

372

TIECELIN: Hang him!

   (Ysengrin pulls the rope, experimentally. At this moment, there is the sound of a hunting-horn.)

BRUN: Men!

EPINARD: *(Rushing to look.)*   They have stopped dancing?

   (An outbreak of dog-barks, offstage.)

YSENGRIN: Dogs!

BRUN: On the chase!

   (A dramatic explosion of rapid-fire, staccato bangs.)

EPINARD: It is the hunt!

NOBLE: The hunt is on: Take cover!

   (Noble flees.)

TIECELIN: Escape if you can!

   (Exit, flying. General flight.)

YSENGRIN: *(Holding Reynard's hanging-rope.)*   Wait! Wait! We must hang him!

BRUN: Come! Do you wish to get pulled apart by dogs?

   (Exit.)

YSENGRIN: *(Torn, he starts off, hesitates.)*   But —

   (Another burst of rapid-fire bangs, accompanied by barking.)

   Farewell, Master Reynard. The dogs will take care of you.

   (Exit.)

REYNARD: *(Alone.)*   Lendore was a true friend.

   (Lendore enters, beating a saucepan, blowing a hunting-horn, and barking.)

LENDORE: Woof! Woof! Bow-wow! Bow-wow!

   (She laughs.)

   Ha, ha, ha! I never saw them run so fast!

REYNARD: Thanks, my dear. It was high time.

LENDORE: *(Releasing him from the rope, and untying his bonds.)*   You'll never know the trouble I had to find this horn, and this saucepan.

373

REYNARD: My good friend, I must be off.

LENDORE: Where will you go?

REYNARD: I will have to make for the outer edge of the woods.

LENDORE: *(Concerned.)*   But that is where the men do their hunting.

REYNARD: If I can elude this pack of rascals, I can surely stay out of the reach of men.

LENDORE: Take care, Reynard.

REYNARD: I will need a little time to get away. If you will be good enough to keep up the music a few moments —

LENDORE: Oh, gladly!

REYNARD: Good bye, old friend.

(Lendore gleefully beats, blows, and barks, though her barking turns a little plaintive, as she watches Reynold go. As she goes out the opposite side, her noise retreats, and soon gives way to the renewed sounds of celebration in the distant vineyard. Lights dim slowly, leaving the empty stage in twilight. Cautiously, Tiecelin peers around a bush, then creeps in.)

TIECELIN: *(Alone.)*   The rope is empty. Reynard is gone. But where is the hunt?

(Music and laughter from the vineyard, Tiecelin runs to look.)

They are dancing again. Ah-h-h! It was all a hoax! There were no hunters. There were no horns. There were no dogs. There was only noise. Reynard has fooled us once again. Oh, that wily Fox! He has out-tricked Ysengrin. He has out-tricked Brun. But he will not out-trick me. I still have my book. And this will make his twenty-third crime!

(Exits. A moment of music. Night falls. Semi-darkness with light background, so that the following scene may be played in silhouette. Ysengrin enters, right side, with stick.)

YSENGRIN: This is the place where Reynard told me to look for that hen. Kikikiki —

(Brun enters, left side, armed with club.)

BRUN: Cluck, cluck, cluck —

YSENGRIN: Kikiriki —

(They advance slowly toward each other.)

BRUN: Hold still, you rooster!

YSENGRIN: Rooster? How dare you call me a rooster! Take that, you miserable hen!

BRUN: Hen? Is this a hen stroke?

(They fight in earnest, and quickly discover each other at the same time.)

Ysengrin! So you want to fight, do you?

YSENGRIN: Brun! What are you beating me for?

BRUN. *(Chasing him.)*   I'll show you what a beating is.

YSENGRIN: *(Fleeing.)*   Help! Help!

(From the distant vineyard comes a burst of laughter.)

End of Scene Three

(Music. Wind. In the distance the howling of the Wolf can be heard. Stage lights come up slowly. Tiecelin, shivering, is stamping his feet. Brun enters, muffled up in his fur.)

TIECELIN: It is winter, Master Brun.

BRUN: You don't have to tell me.

TIECELIN: Here we are, huddled together in a tight little circle, with fortifications all around us. We don't even have any place to run, to keep warm.

BRUN: Hug yourself with your feathers.

TIECELIN: I have tried that, but my feathers are cold, too. And the frost has made the ground so hard that it doesn't provide food any more. I am hungry, Seigneur Brun, and I am not the only one. Listen to the Wolf. What bitter cold! The pool is covered with ice, and even my tongue is frozen, and stiff as a stick.

BRUN: If you kept your mouth shut, this wouldn't happen.

TIECELIN: I would gladly shut it on some food, wouldn't you?

(Lendore crosses slowly, pillow under her arm, overwhelmed with sleep.)

Where are you going?

LENDORE: To sleep.

(Noble enters, overcome by a comic cough.)

NOBLE: Find me a doctor. Promise him a fourth, even half of my kingdom, but let him release me from this awful cough.

TIECELIN: A doctor? Where are we to find a doctor?

BRUN: We are holed up here like fugitives.

TIECELIN: Beyond the barricade, hunting dogs are waiting to pounce on us.

BRUN: And behind them are the hunters with their guns.

TIECELIN: None of us dares to stick our nose beyond the barricade.

NOBLE: But this is a matter of life or death.

TIECELIN: Your Majesty only has a bad cold.

NOBLE: Bad cold? Your King is dying of pneumonia, and there is no one here to lift a finger. Oh, where is Reynard!

TIECELIN: Reynard? The redhair!

NOBLE: Yes. Oh, my good Reynard, if you were only here!

BRUN: He'd better not show his face around here.

NOBLE: Find him. Search the kingdom!

TIECELIN: Outside the barricade, where the dogs are lurking?

NOBLE: Even to the edge of the forest!

BRUN: The edge of the forest, where men are waiting with their guns?

TIECELIN: Would you have us risk our lives?

NOBLE: Yes! Bring me Reynard.

TIECELIN: Your Majesty, Reynard is in hiding. He would not dare to come.

BRUN: He knows a hanging is waiting for him.

NOBLE: Tell him I will forgive him everything, if he will only come back.

(Lendore exits quietly, but purposefully.)

BRUN: Forgive him?

TIECELIN: Forgive him all the crimes he has committed against us?

BRUN: Forgive him this rope?

TIECELIN: It is beyond your power, Sire. My book is full of indictments against him — twenty-four, to be exact.

NOBLE: Then I am doomed. Only Reynard can find a way to save me.

(Ysengrin enters, starving, violent.)

YSENGRIN: Give me something to eat — no matter what, but something.

NOBLE: I am sick, Ysengrin.

YSENGRIN: And I am hungry, Sire.

TIECELIN: Be patient, Sire. Don't die yet. When good weather returns, you will be well again.

NOBLE: I shall not last that long, my friends. My kingdom! Who will save my kingdom?

BRUN *and* YSENGRIN: *(At the same time.)* I! Me!

377

TIECELIN: Gentlemen.

YSENGRIN: *(Pushing Brun back.)* I can take your place, Sire. Don't be afraid to die.

BRUN: *(Elbowing Ysengrin away.)* I can do it, Sire. You may trust me.

TIECELIN: Don't die, your Majesty, or these two will kill each other to take possession of your throne.

NOBLE: Death is inexorable, my friends. There is only one who can help your poor, unfortunate King, and he is not here.

(Outbreak of savage barking.)

Listen!

BRUN: It is the dogs!

YSENGRIN: The dogs have broken through!

TIECELIN: The hunters have found us!

BRUN: They are coming!

YSENGRIN: We are trapped!

NOBLES *(Struggling weakly to his feet.)* My friends, gather round me. We shall die together.

(Cowering together in a close huddle, they await the enemy's approach. Lendore enters, followed by Reynard, disguised as a Minstrel.)

LENDORE: Your Majesty —

NOBLE: Lendore!

TIECELIN: Lendore? It is not the hunters?

LENDORE: Hunters? It is only a poor Minstrel I found hiding beneath the barricade, to escape the dogs. I thought he might be able to help you.

BRUN: If he led the dogs to our stronghold, we are all done for.

TIECELIN: How did you get by the hunters?

REYNARD: *(Minstrel accent.)* Perdone, Senor. I no understanda very well.

YSENGRIN: Who are you, who plays the guitar while our King is dying?

BRUN: Cease your music, vagrant.

REYNARD: No de musique? Porque?

TIECELIN: The King is dying.

NOBLE: Let him approach. Who are you?

REYNARD: Un troubadour, from Andalusia d'Espagne, my gran Senor.

NOBLE: Can you play and sing?

REYNARD: Si. Very good player and singer. And very good doctor, too.

NOBLE: What? You are a doctor? Can you cure my pneumonia?

REYNARD: Si, Senor. I can cure anychosa.

BRUN: Beware. He is a spy.

REYNARD: I can save el gran Senor.

YSENGRIN: Get away.

REYNARD: I can kill la pneumonia, just like that — crac!

NOBLE: Do you really have a remedy?

REYNARD: Si, Senor, un gran remedia.

NOBLE: Relieve me of this cough, and you shall become my prime minister.

BRUN: Allow me, Sire —

NOBLE: I have spoken.

YSENGRINN: What remedy do you recommend?

REYNARD: *(Showing a bottle.)* Esta boteilla, gran Senor. Vino. Good vino. Vino grandissimo to kill la pneumonia.

NOBLE: Give it to me.

REYNARD: Ma, que, but it is not enough by itself. Needa still some otrechosa.

NOBLE: Some other things, such as what?

REYNARD: *(Makes gesture of pulling his moustache.)* Some chosa like this, but bigger, moocha bigger.

NOBLE: A big moustache?

REYNARD: Moustachio, si, yes. Yes, moustachio! Like that!

(Points to Brun.)

379

BRUN: My moustache?

REYNARD: Si, Senor. Si. Gracias.

NOBLE: Has it got to be cut?

REYNARD: Cut? Si, yes. That is of the most importance. It goes in la pocha —

(Shows his leather pouch.)

— and then on la cabeza, there.

(Indicates the King's head.)

NOBLE: Brun, your moustache.

BRUN: But Sire, it is impossible.

NOBLE: *(Stern.)* Your moustache.

BRUN: I shall be disgraced.

NOBLE: It is your King's life.

YSENGRIN: You cannot refuse, my dear Brun.

REYNARD: *(Scissors ready.)* Cut?

BRUN: Sire?

NOBLE: I am waiting.

YSENGRIN: Go ahead, troubadour.

(Reynard cuts off half of Brun's moustache.)

BRUN: Let Heaven be the witness of my disgrace!

NOBLE: It is for your King's welfare, Seigneur Brun.

REYNARD: It is truly un gran moustachio, Senor the Majesty. Half will be enough. No cut la otre. No wish to rob the fat senor.

BRUN: But Sire, I look ridiculous.

NOBLE: You will wear the half-moustache in remembrance of your self-sacrifice.

REYNARD: *(Putting moustache in his pouch.)* Ah, that is good, so far. But gran senor, that is not all.

NOBLE: You need something else? What is it?

REYNARD: A ball of white fur.

NOBLE: White fur?

REYNARD: Si. Oh, a very little ball. Perhaps no more than that.

(Points to Ysengrin's ears, which are lined with white.)

YSENGRIN: My ears? Oh, no!

(Frantically seeks a means of escape.)

REYNARD: Not the ears, senor. Only the white lining of them.

NOBLE: How lucky! Use your scissors, troubadour.

YSENGRIN: But Sire, I need my ear-linings!

BRUN: You cannot refuse, my dear Ysengrin.

NOBLE: This is for your King.

YSENGRIN: I shall never be the same!

NOBLE: Go ahead, Minstrel.

YSENGRIN: My ears! My ears!

REYNARD: *(Cutting.)* If the senor would only stand still — I do not wish to hurt the senor.

YSENGRIN: Ouch! He is taking my whole ear, Sire! Tell him to — Ouch!

REYNARD: Ah! Since the senor is so unhappy to lose a little bit of fur, we may content ourselves with this one piece.

(The ear he has trimmed has lost its erectness, hangs down ludicrously over one eye. The other ear stands up.)

YSENGRIN: But my ears will not match!

REYNARD: Small matter. We do not wish to ask too great a sacrifice of the senor.

YSENGRIN: I am lop-sided!

NOBLE: In the service of your King, Seigneur Wolf. You are sure you have enough white fur for the remedy, troubadour?

REYNARD: Oh, si, gran senor.

NOBLE: And now do you need anything else?

REYNARD: Only one otrechosa, Sire.

NOBLE: And what is that?

REYNARD: We must have three black feathers.

(Tiecelin starts creeping out.)

NOBLE: Tiecelin!

TIECELIN: You c-c-called me, Sire?

REYN(RD: Ma, que, such beautiful, glossy black feathers!

NOBLE: Tiecelin, we have need of some feathers.

TIECELIN: But I have no feathers to spare, Sire.

REYNARD: Ah, si, si. On this side, too short. In front, too soft. On this side, the colour is not true. But ah, the back is just right.

(He seizes Tiecelin by the tail feathers.)

TIECELIN: Sire! He would not take my tail!

NOBLE: Do you find there what you require, troubadour?

REYNARD: Ah, si, si, Senor the Majesty.

TIECELIN: Help! Help! My beautiful tail!

YSENGRIN: Your tail is no better than my ear, Tiecelin.

BRUN: Or than my moustache.

REYNARD: *(Plucking.)*   One!

TIECELIN: Aie!

NOBLE: It is for your King's life, Tiecelin.

REYNARD: Two!

TIECELIN: Aie!

YSENGRIN: At least you will not be one-sided.

REYNARD: Three!

TIECELIN: Aie! Oh, I am so undressed! Sire, I shall take my death of cold.

(He does indeed look odd, with his stub tail.)

REYNARD: *(Placing feathers in the pouch.)*   I regret any inconvenience this may cause the little senor. Now, your Majesty, all is ready. Gran senor. On la cabeza. There.

(He places the pouch inside Noble's crown.)

NOBLE: Are you sure this will cure me?

REYNARD: Oh, very sure, gran senor.

NOBLE: And if your remedy doesn't work?

REYNARD: Then we shall have to resort to extreme measures. But let us hope for the best.

NOBLE: No extreme measures. This will cure me. I can feel it. Give me that bottle.

REYNARD: Ah, si. This is the wine that gives life.

NOBLE: The moustache, what is it for?

REYNARD: Strength. It is the strength of the fat senor.

NOBLE: And the fur?

REYNARD: Warmth. It will dissolve the cough.

NOBLE: And the feathers?

REYNARD: It is a cover, to hold the strength and the warmth in. With the wine, it will spread through the body, and give new life. Drink.

(Noble drinks. All watch with suspense.)

TIECELIN: How does your Majesty feel?

NOBLE: To tell the truth, I don't feel any difference.

REYNARD: Ah, then, we shall have to use the last resort. For this I shall need three needles.

NOBLE *(Alarmed).* Needles? What for?

YSENGRIN: Needles? The Reverend!

BRUN: Of course. Epinard.

TIECELIN: I'll fetch him.

(Exit.)

NOBLE: What are these needles for?

REYNARD: Ah, Senor the Majesty is so very fortunate, to have such willing subjects to supply every need.

NOBLE: But what do you propose to do with these needles?

(Tiecelin returns with Epinard.)

EPINARD: Peace be with you, Master Troubadour.

REYNARD: Ah, si. I can see that he has needles to spare.

EPINARD: *(Bristling.)* Needles? What is this about needles?

NOBLE: That is what I want to know.

REYNARD: We wish to request a small favour of you, Reverend, with your permission.

YSENGRIN: With or without your permission, his Majesty desires you to give up three needles to this troubadour here.

EPINARD: But my needles are my protection!

BRUN: Don't be stingy. You have plenty of them.

(Reynard has circled him, and selected three choice needles, between his ears.)

EPINARD: But your Majesty, I am not — Ow! Have some respect for my — Ow! Will you give me a chance to — Ow! Oh, I am unfrocked!

TIECELIN: It is for your King, Reverend.

REYNARD: Here are three needles, gran senor — nice and long and sharp.

NOBLE: Wait! I demand to know what you intend to do with these needles.

REYNARD: Why, if the first remedia has not cured you, it will be necessary to bleed you, Senor the Majesty.

NOBLE: Oh, no!

REYNARD: First in the arm —

NOBLE: Wait!

REYNARD: Then in the leg —

NOBLE: Stop!

REYNARD: And then, of course, in the — ah — underneath the — ah —

NOBLE: Enough! It is not necessary. I feel better now.

REYNARD: Ah, the remedia is taking effect?

NOBLE: I feel perfectly well. Throw those needles away.

REYNARD: My congratulations, Sire. The King is saved, gentlemen.

ALL: Long live the King!

NOBLE: Thank you. As for you, troubadour, I wish to reward you.

YSENGRIN: Are you going to make him your prime minister?

NOBLE: Did I say that?

BRUN: It is impossible, Sire. A Minstrel — a guitar-player —

NOBLE: Did I really promise it?

TIECELIN: According to law, Sire, a stranger cannot hold office in the animal kingdom.

NOBLE: Ah! You hear, Troubadour. The law prevents it.

REYNARD: The gran senor is cured, that is good. The povre Minstrel is not minister, that is also good. I ask only the gift of your royal favour in the country of los animalos.

NOBLE: Granted. Take this.

YSENGRIN: Your ring, Sire!

BRUN: The King's diamond!

TIECELIN: It is worth a million at least.

NOBLE: Is this too high a price for my life?

TIECELIN: No, indeed, indeed.

NOBLE: This ring will be the token of my royal protection. Whenever you show it to anyone in my kingdom, help and assistance will be granted you.

REYNARD: The senor is gran, gran como la luna. I am his servitor.

NOBLE: Do you wish anything else?

REYNARD: Only la pocha, there.

BRUN: My moustache!

NOBLE: Half of your moustache.

YSENGRIN: My ear!

NOBLE: The lining of one ear.

TIECELIN: My tail!

NOBLE: Three paltry feathers.

EPINARD: (As Reynard tucks his quills into the pouch.)   My quills!

NOBLE: We wish you good luck, Minstrel.

REYNARD: Gracias, Senor the Majesty. Now I must go.

BRUN: Go? Out there?

TIECELIN: Sire, if he so much as snaps a twig going through the barricade, the dogs will be upon us in a flash.

REYNARD: Ma, que, Senors, the dogs will be upon me, not you. But have no fear, Majesty. I know how to escape the dogs.

NOBLE: Just the same, it would seem only wise for us all to take cover, until you are safely away. Follow me, gentlemen. Good bye, my good fellow.

REYNARD: The gran senor is good also. Viva, olle the gran senor. And gracias for the so beautiful ring.

(Noble exits, followed by Brun, Ysengrin, and Epinard. Tiecelin pretends to follow, but lags behind, as Reynard prepares to leave. Lendore has fallen asleep.)

TIECELIN: One moment, my friend.

REYNARD: The little senor said "my friend."

TIECELIN: I said "One moment." It is customary, in cases of audience with the King, to leave an expression of your thanks with me.

REYNARD: Ma, que, I did not know.

TIECELIN: Doubtless you do not know that I am the King's Registrar, and that I regulate, manage, and organize everything in the animal kingdom.

REYNARD: Hombre, que, I thought the gran Senor King did it all.

TIECELIN: He does what I command. When I say "Here comes the King," he comes. I say "The King sits down." He sits down. 'The King drinks." He drinks. "The King gets up." He gets up. He can do nothing without my order. Without me there would be no King of the animals any more.

REYN(RD: Ha, que, how about that! The little senor is a very important persona. It is a pity that he had to sacrifice his so beautiful tail plumage to the King's health.

TIECELIN: It is nothing less than a disgrace.

REYNARD: Ah, yes. Your costume is now a little lacking in dignity for a so important persona. Wait! I have a chosa in la pocha, to make him look more gran. Look. Would the senor do me the great honour to accept this, in place of the feathers he has lost?

(He takes out three peacock feathers.)

TIECELIN: They are peacock feathers, aren't they?

REYNARD: Si. The feathers del peacock. The very marvelosa bird que outshines the sun a hundred times, in his brilliance.

TIECELIN: He is a very beautiful bird indeed, but he is stupid.

REYNARD: Ma, que. but this is the tail, not the head. The little senor with the plumage del peacock, and his own gran intelligencio, will make the greatest bird of all, the very gran Phoenix of the occupantos of these woods.

TIECELIN: Do you think so?

REYNARD: Que, it is the truth. It is the thanks del troubadour to the gran persona del little senor.

TIECELIN: I accept the very humble present you give me. Now you may go.

REYNARD: Ah, si. Adios, senor.

TIECELIN: Take care, as you leave, not to draw the attention of the dogs.

REYNARD: Trust me, senor. Servitor, gran Phoenix. Servitor.

(Pretends to leave, but conceals himself on one side. Lendore stirs on the other side.)

TIECELIN: *(Listens tensely a few moments, for any possible disturbance caused by Minstrel's departure.)*   Ah, he is safely away.
(Not noticing Lendore, he adorns himself with the peacock feathers.)

I can feel myself becoming very beautiful, very beautiful indeed. The King is far behind me when it comes to grace, charm, bearing, and elegance. I am really a Phoenix. The Minstrel said so. When the others see me, they will say "Look at the Crow!" And they will be green with envy. They will say "Look at the Crow!" And the echoes of the forest will endlessly repeat — "Look at the Crow!" "Look at the Crow!"

REYNARD: *(Echoing.)*   Oh!. . . Oh! . . . Oh! . . . Oh!

TIECELIN: How beautiful, beautiful, beautiful. How very beautiful! More beautiful than the Wolf, more beautiful even than the Lion. *(Shouts.)*   More beautiful than the King!

REYNARD: *(Echoing.)*   . . . Ing! . . . Ing! . . . Ing! . . . Hee — hee — hee!

(Lendore takes it up, and the echo gradually changes into a laughter which is curiously prolonged.)

LENDORE: Hee — hee — hee — Hi — hi — hi —

TIECELIN: *(At first taken aback, stops and wonders.)*   What? Hush, Echo.

REYNARD: Ho — ho — ho — ho —

387

LENDORE: Ho — ho — ho — ho —

TIECELIN: Instead of laughing, look at the Crow!

REYNARD: Ho — ho — ho — ho —

LENDORE: Ho — ho — ho — ho —

TIECELIN: *(In a rage.)* Are you almost through?

REYNARD: Hou — hou — hou — hou —

LENDORE: Hoo — hoo — hoo — hoo —

TIECELIN: You laugh at me?

REYNARD and LENDORE: Hee — hee — hee — hee —

(The laughter seems to come from everywhere at once.)

Ha — ha — ha — ha! Hee — hee — hee — hee! Look at the Crow! Ho — ho — ho! How beautiful is he! Hee — hee — hee! Ho — ho — ho! Ha — ha — ha! Hohoho! Hahaha! Hihihi! Hohohohahahahihi! Hohohohahahahihi!

(In shame Tiecelin divests himself of the peacock feathers, but the laughter continues to grow in volume.)

TIECELIN: *(Finally manages to top the laughter.)* Enough! Stop!

(Reynard stops, but Lendore, unaware of danger, continues, convulsed with genuine laughter.)

There is more to this than echoes.

(Creeping quietly across he discovers and seizes Lendore.)

Lendore! You were making fun of me!

LENDORE: — — I — Oh, Tiecelin, you were oh, so funny!

TIECELIN: Nobody is going to laugh at me, and live to tell it.

LENDORE: H — H — H — Stop! You are strangling me.

TIECELIN: *(Choking her.)* I am going to do more than that. I am going to feed you to the Wolf!

LENDORE: *(Struggling in his grasp.)* H-h-help! H-h-h-help!

(Reynard steps out of hiding, discarding his cape.)

REYNARD: Let her go.

TIECELIN: *(Frozen.)* I have surely heard that voice before.

REYNARD: Ma, que, senor, your costume is a little lacking in dignity —

388

TIECELIN: *(Trying shamefully to cover up his stub tail.)* Reynard! It is you!

REYNARD: At your service, Tiecelin.

TIECELIN: You, the Minstrel! I might have known it.

REYNARD: *(Placing peacock feathers at his tail and mimicking Tiecelin.)* Am I not beautiful? The most beautiful of all? Am I not the great Phoenix of the deep woods?

TIECELIN: You will pay for this. It is your last trick. Everybody! Come! It is Reynard! It is his twenty-fifth crime! Trumpets! Trumpets!

REYNARD: Am I not splendid? Am I not the best-looking, the most intelligent —

(Trumpets. At the sound, Reynard breaks off short.)

TIECELIN: Everybody come! It is Reynard! Trumpets!

(Reynard runs desperately in all directions, seeking an escape. Trumpets.)

Twenty-fifth crime! Trumpets!

(Trumpets.)

VOICES: *(Off.)* Reynard! Twenty-fifth crime! *(The Epilogue follows immediately, without break.)*

End of Scene Four

EPILOGUE

TIECELIN: By order of the King, his Majesty Noble the Lion —

REYNARD: All right. I know what is coming next.

(He tries to leave at right, but encounters Noble, entering, and has to bow.)

Sire.

NOBLE: Reynard.

(Reynard tries to leave at left, but Brun and Ysengrin enter there.)

REYNARD: Uncle Brun. Cousin Ysengrin.

BRUN: The rope is still in place.

YSENGRIN: We have kept it waiting for you.

REYNARD: I am in no hurry.

NOBLE: This time, Reynard, you have put the noose around your own neck.

LENDORE: Why did you let yourself get caught? Oh, Reynard, I cannot watch this!

(Exit. Epinard enters.)

EPINARD: What brings on this new disturbance? Ah, it is you, Reynard. You must be out of your mind.

NOBLE: Gentlemen.

TIECELIN: The King is about to speak. Trumpets!

(Trumpets.)

NOBLE: We are now at the end of the year of mercy granted to Reynard the Fox. What are the grievances charged against him now?

TIECELIN: A book full, your Majesty. Twenty-five crimes.

(He reads.)

The Knight Reynard, called Reynard the redhair, is accused —

NOBLE: Never mind, Tiecelin. You have all witnessed Reynard's misdeeds. So you will judge if he deserves to hang, or if he should be granted mercy. How do you feel about it?

YSENGRIN: I demand his hanging.

TIECELIN: He must hang!

BRUN: Hang him!

EPINARD: May Heaven forgive me, let him hang.

NOBLE: You hear, Reynard?

REYNARD: Nevertheless, your Majesty, I have the right to present my defense, I presume?

YSENGRIN: There is no defense.

TIECELIN: He has committed twenty-five crimes.

NOBLE: Have you any defender?

REYNARD: Yes, your Majesty.

NOBLE: Who is it?

REYNARD: You yourself, Sire.

NOBLE: I?

REYNARD: Doesn't this ring remind you of anything. *(Minstrel accent.)* The gran senor has lost la pneumonia. El troubadour has cured the gran senor.

NOBLE: So, it was you?

REYNARD: It was me, Sire, at your service.
(All the animals cry out with rage.)

BRUN: He has cut off half my moustache!

YSENGRIN: My ear!

EPINARD: My quills!

TIECELINS *(Writing furiously.)* My feathers! And all this is going in the book!

BRUN: The bumble-bees have stung me all over!

EPINARD: He made away with my ham!

NOBLE: An end to this! Stop! Enough! Silence!

TIECELIN: Let the King speak.
(But the silence is broken by the sound of a hunting-horn, offstage. Lendore flies in, frantic.)

LENDORE: The hunters! The hunters are coming!
(The hunting horn is repeated from a different direction, and again from another. Everyone is electrified.)
They are closing in, from all sides of the woods!

BRUN: This has happened once before.

YSENGRIN: Is this rascal going to escape us again?

TIECELIN: The rope is ready.

BRUN: Let's not wait any longer. Hang him!

(Genuine rifle shots off-stage.)

EPINARD: This is no joke!

NOBLE: We are caught!

(All make a grand rush for the left. The fanfare breaks out on that side, with renewed vigor.)

Tiecelin, go and see what is going on.

TIECELIN: B-b-b-but —

NOBLE: Go and see, I tell you.

EPINARD: It is no use, Sire. We are surrounded.

LENDORE: *(At right.)*   There are more than twenty.

YSENGRIN: *(At back).*   They are coming this way, too.

BRUN: *(At left.)*   And this way.

NOBLE: This time, my friends, we shall not escape the men. Let each one of you show your courage, and defend your life at a high price.

TIECELIN: Sire, I wish you a very gallant death. As for me, I have wings. Allow me to make use of them.

(Exit. His flight is hailed by shouts and rifle shots.)

BRUN: There goes our brave Phoenix.

YSENGRIN: What shall we do with the prisoner?

NOBLE: We are all prisoners, Seigneur Ysengrin.

REYNARD: I can save you, Sire.

BRUN: Don't listen to him. He is only trying to escape.

NOBLE: How can you save us?

REYNARD: Don't move from here. Stay under cover. I will go out of the woods. The fortifications will hold them until I can get out.

YSENGRIN: You see, he is only trying to get away.

REYNARD: I will let the hunters see me, willingly, in the open. The

392

REYNARD THE FOX

dogs will jump for me, and follow my tracks, and the men will follow them. I will lead them out of the woods, to the other end of the plain.

NOBLE: You will lose your life doing that.

REYNARD: It is possible — but it will save yours.

NOBLE: Release him. May Heaven help you!

REYNARD: Farewell, Sire. Farewell, my friends.

(He takes time to choose his exit point with care, then leaps out, to be greeted by furious dog-barking, men's shouts, and rifle shots. Ballet-mime, as the animals left onstage follow the progress of the chase. The cries, the barks, the shots, and the horn-calls intermingle. Cries and yells, close at first — "The fox! The fox! Loose the dogs! Shoot! Shoot!" By some means, possibly by amplifying, there should be a noticeable difference between the human voices and the animal voices. At first the animals huddle together, frozen with terror, silent, distressed, listening intently. As the offstage sounds retreat, they relax enough to register their fear, stopping up their ears, covering their heads, running for shelter, cowering under rocks, bushes, stumps. Eventually the noises fade away in the distance, indicating that Reynard is leading the chase far away. They begin to express their relief, and then their absolute joy, as the hunt moves further away, leaping with elation, embracing each other, dancing in triumph.)

LENDORE: *(Hopping up and down.)* He has done it! He has done it! *(One last, distant, terribly final shot, then a distressing silence.)* Oh, no!
(All are suddenly sobered.)

BRUN: And so, Sire, this is the end of Reynard.

EPINARD: May Heaven welcome his soul.

YSENGRIN: And the hunters his skin.

LENDORES *(Who has rushed to the overlook.)* He is nowhere in sight.

YSENGRIN: Of course not. The dogs have got him.

NOBLE: He could outrun the dogs.

BRUN: But not the bullets, Sire.

YSENGRIN: The hunters have saved us the trouble of hanging him.
(Tiecelin returns, very cocky and proud.)

BRUN: Ah! Now that the danger is over, our valiant Crow returns.

TIECELIN: Sire, you are saved.

NOBLE: Where do you come from?

TIECELIN: From a tree, Sire. When I left here, I risked thousands of rifle shots — and look. Not a scratch.

LENDORE: Have you seen Reynard?

TIECELIN: He is dead. I saw him fall, covered with blood, and crawl under a hazelnut bush.

LENDORE: No!

NOBLE: The brave fellow!

TIECELIN: The dogs will catch up with him shortly. But they will find him dead. So will the hunters. I am the only one who saw his end.

YSENGRIN: Oh, stop your bragging. Reynard is dead, and that is all that matters.

LENDORE: *(Weeping.)*   Poor redhair!

BRUN: We finally got rid of him.

EPINARD: Since he is gone, let him rest in peace.

NORLE: At least he died like a hero — not by hanging.

(Reynard staggers in, tattered, exhausted, faltering, exaggerating his condition dramatically.)

REYNARD: Sire, my King —

TIECELIN: *(Hastily scrambling up his tree.)*   What! You are not dead?

REYNARD: I . . . fulfilled . . . my promise —

(He staggers.)

NOBLE: Yes, good fellow. You have our undying gratitude.

LENDORE: Are you wounded?

REYNARD: No, it is nothing . . . no, nothing —
(He collapses.)

LENDORE: Reynard!

EPINARD: This time, Sire, beyond any doubt, he is really gone.

YSENGRIN: So much the better.

TIECELIN: Beware. He has more than one trick up his sleeve.

BRUN: Oh, no. Look.
(He lifts one leg, which falls back limply.)

TIECELIN: He did that to me once before.

(But he ventures down from his perch, nevertheless.)

EPINARD: *(Lifts one arm, which falls back, lifeless.)*   He has undoubtedly passed away.

YSENGRIN: *(Lifts the tail, which falls back, a dead weight.)*   There is no doubt indeed.

LENDORE: *(Sobbing.)*   He was so good.

EPINARD: He was a rogue.

LENDORE: So witty.

YSENGRIN: He was a scoundrel.

LENDORE: So clever.

BRUN: He was a villain.

LENDORE: So full of fun.

TIECELIN: He was a cheese robber!

EPINARD: A ham robber!

BRUN: A moustache robber!

YSENGRIN: An ear robber!

TIECELIN: A tail robber!

EPINARD: A quill robber!

TIECELIN: And it is all down in my book. See, my book? Here are all his crimes.

NOBLE: Yes — and here is he. We live, because of him. Give me your book, Tiecelin. Let the accusations against him be buried with Reynard.

(He tears out pages, letting them fall on Reynard.)

TIECELIN: My book! My book!

(Silence. Reynard stirs.)

REYNARD: What gentle winds have blown this soft covering over my poor body? Ah, it is my noble King.

(He gathers loose pages and tears them across.)

What a relief it is to know that your royal person is safe from the hunters!

(He rises.)

BRUN: He lives!

LENDORE: Reynard, my friend!

YSENGRIN: He is alive!

TIECELIN: My book! My book!

REYNARD: Ah, you are concerned about your book, Tiecelin? Allow
me to return it to you — at least part of it. And a part for you,
Uncle Brun. And some for you, Ysengrin.
*(Gaily he pelts them all with torn fragments. Tiecelin, driven to
despair by this desecration, scrambles out frantically, trying to
gather them up.)*

BRUN: Sire, he lives — and there goes all the evidence against him.

REYNARD: Indeed. Then we shall have no use for this grim thing.
Let us use it for a gayer purpose.
(He snatches down the hanging-rope, jumps rope for a few steps.)
Come, my faithful friend Lendore, it is a moment to rejoice. If
you will hold this end, perhaps the Reverend will be good enough
to hold the other?

TIECELIN: *(Picking up torn pages.)*   My book! My book!

YSENGRIN: Sire, he is free to start his crimes all over again.

NOBLE: Reynard, you are really a very bad fellow.

REYNARD: I know, Sire. We all have a little bad in us, don't we?
Reverend, can't you turn a little faster?

EPINARD: Reynard, you have not changed one bit.

REYNARD: Faster, Lendore. Sire, won't you join me?
(He takes Noble's hand, and leads him into the game.)

LENDORE: Reynard is alive!
(And as the rope twirls faster, all take up the refrain.)

BRUN: *(Grumpy.)*   Reynard is alive.

YSENGRIN: *(Bitter.)*   Reynard is alive.

EPINARD: *(Resigned.)*   Reynard is alive.

TIECELIN: *(In tears with frustration.)*   My book! My book!

NOBLE: *(Amused.)*   Reynard is alive!

LENDORE: *(Joyful.)*   Reynard is alive!

REYNARD: *(Triumphant.)*   Reynard is alive!

The End

ANDROCLES AND THE LION

by

<small>AURAND HARRIS</small>

A play for the young, based on the Italian Tale of "Androcles and the Lion," and written in the style of Italian Commedia dell'arte.

ANDROCLES AND THE LION

by

AURAND HARRIS

ANDROCLES AND THE LION

The children's theatre field in the 1960's was characterized by growing diversity as writers began to explore themes, styles, and subjects not traditionally associated with theatre for young audiences. Aurand Harris' *Androcles and the Lion*, which was first presented in New York in 1963, figured prominently in this new movement. The fable of the slave and the lion has long been a popular source of material for children's playwrights; thus, when Harris' version of the story was first presented, audiences found the story very familiar, but they also found this dramatization refreshingly entertaining.

Prior to the premiere of Harris' *Androcles and the Lion*, the best-known dramatization of this tale was the version written by George Bernard Shaw in 1912. Shaw, who reportedly wrote this play as a direct reaction against what he saw as condescension in Barrie's *Peter Pan*, expands the lion and slave fable into a discussion of Christianity and martyrdom. Shaw's play has been produced periodically for child audiences since 1912, but it has never been received with the same interest and excitement as has Harris' dramatization. Although these plays are based on the same fable, they are as different as the children's theatre field as a whole at the time when each of them was written. Where Shaw's play is restrained and intellectual, Harris' version is flamboyant and action-oriented; where Shaw's play reinforces the melodrama and the moral of the fable, Harris' dramatization emphasizes the conventions of farce over story or theme.

Harris' *Androcles and the Lion* has become one of the most popular plays of the modern era, primarily because it reflects none of the preconceptions of theatre for children that have governed the work of many playwrights in the past. It is neither moralistic nor predictable. It is, very simply, good theatre. With this play, Harris is successful in capturing the essence of farce, one of the oldest, most difficult, and most popular of all theatre forms.

Harris firmly establishes a comedic tone for this play by first subordinating the essentially serious fable to the conventions and characters of the *commedia dell'arte* troupe — a group that is ostensibly performing the play. The work thus becomes a play-within-a-play with no more noble purpose than to entertain in the tradition of such masters as Goldoni and Moliere.

The *commedia* troupes of the sixteenth century traveled throughout Europe performing improvised comedies based on scenarios and including stock characters. In some instances, speeches for these plays were written out, and directions for the *lazzi* (slapstick comedy routines) were formalized, but they always had at least the appearance of spontaneity as troupes often altered their fare to suit the audiences they were playing. Since these performances were not based on scripts, they came to be comprised primarily of the comic interaction among the stock characters. The emphasis was on witty repartee, broad physical humor, and fast-paced, fluid action. Although not one of these elements can be found in the original tale, or in George Bernard Shaw's dramatization of the story, they are the basic fabric of Harris' play.

In this play the fable is altered significantly to accommodate several of the stock *commedia* characters. The servant character, often the major focus in *commedia* scenarios, very naturally fits into the slave role in the play. Since there is not an appropriate *commedia* character for the role of the lion, Harris side-steps this problem by having the actor who delivers the prologue (introduces the play in the style of the *commedia*) portray the lion. All of the other characters in the play (the foolish young lovers, the braggart warrior, and the miserly old man) are taken directly from the *commedia* tradition, and, where appropriate, Harris has added scenes to the original tale so that these characters can play out their typical *lazzi*. The interaction between the characters thus becomes as important a part of the play as the story of the slave and the lion.

The original fable is an epigrammatic tale with a very pointed moral. Shaw elected to use this moral as the basis for an extended polemic; Harris chose to use this moral as the basis for a light-hearted anecdote. In the spirit of the *commedia dell'arte* the humor of the play is predicated on developing a non-illusionistic relationship between the actors and the audience. From the introduction of the characters, through the narrated exposition and comic aides, to *Androcles'* farewell speech, the characters invite the audience to join them in poking fun at themselves and their world. When a character has to consult the scenario to find his place in the action, the audience members are reminded that they are in the theatre. When Androcles "hides" behind a non-existent tree to escape from the lion, the audience members freely allow him that convention. It is a zany world that creates its own logic: the logic of farce.

A very important part of this farcical world is the language spoken by the larger-than-life characters. The melodic dialogue, which includes various combinations of rhythm and rhyme, is in hilarious contrast to the seriousness with which each character pursues his or her goal. In some instances Harris interperses rhymed couplets with long lists of rhyming words. He also uses multiple rhymes within a single speech, as well as sometimes having one character's line complete the rhyme scheme begun in the line of a different character. Within the lines themselves one finds assonance, consonance, alliteration, and virtually every other combination of sound and sense. Some lines flow easily, while others have a deliberate halting effect that is humorously capped with a seemingly forced rhyme. Harris uses these techniques with a skillful unpredictability, and the audience is invited to laugh at the techniques of writing as well as the nonsense of the word-play.

The characters of this play are types that have their roots in the New Comedy of ancient Greece, and that have been perfected through appearances in centuries of farcical drama. The modern audience knows these characters and their predictable antics very well, and the audience savors the anticipation of this behavior more than any suspense that might be created in the story. When Androcles hides in the cave, not knowing he is sharing it with the lion, the spectators know that Androcles will not be harmed; they also know that at any moment he will discover the lion and burst from the cave screaming in exaggerated comic fear. Audiences wait expectantly for this action and howl at the precision with which it is carried out.

Such buffoonery and slapstick humor can be found in all of the characters and character interaction in this play. The frenzied chase scenes, the exaggerated proclamations of love, and the ridiculous behavior of the inept soldier are all a part of the language of farce. It is a language that Harris uses very well.

Since its inception in the ribald rituals of ancient cultures, farce has been the drama of the common people; throughout the history of the theatre, when children have been allowed to witness theatre events, it was most often farcical dramas that they saw. Through a broad spectrum of theatre — from Dionysiac revels, to the folk drama of the middle ages, to the traveling *commedia* players, and even to such television fare as "I Love Lucy" — farce has appealed to audiences of all ages because it reduces human foibles to recognizable and hilarious common denominators.

Given the importance of farce in the history of the theatre, it is surprising that very few farces have been written specifically for child audiences. Many plays in the history of dramatic literature for children include broad physical humor, but most often as a device to make the antagonist appear foolish at the point of his downfall, and then only as a small part of a very serious world. Madge Miller's *The Land of the Dragon* is important as one of the few plays written before mid-century that is constructed primarily in the tradition of farce, but even this work includes characters, language, and a story that are much like those of the ubiquitous fairy tale dramas.

With *Androcles and the Lion*, Harris effectively breaks away from many of these delimiting traditions of theatre for children. The play includes one-dimensional characters and a simple story with a predictable happy ending, but Harris uses these traditional elements very much to the advantage of the play. While it is a good play for children, in the true tradition of farce, this play speaks to all ages in terms that are timeless in their simplicity and hilarious in their execution.

AURAND HARRIS was born in Jamesport, Missouri, on July 4, 1915. He attended the University of Kansas City (A.B. 1936), Northwestern University (M.A. 1939), and Columbia University (John Golden Prize 1945). Harris has worked as a teacher at Grace Church School in New York City, in addition to serving short terms as playwright-in-residence at several universities throughout the country. He was a recipient of the Chorpenning Cup from the Children's Theatre Association of America in 1967, and a National Endowment for the Arts Grant in 1976.

Harris is currently America's most-produced children's theatre playwright. Although his career has also included writing plays for adults, since 1955 his focus has been an dramatic literature for children. His plays range from dramatizations of traditional material, such as with *The Plain Princess* and *The Brave Little Tailor*, to plays based on original material, such as *The Arkansaw Bear*.

A more complete summary of Harris' life and work can be found in *Six Plays for Children by Aurand Harris*, with biography and play analyses by Coleman Jennings (Austin, Tx: University of Texas Press, 1977).

ANDROCLES AND THE LION

Adapted by

AURAND HARRIS

CAST

ANDROCLES

PANTALONE

ISABELLA

LELIO

CAPTAIN

LION AND PROLOGUE

SCENE

The improvised stage of a Commedia dell'arte troupe of strolling players. Sixteenth Century, Italy.
The play is in two parts.

The following is a copy of the programme of the first performance of
ANDROCLES AND THE LION, presented at the Forty-First Street
Theatre in New York City, 7 December, 1963:

Expore, Inc. Presents

Stan Raiff's Production of

ANDROCLES AND THE LION

*A Play With Music in the Style of
Commedia dell'Arte*

by

AURAND HARRIS

Directed by Stan Raiff

Musical Score	*Choreography*	*Costumes and Settings*
Glenn Mack	Beverly Schmidt	Richard Rummonds

ANDROCLES .... Joseph Barnaba

LION .... Richard Sanders

PANTALONE .... Leonard Josenhans

CAPTAIN .... Eric Tavares

ISABELLA .... Jacqueline Coslow

LELIO .... Christopher McCall

Assistant Director: Montgomery Davis

Assistants to Mr. Rummonds: Maryet Ramsey and Charles McNab

For

Stan Raiff

who first produced and directed

ANDROCLES AND THE LION

MUSIC NOTE

The music for *Androcles and the Lion* covers a wide range of styles. In order to enhance the character of the Commedia dell'arte form of the play, we chose to begin and end *Androcles* with music that is reminiscent of the early Renaissance.

Thus, the Overture, Finale, and some of the incidental music utilize rythmic modes, short melodic fragments built from modal scales, and improvised percussion sounds executed by the players, on such instruments as hand drums, bells, and cymbals.

As each of the players is introduced, he is given a musical theme, to help emphasize his character in the play. Some of this material is then used in the songs.

The songs are simple, and were composed with the playwright's co-operation. Their purpose is to bring out the dramaitc quality of various situations. They range from a work-song for Androcles, to a lament for Isabella, and a mock funeral march as the Captain and the Miser march Androcles into the pit.

There is also a chorus for everyone to sing. This, and the Lion's song, which end the first act, invite audience participation.

—Glenn R. Mack
New York City

406

ANDROCLES AND THE LION

ACT ONE

(The curtains open on a bare stage with the cyclorama lighted in many colors. There is lively music and the Performers enter, playing cymbals, flute, bells, and drums. They are a Commedia dell'arte group.

Arlequin, dressed in his traditional bright patches, leads the parade. Next is Lelio and Isabella, the romantic forever young lovers. Next is Pantalone, the comic old miser. Next is the Captain, the strutting, bragging soldier. And last is the Prologue who wears a robe and who later plays the Lion.

After a short introductory dance, they line up at the footlights, a colorful troupe of comic players.)

PROLOGUE. Welcome!
　　　Short, glad, tall,
　　　Big, sad, small,
　　　Welcome all!

(Actors wave and pantomine "Hello".)

We are a troupe of strolling players,
With masks, bells, and sword,

(Actors hold up masks, ring bells, and wave sword).

A group of comic portrayers
Who will act out upon the boards
A play for you to see—
A favorite tale of Italy,
Which tells how a friend was won
By a kindness that was done.
Our play is—"Androcles and the Lion."

(Actors beat cymbals, ring bells).

The players are: Arlequin—

(Arlequin steps forward).

Who will be Androcles, a slave.

(Arlequin bows, steps back, and Pantalone steps forward.)

Pantalone, stingy and old.
Who thinks only of his gold.

(Pantalone holds up a bag of gold, bows, steps back; and Isabella and Lelio step forward and pose romantically).

Isabella and Lelio, two lovers
Whose hearts are pierced by Cupid's dart.

(They bow, step back, and Captain marches forward).

It is the bragging Captain's lot
To complicate the plot.

(Captain waves his wooden sword, bows, and steps back).

There is one more in our cast—
The Lion! He, you will see last.
Set the stage—

(Actors quickly set up small painted curtain backdrop).

Drape the curtains—raise the platform stand!
Here we will make a magic circle—
Take you to a magic land—
Where love is sung, noble words are spoken,
Good deeds triumph, and evil plots are broken.

(Holds up a long scroll).

Our story is written on this scroll which I hold.
What happens in every scene here is told.
(Hangs scroll on proscenium arch at L).
Before we start, I will hang it on a hook
So if someone forgets his part
And has the need, he may have a look
And then proceed.
All the words in action or in song
We will make up as we go along.
All is ready! Players, stand within.

(Actors take places behind curtain).

For now I bow and say—the play—begins!

(He bows).

In ancient Rome our scene is laid,
Where the Emperor ruled and all obeyed.

(Points to curtain which is painted with a street in the middle and with a house on either side).

A street you see, two chariots wide,
With a stately house on either side.
In one lives Pantalone—rich, stingy, sour,

(Pantalone leans out the window-flap on the house at R and scowls).

Who counts and recounts his gold every hour.

(Pantalone disappears).

With him lives his niece, Isabella, who each day

(Isabella leans out the window).

Looks lovingly—longingly—across the way

(Lelio leans out the window of the house at L).

At the other house, where Lelio lives, a noble sir, who looks across lovingly—longingly—at her.

(Lelio sighs loudly. Isabella sighs musically, and they both disappear. Androcles enters from R, around the backdrop with broom).

And all the while Androcles toils each day.
A slave has no choice but to obey.

(Prologue exits at R).

ANDROCLES *(Music. He sweeps comically, in front of the door, over the door, then down the "street" to footlights. SINGS).*

Up with the sun
My day begins.
Wake my Nose,
Shake my toes,
Hop and never stop.
No, never stop until I—
Off to the butcher's,
Then to the baker's
To and from the sandalmaker's.
Hop and never stop.
No, never stop until I—
Spaghetti prepare
With sauce to please her.
Dust with care
The bust of Ceasar.
Hop and never stop.
No, Never stop until I—drop.

Some masters, they say, are kind and good. But mine...! He cheats and he beats—he's a miser. Never a kind word does he say, but shouts, "Be about it!" And hits you a whack on the back to make sure. I'm *always* hungry. He believes in under eating. I'm fed every day with a beating. I sleep on the floor by the door to keep the robbers away. My clothes are patched and drafty because my master is stingy, and cruel, and crafty! When—oh when will there ever be a Roman Holiday for me!

(SINGS).

Will my fortune always be,
Always be such drudgery?
Will hope ever be in my horoscope?
Oh, when will I be free?

PANTALONE *(Enters around R of backdrop, counting money).*
. . . twenty-two, twenty-three, twenty-four, twenty-five . . .

(Androcles creeps up behind him, and playing a trick, taps Pantalone on the back with broom. Pantalone jumps).

Who is there?

ANDROCLES.   Androcles.

PANTALONE.   Be about it! Be off! Go! Collect my rents for the day. Everyone shall pay.

(Androcles starts R).

Lock the windows tight. Bolt the doors.

(Androcles starts L).

My stool! Bring me my stool.

(Androcles exits R).

Lazy stupid fool! There will be no supper for you tonight. Oh, I will be buried a poor man yet—without a coin to put in my mouth to pay for ferrying me across the River Styx.

(Androcles runs in R with stool).

My stool!

ANDROCLES *(Places stool behind Pantalone and pushes him down on it roughly. Pantalone gasps in surprise).*

Yes, my master.

PANTALONE.   Go! Collect my rents. Make them pay. Bring me—my gold. Away!

ANDROCLES.   Yes, oh master. I run!

(He starts "running" to L at top speed, then stops, looks back impishly, and then slowly walks).

PANTALONE *(Brings out bag and starts counting).*

Twenty-six, twenty-seven, twenty-eight, twenty-nine, thirty . . .

ISABELLA *(At the same time, she leans out the window, calls, stopping Androcles).*

410

Androcles . . . Androcles!

(He runs to her U.R. She gives him a letter).

For Lelio. Run!

(Androcles nods and smiles, pantomimes "running" to painted house on curtain at L, pantomimes knocking. There is music during the letter scene).

LELIO *(Appears at his window, takes letter).*

Isabella!

(Androcles smiles and nods. Lelio gives him a letter. Androcles "runs" to Isabella who takes letter).

ISABELLA. Admired!

(Gives Androcles another letter. He "runs" with leaps and sighs to Lelio who takes it).

LELIO. Adored!

(He gives Androcles another letter. He "runs" enjoying the romance, to Isabella who takes it).

ISABELLA. Bewitched!

(She gives him another letter—they are the same three sheets of parchment passed back and forth—which he delivers. This action is continued with a letter to each lover, and with Androcles "running" faster and faster between them).

LELIO. Bewildered!

ANDROCLES. And she has a dowry. The gold her father left her.

("Runs" to Isabella with letter).

ISABELLA. Enraptured!

LELIO. Inflamed!

ISABELLA. Endeared!

(Holds letter).

LELIO. My dear!

(Holds letter).

ANDROCLES. My feet!

(Androcles sinks exhausted to ground. Isabella and Lelio disappear behind the window flaps. Music stops).

PANTALONE *(Picks up the dialogue with his action, which has been continuous).*

...One hundred three, one hundred four, one hundred five, one hundred six...

(Bites a coin to make sure).

one hundred seven...one hundred...

LELIO *(Enters from L, around backdrop).* Signor Pantalone.

PANTALONE *(Jumps from stool in fear).* Someone is here!

LELIO. A word with you, I pray.

PANTALONE *(Nervously hides money).* What—what do you wish to say?

LELIO. I come to speak of love. I come to sing of love!

(Reads romantically from a scroll he takes from his belt).

"To Isabella."

PANTALONE. My niece?

LELIO. "Oh, lovely, lovely, lovely, lovely flower,
Growing lovelier, lovelier, lovelier every hour...
Shower me your petals of love, oh Isabella,
I stand outside—with no umbrella."
Signor, I ask you for Isabella. I ask you for her hand in marriage.

PANTALONE. Marry—Isabella?

LELIO *(Reads again).*

"My life, my heart, revolve about her,
Alas, I cannot live without her."

PANTALONE *(Happy at the prospect).* You will support her?

LELIO. I ask you—give me, Isabella.

(Pantalone nods gladly.)

Give us your blessing.

(Pantalone nods eagerly and raises his hand).

Give her—her dowry.

PANTALONE *(Freezes).* Money!

LELIO. The gold her father left her.

PANTALONE. Gold! It is mine—to keep for her.

LELIO. But hers when she marries.

PANTALONE. How did he find out? No. She shall not marry you. Never! Part with my gold! Help! Androcles!

(Androcles runs to him).

LELIO. Part with Isabella? Help! Androcles!

(Androcles, between them, runs from one to the other as their suffering increases).

PANTALONE. My heart is pounding.

LELIO. My heart is broken.

PANTALONE. Quick! Attend!

LELIO. Lend!

PANTALONE. Send!

LELIO. Befriend!

ANDROCLES *(To Lelio).* There is hope.

PANTALONE. I am ill.

LELIO. Amend!

ANDROCLES *(To Lelio).* Elope!

PANTALONE. I have a chill!

LELIO *(Elated with the solution).* Transcend!

(Exits around L of backdrop).

PANTALONE. I will take a pill!

(Exits around R of backdrop).

ANDROCLES *(To audience.)* The end!

(Comes to footlights and SINGS).

They are my masters and I obey.
But who am I? I often say.
"Androcles!" They ring.
"Androcles!" I bring.
But who am I?
A name—I am a name they call,
Only a name—that's all.

(Speaks simply and touchingly).

My father's name was Androcles. We lived on a farm by the sea. Free to be in the sun—to work the land—to be a man. One day when my father was away, a ship came in the bay. "Pirates," my mother cried. I helped her and my sisters hide, but I was caught and brought to Rome—and sold—for twenty pieces of gold. I thought I would run away! But when they catch a slave they decree a holiday. The Emperor and everyone comes to watch the fun of seeing a run-away slave being beaten and eaten by a wild beast. Personally I don't feel like being the meal for a beast. So I stay . . . just a name . . .

(SINGS).

"Androcles!" They ring.
"Androcles!" I bring.
But who am I?
If I were free
Who would I be?
Maybe . . . maybe . . .
A doctor with a degree,
A poet, a priest, a sculptor, a scholar,
A senator—emperor with a golden collar!
I want to be free
So I can find—me.

PANTALONE *(Calls off, then enters U.R.)*   Androcles! Androcles!

ANDROCLES.   You see what I mean.

PANTALONE.   Androcles!

ANDROCLES   Yes, my master.

PANTALONE.   Quick! Answer the bell. Someone is at the gate.

(Androcles picks up stool and crosses to R).

Then come to me in the garden by the wall.

(Holds up a second bag of gold, different colors from the first)

I am going to bury—to plant—this bag of—stones.

ANDROCLES.   Plant a bag of stones?

PANTALONE.   Be off! To the gate!

(Androcles exits D.R. Pantalone holds up bag, schemingly).

Ah, inside this bag are *golden* stones! It is Isabella's dowry.

(There is a loud crashing of wood off R, announcing the entrance of the Captain).

Who is at the gate? I have forgot.

(Hurries to scroll hanging by the proscenium arch, reads—announcing in a loud voice).

"The Captain enters!"

CAPTAIN *(He struts in D.R., wooden sword in hand. His voice is as loud as his look is fierce).* Who sends for the bravest soldier in Rome? Who calls for the boldest Captain in Italy?

PANTALONE. I—Pantalone.

(Goes to him, speaks confidentially).

I will pay you well—

(Looks away. It breaks his heart.)

—in gold—

(Then anxiously. Androcles peeks in at R).

to guard my niece. I have learned today she wishes to marry. You are to keep her lover away. Stand under her window. Station yourself at the door. Isabella is to be kept a prisoner forever more.

(No reaction from Captain).

ANDROCLES. A prisoner? She will be a slave—like me.

PANTALONE. What do you say?

CAPTAIN *(pompously).* I say—she who is inside is not outside.

ANDROCLES *(To audience).* I say—no one should be held a slave. This is treachery!

(Exits U.R. around backdrop).

CAPTAIN *(Struts).* I have guarded the royal Emperor. I have guarded the sacred temple. I can guard one niece—with one eye shut.

(Shuts one eyes and marches L)

PANTALONE. No, no. The house is over there.

(Points R).

And that is her window.

(Isabella leans out of window).

CAPTAIN. Someone is there! Death to him when he tastes my sword!

(Advances with sword waving).

PANTALONE. No. No! It is she! *(Whispering).* It is—Isabella.

415

ISABELLA (*SINGS happily*).

> Oh, yellow moon
> Mellow moon
> In the tree,
> Look and see
> If my lover
> Waits for me.

PANTALONE (*Softly*). Keep watch. Keep guard. She must not meet her lover.

(Captain salutes, clicks his heels, turns and with thundering steps starts to march. Androcles slips in from around backdrop U.L. and listens).

Sh!

(Captain marches with high, silent steps to window and stands at attention. Pantalone speaks to audience).

I must go to the garden! In this bag is the gold her father left her. I gave my oath to *keep* it—for her. To keep it safely—and for me. I will bury it deep, deep in the ground. Never to be found.

(He hurries off D.L.)

ANDROCLES (*To audience*). More trickery that's wrong. The gold belongs to Isabella.

ISABELLA (*Aware someone is outside*). Lelio?

CAPTAIN (*Laughs*). Ha ha ha—no.

ISABELLA. Oh!

CAPTAIN. I am the Captain!

ISABELLA. Oh?

CAPTAIN. I guard your door. You cannot come or go.

ISABELLA. Oh.

CAPTAIN. Do not despair. I will keep you company. Observe how handsome I am—fifty women swooned today.

ISABELLA (*Calls softly*). Lelio . . .?

CAPTAIN. Know how brave I am—on my way to the barber two dragons I slew!

ISABELLA. Lelio . . . . .?

CAPTAIN. Hear what a scholar I am—I say, "He who is sleeping is not awake."

ISABELLA.   Lelio-o-o-o.

(Cries daintily. Captain makes a sweeping bow to her).

No!

(She disappears, letting the flap fall).

CAPTAIN.   She sighs.

(Louder crying of musical "o's" is heard).

She cries. Ah, another heart is mine! Fifty-*one* women have swooned today!

(Poses heroically).

ANDROCLES.   I must do something! She cannot be put in bondage. No one should be. Everyone should be free. But how—

(Beams with an idea, looks at scroll by proscenium arch and points).

Ah, look and see!

(He quickly reads scroll at side).

Oh lonely moon,
Only moon,
Do you sigh,
Do you cry
For your lover
As—as I?

ANDROCLES   Yes, here is the plan I need!

(Clasps hands and looks up in prayer).

Oh, gods of the temple, please give me the courage to succeed.

(Makes a grand bow to Captain).

Signor Captain!

(Captain jumps).

It is said you are so fierce the sun stops when you frown.

CAPTAIN.   That is true.

(Makes a frightening frown, turns, and frightens Androcles).

ANDROCLES   And that the tide goes out whenever you sneeze.

CAPTAIN.   That is true.

417

(Screws up his face comically, puffs up and up his chest, then sneezes).

A-a-a-achew!

ANDROCLES *(Circling in front of Captain, going to R, toward window).*

Ah, brave and mighty Captain, I shake before you.

(Bows, back to audience, shaking).

CAPTAIN. Yesterday I swam five hundred leagues.

ANDROCLES. I heard you swam one thousand.

CAPTAIN. One thousand leagues I swam into the sea.

ANDROCLES. I heard it was the ocean.

CAPTAIN. The ocean! To meet a ship—

ANDROCLES. A fleet of ships.

CAPTAIN. To meet a fleet of ships!

(Captain suddenly huffs and puffs as he starts pantomiming how he swam in the ocean, his arms pulling with great effort).

ANDROCLES *(At the same time, whispers to Isabella).* I have a plan to set you free, listen—carefully.

(Whispers, pointing to Captain. Pantomimes dropping handkerchief and fanning himself).

CAPTAIN *(Suddenly starts coughing and waving his arms).* Help! Help! I am drowning! Drowning!

ANDROCLES *(Rushes to him, hits him on back).* Save him. Throw out a rope. Man overboard!

CAPTAIN *(Sighs in relief, then dramatically continues with his adventure).* I was saved by a school of mermaids—beautiful creatures —and all of them swooned over me.

ANDROCLES. Then you swam on and on—

ANDROCLES *(Pushing him to exit).* And on—

ANDROCLES *(Pushing him to exit).* And on—

CAPTAIN. And on—

ANDROCLES. And on—

CAPTAIN. And on—

(Exits L, "swimming").

418

ANDROCLES *(Quickly speaks to Isabella).* Do as I say and you can escape. We will trick the Captain. Wave your handkerchief. Get his attention. Then say the night is so warm—fan yourself. As he becomes warmer, he will shed his cap and hat and sword—and you will put them on. You will be the Captain.

ISABELLA. I?

ANDROCLES *(On his knees).* Try.

ISABELLA. The Captain's cape and hat will cover me, and I will be free to go—to Lelio.

CAPTAIN *(Re-enters at L).* After I had sunk the fleet of ships—

ANDROCLES. And brought the treasure back.

CAPTAIN. Treasure?

ANDROCLES. You awoke.

CAPTAIN. Awoke?

ANDROCLES. And found—it was but a dream.

(Isabella waves her handkerchief, then drops it coyly. Captain sees it and smiles seductively).

CAPTAIN. Ah! She signals for me to approach. Signora—your servant.

(Androcles, behind him, motions for Isabella to begin the trick).

ISABELLA *(Accepts handkerchief with a nod).* The night is so warm. The air is so still, so stifling. There is no breeze.

CAPTAIN. I will command the wind to blow a gale.

ISABELLA. The heat is so oppressive.

CAPTAIN. I will command the wind to blow a hurricane!

ANDROCLES My nose is toasting.

CAPTAIN. I will call the wind to blow a blizzard!

ANDROCLES. My ears are roasting.

ISABELLA. The heat is baking.

(Captain, between them, looks at each one as each speaks. Captain becomes warmer and warmer. The dialogue builds slowly so the power of suggestion can take the desired effect on the Captain).

ANDROCLES. Sweltering.

ISABELLA. Smoldering.

ANDROCLES. Simmering!

ISABELLA. Seething.

(Captain begins to fan himself).

ANDROCLES. Stewing!

ISABELLA. Parching!

ANDROCLES. Scalding!

ISABELLA. Singeing!

(Captain takes off his hat, which Androcles takes, as Captain mops his brow).

ANDROCLES. Scorching!

ISABELLA. Smoking!

ANDROCLES. Sizzling!

ISABELLA. Blistering!

(Captain, growing warmer and warmer, removes his cape and sword which Androcles takes).

ANDROCLES. Broiling!

ISABELLA. Burning!

ANDROCLES. Blazing!

ISABELLA. Flaming!

CAPTAIN. Help! I am on fire! Blazing! Flaming! I am on fire!

(Captain goes in a circle, flapping his arms, puffing for air, fanning, hopping and crying, "Fire! Fire!" At the same time, Androcles quickly gives hat, cape, sword to Isabella).

ANDROCLES *(Comes to Captain, who is slowing down).* Throw on water! Throw on water!

CAPTAIN *(Stops, dazed).* Where am I?

(Isabella dressed in Captain's hat, cape, and sword, marches from R and imitates Captain with comic exaggeration).

ANDROCLES *(Salutes her).* Signor Captain! What is your philosophy for the day?

ISABELLA *(Poses and speaks in low loud voice).* I say—he who is outside—is not inside.

420

ANDROCLES.   Yes, my Captain.

CAPTAIN.   Captain?

ISABELLA.   I am off to fight a duel. Fifty-four I slew today. Fifty more I will fight—tonight!

ANDROCLES.   Yes, my Captain.

CAPTAIN.   Captain? Captain! *I* am the Captain.

   (They pay no attention to him).

ANDROCLES.   Your horse is waiting.

   (Pantomimes holding a horse).

   Your horse is here. Mount, O Captain, and ride away.

   (Isabella pantomimes sitting on a horse, holding reins).

CAPTAIN.   I am the Captain!

ISABELLA.   Did you hear the wind blow?

CAPTAIN.   I am the Captain!

ANDROCLES *(Listening and ignoring Captain).*   No.

ISABELLA.   I will ride a thousand leagues—

ANDROCLES.   Two thousand—

ISABELLA.   Three—

CAPTAIN.   I am the Captain!

ISABELLA.   Is that a shadow—there?

   (Points sword at Captain).

ANDROCLES.   A shadow . . .?

   (Takes sword and slashes the air, making Captain retreat fearfully).

   No one is here . . . or there . . . or anywhere.

CAPTAIN *(Almost crying).*   But I am the Captain.

ANDROCLES.   To horse! Away—to the woods.

ISABELLA.   To the woods!

ANDROCLES.   But first, a bag of stones—by the garden wall, yours to take before you go.

ISABELLA.   And then—to Lelio!

ANDROCLES. Yes, my Captain.

CAPTAIN (*Crying comically*). But I am the Captain. Look at me. Listen to me.

ISABELLA. To the woods!

(Starts pantomiming riding off L).

Ride, gallop, trot, zoom!

ANDROCLES. Hop. skip—jump over the moon!

(They "ride" off U.L.)

CAPTAIN (*Crying*). But I . . . I am the Captain.

(Then horrified).

If that is the Captain—then—who—who am I?

PANTALONE (*Enters D.L.*) Captain . . . Captain.

CAPTAIN. Some one calls. Oh, Pantalone . . . Pantalone! Can you see me?

(Waves his hands in front of Pantalone, then shouts in his ear).

Can you hear me?

PANTALONE. Yes.

CAPTAIN. Am I . . . I here?

PANTALONE (*Peers at him*). Yes.

CAPTAIN. Ah, I live. I breathe again.

(Breathes vigorously).

I am the Captain.

(Struts).

Look on my hat and shudder. Look at my cape and shiver. Feel my sword—

(Realizes he has no hat, cape, or sword).

It is gone! Ah, your slave took it. Androcles! It was a trick of his. After him!

PANTALONE. My slave? Ha, ha, a trick on you.

CAPTAIN. And another one dressed in my clothes!

PANTALONE (*Laughing, stops immediately*). Another one?

422

CAPTAIN. One who came from your house.

PANTALONE. From my house?

(Runs to house U.R., then turns).

Isabella!

CAPTAIN. Ha, ha, a trick on you.

PANTALONE *(In a rage).* Fool, stupid, simpleton! You have set Isabella free!

CAPTAIN. I let Isabella free?

PANTALONE. Fathead, saphead, noodlehead! It was she who left the house in disguise—and is off to meet her lover. Stop them! Which way? Which way?

CAPTAIN. He said—

(Thinks, which is difficult).

to the woods!

PANTALONE. Bonehead, woodenhead, block head! Quick! Save her! Before she is wed! To the woods!

(Starts R).

CQPTAIN. He said—

(Thinks).

first, take a bag of stones by the wall.

PANTALONE. A bag of stones—the gold! Muttonhead, pumpkin head, cabbage head! To the garden! Before he finds it.

(Starts to L, as Captain starts R.).

Forget Isabella. Save the gold!

(Pantalone exits D.L. Captain salutes and marches after him. Lights may dim slightly. There is music as the Wall enters D.R. and crosses to C. Wall is an actor (LION) with a painted "wall" hanging on his back and short enough to show his feet. The back of his head is masked by a large flower peeping over the wall. He stands at C, feet apart, back to audience. He puts down a bag of gold and then puts a rock over it.

Androcles, followed by Isabella, tiptoes in U.L. They circle around to D.R. Androcles starts feeling for the wall).

ANDROCLES. The gold is buried—by the wall—

423

(Flower on the wall nods vigorously).

buried under a stone—

(Flower nods again).

Look—feel—find a stone—a stone—a stone—

(Wall stomps his foot, then puts foot on top of stone, but Androcles passes by it).

ISABELLA *(Wall again taps foot and points it towards stone. Isabella sees stone and points to it).* A stone!

ANDROCLES. Ah, I see it! Pray that this will be it!

(Slowly lifts stone).

Behold!

(Holds up bag).

A bag of gold!

(Jumps up, sings and dances).

We've found it! We've found it! We've found the gold! Yours to keep! To have! To hold!

ISABELLA. Sh!

ANDROCLES. You are free—go! Off to Lelio, who implores you—adores you. Quick, do not hesitate. Run—before it is too late.

ISABELLA. Thank you. Some day may you be set free, too.

(Kisses her fingers and touches his nose with it).

Good bye.

(Exits D.L.)

ANDROCLES *(Thrilled that she has touched him).* Fly—arreviderci.

(Sees he has the gold).

Wait! The gold! Isabella forgot the gold! Isabella! Isabella!

(He exits after her D.L. At the same time, Pantalone, followed by Captain, tip-toes in U.L., circling D.R. where they stop).

PANTALONE *(Peering and groping).* It is so dark I cannot see.

CAPTAIN *(Also peering and groping).* Wait . . . wait for me.

PANTALONE. The gold—by the wall—under a stone—find—find—

CAPTAIN. You look in front. I'll look behind.

PANTALONE *(He turns R, Captain turns L. Each peers and steps in the opposite direction on each word).* Search—scratch—dig around it.

CAPTAIN *(Still peering, they now step backwards toward each other on each word).* Feel—touch—crouch—

(They bump into each other from the back).

PANTALONE. Ouch!

CAPTAIN *(Grabs and holds Pantalone's foot).* I've found it! I've found it!

PANTALONE. Knucklehead of soot! You've found my foot!

(Kicks free and creeps toward C).

Here . . . there . . . oh, where . . . where is my gold? The stone . . . the stone . . . where has it flown? Quick . . . on your knees . . . search . . . find . . . use your nose . . . and not to sneeze.

(He and Captain, on their knees, comically search frantically).

Pat . . . pound . . . comb . . . the ground . . . chase . . . race . . . find the place.

(He finds stone).

I have found it! Ah, to gods in prayer I kneel. The stone is here. My gold is back.

(Reaches between feet of Wall, then freezes in panic.)

What do I feel? There is no sack!

(Rises in a frenzy).

I have been robbed! Thieves! The gold is gone!

CAPTAIN *(Rises).* It was the slave who took it! Androcles!

PANTALONE. He is a robber. He is a thief! He will pay for this—with his life!

CAPTAIN. I will find him . . . bind him . . . bend . . . make an end of him!

PANTALONE. He has run away! To the woods! Catch him! Hold!

(Captain stomps to R).

To the woods! Before his tracks are cold.

(Captain stomps to L).

Follow! Follow! My bag of gold!

(Pantalone exits D.L. Captain salutes and follows him. Wall picks up stone, then he pulls the street scene curtain to one side, revealing another curtain behind it and painted like a forest. Over his shoulder, back still to audience, Wall announces, "The forest," and exits quickly at R.

Chase music begins. Isabella and Lelio run in from L, look about).

ISABELLA.   The forest paths will guide us.

LELIO.   The forest trees will hide us.

(They exit U.R. around the backdrop).

ANDROCLES *(Runs in from L).*   Isabella! Lelio! I cannot find you. You have left the gold behind you.

(Exits off U.R. around backdrop).

CAPTAIN *(Enters D.L.).*   After them! I say—follow me! This way!

(Exits U.R. behind backdrop).

PANTALONE *(Enters, wheezing, trying to keep up, from L).*   We are near him. I can hear him—and my gold.

(Pantalone exits U.R. around the backdrop. Isabella and Lelio run in U.L. from behind the backdrop, start to R, but suddenly stop frightened at what they seee offstage R).

ISABELLA.   Oh, what do I see?

LELIO.   It is a — quick! We must flee!

(Isabella and Lelio exit U.R. behind the backdrop. Captain enters U.L. around the backdrop, starts to R).

This way! This way! Follow me! Onward to—

(Stops horrified at what he sees off-stage R).

What is that behind a tree? It is a—Oh, no! We must never meet. The order is—retreat!

(Captain runs off U.R. behind backdrop. Pantalone enters U.L. around the backdrop).

PANTALONE.   Find him. Fetch him. Catch him. My gold has run way.

(Stops and looks off-stage R).

What is that? Can that be he?

(Starts to call).

Andro—No! It is a—Help! It's a lion—coming after me!

(There is a loud roar off R. Pantalone sinks to his knees and quickly walking on his knees, exits L.

Music of Lion's song. Lion enters at R, a most appealing creature. he dances to C and SINGS).

LION.   Have you roared today,
    Told the world today how you feel?
    If you're down at the heel
    Or need to put over a deal,
    Happy or sad
    Tearful or glad
    Sunny or mad,
    It's a great way
    To show the world how you feel!
    Without saying a single word
    Your meaning is heard,
    "Good morning" is dull,
    But a roar is musical!
    Happy or sad
    Tearful or glad
    It's a great way
    To show the world how you feel!

(He gives a satisfied low roar, then looks about and speaks.)

The sun is up. It is another day—

(Yawns).

to sleep. Hear all! The King speaks. No birds are allowed over my cave—chirping and burping. No animals are allowed near my cave—growling and howling. Silence in the woods. The King is going to sleep.

(Actors off-stage imitate animal sounds, loud buzzing, barking, etc. Or actors may in simple disguise with masks enter as animals, dance and make sounds).

Silence!

(All noise and motion stops).

The King says, "Silence."

(Noise and motion increases, Lion becomes angry, puffs up and roars like thunder, stalking about in all directions).

R-r-r-r-r-roar!

(There is absolute silence. If actors are on stage, they run off).

You see—

(SINGS).

A roar's a great way
To show the world how you feel!

(He roars and exits majestically into cave—a split in the painted backdrop).

ANDROCLES *(Enters from around backdrop U.R. He runs to C. He looks anxiously to R and to L, and calls softly).* Isabella . . . ? Lelio . . . ? They are lost in the woods. *I* am lost in the woods. I have run this way—I have run that way—I have run—

(A terrible thought strikes him).

I have run—away! I am a run-away slave! No!

(Calls desperately).

Isabella! Lelio! Where will I go? My master will hunt me. He will track me down. He will take me back. I will be thrown to the wild beasts!

(Sees bag he holds).

The gold—my master will say I stole it. A run-away slave—and

a thief! No, I was only trying to help.

(calls).

Isabella! Help *me*, Lelio.

PANTALONE *(Off L, loudly).* Oh, beat the bushes. Beat the ground. Find my slave. Find my gold!

ANDROCLES. My master! What shall I do? Where shall I go? Hide—

(Runs behind imaginary tree R).

Behind a tree—

(Runs to imaginary bush U.L.)

Under a bush—he can see.

(Points at cave).

What is that? Ah, a cave! I will hide—inside the cave and pray he never finds me.

(Quickly he goes into cave, gives a loud "Oh!," and quickly backs out again).

428

It is someone's house.

CAPTAIN *(Off)*.   Follow me. I say—this way!

ANDROCLES *(Knocks at cave in desperation)*.   Please! Please may I come in? I am—

PANTALONE *(Off)*.   I think—I hear him!

ANDROCLES.   I am—in danger.

(Androcles quickly goes into cave. Pantalone enters U.L. followed by Captain. They are in hot pursuit).

PANTALONE *(Crosses to R)*.   My gold! Find the slave. Bind him! Bring him to me.

CAPTAIN *(Circles D.C.)*.   I will look in every brook and nook and hollow tree!

PANTALONE.   Fetch—catch my gold!

(Exits D.R.).

CAPTAIN.   Follow me!

(He exits D.L. From inside the cave, a long loud roar is heard, and Androcles calls, "Help!" Another and louder roar is heard. Androcles runs out of cave to D.L. and cries "Help . . . help!" Lion runs out of cave to D.R. and roars).

ANDROCLES.   It is a lion!

LION.   It is a man! He will try to beat me.

ANDROCLES.   He will try to eat me.

(They eye each other. Lion springs at Androcles with a roar. Androcles backs away).

I am sorry I disturbed you.

(Lion roars. Androcles holds up bag).

I—I will have to hit you if you come closer.

LION.   Hit—hit until he kills—that is man.

ANDROCLES.   Leap—eat—that is a lion.

(Lion roars and then leaps on him. Androcles struggles and fights, but soon he is held in a lion-hug).

Help! Help!

(Lion roars. Androcles gets his arm free and bangs Lion on the back with bag of gold. Lion roars with surprise and releases An-

drocles. Androcles, thinking he is free, starts off, but Lion holds on to his pants. Androcles, at arm's length, runs in one spot. Androcles gets loose, turns, lowers his head and charges, butting into Lion's stomach. Lion roars. Androcles runs to L and hides behind imaginary tree. Lion, angry, roars and slowly starts to creep up on him. Androcles looks around "tree," one side, then the other, shaking with fearful expectation. Lion springs at him in front of "tree." Androcles leaps and runs back of "tree." Lion turns and runs after him. Androcles tries to escape, running in figure-eights around the two "trees." They stop, each facing opposite directions, and start backing toward each other. Androcles turns, sees Lion, jumps, then cautiously tip toes toward him and kicks the bent over approaching Lion. Lion roars and circles. Androcles laughs at his trick. Lion comes up behind him and grabs him, holding Androcles around the waist and lifting him off the ground. Androcles kicks helplessly. Lion throws Androcles on ground. Lion, above him, roars, raises his paw, and gives a crushing blow. But Androcles rolls over and the paw hits the ground. Lion immediately roars and waves his paw in pain. Androcles cautiously slides away and is ready to run. He looks back at Lion who, with tearful sob-roars, is licking and waving his paw).

ANDROCLES.　　He is hurt. I can run away.

(He starts, but stops when Lion sobs).

He is in pain. Someone should help. No one is here. No one but one—*I*—am here.

(Lion roars in frustration. Androcles turns away in fear. Lion sobs sadly. Androcles looks back at him).

If I go—I maybe can be free! If I stay—

(Lion growls at him).

he may take a bite out of me!

(Androcles starts to leave. Lion sobs. Throughout the scene the Lion "talks" in grunts and groans almost like a person in answering and reacting to Androcles. Androcles stops).

When someone needs your help, you can't run away.

(Trying to be brave, he turns to Lion, opens his mouth, but can say nothing).

I wonder what you say—to a lion?

(Lion sobs appealingly).

Signor—

(Lion looks at him. Androcles is afraid).

My name is Androcles.

(Lion roars, looks at his paw and roars louder).

Have you—have you hurt your paw?

(Lion grunts and nods).

If you—will sit still—I will try to help you.

(Lion roars defiantly. Androcles backs away).

Wait! If we succeed, we will need to—cooperate!

(Lion looks at him suspiciously and grunts).

You don't trust me—

(Lion roars).

and I don't trust you. But someone must take the first step—greet the other, or we will never meet each other.

(Cautiously Androcles takes a step sideways, facing audience. Lion cautiously takes a step sideways, facing audience).

That is a beginning—

(Lion roars. Androcles holds his neck).
But what will be the ending?

(Each raises a leg and takes another sideways step toward each other).

I don't want to hurt you. I want to help you.

(He slowly holds out his hand. Lion "talks" and slowly shows him his paw).

It's a thorn. You have a thorn stuck in your paw.

(Lion breaks the tension, crying with the thought of it and waving his injured paw).

I know it hurts.

(Talks slowly as if explaining to a small child).

Once I stepped on a thorn. My father pulled it out.

(Lion grunts and reacts with interest).

My father—on the farm—by the sea. I will pull it out for you—as my father did—for me.

(Lion grunts undecidedly, then slowly offers his paw. Androcles nervously reaches for it).

431

It—it may hurt a little.

(Lion draws back and roars in protest).

I thought a lion was brave—not afraid of anything.

(Lion stops, then grunts in agreement and with great bravery thrusts out his paw).

Now—hold still—brace yourself.

(Lion begins to tremble violently).

Get ready—

(Lion shakes more).

One—

(Lion shakes both of them).

Two—

(Lion cries and tries to pull away. Androcles is stern, with pointed finger).

Don't move about!

(Lion tries to obey, meekly).

Three!

(Lion steps backwards).

It's out!

LION *(Looks at his paw, looks at Androcles, then roars joyfully and hops about. SINGS).*

Let me roar today
Let me say today
We feel great!
Celebrate!
Exhilarate!
Congratulate!
It's a great way
To show the world how you feel.

ANDROCLES *(Lion rubs against Androcles and purrs softly. Androcles, being tickled by Lion's rubbing, giggles and pets him).* You—you are welcome.

LION *(To audience).* He looks tired. I will get a rock.

(Quickly picks up a rock off R and holds it high).

ANDROCLES. He is going to crush me!

432

(He starts to defend himself, but Lion shakes his head and grunts, and shows Androcles that he should sit).
For me?

(Lion nods, trying to talk, and dusts the rock with his tail).

He wants *me* to sit.

(Lion, delighted, grabs Androcles to help him and seats him roughly).

Thank you.

LION *(To audience).*   He looks hungry.

(Roars, shows teeth, and chews).

ANDROCLES.   He is going to eat me!

(Lion shakes his head and "talks," points to Androcles and indicates from his mouth down into his stomach).

He wants *me* to eat.

(Lion agrees joyfully).

I am hungry. I am always hungry.

LION *(Thinking).*   What was for breakfast today? A man's skull in the cave—his liver down by the river—

(Embarrassed at what he has thought).

Oh, I beg your pardon.

(Roars with a new idea, motions Androcles to watch. Lion hums and purrs lightly as he comically pantomimes picking fruit from a tree and eating and spitting out the seeds).

ANDROCLES.   Fruit!

(Lion, encouraged, purrs happily and hops about pantomiming filling a basket with berries from bushes).

Berries!

(Lion, elated with his success, buzzes loudly and dances in ballet fashion like a bee).

What?

(Lion buzzes and dances bigger).

Honey from the bee!

(Lion agrees loudly).

Oh, that will be a banquet for me.

LION *(Speaks to audience).* A new twist in history! Man and beast will feast together. Celebrate! Sit—wait! I'll be back with cherries and berries for you—and a bone or two, before you can roar—*e pluribus unum!*

(Roars happily and exits R).

ANDROCLES *(Sits alone on rock, looks around, smiles, and speaks quietly). I* am sitting down. I am being served. I am being treated like a person. I—I have a friend. This is what it is like to be free. To be—maybe—

(SINGS).

Maybe
A doctor with a degree,
A poet, a priest, a sculptor, a scholar,
A senator—emperor with a golden collar!
I want to be free
So I can find—me.

PANTALONE *(Off).* Hunt—hunt—search and find my slave. Find my gold!

ANDROCLES. My master has come. My freedom has gone.

PANTALONE *(Off R).* Ah, his footprints are on the ground! I have found him!

ANDROCLES *(Calls quickly).* Oh, Lion, I must be off before we have fed. I must run—or it is off with my head!

(He starts D.L. but sees Captain).

Oh! The Captain! Where will I hide? In the cave!

(Quickly hides in cave).

CAPTAIN *(Enters L with fishing net and a slap-stick).* Beware slave, wherever you are. I shall leap and keep and capture you. In this net—I will get you.

(Holds net out ready).

PANTALONE *(Enters R, peering at the ground, crosses to L).* His footprints are on the ground. Toe-heel, heel-toe. This is the way his footsteps go.

CAPTAIN *(To audience).* The trap is set.

PANTALONE. Lead on—lead me to him.

CAPTAIN. Ha, caught in the net!

(Throws net over Pantalone who has walked into it).

PANTALONE.   Help! Help!

CAPTAIN.   You stole my hat!

(Hits Pantalone over the head with slap-stick).

PANTALONE.   Oh!

CAPTAIN.   My sword.

(Hits him again).

PANTALONE.   No!

CAPTAIN.   My cape?

(Hits him again).

PANTALONE: Let me loose!

CAPTAIN.   What?

PANTALONE.   You squawking goose!

CAPTAIN.   Who speaks?

PANTALONE *(Pulling off the net).*   I—Pantalone.

CAPTAIN.   Pantalone? Oh, it was my mistake.

PANTALONE.   It was my head!

CAPTAIN.   Where is the slave? The runaway? Where is Androcles?

PANTALONE.   He is—with my gold.

CAPTAIN *(Struts).*   I will drag him back to Rome. The Emperor will honor me—decree a holiday—so all can see the slave fight a wild and hungry beast. And after the fun is done and the slave is eaten, all will cheer the Captain of the Year.

PANTALONE.   Before you count your cheers, you have to catch one slave—Androcles!

CAPTAIN *(They start searching, a step on each word. Captain circles to L and upstage. Pantalone circles to R and upstage).*   Search.

PANTALONE.   Seek.

CAPTAIN.   Track.

PANTALONE.   Trail.

CAPTAIN.   Use your eyes.

PANTALONE.   Scrutinize!

CAPTAIN *(Stops).*   Think—if you were a slave . . . ?

PANTALONE.   I?

CAPTAIN.   Where would you hide?

PANTALONE.   Inside.

CAPTAIN *(Sees and points).*   A cave!

   (They tip-toe to entrance, hold net ready, whisper excitedly).

   Clap him.

PANTALONE.   Trap him.

CAPTAIN *(Nothing happens).*   The problem is—how to get him to come out.

PANTALONE.   Poke him?

CAPTAIN.   Smoke him?

PANTALONE.   I have a great idea! You will call him in a voice like Isabella.

CAPTAIN.   I—I speak like Isabella?

PANTALONE.   You will cry for help in a soft sweet voice. He will think you are her. He will come to Isabella.

CAPTAIN *(In high voice, comically).*   Help! Oh, help me! I am Isabella

   (They look at cave entrance).

   I heard—

PANTALONE.   Something stirred.

CAPTAIN *(Falsetto again).*   Andro-o-cles. Come out, ple-e-ese.

   (They look at cave and excitedly hold net ready).

   Ready.

PANTALONE.   Steady.

   (Androcles, behind backdrop, roars—long and loud!).

   It is a lion in the cave!

   (Runs D.R. and hides behind a "tree").

CAPTAIN *(Androcles roars again, up and down the scale, louder and louder. Even the backdrop shakes. Captain jumps and runs to*

436

Pantalone and hides behind him). It is *two* lions in the cave!
(They stand shaking with fright).

ANDROCLES *(Peeks out of cave, then comes out).* They have gone.
Ran away from a noise. I have learned that a roar is a mighty
thing. No wonder a lion is a king.

(He enjoys another roar).

PANTALONE *(Still hiding).* We are undone!

CAPTAIN. Run! Crawl!

PANTALONE. I cannot move at all.

(Androcles roars again with joy).

I have an idea. You—you will call in a voice like a lion. He will
think you are another lion—a brother.

CAPTAIN. I—roar like a lion?

PANTALONE: Our only chance is to answer back.

(Captain gulps, and then roars).

ANDROCLES *(He is startled. He hides behind "tree" at L).* It is another lion.

(Pantalone, helping, gives a roar).

It is two lions!

(With an idea, he roars back).

Ro-o-o-hello.

CAPTAIN *(He and Pantalone look at each other in surprise. Captain
answers).* Ro-o-o-hello.

ANDROCLES *(Now Androcles looks surprised).* Ro-o-o-lovely-da-a-ay.

CAPTAIN *(He and Pantalone look at each other and nod, pleased with
their success).* Ro-o-o-have-you-seen—ro-o-o-ar-a-runaway slave?
(Androcles is startled, then he peeks around "tree").

PANTALONE. Named-Andro—

(Captain nudges him to roar).

—roar—cles?

ANDROCLES. It is my master and the Captain. They have come for
me.

(He roars loudly).

Ro-o-oar-he-went—roar-r-r-r-that-away.

CAPTAIN *(They nod).*   Ro-o-o-thank-you.

(He and Pantalone start to tip-toe off R).

ANDROCLES *(Too confident.)*   Ro—o-ar. You are welcome.

PANTALONE.   It is his voice. It is my slave, Androcles.

CAPTAIN.   It is another trick of his.

PANTALONE.   Nab him.

CAPTAIN.   Grab him.

(They start back to get him).

ANDROCLES *(Unaware he has been discovered, continues to roar gaily).*
Ro-o-ar. Goodbye. Ro-o-o-ar. Happy eating.

PANTALONE *(Confronts Androcles on R).*   Eat, cheat, thief! I will
beat you!

(Androcles turns to L and walks into net held by Captain).

CAPTAIN.   Slide, glide, inside. I have you tied!

(Androcles is caught in the net over his head).

PANTALONE *(Grabs his bag of gold).*   My gold!

CAPTAIN.   My captive!

ANDROCLES.   Help! Help!

CAPTAIN.   You stole my hat!

(Hits Androcles over the head with slap-stick).

You stole my sword!

(Hits him).

You stole my cape!

(Hits him).

This time you will not escape.

PANTALONE *(Takes stick from Captain and swings it).*   Robber, Traitor. Thief! Let me hit him.

(Pantalone, in the mix-up, hits Captain several times on his head).

CAPTAIN.   Help!

(He drops the rope of the net).

ANDROCEES *(Runs to R)*. Help!

PANTALONE. Help! He is running away!

CAPTAIN *(Quickly catches Androcles and holds the rope)*. Back to Rome. To the Emperor you will be delivered!

PANTALONE. Into the pit you will be thrown.

CAPTAIN. Where the wild beasts will claw, gnaw, and chew you!

(They start to lead him off, marching—Captain, Androcles, and last Pantalone).

Munch!

PANTALONE. Crunch!

ANDROCLES. I will be eaten for lunch! Help! Lion! Signor Lion, set me free. Come and rescue me! Oh, woods echo my cry for help. Echo so the Lion will know I am in trouble. Roar—roar with me. Echo from tree to tree!

(He roars and the Ushers—and the children—help him roar, as he is led off L).

Roar! Roar!

LION *(He leaps in at R and roars)*. Someone roars for help? Androcles!

(Off, Androcles cries "Help!")

He calls for help.

(SINGS).

Oh, roar and say
Shout out without delay,
Which way, which way, which way?
Oh, roar me a clue,
Roar me two.
I have to know
Which way to go before I start.
Oh, roar, please,
An-dro-cles.
Give a sigh,
Give a cry,
Signify!
I'll sniff—I'll whiff—
Smell *(Sniffs)* — Tell *(Sniffs)*
Fe, fi, fo, fum.
Here —

(Shouts).

I come!

(He exits L).

ISABELLA *(She and Lelio run in from R).*   Oh, Androcles, what has happened to you?

LELIO *(To audience).*   That you will see in Act Two. Now—we must bow and say, "Our play is half done." This is the end of Act One. *(They bow).*

The Curtains Close.

A short intermission.

(Or if played without an intermission, omit the last speech of Lelio's and continue with his first speech in Act Two).

440

ANDROCLES AND THE LION
ACT TWO

(Music: Reprise of "Oh, Roar and Say." The curtains open. The scene is the same. Isabella and Lelio stand in C. Music dims out).

ISABELLA. Androcles. What has happened to you?

LELIO. I heard his voice, calling in the woods.

ISABELLA: He has followed us to bring the gold—my dowry which I left behind.

(Calls).

Androcles?

LELIO. Androcles!

(Lion roars as he enters U.R. He sees the lovers and watches).

ISABELLA. It is a lion!

LELIO. Do not fear.

ISABELLA. Androcles is alone—unarmed. What if he should meet a lion! Androcles! Androcles!

LELIO. Androcles!

LION. Someone else roars "Androcles." I will stay and hear who is here.

(Lion hides his head behind the small rock).

ISABELLA. Androcles! Androcles!

LELIO. We are alone.

(Lion's head pops up behind rock).

Together. It is time to speak—to sing of love!

(He turns aside, takes scroll from belt).

ISABELLA *(Not looking at him).* Please, speak no prepared speech, but sing true words that spring freely from your heart.

LELIO *(Looks surprised, glances again at scroll, then SINGS).*

Oh, lovely, lovely flower,
Growing lovelier every hour,
Shower on me, petals of love, Isabella—

(Lion, enjoying the music, nods his head in rhythm).

441

ISABELLA.   So unrehearsed—so sincere.

LELIO *(SINGS)*.

> My life, my heart revolve about you.
> Say yes, I cannot live without you.
>
> *(Lion, unable to refrain, lifts his head and roars musically on Lelio's last note—unnoticed by the lovers—then hides his head behind the rock).*

ISABELLA.   Oh, Lelio—

> *(Turns to him and speaks or SINGS).*
>
> My answer is—can't you guess?
> Yes, yes, yes, yes, yes!

LELIO *(In ecstacy).*   Oh, woods abound with joyous sound! Melodies sing in the trees—

> *(Music sound. Lion raises up and listens to R).*

Bells ring in the breeze—

> *(Music sound. Lion stands up and listens to L).*

Let the lute of the lily lying in the pond—

> *(Music sound. Lion stands and begins to move his arms like an orchestra conductor).*

Let the flute of the firefly's fluttering wand—

> *(Music sound. Lion motions to R).*

And let the flight of the nightingale—

> *(Music sound. Lion motions L).*

Harmonize!

> *(Music sounds blend together. Lion holds up paw ready to begin directing an orchestra).*

The moment we will immortalize!

> *(Music of all sounds play a folk dance. Lion leads, dramatically, the unseen musicians. Isabella and Lelio do a short dance. At the conclusion, they hold their pose and Lion bows to audience).*

ISABELLA *(Points to ground).*   Look! Footprints—boots and sandals.

LELIO *(Examines them).*   The Captain's boots—Pantalone's sandals. The Captain and Pantalone were here—following us—following Androcles.

ISABELLA. His cry was for help. He ran away. He is—a runaway slave! And they have found him—

LELIO. Bound him—

ISABELLA. Taken him back to Rome.

LELIO. To the pit!

ISABELLA. We must stop them.

LELIO. If we can.

ISABELLA. We must help him.

LELIO. All we can.

LION (*Jumps on rock heroically*). And—we can! (*Roars*).

ISABELLA. Help!

LELIO. Run!
(*Lovers run off D.R.*).

LION. Lead the way. I will follow you. To Androcles! To—the rescue! (*Lion roars, picks up rock, and runs off D.R. Chase music begins —repeated. But the running is reversed, going around in the opposite direction. Lovers enters from U.R. and run across. At C, they look back, "Oh!" and exit U.L. behind backdrop. Lion runs in U.R. At C, roars, and exits U.L. behind backdrop. Lovers enter U.R. from behind backdrop, running faster. At C, they look back in great fright, "OH!" and exit U.L. behind backdrop. Lion follows. At C, roars majestically, and shouts: "Andr-roar-cles! Here we come!" Lion exits after lovers. Lovers enter U.R. from around backdrop. Lelio pulls the curtain of the woods scene back to L, showing the street scene again. Chase music dims out*).

LELIO (*Breathless*). Safe at home—I hope. What does the scroll say?

ISABELLA (*Reads scroll on proscenium arch*). The next scene is—a street in Rome.

LELIO. Ah, we can stay.

ISABELLA (*Reads, announcing*). "The Captain enters."

(*Clashing of slap-stick is heard off L, Isabella runs to C*).

He will find us here.

LELIO. Do not fear. We will hide—behind a mask. Quick! We will hide behind another face, and re-appear in the Market Place.

(*They exit R*).

CAPTAIN *(Enters at L)*. Make way, make way for the hero of the day! Bow, salute, kneel and gaze upon the hero. Raise your voice with praise for the hero. The hero passes by. The hero is—I!

(Lelio and Isabella enter R. Each holds a long, sad beggerman's mask on a stick in front of his face. They walk and act and speak like beggars).

LELIO. Help the poor. Help the blind.

ISABELLA. Alms for the cripple. Alms for the old.

CANTAIN. Away beggars! The emperor comes this way. It is a holiday!

LELIO. What Senator has died? What battle have we won?

CAPTAIN. None! We celebrate today the capture of a runaway.

ISABELLA. A slave?

(They look at each other and speak without their masks; and at the same time, the Captain speaks. They all say together, "Androcles!").

CAPTAIN. Today all Rome will celebrate! A wild beast was caught outside the wall, clawing the gate as if he could not wait to come into the City. Now in the pit the beast is locked and barred, waiting to be released—waiting to eat a juicy feast.

LELIO AND ISABELLA *(They nod to each other and say:)* Androcles!

CAPTAIN. Ah, what a sporting sight to see—a fight—man eaten by a beast. Then I, who caught the slave, will appear. Women will swoon, men will cheer, and I will be crowned the hero of the year!

(Shouts rapidly and marches quickly).

Hep, hep, ho! Step, step, high. Hail the hero. I, I, I!

(Exits R).

ISABELLA *(They take their masks away)*. Poor, poor Androcles.

LELIO. We must try and save him. Quick, before it is too late. We will go to the Arena—

ISABELLA. Yes!

LELIO. We will go to the Royal Box! Implore the Emperor with our plea!

ISABELLA. Yes!

LELIO. For only he by royal decree can save—our Androcles.

(Lelio and Isabella run off L. There is music. Captain, leading Androcles by the rope, and Pantalone following, marches in from R. As they march, they SING).

PANTALONE AND CAPTAIN.   Off to the pit we three. Who will be left?

ANDROCLES.   Just me.

PANTALONE AND CAPTAIN.   Who will be left alone, shaking in every bone?

PANTALONE.   Just—

CAPTAIN.   Just—

ANDROCLES.   Me!

CAPTAIN AND PANTALONE.   Off to the pit we three. Who will be left?

ANDROCLES.   Just me.

CAPTAIN AND PANTALONE.   Who will the animal meet? Who will the animal eat?

PANTALONE.   Just—

CAPTAIN.   Just—

ANDROCLES *(Shouts)*.   Just a minute! I want to be an absentee!
(Music ends as he speaks).

I want to be free—to be————just me!

CAPTAIN.   To the Arena! Forward march!
(Music: Reprise of Introductory Music of Act One. Captain, Androcles, and Pantalone march across the front of the stage or across down in the orchestra pit. At the same time, Lelio and Isabella, disguised with masks, dance in U.L. carrying colorful banners, one in each hand, and on stands. They set the banners down in a semi-circle in front of the backdrop to indicate the Arena. They dance off as the music stops, and the three marchers arrive in the middle of the scene).

CAPTAIN.   Halt! We are at the Arena! The slave will step forward.

PANTALONE.   Step forward.

ANDROCLES   Step forward.
(Frightened, he steps forward).

CAPTAIN.   The slave's head will be covered.

(He holds out left hand to Androcles, who holds out left hand to Pantalone).

PANTALONE. Covered.

(He gives a cloth sack to Androcles, who gives it to Captain, who puts it over Androcles' head).

CAPTAIN *(Trumpets sound).* The Emperor's chariot draws near.

(Trumpets).

The Emperor will soon appear.

(Trumpets).

The Emperor is here!

(A royal banner is extended from the side D.L., indicating the Royal Box).

Bow!

PANTALONE. Now!

(Captain and Pantalone bow low toward Royal Box, facing D.L. Androcles groping with his head covered, turns and bows facing R).

Turn around!

(Androcles turns around).

To the ground!

(Androcles bows to ground).

CAPTAIN. Most noble Emperor—

(Pushes Androcles' head down, making him bow).

Most honored Emperor—

(Pushes Androcles, who keeps bobbing up, down again).

Most imperial Emperor—

(Pushes Androcles down again. He stays down).

The guilty slave stands before you. Stand!

(Androcles quickly straightens up).

As punishment for a slave who runs away, he will today fight a wild beast in the Arena for all Rome to see.

(Androcles shakes his head under the sack).

He will battle for his life—to survive. There will be but one win-ner—the one who is left alive.

(Androcles, courageously, draws his fist and is ready to strike. Captain, growing more eloquent, begins to strut).

I have fought and slain a hundred wild beasts.

(Androcles, visualizing the animals, starts hitting the air).

With fiery eyes, with knashing teeth, they charged at me. Fight! The crowd cried, fight!

(Androcles, ready, starts to fight, hitting wildly for his life, hitting the Captain who is near and whom he cannot see).

Help! Stop! I am not the wild beast.

(At a safe distance, he regains his bravery).

I—I am the Captain, the boldest, bravest fighter in Rome—in all Italy! Go—stand at the side. Appear when you hear the trumpets blow.

(Captain points to L. Androcles starts to R).

No. The other way!

ANDROCLES *(He turns and starts to L. Loud trumpets blow. He stops, faces R, ready to fight).*   The trumpets! Now?

PANTALONE.   No!

(Androcles, groping, exits U.L. Pantalone bows to Royal Box).

Most Imperial Emperor, I am Pantalone, Master of the slave. From me he ran away. From me he stole. I am told you plan to reward me for this holiday with a bag of gold.

CAPTAIN.   I tracked and captured him. I am sure you will confer a title of bravery on me.

(Trumpets blow).

ANDROCLES *(Enters U.L., ready to fight).*   The trumpets! Now?

CAPTAIN.   No!

(Androcles turns and exits).

Ah, the Emperor waves. It is the signal. Open the gates. Let the wild beast in!

PANTALONE.   Let the entertainment begin!

(Captain and Pantalone quickly go D.R. where they stand. Drum rolls are heard. Then loud roars are heard off U.R. Lion, roaring, angrily stalks in from U.R.).

447

LION. Barred—locked—caged! I am—outraged!

(Roars and paces menacingly).

PANTALONE. What a big lion! I am glad he is below.

CAPTAIN. I could conquer him with one blow.

LION. Captured! Held in captivity! Robbed of my liberty! Only man would think of it. Only man would sink to it. Man—man—little —two legged—tailless thing. Beware man, I am a King!

(Roars).

The first man I meet I—will eat!

(Trumpets blow).

ANDROCLES *(Enters, head still covered).* The trumpets! Now?

LION *(Sees him).* Ah, a man! A chew or two and a bone to pick. *(Roars).*

ANDROCLES *(Frightened and groping).* Oh! I am not alone. I must get out quick.

(Drum starts beating in rhythm to the fight. Androcles starts walking, then running, the Lion after him. The chase is a dance-mime, fast, comic, with surprises and suspense. It ends with Lion holding Androcles in his clutches).

LION. Caught! Held!

(Shakes Androcles like a rag doll).

Flip—flop. I will start eating at the top!

(Takes off Androcles' headcovering).

ANDROCLES No hope ever to be free. This is the end of me!

(Lion looks at Androcles, is surprised and roars questioningly. Androcles, frightened, freezes, then slowly feels his neck, his face and nose. He looks at Lion and he is surprised. Lion tries to "talk").

You?

(Lion nods and roars, pantomimes pulling out a thorn from his paw, and points to Androcles who nods).

Me.

(Lion "talks" and points to himself).

You!

448

(Lion nods and roars happily).

Signor Lion!

(Lion "talks" and roars, and they embrace each other joyfully).

PANTALONE.   Let the fight begin! Beat him!

(Lion stops and looks at Pantalone).

CAPTAIN.   The Emperor waits to see who wins. Eat him!

ANDROCLES   He is my master—who bought me. He is the Captain—who caught me.

LION.   Slave makers! Taker of men! I will beat you! I will eat you!

(Roars and starts to C).

PANTALONE.   Help! The lion is looking at me. Draw your sword!

(Hides behind the Captain).

CAPTAIN *(Shaking).*   I am afraid his blood will rust my blade.

PANTALONE.   Show you can do what you say—slay him with one blow!

CAPTAIN.   I suddenly remember—I have to go!

(Starts off R. At the same time, Lion leaps with a roar and attacks the two).

PANTALONE.   Help! Guards! Save, attend me!

CAPTAIN.   Help! Somebody defend me!

(There is an exciting and comic scramble, with Lion finally grabbing each by the collar and hitting their heads together. Then he holds each out at arms length).

LION.   Listen and learn a lesson: only a coward steals and holds a man.

(Roars. Shakes Pantalone).

Only a thief buys and sells a man. And no one—can—own another man!

(Roars).

The world was made for all—equally. Nod your heads if you agree.

(Lion shakes them and makes their heads nod violently. Then he releases them, and the two drop to the ground).

449

The vote is "Yes"—unanimously!

(Trumpets sound. Off-stage voices shout, from R and L and from the back of the auditorium: "Kill the lion. The lion is loose. Club him. Stone him. Kill the lion. Kill! Kill! etc." Captain and Pantalone crawl to R. Hands appear off R and L shaking clubs and spears. This is a tense moment. The Arena has turned against the Lion. Lion is frightened. He crouches by Androcles who stands heroically by him).

ANDROCLES. Stop! Stop! Hold your spears and stones and clubs. Do not kill the lion. You see—he is not an enemy. He remembers me and a kindness which I did for him. Today that kindness he has returned. He did not eat my head, which would have been the end. Instead—he is—my friend.

(He offers his hand to Lion. Lion takes it. Music begins and the two start to waltz together. Pantalone and Captain crouch and watch in amazement. Hands and weapons disappear from the sides at R and L. Androcles and Lion waltz bigger, funnier, and happier. Trumpets sound. Music and dancing stops. Lelio enters D.L. by royal banner).

LELIO. The Emperor has spoken. His words will be heard.

(All bow low toward the Box as Lelio holds up a royal scroll).

The Emperor is amazed, astounded, and astonished—with delight —at this sudden sight. A fight unlike any in history. Indeed it is a mystery. Two enemies—man and lion—dancing hand in hand! To honor this unique occasion, the Emperor has issued this command: today shall be, not one for fighting, but of dance and revelry!

(Trumpets play and people cheer).

The Emperor gives to the Master of the slave—

PANTALONE. That is I, Pantalone. How much gold does he give?

LELIO. The Emperor gives this order; *you* will give twenty pieces of gold to Androcles.

ANDROCLES. To me!

LELIO. A sum he has well earned.

PANTALONE. Give twenty pieces of gold! Oh, I shall die a poor man. No. No!

(Lion starts toward him and growls loudly).

Yes—yes, I will pay.

(Quickly takes a bag from pocket and begins counting).

One—two—three—

LELIO.   Furthermore: the Emperor decrees to the Captain who caught the slave—

CAPTAIN.   Ah, what honor does the Emperor give to me?

LELIO.   You will command a Roman Legion in a distant land. You will sail to the Isle of Britain where even the boldest man must fight to keep alive, where it is so dangerous only the bravest survive.

CAPTAIN *(Shaking violently).*   Danger? Fight? Me?

LELIO.   Because of your boasted bravery.

CAPTAIN.   I would prefer to stay, please. A cold climate makes me sneeze.

(Lion starts and roars loudly).

I will go.

(Lion follows him roaring).

I am going! I am gone!

LELIO.   And to me—the Emperor has given me the lovely, lovely Isabella—

(Isabella enters D.L.).

and has blessed our marriage which soon will be.

ISABELLA.   For me the Emperor decreed, Pantalone shall pay without delay my dowry which he holds for me.

PANTALONE.   Pay more gold! Oh, no—no!

(Lion roars at him loudly).

Yes—yes. I will pay. It is here, my dear.

LELIO.   And finally:

(Trumpets blow).

The Emperor has ruled that both lion and slave today have won a victory unequalled in history. So—both lion and slave are hereby—set free!

ANDROCLES.   Free? I am free.

LION.   The way the world should be!

ANDROCLES.   Free—to find my family—to work the best I can—to raise my head—to be a man. To find out—who I am!

451

(Music. They all SING).

Let us roar today,
Let us say today
We feel great.
Celebrate!
Exhilarate!
Congratulate!

PANTALONE AND CAPTAIN *(Dejected).* We don't feel great.

ALL. It's a great way
To show the world how you feel.
When in need—find a friend.
Laws will read—have a friend.
We feel great.
Don't eat, but meet.
Why wait, make a friend.
Extend!
Do your part, make a start.
Roar today. Show the world today.
It's a great way
To show the world how you feel.

(All the actors bow, then Androcles comes forward).

ANDROCLES. Our story is told. The lovers are joined in happiness.
The bragger and miser are undone. And a friend was won by
kindness. Our masks and bells and curtains we put away for
another day. And we go our way—a group of strolling players.
We say—

LION *(Points at audience).* Be sure you roar today!

ALL. Arrivederci!

(They all bow low and the music swells).

The curtains close.

THE ICE WOLF

by

JOANNA HALPERT KRAUS

A TALE OF THE ESKIMOS

A Play for Young People in Three Acts

THE ICE WOLF

by

JOANNA H. KRAUS

Copyright c, 1963, Joanna M. Halpert.

Reprinted by Permission of New Plays, Inc., Box 273,

Rowayton, CT. 06853.

THE ICE WOLF

The Ice Wolf, Reynard the Fox, and *Androcles and the Lion* are a part of a small group of plays written after mid-century that did much to encourage a new perspective on writing for child audiences. These plays are well written works that reflect more emphasis on artistic inspiration and writing skill than on rules and formulas for writing children's plays. *The Ice Wolf* has few elements of the well-made plays of the past. It is a wholly original work that, like *Reynard the Fox,* is thought-provoking and controversial and, like *Androcles and the Lion,* makes effective use of the theatre medium.

The Ice Wolf is a complex play that operates on many levels simultaneously. On one level the viewer is presented with a surprisingly realistic portrayal of a young girl, Anatou, who must deal with very real feelings of anger, fear, and the desire for revenge. On a second level, this same young girl is presented as a quasi-mythological character who freely interacts with animals and with gods, and who undergoes a transformation from a human to a wolf. The play tells the story of Anatou's life, while offering a larger view of time, a culture, and the primal fears that ruled that culture. As *Androcles and the Lion* presents an exaggerated view of the foibles of human nature, *The Ice Wolf* presents an intense view of the tragic happenings of Anatou's life and world.

In the story of the play Anatou is born into the Eskimo culture with fair skin and light hair. Because she is so different she is feared and hated by the people of her village, and she is made the scapegoat for all of their problems. The play follows Anatou's entire life — from birth to death — as she grows up amid the suspicion of the villagers, as she is forced to flee the village, as she petitions the Wood God to transform her into a wolf, as she succumbs to her desire for revenge, and as she dies trying to save her friend. It is a very serious story of prejudice, revenge, death and redemption that is played out in a world where "the spirits and the Shaman ruled."

The story is revealed through a series of episodes, each of which is framed by remarks of the storyteller, who guides the audience through the chronology of events, while setting the appropriate mood for each scene. With this technique, Kraus rapidly moves the action forward in time without losing continuity in the story — and with the added effect of making it appear as if the audience is viewing Anatou's life from afar and is allowed glimpses of only the climactic moments in her life.

Kraus is particularly skilled at creating mood, atmosphere, and even detailed characterizations (at least with Anatou) with little dialogue. This appropriately generalizes the tale, but the simple truthfulness of Anatou's conflict — her anguish at being persecuted because she is different — makes the action very meaningful.

The play contains two separate parts — almost two separate plays — that are reconciled in the end. The first part focuses specifically on Anatou's struggle against the villagers. This conflict is primarily external, almost melodramatic, as it places Anatou in opposition to a clearly defined antagonist, represented by the chorus of villagers. Anatou is the voice of reason in this struggle, but she loses this fight and is driven from the village. This punishment is harsh by contemporary standards, but made very plausible in the context of the superstitious world of the play. And although the conflict and the opposing forces in the conflict are clearly defined, the resolution is anything but melodramatic.

The struggle is made more poignant by the characterization of Tarto, the only character in the play besides Anatou that is not strictly one-dimensional. Tarto is torn between the superstitions of the village people and his world and his fondness for Anatou. With this character, Kraus captures the essence of the conflict, which is far more complex than the simple story the play suggests. We see in Tarto a sincere and caring individual who honestly does not understand why Anatou is different or just what power she is exercising over their lives. When he asks Anatou to "say another spell" so they can "all eat," the fear, superstition, and confusion of his world is made painfully clear to Anatou and to the audience.

The first part of the play is concluded with Anatou's exile into the forest. The conflict between Anatou and the villagers is not fully resolved by this action, but it is then made secondary to Anatou's conflict with herself. Anatou goes into the forest and asks the Wood God to change her into a wolf so that she can escape the pain of her life as an Eskimo. This transformation, which is made through a ritualistic dance presided over by the animals of the forest, does not diminish Anatou's pain, but merely redirects it; from that point on in the play the character of Anatou is treated somewhat like a tragic hero, who is consumed by internal passions that ultimately bring about her own death.

The persecuted victim becomes the persecutor as Anatou reacts in a wolf-like manner by killing one of the humans. Anatou gradually comes to acknowledge that "she has worn a thick coat of hate," but by that time the people of the village have risen up against her once again. However, Wood God assures Anatou that if she can show that her "heart is empty of all its hate and cruelty" her "spirit will not die."

Kraus brings together the two worlds of the play in the final scene where Anatou gives her life to save her human friend, and the play ends with a vision of Anatou's spirit rising above the repentant villagers.

Anatou's death is a logical outgrowth of the action of the play, and it is neither the end of the play, nor the major thematic element of the story. Like many heroes in dramatic literature for children, Anatou appears to be an innocent victim, but when one views this play from that perspective, it can only be considered as a play of pathos that does not even fulfill the early suggestions of a melodramatic structure. The play has more significance than that, however, because Kraus constructs a character that must take some responsibility for the tragic happenings of the play.

Anatou kills and Anatou dies, more because of her own quest for revenge than because of the persecution of the villagers. It is a thought-provoking idea that makes this play very different from the melodramatic children's plays of the past.

Anatou, though initially just the innocent victim, initiates an action that causes suffering and death, and, within the world of the play, the logical resolution to this action is Anatou's own death. It is a harsh world, but it is a just world; through her suffering Anatou not only redeems herself, but stands as a symbol to the people of the village who come to recognize that they were wrong. It is a poignant and positive ending that is made even more moving by the empathy that the audience feels for the persecuted child who dies.

This play is first, and most importantly, an interesting story. Kraus creates Anatou without elaborate detail of character and situation, yet the audience quickly comes to know her and to care about her problems. With similar simplicity Kraus leads Anatou through feelings of loneliness, fear, anger, and contrition — feelings which are very much a part of every child's life.

The play is written in the idiom of an ancient folk tale, but its dramatization is very modern. The language is highly poetic and, except with the scenes between Anatou and the Wood God, the moralistic elements of the story are generally implied more through the action than made explicit in the dialogue. The protagonist of the play, Antou, is drawn with far more elaborate detail than characters like Cinderella, Sara Crewe, or Zar and Zan, and the actions of this play have ramifications far beyond the narrow world of the story. Fairy and folk tale characters are often passive individuals that overcome their difficulties through the intervention of another person — a person who has magical powers. In *The Ice Wolf*, Anatou petitions to the Wood God for help, but he tells her clearly that she must take the responsibility for her own actions in order to solve the problem. Anatou grows to a nearly heroic stature, not because of her actions or deeds (which are a result of this stature), but because of an internal growth of mind and spirit. Kraus thus makes a statement that is literally larger than life, a statement that relates to a child's everyday activities and, like a true folk tale, to more primal hopes and fears.

The Ice Wolf is not a modern problem play. Anatou and her world are sufficiently distanced to allow the audience to accept the harsh actions in the play. But more than Cinderella, the Infanta, or even Sara Crewe, Anatou is invested with life-like qualities that a contemporary audience can understand. *The Ice Wolf* has a depth and sophistication that cannot be found in the fairy and folk tale dramatizations that have dominated the literature in the past, and it stands today as an important and influential example of serious theatre for child audiences.

JOANNA HALPERT KRAUS was born in Portland, Maine, on December 7, 1937. She attended Sarah Lawrence College (A.B., 1959), University of California, Los Angeles (M.A., 1963), and Columbia University (Ed.D., 1972). Kraus is currently an Associate Professor of Child Drama and Co-ordinator of the Arts for Children program at the State University of New York, College at Brockport. Active in the Children's Theatre Association of America, she is best known for her literary work that includes stories, articles, and plays for young audiences. In 1971 she was awarded the Chorpenning Cup by the Children's Theatre Association for achievement in playwriting. Her latest play, *Circus Home*, was written on a Creative Artists Public Service Fellowship. Other plays by Kraus include *Mean to be Free*, *Vasalisa*, and *Two Plays From the Far East*.

458

The Characters

STORYTELLER

ANATOU, *a girl born to Eskimo parents. Her skin is pale and her hair blond; a phenomenon in the village.*

KARVIK, *her father*

ARNARQIK, *her mother*

TARTO, *her best friend, a village boy*

KIVIOG, *Tarto's father*

ATATA, *an old man of the village but a good hunter*

SHIKIKANAQ, *a village girl*

MOTOMIAK, *a village boy*

VILLAGER 1, *a woman*

VILLAGER 2, *a man*

WOOD GOD, *the God of the Forest*

A BEAVER

A FOX

AN ERMINE

Place and Time

The entire action of the play takes place in a small isolated Eskimo village, Little Whale River, and the forest, a few days inland. It is located in the Hudson Bay area of Canada.

The time is long before the missionaries established their settlements, long before white man had been seen, a time when the spirits and the Shaman, or the Wise Man, ruled.

PROLOGUE

It is the end of January. In the foreground we see an expanse of white spread out. It is broken in a few places by hillocks which rise up like seal's heads from the plains. There is an atmosphere of cold beauty and awesome space.

The STORYTELLER *enters on the apron of the stage. He is dressed, as all the Eskimos, in the attire of the Hudson Bay Eskimos, but somehow there is the quality about him of excitement. He is no ordinary hunter.*

STORYTELLER.
Far beyond the world you know —
Of sun, rushing rivers, and trees
Is the Northland
Where the winter snow is gray,
There is no sound of birds
Nothing but the stillness of space
Of endless snow
And endless cold.
There, the child Anatou was born
In the village of Little Whale River
It was small, beside the sea
But the search for food never ended.

(Lights up on igloo, Eskimos in circle, one beating drum, chanting)

Aja, I remember. It was one of the coldest nights of the year, so cold the dog team had buried themselves in the snow.

ATATA.   And the seal-oil lamps trembled before the Great North Wind.

KARVIK.   Just before dawn, when the baby came, Karvik had to go out and repair their home. His fingers seemed to freeze at once. Never had there been such a storm in Little Whale River.

(Lights up on KARVIK *cutting a snow block and fitting it into dome)*

ARNARQIK.   Inside Arnarqik sewed the caribou skins she had chewed. She was making new clothes for Karvik. Only once did she dare look at the small child beside her wrapped in skins. It was strangely still, strangely quiet. It was unlike any child Arnarqik had ever seen.

STORYTELLER.   Atata was by the seal's breathing hole . . .

(Lights up on ATATA *crouched by breathing hole, poised, ready with harpoon)*

. . . waiting . . . waiting . . . waiting until the seal came up for air. For days there had been no food in Little Whale River.   He

460

thought the birth of a new child might bring him luck! Then . . .
he struck with his harpoon!

(ATATA *harpoons seal*)

ATATA.   Aja, Nuliayuk, now everyone will eat!

STORYTELLER.   He took the choice bit of meat, the seal's liver to return to the seal goddess, Nuliayuk. The Shaman, the wise man,
had told him to do this so she would feast on it and then remember
to send more seals to the hunters of Little Whale River. Atata
rushed back. Now there was something to celebrate. A new child,
a fresh caught seal. There would be drum chants and dancing and
stories in the long white night.

(*Drum Chants begin. They break off abruptly*)

But there was no singing or dancing.

KARVIK.   It was long ago . . .

ARNARQIK.   Just about this time.

STORYTELLER.   It was a pale dawn . . .

ATATA.   Like this one . . .

STORYTELLER.   When Anatou was born.

461

ACT I, *Scene 1*

The interior of Karvik and Arnarqik's home in Little Whale River. Masses of thick, heavy caribou skins are spread about. Seal-Oil lamps, made of soapstone, light the home.

At rise, the sound of Eskimo dogs howling. A strong wind is blowing. Villagers come in from all sides dressed in their habitual furs. They crawl through the passageway and lights come up in the interior of the igloo. Karvik and Arnarqik are seated. Their new child is beside Arnarqik on a caribou skin not visible from the entrance.

KARVIK.   Welcome! Welcome all of you!

VILLAGER 2.   Aja! Your first child. Of course we'd come.

(To others)

We must sing many songs to welcome it.

KIVIOG.   And if it's a man child, Karvik will already have made him a harpoon, and a whip.

VILLAGER 1.   By the next moon he will be able to use them. Wait and see!

(They laugh)

VILLAGER 2.   Good, he can hunt a seal with us this winter and the caribou next fall. If he's as good a hunter as Karvik, we'll get twice as much.

KIVIOG.   And he'll be a companion for my son, Tarto, born under the moon.

(They all laugh except KARVIK *and* ARNARQIK *who are strangely quiet)*

VILLAGER 1.   Karvik! Arnarqik! You are silent. Show us the man child. We've come a long way to see him.

*(*ARNARQIK *moves slowly)*

ARNARQIK.   It is a girl child . . . but we are glad.

KARVIK.   She will be good.

ARNARQIK.   It is true. There is joy in feeling new life come to the great world.

VILLAGER 1.   A girl! Ah-ah. That means more care.

VILLAGER 2.   And more attention.

KIVIOG.   She cannot hunt.

462

VILLAGERS *(Politely).*   But let us see her anyway.

   (Arnarqik moves away troubled, then points to the caribou skin)

ARNARQIK.   There, look for yourself.

   (KARVIK *has turned away. Villagers crowd around the child, move back abruptly, and whirl on* KARVIK *and* ARNARQIK).

VILLAGER 1   *(In low horror).*   Her hair is white!

VILLAGER 2.   Her face is pale.

KIVIOG.   She cannot be an Eskimo.

VILLAGER 1.   She cannot be one of us!

KARVIK.   Of course she is. Her hair will get darker. Wait.

VILLAGER 2.   But her face. Look at it. No Eskimo child was ever born as pale as that.

VILLAGER 1.   She's a devil.

ARNARQIK.   No!

VILLAGER 1.   She will not live one moon.

ARNARQIK.   She will live.

VILLAGER 1.   She will bring bad luck.

ARNARQIK.   She's only a baby.

KIVIOG.   Put her out in the snow now, before she turns the gods against us.

VILLAGER 2.   And our stomachs shrink.

VILLAGER 1.   And our dishes are empty.

VILLAGER 2.   It's happened before. We all know it. Get rid of the child before it's too late.

KIVIOG.   She will offend Nuliayuk, the goddess of the seals. Nuliayuk will stay at the bottom of the sea, and keep the seals beside her, and we will all go hungry. Put the child out into the snow or we will die of famine!

ARNARQIK.   No! She will be a good Eskimo.

VILLAGER 2.   Then let her grow up in another village. We don't want her here.

KIVIOG.   She doesn't look like us. She won't think like us.

VILLAGER 1.   She doesn't belong here.

KARVIK. Then where does she belong? Where should she go?

VILLAGER 1. Put her out in the snow.

(Starts to grab her)

ARNARQIK. No! No! No, I can't. Don't you understand? She is our child.

VILLAGER 2. Then leave our village in peace. Don't anger the spirits of Little Whale River.

KARVIK. But this is our village and you are our people. How can we leave it? Wait! She will be like the others. You'll see. She'll sew and cook just as well as any Eskimo girl. Better! Arnarqik will teach her.

KIVIOG *(Holds up his hands)*. Very well. We will watch and wait. Perhaps you are right, and we will see her hair and cheeks grow darker. But we have no gifts or good wishes to welcome a white-faced child — a white-faced girl child!

(Villagers exit. Arnarqik tries to run after them)

ARNARQIK. Come back! Wait! Please wait. Don't go yet. Oh, Karvik, what will we do?

KARVIK *(Slowly)*. Her hair should be as dark as the raven's wing.

ARNARQIK. It is as white as the caribou's belly. Karvik, what if they are right? She is different. Karvik, why is her hair pale? Why doesn't she cry? She is so still! It's not natural.

KARVIK. She is frightened already. The Fair One will have a hard journey.

(Looks out the passageway)

Arnarqik, the villagers spoke wisely.

(Looks for a long time at his wife)

She would never know. It would not hurt her in the snow now.

ARNARQIK. No, Karvik! You mustn't ask me to.

KARVIK. But if we leave, will the next village think she looks more like an Eskimo?

ARNARQIK *(Shakes her head)*. No, she is Anatou, the Fair One — she will not change. But I will teach her, Karvik. She will be a good Eskimo girl!

KARVIK. But will they ever think she is like the others?

ARNARQIK. Yes. Yes. Of course they will. Let us stay here. Who knows what is beyond the snow?

KARVIK. Then we must be strong. We must teach Anatou to be strong. Only then will our home be her home and our friends her friends.

It won't be easy, Arnarqik.

(Arnarqik is beside the baby)

ARNARQIK. Oh Karvik, I couldn't leave her. Not like that!

(Abruptly she changes)

Look, Karvik . . . she is smiling.

(Picks her up)

Oh, Karvik, we mustn't let them hurt her. We must protect her.

KARVIK. Sing, Arnarqik, sing the morning song. Bring Anatou luck. She will have a hard journey.

ARNARQIK. *(Sits, sings or chants)*

I rise up from rest
Moving swiftly as the raven's wing
I rise up to greet the day
Wo-wa
My face is turned from dark of night
My gaze toward the dawn
Toward the whitening dawn.

(Lights fade)

STORYTELLER. But her hair did not grow dark as the raven's wing. Instead, each day she grew fairer. They called her the "different one," and when the blinding snow swept across the North or when the hunters returned with empty sleds, the villagers whispered, "It's Anatou. She's the one."

ACT I, *Scene 2*

The village. Tarto, Shikikanaq and Motomiak are playing an Eskimo game, a combination of Hide-and-Seek and Touch. Motomiak is just dashing for the goal pursued by Shikikanaq. Tarto is at the goal watching and laughing.

TARTO. Hurry up, Motomiak. She's right behind you. Shikikanaq is right behind you!

(Motomiak turns to look, still running. Anatou enters. She sees the race but moves out of the way too late and they collide. Motomiak falls and Shikikanaq tags him)

SHIKIKANAQ. There! I won!

MOTOMIAK. That wasn't fair. You made me lose the game, Anatou. I've never lost before — not to a girl! See what you made me do. Clumsy!

ANATOU. I'm sorry. I tried to get out of the way. I didn't see you in time.

SHIKIKANAQ *(Whispering).* You better not say anything more, Motomiak, or Anatou will put a spell on you — the way she did the seals.

TARTO. What are you talking about? You know that isn't true.

ANATOU. Oh, I'm sorry I spoiled your game, Motomiak, but couldn't you start again?

SHIKIKANAQ. No. I won. Tarto saw. Didn't you, Tarto?

(He nods).

MOTOMIAK. Beside, we don't want to play in front of a freak.

(Anatou gasps)

TARTO. Who's a freak?

MOTOMIAK. She is. The whole village says so.

ANATOU *(Furious).* No, I'm not! I'm an Eskimo just like you.

SHIKIKANAQ *(Doubtfully).* Ohh . . . .

MOTOMIAK. Well, her face is different enough.

(Anatou touches it)

TARTO. Why, what's wrong with it? It has two eyes, a nose and a mouth just like everyone else's.

SHIKIKANAQ. But it's white, Tarto — like snow. I bet if you put her in the sun she'll melt and that's why she stays inside all the time.

TARTO. You're just jealous because she's prettier than you, Shiki-kanaq.

ANATOU. Stop it. Stop it, all of you.

(She is crying)

Leave me alone.

(Starts to go)

TARTO *(Furious)*. Now see what you've done. If she were made of snow, Shikikanaq, she couldn't cry.

(Crosses to her)

Come on, Anatou. They didn't mean it. Please come back.

(To others)

Let's have another game — all four of us.

SHIKIKANAQ. Well . . . all right . . . if she'll tell us why she looks that way.

TARTO *(Sharply)*. What way?

SHIKIKANAQ. I mean her eyes and her hair. They're such funny colors. There must be a reason.

ANATOU *(Desperate)*. I don't know. Each time you've asked me I said I didn't know.

SHIKIKANAQ. I bet if you asked your mother and father they'd know. It must be something terrible or they'd tell you.

MOTOMIAK. Maybe the wood god from the forest put a spell on an animal and sent it back here. No one else in Little Whale River looks like you. Maybe that's why you look so funny. They say he has the power to make an animal appear like a human.

SHIKIKANAQ. And he can make people look like animals too . . . just by saying a spell! My father says that's why no Eskimo should go into the forest.

ANATOU. No! No! It's not true. I'm just like you are!

MOTOMIAK. Then, maybe, some devil spirit looked at you and it took all the color away.

SHIKIKANAQ. Yes, that's it. And why do you always sit inside and sew?

467

ANATOU (*Lying*)   There's a lot of work. It has to get done.

TARTO (*Quickly*).   She can sew better than any woman in the whole village! Show them, Anatou.

(*He points to her dress which is carefully and beautifully stitched. Shikikanaq examines it*)

SHIKIKANAQ.   It is beautiful. There aren't any mistakes at all.

ANATOU (*Can't believe her praise*).   My mother taught me and she is very good and careful.

SHIKIKANAQ.   Can you make anything else?

ANATOU.   Two snows ago, I made warm boots for my father. Very special boots and he's worn them ever since.

MOTOMIAK.   Then how come he's lost in the snow right now, if the boots you made were so special.

ANATOU.   He went to look for food. Both my mother and father did. That's all I know.

MOTOMIAK.   There's barely any food left in the village. For three days the hunters have returned with empty sleds.

ANATOU.   Famine is everywhere. Not just here. I heard my father say so before he left. That is why he said he was going far away to look.

MOTOMIAK.   You made those boots your father wore. I bet you put a charm on them. Shikikanaq and I saw you talking to them once and blowing on them.

ANATOU.   No! That's not true. I was cleaning them.

MOTOMIAK.   But you were talking too, you were putting a charm on them, weren't you?

ANATOU.   Don't you see? If I did have any magic powers, I'd bring them back. They're my parents. I love them. They're the only ones who've been good to me.

(*Softly*)

I couldn't stay in Little Whale River if it weren't for them.

SHIKIKANAQ. (*Cruelly*).   Well, they're gone now. So you can go too.

ANATOU.   What do you mean? They're coming back. I know they are.

MOTOMIAK.   Maybe. But my father says you killed your own parents.

ANATOU (*With a cry*).   No!

468

TARTO *(Challenging him and pinning his arm back).* Take that back or else!

MOTOMIAK *(Stubbornly).* That's what my father said.

TARTO *(Knocking him down).* Well, he's wrong.

(A fight starts. Shikikanaq shrieks and Anatou watches horrified. Three villagers rush in).

SHIKIKANAQ *(Quickly).* She started it. It's all her fault. Anatou's fault!

KIVIOG *(To Anatou).* Get away from our children.

(Villager 2 has separated the boys)

TARTO. Anatou wasn't doing anything.

KIVIOG. Be still!

VILLAGER 1. She's brought nothing but trouble since the day she was born.

TARTO *(To Kiviog).* But it's not fair, Father, she . . .

KIVIOG. Silence! For days we have searched for Karvik and Arnarqik. They are good peope. Karvik was the best hunter we had. But no man can fight off charmed boots.

VILLAGER 2. No wonder they got lost in the blizzard.

VILLAGER 1. Look at her. She doesn't care her parents are gone.

ANATOU *(Suddenly).* I don't understand. Do you mean they're . . . dead?

(Kiviog nods)

How can you be sure?

KIVIOG. If they haven't frozen, they have starved. We cannot find them anywhere.

VILLAGER 1. You're to blame. You and your witchcraft.

VILLAGER 2. Look, she doesn't even care.

ANATOU. Don't you think I want them here? Don't you think the fire is colder without my mother's face and lonesome without my father's singing? They went to look for food . . . for all of us. I'm hungry too . . . just like the rest of you.

VILLAGER 1. Then why do you anger the Seal Goddess? We used to have days of feasting.

VILLAGER 2. Pots boiling . . .

KIVIOG. But since the same day you were born, the hunters have had to work twice as hard — twice as hard for the same amount!

VILLAGER 2. We used to thank the Seal Goddess, bow down to her and give her seal liver. Now there is none to give her and she is angry — at the bottom of the sea. Our harpoons break in our hands.

ANATOU. It is the bitter cold.

VILLAGER 2. Why is there blizzard after blizzard if the gods aren't angry?

VILLAGER 1. Why is there a famine if the gods aren't angry.

KIVIOG. It's your fault.

VILLAGER 2. You're to blame.

KIVIOG. We have kept silent for the sake of Karvik and Arnarqik, but now they are no longer here.

VILLAGER 1. They took care of you and see what it brought them to!

ANATOU (Sobbing). But I am all alone too.

VILLAGER 2. There is no more to eat.

VILLAGER 1. No oil to burn.

VILLAGER 2. We fear sickness.

KIVIOG. And the souls of the dead.

VILLAGER 1. The souls of animals and men.

VILLAGER 2. We know the spirits of the earth and the air are angry with us.

ANATOU. What am I to do? What do you want of me?

KIVIOG. Leave here. Leave us!

ANATOU. But I haven't done anything. Where will I go? I'll never find my way alone.

KIVIOG. If you stay, you will get no help or protection from us, Anatou. From now on, find your own food and eat with the dogs. No one else will eat with you.

VILLAGER 2. And from now on, speak to yourself. No one else will listen.

(Adults start off)

VILLAGER 1. Go home, children, all of you. Go home quickly.

KIVIOG. Don't talk to that one. That one is evil. Leave her alone.

(They leave. Anatou has turned away. Tarto looks back before exiting but she doesn't see it. Anatou sinks down, unable to bear it)

ANATOU. It isn't true! I loved my parents. Even Tarto believed them. He didn't say a word — he didn't even say good-by. Oh, Moon God, is there nothing I can do.

(She is crying. Tarto reappears, puts his hand out to touch her hair, then in fear withdraws it)

TARTO *(Gently)*. What are you going to do? Where will you go?

ANATOU *(Jerks her head abruptly but doesn't turn around)*. All right! All right! I'm leaving. Are you satisfied now?

TARTO. But it's me, Anatou — Tarto. I want to say good-by.

ANATOU *(Turns around)*. Tarto, you came back!

TARTO. But I can't stay. If they catch me . . . I'll . . . I'll get into trouble. I brought you some food Anatou. It's just a little, but I thought . . .

ANATOU. Thank you, Tarto.

(Suddenly she takes off an amulet that she is wearing)

Tarto. you're the only friend I have now. I want you to keep this to remember me. The Shaman gave it to my mother before I was born. It's to bring good luck, but it was really always meant for a boy child, not a girl.

(He takes it)

Tarto, I wish I had something special to give you, but it's all I have.

TARTO. Then it is special, Anatou. I'll always keep it. I won't forget you. I promise. And when I am older, Anatou, I'll harpoon my own seal. I'll be the best hunter in the village and the men will do anything I say because I'll know all the hiding places of the seals. Then they'll listen to me and . . .

(Breaks off and slowly asks what he has always wondered)

Anatou, why is your hair so light?

ANATOU *(Pierced by the question)*. Tarto, why is the sky gray in the winter? I don't know. All I want is to be like the others, to play with you and sing with you, and I want to see my mother and father again. I love them. Do you believe me?

(He nods)

I want to be friends with the villagers, but they won't let me. You're the only one who tries to understand. I used to wake up and say, "Today will be different." My mother said, "Anatou, every day is the beginning of some new wonderful thing." But it wasn't true! Each day ended the same way and each dawn I was frightened again. And then today . . . today it was the worst of all.

TARTO.   I'm sorry, Anatou.

ANATOU.   Tarto, you were brave to come back here. You know they'll be angry if they find you here.

TARTO.   I know.

ANATOU.   You will be a fine hunter, Tarto . . . the finest of the whole village one day. Tarto, why did you come back?

TARTO.   I am your friend, Anatou. I always will be even if . . .

ANATOU.   Even if what, Tarto?

TARTO.   Anatou, listen. My father said . . . that . . . well, he said . . .

(Gulps)

. . . He said you put spells on the seals so they couldn't come out of the water. Anatou, couldn't you say another spell so we could all eat? Then it would be all right again, Anatou.

ANATOU *(Horrified)*.   Do you believe that, Tarto?

TARTO *(Miserably)*.   Well, first I said it wasn't true! But today . . .

ANATOU.   Tarto, listen. There's nothing I can do. I can't make a spell like a shaman, like the wise man. I'm hungry, too, just like you. Even if I wanted to, there is nothing I can do.

TARTO *(Slowly)*.   Don't you want to? Don't you want to help us, Anatou?

ANATOU.   Don't you believe me either, Tarto? Doesn't anyone? I'm not any different. I don't have any magic powers. I'm just like anyone else.

TARTO.   Your skin is white, mine is brown. Your hair is pale like the dawn, mine is dark like the night.

(He is colder now)

You're not like anyone I've seen.

(A long pause)

ANATOU. I've never heard you say that before. Everyone else, but you! You never seemed to care. You made up for all the others.

(Sound of Eskimo dogs)

TARTO *(Uncomfortably)*. I have to go, Anatou . . . it's late. What will you do?

ANATOU *(With a horrible realization)*. I know I can't stay here now. Tarto, when you lose everything at once, your choice has been made. You can only follow it.

TARTO. But where will you go? What will you do?

ANATOU *(Pauses, making difficult decision)*. The forest, Tarto. It's only a few days from here. I've heard about it from the old men and the Shaman.

TARTO *(Impulsively)*. But you can't. Don't you know about it? It's a place of whispers in the night, of strange whines. They say the trees are living beings but they can't speak. It's not safe for an Eskimo to spend a night in the forest. What if the Wood God changes you into a wolf or another animal?

ANATOU *(Slowly)*. Yes . . . what if he changes me into a wolf?

TARTO *(Continuing without hearing her)*. It's dark and mysterious, Anatou. It's a place where Eskimos never go.

ANATOU. But, don't you see? That's just why. There is no place else!

(Pauses)

Maybe the Wood God won't care if my hair is pale . . . like the dawn!

ACT II, *Scene 1*

Outside the forest at night. Late March. The opening of this scene is mimed and the audience sees Anatou's silhouette.

STORYTELLER.   Anatou ran. It was dark and frightening. The only sound she heard was the wind whipping the snow around her.

(Anatou drops from exhaustion. She is crying but she must continue)

ANATOU.   Where shall I go?

STORYTELLER.   No one could hear her cry. There was no one but the wind. Anatou knew if she stopped too long she would freeze in the fierce cold. Then suddenly she saw the place where no one had ever been.

(Part of the forest appears stage right. Anatou stops stage left)

ANATOU.   The forest! I remember the old men used to tell each other tales by the fire. What did they say? No Eskimo must ever go into the forest. You must never spend the night there. But that's where the Wood God lives.

(She starts to move toward the forest)

I must go. I must ask him.

(Rest of forest scrim appears as Anatou runs first to stage right, then to stage left, stopping at center stage. Exhausted, she sinks to the ground. She is trembling with fear and slowly rises to her knees. Softly)

Wood God!

(Louder)

Wood God!

(Looks all around her)

Wood God . . . help me.

(The Wood God enters. He appears, as the spirits are reputed to, in the shape of an animal. He has chosen the shape of an awesome owl which is white in color)

WOOD GOD.   Who dares to come into my forest where the wind and snow cry into the darkness?

ANATOU *(Draws back)*.   Are you the Wood God?

WOOD GOD.   I am! And will be till the end of time! Who said you could enter my forest?

474

ANATOU *(Terrified).* No one.

WOOD GOD. Where do you come from?

ANATOU. I come from Little Whale River.

WOOD GOD. Are you an Eskimo?

(She nods)

Then why did you come here? Don't you know no Eskimo comes into the middle of the forest and dares to disturb my sleep? Leave my kingdom now and be glad you still have your life.

ANATOU *(Pleading).* No! You don't understand. Please don't send me away.

(Crying. The Wood God comes closer and as he approaches, moonlight shines around them both.)

WOOD GOD. Ah-ah. Even in the darkness your hair shines. Is it the moon, child?

ANATOU *(Desperate).* Wood God. Wood God, can't you see? Even hidden here it shines and glitters. If I were to crawl into a cave it would be the same .

WOOD GOD *(Lifts her face and peers into it.)* Your face is as pale as ice.

(Softer)

And your eyes are red from crying.

(Shakes his head)

That's too bad. It means you're human.

ANATOU. I am an Eskimo. But they don't believe me. Nobody does. Help me. Wood God, help me!

WOOD GOD. How can I help you? Are you hungry, child? Is that why you came here?

ANATOU *(Nods).* We all are . . . no one has eaten in days. But it is not my fault . . . they blame me because my hair shines, because it isn't like the raven's wing. But I am hungry too. I can't go any further . . . I can't.

WOOD GOD. We have no food to give you child. You must leave. Your people will be worried.

(He starts to exit)

ANATOU. Wait! Wait and hear me, Wood God. It is not food I want.

It is not food that made me wake the great spirit of the Wood God.

WOOD GOD. What then?

ANATOU *(Slowly)*. I want what only your powers can grant. But first, Wood God, hear my story.

WOOD GOD. Begin. Quickly, child. You mustn't savor what tastes bitter.

ANATOU. Aja. It is true. You do see much.

WOOD GOD. Begin from the beginning; when you were born.

ANATOU. Even though I was a girl, my parents were happy, or at least they seemed to be. Even though I couldn't hunt . . . even though . . . even though I was different.

WOOD GOD. Why? You have two arms, two legs, and a face with two eyes and a mouth.

ANATOU. But a face that people were afraid of and hair that grew lighter instead of darker. They named me Anatou, the Fair One.

WOOD GOD. So you are Anatou. Then not all the spirits of the earth and air can help you. You are as you are.

ANATOU. But you can help me, Wood God. Please. You must.

WOOD GOD. Go home, fair child. I can do nothing. I cannot turn your pale hair to the dark of the night or your fair skin brown. I cannot teach them to like you. You must do that yourself. Go home to your parents. Go home where you belong.

ANATOU *(Blurts out)*. I can't. They'll kill me if I do.

WOOD GOD *(Puzzled)*. Who will? Your parents, too?

ANATOU. No, they are spirits now. They were the only good people I ever knew. I did love them, Wood God. Some people say that I am a witch and that I cursed my parents, that the Seal Goddess is angry with me. They say that is why there is no food. But it isn't true, Wood God! It isn't true!

WOOD GOD. My power would only hurt you, Anatou. You are young. Go back.

ANATOU. I've heard you can make a seal seem like a man or a girl seem like a wolf. Is that true?

WOOD GOD. I can.

ANATOU. Then, Wood God . . .

476

WOOD GOD. *(Interrupts).* Think Anatou. Is it so terrible to be an Eskimo girl, to learn to laugh and sing, or sew or cook.

ANATOU. Wood God, my father and mother taught me to sew and cook, but not to laugh and sing. I don't know what that is.

WOOD GOD. But what about the villagers?

ANATOU. They only taught me one thing — to hate. When my parents were gone, they wanted me to eat in the passageway with the dogs. They would not give me a skin to sew. Everywhere I went they turned away.

(Softly)

Even Tarto.

WOOD GOD. Tarto?

ANATOU. My best friend.

WOOD GOD. Where is he?

ANATOU. Wood God, they all say I'm planning evil, and now even Tarto thinks so, too. Wood God, Wood God, there are more ways of killing than with a harpoon!

WOOD GOD *(Pauses before he speaks).* What do you wish, Anatou?

ANATOU. I don't want to be human any more. It hurts too much. I want you to turn me into a wolf. Then they'll be afraid of me. Then they'll leave me alone.

WOOD GOD. Think, Anatou, think! An animal cannot . . .

ANATOU. Is a wolf's face white like mine?

WOOD GOD. You know it is not.

ANATOU. Then quickly change me into a beast.

WOOD GOD. An animal is hungry.

ANATOU. I am used to that.

WOOD GOD. He tears with his teeth to eat. A wolf is alone.

ANATOU. I am alone now.

WOOD GOD. Anatou, there is no return. What if you miss your village?

ANATOU. Miss them! When you take a thorn out of an animal's paw, does it miss it? When you fill an empty stomach, does it miss the ache? When you cannot remember pain, do you miss the tears? What would I miss, Wood God, but all of these things.

477

WOOD GOD.   Once it is done, you cannot change your mind.

ANATOU.   I will not want to.

WOOD GOD.   You will never be an Eskimo girl again, not until you are about to die. Not 'till then. Are you sure? Are you sure, Anatou?

ANATOU.   Will I forget everything? I want to forget everything. Now.

WOOD GOD.   No, Anatou. Not at first. As time goes by, you'll forget more and more and only remember your life here.

ANATOU.   No! I want to forget everything now. Everything, Wood God. I want to forget I was ever Anatou, the Fair One.

WOOD GOD.   But you can't escape pain, Anatou. Even a wolf can't escape that.

(She pauses to think, she looks up. He watches her closely)

Are you ready?

ANATOU.   Yes.

(Suddenly frightened)

Wood God, will it hurt much?

WOOD GOD.   Listen to my words. Hear them well.

(Lifts his arms so it appears as though his spirit, in the shape of a white owl, were commanding the universe. Drum beat begins)

Come spirits of earth and sky.
Rise through the snow.
Speed over the ice.
Encircle this child in a coat of thick fur.

(Three forest animals appear — a fox, a beaver and an ermine — and form a circle around Anatou)

FOX.   Night protect it.

BEAVER.   Forest watch it.

ERMINE.   Nothing harm it.

WOOD GOD.   As long as it remembers . . .

FOX.   As long as it remembers . . .

BEAVER.   As long as it remembers . . .

WOOD GOD.   To stay in the forest far from man.

ERMINE.   Far from man.

FOX *(Echoes).*   . . . from man.

(There is more dancing. Animals close in. Their movements become more intense, then with a cry, they disappear and we see the wolf)

FOX.   It is done!

ERMINE.   Now you are a wolf!

BEAVER.   A wolf!

(This should not be a realistic representation, but rather done with masks and a costume, lean and sleek, that would be worn under the eskimo dress, removed and disposed of at the end of the enchantment with a momentary darkening of the stage and more intense beating of the drum. There should be a marked difference in the movement once Anatou has been changed into a wolf)

STORYTELLER. All that winter Anatou lived with the animals enjoying the forest. She made friends with the beaver, fox and ermine. She forgot she had ever been Anatou, the Fair One — an Eskimo. Then one morning she woke up to a spring sun. It warmed the air and touched her fur.

(Spring in the forest. Early dawn. Anatou wakes, stretches, and smells the air with curiosity.

ANATOU. Whorlberries. That's what I smell. And sunlight! Even the forest can't shut it out.

(She puts a paw down on a patch of melting snow)

Beaver! Fox! Wake up. The snow's melting.

(They enter)

FOX. Did you have to wake me up and tell me that? It happens every spring.

ANATOU (With growing excitement). But there are at least a thousand things to see and smell and hear. Come on. I'll race you through the forest and we'll explore the other side.

BEAVER *(Slowly)*. What do you mean by the other side? We've never gone beyond the edge.

ANATOU. Oh, that was all right in the winter time. But now it's Spring. I want to leave the forest today, see what else there is.

FOX *(Sharply)*. No, Anatou.

BEAVER. I thought you liked it here in the forest.

ANATOU. Of course I do, but . . .

(Reluctant to speak of it)

. . . But last night I had a strange dream. I can't remember it now. But it was something out there. There's something I have to see.

BEAVER. Outside the forest?

FOX. Don't go there, Anatou.

ANATOU. Why not?

FOX. Don't go or you'll be sorry.

ANATOU. I just want to look. It's a beautiful day. I want to run in the sunlight and explore.

Fox. If you leave, the Wood God will be furious.

Anatou. The Wood God? Why? I'll be back tonight, I promise. What's there to be afraid of.

Fox *(Quietly)*. Danger.

Beaver. Danger.

Anatou. Maybe there's something dangerous for little animals like you, but I'm strong. I've got sharp teeth and claws.

(Boasting)

Nothing can hurt me.

Fox. You're a fool!

Anatou. *(Angry)*. Wait and see. I'll be back without a scratch on me. I'm not afraid like the rest of you.

Beaver. Listen to her! We'll let her go if she wants to.

Fox. For the last time. We're warning you. Don't go. There'll be trouble if you do.

Anatou. I must go. I don't know why, but I must. Don't try to stop me.

Fox. Remember, we warned you!

Beaver. You wouldn't listen.

Anatou. I can't help it. It's something inside.

(Lights fade, animals exit. Forest scrim rises and Anatou mimes her journey through the forest. She stops at the edge. The hilltops are brown, and there are black willow twigs with new buds)

Willow trees! And sunlight everywhere. Wood God, what a beautiful world outside your forest.

(Her journey continues in dance movement. The lights fade to indicate twilight. She stops worn-out)

Loons on the water. It's so peaceful here.

(Enjoying it)

I'm all alone in the world.

(She prepares to settle down when lights begin to come up on a summer village tent and we hear the sharp sound of an Eskimo dog howling. Anatou peers at the tent and moves in cautiously, closer and closer. The tent should be a movable unit that glides)

on. As Anatou gets closer, we hear the sound of Eskimo singing or chanting. Anatou realizes what it is and cries out)

Eskimos! Wood God! Wood God! Wood God! I'd forgotten.

(As she watches, Kiviog and Tarto cross stage to tent)

Tarto. And he still has the charm I gave him. He still has it.

KIVIOG.   Tarto, we'll never have to worry with you as a hunter. All the pots of the village will boil this spring. Aja, since Anatou left, there's been plenty to eat.

TARTO.   There'd be enough for her, too, if she were here.

KIVIOG.   Forget about her Tarto.

(They go inside)

ANATOU *(Creeping closer).*   Look at them eating, laughing and singing. "Let her die in the snow." That's what they said. I'll show them. I'm strong now. I'll get even. If it's the last thing I do, I'll get even.

(She moves nearer the tent and sees a piece of meat outside)

I'll take some back to the forest.

(But the dogs hear her and they start howling. The singing stops and a villager runs out with his bow and arrow. Anatou sees him and runs, but not before he shoots an arrow at her. Anatou falls and the man disappears into the tent. Anatou is hurt but gets up, limping to the side of the tent)

That one! That one used to call me names. He hurt my mother and father.

(In pain)

I'm remembering. His arrow cut through my heart!

(Villager comes out to check whether the animal is dead or not and he carries another weapon. He looks about)

He'll kill me! Unless . . .

(Anatou springs. There is a short struggle and the man falls without a sound.)

Who is stronger now, Eskimo? Who's stronger now?

(Anatou leaves.   Curtain)

ACT II, *Scene 3*

In the forest. Anatou goes toward Fox. Fox retreats. Anatou approaches Beaver. He moves away in fear.

WOOD GOD.   You must leave man alone.

ANATOU.   He did not leave me alone. Why should I?

WOOD GOD.   Man has a bow, harpoons, knives, spears. You will see, Anatou. He will hunt you out. Stay away! Do not hurt another human.

ANATOU.   But he wounded me.

FOX.   You shouldn't have gone near his tent.

BEAVER.   You don't deserve to stay in the forest with us.

ANATOU.   But the wound hurt.

(Softly)

And then . . .I saw his face. I remembered. I remembered everything before then!

WOOD GOD.   That wound will heal, Anatou. But will this new wound heal? Your hatred is more chilling than the ice caves near the sea. It will grow if you don't kill it now, Anatou. It will grow and freeze your heart.

FOX.   You are a disgrace to the animals.

BEAVER.   Animals kill because they must eat.

FOX.   They must survive.

WOOD GOD.   It's the law of the forest. But you, Anatou, killed out of hate. Men do that, not the animals!

ANATOU *(with awful realization)*.   Wood God . . . when I saw him, and I saw the tent, and I remembered how they made me leave the village, and the arrow pierced me . . . I felt something . . . something I had forgotten. I had to get even!

WOOD GOD *(Sternly)*.   Live in peace with man, Anatou, or leave the forest forever.

(He sweeps off with the animals. Curtain)

Act II, *Scene 4*

The interior of a snow house. Drums are beating. Three village hunters are assembled in a circle. In the distance there is the piercing cry of a wolf. They shudder.

KIVIOG *(Arises).* We must try again. The wolf must be stopped.

ATATA. Never was a wolf spirit so hungry for men's souls.

VILLAGER 2. Hunter after hunter has gone and not returned. What can we do?

ATATA. Aja! But what good is a bow and arrow?

VILLAGER 2. What good are knives if we live in terror in our own houses?

KIVIOG. The great North is no longer safe. We mustn't let the wolf escape this time. Since Spring, he has not let us alone. At night he always disappears into the forest . . . where no Eskimo ever goes.

VILLAGER 2. Even if it does go into the forest, we must find it and put an end to this.

ATATA. But if we go into the forest, we'll be trapped.

KIVIOG. We are trapped in our own homes now!

ALL. Aja! Aja!

ATATA. Never has there been a wolf like this. Its howl makes the fire die and the seal-oil lamp tremble.

VILAGER 2. We must hunt till we find it.

ATATA. We have lost many good hunters.

VILLAGER 2. They have all failed.

KIVIOG. But we must find it.

TARTO *(Has been sitting there all the time unnoticed by the others).* I have hunted before. Let me go, Father.

KIVIOG. Tarto! This is a council for our best hunters. Go outside. You should not be here. You're too young.

VILLAGER 2. He is so small that we don't notice him. It's all right, Kiviog.

ATATA. Perhaps he is so small that he could creep upon the wolf and he wouldn't notice him either.

(They all laugh)

484

TARTO. Please, Father. Please, I'm strong.

KIVIOG. No. We go too far. You will be tired.

TARTO. I won't. Wait and see.

KIVIOG. The men of Little Whale River are going to the forest, Tarto. It's dangerous.

TARTO. Then I will find the wolf's hiding place.

VILLAGER 2. He is swift, Kiviog. His eyes are sharp. He is as good a hunter as the men. If he wishes, let him come.

(Kiviog thinks, then nods to Tarto. Tarto beams)

KIVIOG. We must cover the great North and not stop till the snow is free of the wolf's tracks.

VILLAGERS. Aja! Aja!

VILLAGER 2. We must hunt towards the great plains.

KIVIOG. And hunt towards the forest.

ATATA. And by the caves along the sea.

KIVIOG. We've no time to waste. Harness the dogs!

(Drums increase. Men leave to get dog teams and begin the hunt. Interior fades)

ACT III, *Scene 1*

The forest. There is snow on the ground and a rock unit has been added left center. There is a group of tangled trees that have been blown down in the winter near right center. Anatou sleepily comes from behind the rock. She sniffs the air casually, then her body tenses.

ANATOU *(Calling with increasing alarm).* Wood God! Wood God! Wood God! I smell danger.

(Beaver and fox appear)

FOX. The hunters are here.

BEAVER. The hunters.

ANATOU. But the Eskimos are afraid of the forest. Why do they come here?

FOX. They hunt the wolf.

BEAVER. They hunt you.

FOX. Anatou.

WOOD GOD *(Entering).* I warned you, Anatou. You have hurt too many of them. They are angry, angry enough to enter the forest and to hunt you out.

ANATOU. I'm frightened, Wood God. Please help me.

WOOD GOD. You hate and so you killed. You deliberately disobeyed me after I first sheltered you. I cannot protect you now.

ANATOU. Was I wrong to defend myself, Wood God, to wound when I was wounded?

WOOD GOD. You've been cruel, Anatou, and hate is like a disease spreading through your heart. If you strike an Eskimo, how does the Beaver know that you won't strike him, too, when he sleeps in the night?

ANATOU. No! I'd never do that. You know that, Wood God.

WOOD GOD. How do I know? I only see what you do. That speaks for itself.

ANATOU *(Ashamed).* I won't leave the forest again, Wood God. I have been wrong.

WOOD GOD *(Angry).* It's too late for that, Anatou. The hunters are here.

FOX. They're coming closer.

486

BEAVER. Closer.

ANATOU *(Panicked)*. Wood God, what should I do?

WOOD GOD *(Harshly)*. Replace the hunters you made them lose. Erase the terror you've caused them. Anatou, even the animals have been frightened of you.

ANATOU. But I didn't mean them. They've been good to me. I didn't want to hurt the animals.

WOOD GOD *(Watching her intently)*. If you cannot live in peace with man, Anatou, then one day you will have to face his bow and arrow. There is no law of the forest that can protect you from that time.

ANATOU. Wood God, why didn't you warn me? Why didn't you stop me? I have worn a coat of thick hate — so thick it stopped my feeling or seeing anything else.

WOOD GOD. We tried, Anatou, but before you weren't ready to hear our words.

ANATOU. I am now, Wood God. Please, please, animals.

FOX. Hurry, Anatou. They are closer.

ANATOU. What should I do?

WOOD GOD. Run, Anatou. There is no time. If the hunters find you.

ANATOU. I know.

WOOD GOD. But remember this if you are truly sorry, if you know what understanding means, if you can show me your heart is empty of all its dark hate and cruelty, no matter what happens, your spirit will not die. It will live forever and teach others. Remember that.

ANATOU. Thank you, Wood God.

WOOD GOD. Now run, Anatou.

ANIMALS. Run, Anatou, run.

(Anatou exits across the stage. Village hunters enter. They are frightened. Suddenly a wind comes up)

VILLAGER 2. Aja! The wind is alive.

ATATA. Let's leave. No Eskimo should be here.

KIVIOG. No! We have promised our village.

TARTO. We cannot return 'til the wolf is found.

KIVIOG. Look! His tracks are here.

VILLAGER 2. Follow them!

KIVIOG. Sh-h-h-h. Fresh tracks. Quickly, carefully.

(There is silence as they begin the serious search)

ANIMALS *(Whispering).* Hurry, Anatou. Hurry.

(Anatou streaks across the stage. They see her)

VILLAGER 1. Follow it! Follow it!

(They rush off left. Tarto, who is behind them, gets trapped in the fallen trees: his bow and arrow fly to the side. Tarto tries to escape, but is caught fast.)

TARTO. I can't get out!

(Trying to free himself)

I'm trapped!

(There is deathly silence around him)

Where did they go? I can't even hear them.

(Shouting)

Father! Father, come back. Hurry!

(Sees his bow and arrow, but he can't reach it. Anatou runs on right. She stumbles on bow and arrow and in so doing kicks it to other side. Tarto is terrified. He whispers horrified)

The wolf. What'll I do?

(He tries to struggle out, but he can't. Anatou comes closer. Tarto is wearing the charm she gave him. She half turns away)

ANATOU. It's Tarto! I've got to help him.

(Anatou moves in. Tarto thinks she is going to attack him. He becomes more and more terrified)

TARTO. No! No! Father! Help! Help!

(He covers his face instinctively, afraid to watch, but then forces himself to look. She pushes with all her might and finally the pressure is released and Tarto is out of the trap. He is amazed and does not understand what happened. As soon as Tarto is free, Anatou starts to run, but is too late. Just as she is passing the rock unit, we hear the whiz of an arrow and Anatou falls behind the rock unit)

No! He set me free. Don't kill him. He set me free.

(Kiviog, Atata and Villager 2 rush in)

KIVIOG.   Tarto, what happened?

TARTO.   I got trapped over there in the logs . . . and then the wolf . . . he set me free.

KIVIOG.   What?

TARTO.   The wolf, Father, the wolf. That's the truth. He pulled the log away so I could get out. I thought he was going to kill me.

KIVIOG.   Where is your bow and arrow?

TARTO.   There! I couldn't reach them. But Father, he saved my life. He pushed the log away.

ATATA.   The forest is alive with things we can't understand.

KIVIOG.   Where is he now?

TARTO.   The arrow hit near the rock . . . but . . .

(They look. She is not there)

He's not there. Where did he go?

ATATA.   It may be a trick.

VILLAGER 2 *(Advancing cautiously).*

Here's a fresh footprint.

ATATA.   Watch out.

(They move cautiously)

TARTO. *(With a cry).*   It's . . .

(Turns to Kiviog)

Anatou. It's Anatou, Father. We've hurt her.

(They all stare amazed by the sight of the girl. Tarto kneels down by the rock unit. Anatou's spirit appears above. This can be done by seeing her through a scrim on a higher level so that she looks the same but paler, as though in a dream)

ANATOU.   Tarto . . . don't cry.

TARTO *(To himself)*   Anatou. You were my best friend.

(To her)

I didn't mean to hurt you. Do you understand. We didn't mean . . . *(He can't say it. Tarto tried to hold back the anguish inside)*

489

ANATOU. I do, Tarto, I do. Oh, Wood God, they can't hear me.

TARTO. She could have killed me, Father, but she didn't. She saved my life instead.

VILLAGER 2. Aja. She was brave.

KIVIOG. Braver than all the hunters of Little Whale River. None of us would have done what she did.

(He puts his hand on Tarto's shoulder, but he can't say what he'd like to)

VILLAGER 2. But why did she run into the forest?

TARTO. Don't you see? She had no place else to go. We chased her here.

(This is the most painful of all)

Anatou, even I chased you away.

KIVIOG. We would not speak or smile at the different one, remember. Our silence was worse than a hundred harpoons.

TARTO. Will she forgive me, Father?

KIVIOG. The spirits of the dead know our hearts, Tarto. You cannot keep a secret from them.

TARTO. But will she forgive me?

KIVIOG. We are all to blame.

TARTO. But I want to know! I have to know! She saved me, Father, and then the hunters shot an arrow when she finished.

KIVIOG. She had a bigger heart than you or I, Tarto, but if she is angry we'll be trapped by the snow and the wind and lose our way. No Eskimo should ever enter the realm of the forest. If she forgives us our way will be safe.

(They prepare to leave)

ANATOU. Wood God! Please let me help them.

WOOD GOD *(Pleased)*. 'Til the end of the forest and then I will guide them.

ANATOU. Do they understand, Wood God? How will they remember?

WOOD GOD. Tarto will tell your story tonight, the first time, and they will tell it for many nights. They will remember, for someone will always tell the story of Anatou, the Fair One.

VILLAGER *(Goes over slowly and picks up the arrow, holds it thoughtfully)*. I shot it! I killed her!

KIVIOG. No, we all killed her. But when? Today or long ago?

End

THE TINGALARY BIRD

by

MARY MELWOOD

THE TINGALARY BIRD

by

MARY MELWOOD

THE TINGALARY BIRD

The history of dramatic literature for children in this country has included very few plays that can be considered truly experimental in form or style. Such contemporary works as *The Arkansaw Bear* and *The Ice Wolf* are very different from *Peter Pan* and *The Little Princess*, but these differences are a result of a slow and steady evolution in the literature, rather than the influence of experimental trends. Each successive generation of playwrights has built upon the works of the past so that even plays that include modern themes and styles share some similarities with the more traditional works of the past.

The Tingalary Bird, by British playwright Mary Melwood, cannot be classified easily into such a pattern of evolution. It is a totally bizarre play that uses few of the elements that have been typical of the literature of the past. It thus represents a significant step in the development of the field, but a step that seems to have been made independent of the traditional influences. The play, which is based on an original story that falls somewhere between a modern problem play and a fairy or folk tale dramatization, has a primarily non-linear plot structure, language that is often used more for sound than for sense, and a well-orchestrated pattern of aural and visual spectacle. For these reasons, and others, it appears to be more directly related to experimental forms from the adult theatre than to any antecedents in theatre for children.

One of the more fascinating aspects of this play is that it is both an outrageous fantasy about two old people and a magical bird, and a serious work that offers an intense look at a very unhappy couple. That two such different perspectives can be reflected in the same work is a tribute to the remarkable sophistication of this play.

The play is constructed around a simple story that, when taken from the context of the world of the play, seems almost silly. Melwood has created a "poor old man" and a "mean old woman" who spend all of their time together arguing. We gradually learn that the woman, who appears to dominate the old man, has driven all of the guests away from their inn through her obsession with hoarding food and money for a "rainy day." The old man wants only to be warm, to have something to eat, and to enjoy the comradery of guests in the inn. In the midst of this bickering, a majestic bird makes a mysterious entrance onto the scene. The bird jousts with the old woman and uncovers a bag of coins that she has hidden in the chimney. In the end, the bird subdues the old woman so that the old man once more opens the inn and greets the new day with a cheery welcome.

Because Melwood offers only minimal exposition about characters, character motivation, and the situation, the story is played out in a mysterious world that is both bewildering and fascinating. At the beginning of the play, Melwood cautions (through the sailor's song) that "if you believe" this story, then perhaps it is told too well, but she begins the play with at least a facade of realism that teases the audience to accept the world as real. This perspective is soon altered, however, as the realistic world is gradually dismantled by the situations and behavior that become increasingly fantastic: the old man reminisces about the bird who escaped from the cage made of string, the old woman irons with a cold iron because "anyone can iron with a hot one," the old people dine on a large bone, the old man plays music on his string cage, and the one-handed clock strikes "preternaturally." And all of this action seems to be orchestrated by the god-like Tingalary bird.

The Tingalary Bird does not convey meaning in a traditional way. Characters do not argue philosophical ideas, such as in *The Ice Wolf* or *Reynard the Fox*, nor does the play itself present the message explicit in the downfall of an evil protagonist, such as in *The Emperor's New Clothes*. The play offers a child-like view of the world, complete with contradictions, anachronisms, and a distracted sense of time and place, and, with this perspective, Melwood *demonstrates* rather than discusses the thematic elements of the work as a whole.

The story begins at dusk when the world of the play is in chaos; it ends at dawn when the world of the play is in a state of equilibrium. But, the play does not progress in a typical cause-to-effect pattern between these two points. Although the story does not contain a through-line of action, Melwood, rather than underscoring the traditional elements of exposition, complication, and denouement, presents the story more like a collage of sound, sense, and action given life through the combination of many disparate elements. Very little actually *happens* in the play from the beginning to the end, but the manner in which the sights, sounds, characters, and situations are orchestrated together constitutes the essence of the play. Because of this, an attempt to clarify the many ambiguities and contradictions in the play does little to provide insight into the work as a whole. Melwood poses many questions, and she supplies few answers. This lack of information about the characters and situations is very much to the point of the story, and it makes the play even more fascinating. The characters are at cross-purposes to one another, and, as they focus on their individual, childlike obsessions, the absurdity of their world is clearly revealed.

In keeping with this form, language is not always used just to further the story line. It is characterized by non sequiturs, long pauses, rambling discussions, and intellectual decrees. The woman, for example, at one point in the play babbles on about the proper way of ironing clothes, while at another point, she deftly parries a request from her husband with a seemingly meaningless reply that very succintly characterizes the whole world of the play:

> WOMAN: What do you mean? Go on. Say what you mean
> —if you know what you mean . . . Which I often doubt.
>
> MAN: I don't know what I mean.
>
> WOMAN: There you are!
>
> MAN: I just *feel* what I mean.

It is obvious that Melwood wants her audience, like the old man, to feel what she means as much as to know what she means. The world of the play rejects logic and causes one to muse—in the words of the old woman—why "all this fuss about a word—and a bird."

The Tingalary Bird has often been compared with the absurdist plays for adult theatre — an appropriate comparison considering Melwood's use of many absurdist techniques. The absurdists, however, attempted to portray man's entrapment in an illogical, hostile, impersonal, and indifferent existence. There are no such pretensions in *The Tingalary Bird*; it is more fantastic than brooding, more humorous than menacing.

The play is sometimes farcical, sometimes restrained and poignant. At times there is a clear and heightened aesthetic distance between actors and audience, while at other times Melwood breaks this line and has actors speak directly to audience members, engaging them in songs and games. The characters are not particularly happy, but the play is not negative. It is an alternately happy, sad, moving, and comical world in which the dawn does bring a new and cheerful perspective.

This topsy-turvy world is best perceived and understood by a child audience — one that is not yet constrained by expectations of form and structure, and one that willingly suspends disbelief to follow Melwood through this fantasy. The play demands work from the child audience; but it also generously rewards that work with large servings of laughter, surprise, and pure theatrical fun. And through it all Melwood does not patronize her young audience. *The Tingalary Bird* reflects truthful insight into the human condition, a respect for the intelligence of young people, and a marvelous free-for-all style.

The Tingalary Bird was first published in this country in 1969, a time when the repertoire was becoming increasingly less traditional in its orientation. The success of this play, in turn, is one of the many influences that has stimulated diversity in the field. Although initially greeted with skepticism by the children's theatre community, the play has now assumed a position of prominence in the repertoire. In the context of some of the contemporary trends in dramatic literature for children — such things as participation theatre, story theatre, and improvisational drama — *The Tingalary Bird* no longer stands out as being so different from other plays. It is, however, still very much one of a kind.

MARY MELWOOD was born in Carlton-on-Lindwick, Nottinghamshire. She was educated at Retford County High School for Girls, Nottinghamshire, and currently resides at Brighton, Sussex.

Melwood has written several plays for children, two of which have been published in the United States: *The Tingalary Bird* and *Five Minutes to Morning*. When *The Tingalary Bird* was performed at the Arts Theatre London in 1964 it became the first children's play to receive a British Arts Council award. In the following year a similar award was given to *Five Minutes to Morning*.

Melwood's children's novels included *Nettlewood* (London: Andre Deutsch, 1974) and *The Watcher Bee* published by Andre Deutsch in 1982.

THE TINGALARY BIRD

Characters

THE OLD MAN

THE OLD WOMAN

THE SAILOR

THE TINGALARY BIRD

"The Tingalary Bird" was first presented with the Unicorn Theatre for Young People at the Arts Theatre in London on December 21st, 1964.

SCENE

The interior of an old inn, fallen into disuse.

ACT I

A poor room in a small inn at the edge of a forest. It is a winter evening and growing dark, but the shapes of twisted old trees can be seen crowding the dwelling.

Above the door of the inn is a battered sign upon which is written "The-Come-and-Sit Down-Inn." Some of the words have been crossed out and others written above them, so that the message of the sign is now "Stop-Outside-and-Go-Away." Just outside the door is a small clearing amidst the trees where stands a signpost. One of its arms is pointing backstage and saying "To the Village." The other points forward and says "To the Sea."

The room, which occupies the left part of the stage, has been the bar-parlor of the inn. In the middle of the left-hand wall is an old-fashioned fireplace choked with pieces of wood. Over it is a chimney-piece crowded with things. At the end nearest the audience from a rail in the wall hangs a much larger than life-size pair of spectacles. At the far end is a large hairbrush and comb like a rake. The side nearest the audience belongs to the POOR OLD MAN and there his rickety three-legged stool is placed. The side farthest from the audience belongs to the MEAN OLD WOMAN and there is her wooden rocking chair with a yellow cushion in it, and a bright woolen shawl folded over the back. On the wall by the fire and near her chair hangs a copper warming pan, and near to this, her broomstick is propped up. Behind her chair, to the left, is a hidden door through which she makes her entrance. On the center wall backstage is a cupboard and above it a wall clock with only one finger. At certain times during this play the tick of the clock is preternaturally loud.

To the left of the cupboard is the window, which looks out into the trees. A small empty birdcage made of string hangs limply from a hook. There are shutters instead of curtains.

To the right of the cupboard a half-opened door allows a glimpse into a crowded little lean-to room which is bursting with washday paraphernalia — an old-type washtub, for instance, and dolly-legs, mangle and scrubbing board. There is an iron pump with a curly handle.

The door into the forest is in the center of the wall which makes a right-angle with the back wall of the room. To the right of this door, nearer the audience, is a shelf over which is printed in shaky, childish writing "For a Rainy Day." It is full of assorted jumble amongst which can be seen a rusty, dusty watering can and a dented old tin marked "Buns." In the middle of the stage is a bare wooden table with a chair at either end. Various small signs that this cottage has once been an inn can be imagined.

When the play begins the left side of the stage is in darkness, the room and its objects being only vaguely seen. Along the path through the trees, at the right side of the stage, comes the SAILOR *from the village. He seems to know the inn, and notices the sign over the door with a wry smile. He comes front stage to sing his song to the audience.*

SAILOR *(singing):*

> I'm a wandering sailor,
> With a story to tell,
> And if you believe it,
> P'raps I've told it too well.

> This poor little dwelling
> Is cold and unkind,
> And over its threshold,
> No welcome I'll find.

> So out in the forest
> I'll go on my way,
> And see you no more till
> The end of the play!

(When the SAILOR *has finished his song he walks over to the left and makes his exit. As he does so, he is seen to carry on his back a small wicker birdcage covered by a black cloth. Now the forest darkens and the light increases on the left side of the stage to show the room of the inn. The* POOR OLD MAN *is struggling, with the help of a pair of wheezy bellows, to make the fire burn. The wind grows stronger, rattling the doors and windows, and puffing smoke and soot down the chimney into the room.)*

POOR OLD MAN *(Recoiling):* Smoke! Smoke! Nothing but smoke— except soot. What a mess! She'll be furious. *(He takes the broom and tries to clear up the hearth.)* No wonder we never get a decent fire with all this soot in the chimney. *(He puts the broom aside and cranes his neck up the chimney. Another gust of wind blows a puff of smoke into his face. He coughs and chokes. Doors and windows rattle violently.)* Go away! Go away, Wind! Can't you read the sign, "Stop-Outside-and-Go-Away"? Go and blow somewhere else before we're smothered with soot. *(He picks up the broomstick again and tries to tidy around the hearth, muttering to himself.)* I don't know *what* she'll say . . . all this mess. . . . 'Tisn't my fault, I'm sure. . . . And it's *SO* cold. . . . *(For a moment forgetting what he is doing, he sits on the rocking chair and folds the shawl over his shoulders for a minute's repose, leaning over the dead fire and rubbing his hands together. Then he quickly jumps up, guiltily shakes out the yellow cushion with sooty hands, then blows the soot from it. He rearranges the shawl*

*on the back of the chair and props up the broomstick close by,
always treating these properties with a mixture of sly respect and
envy. He bends down, blowing soot from the chair and cushion,
with much tut-tutting to himself.)* Oh dear, oh dear! I shouldn't
have sat in it. I've got my own nice comfortable stool, haven't I?
I can draw it right up to the fire . . . close *(draws up stool and
huddles over fire),* so close to it I'd burn—if there was any fire.
. . . Why, I remember . . . *(He breaks off as a tremendous gust
of wind rattles the door and blows in his wife, the* MEAN OLD
WOMAN, *from the hidden door at the back. This entrance must
come as a dramatic shock. The* MEAN OLD WOMAN *is wrapped
up in a red blanket, entwined by a clothesline which is dangling
from a huge basket of washing which she is carrying. An enormous iron, perched on top of the piled up clothes in the basket,
trails a long flex, which of course is not destined to connect with
anything but is there just for the absurdity of it and to trip her up.
Her hair is blown-about and she has pinned clothes pegs in it,
like hairpins. As she bursts in, a huge scrubbing brush falls from
underneath the blanket and is followed by a shower of pieces of
soap and lumps of washing soda.)*

MEAN OLD WOMAN: Whew! What a wind! It's nearly blown my hair
right off! *(She puts down her basket, etc., in the doorway of the
lean-to shed, removes her red blanket and puts it on top of the
washing. Picking up objects she has dropped and at the same time
scattering clothes pegs all about her, she moves toward the* OLD
MAN.) I'm *so* glad to be safe indoors in my dear little home with
my dear little—*(Her voice changes so abruptly that the* OLD MAN
jumps.) What have you been doing up that chimney again, HEY?

OLD MAN: Ch-chimney? I . . . I haven't . . .

MEAN OLD WOMAN: Look at the soot! Look at *you.* Oh, what a
mess!

OLD MAN: It's the wind. . . . It keeps blowing . . .

MEAN OLD WOMAN: Of course it keeps blowing. . . . That's what
wind is *for.*

OLD MAN: . . . the soot down the chimney. You should have the
sweep in, like I keep on saying.

OLD WOMAN *(To audience)*:   There he goes again. Nothing to do all
day but think of ways of spending money. There's nothing like it
for passing the time. *(To* OLD MAN.) The sweep indeed! I'll sweep
the chimney myself . . . in the spring. You just leave things alone
. . . *(She is looking sharply around the hearth with darting
glances..)* and don't go *touching* things. *(With a lightning gesture
she seizes her broomstick and with a few swift sudden strokes she*

500

sweeps the soot into the hearth and the OLD MAN *away from it up onto his stool. From one of her pockets—and her apron seems to have any amount of them—she takes a garment with which she proceeds to dust about the chimneypiece, grumbling all the time.)* Sooty fingerprints everywhere . . . *and* footprints. Here, dust yourself with this. *You're* as black as a boot. *(She throws her duster at the* OLD MAN *who begins to dust himself with it. She sees that it is a garment from her washing basket, seizes it from him crossly and holds it up.)* Now see what you've done! Who's going to wear that now, I'd like to know. *(Before the* OLD MAN *can get out an answer another puff of wind sends smoke down the chimney again, and his words change to a cough. The* OLD WOMAN *stuffs her duster into one pocket and feels through the others.)* About that cough of yours. I've been to the A-cough! the A-cough! —*A-COUGH-e-pary (She brings out the word like a sneeze.)* and he says—*(this must be gabbled at great speed.)*—What-sort-of-a-cough-is-it-and-I-says-the-sort-that-keeps-ME-awake-all-night-and-he-say-This-is-the-stuff-as'll-do-the-trick-Give-it-him-strong-he-says and-here-it-is-Open your mouth! *(She has taken a large greeny-black bottle from one pocket and a big spoon from another and with the last words of her speech she seizes the* OLD MAN'S *nose, jerks his head back and rams a spoonful of medicine down his throat, all in movements as quick as possible. The* OLD MAN *chokes and nearly falls off his stool.)* There! That'll do you good. *(To audience.)* I don't know what he'd do if he hadn't ME to look after him. *(She puts spoon and medicine on chimneypiece. She then glances into the warming pan as into a mirror, takes her brush and comb for a quick scrape at her hair, puts herself to rights and sits down in her rocking chair, folding her shawl about her shoulders.)* Now! Aren't you glad to see me after being alone all day? I expect you're longing for a-nice-little-chat. *(The* POOR OLD MAN *has hardly recovered from the effects of drinking his medicine, but he manages to say, although with a tinge of apprehension—)*

OLD MAN: Ch-Chat! *(He becomes aware of her inquisitorial gaze and nervously gets up from his stool. She grabs him and puts him back.)*

OLD WOMAN: Yes. Chat. We'll have a little chat, shall we? *(Amiably).* A little bit of talk is what makes these long winter evenings so cosy—*(snaps suddenly)*—and I want the truth, remember . . . and see that *your* idea of the truth is *my* idea of the truth, which isn't always the case. *(Pause.)* Has anybody been here today while I've been out earning our living?

OLD MAN: Who wants to come here anymore? What is there to make them welcome nowadays?

OLD WOMAN: Keep to the point . . . and answer the question. Has anybody been in this room?

OLD MAN: Yes. *(Pause.)* I've been in it.

OLD WOMAN: Any callers? Any travelers? Any of your disreputable friends, otherwise called customers?

OLD MAN: You know I haven't any friends . . . customers . . . since you sent them all away.

OLD WOMAN: We can't afford friends—or customers either. And don't think I haven't noticed that you've dodged the question. *(She picks up her broomstick.)* Remember, *I* like plain Yeses and Noes.

OLD MAN: No, then.

OLD WOMAN: No, what?

OLD MAN: No, your Majesty. *(He cannot help laughing. She gives him a poke with her stick. His laughter stops.)* I mean, no, nobody's been here.

OLD WOMAN *(Suspiciously)*:   No nobodies . . . no nobodies. . . . If two noes make a yes as some people seem to think.

OLD MAN: Nobody's been here but me—*(pause)*—except for—*(He breaks off.)*

OLD WOMAN: So there *was* somebody. I thought as much. Quick! Tell me! Who was it? You and—

OLD MAN: My little bird.

OLD WOMAN: Oh, The bird. *(She glances at the empty cage hanging in the window.)* Hullo! Where is it? *(The* OLD MAN *is silent.)* So it's gone. I told you it was a silly idea to make it a cage of string. Might as well not have put it in a cage at all.

OLD MAN: It needed somewhere of its own . . . and string doesn't hurt little wings as wires do.

OLD WOMAN: And you left the door open all the time. No wonder it flew away.

OLD MAN: It didn't fly away. *(Pause.)* It died.

OLD WOMAN: So it died, did it? Moody little thing. It died of sulks, I suppose.

OLD MAN: It died of No-fire-and-not-enough-crumbs. *(Pause.)* I don't know *what* I'll tell the Sailor if he comes back for it. He let me look after it as a favor.

OLD WOMAN: Favor! And not a penny toward its keep!

OLD MAN: He told me to take good care of it.

OLD WOMAN: I'll take good care of *him* if he dares to come here again. The Pirate! Coming here and cheating us of our hard-earned victuals.

OLD MAN: It wasn't his fault he'd lost all his money.

OLD WOMAN *(Mockingly)*: Oh no!

OLD MAN: And he was *very* hungry.

OLD WOMAN: Oh yes!

OLD MAN: And he promised to bring the money the next time he came.

OLD WOMAN: Next time he'd come to rob us, simpleton. I saw him staring all around with his sharp black eyes! It was a good thing *I* came home when I did and made short work of him. *(She chuckles.)* Oho! He won't forget my trademark in a hurry. *(She brandishes her broomstick.)* So his bird died, did it? And a good thing, too!

OLD MAN: All the same . . . *(He breaks off.)*

OLD WOMAN: All the same? *(She gets up, walks over to the birdcage and takes it down. She stands, thoughtfully, turning it over in her hands.)*

OLD MAN *(Anxiously)*: You're not going to throw it away, are you?

OLD WOMAN: Do I ever throw anything away? *(She walks front stage to face audience standing at the left side of the stage. The* OLD MAN *walks front stage, stands at the right.)* There *must* be something we could use it for.

OLD MAN: We could put another bird in it.

OLD WOMAN: What do we want with a bird, eating us out of house and home? Think of something that doesn't cost money. Quick. Any ideas? *(She invites the audience holding up the cage.)* What's that? A toast rack.

OLD MAN: A toast rack? But we never have any toast.

OLD WOMAN: We may have some day—when we can afford it. *(She leaves the front of the stage, goes to the table and picks up one of the chairs.)*

OLD MAN: Not while we have fires like this. *(He goes to the fireplace.)*

OLD WOMAN: That's a good fire. Look at all the wood in it.

OLD MAN: Yes, but it don't burn.

(The OLD WOMAN carries the chair and puts it beneath the Rainy Day shelf. She climbs up to put the birdcage away with the other jumble. From her perch she looks down at the OLD MAN and says in an explanatory manner as if to a child):

OLD WOMAN: It's a wood fire . . . but if the wood burned there wouldn't be any wood on it, would there? So—it wouldn't *be* a wood fire . . . and it couldn't be a good fire . . . so you'd still have something to grumble about, wouldn't you? *(She gets down with the air of having triumphantly proved her point. While the OLD MAN is turning over her words in his mind, she puts back the chair, then goes to the lean-to room, takes the red blanket from her washing basket and drapes it over the table. Then she goes for her big iron, and comes back, trying to disentangle it from its flex.)*

OLD MAN *(To audience):*   Hurrah! She's going to iron! Now we'll have to have a good fire. *(Begins to poke the wood on the fire.)*

OLD WOMAN: Stop poking the fire. The kind of ironing *I'm* going to do can be done with a cold iron, thank you very much. Anybody can iron with a *hot* iron.

(Disappointed, the OLD MAN sits on his stool and watches the OLD WOMAN as she proceeds to do the ironing. She brings her clothes basket up to the table, then takes her stance with the iron. She twirls the loose flex round and round above her head, then throws it, like a lasso around the OLD MAN. She takes from the pile of washing an outlandish garment, which she holds up so that the audience can have a good look.)

OLD MAN: What's that?

OLD WOMAN: Don't be impertinent. I don't ask my clients what they are wearing.

OLD MAN: That'll take a bit of straightening out with a cold iron. *(The OLD WOMAN leans heavily on the iron for some time.)*

OLD WOMAN: It's all a question of weight . . . and waiting. . . . Haven't you ever heard of patience? *(She leans on the iron, and waits . . . and waits . . . The OLD MAN watches her . . . and the clock's tick is heard . . . and then the wind blows . . . and blows. The OLD WOMAN at last removes the iron and hopefully holds up the garment. It is more creased than ever. The light in the room is gradually fading.)* There! You see!

OLD MAN: I can't see. Let's have a candle. *(Jumps up.)*

504

OLD WOMAN (*Picks up the lasso and jerks it*):   I'll get it. You make yourself useful and put all this away. (*The* OLD MAN *gets out of the lasso—and begins to gather up the ironing things while the* OLD WOMAN *goes to the cupboard. She takes a key from her pocket and with the air of gravest secrecy unlocks the cupboard door, taking care that the* OLD MAN, *who is watching every movement, cannot peep over her shoulder and see inside. She takes out a candle in a candlestick and locks up again. She carries the candle to the table and lights it with a match taken from her apron pocket. The* OLD MAN *claps his hands as if at a performance—and the candle goes out.*) Now see what you've done. (*The* OLD MAN *looks crestfallen. The* OLD WOMAN *goes to the cupboard and the whole procedure occurs again. At last the candle is lighted and burning steadily in the center of the table. Then the wind blows vehemently, and the doors and the windows rattle. Putting her hand round the flame.*) Drat the wind. Go and close the shutters— or the draft will put the candle out. Go on, silly, do you think I'm made of matches?

(*The* OLD MAN *goes to the window but before he fastens the shutters, he peers outside into the wood.*)

OLD MAN: What a noise the trees are making? I'm sorry for anybody who is out tonight. (*Hesitates, looks at the* OLD WOMAN.) It's nice to see a candle shining—if you're outside in the dark.

OLD WOMAN: I'm *not* outside but I might as well be in this draft. Close the shutters.

OLD MAN (*Still hesitating*):   It's a pity we're out of business. It's just the night for customers.

OLD WOMAN: Customers! I've had enough of them, thank you very much. Shoo! to customers! Let them stay at home, say I . . . and if they're the sort of customers who came here before—we'll be all the better off. Now close the shutters. . . . (*The* OLD MAN *does so, at last.*) And bolt the door as well. Make sure nobody gets in.

(*The* OLD MAN *potters about locking up and the* OLD WOMAN *goes to her rocking chair. The* OLD MAN *comes back to her.*)

OLD MAN: All's bolted and barred. *We're* locked in and *they're* locked out.

OLD WOMAN (*Jumping*):   Who! Who are you talking about?

OLD MAN: Why, nobody. Anybody.

OLD WOMAN: You just be careful . . . that's all. . . . With your nobodies and anybodies. Thank goodness there's only the two of us.

(The OLD MAN sits down on his stool at the other side of the fire.)
Just you and me in our cozy little home—

(The wind blows harder than ever and she breaks off. Smoke puffs down the chimney. They both jump back.)

OLD MAN: There's the soot again. That's the end of the fire.

OLD WOMAN: It's bedtime then. *(She jumps up as if ready to go.)*

OLD MAN: Bedtime? What about supper?

OLD WOMAN *(To audience)*:   There he goes again. I never knew such a man for extravagant ideas.

OLD MAN: I'll lay the table. *(He speedily gets tablecloth, knives, etc. from drawer in the table and sets the table in a rush.)*

OLD WOMAN *(Seeing table)*:   What makes you think it's knives and forks? It's not Christmas. *(She goes to the cupboard, which she unlocks, standing with her back to the audience.)*

OLD MAN *(Drooping)*:   Only spoons . . . *again?*

OLD WOMAN: Knives and forks if you like. *(She whips around to face the audience and is carrying a huge bone on a dish and a piece of bread. She comes to the table and puts them down on it.)* I don't care *how* you tackle it.

OLD MAN *(Dismayed)*:   The Bone! Again!

OLD WOMAN: Sit down—or you won't get any!

OLD MAN: What a meal it must have been for the lucky people who had it first. *(The OLD WOMAN takes a pair of carvers and sharpens the knife. The OLD MAN goes to the fireplace and takes down the pair of spectacles; returns to the table wearing them. He looks at the audience and says)*: The bigger the spectacles the more you see.

OLD WOMAN *(Carvers poised)*:   Ssh. Listen. I thought I heard something.

OLD MAN: You heard my stomach rumbling. It's so empty. Go on. Carve the Bone. *(He puts his elbows on the table and peers over his spectacles as the OLD WOMAN ceremoniously performs with the carving knife and fork. He almost believes that her flourishes are part of a magic ritual that might put meat on his plate. The OLD WOMAN listens again.)*

OLD WOMAN: There it is again. Ssh!

OLD MAN: It's the wind blowing through the keyhole.

OLD WOMAN *(Low voice)*: It doesn't sound like the wind.

OLD MAN: What does it sound like?

OLD WOMAN *(Concentrating)*: Like—like—singing.

OLD MAN: No harm in singing. *(He hums the* SAILOR'S *tune.)*

OLD WOMAN *(Excitedly)*: That's it. You! It was you!

OLD MAN: No, it wasn't.

OLD WOMAN: You've just sung it. That's what I heard.

OLD MAN: That was the song the Sailor taught me to play on my little harp before you took it away and sold it for fourpence.

OLD WOMAN: Well, I don't like it, so don't sing it.

OLD MAN: I tell you I wasn't singing—

OLD WOMAN: I tell you you were. Oh, eat your supper and be quiet. *(She puts the bone on his plate.)*

OLD MAN: Hey! You've got all the meat.

OLD WOMAN: Those that work the hardest must eat the most.

OLD MAN *(Pushing chair back)*: I'm going to have one of my fainty fits.

OLD WOMAN: Then you're better off without any supper. Nobody should faint on a full stomach. *(As quick as lightning she whips the bone from his plate onto the dish and the dish in the cupboard and the door locked again. The* OLD MAN *gets up disconsolately and goes to the window. The* OLD WOMAN *goes back to the table and resumes her supper. But the wind roars terribly now, and the house rattles violently.)*

OLD MAN *(Peeping through the shutters)*: It's raining now. Torrents of rain. It's just the sort of night . . . not to get lost in.

OLD WOMAN: It's just the sort of night to appreciate the difference between outside and in. *(More gusts of wind.)* When I hear all that noise outside I feel so snug and dry I could laugh. *(She begins to laugh, but her laughter ends in a cry as she drops her knife and fork with a clatter as the* SAILOR'S *Song is heard loud and clear.)*

SAILOR'S VOICE *(Singing)*:

> Oh, people with houses
> Are lucky and dry.
> They carelessly smile as
> The homeless go by.

(She stares at the OLD MAN, *who is dreamily looking through a chink in the shutters.*

OLD MAN: It's a bad thing to be homeless on a night like this.

OLD WOMAN: So it wasn't you! That wasn't your old croak!

OLD MAN: What's the matter? Has something gone down the wrong way?

OLD WOMAN *(Hoarsely)*: I heard it again. The same song—only closer —and if it wasn't you—*WHO WAS IT?*

OLD MAN: Noises in the ears! That's what you've got! You must ask that A-cough, A-cough, A-cough—that person who sells cough mixture if he's got any ear mixture. Or you can try a drop of *my* medicine if you like. *(He moves toward the chimneypiece, but the* OLD WOMAN *stops him.*

OLD WOMAN *(Terrified)*: Stop! Don't move! Keep quiet! Somebody's outside and going to rob us. That's what it is. *(Shrieks.)* Help! Help!

OLD MAN: Who could rob us? We haven't got anything.

OLD WOMAN: Help! Help!

OLD MAN: And who could help us, either, here in this wood?

OLD WOMAN: Don't—don't . . . make it worse.

OLD MAN: If only you hadn't sold my little harp for fourpence, I'd have played you a tune to calm your nerves. Fourpence was such a silly price.

OLD WOMAN: It paid for the food and drink that rascally Sailor had for nothing. *(The sound of the storm grows more and more violent. The light dims. There is a great crash at the door. The candlestick on the table falls over, the light goes out. The stage is dim. There is great commotion.)* Don't tell me *that's* nobody. Help! Help!

OLD MAN *(calmly)*: It's somebody knocking to ask the way. After all, this *is* an inn . . . or used to be. *(He begins to walk toward the door, but the* OLD WOMAN *runs after him and stops him.)*

OLD WOMAN: Wait! Wait! What are you going to do?

OLD MAN: Open the door of course.

OLD WOMAN: You must be out of your senses. *(Calls.)* We're not open. . . . We're closed. . . . Go away. . . . We don't want any customers. . . . Nobody's welcome. *(There is another great crash at the door.)* Oh, bless and preserve us! Don't open the door.

(Another great bang at the door.)

OLD MAN: Whoever it is will knock it down, seemingly if I don't *(He walks calmly toward the door.)* Wait a minute, whoever you are, I'm coming.

(The stage now darkens so that the action cannot be seen. There is a sound of footsteps, then another crash, then the sound of the door being unbolted. There is a Whooosh of air rushing into the room, a gasp from the OLD WOMAN, then a pause followed by the sound of the door being closed and bolted. All these actions are followed by the ear, in darkness.)

OLD WOMAN *(Calling)*:   Who is it? For Mercy's sake, *tell* me who it is. *(Sound of footsteps. Then silence.)* Where are you? Are you there? Have you gone and left me? *(Her voice rises in fright.)*

OLD MAN: Here I am. *(The stage goes a little lighter but is still dim. Now it can be seen that the OLD WOMAN is crouching under the table. She has lighted the candle and is holding it in a shaking hand, gradually finding the courage to put out her head and peer about. The OLD MAN is standing strangely still between her and the door in such a position that he is able to conceal something behind his back, a shape vague but large. It is still too dark for her, or the audience, to see what it is.)* What are you doing under there? Come out.

OLD WOMAN: Who was it?

OLD MAN: Nobody.

OLD WOMAN *(Crawling from under the table)*:   Why didn't you say so straightaway? All that noise must have been a tree falling.

BIRD: CRAWK!

OLD WOMAN *(Frozen)*:   What's that? *(Pause.)* Why—why—are you standing so still? . . . Move away. *(Her voice falters.)* What are you hiding? *(The OLD MAN partly moves. The light flashes, then grows dim. The candle drops from the OLD WOMAN's hand and goes out. She gives a terrified cry. Noise of thunder and wind. Vivid flashes of lightning. Shrinking away.)* What is it? What's that— behind you?

(The OLD MAN moves aside. Behind him, between the flashes of lightning, can be seen a big, black, covered object, absolutely still and dark. Lightning flashes again and again, then the stage grows completely dark. The OLD WOMAN cries again in fear, and the BIRD, through the blackness, speaks.)

BIRD: CRAWK! CRAWK!
   (Darkness.)

ACT II

As the light slowly fills the stage, the OLD WOMAN *is discovered at the left side of it, cringing behind her broomstick. The* OLD MAN, *holding a lighted candle, is standing near the birdcage, which is at the right side of the room and covered by a black cloth. The scene is held thus for a few minutes as if the characters are under a spell. Then the* OLD MAN, *like a statue struggling from its immobility, makes a movement toward the cage. The* OLD WOMAN *stops him with a hoarse cry when she sees that he is about to lift off the black cover.*

OLD WOMAN: Stop! Wait! You—you don't know what's underneath that.

OLD MAN *(Calmly):*   I shan't know until I look, shall I? *(He makes another movement to lift up the cloth. This time the* OLD WOMAN *stops him with a fierce rap of her stick upon the floor.)*

OLD WOMAN: Stop a bit. *(He pauses.)* Think! Whenever you see anything new always stop and ask yourself—
Will it bounce?
Will it bang?
Will it burst?

OLD MAN *(Obediently):*
Will it bounce?
Will it bang?
Will it burst?

OLD WOMAN: Better poke it and see. Stand . . . away! *(With a sudden loud cry she darts across to the cage and gives it a poke with her stick. The* OLD MAN, *startled, nearly drops the candle. There is a great disturbance underneath the cloth. The* OLD WOMAN *hastily draws back.)* Sakes alive! What is it?

(The OLD MAN *holds the light and draws away the cloth from the cage.)*

OLD MAN: It's a bird in a cage. That's all.
(Silence. They absorb the sight before them. The great BIRD *droops in the cage.)*

OLD WOMAN: That's all? A bird . . . *all* of it? *(She tentatively walks around the cage, keeping her distance from it by making a wide circle. The* OLD MAN *puts the candle down on the table.)*

OLD MAN: Some of it's cage, of course. *(He touches the wicker bars.)* Good strong cage, too; no string here.

OLD WOMAN: Where did you find it? Where was it?

OLD MAN: On the doorstep.

OLD WOMAN: The doorstep? How did it get there?

OLD MAN: P'r'aps it flew.

OLD WOMAN: Cages can't fly. *(The* BIRD *is still silent. The* OLD WOMAN *looks at it dubiously.)* Somebody must have put it there.

OLD MAN: Hooray! Somebody's left us a present.

OLD WOMAN: Why should anybody do that, blockhead?

OLD MAN: P'r'aps somebody likes us. P'r'aps somebody's paying us back for a kindness we've forgotten about.

OLD WOMAN: Nonsense. If I'd ever done a kindness *I* wouldn't forget it.

BIRD: CRAWK!

OLD WOMAN: And it's not much of a kindness to leave *that!*

BIRD: CRAWK! CRAWK! CRAWK!

OLD WOMAN: It can't even sing! Quick! Open the door and put it outside again!

OLD MAN: Poor thing'll get soaked through.

OLD WOMAN: Don't stand there. Get rid of it. Whoever put it there can take it away again. Somebody's hanging about outside, you may be sure. *(She goes to the window, opens the shutters and peers outside, rubbing the glass to see better, and making threatening gestures with her fists.)*

OLD MAN: Can you see somebody?

OLD WOMAN: No. It's too dark . . . and too wet. But be sure they can see me! *(More gestures.)* Be off! You don't frighten me! Whoever you are! *(Comes from the window, leaving shutters open.)* Take it outside. Present indeed! That's not the sort of present I like. *(The* OLD MAN *steps nearer the cage, half fearful, half fascinated. The* BIRD *stirs and flutters his wings. The* OLD MAN *steps back.)* Go on. Out with it. What are you afraid of? *(The* OLD MAN *makes a tentative gesture towards the* BIRD.) Wait a bit, though, it's a good wicker cage. I could use it for a clothes basket. *(Pause.)* I'll keep the cage. Take it to the doorstep . . . then let the Bird out. It'll fly away.

(Pause. They look at the motionless silent BIRD *as it broods in its cage. An expression of sly mischief struggles through the look of fear on the* OLD MAN'*s face.)*

OLD MAN *(slowly)*: Supposing it doesn't.

OLD WOMAN: Doesn't what?

OLD MAN: Fly . . . away. . . .

OLD WOMAN: Of course it'll fly away. It's the nature of birds to fly away. *(Pause, while her confidence begins to trickle away.)* Isn't it?

OLD MAN: Suppose-this-isn't-a-natural-sort-of-Bird-somehow.

OLD WOMAN: What do you mean? *(The OLD MAN is silent. They both look at the quiet BIRD. The OLD WOMAN slowly and thoughtfully walks around the cage again, and comes back to where she started from. Crossly.)* Go on. Say what you mean—if you know what you mean . . . which I often doubt.

OLD MAN: I don't *know* what I mean.

OLD WOMAN: There you are!

OLD MAN: I just feel what I mean.

OLD WOMAN *(Impatiently)*:   Are you going to move it—or am I? *(The OLD MAN walks close to the cage and nervously lays hands on it. Then he stretches both arms around it as far as he can, then drops them.)*

OLD MAN: It's no use. I can't.

OLD WOMAN: Nonsense. Try again.

(The OLD MAN tries again but gives up.)

OLD MAN: No good. I can't move it an inch.

OLD WOMAN: It can't be any heavier than it was before.

OLD MAN: It seems heavier.

OLD WOMAN *(Sarcastically)*:   Oh, very odd! You can't move it out though you did move it in.

OLD MAN *(With mystery)*:   Or—did *it* move *me*?

(Another pause. They look at each other. Then the OLD WOMAN recovers herself.)

OLD WOMAN: I've had enough of this. Either that Bird goes or *I* go. *(Pause. The OLD MAN does not move.)* Either that Bird goes—or YOU go.

(The OLD MAN puts his arms around the cage again.)

OLD MAN: Take it to the doorstep, you said.

OLD WOMAN: Yes.

512

OLD MAN: Open the cage, you said.

OLD WOMAN: Yes.

OLD MAN: And let it fly away.

OLD WOMAN: *Let* it? *Make* it! And if it won't give it a good hard push—with your foot.

BIRD: CRAWK! CRAWK! CRAWK! *(The* BIRD *flaps his wings, greatly perturbed.)*

OLD MAN: Now see what you've done.

OLD WOMAN: All I can see is a greatly ugly thing that I didn't ask for and don't want—and WON'T HAVE. *(She stamps her feet and bangs her broomstick on the floor.)*

BIRD: CRAWK! CRAWK! CRAWK!

OLD MAN *(Upset)*:   You've gone and offended him now. *(Low voice.)* I believe he can understand every word we say.

OLD WOMAN: HE! HIM! I've never heard such rubbish in my life. If IT doesn't like what *I* say IT can put up with it . . . and take ITSELF off before I . . .

BIRD: CRAWK! CRAWK! CRAWK! *(The* BIRD *makes a huge flapping noise directed at the* OLD WOMAN, *who jumps back from the cage, rather frightened.)*

OLD MAN: What did I tell you? You'd better be careful of your tongue.

BIRD *(More gently)*:   CRAWK! CRAWK!

OLD MAN: Or it'll be getting you into trouble . . . not for the first time, either. *(The* OLD MAN *begins making advances to the* BIRD.) Hullo then! *(He puts out a careful finger and prepares to tickle the* BIRD. *The* OLD WOMAN *screams at the sight, and the* OLD MAN *jumps, pulling his finger back.)*

OLD WOMAN: Careful! It'll have your finger off.
(The OLD MAN *recovers from the fright she gave him and again puts his finger through the bars of the cage, the* OLD WOMAN *watching to say "I told you so." The* BIRD *sidles up to be caressed however, and the* OLD MAN *turns to the* OLD WOMAN *in triumph.)*

OLD MAN: 'Course he won't have my finger off. Look at him. He's quite affectionate. Did he want to have his nice feathers tickled, then, eh?

(Out of the BIRD's *eyes now beam two great golden lights as he*

looks at the OLD MAN. *The* OLD WOMAN *gasps—the* OLD MAN *goes on fondling the* BIRD. *Now the* OLD WOMAN, *jealous of the* OLD MAN's *success, also approaches the cage, jostling the* OLD MAN *aside. She puts out, not her finger, she will not risk that, but the handle end of her broomstick, to give the* BIRD *a poke. She comes too near for the* BIRD's *liking, and he rears up in the cage. His beautiful yellow eyes turn to a vivid green and send out a baleful stream of green light upon her. She screams, and retreats.)*

OLD WOMAN: Mercy on us! It's a monster!

(But the OLD MAN *coos and fondles the* BIRD.)*

OLD MAN: Pretty Bird. Oh, he's a pretty fellow! Pretty Dickeybird.

OLD WOMAN *(From a safe distance)*:   Pretty he calls it . . . it's as ugly as sin.

OLD MAN *(Bending to the* BIRD):   She says you're ugly, Dickeybird.

OLD WOMAN *(Shouting)*:   So it is . . . *(to audience)* isn't it?

OLD MAN: Ugly? With such beautiful golden eyes?

OLD WOMAN *(Mocking him)*:   Beautiful golden eyes *(to audience)* when they're green, as green as grass. Let me look . . . just in case I made a mistake. . . . *(The* BIRD *turns green eyes upon her. She jumps away from him, walks up front to face the audience and stands at the left side of the stage. To audience.)* That Bird has green eyes. If I'm wrong you can all . . . Yell!

(Behind her back the BIRD's *eyes turn to yellow for the* OLD MAN, *who looks at them, then walks up front and stands at the right side of the stage, opposite the* OLD WOMAN.)

OLD MAN *(To audience)*:   My Bird has golden eyes. If I'm right you can all CLAP.

(Pause.)

OLD WOMAN: Rubbish! You're *all* wrong. Its eyes are as green as— as rhubarb. *(She dips into her pocket and produces a stick of vivid green rhubarb, which she swishes at the startled* OLD MAN.) Here. Chop this up for your new pet. *(Laughs).* I'm sure that'll be good for its gizzard. P'r'aps it'll make it sing. *(She runs up to the cage and thrusts the rhubarb through the bars. The* BIRD *rises up in anger, the* OLD MAN *follows her.)*

BIRD: CRAWK! CRAWK! CRAWK!
(Its green eyes shoot light over her. She recoils from the cage, her laughter cut short, trying in dumb show to tell the audience that she was right about the eyes being green. The OLD MAN

514

moves to the cage to quiet the BIRD. It is silent now and its eyes *are normal. The* OLD MAN *and the* OLD WOMAN *stare at it.)*

OLD WOMAN: And another thing. . . Look at the size of it. But perhaps *you're* going to say it's a *little* bird.

OLD MAN: Oh no! I'm not going to say it's a little bird. I'm going to say it's Big . . . as Big as . . . as Big as a Boy.

OLD WOMAN *(Moving up front stage, left side)*:   As Big as a Boy? *(Pause.)* Then I'll say—it's as Big as a Bear!

(The OLD MAN *moves up front stage right. They both face the audience).*

OLD MAN *(As if playing a game)*:   I'll say—it's as Big as a—Battleship.

OLD WOMAN: I'll say—it's as Big as—as Big as a Baboon.

OLD MAN: It's as Big as—a Barn.

OLD WOMAN: As Big as a—Bandit.

(Their excitement mounts up.)

OLD MAN *(Thinking hard)*:   As Big as . . . as Big as . . . as Big as . . .

OLD WOMAN *(Bursting in and thinking she is winning)*:   —As a Ballroom—as a Bank—as a Barge!

OLD MAN *(Getting a word out at last)*:   —As a Bantam.

(The OLD WOMAN *hoots with laughter.)*

OLD WOMAN *(To audience)*:   Bantam, he says. Bantams aren't big, stupid.

OLD MAN *(Ideas nearly played out)*:   As Big as a Birdcage, then.

OLD WOMAN: No, it isn't. Or it couldn't have got inside it in the first place, could it? Now it's my turn. It's—it's—*(with an air of finality)* It's as—Big—as a Beast. I've won! I've won! *(She faces the audience triumphantly and claps her hands for herself. The* OLD MAN *slyly sidles away to the birdcage and puts his head down to whisper to the* BIRD.)*

OLD MAN: She called you a Beast, Dickeybird.

BIRD: CRAWK! CRAWK!

OLD MAN: Yes . . . *and* a Barge . . .*and* a Baboon . . . and a . . . and a . . .

OLD WOMAN *(Seeing what he is up to)*:   BRUTE !

OLD MAN: Yes—*and* a Brute

BIRD: CRAWK! CRAWK!

(The OLD MAN *strokes the* BIRD *appeasingly.)*

OLD MAN: But *I* say you're Big, Beautiful and—

OLD WOMAN *(Scornfully)*: Go on.

OLD MAN: —and—Bituminous.

OLD WOMAN *(Incredulously)*: Bitu—Bitu—

OLD MAN: Bituminous.

OLD WOMAN: You don't know what that means.

OLD MAN: Yes, I do. I know more than you think I know.

OLD WOMAN: What does—Bitu—bituminous mean, then?

OLD MAN: Find out for yourself. *(To audience.)* That's the best way. Look it up in the dictionary.

OLD WOMAN: I haven't one.

OLD MAN: Find one.

OLD WOMAN: There isn't such a thing as a dictionary in the house.

OLD MAN: Then there should be. Every house should have a dictionary in it. A dictionary's—most important—like the foundations of this desirable property—or the roof—or the chimneys.

OLD WOMAN *(Instantly suspicious at the word)*: Chimneys? What's it got to do with chimneys? *(To herself.)* Looking things up in dictionaries, looking things up in chimneys. *(To* OLD MAN.*)* I keep telling you to keep away from my chimney. *(She walks over to the fireplace, very uneasy in her mind, and begins to look about.)* I believe you do know more than I think you know.

OLD MAN: Of course I do. But go on looking. You're getting warm. That's right. Just keep near the chimney.

(The OLD WOMAN *begins to examine the fireplace.)*

OLD WOMAN *(Speaking to herself)*: Chimney! Chimney! Why so much about chimney? Eh?

OLD MAN *(Laughing)*: That's a clue of course. I'm just giving you a clue.

OLD WOMAN: Clue? *(She is more uneasy than ever.)* I don't know what you're getting at. *(Pause.)* Has it anything to do with—soot?

(She brings out the word "soot" very carefully, trying him.)

OLD MAN *(Considering)*: It might have. Let me see. You get soot in the chimney . . .

OLD WOMAN: Soot in the chimney . . . !

OLD MAN: Soot in the chimney when you burn COAL . . . COAL . . . see? Oh, I'll give it away. Coal—is *Bituminous.* There now. You know what it means.

OLD WOMAN: Oh!

OLD MAN: And my Bird is Bituminous because it is coal-BLACK.

(He goes to the cage.)

OLD WOMAN: Oh, Whew! *(Almost collapsing; fans herself.)* All that fuss about a word—and a bird. I shall have to sit down a bit.

(She goes to sit down.)

BIRD: CRAWK! CRAWK! CRAWK! *(The BIRD shuffles and stretches inside the cage, as if pressed for room.)*

OLD MAN: He hasn't enough room inside that cage. *(Pause.)* Let's have him out.

(The OLD WOMAN jumps up in horror.)

OLD WOMAN: Out. That thing—loose! *(She looks at the BIRD in horror.)*

OLD MAN: I thought you said—let it out.

OLD WOMAN: I meant outside. Not in here. There isn't room.

OLD MAN *(To the BIRD)*: It'd be a bit of fun though, wouldn't it? *(The BIRD bridles under the OLD MAN's attentions, then squawks and flutters. The OLD MAN laughs with pleasure.)*

OLD WOMAN: Get it out of the house at once. Nobody's house should have a thing like that in it. *(She gives a sudden shriek.)* Its eyes! Look at its eyes. They've turned on again.

(The BIRD's eyes are a baleful green again. They play on the OLD WOMAN like a green searchlight.)

OLD MAN: You've got to go, Dickeybird. She don't like your eyes.

OLD WOMAN: Eyes like a crocodile . . . and I bet it eats like a crocodile, too.

OLD MAN *(whispering to BIRD)*: You're a crocodile now, Dickeybird.

BIRD: CRAWK! CRAWK!

OLD MAN: He's hungry. Why didn't I think of it before? Here Dickeybird. *(Darts to the table and picks up a crust.)* Have a bit of bread.

OLD WOMAN: Bread!

OLD MAN: It's only the bit I didn't eat for supper. Goodness! All gone!

OLD WOMAN: What did I tell you? Eats like a crocodile. *(She wrings her hands in despair while the* BIRD *scuffles and squawks.)*

BIRD: CRAWK! CRAWK! CRAWK!

OLD MAN: He don't like the way you keep on about crocodiles.

BIRD: CRAWK! CRAWK!

OLD MAN: He'd like some more bread, though. Oh, he's clever.

OLD WOMAN: It'll eat everything we've got. There's nothing clever about that.

BIRD: CRAWK! CRAWK! CRAWK!

OLD WOMAN *(Shaking her fist at the* BIRD*)*: And stop that silly noise!

OLD MAN: He's singing for his supper. That's his way of saying, "More Bread, Please." Say it again, Dickey.

BIRD *(Furiously)*: CRAWK! CRAWK! CRAWK!

(The OLD MAN *is charmed. He turns to the* OLD WOMAN.*)*

OLD MAN: Come on. Give me the key to the cupboard. I know there's more bread in there. *(The* OLD MAN *goes demandingly up to the* OLD WOMAN, *who backs away from him, clutching the pocket of her apron. She tries to fend him off with her stick, but he is not so frightened of it now.)*

OLD WOMAN: That's not for eating.

OLD MAN: What is it for, then?

OLD WOMAN: It's for keeping.

BIRD: CRAWK! CRAWK! CRAWK!

OLD MAN: Don't worry, Dickeybird. *That* loaf isn't going on the Rainey-Day shelf. *(To* OLD WOMAN.*)* Come on. The key, if you please. Quick. You can see he's getting impatient. *(The* BIRD *scratches at the bars of the cage, flaps his wing and makes rasping bird noises. The* OLD WOMAN *has been driven into a corner by the* OLD MAN *and though she tries to swipe at him with her*

518

broom, he nimbly jumps over it every time she lunges at his legs. He finally pushes it aside and holds out his hand.) The key, please.

OLD WOMAN: You shan't have it. I *WON'T* be bamboozled by a bird.

BIRD *(Furiously)*: CRAWK! CRAWK! CRAWK!

OLD MAN *(Calmly)*: Better hand it over. Look . . . he's pecking through the bars. *(She quietly gives up the key.)* Thank you. *(The OLD MAN walks firmly to the cupboard, unlocks the door, has a good leisurely look inside, then takes out a loaf. He does not re-lock the cupboard when he shuts the door. When the OLD WOMAN holds out her hand for the key, he makes as if to give it to her, then thinks better of it, and puts it in his pocket. With a baffled look, she lets her hand fall to her side, while he walks to the cage and, standing with his back to the audience, so as to hide the BIRD, he thrusts the loaf through the bars.)* Here you are, Dickeybird.

BIRD: CRAWK! CRAWK! *(Muffled.)* CRAWK!

OLD WOMAN: A whole loaf. We're ruined.

OLD MAN: He's ever so grateful. *(He moves so that the audience can see the BIRD, who is rubbing against the bars of the cage, and affectionately nuzzling the OLD MAN's hand.)*

OLD WOMAN: Grateful! So he should be. That's a week's breakfasts gone down its gizzard.

OLD MAN: Who cares about breakfasts!

OLD WOMAN *(To audience)*: How noble he feels—giving away *my* breakfasts.

BIRD: CRAW-W-W-K!

OLD MAN: More bread? Sorry, Dickeybird. Cupboard's empty. *(Walks to the cupboard.)* See for yourself *(Opens the cupboard door.)*

BIRD: CRAWK! CRAWK!

OLD MAN *(Turning to OLD WOMAN)*: You see how reasonable he is. *(To BIRD.)* You understand we can't give you what we haven't got, don't you, my pretty? Good, Dickeybird.

OLD WOMAN *(Front stage to audience)*: Did you ever hear such a fool? Good Bird—kind Bird—for eating our last crumb. *(She whirls on the OLD MAN.)* Out with the wretched thing before I take my broomstick to it.

OLD MAN: Ooh! The broomstick.

BIRD: CRAWK! CRAWK! CRAWK!

OLD WOMAN: And not so much of your Crawk! Crawk! Crawk! You don't frighten me.

(The BIRD jumps about in his cage, as if he will tear it apart.)

OLD MAN: You know how to get his feathers up, I will say that. He wouldn't half come for you, if he could.

OLD WOMAN: Make sure the cage is fastened then. Quick!

BIRD: CRAWK! CRAWK! CRAWK!

OLD MAN *(His ear to the cage)*:   He says he'd like a little stroll.

(Begins to unfasten the cage door.)

OLD WOMAN *(To audience)*:   Was ever woman cursed with such a duffer? I said, Fasten it *in*, not let it *out*. *(She raps the OLD MAN's fingers with her stick.)* Out of my way. I'll see to it myself. Who's frightened of a Bird, especially a Beastly, Bad, Bi—Bituminous Bird like this. *(She elbows the OLD MAN out of her way and, standing with her back to the audience, bends toward the cage.)*

BIRD: CRAWK! CRAWK! CRAWK! CRAWK!

(Sound of much scratching and flapping. The OLD WOMAN screams and hops about in pain, one finger in her mouth.)

OLD MAN *(Mildly)*:   You went a bit too close my dear.

OLD WOMAN: Oh, my finger! my finger! *(The BIRD cackles. The OLD MAN turns away to hide a smile, the OLD WOMAN sucks her finger . . . and thinks. The OLD MAN stands by the cage, gently stroking the BIRD, which caresses his hand. A sly look comes onto the face of the OLD WOMAN. She tiptoes into the lean-to room where all the washing things are stored, and disappears. Soon there is the sound of things being moved about, then of pots clattering and breaking. Eventually she struggles out of the room, heated and disheveled, her arms clasped around an enormous brown stewpot, which she tries to hide from the BIRD by walking sideways with her back turned to the cage. She staggers front stage, left side, and dumps the pot, looking with great significance from it to the BIRD, from the BIRD to the pot, with a measuring eye. She tries to attract the OLD MAN's attention, but he is engrossed with the BIRD and takes no notice of her. At last she calls to him in a loud, impatient whisper.)* Husband!

OLD MAN *(At last)*:   Yes, my dear.

OLD WOMAN *(Gestures to him to come over)*:   I want to tell you something—in private . . . so that—IT—can't hear me. Psst. Are you deaf?

OLD MAN: What d'you say?

OLD WOMAN: Come over here—it's a secret. *(She is seething with impatience but tries to be pleasant.)*

OLD MAN: Call him a pretty Bird, then.

OLD WOMAN *(Small voice)*:   Pretty Bird.

OLD MAN: So that he can hear.

OLD WOMAN *(Savagely)*:   PRETTY BIRD—*(To audience)* DRAT IT. *(The* BIRD *preens in his cage and the* OLD MAN *smiles.)* Come on then. Don't take all night. *(Curiosity gets the better of the* OLD MAN *and he tiptoes over to the* OLD WOMAN *and stands front stage, opposite to her, facing audience. In a whisper.)* How would you fancy a nice fowl pie?

OLD MAN *(In loud voice)*:   A FOUL Pie? Of course, I wouldn't fancy a foul pie. Who likes foul food? Oh, a FOWL pie. That's different. *(The* OLD WOMAN *dances about with exasperation.)*

OLD WOMAN: Keep your voice down, stupid. I bet it's a scraggy thing for all it's so big, more feather than flesh, you may be sure. But— *(She breaks off. There is a significant pause. Her meaning slowly dawns on the* OLD MAN *as she gestures toward the* BIRD *and points to the big stewpot.)*

OLD MAN *(Looking first at the* BIRD, *then at the pot)*:   You mean?

OLD WOMAN: I dare say there's a good picking on it . . . and I think it'd just go in . . . with a bit of maneuvering.

OLD MAN *(Dazed)*:   Maneuvering?

OLD WOMAN: Of course . . . it might taste a bit strong . . . but I'd make a nice gravy.

OLD MAN: Gravy?

OLD WOMAN: So . . . go on. *(She pushes him toward the* BIRD.) You just wring its neck and I'll stew it in . . . *(She points to the pot.)* It may stew quite tender if I put a lump of soda with it.

OLD MAN: Wring its neck . . . stew it! . . . sssoda?

OLD WOMAN: Sssh! *(*BIRD *squawks.)* Now see what you've done, you good-for-nothing old duffer. Now it knows what we're going to do.

OLD MAN: We! I like that! *I'm* not going to do anything. I'm not going to wring his neck . . . *I'm* not going to stew him and . . . THAT—for your big brown pot. *(He gives the pot a kick and*

521

sends it skidding off stage.) Eh, Birdie? *(He walks over to the* BIRD.*)*

BIRD: CRAWK! CRAWK! CRAWK! CRAWK!

(The OLD MAN *puts a protective arm about the cage and turns to the* OLD WOMAN.*)*

OLD MAN: You've unsettled him now and no mistake. *(To the* BIRD.*)* It's all right, my precious, nobody's going to eat you. As for me . . . I wouldn't pull one little feather from your beautiful tail.

OLD WOMAN *(Shouting)*:   Well, I would. I'll pull his tail right off if I get the chance. I'll—I'll stuff cushions with it. *(She rushes to find her broomstick and seizes it, her confidence flooding up again.)*

BIRD: CRAWK! CRAWK! CRAWK!

(The OLD WOMAN *advances upon the birdcage with her broomstick.)*

OLD WOMAN: I'll give you CRAWK! CRAWK! CRAWK! *(The* OLD MAN *intervenes.)* And you as well if you don't get out of my way. *(Threatening him with broom.)*

OLD MAN: Watch out, Dickeybird. *(He tries to stop the* OLD WOMAN's *attack. They fall into fencing positions. She has her stick and he has only his right arm to use as a foil, but he parries her blows with it.)*

OLD WOMAN *(Mimicking the* OLD MAN's *voice)*:   Watch out, Dickeybird . . . because I'm going to give you a wallop right on your ugly head. *(The* OLD MAN *is weakening now and losing his position. She is almost at the point of victory, ready to trample down the* OLD MAN *and attack the cage when the lights go out, there is a strange long-drawn-out call from the* BIRD *and an anguished yell from the* OLD WOMAN. *Then a clap of thunder reverberates around the stage and the auditorium. Silence and darkness follow. A Pause. The lights come on to reveal the* BIRD *in all his glory. His big beautiful tail is spread out to show iridescent colors, his eyes are blazing green and golden lights. He is out of his cage and in command of the stage, calm, magnificent, possessive, like a Bird-god. The* OLD MAN *seems to have dwindled. He stands humbly, almost blinded by the beauty of the sight. The* OLD WOMAN *is cowering upon the table, her hace hidden by her apron, a picture of abject terror. The scene is held thus for a few seconds, then the* OLD WOMAN, *peeping from under apron, raises her head to give a trembling cry.)* Help me, husband. Help me!

OLD MAN: Oh, wonderful Sir!

OLD WOMAN: Husband, husband . . . help me!

522

(The OLD MAN *behaves as if he is awakening from a dream. He slowly turns and looks at the* OLD WOMAN.*)*

OLD MAN *(Bewildered)*:   Why . . . what are you doing up there?

OLD WOMAN *(Whispering)*:   I'm keeping away from the Monster.

BIRD: CRAWK! CRAWK! CRAWK! *(The* BIRD *moves forward. The* OLD WOMAN *thinks that he is coming for her. She screams and hides under her apron, but he is merely stretching his legs, trying out his wings first separately, then together, bending and stretching, with a noble dignity.)*

OLD MAN *(Tremulously)*:   Beautiful, wonderful Sir!

(The OLD WOMAN *now lifts up her head. The* BIRD's *tail closes up so that its colors are hidden.)*

OLD WOMAN *(Whimpering)*:   I want to get off this table.

OLD MAN *(Making obeisance)*:   What country do you come from, beautiful Sir? What marvelous place can be your home?

OLD WOMAN *(To audience)*:   Bowing now! What next? *(To* OLD MAN.*)* Give me my broomstick.

OLD MAN: Never mention that dreadful word! *(The* OLD WOMAN *bends all ways trying to see where her broomstick is. It is only just out of reach. She does not see when the* BIRD *again spreads out its tail for the* OLD MAN.*)* Have you ever seen the like? A peacock is a dull bird compared to this. All the colors of the rainbow.

OLD WOMAN *(To audience)*:   A plain black bird and he sees all the colors of the rainbow in it.

(The BIRD *comes out front stage and standing so that the* OLD WOMAN *still cannot see, he shows the audience the full extent of his colored tail feathers.)*

OLD MAN *(Coming front stage)*:   You see.

OLD WOMAN: *You* see what *you* want to see and *I'll* see what *I* want to see . . . and I see a black bird . . . and I'm not going to see any different if I stay here till Doomsday. *(The* BIRD *closes his tail and strolls toward the* OLD WOMAN, *who nervously crouches away from him on the extreme edge of the table. With a last vestige of bravado she picks up her apron and flaps it.)* Shoo! Husband, save me!

(The OLD MAN *makes a wheedling noise to the* BIRD, *who turns away from the* OLD WOMAN. *Behind his back she makes a sly move to pull her leg off the table. The* BIRD *immediately turns*

round on her. She draws her leg up. The BIRD *moves away again. She creeps forward on the table as if going to spring off. The* BIRD *spins round to her—she draws back. They repeat this several times in a sort of rhythm. The* OLD MAN *begins to clap his hands in time.)*

OLD MAN: If only we had some music! . . . You see, you shouldn't have sold my little harp for fourpence. But wait a minute, Birdie, noble Sir. (*The* OLD MAN *takes up a chair from the table, puts it beneath the Rainy-Day shelf, climbs up and rummages about until he finds the string birdcage. The* OLD WOMAN *looks from him to the audience as if saying, "Whatever is the silly fellow going to do next?" The* OLD MAN *sits on the chair back, a pleased smile on his face as he fingers the strings of the birdcage.*)

OLD WOMAN (*As if making a good joke*):   What are you going to do now—play that?

OLD MAN: Why not? There are plenty of chords on it. (*He strikes a magnificent chord, as if it is a harp. When it responds, a look of delight spreads over his face.*) Whyever didn't I think of this before? (*He sits on the back of the chair and draws his fingers across the strings as he must have done many a time on his little harp. At first he plays hesitantly, wonderingly. The* OLD WOMAN, *unbelievingly, and the* BIRD, *approvingly, look on. Soon he begins to play more confidently. He smiles to the audience.*) And I've never had a birdcage lesson in me life. (*He plays on. Music seems to come from all around him, tumbling from the rafters, coming from all corners of the stage and auditorium, rising, falling, echoing. He stops, overcome.*) All that music in this little cage! (*He plays again. The* BIRD *listens in high appreciation, gravely nodding his head, twitching a wing in time, moving his feet as if longing to dance; the* OLD WOMAN *puts her hands over her ears and rocks in agony.*)

OLD WOMAN: Oh my nerves, my nerves! Ten thousand screaming cats, my poor nerves!

OLD MAN (*Calling out in excitement*):   Now, Birdie, dance. (*And so, to the* OLD MAN'S *music, the* BIRD *dances, a beautiful, stately, magical dance. His tail spreads out and closes again. Sometimes it is all black, sometimes shining in rainbow colors, and all the time the* BIRD *goes round and round the table in such a way that the* OLD WOMAN, *though waiting for the opportunity, dare not try to climb down. The lights on the stage change then change again. At last the* BIRD *shows the* OLD MAN *that he wishes to have him for a partner. The* OLD MAN *bashfully demurs at first as if overcome by the honor, then he takes the floor, holding delicately onto a wing tip of the* BIRD.) What about the music,

524

though? I know. Here. *You* can play it. *(He throws the birdcage he has been playing to the* OLD WOMAN.*)*

OLD WOMAN: Me? *I* can't play.

OLD MAN: Yes you can. You'll pick it up. Just think of a tune, it'll come by itself tonight. *(The* BIRD *gives a warning flap of his wing toward the* OLD WOMAN, *who hastily strikes a chord; not a very good one. They all grimace.)* Try again. You'll improve with effort. *(She tries again, pulling faces at the audience at the discords.)* You're not thinking of what you're playing. You're thinking how you can get off the table. *(She tries again.)* Practice makes Perfect. *(She plays again.)* You've got quite a nice touch, I do declare.

OLD WOMAN *(Flattered)*:   Have I really? *(She continues to play.)* If this is all there is to it, it's quite easy. All that fuss people make about practice. *(She strums away and the music improves. The* OLD MAN *and the* BIRD *bow to each other. Then they try the dance—not without mistakes.)*

OLD MAN:
You hop.
I hop—
Then we'll hop together.
You hop—
And never lose a feather.

(The BIRD *and the* OLD MAN *go into a dance to the* OLD WOMAN's *music. She is sitting quite engrossed in her playing, in the middle of the table. The lights flash, and grow dim, and change color. A big silver moon appears in the window and its rays stream into the room. Suddenly the* OLD WOMAN's *mood alters. A strange chord, a dissonance, changes the tone of the music and the happy, magical mood of the dance. Now, the* OLD WOMAN, *still playing, stands up on the table and cavorts about. There is irony in her music, there is bad temper in it, there is the iron-hand-in-the-velvet-glove in it ... and more iron than velvet the longer she plays. Faster and faster beats her music until it seems the* OLD MAN *and the* BIRD *are in its power, they are so captivated by its fantastic spirit. At last, as they whirl about her, in wider and wider circles around the table, she slyly puts her leg down to the floor, her toe nearly touches the floor —then there is a clap of thunder, the lights flash, the* BIRD *gives a cry and rushes toward her. As quick as possible she is up on the table again, and throws the birdcage at the* BIRD. *It bounces on the floor with a tuneless twang. The music is all gone. The magic has fled. The stage is full of ordinary light.)*

OLD MAN: Now you've spoiled everything.

OLD WOMAN: You don't think I'm going to stand on this table for-ever do you?

OLD MAN: Why did you have to spoil the dance?

OLD WOMAN: Dance? I never saw such a shimble-shamble in all my life. *(She turns to the* BIRD *and begins to flap her apron.)* Go back into your cage, you . . . creature, whatever you are. Shoo! Do something useful . . . lay an egg, or better still, fly away. We don't want things like you around here. We're *respectable.*

BIRD: CRAWK! CRAWK! NAUGHTY. NAUGHTY.

OLD MAN: What! What did he say?

OLD WOMAN: Shoo! Shoo!

OLD MAN: He talked! He talked!

OLD WOMAN *(To audience)*: Right off his head, even worse than usual. Just wait till I get off this table. I'll teach him a lesson *(She marches up and down the table. The* BIRD *approaches her.)* Get away, Fowl!

BIRD: Naughty girl! Naughty girl! Tell him! Tell him!

OLD WOMAN: Go away! Shoo!

OLD MAN: He talked again!

OLD WOMAN: Oh, shove it into its cage—for goodness' sake.

OLD MAN: He talked—oh, marvels and wonders! Oh, now I can be-lieve in anything I like—in miracles and mermaids—and happy endings—

OLD WOMAN: I'll end you when I get off this table.

BIRD: CRAWK! CRAWK! CRAWK!

OLD WOMAN: *And* you. Crawk, crawk, crawk! D'you call *that* talk-ing?

BIRD: Tell him where you put it. Tell him where you put it.

OLD WOMAN: Trying to sing now, are you?

BIRD: Naughty girl! Naughty girl! Tell him where you put it, CRAWK CRAWK CRAWK.

OLD WOMAN: If you don't shut that beak of yours, I'll—

BIRD: CRAWK! CRAWK! TELL HIM! TELL HIM!

OLD WOMAN: I'll smother you with my apron.

OLD MAN *(Thoughtfully):*   Tell *him.* Tell who? Does he mean—me?

BIRD: CRAWK! CRAWK! CRAWK! CRAWK!

OLD MAN: Yes, he does.

BIRD: CRAWK! CRAWK! TELL. TELL. TELL. TELL.

OLD MAN: Tell what, Dickeybird?

BIRD: CRAWK! CRAWK! Naughty girl. Tell where you put it.

OLD MAN *(To* OLD WOMAN*):*   Go on, then. Tell me where you put it.

OLD WOMAN *(Astonished):*   What?

OLD MAN: I don't know what. It's just wnat he keeps on saying—so tell me where you put it.

OLD WOMAN: So you *have* been peeping and prying.

BIRD: Tell him ⎫
OLD MAN: Tell him ⎬ where you put it *(together).*

(The OLD WOMAN *shrieks and stamps her feet on the table.)*

OLD WOMAN: I won't! I won't! I won't! *(The* BIRD *and the* OLD MAN *look at each other and hesitate. The* OLD WOMAN *leans over and manages to grab her broomstick, which has been kicked nearer to her during the dance. Then she gives a wild red Indian yell and points behind them. They both involuntarily turn their heads. During this moment, holding on to her broomstick, she gives a great leap into the air, almost up to the ceiling, then with a whoosh and a scream she flies right over their heads and stands opposite to them, behind the stick, all her strength and confidence recovered. Again she is at the left side of the stage and they are at the right. To audience.)* Now I'll show 'em. I'll have 'em both out of the house, I will. *(She rushes at the* BIRD, *but he spreads his wings and rises up to the ceiling. She hesitates, then, not to be outdone, she gives one, two, three leaps in the air and at the third leap achieves flight. Mad with joy and excitement at being aloft—she is not used to flying as she is not really a witch— she goes for the* BIRD *with a lot of hasty, excited little blows which never really amount to much. The* BIRD *is never vicious or excited. He merely parries her ridiculous frenzy with calm and powerful wings, almost benevolently as one fends off an excited puppy. As she withdraws for another attack he suddenly seems to weary of her nonsense and drops down to the hearth, leaving her aloft. For a second or two she loses him and cries in triumph.)* I've won! I've won!

(Down below the OLD MAN, *who has been gazing upwards in*

wonder at the battle, now recovers himself to speak to the BIRD, *who is investigating the chimney.)*

OLD MAN: Mind the chimney, Dickeybird. Your pretty feathers'll be all over soot.

OLD WOMAN *(Still aloft)*: Soot! Chimney! *(Now she sees what the* BIRD *is doing and struggles to get down to floor level, waving her arms and legs about like a poor swimmer.)* Get away from there! Get away from that fireplace! You fiend! *(She is down at last and, quite demented, rushes at the* BIRD.) Oh, the soot! Look at the soot! I'll kill it! I'll kill it! *(Commotion. The* OLD MAN *gets in the way, but she pushes him aside and hangs on to the* BIRD, *who seems intent upon going up the chimney. Beside herself.)* Now I'm going to wring your wicked neck!

OLD MAN: No! No! No!

OLD WOMAN: Yes! Yes! Yes!

BIRD: CRAWK! CRAWK! CRAWK! *(There is a crash and a flash . . . and a tinkling shower of coins spills all over the floor.)* CRAWK! CRAWK! CRAWK!

OLD WOMAN: Oh, the soot, the soot! I'm choking! I'm dying!

(Silence.)

OLD MAN *(Wonderingly)*: It's all come down. So *that* was the soot in the chimney. *(He takes up a handful of coins and lets them trickle through his fingers.)*

BIRD *(Very gently, as if he knows his work is done)*: CRAWK! CRAWK! CRAWK!

(Darkness.)

ACT III

When the scene opens the OLD WOMAN *is crawling about the floor feverishly picking up the spilled money. The* OLD MAN *is sitting on the table, center stage, dreamily trickling coins from one hand into a leather bag which he holds in the other. The* BIRD *has withdrawn to the back of the stage, where he stands with benevolently inclined head and folded wings, watching the couple.*

OLD MAN: Well, I never!

BIRD *(Mildly)*:   CRAWK! CRAWK!

OLD MAN: All this money! Whose is it?

(The OLD WOMAN *lifts up her face. It is all over soot.)*

OLD WOMAN *(From the floor)*:   Mine.

BIRD *(Disturbed)*:   CRAWK! CRAWK! CRAWK!

OLD WOMAN: Ours, then, though, begging *its* pardon. *(Gestures toward* BIRD.*)* I'll venture to remind you that *I* was the one who saved it.

OLD MAN: Is it real?

OLD WOMAN: Of course it's real, stupid. Don't you know real money when you see it?

OLD MAN: It's such a long time since I saw any. When I was in business my customers never seemed to have any.

OLD WOMAN *(Very cynically)*:   Hmmph!

OLD MAN: Then, you see, Dickeybird, the strength went out of my arms—*and* legs—and my poor wife had to earn the living for both of us.

OLD WOMAN: Scrubbing and cleaning—

OLD MAN: Yes.

OLD WOMAN: Washing and ironing—

OLD MAN: Yes, yes!

OLD WOMAN: Baking and aching—

OLD MAN: Tut-tut. You don't have to go over all *that.*

OLD WOMAN: Trying to save a bit here and there for a rainy day.

OLD MAN: Oh, that rainy day! It's all up there, you know. *(Points impatiently to the Rainy-Day shelf)*

OLD WOMAN: There'll be plenty of rainy days now we're old.

OLD MAN: What about all those fine days we could have enjoyed so much more than we did? *(Trickles money from hand to hand.)* Oh, the fun we could have had?

OLD WOMAN: All the same . . . you'll admit you've got a thrifty little wife . . . to save such a nice little nest egg. *(Crawling about the floor the* OLD WOMAN *has come to rest beneath the* OLD MAN's *feet as he sits on the table. She squats on her knees and looks up at him now.)*

OLD MAN: All the same we could have enjoyed a bit more company . . . and we could certainly have spared a meal for a hungry traveler without bothering about the bill.

OLD WOMAN: All the same, you won't say "No" to *this*, I'm sure.

(She gets up from the floor and goes to put the coins which she has collected into the bag the OLD MAN *is playing with. She tries to take the bag, but to her surprise the* OLD MAN *retains a firm hold on it.)*

OLD MAN: All the same—you needn't have sold my little harp for fourpence . . . and you needn't have thrown out the Sailor for not having any money. And you needn't have hit him over the head with your broomstick. He told the best tales I've ever heard in my life. . . .

OLD WOMAN *(Interrupting)*: I'm sure he did! *(She pulls at the bag.)*

OLD MAN *(Also pulling the bag)*: It was worth a lot of suppers just to sit and listen to him. All the same—

OLD WOMAN *(Tugging the bag)*: All the same—

OLD MAN *(He has pulled the bag away from her)*: All the same—

(He makes a stream of coins from bag to hand and vice-versa).

All the same. I can buy another harp, a bigger one, and my friends will soon be around when they hear about this.

OLD WOMAN: *That* you may be sure of.

OLD MAN *(Jumping up and retaining the bag)*: And now there's no soot in the chimney, we can have a roaring fire before we go to bed. Let's have the matches. *(Hesitating slightly, she at last produces a box of matches from her apron, which is all sooty now. He lights the fire.)* Burn fire, burn! *(A flame shoots up in the fireplace. The* OLD MAN *rubs his hands and dances about with glee, the money bag jingling.)* Don't look so glum. There'll be plenty of firewood lying about outside after the storm. You can

530

be out nice and early a-picking it up. *(He sings.)*

A-picking-it-up.
A-picking-it-up.

(Money drops out of the bag. The OLD WOMAN *bends to pick it up. The* OLD MAN *ignores her and pokes the wood on the fire.)*

OLD WOMAN: I knew it. Throwing the money around already. We're ruined. Drat you, Bird, if it hadn't been for you—*(She breaks off; looks round in surprise.)* Why, where is it?

OLD MAN: Where's what? *(Looks around.)* What d'you mean?

OLD WOMAN: The Bird. It's gone.

OLD MAN: Gone? *(He is bewildered.)* Gone? Gone where? *(Runs to her.)* What have you done with him?

OLD WOMAN: Me? I haven't done anything. It's gone, that's all.

OLD MAN: Gone? I don't believe it. He can't have gone. He wouldn't go—like that—without so much as a cry . . . *(The* OLD MAN *rushes around the room, trying window and door, looking up the chimney. He forgets to bother about the money bag, which falls to the floor. He finds that the door into the forest is unlocked. He looks accusingly at the* OLD WOMAN.*)* You've done it! It's your fault! You opened the door.

OLD WOMAN: I swear I never! *(Her eye is on the money bag. The* OLD MAN *runs through the door into the forest.)*

OLD MAN *(Crying)*:   Come back, beautiful Bird.

OLD WOMAN: He's gone. Cage and all. *(She cannot disguise her satisfaction.)*

OLD MAN: Cages can't fly.

OLD WOMAN: Find it, then.

(The OLD MAN *comes back into the room and starts looking for the cage.)*

OLD MAN: Not even a goodbye. I can't believe it. Gone! Gone! Gone!

OLD WOMAN: Shut the door quick in case it comes back. *(She darts to the door and bolts it, then turns around to face the* OLD MAN, *looking much more like her old self. The* OLD MAN *is a picture of grief.)*

OLD MAN *(Wringing his hands)*:   If only I'd taken more care of him! *(The* OLD WOMAN *calmly goes and picks up the money bag.)*

OLD WOMAN: Never mind about the bird. Let's count the money.

OLD MAN *(Bitterly)*:   The money! If it hadn't been for the money I'd still have *him*. Oh, I always wanted a talking bird.

OLD WOMAN *(Busy with the money)*:   You've got me, haven't you? *I* talk, don't I?

OLD MAN: Anyone can have a talking wife.

OLD WOMAN: Not one like me. *(Her voice has now such a grim note in it that he is startled. He realizes that the atmosphere has changed. He looks around, as if seeking help.)* No use staring around in the air. Look on the floor and make sure we haven't lost any money. *(She empties the money bag onto the middle of the table and begins to count up, very much in possession of the situation.)*

OLD MAN *(Bewildered)*:   What's happening? *(To audience, front stage.)* Everything's going wrong. If only the Bird had stayed!

OLD WOMAN *(Deliberately)*:   What bird? *(The OLD MAN stares at her, dumbfounded. Then he stares at the audience.)* I said . . . What bird are you talking about? If you mean the miserable little thing that died . . . here's his cage. *(She finds the discarded string birdcage which she threw at the BIRD earlier on. She throws it now, contemptuously, at the OLD MAN. She is feeling more and more like her old self. The OLD MAN picks up the cage. He holds it like a harp, and tries to play it. The OLD WOMAN goes up front stage left.)*

OLD MAN *(Trying the strings)*:   I can't play it.

OLD WOMAN: He's trying to play a birdcage. *(Doubles up with laughter.)* Did you ever? *(She begins mockingly to copy his gestures.)* You look like the Old Tingalary Man. *(She begins to play an imaginary violin.)* Only *he* had a fiddle! *(She begins to sing, fiddling vigorously.)*

Tingalary, O me Sary?
Ting-a-lary Man!

(Now she has caught the OLD MAN's attention. She changes her fiddle-playing gestures to harp-playing ones like his, and he quickly changes to playing the fiddle, sawing with one arm over the other, and dropping the birdcage. Singing rapidly.) Join in—"I'll do all that ever I can!"

(They both sing together.)

I'll do all that ever I can
To follow the Tingalary Man.

(They go dancing round the room, each playing the imaginary harp and fiddle, changing and rechanging instruments and singing together.)

Ting-a-lary! O me Sary!
Ting-a-lary Man!
I'll do all that ever I can
To follow the Tingalary Man!

(It is possible for the audience to join in this game, which goes in this way. The one who is Tingalary [the OLD MAN] pretends to play the fiddle. Different instruments are chosen by other people. [The audience could be divided into sections, each section with one instrument.] When Tingalary changes from his fiddle to one of the other instruments, the players of that all quickly change over to the fiddle. When Tingalary changes back to the fiddle, the other players quickly resume their own instrument. The point of the game is to make the changeover quickly, or take the place of Tingalary. The traditional tune is simple and quickly picked up. A word sheet could be lowered.)

(At last the OLD MAN and the OLD WOMAN finish the game. The OLD WOMAN flops down, fanning herself, but the OLD MAN goes back to the birdcage and picks it up.)

OLD WOMAN: Whew! That's done me a lot of good, I'm sure! Why, it's I don't know how many years since I played that.

OLD MAN *(Shaking the cage)*: It's not long since *I played* it, though! Why can't I play it now, I wonder?

OLD WOMAN: If you can't understand why you can't play a birdcage, you'll never understand anything in this world! Whatever next!

OLD MAN: Next, I suppose you'll be saying *you* didn't fly.

OLD WOMAN: I? Fly? *(She jumps up and shrieks with laughter.)*

OLD MAN: Yes. Up there! Right up to the ceiling!

OLD WOMAN: Up there? Me? Curi-oss-ities and Fabul-oss-ities—I! Fly! The only flying I ever do is in my dreams. *(She goes away on a flounce around the room. The OLD MAN steps up front stage.)*

OLD MAN *(To audience)*: Oh dear—and I was *so* hoping A.B. was going to be nicer than B.B.

OLD WOMAN *(Also stepping front stage)*: A.B.? B.B.?

OLD MAN *(Still speak to audience)*: Everything seemed to be getting so much more pleasant—A.B.

OLD WOMAN *(To audience)*:   A.B.? B.B.? He means A.M. and P.M.

OLD MAN: What *is* A.M.?

OLD WOMAN: What *is* A.M.? Oh, you ignoramus! *(Pause.)* A.M.'s
ALL MORNING, of course. And P.M. is—

OLD MAN *(Quickly)*:   Past Morning.

OLD WOMAN: Naturally.

OLD MAN: Then I *don't* mean A.M. and P.M. I mean A.B. and B.B.
(To audience.) You know what I mean, don't you? *(Pause.)* B.B.
means Before the Bird. A.B. means After the Bird. And I've got
a feeling that A.B. is going to be worse than B.B.

OLD WOMAN: A.B. B.B. How he goes on. (Yawns.) It's A.M. now.
(Looks at clock.) Five minutes to something. We'd know what if
you'd only put a new finger on the clock instead of dreaming so
much.

OLD MAN: Dreaming? It's not true.

OLD WOMAN: That's what I'm telling you. Of course it's not true.
Magic bird my eye! It's not more true than—than Tingalary.

OLD MAN: That's only a game . . . only pretending.

OLD WOMAN: So is your Magic Bird . . . it's just a—Tingalary Bird.
. . . It doesn't exist.

OLD MAN: But . . . *(groping)* what about the money then?

OLD WOMAN: The money?

OLD MAN *(Excitedly)*:   It was the Magic Bird who told me about it.

OLD WOMAN: Pooh. Nothing magic about that! Little birds are always telling me things . . . especially things other people don't
want me to know about. *(Pause.)* You must be sensible, you know.

OLD MAN: Must I?

OLD WOMAN: You don't want to be insensible do you? 'Cos if you
do it won't take a minute. *(She picks up her stick as if to hit
him.)*

OLD MAN *(Quickly)*:   I'll be sensible, I suppose.

OLD WOMAN: That's better. Now let's reason it out. *I* put the money
in the chimney myself. . . . The only miracle about *that* is that
you didn't find it before with all your poking and prying about.
There's no magic about it.

OLD MAN: No magic?

OLD WOMAN: There's no magic at all.

OLD MAN: I don't believe it. . . . *(Indicates audience.)* And they don't believe it either. *(To audience.)* Do you? There, you see.

OLD WOMAN: See? See what? See whom? *(She peers outwards to the auditorium, hand shading eyes.)* I don't see anything . . . at least I only see what I want to see. That's far the best way, you know. *(The OLD MAN looks flabbergasted. The OLD WOMAN goes demandingly up to him and holds out her hand. He looks uncomprehending.)* Come on. Give it to me. *(Pause.)* The key to *my* cupboard. *(Pause.)* Don't think I've forgotten where it is . . .*(The OLD MAN fumbles through pockets.)* It's in *that* pocket . . . there. *(She points to the pocket where he put it. He takes out the key and, thoroughly intimidated, gives it to her.)* That's more like it. I feel better now. Better and better. And I'll feel better still when I've got the money safely locked up. *(Up to now the money bag is still on the table where she put it. She now goes up to it, but before she puts her hand on it she says to the OLD MAN):* Still being reasonable. *I'm* the one who can look after it properly and if money doesn't belong to those who can look after it—it ought to. *(She puts out her hand to pick up the money but before she can do so, the stage darkens, claps of thunder are heard again, and the wind howls.)* Mercy! I thought that was all over!

(Lightning flashes. There is the sound as of great wings rushing overhead, then scratching at the window. The OLD MAN rushes to the window in great joy.)

OLD MAN: He's come back! He's here.

BIRD *(Off)*:   CRAWK! CRAWK!

OLD WOMAN: The money! It's yours, husband. Take it—take it for mercy's sake, but DON'T — DON'T — DON'T LET THAT — THAT TINGALARY THING in again.

(The OLD MAN is not listening. He is trying with frantic haste to open the window. Lightning flashes and thunder rumbles all the time.)

OLD MAN: Don't go away! Wait! Wait for me! Come back! Come back! *(He has opened the window at last—and crying, "Come back," he is halfway out himself, stretching out his arms—straining outwards as if in response to some invisible power. The OLD WOMAN grabs his coat tails and she echoes his cry of "Come back!)*

OLD WOMAN: Come back! Come back!

OLD MAN *(Calling)*:   Wait for me! Take me with you! Take me with you—*(His voice echoes strangely. The* OLD WOMAN *hangs grimly on to his coat tails. The thunder and lightning intensify—then subside. The* OLD MAN *sags back into the room. The* OLD WOMAN *falls onto the floor. SILENCE. Then:)*

OLD WOMAN *(To audience)*: I should have missed him if he'd got away! *(Anxiously, after a pause.)* Has it gone?

(The OLD MAN *has his head in his hands.)*

OLD MAN: I was too slow, too slow! It's too late! He's gone.

OLD WOMAN *(Sotto voce)*: Thank goodness. *You* can have the money, husband dear. It's all yours.

OLD MAN: *Now* you won't say he wasn't here? You won't ever again disbelieve in my beautiful talking Bird?

OLD WOMAN: Well . . . it's true that *I'm* here. And it's true that *you're* here. *(She has hold of his coat.)*

OLD MAN: He is truer than true! My beautiful, talking Bird is truer than true. *(The* OLD MAN *pulls away from the* OLD WOMAN, *muttering to himself as he goes around the room.)* Truer than true! Truer than me! Truer than you! And look at this—*(He has spotted the black cloth that covered the wicker birdcage, and holds it up.)* I *knew* there was something to prove it. Now you won't be able to say the Magic Bird wasn't here. This proves everything. . . . The Bird *was* here . . . I *did* play the little bird-cage and you *did* fly—right up there with your broomstick!

OLD WOMAN: I'm not quite sure that I like what *that* remark might imply.
(The OLD MAN *tosses the black cloth to her; she drapes it around herself like a cloak. The* OLD MAN *goes to the wide-open window and looks out.)*

OLD MAN: Goodbye, Beautiful Bird, Goodbye!

OLD WOMAN: That air's too fresh. It'll make you sneeze. Close the window. *(She preens and fancies herself in the black cloak.)*

OLD MAN: Adieu! and Farewell!

OLD WOMAN: And close it tight! Dear me, this is just the thing for these dark nights.

(The OLD MAN *shuts the window and comes into the room.)*

OLD MAN: Vanished!

OLD WOMAN: Have I really? I thought you meant me. Never mind, it'll come in useful for a rainy day. *(Folding up the cloth, she takes a chair and puts it beneath the Rainy-Day shelf. As she reaches up to put the cloth away with the other things, the shelf falls down and the piled-up rubbish scatters about all over the floor. The tin of buns bursts open and scatters stale buns that burst like splashes of plaster over the floor. Agonized.)* Oh, my shelf! My treasures! My rainy-day things! My darlings! My beauties! *(She runs this way and that, quite distracted. The* OLD MAN *begins to pick up things. He tries a bun with his teeth, then throws it outside in disgust. He picks up a wooden cradle and brings it forward.)*

OLD MAN: What's this?

OLD WOMAN *(Passionately)*:   Leave it alone! Give it to me! *(She grabs it from him, blowing off the dust.)*

OLD MAN *(Bewildered)*:   But we haven't any children.

OLD WOMAN: We might have had. *(She puts the cradle on the table and rocks it.)*

OLD MAN: How many . . . might we have had?

OLD WOMAN *(Promptly)*:   Three. Tom. Harry. And Elsie-May.

OLD MAN: That's four.

OLD WOMAN: Elsie-May is all one-and-the-same . . . might have been. This was hers . . . would have been. *(She puts her hand into the table and takes out a dusty rag doll. She holds this in her arms, then abruptly turns her back to the audience. The* OLD MAN *examines the cradle. The* OLD WOMAN *turns around and sings these words to the traditional tune of "Rock-a-bye-Baby," standing front stage with doll.)*

Rock-a-bye-Baby, dear Elsie-Mae,
Stay in the treetop all through the day,
No use to whimper up there at the top
Hardworking Mother's too busy to stop!

That's what I used to sing . . . or would have sung! *(She throws the doll to the* OLD MAN, *who takes up the song.)*

OLD MAN *(sings)*:
Rock-a-bye Baby, dear Elsie-May,
Mother is busy, but Father can play.
Up in the treetop, no need to yell,
Father will climb up and rock there as well.

OLD WOMAN: Spoiling things as usual! *(She snatches the doll, begins to rock it in her arms, and waltzes around the room as she sings.)*
Rock-a-bye Baby, dear Elsie-May,

Mother won't spoil you, whatever folks say.
When evening comes, from tree at the top,
Right to the bottom, dear Baby can drop!

(She joins the OLD MAN *front stage.)*

OLD MAN: What a nice family. I'm glad I've joined in!

OLD WOMAN: Too late! Too late! They've gone. *(She puts the doll away in the cradle.)*

OLD MAN: Why? What's happened to 'em?

(They stand together front stage, each with a hold on the cradle.)

OLD WOMAN *(Giving a tug)*:   Same as happens to other people's families. They've all grown up and flown away. It's the nature of families to fly *(The* OLD MAN *gives a tug. The cradle breaks in two and falls to the floor, with the doll.)* So that's that! *(She picks up the doll and puts it on the table. She goes for her broomstick to sweep up the bits. As she begins to sweep she cannot resist a few surreptitious attempts to make it fly, but it does not respond. She shrugs her shoulders and begins to sweep the room. The* OLD MAN, *who is also tidying things, stops.)*

OLD MAN: There's something yellow on the floor.

OLD WOMAN *(Pouncing)*:   Gold! you must have dropped it! Quick! Put it in the bag! *(She searches the floor.)* I can't see anything! Where is it?

OLD MAN: Here . . . and here . . . and here. It's everywhere. The room's filling up with it.

(The room is slowly filling with warm, yellow light.)

OLD WOMAN: Daylight! That's all it is! It's morning—and we haven't been to bed.

(The OLD MAN *goes to the open door, into the forest.)*

OLD MAN: How beautiful the forest looks after the storm.

(The OLD WOMAN *follows him to the door with her broom, but she sees a drift of dead leaves around the doorstep and crossly begins to sweep them away.)*

OLD WOMAN: The trouble with forests is—trees, and the trouble with trees is—leaves, and the trouble with leaves is—they fall off— and *I'm* the one who has to sweep them up. It isn't fair! It isn't fair! It isn't fair! *(She throws her broomstick away. Perhaps it is a gesture of abdication.)* I'm sick of trying to keep this forest tidy.

I'm going to bed. Goodnight! *(She marches inside—and goes to the door at the left.)*

OLD MAN: Good *DAY!*

OLD WOMAN: How do you know it's going to be a good day? If it's anything like the night we've had, *I* don't want it! *(Yawns.)* Don't forget to wind the clock up. *(The* OLD MAN *picks up her broom and props it outside the door. The* OLD WOMAN *hesitates, sees that the* OLD MAN *is still outside looking out toward the sunrise. She looks at the money bag, which is still on the table. She walks up to it. Her fingers itch to be on it. She stretches out her hand, looking stealthily about as she does so. Her hand descends. There is an almost inaudible note of thunder. She draws back her hand, not quite sure if she really heard anything. She tries again. This time her hand is actually upon the bag when there is a real crash of thunder which makes her leap in the air.)* Whew! I'm going. *(She exits left. The* OLD MAN *is still outside. The* OLD WOMAN *puts her head into the room and calls to him.)* Don't forget to put the money away! *(She disappears for an instant, then comes back. When she sees that the* OLD MAN *is still outside and unaware of her, she steals up to the table, reaches out her hand, picks up the rag doll and goes out with it, left. Silence. The clock's tick is heard again. The* OLD MAN *sits on the doorstep and idly picks up a handful of dead leaves. He begins to send them away one by one.)*

OLD MAN:
This day, next day, sometime—never!
This day, next day, someday—

(He comes to the last leaf.)

Someday you'll come back, Beautiful, glorious Bird.
Someday you'll come back.

(He comes into the house, goes into the lean-to room and disappears. There is the sound of things being moved about, then the OLD MAN *comes out, carrying a newly painted inn sign. This says, "The Come-Inn-and-Welcome." He props it up and looks at it very proudly. He carries it outside, climbs up, takes down the unfriendly sign and puts up the new one. With great satisfaction.)* Come in and welcome! Don't know what sort of a day you're going to be. . . . *(Turns out toward sun.)* But whatever you're going to be—come in and welcome, Day! *(The* OLD MAN *comes into the room, setting the door open for the sun to shine in. He stands center stage, caught in a ray of sunlight and still looking through the open door into the distance. At last he moves out of the stream of light. The clock's tick reminds him he must wind it up. Now he stands scratching his head and trying to remember*

what else he is supposed to do. *The children in the audience
really end this play. All through the performance they have repeatedly taken part in it. The* OLD WOMAN *has left the money
bag on the table and has told the* OLD MAN *to take care of it.
But his mind is on the* BIRD, *not on the money. Yawning sleepily
he begins to go on his way to bed. He remembers that he has to
remember something. But what? He begins to play a game with
the children in the audience,* HOT *or* COLD, *touching first this
object, then another. If the children mean him to do so, he will
pick up the money bag and go to bed. If not, he will go quite
happily without it. There is a pause. The whole stage is bathed
in light. Birds sing. Along the path from the village the* SAILOR
*comes on his way to the sea. He passes the inn door, noticing the
new sign with a smile. He comes up to the front of the stage and
sings his farewell song to the audience.*)

SAILOR:

> I'm a wandering Sailor,
> My story is told,
> Old Man and Old Woman
> I'll leave with their gold.
>
> This dear little dwelling
> Has door opened wide,
> The weary and hungry,
> May rest there inside.
>
> Let Friendship and Laughter,
> Create from today,
> A new way of living,
> In work and in play.
>
> I'm a wandering Sailor,
> With no more to tell,
> So I'll love you—and leave you—
> And bid you—Farewell!

(*When the* SAILOR's *song is over and he has made his bow to the
audience, he turns to make his exit. It is seen that the small
wicker birdcage which he carries on his back is now uncovered—
and that it contains a replica in miniature—of the Tingalary Bird.*)

ALADDIN

A PARTICIPATION PLAY

by

MOSES GOLDBERG

ALADDIN

by

MOSES GOLDBERG

ALADDIN

The adult theatre of the 1960's was characterized by experimentation both in the types of plays written and in the manner of their presentation. The field included such things as agit-prop, street drama, drama that reflected the concerns of various sub-cultures, and environmental theatre productions that sought to break down the aesthetic distance between actor and audience and involve the audience directly in the performance. It was a time when virtually all of the accepted standards and traditions of the theatre were challenged, as stories, language, and conventions that were considered inappropriate for the theatre prior to that time became very common on stages throughout the country.

The children's theatre field was far less adventurous than the adult theatre, but the growing popularity of such plays as *The Tingalary Bird, Reynard the Fox*, and *The Ice Wolf* pointed toward significant changes in the literature. Concurrent with this movement toward plays with more relevant themes and stories, the field also began to accommodate — and in some cases encourage — participation theatre, a form of theatre production much like the environmental theatre movement in the adult drama. The aim of participation theatre and participation plays is to minimize the actual and aesthetic distance between the actors and the audience, and to encourage participation in the plays by the audience members.

The movement toward participation theatre for children gained particular impetus during the 1960's, but it was not completely new to the field. One of the most famous of all moments of theatre participation occurs in Barrie's *Peter Pan*, when Peter solicits help from the audience to save Tinkerbell. Peter asks all of the people who believe in fairies to clap their hands, and the predictable applause that follows ostensibly affects the outcome of the play. But prior to mid-century such incidents of participatory theatre were very rare, and those that did exist were usually a part of very traditional "distanced" performances. Even in some very presentational plays, such as Miller's *The Land of the Dragon*, where characters talk directly to the audience, participation is ruled out when the audience is not encouraged to talk back.

The roots of the participation theatre movement in this country are many and varied. They range from forces in the adult theatre that were breaking down aesthetic barriers to a desire among children's theatre writers to make more use of a child's natural desire to become a part of the play. Regardless of the philosophies that informed the movement, the first important specific influences came from the work of the British playwright, Brian Way. Way wrote a large number of participation plays, designed for a wide variety of age groups and situations. These works became very popular in this country during the 1960's, and they subsequently influenced many American writers.

One of the most successful of the American writers to work with participation theatre has been Moses Goldberg, and one of the most popular of his participation plays is *Aladdin*. Like most participation plays, *Aladdin* is designed to be performed before a relatively small audience. Goldberg specifies that this audience should include no more than 250 children between four and nine years of age. In his preface to the original published version, Goldberg notes that participation theatre is particularly appropriate for children of this age because they have a tendency to want to become directly involved in the action of the play. According to Goldberg, a play that acknowledges this tendency and invites and structures audience participation, can teach a child to substitute aesthetic participation for active participation.

All of the elements of *Aladdin* are constructed and arranged to minimize the aesthetic distance, a factor which is particularly apparent in the basic structure of the play. The work consists of a play-within-a play wherein a family of peddlers decides to enact some of the adventures of Aladdin and his magic lamp. Two levels of "reality" are thus presented, both of which serve important functions in encouraging and directing audience involvement.

The action that occurs prior to the beginning of the play-within-the-play is designed to develop a close bond between the actors and the audience. Goldberg suggests that the actors should assemble in the playing space before the audience enters, meet each of the children personally, and show them to their seats. The dialogue used with this business is improvised, but it is still a very important part of the play itself. Once personal contact has been made with each audience member, the action progresses to the play-within-the-play; it is within this context that the audience is asked to participate. But, it is important to note, this does not occur until the audience sees the actors themselves (as the family of peddlers) "participating" in the enactment of the Aladdin story. It is a subtle device that effectively directs the audience toward their own participation.

The participation activities called for in this play range from simple vocal responses to more elaborate pantomime, all of which the children can do without leaving their places. Most of these actions are used to help one of the main characters deal with a complication, and, when it is done well, the audience is made to believe that they actually exercise some control over the story. For example, when Aladdin asks the audience where the Magician took the princess, the audience is eager to intervene on the princess' behalf. In those instances where the expected participation does not occur, the actors must be prepared to improvise their way through the complication, because, regardless of the participation of the audience, there is very little flexibility in the through-line of the story.

Aladdin requires no scenery, minimal properties, and simple costumes. Costume changes, shifts in locale, and the distribution of properties are all accomplished in full view of the audience. These conventions greatly simplify the technical requirements of the play; more importantly, they allow the audience to share in the actual process of putting on the play. The simplicity of the world of the play also makes it easier for the children in the audience to cross over that aesthetic line and imagine themselves (dressed as they are and still seated in the same place) very much a part of the action.

This play presents a world more akin to a story-telling session with the audience involved in the telling of the story, than a world of illusion that transports the audience to a different time and place. For this reason, an analysis of *Aladdin* in terms of elements found in more conventional dramatic literature reveals little about the unique qualities of participatory drama in general or *Aladdin* in particular. The story is simple, the characters are one-dimensional, and the dialogue is prosaic. Emphasis has clearly been placed on creating a style of performance that literally leads the audience into the world of the play, and on developing a structure within the play that encourages and supports that audience involvement.

Participation plays have been a controversial addition to the repertoire, and their presence has further sharpened the debate among theatre artists about the nature and purpose of dramatic literature for children. Participation theatre has been a popular theatre form; it has been a much-abused theatre form as well. Many writers have created these plays out of a sincere desire to enrich the theatre experience for the children in the audience, while others have entered the field because these plays provide many easy ways to involve the audience in the action — even if this involvement is only superficial. Writers in this latter category generally emphasize the audience involvement at the expense of the play itself, and this imbalance weakens both the aesthetic impact of the work and the participation activities.

Aladdin provides an appropriate balance between viewing and participating. The participation — which grows believably from the story — becomes more complex as the play progresses and as the psychological involvement of the participants increases. In addition, the play is interesting, entertaining, and inviting.

The popularity of participation drama has decreased somewhat during the last decade, although several writers continue to experiment with the form. It is difficult to judge the impact such plays have had on the repertoire, primarily because participation plays have usually been considered as a totally separate entity within the field. But it is clear that the importance of a work such as *Aladdin* does not rest with literary considerations; the play is straightforward in construction, the story is very familiar, and there are no new perspectives offered in the work as a whole. What the play does offer is a style of production that breaks down the aesthetic distance between actors and audience and demonstrates various strategies for involving the audience in the action. Although such strategies are not directly applicable to more traditional theatre situations, these experiments with audience/actor relationships have done much to free modern writers from the restrictive, representational styles of the past. More importantly, these plays have also offered children a unique theatre experience.

MOSES GOLDBERG currently serves as Artistic Director for Stage One in Louisville, Kentucky. In addition to teaching at Florida State University and Southwest Texas State University, Goldberg has directed professionally at the PAF Playhouse in New York, the Asolo State Theatre in Florida, The Delaware Summer Festival, A Contemporary Theatre and Poncho Theatre in Seattle, and the Peppermint Tent in Minneapolis. Goldberg has written several plays for child audiences, and his textbook, *Children's Theatre: A Philosophy and A Method* (Englewood Cliffs, N.J.: Prentice Hall, 1974), is currently used in many colleges and universities. In 1980 Goldberg was awarded the Chorpenning Cup by the Children's Theatre Association of America for outstanding work as a playwright for young audiences. Other published plays by Goldberg include *The Analysis of Mineral #4*, *The Men's Cottage*, *The Outlaw Robin Hood* and *The Wind in the Willows*. Forthcoming from Anchorage Press is his latest participation-play *Rumpelstiltskin*.

ALADDIN,

A PARTICIPATION PLAY

Created by

Moses Goldberg

and

The Original Acting Company

BURGUNDO	Doug Kaye
CORDOVA	Victoria Wells
DAHLIA	Kerry Shanklin
DOMINO	Morris Matthews
ZAMPANO	Richard Jacobs
PICO	Burton Clarke

with special acknowledgements to

Henson Keys

ALADDIN: A PARTICIPATION PLAY

PREFACE

The fact that this play carries the subtitle, "A Participation Play," is not to suggest that other plays are not participatory. All plays, if they move an audience, can be said to be participation plays. In fact, few people would ever become actors if it were not that they crave the sense of being the focal point for the projected energies of an enthralled audience. That focused energy, which shapes the performance from night to night, is the audience's participation. But it is an "aesthetic" participation — it takes place at a remove; through the audience's ability to perceive the truth of the world of the play, while simultaneously holding onto the other truth, that they are sitting in a theatre and watching a rehearsed sequence of lines and gestures.

In recent years, however, producers of children's theatre have used the term "participation theatre" to mean a different kind of event; not the aesthetic participation of sophisticated audience members, but a less sophisticated, perhaps more natural, kind of response: an *active* participation. This event takes advantage of the fact that the young child has not yet learned to delegate the task of playing out his fantasy to the "actor," but tends to want to play out the conflicts himself. In my work, I have generally seen the role of these kinds of plays as actually helping the child to learn not to participate; or — more correctly — of teaching him to substitute *aesthetic* participation for his natural *active* participation. By giving him a chance to respond actively at some points in the play, we are helping him to distinguish moments in the play when active help is not appropriate. By the time the child is nine or ten, he should have developed his ability, and therefore outgrown his need for this kind of play.

But during those critical years, from approximately four or five to eight or nine, it is ideal to capitalize on that transition from active to aesthetic participation by presenting plays of this type. It is also desirable that these same plays subtly teach the new audience member some of the conventions of our theatre tradition. In *Aladdin: A Participation Play* we have tried to incorporate — in an enjoyable way — concepts like onstage *vs.* offstage, the use of costumes to set mileau; changing of locales by changing scenery; the process of the actor; etc. Of course, the main purpose has been, and should remain in the production, to entertain the children.

In my conversations with producers of this or other of these participation plays, several points invariably emerge, and perhaps it will be of some benefit to list them here for those considering production of this script:

1) Once the convention is established that the audience can effect

the course of the play's action, that convention cannot be changed. Should a significant portion of the audience respond at times or in ways not planned, those responses must be dealt with — either actually incorporated into the show, or, at the least, acknowledged. The audience must be thought of by the company as the seventh member of the cast; which means, among other things, that the same honesty that goes into communication between actor and actor must be present in all actor-audience communication.

2) The direct involvement of the audience is best achieved when the performance is in-the-round with a maximum attendance of 250 children. In such a setting, no child need be further than four or five rows from the acting area. Before the dialogue in the script begins, it is especially desirable that the actors (the family of peddlers) move among the children — seating them, engaging them in conversation, etc. The performance should not start until each individual child has been "looked at particularly" by at least one of the actors. Resist all inducements to bring in more than 250 children; no matter how it is handled it always weakens the bond of intimacy on which this kind of play depends.

3) When the moment for active participation arrives, the actors must:

a) need help (sincerely),

b) provide security (make sure they know what they are asked to do, what the limits are, when to start),

3) encourage creativity (reward, by mentioning, the most different, novel, or unusual solutions to the problem), and

d) end the active participation before going on (resolve the need for help and thank the audience).

These steps are detailed in the text where appropriate, but it may help the actors to actually be aware that there is a sequence of these four steps behind each of these moments.

4) This kind of play is basically an actor's theatre. Simple, but effective, costumes, and a minimum of props are all that is needed from the technical department. The fullest resources should be committed to casting creative actors who can relate honestly to children and each other, who can think on their feet, and who can find ways to physicalize their characters or thoughts. The primary values of the theatre — dynamic actors in an intimate relationship with a participating audience — have helped this script to enjoy its previous successes; and I hope those values will continue to be there whenever it meets its audience of young theatre patrons.

MOSES GOLDBERG
Huntington, New York
January, 1977

ALADDIN

The audience arrives to discover the Prologue characters in the final process of setting up the area in which they will operate. This consists of a square about 15 feet on a side, with aisles in the four corners. The audience is separated from the "stage" by bright ribbons marking the aisles and sides of the square. As the audience comes in they are seated by members of the company, who chat with them, and then try to show off their wares, hoping for a sale. These wares all come from a huge trunk presided over by *Pico*, who never speaks. Among them we see silks, jewelry, a few lamps, etc.— all the articles which eventually become props or costumes for the play. Next to the trunk is a set of three brightly painted nesting wooden cubes (20″, 18″, and 16″ are the right sizes.) These will become the set of the play. Now the actors use them as stands on which to display merchandise. *Burgundo* is the nominal head of the troupe, and eagerly tries to interest the children in his goods; but *Cordova*, his wife, spends more time criticizing *Burgundo* than selling. *Burgundo* takes most of her abuse mildly, perhaps confiding in individuals in the audience of his need to stop being bossed so much. *Domino* is the lazy son of this pair, and he comes in for much abuse from his Mother, too. *Dahlia*, his sister, is quiet and helpful — she serves to protect her brother and father from Cordova. *Zampano* is *Cordova's* brother, and largely ignores her — which of course is the best thing to do with a bully. *Pico*, the mute, is *Zampano's* sidekick, from so long ago that neither remembers how they met. He could be played as female, but was male in the original production. He must be careful never to speak when there is anyone present from outside the company.

By the time the audience, which should be limited to 250 for best results, is assembled, the members of the company have made some sort of personal contact with each child. This rapport is essential to the success of the play. The Prologue characters, although strange types, must be realistic human beings, who can interest the audience in the lives they lead as itinerant peddlars with real family relationships. When the audience is assembled and the signal given, *Burgundo* renews his efforts to sell some cloth to a group of audience members. *Cordova* comes to him and again is criticizing his display methods, his sales pitch, everything about the poor man. Finally *Burgundo* erupts, loudly enough to signal everyone else that a significant action has begun.

BURGUNDO.   All right! I'm not going to sell any more of this junk! You are always telling me I'm doing it wrong. OK. I'm not going to sell anymore, so there. From now on, I'm going to do what I want to do!

CORDOVA.   No!

BURGUNDO.   Yes! What I want to do!

DAHLIA and DOMINO.   No. Papa. *(Burgundo sets his jaw.)*

BURGUNDO.   I said, "What I want to do," and that's it!

DAHLIA.   Papa, what do you want to do?

DOMINO.   Yeah, Papa, if you don't want to sell things?

BURGUNDO.   Well . . . you won't laugh?

DAHLIA.   I won't laugh, Papa.

BURGUNDO.   I've always wanted to be an actor . . . *(Cordova's snort cuts him off.)* Yeah! And do plays.

DOMINO.   Hey, that sounds like fun — doing plays.

ZAMPANO.   Come on and do a play, Burgundo. *(They watch him eagerly.)*

DOMINO.   Do a play, Papa?

BURGUNDO.   No, no. I can't do it alone. I need some help. *(blank looks)* I need other actors to help me do a play.

DOMINO.   Oh. I'll help you, Papa.

DAHLIA.   Me too.

ZAMPANO.   And I'll help you, Burgundo.

PICO.   *(Indicates he will help too.)*

BURGUNDO.   OK, all right.

DAHLIA.   Well, what play are we going to do?

BURGUNDO.   Oh. Well *(gathers courage)* I've been reading this book and it's full of magic and faraway places — Aladdin, the story of Aladdin.

DOMINO.   Wow! *(The others ad lib agreement)*

CORDOVA.   *(tired of being ignored)* And what sort of a part could there be in that for a marshmallow like you?

BURGUNDO.   You . . . or . . . that is . . .

DOMINO.   *(he and Dahlia have taken the book)* Hey, look!

DAHLIA.   There's a Sultan in here — a Father. I think Papa would make a good Sultan.

BURGUNDO. Yeah, I can play a Sultan. And the Sultan needs a beautiful daughter — the Princess.

DOMINO. Dahlia! *(spoiling Cordova's attempt to offer herself)*.

BURGUNDO. Dahlia, you can be the Princess. And Domino, you can play Aladdin.

DOMINO. Aladdin!

BURGUNDO. Yes. Oh, it's a really great part for you; he's really lazy! And Zampano, the Evil Magician. And you're the Mother.

CORDOVA. The Mother! I'm not going to be in this play.

BURGUNDO. Oh, yes you are. *(somewhat hesititatingly)*

DAHLIA. *(still with the book)* Papa, there's a Genie of the Lamp here.

BURGUNDO. Oh, a Genie. Well, I can play the Genie of the Lamp. I can play the Genie and the Sultan.

CORDOVA. Two parts! Well, if you get to play two parts, I get to play two parts.

DOMINO. Papa, there's a Genie of the Ring.

BURGUNDO. *(Making peace)* Would you like to play the Genie of the Ring? The *beautiful* Genie of the Ring?

CORDOVA. Do I get to play both parts?

BURGUNDO. Yes, yes you can.

CORDOVA. Well, if you really need me so much.

EVERYONE. You'll do it? Hurray! Thank you. (etc.) Let's get ready!

ZAMPANO. Wait a minute! What about Pico? Pico doesn't have a part.

DOMINO. *(shows in book)* Well there are all kinds of other parts. Pico can do all of these.

BURGUNDO. Would you, Pico? *(He agrees)*

ALL. Let's get ready! *(they all scurry about and exit, leaving Domino.)*

DOMINO. Get ready? Oh, well. I'm already ready. I'll just take a nap before the play starts. *(curls up on floor for a nap.)*

PICO. *(is horrified to find Domino sleeping, nudges him with foot.)*

DOMINO. Huh? What? What do you want?

PICO. *(get up)*

DOMINO. No, Pico, I'm trying to take a nap before the play starts.

552

PICO. *(let's do some warm-up exercises.)*

DOMINO. You want me to do exercises? What for? Oh, warm-up exercises. No, Pico, I'm playing Aladdin and he's really lazy. I don't have to do exercises. You do the exercises and wake me when its time for the play.

PICO. *(thinks, then walks around him nudging him and kicking him.)*

DOMINO. *(sleeping)* Wake me when it's time for the play. No, Pico, wake me when it's time for the play. *(getting madder)* I said, wake me when it's time . . . *(jumps up)* WAKE ME WHEN IT'S TIME FOR THE PLAY!

PICO. *(put up your dukes!)*

DOMINO. Oh, you're going to get tough about it, eh? Wanta fight a little bit, huh? put 'em up, put 'em up! *(They spar quite actively, just out of range of each other.)*

DOMINO. What are you . . . Pico, you tricked me into warming up for the play. Come on, come on! *(They mock fight some more.)*

CORDOVA. *(entering)* You boys stop this, this instant.

(Domino and Pico laugh at Cordova and exit together)

CORDOVA. Now, What was that all about? *(goes to trunk and rummages)*

ZAMPANO. *(enters singing and goes to box opposite trunk where the magician's costume is still on display. He is singing to himself.)* Oh, I'm Zampano — tre, la, la, and I need a costume for the Evil Magician. Oh, this turban should be perfect. It is! Now, I need a robe, and I think this one's a beauty. Look it even has stars on the sleeves. That way everyone will think I'm the star of the play! *(spots Cordova)* I think I'll try it out on Cordova. *(taps her and jumps back in grotesque pose.)*

CORDOVA. *(screams)* Zampano! What are you doing in that get-up?

ZAMPANO. This is my costume for the Evil Magician. Don't you think I look evil?

CORDOVA. Yes. Yes, you do. Stay away from me!

ZAMPANO. Where's your costume for the Mother, Cordova?

CORDOVA. I already am a mother; I don't need a costume.

ZAMPANO. No, Cordova. No, no, no. It's the wrong style, the wrong country, no. Go over there and try something on.

CORDOVA. *(goes to trunk and pulls out Genie's turban)* I always wanted to wear this.

ZAMPANO.   Oh Cordova, that looks ridiculous on you. Here, try this
on, it looks pretty to me. *(helps her on with the Mother's over-
skirt.)*

CORDOVA.   Oh, it's stunning!

ZAMPANO.   It's going to be perfect. *(they get it on, she poses.)*
That's just how Aladdin's mother should look. *(she moves)* But no,
no, no. That's not the right way to walk. This play is in a different
country, remember. Let me show you; just follow me. Place your
right foot out, your left foot down, up, right, in, in, out, up down.
(He has her doing impossible steps) That's right, you're doing fine.
Up, in, right, down . . . *(they exit together.)*

BURGUNDO.   *(enters, finds Genie's turban and puts it on.)*

DAHLIA.   *(entering)* Papa, what are you doing?

BURGUNDO.   Oh, I'm practicing to be the Genie of the Lamp.

DAHLIA.   Oh! Well, let me watch you practice, Papa. I know! I can be
Aladdin and rub the lamp, and then you jump out!

BURGUNDO.   Oh, OK. Er . . . uh . . .

DAHLIA.   *(with lamp from display table)* Here goes *(rubs it)*

BURGUNDO.   *(very much himself)* Excuse me. I am the Genie of the
Lamp. How's that?

DAHLIA.   *(with astonishment)* Oh, that was good . . . But, it might be
a little better if you were, well, taller. You know? Hold your shoulders back, stick your chest out?

BURGUNDO.   Oh, look strong! I've got it. How's this? *(He looks strong,
but still speaks weakly)* Hello, I'm the Genie of the Lamp.

DAHLIA.   Yes, Papa, but you have to be real loud so everyone can hear
you.

BURGUNDO.   Oh, loud. HELLO, I'M THE GENIE OF THE LAMP.

(Still no power.)

DAHLIA.   Yes, but you have to say it like you mean it, Papa. You have
to sound strong, too.

BURGUNDO.   Like I mean it. (Practicing to self) I'm the Genie . . . I
am the Genie . . .

CORDOVA.   *(enters laughing at him)* Who do you think you are?

554

BURGUNDO. *(snaps at her)* I am the Genie of the Lamp! *(Cordova wilts and exits.)*

DAHLIA. Yes! Papa, that's right!

BURGUNDO. *(advancing on her)* I am the Genie of the Lamp! *(she exits, he follows her in character.)*

ZAMPANO. *(enters)* Genie of the Lamp? Genie of the Lamp? Oh, I feel so evil already. Would you all like to take a peek at that little Genie of the Lamp before anyone else does? *(Like all direct addresses in the play, this is an honest question. If they say "No," Zampano has to say "Well, I do.")* All right, all you have to do is rub the lamp. *(he does.)* Hmm? I'll rub the other side. *(Still nothing.)* Hmmm? Genie? He's not coming out! *(Getting frantic)* Genie? Oh no? There's no Genie in the magic lamp. Now we can't do the play! What are we going to do? Genie, Genie, Genie, Genie, Genie, Genie? Pico! *(who is watching all of this, having just entered.)* There's no genie in the magic lamp. Now we can't do the play!

PICO. *(laughs at him)*

ZAMPANO. What's so funny?

PICO. *(Don't worry, I'll take care of the Genie.)*

ZAMPANO. You're going to put the Genie in the magic lamp?

PICO. *(of course)*

ZAMPANO. Hah! I'd like to see that trick!

PICO. *(Stand back. Warms up and with a series of contortions, leaps, spins — "puts" the genie in the lamp.)*

ZAMPANO. Is he in there?

PICO. *(Sure. He looks in, not expecting much, and is shocked to discover that there is now a genie in there!)*

ZAMPANO. He's really in there? Well, let me see the Genie. I want to see the genie. Show him to me.

PICO. *(No. He's asleep)*

ZAMPANO. What? He's sleeping? Well, I'll be quiet. Let me take a look at him.

PICO. *(hands him over gently and opens lamp for Zampano)*

ZAMPANO. *(too loud)* Lullaby!

PICO. *(quickly pulls the lamp away and closes it up.)*

ZAMPANO. *(Amazed)* He really put the genie in the lamp! Hey, Pico. Will you be able to wake him up by the time we need him in the play?

PICO. *(I think so)*

ZAMPANO. Well, we're depending on you.

BURGUNDO. *(entering with the book)* Why don't you guys have the set up? Come on, hurry up! Here's the book. See what the first scene has to be. Pico, help him! *(exits)*

ZAMPANO. The first scene takes place outside Aladdin's house. We need a step. *(Pico sets up two boxes opposite the trunk to make a step.)* Yeah, I think that's perfect. Now, will you be able to change that for scene two? *(Pico nods and they start out)* Scene two takes place in a cave, so we'll need . . .

DAHLIA. *(enters and picks up remaining costumes and props, putting them in trunk. Cordova enters practicing her walk.)*

CORDOVA. Now that Zampano has taught me how to walk right, I must look very beautiful. Dahlia?

DAHLIA. *(turns, and manages to keep from breaking into hysterics.)* Mama? Oh, oh! You've been practicing! Oh, you look . . . beautiful.

CORDOVA. Look at this. *(a fancy turn)*

DOMINO. *(enters, and seeing his mother's antics, begins to laugh and scream at the sight. Dahlia fails to stop him until it is too late.)*

CORDOVA. What is he laughing at? I'm ugly? You think I look ugly! I'm not going to be in this play! I look ugly! *(In tears, retreats to the "step")*

DAHLIA. *(Simultaneously with above)* I don't know Mama. No, Mama! Domino, be quiet. Mama, you don't look ugly. *(Catching hold of Domino.)* Now look, you've hurt her feelings.

DOMINO. I didn't mean to hurt . . .

DAHLIA. Well, go give her a compliment and tell her she looks pretty.

DOMINO. OK. Aw, Mama, you look pretty.

CORDOVA. *I don't believe you! (Still in tears, and not hearing the following)*

DOMINO. She doesn't believe me. Now what are we going to do? We can't do the play without Mama.

DAHLIA. We need more compliments. More people to tell her . . .

DOMINO. Dahlia! *(indicates audience)* Hey, maybe they . . . Will you help us? *(Must be asked honestly so the audience knows they have the answer. If they don't reply, ask again, specific individuals if necessary and working up to the whole crowd; but don't make it seem automatic, they will help only if they believe you really need them to. So really need them to, because the play can't go on til they say "Yes".)*

DOMINO and DAHLIA. *(simultaneously talking to half the audience)* Everybody think of all the different nice things you could say to Mama to make her feel better, and when we count to three, you shout out your best compliment. Shout it to Mama as loud as you can. And say it like you really mean it, all right? The nicest thing you can think of. Are you ready? *(The two actors playing Domino and Dahlia have to judge the length of this by the physical readiness of the audience to shout. It must last until they all understand what to do, but no longer, since that would dampen enthusiasm. Throughout the play the same sense of timing is necessary to know when to give the signal for the audience to start. Lines may need to be added or cut to adjust to the audiences' tempo.)* One, Two, THREE! *(They shout, and Cordova responds to the main thing(s) she hears.).*

CORDOVA. I look pretty? *(or whatever)* Oh, do you really think so? Well, what are we standing around for? Let's do the Play!

DOMINO and DAHLIA. Hey, it worked! Thank you!

DOMINO. Say, if we need your help again later, will you help us then? Thanks!

(By now the others have entered and all take their places for the overture. In the original production we used a guitar, several kazoos, a xylophone, cymbals, kalimba, etc., but any rudimentary orchestra will suffice — even all kazoos and percussion. The company "tunes up" until Zampano stops them with a tapping sound.)

ZAMPANO. The Overture! *(Immediately afterwards, they all exit except Aladdin, who begins the play sprawled on the ground of his front yard, and Pico, who is now invisible to all the company, and sits on top of the trunk from which he obtains the props he needs.)*

MOTHER. *(offstage)* Aladdin!

ALADDIN. Oh, there's my mama. She probably has some work for me to do. Oh oh, she's coming out. I better hide behind this tree. *(The word "tree" is Pico's cue, and on it he snaps into place as the tree, holding up a stylized branch.)* ⟩

MOTHER. Aladdin, where are you? Where is he? *(the audience may*

557

tell. If so the mother goes right to the tree.) Aladdin? *(She hunts around finally spotting him. She sneaks around the tree and he stays ahead of her till the "tree" helps out by snagging his clothes and she catches him. Instantly the tree is finished with, so it disappears, and Pico goes quickly back to the trunk.)*

ALADDIN. Aw, Mama. Mama, I heard you calling but I was sitting over there by this big tree and right before you came out the roots started climbing out of the ground like big snakes, and then they got me around the ankles and they started choking me and I couldn't breathe and . . . *(acting it out, of course.)*

MOTHER. Aladdin, you've been telling stories again.

ALADDIN. No, Mama. It's true.

MOTHER. Now, I want you to help me today.

ALADDIN. Help you?

MOTHER. Now, I have this robe *(On the word, Pico places the robe in the Mother's hand. None of the actors see Pico performing this function.)* and I have to sew the emblem on it.

ALADDIN. But I have to go elephant hunting . . .

MOTHER. *(grabbing his ear)* You're not going elephant hunting or mosquito hunting, or anything else. Now, I want you to help me and hold this robe.

ALADDIN. I don't know anything about how to do this.

MOTHER. Now where did my needle go? *(Aladdin throws the robe over her head and hides behind her.)* Aladdin? Aladdin! *(She turns quickly and catches him.)* All right, Aladdin.

ALADDIN. *(He reluctantly kneels facing her.)* Aw, Mama, I don't know anything about sewing.

MOTHER. All you have to do is hold it.

ALADDIN. How do I hold it?

MOTHER. Very tightly.

ALADDIN. Very tightly?

MOTHER. Yes.

ALADDIN. OK, here goes. *(he pulls it tightly and there is a ripping sound. All sound effects should be made by the offstage cast members using instruments, etc. This could be a sandblock, or even a piece of muslin which they rip on cue.)*

MOTHER. Oh, Aladdin. Now I have to mend it.

ALADDIN. OK, well, if you need me I'll be down in the woods . . .

MOTHER. And in the meantime you can polish the porch steps.

ALADDIN. Polish the porch steps?

MOTHER. That's right, and I want you to polish them so you can see your face in them. *(Pico provides a rag.)*

ALADDIN. See my face!

MOTHER. Your face. *(exits)*

ALADDIN. Aw, Mama. She's always making me work. *(rubbing the step.)* I don't see my face, but I know what I do see standing over me! A big dragon! Aaaah! *(he acts it out)* Four big feet, sharp, sharp claws sticking out, and a long green tail waving in the air, and fire coming out of his mouth like this: Aaaaah! Aaaaah!

MOTHER. *(offstage)* Aladdin!

ALADDIN. *(in dragon voice)* Yeaaaaah? *(As the "hero")* Watch out, Aladdin! Before he eats you up. Get out your sword and get ready to . . . . *(His Mother has entered and he almost runs her through)* Ma'am? *(She points to the step and exits)* Aw, Mama. I don't want to clean this old step. *(Hits it)* Hey, it's like a drum! You want to play with me? *(Waits for an answer)* I'll play the first part of a rhythm on my drum, and you can play the ending by clapping your hands, OK? You wait till I do mine, and then you figure out what the ending is. Here goes. *(He taps a simple rhythm, and waits for the audience to complete it. If they don't get it, he may have to repeat the instructions. It doesn't matter if the audience is all together or not — he may even tell them "You don't have to all do the same thing, clap the way you think it ought to end." After three or four exchanges the Magician enters, sneaking very slowly on all fours, hiding in broad daylight and in the middle of the road from something or other.)*

MAGICIAN. Where is it? Where is it? I have been looking for it a year. *(Mumbles away. Aladdin spots him and motions the audience to hush. Then he sneaks up behind the Magician and taps his shoulder. The Magician yelps and collapses.)*

ALADDIN. Hello.

MAGICIAN. *(trying to regain poise as he rises.)* Hello.

ALADDIN. Can I help you?

MAGICIAN. Hmm. Maybe you can. You may have noticed that I have been looking for something. The House of Moustapha the Tailor.

ALADDIN.   The House of Moustapha the Tailor?

MAGICIAN.   Yes, the House of Moustapha the Tailor.

ALADDIN.   Well, I know where that is.

MAGICIAN.   You do! Could you tell me where it is?

ALADDIN.   Sure. The House of Moustapha the Tailor, huh? Let me see now. The House of Moustapha is over there. *(He points quickly in a circle, whirling about.)*

MAGICIAN.   Where?

ALADDIN.   Over there. *(same business.)*

MAGICIAN.   Where??

ALADDIN.   Over There! *(same business.)*

MAGICIAN.   Perhaps if I gave you a little reward *(Pico provides a coin)* you might take me to it.

MAGICIAN.   Silver. Real Silver. *(Moves the coin hypnotically)*

ALADDIN.   *(slightly entranced)* The House of Moustapha the Tailor is right there.

MAGICIAN.   *(returning coin to his hand through slight of hand)* Thank you very much.

ALADDIN.   *(comes to)* Hey! Moustapha's dead, though.

MAGICIAN.   No! Well, what about his son, Aladdin? Tell me where is his son, Aladdin?

ALADDIN.   I'll tell you where Aladdin is if you'll give me that piece of silver.

MAGICIAN.   All right. *(gives it to him)*

ALADDIN.   OK. Well, you stand there and don't turn around, and I'll get Aladdin. Wait until I tell you to turn around. *(Poses)* OK, you can turn around now. *(pause, Magician is confused.)* I'm Aladdin!

MAGICIAN.   Ha. ha. ha. How silly of me not to notice that you were Aladdin. You little brat, give me that coin and don't try to trick me! *(grabs Aladdin's ear and wrests coin from him.)*

ALADDIN.   But I am Aladdin. I'm not trying to trick you. I can prove it to you. Mama, hey, Mama!

MOTHER.   *(entering)* Aladdin, now you haven't . . .

MAGICIAN. *(hearing the name)* AAh! *(Throws coin to Aladdin)* Then you must be the widow of dear Moustapha! *(Aladdin tosses the coin up and catches it several times; finally Pico snares it and it simply disappears.)*

MOTHER. Yes.

MAGICIAN. Well, don't you recognize me?

MOTHER. No.

MAGICIAN. I am Moustapha's brother, your brother-in-law!

MOTHER. *(reaching out to him)* Brother!

MAGICIAN. Sister!

MOTHER. *(almost in his arms)* Wait a minute! My husband never had a brother. Come along, Aladdin.

MAGICIAN. Your husband never told you about his rich brother?

MOTHER. *(stopping)* rich?

MAGICIAN. *(nearly in tears)* Why, on his deathbed dear little Musty made me promise that I would give his son, Aladdin, a great opportunity.

MOTHER. For what?

MAGICIAN. For wealth such as mine. *(flashes ring)*

MOTHER. Brother?

MAGICIAN. Sister?

MOTHER. Brother?

MAGICIAN. Sister!

MOTHER. Oh, Brother?

MAGICIAN. Oh, Sister! *(they embrace)* We must have a great reunion feast. Take this purse! *(Pico provides it on the word)* Go into the town and buy us all kinds of tasty treats.

MOTHER. Oh, Brother!

MAGICIAN. Oh, Sister!

MOTHER. *(exiting)* Oh, Brother.

MAGICIAN. Aladdin. *(A complete change comes over him)*

ALADDIN. Uncle?

MAGICIAN. Are you ready to get your great wealth? Right now?

561

ALADDIN.   Great wealth?

MAGICIAN.   Great jewels?

ALADDIN.   *(becoming entranced)* Jewels?

MAGICIAN.   Riches?

ALADDIN.   Riches?

MAGICIAN.   Power?

ALADDIN.   Power.

MAGICIAN.   Happiness?

ALADDIN.   Happiness!

MAGICIAN.   Yes, they are all waiting for you at the Treasure Cave.

ALADDIN.   The Treasure Cave!·

MAGICIAN.   Are you ready for a great adventure at the Treasure Cave?

ALADDIN.   A great adventure!

MAGICIAN.   Well, then, let's go right now before your mother comes
back. To the Treasure Cave!

ALADDIN.   To the Treasure Cave! *(they exit to music.)*

*(Pico quickly changes the scene to the Cave. Two boxes are side-by-
side in one corner, with the smallest box opposite them, for the lamp
to be on. Pico then becomes, with the aid of a huge beak, the Guardian
Vulture of the Cave. The Magician and Aladdin enter from the aisle
blocked by the two boxes.)*

MAGICIAN.   Now come quickly, Aladdin, and get our money!

ALADDIN.   It's awfully dark, Uncle. Why don't we wait and come
back in the morning?

MAGICIAN.   No, Aladdin, it has to be done right now! Here's the Cave.

ALADDIN.   *That's the cave? (The Vulture awakes and menaces them)*

MAGICIAN.   The Guardian of the Gate! I forgot about him! The only
thing that will make him stop, and put him to sleep is the roaring
of tigers. Roar, Aladdin! *(they roar, to no avail.)* We're not loud
enough! Roar!!

ALADDIN.   Not loud enough? Help us? *(if they haven't already started)*
Roar! *(The Vulture is put to sleep by the roaring. Pico removes
the beak and retires.)* It worked! Thank you!

MAGICIAN. Thank you very much! Now Aladdin, open the door of the cave.

ALADDIN. The door! Where is the door?

MAGICIAN. Ha, ha, ha. Say your name.

ALADDIN. You know my name.

MAGICIAN. Say your name.

ALADDIN. Aladdin.

MAGICIAN. Say your whole name!

ALADDIN. Aladdin, son of Moustapha. *(Pico slides the two blocks apart to thunderous crashes of the cymbals.)*

MAGICIAN. It worked!

ALADDIN. Magic?

MAGICIAN. Of course. Now, Aladdin, into the cave!

ALADDIN. I don't know, Uncle. There might be all kinds of monsters in there. Why don't you go in first, and I'll follow you?

MAGICIAN. *(beginning to become impatient)* Anyone named Aladdin, son of Moustapha can enter this cave very safely.

ALADDIN. I think I'll just go home and ask my Mama.

MAGICIAN. No, no, no. Aladdin, I will give you this magic ring. *(ring music)* It will ward off all ghosts, monsters, and spooky things.

ALADDIN. You mean this magic ring will protect me?

MAGICIAN. It will protect you against anything. Now, into the Cave!

ALADDIN. OK, here goes. *(He crawls between the two blocks and under a very tight invisible barrier, barely squeezing into the cave.)*

MAGICIAN. Aladdin, are you in yet?

ALADDIN. I'm almost through, Uncle.

MAGICIAN. Aladdin, tell me what you see. *(In case the audience has become monsters, Aladdin wards them off with the ring; otherwise . . .)*

ALADDIN. Oh, Uncle, I see all kinds of jewels! Diamonds sparkling and shining over here! *(If Aladdin is specific enough, the audience will become jewels.)* Rubies and sapphires over here! And pearls! All kinds of jewels! We'll be rich! *(he picks them, and stuffs his pockets.)*

MAGICIAN. Aladdin. Aladdin?

ALADDIN.   Yes, Uncle?

MAGICIAN.   Will you do me a slight favor?

ALADDIN.   Sure, Uncle. What is it?

MAGICIAN.   In the far corner of the cave there should be an old tarnished lamp. *(On the word, Pico places it, and becomes a spider guarding it.)* Would you bring it to me?

ALADDIN.   What do you want with an old lamp, Uncle?

MAGICIAN.   Uh, it was a gift from your Father; it means a good deal to me.

ALADDIN.   OK, Uncle. Oh, I see the lamp. It's covered with spiders, and it's all dirty. *(Chases away the spiders with the ring).*

MAGICIAN.   Just get it, Aladdin. *(excited and impatient)*

ALADDIN.   All right, Uncle. *(a chime sounds when he touches it)* I have the lamp now — I'm coming out. I've got all kinds of jewels, too! We'll be rich! My mama will be so happy! *(Trying to squeeze out)*

MAGICIAN.   Just bring me the lamp.

ALADDIN.   I can't squeeze through Uncle, with all these jewels and this lamp on me. *(It is hanging around his neck by now, on a length of rope which is tied to it firmly).*

MAGICIAN.   Well, Aladdin, take out the jewels, and bring me the lamp.

ALADDIN.   Wait, Uncle! I've got an idea! I'll take off the lamp and come out with all the jewels!

MAGICIAN.   NO! Don't you dare take off that lamp! Hand it out to me!

ALADDIN.   But, Uncle, we can buy plenty of lamps!

MAGICIAN.   Stop calling me "Uncle" you pernicious little brat, and hand me out that lamp!

ALADDIN.   You're not my uncle?

MAGICIAN.   No, of course I'm not your uncle. Now hand me out that lamp!

ALADDIN.   Who are you?

MAGICIAN.   Never mind who I am. Are you going to hand out that lamp?

ALADDIN.   No, you can't have it.

MAGICIAN.   All right, Aladdin, then I will seal you in this cave forever! See how you like your jewels now! *(He seals the cave with a magic pass and a loud crash, and exits.)*

ALADDIN. You can't have this lamp! *(echoes — lamp, lamp, lamp, etc.)* *(Pause)* Mister? *(echoes)* OK Mister, you win. I'm coming out now. I'm taking off all the jewels and I'll bring out the lamp. Mister! *(echoes)* *(Squeezes through the door and finds it stuck)* Aladdin, son of Moustapha! *(nothing happens)* Help! *(echoes)* Help! *(Pause, he squeezes back into cave, near tears.)* I'm trapped. I'm cold and . . . Oh, what good are magic rings and . . . *(rubbing his hands, trying to keep warm, and in so doing rubs the ring.)*

RING GENIE. *(entering to music)* I am the Genie of the Ring!

ALADDIN. Don't hurt me!

RING GENIE. I serve the holder of the Ring, Master.

ALADDIN. The ring? What do you do?

RING GENIE. I can take you anywhere you want to go.

ALADDIN. You can take me anywhere? I want to go home.

RING GENIE. *(grabs Aladdin and whirls him, as Pico changes the set around them)* Home — Hooooooommmmmmeee! *(Ring Genie exits, and quickly changes back to the Mother)*

ALADDIN. Home! Look, my street, my house. I made it! I'm home! Mama, I'm home!

MOTHER. *(entering, and receiving rag from Pico)* Now where have you been? And you're all dirty! *(dusts him off)*

ALADDIN. Yes, but Mama, that man who said he was my uncle — he wasn't my uncle at all. He was a mean old man and he trapped me in a Treasure Cave. At first we couldn't get in — we had to kill all kinds of monsters and vultures — and I didn't know how to get in. I thought, "Say your name!" Aladdin, son of Moustapha! And then I could squeeze in, and inside Mama, you won't believe what I saw; Look, Mama, we have all kinds of jewels — we'll be rich! *(he, of course, has taken all the jewels off)*

MOTHER. Jewels!

ALADDIN. Diamonds and — oh no! I had to leave them in the cave!

MOTHER. Uh. uh. Aladdin, you are telling stories again.

ALADDIN. No, no, Mama.

MOTHER. When will you ever learn?

ALADDIN. Look, he made me take this old lamp instead of the jewels.

MOTHER. You stole a lamp?

ALADDIN. No. Mama!

MOTHER. Now I know where your Uncle is! He saw you steal this lamp and he realized you were a good for nothing, lazy boy, and now we'll have nothing — nothing. I'll try to polish it up, and then we'll have to find the owner. *(She polishes with the cloth; there is a cymbal crash and the Genie appears behind her.)*

ALADDIN. Who are you?

MOTHER. I'm your mother, who do you think . . .

LAMP GENIE. Who dares to call the Genie of the Lamp? *(Mother screams and faints)*

ALADDIN. (grabbing lamp) I called.

LAMP GENIE. Master, your wish is my command.

ALADDIN. You mean you can take me places, too?

LAMP GENIE. I can do *anything* for he who holds the lamp!

ALADDIN. Anything! All right, Genie of the Lamp, turn this old rag into a piece of golden cloth. *(Aladdin hands it to the Genie who whisks it behind his back, and, in a single motion, whips it back out again as a gold cloth, later used as a shawl by the Mother. Pico, of course, has made the switch.)* Oh, it's beautiful! Hey, Mama, look at this! Ma? Can you put my poor Mother to bed? *(Genie enchants her into rising and wafting off into the house. Aladdin drapes the cloth around her as she goes.)* It's amazing!

LAMP GENIE. I can do anything, Master. To summon me, you need but rub the lamp.

(A Trumpet sounds, and Pico enters, as a Herald from the Palace and waves to Aladdin to depart.)

ALADDIN. The Herald from the palace. What? Someone's coming? Who?

PICO. *(The Princess)*

ALADDIN. The Princess!

PICO. *(Cover your eyes. Go away.)*

ALADDIN. No one must see her. *Go inside. (Herald exits the way he came in.)* No one in the village has ever seen the Princess, but everyone in the palace talks of her great beauty. How I'd love to see her.

LAMP GENIE.   Master, you would like to see the Princess?

ALADDIN.   Oh, yes! Can you help me?

LAMP GENIE.   I can turn you invisible to the eyes of the Princess and her guard.

ALADDIN.   Invisible!

LAMP GENIE.   Then you will be able to see her without being seen. *(Gestures, invisible music)* To become visible again, you need but say your name.

ALADDIN.   Say my name. *(Cymbal, Genie goes.)*

(Herald enters, sees no one, and crosses the stage. The Princess follows sadly. She sings, and does an Oriental Dance.)

PRINCESS.   *(SONG)*
Why am I
So alone?
No one to share the nightingale's song.
Only dreams to comfort me.
No one sees,
No one hears,
No one to brush away my tears,
Only dreams to comfort me. *(end song)*

(sees a butterfly, made of her own hand.) A butterfly! Oh, how beautiful! *(it lands on her finger)* How beautiful it must be to be to be able to fly and — *(it has flown away)* Oh, No! Come back, please come . . . *(Aladdin catches it and brings it back to her)* Oh, yes, little butterfly. I won't hurt you. *(takes it back)* Oh, if only you could speak to me and tell me what it must be like to be . . . *(she breaks off, pause)*

ALADDIN.   Why are you so sad?

PRINCESS.   Oh, you can talk! Maybe you will be my friend?

ALADDIN.   Of course.

PRINCESS.   What is your name?

ALADDIN.   Aladdin. *(Invisible music repeats and she sees him. She starts to leave.)* No, wait! Don't run away from me. I won't hurt you. I'll be your friend. We can laugh together.

PRINCESS.   Laugh together?

ALADDIN.   Yes. You know — like . . . like this. *(He whirls her around till she laughs in spite of herself.)*

PRINCESS.   Who are you? I never met . . . *(pause)*

ALADDIN.   Oh. Well, I'm a great prince. Yes. I was captured by an evil genie . . .

PRINCESS.   You were?

ALADDIN.   And he turned me into a butterfly . . .

PRINCESS.   He did!

ALADDIN.   And you set me free.

PRINCESS.   I did! ! !

ALADDIN.   No.

PRINCESS.   I did not?

ALADDIN.   No. I'm just a poor boy who lives in this house. I just like to dream that I'm a great prince.

PRINCESS.   I like to dream that I'm poor, and no one tells me what to do . . .

ALADDIN.   You mean you dream, too?

PRINCESS.   All the time.

ALADDIN.   Hey, do you ever have any great adventures in your dreams?

PRINCESS.   Oh, yes! In my favorite dream, a huge dragon . . .

ALADDIN.   Yeah, with fire shooting out of his mouth . . .

PRINCESS.   Twenty feet tall . . .

ALADDIN.   and a long tail . . .

PRINCESS.   and scales . . .

ALADDIN.   Yes!

PRINCESS.   He captures me!

ALADDIN.   I'm always coming after you! *(they are enacting it by now)*

PRINCESS.   He carries me to the woods!

ALADDIN.   I have my sword. I'm chopping down trees and killing snakes.

PRINCESS.   Help! Save me!

ALADDIN.   I hear you screaming!

PRINCESS.   Help!

ALADDIN. I run and jump on top of the dragon's back . . .

(simultaneously)

ALADDIN. And I chop off his head! And I take you away!

PRINCESS. And you chop off his head! And you take me away!

TOGETHER. And we live happily . . . *(long pause as they gaze at each other.)*

(Herald enters, sees what is going on, and angrily snaps at Princess)

PRINCESS. Excuse me, I must go. *(turns back)* Goodbye — Aladdin. *(exits with Herald)*

ALADDIN. Goodbye! *(pause)* Mama, Mama!

MOTHER. (Enters, still somewhat dazed) I just had the strangeest dream.

ALADDIN. Mama, the greatest thing just happened! I think I'm going to be married!

MOTHER. Married! Oh, Son! You'll get a job . . .

ALADDIN. To the most beautiful girl.

MOTHER. Who is she, son? Who is she?

ALADDIN. The Princess!

MOTHER. Oh, no! *(cries)* Why must you make your poor mother suffer so?

ALADDIN. No, Mama. It's the truth. She was right here and I . . .You don't believe me, do you? *(Mother shakes her head and sobs)* Mama, where do you think we got this gold cloth? *(she still holds it.)* Don't you remember the Genie?

MOTHER. It wasn't a dream?

ALADDIN. No, it really happened, and I'm going to marry the Princess, I know it. Now you wait here and I'm going to the palace and ask her if she'll be my wife.

MOTHER. Wait, Aladdin! You can't go dressed like that. Oh, and you need a present.

ALADDIN. She doesn't want presents, Mama.

MOTHER. Her father needs the present.

ALADDIN. The Sultan!

MOTHER. Yes. *(He thinks a moment)*

ALADDIN. Flowers!

MOTHER. We don't have any flowers! *(The audience may suggest the Genie. If so he is called and tells them to do it themselves, he has more important problems to save his energy for.)*

ALADDIN. No, but we can get some. *(or "I know how we can get some without him.")* Just watch. Hey, will you help? *(Wait for an answer.)* I need all *different* kinds of flowers to give to the Sultan as a present. So use your whole bodies to grow into flowers, all different kinds of flowers. *(if they are slow starting, add)* Start out as a tiny seed in the ground and grow into all different kinds — kinds no one has ever seen before. Yes, Yes. *(if needed)* But these all look the same. I need something different. Yes, that's good. *(Aladdin should specifically point out a few of the most creative ones, as "This one's really different" or "There's nothing else in the world like this one." After he has a good start, the Mother can join in pointing out creative ones to him. This must be very quick, though, only singling out the best three or four.)* Now, everybody pick your flower and put it into your lap. *(gestures should help them to sit down, holding their flower.)* Now, give them to us when we come around. *(He and Mother collect the flowers.)* Thank you, thank you.

MOTHER. Thank you!

ALADDIN. I'm off to the Palace!

MOTHER. You can't go yourself, Son. I'll have to go for you.

ALADDIN. Why can't I go?

MOTHER. Because you have to send someone witty and charming who can impress the Sultan.

ALADDIN. All right, you go ahead of me and I'll meet you at the Palace.

MOTHER. *(exits putting on the gold shawl)* Wash your face, and put on that little sash I like so much.

ALADDIN. Yes, Mama. See you at the Palace. *(exits into the house as as she saunters out singing, "I'm going to see the Sultan!")*

(Trumpets. Pico changes the scene to the Throne Room — two boxes form the throne. Sultan enters.)

SULTAN. This palace is a mess! Why doesn't anyone ever clean it? *(He starts out by flicking dust away, and ends up down on his hands and knees scrubbing at a spot with his robe. The Princess enters, rushing right by him)*

570

PRINCESS. Papa, Oh Papa!

SULTAN. Princess! *(rising to greet her)*

PRINCESS. Oh, Papa! The most exciting thing has happened to me!

SULTAN. Something special?

PRINCESS. Oh yes! I was walking in the village and . . .

SULTAN. I can see that! You're all dirty. *(brushes her clothes)*

PRINCESS. But listen, Papa. I met this boy who had been turned into a butterfly and he killed a dragon for me and . . .

SULTAN. Princess, please! That's just another one of your stories!

PRINCESS. Oh, no, Papa! This is true!

SULTAN. Princess, now you know that none of your stories are true. Now please, I have visitors coming. You run along and I'll listen to your stories later. Dust yourself off and put that little thing in your hair that I like so much.

PRINCESS. *(deflated)* Yes, Papa. *(bows and exits)*

SULTAN. Visitors! Same old stuff! Do nothing but create more dirt!

(goes back to work on spot on floor. Mother enters and sees him.)

MOTHER. You there!

SULTAN. *(Not noticing her, muttering to self)* more dirt!

MOTHER. You there! *(Kicks him. He falls, then rises and starts swatting at her. She defends herself.)* What do you think you are doing, you puffball?

SULTAN. *(When he can finally speak)* What do you want?

MOTHER. I want to see the Sultan!

SULTAN. I am the Sultan.

MOTHER. *(Instantly contrite)* I have a gift for you.

SULTAN. A gift? What is it? More jewels? More gold?

MOTHER. Flowers.

SULTAN. Flowers? I have flowers.

MOTHER. But these are different.

SULTAN. (Impressed) These are different! I've never seen flowers like this before! They're beautiful! They must be special! I love things

571

that are different — special! You may have a reward. Anything you like.

MOTHER. Anything?

SULTAN. Anything.

MOTHER. Then let my son marry your daughter.

SULTAN. What?

MOTHER. Let my son marry the Princess. You said, "anything." Didn't you say, "anything?"

SULTAN. Who is your son?

MOTHER. Aladdin.

SULTAN. Well, why don't you go out and send him in to me?

MOTHER. Oh, he'll be right here. Don't go away. *(exits.)*

SULTAN. *(deeply concerned)* Aladdin? Hmm. Pretty ordinary name. I always wanted a special extraordinary husband for my daughter. Mmm. I have an idea. *(The Sultan is making up the test as he goes along.)*

ALADDIN. *(enters and bows)* Your Majesty!

SULTAN. Aladdin? Aladdin! Oh, Aladdin, I'm so happy, so happy, so very very sad!

ALADDIN. Why are you sad?

SULTAN. Oh, Aladdin, I promised a long time ago that anyone who wanted to marry my daughter had to be very special, and pass a very special test, a very special and very dangerous test!

ALADDIN. Well, give me a try!

SULTAN. You want to try? Uh, Well, er . . . the test is, the test is . . . you must find a dragon.

ALADDIN. Find a dragon?

SULTAN. And tame him.

ALADDIN. And tame . . . find a dragon and tame him?

SULTAN. Aladdin, if you love the Princess, I'm sure you'll find a way.

ALADDIN. Oh, I do love her!

SULTAN. Oh. Good, by the way, Aladdin, you have three minutes to tame the dragon. *(exits. In the original production we made no attempt to hide the fact that Burgundo has a rather fast change or*

two to make between the Genie and the Sultan. He did the changes
while running madly from one aisle to the other with Cordova
handing him his other robe and turban. The audience loved it. Of
course, he must differentiate completely between the two charac-
ters.)

ALADDIN.   Three minutes! What am I going to do? The Genie! Genie!

(rubs lamp, which he wears throughout around his neck)

LAMP GENIE. *(appearing)* Yes, young Master.

ALADDIN.   Can you help me? I have to tame a dragon in three minutes.

LAMP GENIE.   I can give you the dragon, young Master, but you must
tame him yourself.

ALADDIN.   But I don't know how to . . .

LAMP GENIE.   You must. *(making magic passes)* Here is your dragon.
Good luck. *(the Genie exits and Pico appears as the dragon, spit-*
ing fire) (perhaps a mask and a party blower painted red and
orange)

ALADDIN.   Nice dragon! Good dragon! *(Chase, finally, Aladdin gets*
the dragon dizzy and tickles him, which renders him gentle.) He's
ticklish! This dragon is ticklish! *(He "licks" Aladdin)* Hey! I tamed
a dragon!

SULTAN.   *(entering, not seeing dragon)* Oh, Aladdin, are you still here?
I'm sorry you couldn't find a DRAGON!!!

ALADDIN.   Oh, he won't hurt you. All you have to do is tickle him.

SULTAN.   Tickle him? This better not be a trick. *(He approaches the*
the dragon gingerly.) Nice dragon. *(He tickles the dragon, the*
dragon tickles him!) Oh no, stop! Oh, make him stop!

ALADDIN.   Down, boy!

SULTAN.   Nice dragon. Why don't you go in the yard and I'll send you
out some lunch? *(Dragon licks him and exits)*.

ALADDIN.   Now, your Majesty, I've tamed the dragon, and I can marry
the Princess, right?

SULTAN.   What? Oh, oh yes. You have tamed the dragon, and passed
the first part of the test. Now for the second part.

ALADDIN.   You didn't say anything about a second part!

SULTAN.   I didn't? Well, the second part of the test is a . . . er . . . palace. The Princess must have a palace to live in; and it must be a
very special and very very clean palace made out of something

very special and clean, such as . . . er . . . Light!

ALADDIN. Light?

SULTAN. Yes, light. You must build a palace of light.

ALADDIN. A palace of light? But, that's impossible!

SULTAN. *(exiting)* Oh, Aladdin, you have two minutes to build the palace of light.

ALADDIN. *(rubs)* Genie! Genie!

GENIE. *(appearing)* Yes, Master? Another dragon?

ALADDIN. No, no more dragons! I need to build a palace of light in two minutes.

LAMP GENIE. I can build the palace; but I must have help if it is to be done in two minutes.

ALADDIN. I'll help you!

LAMP GENIE. I need more help than that!

ALADDIN. *(if they haven't offered)* Will you help us? *(get a "yes")*

LAMP GENIE. Very well. First we must make bricks. So mix up mud, and water, and straw. *(Take time for the audience to feel the different textures of the three substances.)* Mix them well. Good. Now, everyone make a brick. Make all different kinds of bricks, different sizes, different shapes, no two should be the same. Do you have your bricks? *(get an answer)* Hold them over your heads. Good. Now throw them in the middle.

ALADDIN. Wait, Genie. These are great bricks, but they're just ordinary bricks. I have to build a palace of light!

LAMP GENIE. Then we must turn these bricks into light. Everyone, with your whole body, turn into your own special kind of light — your favorite kind of light — and shine onto the bricks. Be a special, different kind of light.

ALADDIN. It's working, it's working! *(picks up a brick)* I can even see through this one now.

LAMP GENIE. Now for the palace. Stand back! *(Gestures, cymbals)* And unto the hillside over there! *(He throws the palace out on the hillside)* Young Master, your Palace of Light! *(to audience)* Thank you, thank you. *(exits)*

ALADDIN. Thank you, Genie. Thank you, everybody!

SULTAN. *(entering)* Aladdin! Are you still here? I'm sorry, but your

574

two minutes are up! Good-bye! Good luck! Get out! *(sees Palace, screams)* What is that?

ALADDIN.   It's the Palace of Light you asked for.

SULTAN.   You built that?

ALADDIN.   With some help.

SULTAN.   You built a . . . Oh, ah, uh, ah, ee . . . *(Advances strangely on Aladdin)*

ALADDIN.   *(retreating)* Don't you like it? It's what you asked for. A Palace of Light for the Princess? I thought . . .

SULTAN.   *(embracing him)* I love it! It's beautiful! The only Palace of Light in the whole world! The only one! You wait here. I'll get the Princess! *(Starts out as she starts in)* Princess, oh Princess! I have found you a very special husband!

PRINCESS.   Papa, I can not marry him. I am in love with someone else. *(she doesn't see Aladdin, but he hears and is saddened.)*

SULTAN.   In love? Well never mind that! Here! I want you to meet . . .

PRINCESS.   *(seeing him)* Aladdin!

SULTAN.   Uh, yes. Aladdin, I want you to meet . . .

ALADDIN.   *(Perking up)* Princess!

PRINCESS.   But I thought . . .

TOGETHER.   You want to marry me?

SULTAN.   Let there be a wedding!

SULTAN.   A celebration! *(Music, They sing)*

SULTAN.   I give you . . .

MOTHER.   Take her hand.

SULTAN & MOTHER.   Please care for her/him.

PRINCESS.   I take you

ALADDIN.   I take you

ALADDIN & PRINCESS.   To be my own.

SULTAN & MOTHER.   May they find peace in love.

PRINCESS & ALADDIN.
    May we have joy of heart.
    Oh, may we never part.

SULTAN & MOTHER.   Oh, may they never part.

ALL FOUR.   Now let the new day start.
Now it's time to dance and sing
To celebrate this wedding day.
Come and join our song.

SULTAN & MOTHER.   Dance with me.

ALADDIN & PRINCESS.   Dance with me.

ALL FOUR.
Come and join our happy song
And live in Harmony.

ALADDIN & PRINCESS.
I take you
I take you
To be my own. *(end of song. All four exit, as the Magician comes sneaking in over the trunk.)*

MAGICIAN.   A wedding! How very touching! I don't know how that brat Aladdin escaped from that cave, but it doesn't matter! I will soon have that lamp *and* the Princess in my own possession. *(During this Pico has changed the set to the garden of the Palace of Light — one box is upside down in the center for a fountain, two are piled up in an aisle to make a tree.)* First, for the Palace of Light. Oh, here it is! *(Princess enters humming)* I'll just hide behind this tree, Shh! *(He watches for a few seconds as she plays with the fountain.)* This is my big chance! *(He bends over and disguises his voice)* Princess, Princess!

PRINCESS.   *(seeing him)* What is it?

MAGICIAN.   An urgent message from the Palace! The Sultan wishes to see Aladdin immediately!

PRINCESS.   What is wrong?

MAGICIAN.   I don't know, but he sounded terribly worried! *(He ducks behind tree as soon as she looks away)*

PRINCESS.   Aladdin! My Lord! There is a messenger here . . . my father . . . *(looks in vain for messenger)* You must go to the Palace immediately! I'm afraid something is wrong! *(he enters, without the lamp)*

ALADDIN.   You stay here, and I'll go at once.

PRINCESS.   Yes, hurry, hurry! *(He runs out)*

MAGICIAN.   Ha, ha! Now to get my lamp. All I need is my bag of tricks. *(Pico hands him the scarf trick.)* Magic! Magic! Magic,

magic, magic! *(appears from around the tree, this time as himself — a street magician.)*

PRINCESS. What are you doing here in the Palace Gardens?

MAGICIAN. I am the world's greatest magician. Wouldn't you like to see a trick? I pass my hand over the scarves once. I pass my hands over the scarf twice. I pass my hand over the scarf three times! *(It changes colors.)*

PRINCESS. *(thrilled)* Oh,, but that is wonderful! You are a good magician. Can you do anything else?

MAGICIAN. Of course. *(pretends to think)* I have it, for you I will perform my very best trick.

PRINCESS. Yes. Please.

MAGICIAN. For this trick I must have an old dirty lamp.

PRINCESS. Oh, my husband has such a lamp.

MAGICIAN. He does?

PRINCESS. But perhaps he would rather I didn't use his lamp.

MAGICIAN. But I can change it into a shiny new gold lamp! Won't that be a nice surprise for him?

PRINCESS. Yes, it will. I'll go and fetch it. *(exits into Palace of Light)*

MAGICIAN. Now watch how I fool her with this ordinary lamp. *(Pico hands him a shiny lamp, and strikes the scarf. He hides the new lamp up his sleeve.)*

PRINCESS. *(returning with the magic lamp)* Here it is. It's terribly old and . . .

MAGICIAN. Yes, it's terribly ugly, isn't it.

PRINCESS. You can really change it into gold?

MAGICIAN. Of course. *(He takes the lamp. If the audience shouts for her not to give it up, he "hypnotizes" her as he did Aladdin with the coin.)* Now watch this. One, abracadabra. Two, abacadara. My stars! Look at that! *(Points at sky, and switches lamps when she looks up)* Three, abracadabra! *(He shows the gold lamp!)*

PRINCESS. That is wonderful! You must have a reward. I'll be right back! *(she exits with the new lamp)*

MAGICIAN. At last I have the lamp! Now to get the Genie! *(rubs the lamp)*

LAMP GENIE. *(appearing)* Yes, Young . . . You are not my Young Master.

MAGICIAN. Surprised? You are . . .

LAMP GENIE. The Genie of the Lamp.

MAGICIAN. And you can . . .

GENIE. Do the bidding of he who holds the lamp. *(Magician waves the lamp)*

MAGICIAN. Well, my first bidding is that you dance a victory dance in my honor.

LAMP GENIE. Dance! But it is undignified for Genies to dance!

MAGICIAN. *(rubbing lamp)* Dance, and be happy about it!
(Music, they sing and dance:)
Who's the cleverest man in the land?
Me!

LAMP GENIE. You?

MAGICIAN. Me!
Who has Genies eating out of his hand?

LAMP GENIE. You?

MAGICIAN. Me.

LAMP GENIE. You.

MAGICIAN.
I've tricked and plotted everywhere
To find this lamp divine.
And now I have it you will see,
The whole world shall be mine!
Mine! Mine! Mine!
Mine! Mine! Mine! Mine! Mine!
Palace, Princess, riches, too.
You will see!
All of these will soon belong to
Me! Me! Me! *(end of song)*
All right now, Genie, I want you to take the Princess, and this Palace of Light, and everything in it — including me — to Africa!

LAMP GENIE. *(As they whirl around)* To AFRICAAAAAAAAAAA!
(Pico sweeps the set off, leaving a bare stage)

ALADDIN *(entering with the Sultan, or just ahead of him)* Oh Father, the Princess will be happy to find out that you're all right, and that it was nothing but a mistake.

ALADDIN

SULTAN. Well I'm happy, too. Especially since this is the first time I've been to your Palace of Light and I haven't tripped over the fountain . . . *(doubletake)*

ALADDIN. The fountain?

SULTAN. It's gone! You didn't tell me . . .

ALADDIN. But it's always been right here by the . . . the tree!

SULTAN. It's gone!

ALADDIN. The Palace!

SULTAN. It's gone, too!

ALADDIN. Princess!

SULTAN. She's gone! Aladdin, where are they? Where are they? I want them back! Aladdin, I'll give you till nightfall to have the Princess back or I'll chop off your head! *(exits)*

ALADDIN. I'll get them back! The lamp! The magic lamp! Oh, no, it's in the Palace! *(thinks furiously; the audience may tell him his next line.)* The Ring! The Genie of the Ring! *(rubs ring)* Genie of the Ring!

RING GENIE. *(entering)* I am the Genie of the Ring!

ALADDIN. Genie of the Ring, please bring back my Palace of Light, and the Princess!

RING GENIE. I can not do that.

ALADDIN. You can't do it?

RING GENIE. It is beyond my powers! I *can* take you there, if you wish?

ALADDIN. Quick, take me there!

RING GENIE. Where is it?

ALADDIN. You don't know where it is?

RING GENIE. No.

ALADDIN. Oh, where did they go? *(Usually the audience has told long long before this. One time they didn't remember at all, though, so the Ring Genie had to make a telepathic call to the Lamp Genie to get the location.)*

RING GENIE and ALADDIN. *(as they whirl off, and Pico returns the set of the Palace of Light)* AFRICAAAAA!

MAGICIAN. *(entering, primping himself)* The Princess will be here soon. I must look my best.

PRINCESS. *(entering, she has just come from getting the reward she promised the magician.)* Here is your rew . . . Where am I?

MAGICIAN. Africa.

PRINCESS. *(Sees his grimace and screams)* Who are you?

MAGICIAN. I am your new husband!

PRINCESS. But I don't want a new husband. I already have a husband — Aladdin.

MAGICIAN. How can you speak of that little brat when you have before you the greatest magician that has ever lived?

PRINCESS. But I love Aladdin. (crying) He is the only one who could ever make me laugh.

MAGICIAN. Posh! I can make you laugh harder than Aladdin ever could! Watch this! *(he makes a face, she cries louder.)*

PRINCESS. I want to go home.

MAGICIAN. Hmm, that always used to make me laugh. I know, I know! This will make you laugh. Watch that. *(does his frog imitation)* Knee-deep, knee deep! *(squatting and jumping)*

PRINCESS. Oh, you look like an old frog! *(Kicks him over and hides behind tree.)* I'll never marry you!

MAGICIAN. Yes, you will, my sweetie! *(dusting self off)* You will marry me because . . . because, er, because Aladdin is dead. *(laughs)*

PRINCESS. *(runs from tree and pummels him with her fists)* Dead! Oh, you killed him, you mean old man! I hate you! I hate you! *(he throws her down)*

MAGICIAN. Now, I want you to be calm and composed and ready to marry me by the time I come back! *(exits)*

ALADDIN. *(whirling in)* Africaaa! The palace of light! The tree *(sees Princess weeping, she thinks at first it is the Magician returning)* Princess!

PRINCESS. *(Springing at him)* No! I won't marry you! I told you . . .

ALADDIN. Princess!

PRINCESS. *(seeing him)* Oh; Aladdin; *(embrace)* There's a magician. He wants me to marry him. He said you were dead. *(nearly hysterical.)* He . . .

ALADDIN. *(calming her)* Where's my lamp? My magic lamp?

PRINCESS. Magic? I didn't know! He is wearing it — around his neck.

ALADDIN. We've got to get it back!

MAGICIAN. *(offstage)* Princess!

ALADDIN. He's coming! I'll hide behind the tree. Make him take off the lamp! *(hiding)*

PRINCESS. But I don't . . .

ALADDIN. Get the lamp!

MAGICIAN. *(enters, and Aladdin ducks out of sight)* Well, are you ready to marry me?

PRINCESS. Yes, I am.

MAGICIAN. You are?

PRINCESS. Yes, I have changed my mind.

MAGICIAN. You have?

PRINCESS. I would like to marry you.

MAGICIAN. You would? *(reaching to embrace her)*

PRINCESS. On one condition. *(ducks away)*

MAGICIAN. Grrr! What?

PRINCESS. Well, I've always dreamed that my husband would be handsome and brave and kill dragons for me.

MAGICIAN. You've got him!

PRINCESS. You could kill a dragon?

MAGICIAN. Naturally.

PRINCESS. Oh, show me! Show me how you would look!

MAGICIAN. All right. Watch this. This is how I would look if I were slaying a dragon. *(strikes pose)*

PRINCESS. Oh, that's good.

MAGICIAN. Isn't that beautiful?

PRINCESS. Oh yes, but it would be even more beautiful if your arms were higher.

MAGICIAN. *(obliging her whims)* Like this?

PRINCESS.   Oh, yes! *(becomes more enthusiastic with every change)* Now lift your foot to kick him in the stomach. That's right! And bend forward at the waist. And hold your head back. And your other arm out. And . . . Yes! Yes! Oh, Yes!!

MAGICIAN.   Am I beautiful?!

PRINCESS.   *(deflated)* Oh, no!!

MAGICIAN.   What's wrong?

PRINCESS.   That ugly old lamp is hanging there. It spoils the whole effect.

MAGICIAN.   It does?

MAGICIAN.   Then get it off me! Quickly, I must look beautiful!!

PRINCESS.   Yes, Yes, I must take it off! *(does so)* Oh, yes, that's it!!!

MAGICIAN.   Am I beautiful now?

PRINCESS.   Oh, yes! *(pretends to see something offstage)* Oh, no! Look at that!

MAGICIAN.   Where?

ALADDIN.   *(coming out)* Princess! *(she throws him the lamp. The Magician charges Aladdin before he can use it. Aladdin tosses the lamp to the Princess and there is a short game of "keep-away". Suddenly the Magician grabs his sword [from Pico]. The Princess ends up with the lamp, as Aladdin is forced to grab a sword from the same source.)*

MAGICIAN.   *(threatening with sword)* All right, Aladdin. I'll take care of you.

(They fight a very stylized duel, after the manner of the Peking Opera, where neither sword touches the opponent's. All blows are accompanied by the drum beats of the "orchestra" — Pico and Cordova. Finally, Aladdin "chops" the Magician's head off.)

MAGICIAN.   I'm deeeeeaaaaaaad! *(He runs off screaming, removes his robe quickly, and joins Pico in the orchestra for the finale.)*

ALADDIN.   He's dead!

PRINCESS.   You've saved us!

ALADDIN.   Quick, rub the lamp! *Call the Genie (she rubs and the Genie comes)*

LAMP GENIE.   Yes, Young Master — you're back!

ALADDIN. *(as the Princess tosses him the lamp)* Yes! Genie, please take us home!

LAMP GENIE.   Anything for you, Young Master! Hoooooooome!

ALADDIN & PRINCESS.   *(whirling about until the Genie has changed to the Sultan)* Hooooome! We're back, we're safe, etc.

(Sultan and Mother enter)

ALADDIN.   Mama, mama.

MOTHER.   Son!

PRINCESS.   Papa, oh, Papa!

SULTAN.   Princess! *(Cymbals, wedding music, and they sing:)*

ALL FOUR.
    Now it's time to dance and sing
    To celebrate this victory!
    Come and join our song,

SULTAN & MOTHER.   Dance with me.

ALADDIN & PRINCESS.   Dance with me.

ALL FOUR.
    Come and join our happy song
    And live in Harmony. *(end of song, all freeze except Domino)*

DOMINO.
    We've learned through song and dance and tricks
    That work and play can sometimes mix.
    Our Dad is glad *(Burgundo smiles and waves)*; our ending's happy!
    We'll pack up now . . .

CORDOVA.   *(as they all unfreeze)* And make it snappy! *(all remove costume pieces of Aladdin characters)*

DOMINO.
    But before we go to other lands.
    We'll take a bow. You clap your hands!

(They all bow, pick up pieces of the scenery, and exit.)

ALL.   Thank you! Good bye!

THE END

583

STEP ON A CRACK

by

Suzan Zeder

STEP ON A CRACK

by

SUZAN ZEDER

Copyright, 1976 by
Anchorage Press
P.O. Box 8067
New Orleans, Louisiana 70182

STEP ON A CRACK

One of the many trends in modern literature is manifested in what are called "today" plays, plays that present everyday, real characters confronted with contemporary problems. These plays are, by definition, different from fantasy and folk plays, but so too are they different from the realistic plays of the past. *The Little Princess*, for example ostensibly presents a life-like little girl in a realistic setting. But Sara Crewe is no more like a child of that time than Reynard is like a real fox in a real forest. Sara is the product of a romanticized view of children and childhood, and the realism of her world serves only to underscore the one-dimensional nature of her character.

Two similar plays from later years, *The Ghost of Mr. Penny* (1939) and Chorpenning's *Radio Rescue* (1938), come closer to depicting lifelike children, but no closer to depicting the problems they might face. These plays are adventure stories wherein the children become involved in a series of complications. The characters appear more life-like, primarily because they are shown in *action*, as compared to Sara Crewe, who is depicted as the passive victim of an exaggerated villain.

All three of these plays feature characters who are orphans, and, although the resolutions of each story include finding a home for the children, the hopes, fears, and insecurities that might be a part of such situations are dealt with only superficially. The conflicts of the plays are impersonal; the stories are sentimental.

A comparison of these plays with modern works like *Step on a Crack* clearly reveals how much the literature has changed over the years. The characters in *Step on a Crack* are life-like, the story is timely, the setting is contemporary, and the play is simultaneously serious, humorous, and provocative. This play has little hint of the sentimentality of the past, because the protagonist, Ellie Murphy, has a very real, and a very personal, problem.

The play begins with Ellie chanting a variation of a popular children's rhyme:

> Step on a crack . . . break your mother's back.
>
> Step on a crack . . . break your mother's back.
>
> Step on a crack . . . break your *stepmother's* back.

This rhyme both introduces the basic conflict of the story and sets the stage for the playful spirit and truthfulness that characterize the world of the play.

According to Voice (Ellie's alter-ego), "Ellie Murphy used to be a perfectly good little girl" — that is, until her life changed when her widowed father remarried, and Ellie was confronted with a stepmother. In the play Ellie sees Lucille, her stepmother, as a threat to her own relationship with her father, and retreats into a comforting fantasy world to ease her fear and self-doubt. Max, Ellie's father, wants only to avoid the problem, and refuses to deal directly with Ellie about her misgivings. Lucille, on the other hand, exacerbates the problem by trying to talk with Ellie openly and honestly.

All of this action causes Ellie to become more involved with her zany, fantasy companions, Lana (an aspiring movie actress) and Frizbee (a clown-like friend). Together they play out a series of hilarious situations that comment upon Ellie's real-world life. In one vignette, Ellie sees herself as the abused "Cinderelli" — a characterization that is given full support by her imaginary friends. The climax of this fantasy life comes when Ellie directs her own funeral, "where everybody is real sorry for all the mean things they ever did to you." It is a comical routine that conveys a truthful image of the insecurities of a young girl.

As Ellie becomes more unhappy she attempts to run away. When this does not work out, she returns home, where she overhears a conversation between Lucille and Max that convinces her she is loved. But the resolution to this conflict comes only after Ellie is able to discard her fantasy life and face her problems directly.

It is a serious story, built around a theme that is particularly relevant to the modern generation of children, many of whom are in single-parent families. Although the subject is sentimental, Zeder does not let the play become mired in sentimentality: the fantasy scenes are played for humor rather than pathos, and Ellie's attempts to maintain her relationship with her father are charming and truthful.

Ellie Murphy is one of the most well-developed and believable child characters in all of the literature. Unlike the cherubic Sara Crewe, Ellie is insecure and obnoxious, angry and loveable. She is not a rogue hero, but she is sometimes a brat. Through this behavior she shows us a confused, young girl, struggling to adjust to a major life change. Ellie is not confronted with trials of the same magnitude as Anatou, but neither is she given super-human qualities to combat them. The problems she faces are true-to-life, and Ellie responds to them in a consistent and truthful manner.

Max and Lucille, though less well-developed than Ellie, provide a realistic context within which the problem is played out. It is clear from the beginning of the play that it is not just Ellie's problem; Zeder is successful in portraying three different relationships among the main characters and in showing how each of them has some responsibility in the complications that develop. Max has his own insecurities that cause him to be of little comfort to Ellie. His answer to the problem is for the family to go bowling or out for ice cream. Lucille pictured as sincere but somewhat timid in her new role, and, because she wants to confront the problem directly, she becomes frustrated with both Ellie and Max.

Audiences empathize with Ellie, but they also sympathize with Lucille as she tries to open a line of communication with her new daughter. At the climactic moment when Ellie finally tells the Voice to shut up, audiences are moved to cheer for both Ellie and Lucille. Max, on the other hand, garners little audience interest, and less sympathy.

Step on a Crack is about stepmothers and stepdaughters, but, more importantly, it is about Ellie, Max, and Lucille. Ellie learns to deal with her problems directly; in the process, we are given an insightful portrait of the interaction of a contemporary family.

Although the situations in the story are true-to-life, the play is not presented in a realistic manner. The scenes shift rapidly back and forth from the real world to a fantasy world, from an objective view of the situation to a view of the world as seen from Ellie's perspective. Characters move freely from one world to another, as even Max and Lucille become a part of Ellie's fantasies. It is a playful structure that adds a dimension to the typical exposition-complication-denouement form. The images of a child — the messy room, the knock-knock jokes, the imaginary friends, and the dress-up games — pervade both worlds and add to the truthful depiction of Ellie's situation.

Step on a Crack has no great ramifications beyond the sensitive portrait of a troubled young girl; but in considering the development of the literature such a portrait is very significant. Ellie Murphy is a very real child, with good and bad qualities, who is able to make decisions for herself. The success of the work hinges on the sincerity and truth of the images of Ellie and her world. While fairy tale characters such as Snow White and Cinderella — and even some realistic characters like Sara Crewe and Anatou — are essentially one-dimensional figures that are used in service to a larger story, the characterization of Ellie Murphy *is* the story of *Step on a Crack*.

Traditionally, folk tales and children's literature have portrayed the stepmother as a selfish and evil character, who inflicts pain on her stepchildren. Zeder alters this Cinderella perspective and invests the stepmother with the same sensitivity and vulnerability as she gives the stepchild. It is interesting to note, however, that as this work ages, and as more plays and stories deal with the subjects presented herein, the caring but inept parent and the gentle stepparent have themselves become stereotyped characters.

More than any other play in the repertoire, *Step on a Crack* epitomizes the "today" play, and this form has proven to be very successful. Since the premiere of *Step on a Crack* in 1974, it has received over 300 productions nationwide. Audiences have been charmed by the characters, moved by the story, and entertained by the eclectic style.

SUZAN ZEDER grew up in Greenwich, Connecticut and attended Trinity University in San Antonio, Texas (B.A. 1969), Southern Methodist University in Dallas, Texas (M.F.A. 1972), and Florida State University in Tallahassee, Florida (Ph.D. 1978). Zeder has worked as the Director of the Developmental Drama Program at Florida State University and Director of the Child Drama Program at the University of Washington. Her published plays include *Step on a Crack, Wiley and the Hairy Man,* and *Ozma of Oz: A Tale of Time, The Play Called Noah's Flood.*

Zeder has been the recipient of many fellowships and awards including a Fulbright-Hayes Scholarship to England (1972–1973) and the first Children's Theatre Foundation Playwriting Grant (1980). In 1978 she was awarded the Chorpenning Award presented by the Children's Theatre Association of America for outstanding work in writing plays for young people.

Zeder is currently working on several plays including "Doors," which was commissioned by A Contemporary Theatre in Seattle, Washington, and *Mother Hicks.*

FOREWORD

I offer this play to you with a profound respect for the compelxity of childhood. As a writer, I have tried to confront the child within myself as honestly as possible in order to bring you a child of this moment. A funny, crazy, wildly imaginative child who arms herself with a full-blown fantasy life to fight her way through real life problems. Ellie's difficulty adjusting to her new stepmother is as classic as Cinderella and as timely as tomorrow.

I have been deeply gratified by audience reaction to this play. I remember one day after a matinee performance a child and a young woman sat quietly together in the empty lobby of the theatre. After a few moments the child turned to the woman and said, "That could have been about us." "Yes," the woman replied, "Do you want to talk about it?" The child thought for a moment and finally said, "Okay. Let's go home!"

Perhaps I might offer a bit of advice to potential producers and directors of this play. If a child actress with sufficient maturity, skill, and depth can be found, by all means cast her. But do not let this be a limitation. I have seen this play work equally well with a young adult in this role. Perhaps you might consider a college student with a bit of training behind her. I have even seen an impressive performance by a high school student.

If an adult actress is used I would urge her to spend some time with children; to notice how they move; to listen to the patterns of their laughter; to watch them closely in the whirlwind of temper tantrums, in joyous flights of fantasy, and in quiet moments of frustration and despair. All of these things are part of Ellie. It is my sincere wish that Ellie be played as a real child and not as an adult comment on childhood.

Above all, please have fun with this script . . . I have!

— *Suzan Zeder*

Characters

ELLIE MURPHY: A ten year old girl.

MAX MURPHY: Her father, about thirty-seven.

LUCILLE MURPHY: Her stepmother, about thirty-five.

LANA: Ellie's imaginary friend.

FRIZBEE: An imaginary friend.

VOICE: Ellie's alter-ego.

SETTING

Ellie's house

A bowling alley

The streets

TIME

The Present

The premiere production of STEP ON A CRACK, was presented on March 14, 1974, at Southern Methodist University, Dallas, Texas, with the following cast:

ELLIE .... Martha LaFollette

LUCILLE .... Mary Jo Lutticken

MAX .... Ron DeLucia

LANA .... Jackie Ezzell

FRIZBEE .... John Rainone

VOICE .... Jennifer Glenn

The production was directed by Susan Pearson.

Set Design by .... John Tillotson

Costume Design by .... Nina Vail

Faculty Advisor .... Charley Helfert

The cover graphic is the set as designed for STEP ON A CRACK by John Tillotson

STEP ON A CRACK

by

SUZAN ZEDER

The main playing space consists of two areas: ELLIE's bedroom and a living room. A free standing door separates the two areas. The set should be little more than a brightly colored framework. Each space has a ladder which is hung with the various costumes and props used throughout the play.

ELLIE's room is the larger of the two spaces. It is outlandishly decorated with old pieces of junk, flags, banners, old clothes etc. which have been rescued by ELLIE from her father's junk yard. The room is a mess, strewn with piles of clothes and junk. Up center is a larger box marked 'TOYZ'. At the far side of the room there is a stool surrounded by a simple frame. This frame indicates a mirror. This is VOICE's area. VOICE never moves from this spot until the very end of the play. It would be helpful to have a microphone and P.A. speaker system here. VOICE will make all of the sound effects during the play.

The living room, MAX and LUCILLE's space, is conspicuously neat. A coffee table and a few chairs indicate this area.

At Rise: ELLIE, MAX, LUCILLE and VOICE are onstage. MAX holds one end of a jumprope, the other end is tied to the set. VOICE sits on the stool. LUCILLE sits in the living room area. ELLIE jumps as MAX turns the rope for her. She jumps for a few seconds to establish a rhythm.

MAX: Cinderella . . . Dressed in yeller . . . Went downtown to meet her feller. Cinderella . . . Dressed in yeller . . . Went downtown to meet her feller. *[MAX continues to chant and ELLIE to jump as LUCILLE speaks.]*

LUCILLE: Grace, Grace . . . dressed in lace . . . Went upstairs to wash her face. Grace, Grace . . . Dressed in lace . . . Went upstairs to wash her face.

VOICE: *[Joins in]* Step on a Crack . . . Break your Mother's back. Step on a crack . . . Break your Mother's back. Step on a Crack . . . Break your Mother's back! *[ELLIE jumps out of the rope and hops four times firmly.]*

ELLIE: CRACK! CRACK! CRACK! CRACK! Step on a crack, break your STEPmother's back!

VOICE: Red Light! *[All freeze.]*

593

VOICE: Ellie Murphy used to be a perfectly good little girl. Green Light! *[All come to life for a second.* MAX *and* ELLIE *take a few steps toward each other.]*

VOICE: Red Light! *[All freeze.]*

VOICE: Her mom died when Ellie was just four years old, and everybody felt so sorry for her. They said "Oh you poor little girl." And they brought her extra helpings of cake and lots of presents. Ellie lived with her Pop, Max Murphy, boss of Murphy's Wrecking and Salvage Company. Green Light! *[During the next few lines* MAX *and* ELLIE *play a game of*

ELLIE: Not it!

MAX: Knock, knock . . .

ELLIE: Who's there?

MAX: Banana.

ELLIE: Banana who?

MAX: Knock, knock . . .

ELLIE: Who's there?

MAX: Banana.

ELLIE: Banana who?

MAX: Knock, knock . . .

ELLIE: Who's there?

MAX: Orange.

ELLIE: Orange who?

MAX: Orange you glad I didn't say banana?

VOICE: Red Light! *[All freeze.]*

VOICE: They played tag and went bowling; they ate T.V. dinners and practiced baseball for six years and they were very happy. Green Light! *[*ELLIE *and* MAX *mime practicing baseball]*

MAX: Listen Midget, if I told you once I told you a million times, you gotta keep your eye on the ball. *[He throws an imaginary baseball,* ELLIE *hits it and* MAX *follows the ball with his eyes and sees* LUCILLE.*]*

MAX: Fantastic!

VOICE: Red Light! *[All freeze.]*

VOICE: About two months ago Ellie went to camp and Pop met a pretty lady who taught music. Green Light! *[*ELLIE *and* MAX *hug goodbye.* ELLIE *moves up her ladder and scratches her bottom, she mimes writing.]*

ELLIE: Dear Pop, Today we went camping in the woods and guess where I got poison ivy? *[*MAX *moves over to* LUCILLE.*]*

MAX: *[shyly]* Hi, my name is Max, Max Murphy.

LUCILLE: Pleased to meet you Max, I'm Lucille.

VOICE: Red Light! *[All freeze.]*

VOICE: And Pop liked Lucille and Lucille liked Pop. Green Light! *[Ellie puts a blindfold over her eyes]*

ELLIE: Dear Pop, I can't go swimming today cause I got pink eye.

VOICE: Ellie came back from camp and everything in her whole life was different. *[*ELLIE, MAX *and* LUCILLE *play blind man's bluff.]*

ELLIE: 5, 4, 3, 2, 1 . . . Ready or not here I come.

MAX: We're over here.

ELLIE: Where? Am I getting warmer?

MAX: Naw, you're a mile off.

ELLIE: Am I getting warmer?

VOICE: Red Light! *[All freeze.]*

VOICE: Pop and Lucille got married. Green Light! *[*MAX *and* LU- CILLE *move into wedding positions. They mime an exchange of rings and kiss.]*

ELLIE: I said am I getting warmer? Hey Pop where did you . . . *[*ELLIE *takes off the blindfold and sees them kissing. She claps her hand over her eyes and giggles.]*

VOICE: Red Light! *[All freeze.]*

VOICE: Everything was different. Lucille cooked well balanced meals with vegetables. She kept the house neat and sewed buttons on all Ellie's clothing. Pop liked Lucille a lot, he wanted Ellie to like her too but somewhere deep inside Ellie's head this little voice kept saying . . . Look how pretty she is . . .

ELLIE: Look how pretty she is.

VOICE: Look how neat she is . . .

ELLIE: Look how neat she is.

VOICE: Pop likes her much better than he likes you.

ELLIE: No!

VOICE: Oh yes he does! *[Ellie turns away.]*

VOICE: Ellie Murphy used to be a perfectly good little girl. Green Light! *[MAX exits. ELLIE moves into her room and picks up a Whammo paddleball. LUCILLE moves into the living room area and sets up a music stand and practices singing scales. She has a beautiful voice.]*

ELLIE: *[Hitting the paddle-ball]* 235, 236, 237, 238, 239, 240, 241, 242, 243, 244, 245, 246 . . . *[ELLIE misses, sighs, and starts again.]*

ELLIE: 1,2,3,4,5,6,7,8,9,10,11,12,13,14 . . . *[ELLIE misses, sighs, and starts again.]*

ELLIE: 1, 2, 3, 4, 5, 6, 7, 8, 9, 10, 11 . . . *[ELLIE misses.]*

ELLIE: I'll never make 300! 1, 2, 3, 4, 5, 6 . . . *[ELLIE misses. She crosses to the mirror. VOICE mimes her gestures.]*

ELLIE: If I could make 300 I'd be famous. I'd be the world's champion. I'd be rich and famous and everyone in the whole world would come up to me and . . . How de do? Yes, it was very difficult, but I just kept practicing and practicing. No, it wasn't easy. *[LUCILLE sings louder.]*

VOICE: Considering all the racket SHE was making.

ELLIE: Considering all the racket SHE was making.

VOICE: How could anyone expect to concentrate with all that toot toot de doot?

ELLIE: How could anyone expect to concentrate with all that toot toot de doot.

VOICE: What does she think this is Grand Opree or something?

[ELLIE clutches her throat and mimics LUCILLE, she warbles off-key.]

ELLIE: Laaaaa . . . Laaaaaaa, Laaaaaaa, Laaaaaaa *[LUCILLE hears her and stops.]*

LUCILLE: Ellinor? Did you call me?

ELLIE: No. *[LUCILLE resumes the scales. ELLIE gets an idea. She crosses to the toy box and pulls out a weird assortment of junk; a couple of old hats, a black cloak, a deflated inner tube, silver shoes, and a set of Dracula fangs. ELLIE dresses herself and*

596

makes a couple of menacing passes at the mirror. VOICE *mimics her action.* ELLIE *sneaks out of the room and up behind* LUCILLE.]

ELLIE: I am Count Dracula and I have come to suck your blood!

LUCILLE: *[Startled]* Oh my!

ELLIE: Did I scare you?

LUCILLE: You startled me.

ELLIE: What are you doing anyway?

LUCILLE: I am just running through a few scales.

ELLIE: Do you have to?

LUCILLE: Well, yes. The voice is just like any other instrument, you have to practice every day.

ELLIE: You call that MUSIC? All that toot toot de doot?

LUCILLE: Well, scales aren't exactly music but . . .

ELLIE: *[Singing very off-key.]* "Everybody was Kung Fu Fighting." Uh . . . uh . . . uh . . . uh . . . hu!**

LUCILLE: Well, ummm that's very nice but . . .

ELLIE: *[Lying on her back with feet in the air.]* "I've got tears in my ears from lying on my back crying out my eyes over you."**

LUCILLE: Ellinor, what in the world are you wearing?

ELLIE: Pretty neat huh? I got this stuff from Pop, it's from the yard. He said I could keep it. You should go down there, he's got some great stuff.

LUCILLE: Oh Ellinor, you have such a nice room and so many lovely toys. Why do you keep bringing home all this junk?

ELLIE: This isn't junk! It's perfectly good stuff!

LUCILLE: But people have thrown it away.

ELLIE: That doesn't mean it isn't any good! How would you like to be thrown away?

LUCILLE: When I was your age I had a collection of dolls from all over the world. I used to make clothes for them and make up stories about them. You know I still have those dolls. I gave them

---

**These songs should be constantly changed to songs that are currently popular.

to my brother for his children, maybe I could write to him and we could . . .

ELLIE: Dolls! Ugghhh! I like this stuff better. Besides most of it isn't mine. Most of this belongs to Lana and Frizbee.

LUCILLE: Oh?

ELLIE: This tire is for Frizbee's motorcycle and these hats and beautiful shoes are for Lana. She's a movie star and she needs these things in her work.

LUCILLE: I thought you told me she was a Roller Derby Queen.

ELLIE: She's both! Oh, the Dracula fangs . . . they're mine.

LUCILLE: Just put them away when you are through. Have you finished cleaning up your room yet?

ELLIE: Ohhh I have been busy.

LUCILLE: You promised to do it before your father came home.

ELLIE: Pop doesn't care. He never used to make me clean up my room.

LUCILLE: Look, why don't I give you a hand. Together we can do it in no time.

ELLIE: No way! You'll just make me throw stuff out. [ELLIE *walks back to her room and stands in her doorway.*]

ELLIE: Nobody gets in my room without a pass! [*She slams the door.* LUCILLE *sighs and turns back to her music.*]

VOICE: Red Light! [*All freeze.*]

VOICE: She doesn't like you. [ELLIE *is drawn to the mirror.*]

ELLIE *and* VOICE: Pick up your room you messy little girl. Why don't you play with dolls like normal children? You're freaky and you like junk. You could have such a lovely room if it wasn't such a mess.

VOICE: She could never like a messy little girl like you. Green Light! [LUCILLE *resumes her scales.* ELLIE *listens for a second and begins to mimic her.* ELLIE *leaps to the top of the toy box and warbles in a high squeaky voice.* FRIZBEE *pops up from under a pile of dirty clothes.*]

FRIZBEE: Bravo! Bravo! What a beautiful voice you have! You sing like an angel! You sing like a bird, only better. I kiss your hand. May I have your autograph?

ELLIE: Why certainly young man! [ELLIE *scribbles on his back*]

ELLIE: "To Frizbee from Ellie, the world's greatest opera singer."

FRIZBEE: I will treasure this forever. Here this is for you! *[FRIZBEE pulls a flower from nowhere and presents it to ELLIE.]*

LANA: *[Her voice comes from the toy box.]* Everybody out of my way. *[ELLIE jumps off the box, the lid flies open and LANA pops out.]*

LANA: Ellie Murphy, the great opera singer, do you have anything to say to our viewers at home?

ELLIE: How de do.

LANA: How did you get to be such a great opera singer?

ELLIE: Oh it was very difficult. The voice is just like any other instrument you have to practice every day. *[FRIZBEE presents her with a bowling pin.]*

FRIZBEE: Ellie Murphy I am pleased and proud to present you with this singer of the year award.

ELLIE: Dear friends, I thank you and I have only one thing to say, I deserved it. I practiced every day . . . *[LUCILLE starts to sing a beautiful melody. ELLIE moves toward the mirror.]*

ELLIE: I practiced until my throat was sore from singing and . . .

VOICE: Red Light! *[All freeze.]*

VOICE: You'll never be as good as Lucille. *[VOICE snatches the pin away from her.]*

VOICE: She's a much better singer than you are. Green Light!

ELLIE: *[Grabs for the pin]* This is MY prize and I deserve it! *[They struggle with the pin]*

ELLIE: *[To LANA and FRIZBEE.]* Hey you guys! *[They rush to her aid. The pin is tossed in the air and FRIZBEE catches it.]*

FRIZBEE: Ellie Murphy I am pleased and proud to present you with this singer of the year award.

ELLIE: Thank you for my prize. It is neat! *[There is the sound of thunderous applause. LUCILLE crosses to ELLIE'S door and knocks. The applause stops instantly.]*

LUCILLE: Ellinor? *[LANA and FRIZBEE freeze.]*

ELLIE: Who goes there?

LUCILLE: May I come in?

ELLIE: What's the password?

LUCILLE: Please?

ELLIE: *[Peeking out]* Have you got a pass?

[LUCILLE enters and looks around.]

LUCILLE: Who were you talking to?

ELLIE: Lana and Frizbee.

LUCILLE: *[Playing along]* OH! Are they still here?

[FRIZBEE pops his head up and makes a rude sound, then disappears into the box.]

ELLIE: Sure, Frizbee just did a raspberry.

LUCILLE: Oh? *[LANA crosses in front of LUCILLE making ugly faces at her.]*

ELLIE: And Lana's making faces . . . like this and this and this . . .

[LANA goes into the toy box. LUCILLE crosses to the middle of the room crouches down and speaks into empty air.]

LUCILLE: Were you two helping Ellie clean up her room?

ELLIE: Lucille, they're not here. They went into the toy box.

LUCILLE: *[Playing along a bit too much]* Oh I see. Do they live in the toy box?

ELLIE: *[Nonplussed.]* It's too small to live in there. They just sit there sometimes.

LUCILLE: Oh. Please Ellie, let me help you. We'll have this place cleaned up in no time. Now where does this go?

ELLIE: No deal! You throw out too much!
[ELLIE starts putting things away.]

LUCILLE: Oh, Ellinor, you've lost another button. I just sewed that one on too.

ELLIE: It's a scientific fact that some people are allergic to buttons.

[ELLIE looks hard at LUCILLE]

Hey, Lucille, how old are you?

LUCILLE: *[A bit taken aback.]* Uhhh, well, I'm thirty-five.

ELLIE: *[Very serious]* Boy that's old.

LUCILLE: Well, it's not that old.

ELLIE: Do you use a lot of make-up?

LUCILLE: I use some.

ELLIE: A lot? Do you put that goopy stuff on your eyes to make them look big?

LUCILLE: Would you like me to show you about make-up?

ELLIE: Uhhhgg. NO! Make-up is for girlies and OLD people.

LUCILLE: Come on Ellinor, let's get this room done before your father gets home. *[MAX enters with a football helmet and a feather duster for ELLIE.]*

MAX: Anybody home?

ELLIE: Too late! *[ELLIE runs to greet him and jumps into his arms. He gives her the helmet and duster, as LUCILLE enters ELLIE hides them behind her back and sneaks them into her room.]*

MAX: Hey Midget.

ELLIE: Neato. Thanks.

[LUCILLE approaches to hug him.]

LUCILLE: Hello dear, you're early.

MAX: Be careful, I'm a mess. I gotta wash up. *[LUCILLE gets him a rag. He wipes his hands and then kisses her. He sits down to take off his boots. ELLIE enters with his house shoes.]*

MAX: Hey Ellie, what's the matter with your shirt?

[MAX points to an imaginary spot on her shirt. ELLIE looks down and MAX tweaks her nose.]

MAX: Ha! Hah! Gotcha! Can't have your nose back. Not till you answer three knock knocks . . . Let's see . . . Knock knock . . .

ELLIE: *[With her nose still held.]* Who's there?

MAX: Dwain.

ELLIE: Dwain who?

MAX: Dwain the bathtub I'm dwouning.

ELLIE: Hey, I got one. Knock, knock.

MAX: Who's there?

ELLIE: DeGaulle.

MAX: Degaulle who?

601

ELLIE: *[Crossing her eyes]* De-gaulle-f ball hit me in the head and dats why I talk dis way.

MAX: Ohhhh.

ELLIE: Oh I got another one Pop. Knock, knock . . .

LUCILLE: *[Jumping in]* Who's there? *[ELLIE shoots her a nasty look and turns away.]*

ELLIE: Nobody.

LUCILLE: *[Puzzled]* Nobody who?

ELLIE: *[Insolently]* Just nobody that's all! *[MAX and LUCILLE exchange a look.]*

MAX: I've still got your nose.

ELLIE: *[Back in the game]* Give it back you Bozo.

MAX: Nope you gotta get it. *[MAX pretends to hold her nose just out of reach. ELLIE jumps for it. MAX tosses it to LUCILLE.]*

MAX: Here Lucille, catch! *[LUCILLE, confused, misses it.]*

LUCILLE: Huh? Oh I'm sorry.

[The game is over and Ellie scowls.]

ELLIE: Pop, do I have to clean up my room? Can I get you a beer? Can I watch T.V.? Do I have to throw out all my good stuff?

MAX: Whoa! What's going on?

ELLIE: Can I watch T.V.?

MAX: Sure.

LUCILLE: Max, I have been trying to get her to clean up her room for days.

MAX: Awww it's Friday afternoon.

LUCILLE: Max.

MAX: Clean up your room Ellie.

ELLIE: Awww Pop, you never used to make me.

MAX: Sorry Midget. This ship's got a new captain.

ELLIE: Awww Pop!

MAX: Do what your mother says.

ELLIE: *[Under her breath]* She is not my real mother.

MAX: What did you say?

ELLIE: Nothing.

MAX: Hey, maybe later we'll do something fun.

ELLIE: Can we go bowling?

MAX: Maybe.

ELLIE: Oh please, oh please, oh please! We used to go all the time. Pop and me, we were practically professional bowlers. We were practicing to go on Family Bowl-O-Rama, on T.V.

MAX: Clean up your room and we'll talk about bowling later. *[ELLIE trudges into her room. MAX sits down and LUCILLE massages his back.]*

LUCILLE: You're early.

MAX: Yep, and I have a surprise for you.

LUCILLE: For me, Max? What is it?

MAX: You gotta guess. It's something we've been talking about.

[ELLIE interrupts. She is wearing a long black cape, a tall hat and a scarf. She holds a piece of metal pipe.]

ELLIE: Ta Dah! Presenting the Great Mysterioso! You will see that I have nothing up my sleeve. See this pipe? See this scarf? Here hold this hat lady. *[ELLIE hands the hat to LUCILLE.]*

ELLIE: Now I take this scarf, just an ordinary everyday magic scarf, and I put it over this piece of pipe. Now you both will blow on it.

[MAX and LUCILLE blow on the scarf.]

ELLIE: I say some magic words. OOOOOBLEEEDOOOO OBBBBB-LEEEDAY ZOOOOOBLEEDA! Zap! Zap! Zap! *[ELLIE flips the pipe over her shoulder, it lands with a loud crash. She grabs the hat and places the scarf in it.]*

ELLIE: Presto! No more pipe! Ta Dah! *[ELLIE displays the empty scarf. MAX and LUCILLE clap.]*

MAX: I thought you went to . . .

ELLIE: I found this stuff while I was cleaning. Pretty neat huh?

LUCILLE: That was very nice Ellie.

MAX: Ellie, Lucille and I are talking.

ELLIE: What about?

MAX: ELLIE!

ELLIE: I'm going. I'm going. [ELLIE *goes back to her room.* MAX *takes some folders out of his pocket.*]

MAX: Do you remember that travel agent I said I was going to talk to?

LUCILLE: Oh Max, do you mean you did it?

MAX: Did I talk to him? Ta Dah! Little lady, you and I are going on a honeymoon. We are going to Hawaii.

LUCILLE: Hawaii? Oh Max!

MAX: Just look at this, "American Express twenty-one day excursion to Honolulu and the islands." That's our honeymoon, that is if you want to go.

LUCILLE: Want to? I have always wanted to go to those places. But can we? I mean should we? Right now?

MAX: Why not? I've been saving for a trip and I think I can take about three weeks off. Now's as good a time as ever.

LUCILLE: I'm not sure we ought to leave Ellie right now.

MAX: She'll be fine. I can get someone to stay with her and after all she's in school. There is this lady, Mrs. Dougan, she used to stay with Ellie when I'd go on hunting trips. I'll call her tomorrow.

LUCILLE: I just don't want her to think that we are running off and leaving her.

MAX: Don't worry, I'll talk to her.

LUCILLE: Right away . . . that is if you are serious.

MAX: You bet I'm serious. I got all this stuff didn't I? Look at some of these tour deals. You get everything: air fare, meals, hotel, an air conditioned bus . . .

LUCILLE: Oh look at that sun, and all that sand. What a beautiful beach. [ELLIE *enters clutching T.V. Guide.*]

ELLIE: Guess what! Midnight Spook-a-thon has a double feature tonight! *The Curse of Frankenstein* and the *Return of the Mummy's Hand!* Isn't that neat? Can I watch it Pop?

MAX: [*Hiding the folders*] Uhhh Sure, why not.

LUCILLE: What time does it come on?

ELLIE: [*Nonchalantly*] Oh early.

LUCILLE: What time?

ELLIE: *[Quickly]* Eleven-thirty.

LUCILLE: That's awfully late.

ELLIE: Tomorrow's Saturday. And besides Pop said I could.

LUCILLE: We'll see.

ELLIE: You always say that when you mean no. What are you guys doing?

MAX: We're talking.

ELLIE: *[Seeing the folders]* What's this? *[LUCILLE starts to show them to her and MAX snatches them away.]*

MAX: Papers, papers of mine. Ellie is your room cleaned up yet?

ELLIE: No! Gee whiz! I'm going. I'm going! *[ELLIE crosses back to her room.]*

LUCILLE: Max, why didn't you talk to her?

MAX: Oh I don't know, I just hate it when she yells.

LUCILLE: Yells? I thought you said it was going to be alright.

MAX: It is! I just have to kind of talk to her about it . . . when she's in a good mood.

LUCILLE: If you really think it is going to upset her, let's not do it now. We can always go later.

MAX: I said I was going to talk to her and I will . . . *[MAX crosses to ELLIE'S room. LUCILLE follows slightly behind.]*

MAX: Ellie . . . uhhh

ELLIE: I'm not finished yet but I'm cleaning!

MAX: Looks like you are doing a good job here. Want any help?

ELLIE: Huh? *[ELLIE finds the duster and dusts everything and then starts dusting MAX.]*

MAX: Ellie, umm Lucille and I . . . uhhh we were thinking that it might be a good idea if . . . if . . . we went . . . bowling! Tonight!

ELLIE: Hey, neato!

MAX: After you clean up your room.

ELLIE: I'll hurry. I'll hurry. *[MAX leaves the room with LUCILLE shaking her head.]*

LUCILLE: Why didn't you tell her?

MAX: Let's wait until we know exactly when we're going.

LUCILLE: I don't want her to think that we are sneaking around behind her back.

MAX: I'll tell her. I just want to pick my own time. [ELLIE *starts out the door.*]

VOICE: Red Light! [ELLIE *freezes.*]

VOICE: Something fishy's going on. They don't want you around. They're trying to get rid of you . . . Green Light.

[ELLIE *stares into the mirror.*]

MAX: So that's your surprise. How do you like it?

LUCILLE: Oh Max! [LUCILLE *hugs him.* ELLIE *enters.*]

ELLIE: Ahem!

MAX: What do you want?

ELLIE: I just came to get a shovel.

LUCILLE: What do you need a shovel for?

ELLIE: I'm cleaning! I'm cleaning! [MAX *turns her around and marches her back into the room.*]

LUCILLE: Please Max! [*They all enter the room.*]

MAX: Ellie, I want to talk to you . . . . . [ELLIE *shines his shoes.*]

MAX: ELLIE! [ELLIE *looks up at him and gives him a goofy look.*]

MAX: I just want to tell you . . . . I tell you what! If you clean up your room right now then we'll all go get ice cream or something!

LUCILLE: [*Exasperated.*] I have to stop at the market anyway. I'll go make a list. [LUCILLE *exits.*]

MAX: And now once and for all . . . listen here tough guy . . . you is gonna clean up that room. Okay?

ELLIE: [*Tough guy.*] Oh Yeah? Who is gonna make me?

MAX: I am Louie, cause I am da tough cop in dis town. Now you is gonna get in dat cell and you is gonna clean it up, or else I is gonna throw you in solitary . . . see? [*They tussle for a moment,* MAX *pulls her cap over her eyes.*]

MAX: An I don't want to see you outta there till you is done. [MAX *shuts the door and exits.*]

ELLIE: Darn! Lately this place is really getting like a prison.

VOICE: Red Light! She keeps you locked up like some kind of prisoner.

ELLIE: Yeah! A prison with walls and bars and chains. A dungeon with cold stones and bread and water and rats. Solitary confinement . . . The walls are closing in. You gotta let me out . . . You gotta let me out . . .

VOICE: Green Light! *[Suddenly the toy lid flips open and a shovel full of dirt comes flying out. A shovel appears and on the other end of the shovel is LANA.]*

LANA: Hi yah, Sweetie!

ELLIE: Lana!

LANA: Who else? You think we wuz gonna let you take a bum rap? We dug this tunnel t'bust you outta here.

ELLIE: We?

LANA: Frizbee and me! Right Frizbee? Frizbee? He was right behind me in the tunnel. He must be here someplace. *[They look for FRIZBEE. LANA looks in the toy chest and slams the lid.]*

LANA: Oh no!

ELLIE: What?

LANA: Don't look!

ELLIE: Why not?

LANA: Cave in! The tunnel's caved in.

ELLIE: Oh NO!

LANA: The whole thing. . . . Squash!

ELLIE: Poor Frizbee!

LANA: What are we gonna do?

ELLIE: There is only one thing we can do!

LANA: Yeah?

ELLIE: Blast!

LANA: Blast Boss?

ELLIE: It's the only way. You get the dynamite and I'll get the fuse. *[They gather together junk to make a blasting box, fuse and plunger.]*

ELLIE: First you gotta make the box. Then you gotta put the dynamite in and then stick your fingers in your ears, and count down 10,9,8,7,6,5,4,3,2. . . . 1 BARRROOOOOOOM. *[VOICE makes the sound of the explosion. The lid flies open, a puff of smoke comes out. FRIZBEE'S arms and legs hang out of the box.]*

FRIZBEE: *[Weakly]* Hey you guys . . . . .

[LANA and ELLIE rush to FRIZBEE and lift him out of the toy chest.]

LANA: Are you alright?

FRIZBEE: Sure.

ELLIE: The tunnel collapsed on you.

FRIZBEE: I thought it got dark all of a sudden.

ELLIE: Okay. Youse guys we gotta blow this joint. *[FRIZBEE pulls a handkerchief out of costume and blows his nose, as he pulls another handkerchief comes out and a whole string of handkerchiefs follow to FRIZBEE'S amazement.]*

ELLIE: Great idea Frizbee. Here Lana you take one end and go first, I'll hold this, and Frizbee, you bring up the rear. Goodbye cruel cell. *[LANA and ELLIE dive into the box.]*

FRIZBEE: Goodbye cruel ceeeeeeee . . . . .

[FRIZBEE is pulled in after them. LUCILLE enters wearing a police hat and badge.]

LUCILLE: Calling all cars. Calling all cars. This is the warden speaking! Ellie-the-mess-Murphy has just escaped from solitary confinement. She is messy and extremely dangerous. After her? After her! *[There is a chase. LANA and ELLIE crawl under the bed, and around the stage. LUCILLE crouches behind the bed.]*

LANA: We made it!

ELLIE: Free at last.

LANA: Wow that was close. *[LUCILLE appears.]*

LUCILLE: Have you cleaned up your room yet?

ELLIE and LANA: EEEK! *[There is a short chase. LUCILLE lassos ELLIE and LANA with the scarfs and drags them over to one side of the stage where she crouches down and VOICE makes the sound of a car. LUCILLE mimes driving the paddy wagon. FRIZBEE finally makes it out of the tunnel, sees what's going on, disappears for a second and reappears wearing the football helmet. VOICE makes the sound of a siren. FRIZBEE mimes riding a motorcycle.*

STEP ON A CRACK

LUCILLE *puts on the brakes.* FRIZBEE *gets off the motorcycle, pulls an imaginary pad out of his pocket, licks an imaginary pencil.]*

FRIZBEE: Okay girlie, where's the fire?

LUCILLE: I'm sorry officer, I . . . . just wanted her to clean up her . . .

FRIZBEE: Let me see your license. I'm gonna give you a ticket.

LUCILLE: But officer I . . . .

FRIZBEE: But first I'm gonna give you a . . . tickle. *[*FRIZBEE *tickles* LUCILLE, *she laughs helplessly,* LANA *and* ELLIE *escape.]*

LUCILLE: You can't do that!

FRIZBEE: Oh yeah? I just did!

ELLIE: To the hideout! *[*LUCILLE *chases them off.* ELLIE, LANA *and* FRIZBEE *race back to* ELLIE'S *room. They overturn the benches to make a barricade.* ELLIE *rifles through the toy chest throwing junk everywhere. They put on guns and helmets.]*

ELLIE: Get the ammo and take cover.

VOICE: Come out with your hands up.

ELLIE: Let 'em have it.
[Imaginary battle takes place. They throw things all over the room. FRIZBEE *uses a toilet paper roll like a grenade.* ELLIE *clutches a grease gun like a tommy gun. All make sounds.* LUCILLE *enters dressed in regular street clothes. She is not part of the fantasy.]*

LUCILLE: *[Approaching the door]* Ellinor, are you ready?

ELLIE: You'll never take us copper! *[*LUCILLE *opens the door. All sound effects stop.* LANA *and* FRIZBEE *freeze. The room is totally destroyed.* ELLIE *pretends to be oiling the bed.]*

LUCILLE: *[Dumbfounded]* Ellinor.

ELLIE: I . . . I . . . I. uh, was just cleaning my room.

LUCILLE: Ellinor.

ELLIE: I didn't do it. Lana threw the grenade.

LANA: I did not!

LUCILLE: I certainly hope you don't mean to tell me that Lana and Frizbee made all this mess.

ELLIE: What are you hoping I'll tell you?

LUCILLE: Oh Ellinor.

ELLIE: They made most of it.

FRIZBEE: We did not!

LUCILLE: Are they supposed to be here now?

ELLIE: *[Gesturing with grease gun]* They're right over . . . .

LUCILLE: Ellinor, that's a grease gun . . . . . don't . . . . . *[ELLIE squeezes a glob of grease on the floor.]*

VOICE: Glop!

ELLIE: Uh oh!

LUCILLE: The carpet! A brand new carpet! Grease is the worst possible stain. Oh my lord.

ELLIE: I thought it was empty.

LUCILLE: Now which is it, hot water or cold? . . . . Oh my lord.

   [LUCILLE rushes off to get a rag.]

LANA: Uhhhh so long Boss.

FRIZBEE: Be seeing you around.

ELLIE: Where are you going?

LANA: I just remembered something I gotta do.

FRIZBEE: Yeah and I gotta do it with her . . . . Whatever it is . . . . .

   [They exit into the box. LUCILLE enters and rubs frantically at the spot.]

LUCILLE: It just gets worse and worse . . . It's ruined. A brand new carpet.

ELLIE: Well, I'm your brand new kid.

LUCILLE: Ellinor I knew something like this would happen. This is the last time you bring junk into your room. Oh it just gets bigger and bigger. *[MAX enters, and rushes to help.]*

MAX: What in the world . . . . . .

LUCILLE: Oh Max, Ellinor spilled grease on the carpet.

ELLIE: I didn't mean to.

LUCILLE: The more I rub the worse it gets.

ELLIE: It's not my fault.

MAX: Did you try cold water?

LUCILLE: No, it's hot water for grease.

ELLIE: Hey listen, I don't mind that spot.

MAX: No, I'm sure it's cold water.

ELLIE: Honest, I like that spot just the way it is.

LUCILLE: Max, it's hot water for grease and cold water for blood
stains and ink.

MAX: I've got this stuff in my car.

LUCILLE: Oh it's no use!

ELLIE: *[Shouting]* Would you leave it alone! I like that spot. *[They
both stop and stare at her.]* This is MY room.

LUCILLE: But it is a brand new carpet.

ELLIE: BIG DEAL.

MAX: Ellie, don't talk that way to your Mother.

ELLIE: She is not my real Mother. *[Stiff pause.]* *[To* LUCILLE*]* You'll
never be my REAL MOTHER.

LUCILLE: *[Angry but even]* You know, Ellie. You're absolutely right.
[Pause]

LUCILLE: *[Covering.]* Well if we are going to the market I better get
my coat. *[*LUCILLE *exits.* MAX *is angry and very depressed.]*

MAX: That was nice. . . . that was really nice.

ELLIE: It's not my fault.

MAX: You hurt her feelings.

ELLIE: I have feelings too you know. Just because you're a kid
doesn't mean you're junk!

MAX: Come off it Ellie.

ELLIE: That spot is almost out.

MAX: *[Really down]* Yeah!

ELLIE: Maybe we could put something over it.

MAX: Yeah.

ELLIE: With a sign that says "Don't look here."

MAX: *[With a slight laugh]* Sure.

ELLIE: *[Trying to get him out of his mood.]* Knock, knock.

MAX: Not now, Ellie.

ELLIE: Let's wrestle.

MAX: Uh uh! You're getting too big for me.

ELLIE: Do you think I'm too fat?

MAX: You? Naw you're fine.

ELLIE: Hey Pop, do you remember the time we went camping and you drove all afternoon to get out of the woods? It was dark when we pitched the tent and we heard all those funny sounds and you said it was MONSTERS. Then in the morning we found out we were in somebody's front lawn.

MAX: *[Responding a bit.]* I knew where we were all the time.

ELLIE: Or when we went to the Super Bowl and I got cold, and you said yell something in your megaphone.

MAX: Yeah, and you yelled "I'm cold and I want to go home." *[They both laugh.]*

ELLISS *[Tentatively.]* Hey Pop, tell me about my real mother.

MAX: How come you want to hear about her all the time these days? *[ELLIE sits at his feet and rests against his knees.]*

ELLIE: I just do. Hey do you remember the time it was my birthday and you brought Mom home from the hospital, and I didn't know she was coming that time? I remember I was already in bed and you guys wanted to surprise me. She just came into my room, kissed me goodnight and tucked me in, just like it was any other night.

MAX: *[Moved]* How could you remember that? You were just four years old.

ELLIE: I just remember.

MAX: Your mother was a wonderful person and I loved her very much.

ELLIE: As much as you . . . like Lucille?

MAX: Ellie.

ELLIE: Was she pretty?

MAX: She was beautiful.

ELLIE: Do I look like her?

MAX: Naw, you look more like me, you mug.

ELLIE: *[Suddenly angry]* Why does everything have to change?

MAX: Hey.

ELLIE: How come Lucille is always so neat and everything? I bet she never even burps.

MAX: She does.

ELLIE: HUH!

MAX: I heard her once.

ELLIE: Do you think I'd look cute with make-up on?

MAX: You? You're just a kid.

ELLIE: But Lucille wears make-up. Lot's of it.

MAX: Well she's grown up.

ELLIE: Hey do you know how old she is?

MAX: Sure. Thirty- five.

ELLIE: How come you married such an old one?

MAX: That's not old.

ELLIE: Huh!

MAX: Why I am older than that myself.

ELLIE: You are??

MAX: Ellie, you know how you get to go to camp in the summer. You get to go away all by yourself.

ELLIE: Yeah but I'm not going any more.

MAX: You're not?

ELLIE: Nope, look what happened the last time I went. You and Lucille got to be good friends, then as soon as I get back you get married. Who knows if I go away again I might get back and find out you moved to Alaska.

MAX: We wouldn't do that.

ELLIE: You might.

MAX: Ellie, kids can't always go where parents go. Sometimes parents go away all by themselves.

ELLIE: How come ever since you got married I am such a kid. You never used to say I was a kid. We did everything together. Now all

I hear is, "Kids can't do this," "Kids can't do that," "Kids have to go to bed at eight-thirty." "Kids have to clean up their rooms." Why does everything have to change?

MAX: Nothing's changed. I still love you the same. Now there's just two of us who love you.

ELLIE: HUH!

POP: I just wish you'd try a little harder to . . . . .

ELLIE: To like Lucille? Why should I? She doesn't like me. She likes cute little girls who play with dollies.

MAX: Well she got herself a messy little mug that likes junk. *[ELLIE pulls away.]*

MAX: I'm just kidding. She likes you fine the way you are.

ELLIE: Oh yeah, well I don't like her.

MAX: Why not?
[LUCILLE enters and overhears the following.]

ELLIE: Cause . . . Cause . . . Cause she's a wicked stepmother . . . .
[ELLIE giggles in spite of herself. MAX is really angry.]

MAX: That's not funny!

ELLIE: You shout at me all the time!

MAX: *[Shouting.]* I'm not shouting!

LUCILLE: *[Breaking it up.]* Is everybody ready to go?

MAX: Ellie get your coat.

ELLIE: I'm not going.

MAX: Get your coat. We are going for ice cream!

ELLIE: *[Pouting]* I don't want any.

MAX: Okay. Lucille let's go. Ellie you can just stay at home and clean up your room.

LUCILLE: Max . . . .

MAX: I said let's go!

ELLIE: See if I care.
[They leave the room. ELLIE pouts.]

LUCILLE: Was it about the trip?

MAX: What?

LUCILLE: Were you two arguing about the trip?

MAX: Are you kidding. I didn't even get that far.

LUCILLE: Let's just forget it.

MAX: What?

LUCILLE: Forget the whole thing!

MAX: Oh no, I need this trip. We need it; we have got to have some time for US.

LUCILLE: If you want to go, then let's talk to her and we'll go. If not, let's just forget it!

MAX: Let me work this out in my own way.

LUCILLE: Why does everything have to be a game or a joke? Max, it really isn't fair to Ellie or me. Why can't we just talk?

MAX: This isn't easy for her.

LUCILLE: Well, it isn't easy for me either; and frankly, Max, I have just about had it.

MAX: Lucille . . .

LUCILLE: If we are ever going to be a family, we've got to be able to talk . . .

MAX: Not now! You're angry, she's angry. Let's go to the market, calm down, and we'll talk when we get home.

[They exit.]

ELLIE: Hey, wait a minute. . . Wait, I changed my mind. I want to go. [They have gone. ELLIE turns back.]

VOICE: Red Light! It's all her fault! She didn't want you to go. SHE made it so you couldn't go.

[ELLIE is drawn to the mirror.]

ELLIE and VOICE: Pick up your toys. Make your bed. Do what we say or you won't be fed.

ELLIE: I'll never be pretty. Ugly face, ugly hair and squinty little eyes. If I had my real mother I'd be pretty.

VOICE: You'll never be as pretty as Lucille. Green Light!

ELLIE: They dress me in rags. They make me work all day.

VOICE: Ugly Ellie.

ELLIE: Ugly Ellie, Ugly Ellie . . . [ELLIE *sits on the bed and pulls her cap over her face dejectedly.*]

FRIZBEE: [*Inside the toy box.*] Cinderelli, Cinderelli Cinderelli, [*Lid to the box opens and out pops* FRIZBEE *wearing Mickey Mouse ears and singing the Walt Disney song.*]

FRIZBEE: Cinderelli, Cinderelli, Cinderelli, Cinderelli . . . .

ELLIE: What are you supposed to be?

FRIZBEE: I am just a little Mouse. Who lives inside this great big house. Oh Cinderelli kind and dear, I see what's been going on right here. Your wicked stepmother cruel and mean, Makes you wash and wax and clean. Now she's gone to the ice cream ball, And left you here with nothing at all.

ELLIE: Dear little Mouse you've seen everything?

FRIZBEE: Oh Yes! Everything and more.
Ever since your stepmother came to stay,
I have seen you slave all day.
She gives you crusts of bread to eat.
She pinches your elbows and stamps on your feet.
She gives you rags and paper towels to wear.
She calls you names and tangles your hair.

ELLIE: But what are we to do? I want to go to the ball but I have nothing to wear, my hair is dull, dull, dull, and my face is blah!

LANA: [*From the toy box.*] Perhaps there's something I can do. [*Toy box opens again, we see* LANA's *feet waving in the air.* ELLIE *and* FRIZBEE *pull her out, she is outlandishly dressed in a gold lamé dress, blond wig, tiara, and silvery shoes.*]

LANA: I am your fairy godmother and I have come to make you a star. We have much to do, after all stars are made not born.

ELLIE: Are you going to do a spell?

LANA: Oh no, spells are old fashioned. Today we have something much better . . . money! [LANA *throws a fist-full of money in the air.*]

LANA: First we need a dress.

ELLIE: Hey, I got an idea. Come with me. . . . .

[ELLIE *leads them out of her room to* LUCILLE's *ladder where she gets an elaborate party dress.*]

LANA: Perfect!

FRIZBEE: But that's Lucille's.

616

LANA: Not anymore. We just bought it. [LANA *spears a bill on the hanger and helps* ELLIE *on with the dress over her clothes.*]

LANA: And now the hair! Give her something that simply screams glamour. [FRIZBEE *becomes the hairdresser.*]

FRIZBEE: Would Madame care for a flip?
[FRIZBEE *does a flip.*]

LANA: The hair you dolt! [LANA *clobbers him.* FRIZBEE *makes an elaborate production of messing up* ELLIE'S *hair.*]

LANA: Make-up!/[FRIZBEE *slaps make-up on* ELLIE *and shows her how to blot her lipstick by smacking her lips. He gets carried away with the smacking and gives* LANA *a big kiss.*]

LANA: Oh gross! [LANA *clobbers him.*]

LANA: And now the coach. [FRIZBEE *puts on the football helmet and jumps around being a coach.*]

LANA: THE CARRIAGE!! [FRIZBEE *gets a broomstick horse.*]

LANA: And last but not least. . . . your public! [LANA *throws a fist full of money in the air and there is tumultuous cheering.*]

[ELLIE, FRIZBEE *and* LANA *exit in procession. A fanfare is heard.* FRIZBEE *enters with a roll of paper towels which he rolls out like a red carpet. He stands at attention at the end of the carpet.* LANA *swirls on and down the carpet, she curtsies to* FRIZBEE.]

VOICE: Ladies and gentlemen, the Prince. [MAX *enters dressed in a frock coat over his regular clothes. He bows and stands at the end of the "carpet."*]

VOICE: And now ladies and gentlemen, the moment we have all been waiting for, the star of stage, screen and television . . . the Princess Cinderelli! [*Music plays the Sleeping Beauty Waltz,* ELLIE *enters, a spot light catches her, she sweeps down the carpet to* MAX *who bows. They dance.*]

LANA: [*As they waltz by her.*] Remember darling, your contract is up at midnight. [VOICE *begins to bang on a pot with a spoon, twelve times in all. On the stroke of twelve* LUCILLE *appears, sweeps down the "carpet."* MAX *turns and bows to her and dances off with her leaving* ELLIE.]

ELLIE: Hey wait a minute, what do you think you're doing? [LANA *and* FRIZBEE *exit.*]

ELLIE: Hey, I'm supposed to be the Princess around here. Hey, I'm Cinderelli! Come back. Alright see if I care. I don't need any stupid old prince. I can have a good time all by myself. [ELLIE *sings and dances all by herself. Music out.* ELLIE, *obviously upset, dances faster and faster.* MAX *and* LUCILLE *enter with groceries. They stop at her door and watch.* MAX *bursts out laughing.* LU-CILLE *elbows him.* ELLIE *stops, mortified at being caught.]*

ELLIE: Well what are you staring at?

MAX: What is this, Halloween?

ELLIE: What's so funny?

LUCILLE: I think you look very pretty.

ELLIE: *[Defensively.]* Well I wasn't trying to look pretty! I was trying to look dumb and funny, like this . . . and this . . . and this . . . *[*ELLIE *makes faces.]*

Since I can't be pretty I might as well be funny and dumb. *[*ELLIE *capers around wildly until she stubs her toe.]*

ELLIE: Owwwwwwww!

LUCILLE: What's the matter?

ELLIE: I stubbed my dumb toe. *[*ELLIE *sits and buries her head in her hands.* MAX *starts to go to her.* LUCILLE *stops him by shoving her sack of groceries into his arms.]*

LUCILLE: Max, will you put these in the kitchen for me? *[*MAX *gives her a look, she waves him away and he exits.* LUCILLE *goes to* ELLIE *and helps her out of the dress.]*

LUCILLE: You okay? *[*ELLIE *pulls away and sits on the bed. She shrugs.]*

LUCILLE: Ellinor, if I asked you to help me with something would you do it?

ELLIE: I didn't clean up my room.

LUCILLE: So I see, but that's not what I am talking about. I want you to help me with something else.

ELLIE: Huh! I don't see what I could help you do.

LUCILLE: *[Tentatively]* Well, I never had any children . . . and lots of times I'm not too sure what mothers are supposed to do. So I wanted you to help me.

ELLIE: How should I know? I never really had a mother, not one I remember real well.

LUCILLE: Well, maybe we could help each other. *[*ELLIE *shrugs.]*

LUCILLE: You see, my mother was very strict. She made me pick up my room and practice my voice every day and I loved her.

ELLIE: She was your real mother.

LUCILLE: Yes.

ELLIE: That makes a difference. You have to love your real mother and your real kids.

LUCILLE: But you can choose to love your stepchildren.

ELLIE: But nobody can make you.

LUCILLE: *[Pause.]* That's right.

ELLIE: Well I can tell you a couple of things mothers shouldn't do. They shouldn't try to make their kids different from the way they are. Like if the kid is messy, they shouldn't try to make them be neat. And mothers shouldn't make their kids go to bed at eight-thirty, especially when there's good movies on T.V.

LUCILLE: But what if the mother wants the child to be healthy and she thinks the child should get some sleep?

ELLIE: Who's supposed to be doing the helping around here, you or me?

LUCILLE: Sorry.

ELLIE: Mothers should love their kids no matter what. Even if the kid is funny and dumb and looks like a gorilla; Mothers should make them think they are beautiful.

LUCILLE: But what if the . . . kid won't let the mother. . . .

ELLIE: Mothers gotta go first! That's the rules.

LUCILLE: Ellie . . . I . . .

ELLIE: *[Turning away.]* What's for supper?

LUCILLE: Huh?

ELLIE: I'm getting hungry. What's for supper?

LUCILLE: I thought I'd make a beef stroganoff.

ELLIE: What's that?

LUCILLE: It's little slices of beef with sour cream and. . . . .

ELLIE: SOUR CREAM! UHHHHHH! Mothers should never make their kids eat SOUR CREAM! *[ELLIE clutches her throat.]*

LUCILLE: *[Laughing]* You should try it.

ELLIE: I know, Why don't I make dinner tonight? I used to do that all the time. Pop and I had this really neat game we'd play. First we'd cook up a whole bunch of T.V. dinners and then we'd put on blindfolds and try to guess what we were eating.

MAX: *[Entering]* Did I hear somebody mention food?

LUCILLE: I just had a great idea! Why don't we eat out tonight?

ELLIE: Knock knock. . . .

MAX: Who's there?

ELLIE: Uda.

MAX: Uda who?

ELLIE: *[Singing]* "You deserve a break today" . . . . . .

MAX: *[Joining in]* . . . "So go on and get away to MacDonalds."**
[MAX encourages LUCILLE to join in.]

LUCILLE: But I don't know the words.

ELLIE: It's simple. But you can't sing it in that toot toot de doot voice. You gotta do it like this. . . *[ELLIE belts it out.]*

ELLIE: "You deserve a break today. So go on and get away to Mac-Donalds."

LUCILLE: *[Belting]* Like this? "You deserve a break today. So go on and get away to MacDonalds." *[They all join in on the last line.]*

ELLIE: Not bad, for a beginner.

MAX: Let's go.

LUCILLE: Wait a minute, I have to put the meat in the freezer.

[LUCILLE exits.]

MAX: Hey Ellie, after supper how about a little . . . *[MAX mimes bowling]*

ELLIE: Great! Just you and me, like the old days?

MAX: Ellie?

ELLIE: Oh I bet Lucille doesn't even know how to bowl. I bet she thinks it is a dirty smelly sport.

MAX: Oh, come on.

**This jingle should be constantly updated to any popular theme song of a fast food chain.*

ELLIE: Oh, I guess she can come.

MAX: If she doesn't know you'll have to teach her.

ELLIE: Yeah, I could. Cause if there is one thing I do know it is bowling. [LUCILLE enters.]

MAX: Lucille, would you like to go bowling after supper?

LUCILLE: Oh Max, I was hoping we could all come back here and TALK.

MAX: [Ignoring the hint] Oh yeah, yeah. We can do that afterward.

LUCILLE: Maybe just you two should go. I've never bowled before and I wouldn't want to slow you down.

MAX: Baloney! There's nothing to it. We'll show you. Right Midget?

[ELLIE shrugs and MAX elbows her.]

ELLIE: Sure, sure, it just takes practice, to get good that is. I'll show you.

MAX: Let's go. [They start out.]

ELLIE: Wait a sec, let me get my shoes.

MAX: We'll meet you in the car.

[MAX and LUCILLE exit. ELLIE gets her bowling shoes from under the bed and starts out.]

VOICE: Red Light! [ELLIE freezes.]

VOICE: You aren't going to fall for all that stuff are you?

ELLIE: Huh?

VOICE: All that "Help me be a mother" stuff?

ELLIE: Well. . . .

VOICE: Stepmothers always say that . . . to soften you up. They don't really mean that. And now she's going bowling with you. And after you teach her you know what will happen? She and Pop will go and leave you home . . . alone. Green Light!

MAX: [Off stage] Come on Ellie! [ELLIE hesitates and exits. By minor adjustments in the set it switches to the bowling alley. The sound of balls rolling and pins falling can be heard through the next scene. As soon as the scene is shifted ELLIE, MAX, and LUCILLE enter. ELLIE munches a bag of french fries, they cross to benches set up to indicate their alley. MAX sets up a score sheet, changes his shoes. All bowling should be mimed.]

MAX: Why don't we take a couple of practice shots? Will you show Lucille how to hold the ball while I get squared away?

ELLIE: *[Licking her fingers]* Okay, first you get a ball . . . *[ELLIE points, LUCILLE looks a bit apprehensive but she gets a ball.]*

MAX: *[Under his breath]* Ellie, I want you to be nice.

ELLIE: *[Slaps on a huge smile]* I am being nice . . . SEE? Now you hold the ball like this with three fingers . . . That's good . . . very very good! And you look right at that center pin and bring your hand straight back . . . like this and you just swing through . . . See?

LUCILLE: *[Gamely]* Sure I think so. . .

ELLIE: Well go ahead . . . Try one. *[LUCILLE follows all ELLIE's instructions but the unexpected weight of the ball throws her off balance. Finally she manages to bowl one ball but very badly. There is the sound of a gutterball.]*

ELLIE: *[Much too nice.]* Good! VERY GOOD Lucille. *[ELLIE smirks.]*

MAX: Lucille, that's called a gutterball, and it's not good. Ellie I'll show her. Why don't you take your turn?

ELLIE: Can I have a Coke?

LUCILLE: You just finished dinner.

ELLIE: Pop?

MAX: Yeah sure, here's fifteen cents.

[ELLIE walks away a few steps. MAX moves over to LUCILLE and shows her how to hold the ball, very cozily. ELLIE returns.]

ELLIE: AHEM! I believe it is MY turn. *[ELLIE takes a ball and goes through a very elaborate warm-up.]*

MAX: *[Quietly]* Now you see you just bring the ball straight back and . . .

LUCILLE: Where is the aiming? *[ELLIE bowls just as LUCILLE is talking, she slips a little and is thrown off. There is the sound of a few pins falling.]*

ELLIE: No fair! No fair! You're not supposed to talk! You threw me off!

MAX: *[Writing down the score.]* Uhhh, three! A little to the left.

ELLIE: That's not fair.

MAX: Oh go on, you've still got another ball.

ELLIE: This time NO talking. [ELLIE *bowls. All pins fall.*]

MAX: Fantastic.

LUCILLE: Nice aiming, Ellinor. That was a good shot wasn't it dear?

ELLIE: *[Cocky]* You bet. That's what they call a spare. It is just about the best you can do. Of course it takes hours and hours of practice.

MAX: Nice one Midget! Okay Lucille, it's all yours. Just relax and concentrate. [LUCILLE *starts into the backswing.*]

ELLIE: Hold IT!

[LUCILLE *stops clumsily.*]

LUCILLE: This is the foul line. If you step over it nothing counts. . . . I was just trying to help! [LUCILLE *bowls, very awkwardly. Sound of ball rolling very slowly.*]

ELLIE: *[Watching the ball.]* Don't expect too much, not right at first. After all there is only one thing better than a spare and that's a . . .

[*Sound of pins falling domino effect.* ELLIE'S *face contorts in utter amazement.*]

ELLIE: A STRIKE?????

MAX: Fantastic!

LUCILLE: Is that good?

MAX: You bet it is!

ELLIE: I think I'm going to be sick!

LUCILLE: What does that little X mean up there?

ELLIE: *[Nasty]* It means a strike!

MAX: Not bad, old lady, not bad at all.

[ELLIE *starts coughing real fakey.*]

LUCILLE: Beginner's luck.

MAX: Let's see. My turn now. [ELLIE *coughs.*]

MAX: What's the matter with you?

ELLIE: I don't feel so good.

MAX: Well lie down for a minute.

ELLIE: I don't exactly feel like bowling. [MAX *shoots her a look which silences her.* MAX *picks up the ball and lines up the shot, very machismo. Just as he bowls* ELLIE *coughs and throws him off. He gets a gutterball.*]

MAX: Ellie!

ELLIE: *[Innocently]* Sorry.

LUCILLE: What's the matter Ellinor?

MAX: Nothing's the matter. She's just got a bad case of fakeitus that's all!

ELLIE: By the way, Lucille, that's called a gutterball, it's not good.

MAX: Now, no more talking, noisemaking, sneezing, coughing or anything. [MAX *lines up the shot and* ELLIE *yawns.*]

MAX: One more noise out of you and it's out to the car. [MAX *takes his time lining up the shot,* ELLIE *picks up her Coke can which she opens just as he bowls. The can explodes in a spray of Coke.* MAX *tosses his ball over several lanes. He is furious.*]

ELLIE: Ooops!

MAX: ELLIE!

LUCILLE: Good Lord it is all over everything!

ELLIE: I couldn't help it.

MAX: You did that on purpose 'cause you're a rotten sport.

ELLIE: I did not.

MAX: Out to the car!

ELLIE: POP!

MAX: I said out to the car!

LUCILLE: Dear!

MAX: I am not going to have her wreck our game just because she's a lousy sport.

LUCILLE: Let's go home.

MAX: WHAT?

LUCILLE: I don't really care about bowling.

MAX: Well I do. Ellie out to the car. I said it and I meant it.

LUCILLE: You can't send her out there to wait in a dark parking lot.

624

MAX: Oh yes I can. We are going to finish this game, and Ellie is going to wait for us out in the car. If there is one thing I can't stand it is a rotten sport.

LUCILLE: I will not permit you to send that child out there alone.

MAX: It's just out to the car, do you want me to hire a babysitter?

ELLIE: *[Embarrassed.]* Pop!

LUCILLE: Max, keep your voice down. We'll settle this when we get home.

MAX: Are you telling me how to discipline my kid?

LUCILLE: You? You're a fine one to talk about discipline. Why you're a bigger kid than she is. Why we should all be sitting at home right now having a family discussion. But Oh no! We have to get ice cream. We all have to go bowling first . . . all because you can't even talk to your own child. . . .

MAX: *[Impulsive]* Oh you don't think I can tell her . . . *[MAX crosses to ELLIE. LUCILLE tries to stop him.]*

LUCILLE: Max, not here and not now. . . Let's go home.

MAX: *[To ELLIE]* Ellie, we are going to Hawaii!

[To LUCILLE.] There! Now are you satisfied? *[LUCILLE is horrified. MAX realizes instantly that he has really blown it.]*

LUCILLE: Oh MAX!

ELLIE: What are you guys talking about?

MAX: *[Fighting his way out.]* Uhhh, Ellie, we are going away. . . We're going to Hawaii.

ELLIE: HAWAII?

MAX: Yeah, for about three weeks.

ELLIE: Neato! Do I get to get out of school?

MAX: No Ellie, just Lucille and I are going. I was gonna tell you all about it when we got home tonight, well now you know.

ELLIE: What . . . What about me?

MAX: Well you kind of like Mrs. Dougan and I thought maybe she'd come and . . .

ELLIE: You are going away and leaving me.

LUCILLE: Ellie . . .

ELLIE: *[Getting mad.]* So that's what all that sneaking around was about! So that's what all those papers and secret stuff was about. You guys are going away and leaving me.

LUCILLE: Ellinor, that's not. . . .

ELLIE: *[Turns on her.]* And YOU! All that "Help me be a mother," stuff! That was just to soften me up. Well I'll tell you one thing mothers shouldn't do, mothers shouldn't lie to their kids about all that love stuff and then dump them.

MAX: Ellie, stop shouting.

ELLIE: I should have known. I should have known you didn't really like me. You just wanted to have POP all to yourself. Well go ahead! See if I care!

MAX: Ellie, we are going home. Take off your shoes and wait for me in the car.

ELLIE: You can't just throw me out like the trash you know.

MAX: ELLIE OUT TO THE CAR! *[ELLIE starts to run out. MAX stops her.]*

MAX: Ellie, your shoes! *[ELLIE, furious, takes off her shoes and throws them at him and runs out. LUCILLE looks at MAX for a minute.]*

LUCILLE: Well you certainly handled that one well.

MAX: Lay off! Oh I'm sorry, I didn't mean for this to happen.

LUCILLE: I should hope not. Max, discipline isn't something you turn off and on like hot water.

MAX: I know.

LUCILLE: *[Taking off her shoes and exiting.]* We were just beginning. After two months we were just beginning. *[LUCILLE exits. MAX sits for a minute. He picks up the score sheet and crumples it. He starts out when LUCILLE enters at a run.]*

LUCILLE: Max, she isn't there! She's gone!

MAX: What?

LUCILLE: She's run away. She left this note on the windshield.

[LUCILLE hands MAX a note.]

MAX: *[Reading]* "You win Lucille."

LUCILLE: *[Panicking]* Where could she have gone?

MAX: Anywhere! Let's go, she can't have gotten too far. *[LUCILLE sees ELLIE's shoes.]*

LUCILLE: Oh Max, she hasn't even got her shoes on.

MAX: Come on. *[MAX and LUCILLE exit. Weird sounds begin, the recorded voices of LANA and FRIZBEE and VOICE are heard chanting "Run away." The following scene is a mixture of fantasy and reality. A sound collage of voices and scary music form the background.]*

VOICE, LANA and FRIZBEE: Run away . . . Run away . . . Run away . . . Run away. . . .

[ELLIE enters at a run. LANA and FRIZBEE enter also but they appear as strange menacing figures, such as a stop sign that is knocked over, a staggering drunk, a car that nearly runs ELLIE down.]

VOICE, LANA and FRIZBEE: Run away. Run away. Run away. Run away.
There's a fact you've got to face. . .
Run away. Run away.
That she's taken your place. . . .
Run away. Run away.

VOICE, LANA and FRIZBEE: *[Recorded]* And there's nothing you can do . . . Run away, Run away. Cause he loves her more than you . . . Run away, Run away.

ELLIE: I'll show you. Boy will you be sorry! I'm never going home.

[A cat yeowls and LUCILLE appears dressed in a long black cloak.]

LUCILLE: *[Recorded.]* Mirror, mirror, on the wall, who's the fairest of them all?

ELLIE: I am, you wicked old stepmother! *[ELLIE runs into FRIZBEE who holds a newspaper in front of his face.]*

FRIZBEE: Go home little girl.

ELLIE: I'm never going home. I'll find some new parents.

[ELLIE runs over to LANA who is wearing a farmer's hat and mimes churning butter.]

ELLIE: Will you adopt a poor orphan child?

LANA: *[Malevolently]* My lands, who is this child?

ELLIE: I am just a poor orphan with no father or mother.

FRIZBEE: *[Also wearing a farmer's hat.]* I see the mark of the princess Cinderelli upon her cheek. We will adopt you.

627

ELLIE: I am not a princess, I'm just Ellie, Ellie Murphy.

FRIZBEE: Well, if you are not the princess then get lost. [ELLIE *staggers away from them.*]

ELLIE: I'm not scared. I'm not scared. I'm not scared. Oh, my feet are so cold. [MAX *enters slowly with his back to the audience. He wears a raincoat with a hood.* LUCILLE *enters with her back to the audience, she too wears a long coat.*]

ELLIE: Pop! Is that you Pop? Hey!

MAX: [*Still with his back to her.*] I beg your pardon?

ELLIE: Pop! It's me, Ellie.

MAX: I'm sorry but I don't believe I know you.

ELLIE: Pop, It's me, your daughter! Ellie!

MAX: Who?

ELLIE: Hey Lucille! It's me, Ellie.

LUCILLE: [*Still with her back to her.*] I beg your pardon?

ELLIE: Look at me! It's Ellie!

LUCILLE: I don't believe I know you. [*Slowly they turn to look at her. They wear half-masks which are transparent.*]

LUCILLE: Do you know this child?

MAX: No, I'm sorry little girl.

LUCILLE: Come dear, we have a plane to catch.

MAX: Oh yes, we mustn't be late.

LUCILLE: [*As they exit*] What a strange little girl.

ELLIE: Don't you know me? I'm your child! [*Strange music and recorded voices begin again.* LANA *and* FRIZBEE *step in and out of the shadows moving in slow motion.*]

VOICE, LANA and FRIZBEE: [*Recorded*] You're alone . . . You're alone.

LANA: [*Like a cat yeowl*] Hi ya Sweetie. . . .

VOICE, LANA and FRIZBEE: [*Recorded*] Can't go home. . . Can't go home. . .

ELLIE: Doesn't anybody know me?

LANA: Hi ya Boss. . . .

ELLIE: I'm not the Boss. I'm. . . .

VOICE, LANA and FRIZBEE: *[Recorded]* You're alone . . . You're alone.

FRIZBEE: Singer of the year. . .

ELLIE: I don't want to be. . .

VOICE, LANA and FRIZBEE: Got no home . . . Got no home . . .

ELLIE: I don't want to be an orphan.

VOICE, LANA *and* FRIZBEE: You're alone . . . You're alone . . . All alone . . . All alone. . .

ELLIE: I just want to go home. *[ELLIE runs around the stage, as she does the scene is shifted back to her house. ELLIE enters the living room area and looks around.]*

ELLIE: I'm home! Hey Pop? Lucille? I'm home. I don't want to be an orphan. Pop? LUCILLE? *[ELLIE sighs and goes into her room. She throws herself down on her bed and falls into a deep sleep.] [Soft music begins, a lullabye played on a music box. ELLIE dreams and in her dream MAX and LUCILLE enter wearing dressing gowns. LANA and FRIZBEE enter. They carry windchimes which tinkle softly. During this scene the words must tumble and flow like a waterfall, nothing frightening. It is a soft and gentle dream.]*

LUCILLE: Shhhh. Don't wake the baby . . .

FRIZBEE: What a beautiful baby. . . .

LANA: What a good baby. . . .

MAX: Daddy's beautiful baby girl.

ELLIE: *[Recorded]* I never had a Mother, not one I remember real well.

LANA: Sleep. . . .

FRIZBEE: . . . Dream.

ELLIE: *[Recorded]* Mother? Mother? Where are you? It's dark. I'm scared. *[LUCILLE billows a soft coverlet and covers ELLIE.]*

LUCILLE: Shall I tell you a story? Shall I sing you a song?

ELLIE: *[Recorded]* I can't see myself. I'm messy. I'm mean.

LANA: Sleep. . . .

FRIZBEE: . . . Dream.

MAX: Daddy's pretty Ellie.

ELLIE: *[Recorded]* Mother tell me a story. Mother sing me a song.
         [LUCILLE begins to hum softly.]

LANA: Sleep. . . .

FRIZBEE: . . . Dream.

ELLIE: Can you be my mother?

LUCILLE: Sleep. . . .

ELLIE: Please be my mother.

MAX: . . . Dream.

ELLIE: I want to have a mother!

LANA: Shhh. Don't wake the child.

FRIZBEE: What a beautiful child.

MAX: Daddy's beautiful girl.

LUCILLE: Pretty Ellie. . . .

MAX and LUCILLE: *[Recorded]* Pretty Ellie . . . Pretty Ellie . . .
         Pretty Ellie . . . Pretty Ellie. *[All exit slowly as the recorded
         music and sound continue for a moment. ELLIE tosses and turns
         on the bed. The dream fades and the house returns to normal.
         MAX enters the house dressed as he was at the bowling alley. He
         is upset and in a hurry.]*

MAX: I know I have a recent photograph around here somewhere.
       Lucille you call the police, say you want to report a missing
       person. *[LUCILLE enters.]*

LUCILLE: I just don't understand how she could have gotten so far
       so quickly. Oh Max, what are we going to do?

MAX: I know we had some pictures taken at Woolworths right be-
       fore she left for camp. Where did I put them?

LUCILLE: She's been gone two hours. Anything could have happened.

MAX: Take it easy. We'll find her. She's probably just hiding in a
       restaurant or something. You call the police. I'll go back to the
       bowling alley.

LUCILLE: I can't help feeling this is all my fault.

MAX: Maybe they are in her room. Call the police. *[MAX enters
       ELLIE'S room. He stops dead when he sees her asleep. He is un-
       able to speak for a second and sighs in relief.]*

MAX: *[Very calmly]* Lucille. *[LUCILLE crosses to him. He points to the sleeping figure.* LUCILLE *crouches by the bed.]*

LUCILLE: Thank God.

MAX: Let's let her sleep. She must be exhausted. *[They leave the room and close the door behind them.]*

LUCILLE: She must have walked all this way.

MAX: She must have run.

LUCILLE: *[Still slightly hysterical]* Thank God she's alright. Anything could have happened to her. I don't know what I would have done if . . .

   *[*ELLIE *wakes up, sits and listens.]*

MAX: Hey, calm down. Everything is alright now.

LUCILLE: She could have been killed. What if she'd gotten hit by a car?

MAX: *[Firmly]* Lucille, it is all over now. Take it easy. She's home. I'll get something to relax you, just a minute. *[*MAX *exits.* ELLIE *gets out of bed and starts toward the door.]*

VOICE: Red Light!

   *[*ELLIE *freezes.]*

VOICE: Where are you going?

ELLIE: Out there.

VOICE: Why?

ELLIE: To tell them I'm . . .

VOICE: You could have been killed and it's all HER fault. She almost got rid of you once and for all.

ELLIE: But she really sounded worried.

VOICE: You aren't going to fall for that stuff again are you? She just said that so Pop wouldn't be mad at her. She's trying to get rid of you.

ELLIE: Aww that's dumb.

VOICE: You could have been killed and she'd live happily ever after with Pop. That's how wicked stepmothers are you know.

ELLIE: But . . .

VOICE: You could have been killed. Green Light!
   *[*MAX *enters with a drink for* LUCILLE.*]*

631

MAX: Here, this will calm you down. Everything is going to be alright.

LUCILLE: Thanks. I've been thinking, Max, maybe I should go away.

MAX: What?

LUCILLE: Maybe I should just let you and Ellie work things out alone. I kept hoping it was just a matter of time . . . that gradually she would come to accept me.

MAX: You're just upset.

LUCILLE: I care for both of you too much to see you destroy what you had together. Maybe I should just leave for a while.

MAX: That's crazy. We are a family now and we are going to work through this thing, all of us, together. Your leaving isn't going to help.

LUCILLE: I don't know.

MAX: Well, I do.

LUCILLE: She must have loved her real Mother very much to hate me so.

MAX: She doesn't hate you. She's just mixed up right now. It's late and we are tired. Let's talk about this in the morning.

LUCILLE: No, I really think it would be better for me to leave you two alone for a while to work things out any way you can.

MAX: Let's go to bed.

[MAX *exits.* LUCILLE *picks up the note* ELLIE *left on the windshield and reads.*]

LUCILLE: "You win, Lucille." [*She looks towards* ELLIE'S *room.*] No, Ellie, YOU win. [*She exits.*]

[ELLIE *is disturbed and she starts out the door after them.*]

ELLIE: Hey you guys . . .

VOICE: Red Light! [ELLIE *freezes.*]

VOICE: Congratulations! You won!

ELLIE: But she's leaving.

VOICE: That's what you wanted isn't it? Now you and Pop can go back to having things the way they used to be.

ELLIE: Yeah but . . .

VOICE: After all, she wanted to get rid of you. She wanted you to get killed, and then you could have had a funeral.

ELLIE: A funeral?

VOICE: Yeah a funeral. At funerals everybody is real sorry for all the means things they ever did to you. Everybody just sits around and says nice things about you and they cry and cry and cry.

[FRIZBEE *starts to sniffle.*]

ELLIE: What about Pop?

VOICE: He cries the loudest of all. [FRIZBEE *bursts into sobs.*]

ELLIE: What am I supposed to do?

VOICE: Well, first you gotta have a coffin. [LANA *and* FRIZBEE *move the toy box forward for the coffin.*]

VOICE: You just lie there.

ELLIE: Suppose I want to see what's going on.

VOICE: No, you gotta just lie there.

ELLIE: That sounds stupid. Hey, I got an idea. Why don't you lie there and be me in the coffin.

VOICE: No, I stay right here.

ELLIE: Get in that coffin!

VOICE: Okay . . . Okay . . . Green Light! [VOICE *lies on the box and* ELLIE *takes charge of the microphone.*]

ELLIE: Okay ladies and gentlemen. Let's get this show on the road. Ellie Murphy's funeral . . . Take one! [LANA *and* FRIZBEE *clap their hands like a claque board.*]

ELLIE: Now the parade starts over there. I want a black horse with a plume. [FRIZBEE *puts a plume on his head and neighs.*]

ELLIE: Fantastic! I want music, drums sad and slow! That's right. [LANA *wearing a long black veil falls into a procession behind* FRIZBEE *and they both wail.*]

ELLIE: Now start with the nice things.

LANA: She was so young and so beautiful.

ELLIE: Cut! Lana, honey, more tears . . . that's right cry, cry, cry. Now throw yourself over the coffin. Preacher that's your cue. [FRIZBEE *becomes the preacher.*]

FRIZBEE: Poor Ellie Murphy! Why didn't I tell her how cute she was and what nice straight teeth she had.

ELLIE: Come on preacher, nicer things!

FRIZBEE: Poor Ellie Murphy. Why didn't I tell her how pretty she was, what a good voice she had. She was the best bowler I ever saw!

ELLIE: Pop! You're on! *[MAX enters wearing pajamas and a high silk hat, and black arm bands.]*

MAX: I'm sorry Ellie.

ELLIE: More feeling Pop!

MAX: I'M SORRY ELLIE!!!! How could I have been so blind? I never needed anyone but you. Now my life is empty, bleak, bland . . .

ELLIE: From the bottom of your heart, Pop!

MAX: What a fool I have been and now it is too late!!!

ELLIE: And now for the final touch! Lucille enters up right, rubbing her hand and laughing. *[ELLIE indicates up right. Nothing happens.]*

ELLIE: I said, the grand finale . . .LUCILLE enters up right, rubbing her hands and laughing. *[ELLIE indicates up right again and LUCILLE enters up left. She wears a coat and carries a suitcase.]*

LUCILLE: I have been thinking, Max, maybe I should go away.

ELLIE: No, CUT! Lucille enters up right, rubbing her hands and laughing.

LUCILLE: Maybe I should let you and Ellie work things out alone.

ELLIE: I said, up right!

LUCILLE: I kept hoping that it was just a matter of time.

ELLIE: Cut! Cut! You are not supposed to be saying that!

LUCILLE: I kept hoping that gradually she would come to accept me.

ELLIE: You are supposed to be glad that I'm dead.

LUCILLE: I care for you both too much to see you destroy what you had together. Maybe I should just leave.

ELLIE: You are not supposed to be saying that!

LUCILLE: She must have loved her real mother very much to hate me so. So I'm leaving.

ELLIE: Hey wait, Lucille.

LUCILLE: No Ellie, YOU win.

ELLIE: Wait I didn't mean for it to go this far.

VOICE: Red Light! [ELLIE *freezes.*]

VOICE: Don't call her back. You've won! Now things will be the way they always have been.

ELLIE: Why don't you shut up! You are supposed to be dead! I want a mother and she's a perfectly good one.

VOICE: But she's a wicked step. . . .

ELLIE: RED LIGHT! [VOICE *freezes.*]

ELLIE: Lana, Frizbee, take that thing away. Green Light! [LANA *and* FRIZBEE *move like puppets. They move* VOICE *back to the stool and move the toy box back into its place.*]

ELLIE: Now get in. [ELLIE *helps them both into the toy box. She closes the lid and sits on the box for a second.*]

ELLIE: Lucille! Lucille! Come back! [ELLIE *moves back into bed as* LUCILLE *and* MAX *enter her room. They both wear the dressing gowns seen in the dream scene.*]

MAX: [*Entering first*] Ellie? What's the matter?

ELLIE: Where is Lucille?

LUCILLE: [*Entering*] Right here. What's the matter?

ELLIE: [*Relieved*] Oh . . . uhhh, nothing. I must have had a bad dream.

MAX: Do you want to tell me about it?

ELLIE: I don't think you'd like it.

MAX: Is it alright now?

ELLIE: Yeah. I guess so.

MAX: Well, goodnight Midget.

[MAX *kisses her on the forehead.*]

ELLIE: Goodnight Pop. [MAX *and* LUCILLE *turn to leave.*]

ELLIE: Uhhh Lucille? [MAX *stays in the doorway and* LUCILLE *crosses to her.*]

LUCILLE: Yes?

ELLIE: I'm . . . sorry I ran away.

LUCILLE: So am I.

ELLIE: Well, I'm back now.

LUCILLE: I'm glad.

ELLIE: So am I. *[Pause.]*

ELLIE: Uhhh Lucille, I'm cold.

LUCILLE: Well no wonder, you kicked your covers off. *[LUCILLE billows the covers over her and tucks her in. ELLIE smiles.]*

ELLIE: Uhh. Lucille, knock, knock . . .

LUCILLE: Who's there?

ELLIE: Sticker.

LUCILLE: Sticker who?

ELLIE: Sticker-ound for a while, okay?

LUCILLE: Okay. Goodnight Ellie. Sleep well. *[LUCILLE moves away a few steps and crouches.]*

LUCILLE: Goodnight Lana. Goodnight Frizbee.

ELLIE: Uhhh Lucille, they're not here.

LUCILLE: Oh. *[LUCILLE crosses to MAX and turns back.]*

LUCILLE: Goodnight Ellie.

ELLIE: *[Pulling the covers up and turning over.]* See ya in the morning.

BLACK OUT

THE ARKANSAW BEAR

by

AURAND HARRIS

THE ARKANSAW BEAR

by

Aurand Harris

Copyright 1980,
by

ANCHORAGE PRESS, INC.
Post Office Box 8067
New Orleans, Louisiana 70182

THE ARKANSAW BEAR

The repertoire of plays for children in this country has included so few serious plays that, over the years, children's theatre has come to be almost synonomous with light, superficial dramas with happy endings. Such a conception has a basis in fact, but it is, in reality, only partly true; and in the last few years several dramas have appeared to challenge this stereotype.

Most of the children's plays written over the last century have included serious stories, albeit stories where the seriousness has been greatly reduced by happy endings, liberal doses of comic relief, and characters and situations that are set in a far-off time and place. The fairy tale plays provide a good illustration of this point. *Jack in the Beanstalk* and *Rumpelstiltskin*, for example, each includes wicked and powerful antagonists who threaten the well-being of other characters in the stories: in several instances Jack is in danger of being killed by the giant; and the Princess in *Rumpelstiltskin* is threatened with losing her child — actions that are as serious as one can imagine. Of course, Jack ultimately defeats the Giant, the Princess out-smarts Rumpelstiltskin, and all — except the antagonist — live happily ever after.

Regardless of this action, these two plays are seldom perceived by children as being essentially serious, as the primary audience response is one of emotional titilation from being caught up in the excitement of the struggle between only vaguely recognizable characters. The perils of each situation are dealt with in a generalized manner, and it is left to generalized characters to find a solution to the problem. Audience members have little personal involvement in the situation, and, in the tradition of the popular theatre entertainment throughout the ages, the plays cause more excitement than thought, more thrills than insight.

Such trends in the development of literature have not occurred by chance. The nature of the literature has always been determined by adult perspectives of what children can understand and what is appropriate for them. It is these perspectives that have caused playwrights to make villains look ludicrous and heros wholly good, and it is these perspectives that have brought pressure to bear on playwrights to write happy endings for their works.

This attitude has been quite consistent throughout the history of children's theatre in this country. Of the plays written prior to mid-century, only *The Birthday of the Infanta* (wherein a sympathetic character dies) stands as a notable exception in this regard — but even with this play the action is set in a far-off time and place.

The stylistic and thematic innovations that began to appear in the literature after mid-century have only slowly begun to reflect a change

639

in this attitude about drama for children — a change that has been caused, in part, by the success of a handful of plays that challenge that protective view.

A list of such plays would include *Reynard the Fox* and *The Ice Wolf*, both of which are at the forefront of this movement, and less well-known works, such as Harris' *Steal Away Home* and Fauquez's *Don Quixote of La Mancha*. *Steal Away Home* is a dramatic story of two boys' escape from slavery on the Underground Railroad — the seriousness of which is underscored by the murder of their companion. In *Don Quixote of La Mancha* a well-liked, sympathetic character dies. The death is natural and expected, but its impact is powerful.

Even these modern plays all include at least one of the factors that serve to insulate the audience members from a personal understanding of the seriousness of the action. It has been only in the last few years, with the increased popularity of plays that present real characters in contemporary situations, that playwrights have written serious plays that are not changed substantially by these insulating factors — plays that invite close, personal involvement in an action that is serious, and is told seriously.

The Arkansaw Bear, by Aurand Harris, is just such a play. It is a serious dramatization that focuses on death, a subject seldom discussed in detail with children. In the play Harris reveals the hurt, confusion, and fear experienced by a young girl (Tish) when she is told that her beloved Grandfather is about to die. In contrast to the more traditional literature, the story is placed in a contemporary setting; Tish is portrayed as a modern little girl, the humor in the play does not lessen the impact of the story, and there is no surprise, happy ending.

The play opens with an emotional scene that quickly places the audience in the midst of the conflict. Tish is alone on the stage, talking to her mother and her aunt: characters that we hear but never see. Tish is told that her grandfather is about to die; when she tries to see her grandfather, her mother prevents her from entering his room. Although this action is done to shield Tish from the pain of the situation, it only makes her more confused. Tish does not understand death; she particularly doesn't understand why her grandfather has to die. With minimal exposition, Harris clearly outlines the problem: not that Grandfather has to die, but that Tish must come to some understanding of his death.

Tish runs off to her favorite tree, where she makes a wish on Star Bright, the first star visible that night. Tish asks to know "why Grandpa has to die?" Star Bright does not answer this question directly, but instead unfolds a fantasy world of circus characters wherein Mime, the World's Greatest Dancing Bear, Ringmaster, and Little Bear play out the "riddle of life" for Tish.

THE ARKANSAW BEAR

In this fable, Dancing Bear is about to be called to the Great Center Ring — a metaphor for death. Not wanting to die, Dancing Bear tries to escape from the Ringmaster, who is pursuing him. With Tish's help, Dancing Bear finally accepts his own inevitable death, but only after he has taught his dances to Little Bear, so that these dances might live on after he dies. Dancing Bear thus poignantly demonstrates, as he himself comes to know, that he is a part of what went before, and he will be a part of what is yet to come.

Through her fantasized participation in this fable, Tish also comes to realize that she, like Little Bear, is in a position to carry on where her Grandfather left off. She recognizes that she too is a "chip off the old block," and, although her grandfather has to die, much of him lives on in her. Armed with this new perspective, she breaks out of the fantasy and returns home to say goodbye to her grandfather.

The play includes two separate but related stories; the first shows Tish's interaction with her family, and the second tells of the Dancing Bear's struggle to understand the riddle of life. Although this latter story comprises the major portion of the play — a factor which can be interpreted as shifting the emphasis away from Tish to the Dancing Bear — the two sections of the play are well integrated. The characters in the real world each have counterparts in the fantasy, and it is through the fantasy that Tish learns to cope with her real world problems. Through her experience with the fantasy characters Tish is better able to accept her Grandfather's death, and at the end of the play she declares: "I know everyone . . . everything has a time to die . . . and it's sad. But Grandpa knew the answer to the riddle."

Harris is not subtle about the message of the play, but neither is he overly-sentimental. The theme is stated in positive terms through a variety of symbols including the Ringmaster, the Great Center Ring, and the show-must-go-on philosophy of the circus world. Even Star Bright — who, like Tish's mother, watches over Tish — talks of her place in "the great circle of life" where "in every ending there is a new beginning."

Amid these symbols Harris introduces the Little Bear, a character that embodies everything this play is about. He is "just a country bear, with no schoolin'," yet his homespun philosophy of life reverberates with wisdom. He has "seen a lot of them" [other bears] die, but since there ain't nothin' you can do about it," you go on living. And, as his mama told him (and of course his mama would be a source of wisdom), "you give yourself to the living." The youthful exuberance of the Little Bear, his innocence and his joy of living are quickly recognized, enjoyed, and understood by children.

The difference between this play and the less serious and immediate plays of the past are manifold. The protagonist, Tish, is bright, intelligent, and inquisitive; she is also frightened and vulnerable. She is a very real character with whom audiences can readily identify. Although the play also contains fantasy characters, these are used to push forward the through-line of Tish's action: the pursuit of a real and serious problem. Rather than distance the audience from this action, the fantasy situation allows the riddle to be explained in metaphoric images that can be readily understood by young children.

The play begins in the real world and ends in the real world, with a denouement that is sad, but affirmative and realistic. Tish is not given the magical powers to prevent her grandfather's death, but even though she is a child, she comes to some understanding about death and grows considerably in the process.

This use of the fantasy in *Arkansaw Bear* is similar to that portrayed in *Step on a Crack*, where Ellie comes to some understanding of her problems through interaction with imaginary characters. This technique of moving the action of the play back and forth between real and fantasy worlds is an effective dramatic device that also conveys a realistic image of a troubled child.

The Arkansaw Bear is a relatively new addition to the repertoire, and although it does not, by itself, signal a new trend toward more serious drama for young people, it does point out one area of growth within the field. Plays such as *Step on a Crack*, Kral's *Special Class*, and Kesselman's "Maggie Magalita" — all of which present recognizable child characters confronted with real problems — illustrate both the degree to which playwrights are making more creative use of the theatre medium, and the changing views of children and childhood. The adults who presented *The Little Princess* almost eighty years ago would probably consider the thematic material presented in *The Arkansaw Bear* much too harsh for children and very much beyond their intellectual and emotional powers of understanding.

Plays designed for mindless entertainment still dominate the literature, but *The Arkansaw Bear* demonstrates well that the field is not comprised entirely of spectacle and melodrama. This play, which shows a profound respect for children, presents a serious and complex issue in a manner that entertains without diminishing that seriousness.

THE ARKANSAW BEAR

Cast

TISH

STAR BRIGHT

MIME

WORLD'S GREATEST DANCING BEAR

GREAT RINGMASTER

LITTLE BEAR

VOICES: MOTHER

AUNT ELLEN

ANNOUNCER

SCENE

The present. Somewhere in Arkansas.

(As the house lights dim, there is a glow of light on the front curtain. Over a loud speaker a man's whistling of "O Susannah" is heard. The curtains open. Tish walks into a large spot of warm light at L. The whistling dims out. Tish is a little girl and carries some hand-picked flowers. She listens to the voices, heard over a loud speaker, and reacts to them as if Mother and Aunt Ellen were on each side of her, downstage.)

TISH.   I've come to see Grandpa.

MOTHER'S VOICE.   No, dear. No. You can't go in.

TISH.   But Mother —— ——

MOTHER'S VOICE.   No, Tish! You can't see Grandpa now.

TISH.   I picked him some flowers. These are Grandpa's favorites.

AUNT ELLEN'S VOICE.   *(She is Tish's great aunt, elderly, gentle and emotional)* Quiet, child.

TISH.   But Aunt Ellen —— ——

AUNT ELLEN'S VOICE.   The doctor is here.

TISH.   The doctor?

MOTHER'S VOICE.   Tish, dear.

TISH.   Yes, mother?

MOTHER'S VOICE.   Grandpa had a turn for the worse. His heart —— ——

AUNT ELLEN'S VOICE.   Oh, it's the end.

   (Cries quietly)

TISH.   The end?

AUNT ELLEN'S VOICE.   The doctor said . . . no hope.

   (Tish reacts)

MOTHER'S VOICE.   Don't cry, Aunt Ellen.

TISH.   Is Grandpa going . . . to die?

AUNT ELLEN'S VOICE.   Yes.

TISH.   No! He can't.

MOTHER'S VOICE.   We all have to die, dear.

TISH.   I know. But not Grandpa.

   (Start to move)

644

MOTHER'S VOICE. Stop. You can't go in.

TISH. Why can't he live forever!

AUNT ELLEN'S VOICE. You're too young to understand. To full of life.

TISH. I have to tell him there's a circus coming. I saw a poster with a bear.

MOTHER'S VOICE. It doesn't matter now.

TISH. Yes, it does! Do something!

MOTHER'S VOICE. *(Firmly)* We've done all we can.

TISH. But not enough! I . . . I didn't do enough!

AUNT ELLEN'S VOICE. Quiet. Quiet.

TISH. *(Softly)* Yes, if I'd been quiet so he could sleep. And — Oh! Once when I' was mad, I said . . . I wish he was dead. I didn't mean it, Grandpa. I didn't mean it.

MOTHER'S VOICE. Hush, dear. It's not your fault. Grandpa loved you.

TISH. Then why is he . . . leaving me?

(Pulls away as if being held)

TISH. Oh, let me go!

MOTHER'S VOICE. *(Sharply, becoming edgy with emotion)* Yes. Go put the flowers in some water.

TISH. He liked the pink ones. Now . . . he'll never see them. Oh, why . . . why does Grandpa have to die?

MOTHER'S VOICE. *(Sternly, trying to control and cover her grief)* Run along, dear. Run along.

AUNT ELLEN'S VOICE. Keep away. Away from his door. Away . . . away.

(The voices of Mother and Aunt Ellen overlap and mix together, as they keep repeating, "Run along," "Away," "Run . . . run," "Away . . . away," "Run," "Away." "Run . . . away; run . . . away." They build to a climax in a choral chant, "Run . . . away.)

TISH. I will. I'll run away. Up the hill . . . to my tree . . . my tree.
(She runs, circling to the tree which is at R, and on which the lights come up. The circle of light on the first scene dims out, and the chanting of the voices stop. Tish stands alone by her tree in the soft light of evening. She brushes back a tear, shakes her head, and throws the flowers on the ground)

(She sinks to the ground by the tree, hugs her knees, and looks up. She sees the first star, which is out of sight. Quickly she gets up, points to the star and chants)

Star light, star bright,
First star I see tonight,
I wish I may, I wish I might,
Have the wish I wish tonight.
I wish . . . I wish . . . Oh, Grandpa . . . why?

(Goes back to tree)

Why do you have to die?

(There is star music, tinkling with bells. From above, a small swing starts descending. Magic star light spots on it. Star Bright stands on the swing, which stops in mid-air. Music dims out)

STAR BRIGHT. Repeat, please.

TISH. I wish . . . I wish . . .

STAR BRIGHT. I know you are wishing. That's why I'm here. But WHAT? Repeat please.

TISH. *(Sees and goes near him)* Who are you?

STAR BRIGHT. *(Slowly and proudly)* I am the first star out tonight!

(Happily)

I did it! I did it! I did it again!

(Excitedly)

First star . . . first star . . . first star out tonight!

(To Tish)

It's the early star, you know, who gets the wish. What is yours? Repeat, please.

TISH. Can you make a wish come true?

STAR BRIGHT. I've been making wishes come true for a thousand years.

TISH. A thousand years! You're older than Grandpa.

STAR BRIGHT. *(Sits on swing)* Old? Oh, no. I'll twinkle for another thousand years.

TISH. And then?

STAR BRIGHT. *(Cheerfully)* Then my light will go out.

TISH. Like Grandpa.

STAR BRIGHT. But there will be a new star. It's the great pattern . . .

TISH. I'll never have another Grandpa.

STAR BRIGHT. . . . the great circle of life. In every ending there is a new beginning.

TISH. *(Fully realizing it)* I'll never see Grandpa again. I'll never hear him whistle.

(Begins to whistle "O Susannah")

STAR BRIGHT. Your wish? What is your wish?

TISH. I wish . . . I wish Grandpa could live a thousand years!

STAR BRIGHT. *(Startled)* What? Repeat, please!

TISH. *(Excited)* I wish he'd never die. Nobody would ever die! Everyone live forever!

STAR BRIGHT. Oh, no, no, no! Think what a mixed up world it would be!

TISH. *(Speaks intently)* I wish . . . I wish I knew why . . . why Grandpa has to die.

STAR BRIGHT. That is not a quick one-two-buckle-my shoe wish. No. That is a think-and-show-it, then you-know-it, come-true wish.

TISH. Please.

STAR BRIGHT. *(With anticipated excitement)* Close your eyes. Whisper the words again. Open your eyes. And your wish will begin.

(Tish closes her eyes. Star Bright claps his hands, then motions. There are music and beautiful lights. Star Bright is delighted with the effect.)

Very good! Repeat, please.

(He claps and waves his hand. Again there are music and beautiful lights.)

Excellent! Thank you!

(The swing with Star Bright is pulled up and out of sight. The full stage is seen, lighted brightly and in soft colors. [Never is the stage dark, eerie, or frightening]. It is Tish's fantasy. There are the large tree at R, and open space with beautiful sky.

Mime appears at R. He is a showman, a magician and an accomplished mime who never speaks. He wears a long coat with many colorful patch pockets. He is NOT in white face, but his face is natural, friendly and expressive. He enters cautiously, carrying a

*traveling box, which he sets down at C. On the side the audience
sees, is painted the word, BEAR. On the other side is painted the
word, DANCING. He beckons off R. The World's Greatest Dancing Bear enters R. He is a star performer, amusing, vain and
loveable like a teddy bear. He does NOT wear an animal mask,
nor is the actor's face painted, frightening or grotesque, with animal make up. He wears his traveling hat. He hurries in, worried
and out of breath.)*

BEAR.   I must stop and get my breath.

(Pants heavily)

My heart is pounding.

(Looks about)

Are we safe?

(Frightened)

I don't see him. I don't hear him. Yes, we have out run him.

(Motions and Mime places box for Bear to sit)

Where . . . where in this wide whirling wonderful world . . . do
you think we are? Switzerland?

*(Mime makes pointed mountain with his wrist, runs his fingers
up and down the "mountain," then shakes his head.)*

You are right. No mountains. England?

*(Mime opens and holds up imaginary umbrella, holds hand out to
feel the rain, shakes his head.)*

You are right. No rain. India?

*(Mime leans over, swings one arm for a trunk, then other for his
tail and walks.)*

No elephants.

TISH.   Excuse me.

(They freeze. She comes to them.)

I can tell you where you are. You are in Arkansas.

BEAR.   Quick! Disguise. Hide.

*(He and Mime hurry to R. Mime quickly takes from one of his
pockets a pair of dark glasses and gives them to Bear who puts
them on; then stands beside Bear to hide him.)*

TISH. *(Recites with pride)* Arkansas was the 25th state to be admitted to the union. It is the 27th in size, and the state flower is apple blossom.

BEAR. Who is it?

(Mime pantomines a girl)

A girl?

(Mime pantomimes a small girl)

A little girl? Tell her to go away. To run away.

(Mime pantomimes to Tish. Bear hides behind tree)

TISH. I have. I have run away. Have you run away, too?

(Mime nods)

Why?

(Mime looks frightened off R, then puts finger to lips)

Who are you?

(Mime takes a card from a pocket and presents it to her. She reads)

"A Mime." You never speak.

(Mime shakes his head, and "walks" in one spot and tips his hat.)

"A Magician." You do tricks!

(Mime pulls handkerchief from sleeve)

"Friend." You give help.

(Mime touches handkerchief under her eyes)

Thank you. I was crying because my Grandpa . . . he's going to . . .

(Bear, without glasses steps out from behind the tree, does a loud tap dance step and poses. Mime turns the traveling box around and with a flourish points to the word painted on the side of the box. Tish reads it with amazement.)

Dancing.

(Mime turns box around again. She reads)

Bear.

(Mime motions to Bear who steps forward.)

I've never met a bear. I've never seen a DANCING bear.

BEAR. *(To Mime)*

Should I?

(Mime nods)

Shall I?

(Mime nods)

I will! My Spanish hat.

(Mime jumps with joy and gets hat from box. Bear motions to Tish who sits on the ground.)

Be seated, please.

(Mime holds up handmirror, which he takes from a pocket, holds it up for Bear to look at himself, and fixes the hat.)

To the right . . . to the right . . . Ah, just right!

(Mime motions and a spot light comes on. An announcer's voice is heard over a loud speaker.)

ANNOUNCER'S VOICE.   Ladies and Gentlemen: Presenting in his spectacular special, Spanish dance, the World's famous, the World's favorite, the World's Greatest Dancing Bear!

BEAR.   *(Mime motions and Spanish music is heard. Bear steps into the spotlight. He dances with professional perfection a Spanish dance, but he does not finish. At a climactic moment, he stops, holds his hand against his heart and speaks with short breaths.)*

Stop the music.

(Mime motions. Music stops.)

Dim the light.

(Mime motions. Spot dims out.)

TISH.   What is it?

BEAR.   *(Breathing heavily.)* He is near. He is coming.

TISH.   Who?

BEAR.   He is almost here. Hide. I must hide. He must not find me.

(Mime points to tree.)

Yes, the tree. Hurry!

(Mime helps Bear to tree.)

TISH.   Who? Who is coming?

BEAR.   The box. Cover the box.

(He disappears behind the tree. Mime sits on traveling box. Bear's head appears.)

Talk.

(Mime mime-talks with hands and face.)

Louder!

(Bear's head disappears. Mime motions for Tish to talk.)

TISH.   Talk? What about?

BEAR.   *(Head appears)* Arkansas.

(Head disappears)

TISH.   *(Recites nervously)* Arkansas has mineral springs, natural caves, and . . . and . . . diamond mines.

(Looks off R and whispers frightened)

I don't hear anyone. I don't see anyone.

(Mime motions for her to talk.)

Arkansas was first known as the state of many bears.

(Looks and whispers mysteriously)

There isn't anyone. Nothing. Just quiet, nothing. Who is he running away from?

(Mime motions "Sh," then runs L to R and looks, then motions for Bear to come out.)

BEAR.   *(Comes from behind tree)* He didn't find me. I escaped . . . this time.

(Pleased, but short of breath)

My traveling hat. We must go on.

(Mime takes Spanish hat and gives Bear traveling hat.)

TISH.   Where? Where will you go?

BEAR.   *(Looks off R, afraid)* I must keep ahead of him.

TISH.   Ahead of who? Who!

BEAR.   *(Cautiously)* Never speak his name aloud.

(Looks around)

He may be listening, and come at once.

(Mime gives him hat)

Oh, my poor hat. You and I have traveled together for many a mile and many a year. We are both beginning to look a little weary.

(Puts hat on)

TISH. Grandpa has an old hat.

BEAR. Perhaps, if it had a new feather. Yes! A bright new feather!

TISH. I think your hat is very stylish.

BEAR. *(Pleased)* You do?

TISH. And very becoming.

BEAR. *(Flattered)* Thank you. You are a very charming little girl. What is your name?

TISH. Tish.

BEAR. Tish-sh-sh! That is not a name. That is a whistle. Ti-sh-sh-sh!

TISH. It's short for Leticia. It was my Grandmother's name.

BEAR. Leticia. Ah, that is a name with beauty.

TISH. Grandpa calls me "Little Leticia."

BEAR. I shall call you . . .

(Rolling the "R")

Princess Leticia.

TISH. Princess?

BEAR. All my friends are important. Kings and Queens . . . Command performances for Ambassadors and Presidents . . .

(To Mime)

The velvet box, please.

(Mime takes from a pocket a small box)

I will show you my medals, my honors.

TISH. My Grandpa won a medal.

BEAR. Ah?

TISH. He was the best turkey caller in Arkansas.

BEAR. Turkey caller?

TISH. He won first prize!

BEAR. (To Mime) Pin them on me so she can see. And so that I can remember . . . once again . . . all my glories.

(Royal music begins and continues during the scene. Mime puts ribbons and jeweled medals on Bear as Voice announces each decoration. Two are pinned on. One is on a ribbon which is fastened around Bear's neck.)

ANNOUNCER'S VOICE. The Queen's highest honor, the Royal Medallion.

BEAR. I danced in the Great Hall. It was the Queen's birthday party.

ANNOUNCER'S VOICE. The Diamond Crescent of the East.

BEAR. Fifteen encores. Fifteen encores and they still applauded.

ANNOUNCER'S VOICE. The Royal Ribbon of Honor for Distinguished Service.

BEAR. It was during the war. I danced for the soldiers.

ANNOUNCER'S VOICE. And today, a new decoration. Her Royal Highness, Princess Leticia presents, in honor of her Grandfather, the highest award in the State of Arkansas — the Turkey Feather.

(Mime takes a bright feather from a pocket and gives it to Tish. Bear parades to her, with a few dance steps, and she puts the feather in his hat. Royal music stops.)

BEAR. Thank you. A party! We will celebrate my new honor!

(To Mime)

Food and festivities! Honey bread!

(Mime nods)

Thick with honey spread!

(Mime nods twice, then makes magic motions toward Bear. Suddenly Mime turns and points to Leticia. She puts out her hand which, magically, holds a honey bun.)

TISH. *(Delighted)* O-o-oh! It looks delicious.

BEAR. *(Mime turns and points to Bear who puts out his hand which, also magically, holds a colorful honey bun.)*

A-a-ah! It IS delicious.

(Bear puts finger in it, then licks finger. Mime raises his hand.)

Yes, give us a toast.

(Bear and Tish hold honey buns up. Mime pantomimes "A toast . . ." holds up his hand; "to the winner . . ." clasps his hands and shakes them high in the air; "of the turkey feather," walks like a turkey, bobbing his head, then Mime pulls out an imaginary feather from his hip.)

Thank you.

TISH.   What did he say?

BEAR.   You didn't listen.

TISH.   How can I hear when he doesn't speak?

BEAR.   You listen with your eyes, and then YOU say the words. Listen. He will repeat the toast.

TISH.   *(Mime pantomimes the toast again. She watches and speaks aloud.)* "A toast . . . to the winner . . . of the turkey feather!"

BEAR.   Thank you. Now entertainment!

(To Mime)

You tell us a story.

(To Tish)

You listen and say the words.

TISH.   Me?

BEAR.   And I will eat!

(Wiggles with excitement and sits on box.)

TISH.   *Mime pantomimes a story which Tish, watching him, repeats in words.)* "Once there was . . . a princess. . . a beautiful princess!"

BEAR.   Named

(Sings it)

Leticia.

(Takes a bite)

TISH.   "One day . . . in the woods . . . she met . . .

(Doubtful)

. . . a cat?"

654

(Mime shakes his head. Mimes again)

A . . . goosey-gander?

(Mime shakes his head. Mimes again.)

TISH. A . . . bear!

BEAR. The World's Greatest Dancing Bear!

(Seated, he makes his own vocal music and dances with his feet.)

TISH. "Under a spreading tree . . . they had a party . . . with honey bread, thick with honey spread."

BEAR. (Licks his five fingers, one on each word) Yum . . . yum . . . TO . . . the . . . last . . . crumb.

(Licks his hand and picks and eats crumbs from his lap).

TISH. "Now honey bread, thick with honey spread . . . made the bear very . . . sleepy. He yawned."

(Bear follows action of the story and goes to sleep.)

". . . gave a little sigh . . . and took a little nap."

(Bear snores)

He's asleep. Who . . . who is he running away from?

(Mime goes to sleeping Bear, puts his fingers to his lips then mimes.)

"The World's Greatest Dancing Bear . . . is old and tired . . . and his heart . . . is tired."

(Herself)

Like Grandpa.

(Speaking for Mime)

"He is running away from . . ." Who? "Someone is coming to take him away . . . forever." Does that mean if he's caught, he will die?

(Mime nods)

TISH. Is he running away . . . from death?

(Mime nods)

Oh! I'll help him. Yes, I'll help him.

(Faint music of calliope is heard, Bear stirs)

He's waking up.

BEAR.   *(Slowly wakes up)* Music . . . the calliope . . . circus music of the Great Center ring!

(Rises)

The Ringmaster is coming!

TISH.   *(To Mime)* Death?

(Mime nods)

BEAR.   He is near. I hear the music.

TISH.   I don't hear it.

(To Mime)

Do you?

(Mime shakes his head)

BEAR.   Only I can hear him. Only I can see him. He is coming for me. Quick! We must go.

TISH.   Yes, I'll help you.

BEAR.   This way. Hurry!

(Mime carries box. Led by Bear they start L, but stop when the music becomes louder.)

No! No! The music is here. Quick! Turn! Run the other way.

(They rush to R and are stopped by music becoming louder.)

No! The music is coming from here. It is all around us! Here! There! Look!

(He points off R)

TISH.   What?

BEAR.   The Great Ringmaster. He is there! He is coming . . . for me! *(Ringmaster enters slowly from R. He wears an ornate ringmaster's jacket, boots and a tall hat. He has a friendly face, a pleasant voice, but walks and speaks with authority. He stops. Music stops.)*

Quick! Hide me! Hide me!

(Bear runs L. Tish and Mime follow. He quickly hides behind them when they stop. Bear peeks over Tish's shoulder.)

Tell him to go away.

TISH.   I can't see him. Where is he?

656

BEAR. There.

(Hides)

TISH. *(Bravely speaks, facing front talking into space.)* Excuse me . . . sir. This is my secret place . . . by the big tree. You must leave at once. Go away. Now.

(Whispers to Bear)

Did he go?

BEAR. *(Peeks) No.*

(Hides)

RINGMASTER. *(Distinctly and with authority)* I have come for the Dancing Bear. I have come to take him to the Great Center Ring.

BEAR. Tell him he has made a mistake.

TISH. Excuse me . . . sir. You have made a mistake.

RINGMASTER. *(Opens book)* No. It is written plainly in the book. The date is today. The name . . . is the Dancing Bear.

BEAR. *(Who was hidden by Mime at the side, now steps into view, wearing boxing gloves and a sport cap.)* You HAVE made a mistake. I am a BOXING bear.

(Mime blows a whistle and continues to blow it, as Bear shadow boxes, comically, with a few dance steps and kicks thrown in. He ends in a heroic pose.)

Goodbye.

RINGMASTER. A boxing bear?

(Looks in book)

There has never been a mistake.

TISH. *(Whispers)* Have you tricked him? Outwitted him?

BEAR. *(Nods, then calls loudly)* Yes. Training time. On your mark; get set; ready — talleyho!

(Starts jogging off R)

RINGMASTER. *(Reads)* The book says: His father, born in Russia, a dancing bear.

BEAR. *(Stops, indignant)* Correct that. He was Russia's most honored dancing bear.

RINGMASTER. His mother, born in Spain, also a dancing bear.

BEAR. She was the prima ballerina bear of all Spain!

RINGMASTER. He, only son — —

BEAR. Is the World's Greatest Dancing Bear!

RINGMASTER. Then you are the one I have come for!

BEAR. Yes!

RINGMASTER. Then we will have no more tricks or games.

(Bear realizes he has revealed himself.)

Come. Take my hand.

(Bear always reacts with fear to the Ringmaster's white gloved hand.)

I will show you the way to the Great Center Ring.

BEAR. No! No!

TISH. What is he saying?

BEAR. He is going to take me away.

RINGMASTER. Come. You must. And it is easier if you go quietly.

BEAR. No! I will not go with you. I will fight!

(Holds up boxing gloves)

TISH. Fight him! I'll help you!

BEAR. I have fought all my life. Battled my way to the top. Look at my medals. I will fight to the end.

RINGMASTER. This, my friend, is the end.

BEAR. No! No! Not for me. Not yet! Stay away! I have new dances to do.

BEAR. No! No.

(Savagely)

I will claw! I will eat! I will crush! I will kill! Kill to live!

(Violently throws boxing gloves away)

To live! To live!

RINGMASTER. Everyone shouts when he is frightened of the dark.

BEAR. I WILL NOT DIE!

RINGMASTER. You have no choice.

BEAR. But . . . why? Why me? ME!

RINGMASTER. You are like all the others. Everyone thinks HE will live forever. Come.

BEAR. No! What did I do wrong? What can I do now? To stop it!

RINGMASTER. Death comes to all. It has never been IF you will die. The only question has been WHEN you will die. Now you know.

BEAR. *(Runs)* I will run, I will hide.

RINGMASTER. *(With authority)* You cannot escape from death.

BEAR. *(Bargaining desperately)* More time. Give me more time. I have so much to do.

RINGMASTER. *(Slightly annoyed)* There is always that which is left undone.

BEAR. I don't know how . . . to die. I need to rehearse.

RINGMASTER. No one has to rehearse. It is very simple . . . very easy.

(Holds out hand)

Come. It is growing late.

BEAR. No!

(Desperate for any excuse)

I must write my memories! Tell the world the glories of my life. My life . . .

(Pause. Tish and Mime rush to him as he falters, place box and help him sit.)

it is almost over. And what was it? A few medals that will be lost. There must be more to life. Give me time. Time to find the answer.

TISH. *(Kneeling by him, pleads into space.)* Please . . . let him live.

RINGMASTER. Your life is over. Today is the day.

BEAR. But my day is not over.

(To Tish)

The day is not ended, is it?

TISH. Give him to the END of the day!

BEAR. Yes! To the end. Oh, you are a very smart little girl!

RINGMASTER. Well . . .

(*Looks in his book*)

TISH. What did he say?

BEAR. He's looking in his book.

RINGMASTER. The day you are to die is written plainly. But not the hour.

BEAR. Then give me the full day.

TISH. Please.

BEAR. YES!

TISH. Can you live?

BEAR. YES! Oh, let me shout to the world! I AM ALIVE!

(*To Mime*)

Give me my brightest, my happiest hat!

(*To Ringmaster, who has gone*)

Oh, thank you . . . thank you . . . He is gone . . . for a while.

(*To Tish*)

Oh, let me touch you. Let me feel the warmth . . . the life in you. There is so much yet to do! And so little time. My life . . . it went too fast. I didn't stop to listen . . . I didn't stop to see.

(*Mime waves clown hat in front of Bear*)

Oh, yes! I will be the clown!

(*Puts hat on. To Tish*)

Come. Dance with me! And we will make the world spin round and round with joy!

TISH. Grandpa taught me how to whistle and how to dance a jig.

(*Quickly she whistles "O Susannah," and does a little jig, looking at her feet.*)

BEAR. No, no, no. To dance is a great honor. Hold your head high.

(*He follows his own instructions*)

And first you smile to the right . . . then you smile to the left . . . and you bow to the center . . . and then . . . begin.
(*Mime motions. A spotlight comes on Bear. Music is heard. Bear does a short, charming soft-shoe dance. Spotlight and music dim*)

out. Tish applauds. Bear sits on box which Mime places for him.
Bear is happy, but breathless.)

TISH.   Oh, how wonderful!

BEAR.   Thank you.

TISH.   You're better than Grandpa! He can only do a little jig.

BEAR.   But he taught you?

TISH.   Yes.

BEAR.   And he taught you how to whistle?

TISH.   Yes.

BEAR.   *(Rises)* If I could teach my dances to someone . . . if someone
could carry on the fame of my family . . . All my hats . . . there
will be no one to wear my hats. They, too, will be put in a box
and forgotten. Tell me, are you like your Grandfather?

TISH.   Daddy says I'm a chip off the old block.

BEAR.   You are a part of him. And you will carry on for him in life.

(Excited)

Yes! Yes, that is the answer to the riddle.

TISH.   What riddle?

BEAR.   The riddle of life. I must leave my dances! They will be a part
of me that will live on! But who? Where! How!

TISH.   Make a wish!

BEAR.   A wish?

TISH.   On the first star you see. And it will come true. It will. It will!

BEAR.   *(Wanting to believe)* You are sure it will?

(Tish nods. To Mime)

Do you believe it will?

(Mime nods)

I could try.

TISH.   Quick!

BEAR.   Of course I don't believe in superstitions. But I did get up on
the right side of the bed.

(Mime nods)

I did find a four leaf clover.

(Mime nods)

And I haven't sneezed once.

(Mime shakes his head)

Yes, luck is with me today! So . . . let me knock on wood — three times — and I will do it!

(Mime takes off hat. Bear knocks on Mime's head three times, with sound effects.)

What do I say?

TISH.   Point to the first star you see.

BEAR.   *(Looks about, then points.)* There! I see a bright twinkling one.

TISH.   Say, "Star light, star bright . . ."

BEAR.   *(To Mime)* The rabbit's foot! This wish must come true.

   (Looks up)

   "Star light, star bright."

TISH.   "First star I see tonight."

BEAR.   "First star I see tonight."

   (Takes rabbit's foot from Mime and rubs it vigorously)

   Oh, bring me luck. Make my wish come true.

TISH.   "I wish I may, I wish I might . . ."

BEAR.   "I wish I may, I wish I might" Oh, it won't work. It's nothing but a nursery rhyme.

TISH.   "Have the wish I wish tonight." Say it. Say it!

BEAR.   "Have the wish I wish tonight."

   (Pause)

   Nothing. Nothing. I told you so.

TISH.   Look. Look! It's beginning to happen.

STAR BRIGHT.   *(Star music and lights begin as Star Bright enters on swing. He is joyously happy.)* Tonight I'm blinking. Tonight I'm winking. Wishes are flying past. Wishes are coming quick and fast! I'm twinkling bright and RIGHT tonight!

   (Laughs)

Your wish, please.

BEAR. *(Lost in happy memories)* Look. It is like the circus. The trapeze high in a tent of blue . . . the music of the band . . .

(Mime motions. Soft band music of the circus is heard. Colorful lights play on the backdrop.)

the acrobats; the jugglers tossing, catching bouncing balls . . .

(Mime pantomimes juggling)

the delicious smell of popcorn . . . the dance on the high wire . . .

(Tish holds up an imaginary umbrella and walks on an imaginary tight rope)

the sweet taste of pink lemonade . . . Oh, the beauty, the wonder of life. Let me look at it. The happiness of living . . . Oh, let me feel it. The joy of being alive! Let me keep it. Let me hold it forever.

(Holds out his arms to embrace it all)

STAR BRIGHT. *(Clasps his hands. Music and circus scene stops.)* Your wish. Your wish. Repeat, please.

BEAR. *(Confused, he is led by Mime to Star)* I wish to leave a footprint.

STAR BRIGHT. *(Puzzled)* Repeat, please.

TISH. The answer to the riddle.

BEAR. *(Intently)* I wish to leave with someone my dances so that I . . . so that they . . . will be remembered.

STAR BRIGHT. That is a wish I hear every night . . . every night. A wish to shine on earth . . . and leave behind a trace . . . to learn, to earn the grace . . . of immortality. Of your wish, half I can do. The other half is left for you. But quick! You must start. Because all wishes on a star must be done before the star is over shadowed by the sun.

(He claps his hands. Magic music and lights begin.)

One, two;
Sunset red;
Midnight blue;
The wish you wish
I give to you.

(Magic lights and music end as Star Bright exits up and out of sight. From off L, Little Bear is heard singing. All look to L. Little

Bear enters finishing his song to the tune of "Turkey in the Straw."
He is a small cub, wearing country overalls and a little turned-up
straw hat. Over his shoulder he carries a small fishing pole.)

LITTLE BEAR.   *(Sings)*

> Turkey in the straw, haw, haw, haw;
> Turkey in the hay, hay, hay, hay;
> Bait the hook, give the line a swish;
> Jumpin' jiggers, I caught a fish.

TISH.   A little bear.

BEAR.   *(Little Bear does a few dance steps of joy, and continues walk-*
ing and singing) A little dancing bear.

(To Mime)

Meet him. Greet him. Make him welcome.

(To Tish)

Quick, the handmirror.

(Tish holds mirror which Mime gives her and Bear preens. Mime
hurries to Little Bear and pantomimes a big and friendly greeting.
Little Bear, as if it were a game, happily imitates every movement
of the Mime. It ends with both shaking hands. Then Little Bear
gives a friendly goodbye wave and starts off R, singing)

Stop him!

(Mime rushes in front of Little Bear and turns him around.)

I am ready to be presented.

(Mime, with a flourish, presents Bear.)

LITTLE BEAR.   Howdy-do to you.

BEAR.   You have come from my WISHING on a star.

LITTLE BEAR.   Huh uh. I've come from my FISHING in the river.

BEAR.   Oh, my little one, I am going to give you the treasure of my
life. Bestow on you all my gifts.

LITTLE BEAR.   I could use a new fishing pole.

BEAR.   I am going to teach you all my dances. You will wear all my
hats. Oh-ho! I have never felt so alive in my life!

(He gives a joyous whoop and jumps and clicks his heels. Little
Bear is bewildered. Bear, with the eyes of a dancing master, looks
Little Bear over.)

Yes, you have a good build. Good stance. Relaxed torso.

(Taps Little Bear's waist. Little Bear wiggles and giggles from the tickling.)

Legs sturdy, Up! Leg up. Up!

(Little Bear cautiously lifts leg.)

Up! Up!

(Bear raises Little Bear's leg high.)

LITTLE BEAR.   Whoa!

BEAR.   Point, Point!

LITTLE BEAR.   *(Points with finger)* Point where?

BEAR.   *(Holding Little Bear's foot high)* Point your foot. Ah, feet too stiff . . . too stiff.

(Lets leg down. Little Bear stands in profile, stomach pushed out.)

Stomach flat!

(Taps stomach. Little Bear pulls stomach in, but pushes hips out.)

Rear push in!

(Smacks Little Bear on the bottom. Little Bear pulls hips in, and turns facing audience.)

Stretch . . . up . . . up!

(Pulls Little Bear up who tries to stretch. His face is tense.)

Relax.

(Pats Little Bear on forehead. Little Bear slowly sinks to the ground. Bear lifts him up.)

Smile.

(Little Bear forces a tortured smile.)

Walk! Walk!

(Little Bear starts walking stiffly.)

TISH.   Will he be a good dancer?

BEAR.   He will be magnificent!

(Puts arm out and stops Little Bear's escape.)

He will be — ME! My rehearsal hat. My father's Russian dancing hat!

(He dances a few steps of a Russian dance, and shouts a few Russian words.)

To the dressing room.

(He continues the dance steps and shouting as he exits at R. Mime, with traveling box follows him, imitating the dance steps.)

LITTLE BEAR.   Who . . . who is he?

TISH.   He is the greatest dancing bear in the world.

LITTLE BEAR.   Oh!

TISH.   And . . . he's going to die.

LITTLE BEAR.   Oh.

TISH.   My Grandpa is going to die and I don't know what to do.

LITTLE BEAR.   Up in the hills, I've seen a lot of them die.

TISH.   You have?

LITTLE BEAR.   Old ones, little ones, and big ones, too. And there ain't nothing you can do about it. 'Cause as sure as you're born, you're sure of dying.

TISH.   It's sad.

LITTLE BEAR.   Course it's sad.

TISH.   It's frightening.

LITTLE BEAR.   *(Thinking it out)* No. It ain't dyin' that you're afraid of. It's the not knowin' what comes AFTER you die. That's what scares you.

TISH.   *(Tearfully)* I'll never see Grandpa again.

LITTLE BEAR.   *(With gentle understanding)* You go on. You have yourself a good cry. It'll help you to give him up. And you got to.

(With emphasis)

You got to let him go.

TISH.   No.

LITTLE BEAR.   You have to! 'Cause he gone . . . forever.

TISH.   You don't know what it's like to have your Grandpa die.

LITTLE BEAR.   Yes, I do. My Grandpa died last winter. And my Papa . . . I saw a hunter shoot my Papa.

TISH.   *(Shocked)* Shoot your Papa! Oh, what did you do?

LITTLE BEAR.   First, I cried. Yes, I cried, and then I started hatin' and I kicked and clawed 'cause I felt all alone.

TISH.   *(Nods)* All by yourself.

LITTLE BEAR.   Then my Mama said, "You have to go on living, so . . . do your best. Give yourself to the livin'. 'Cause that's the best way to say goodbye to your Pa." So I made my peace.

TISH.   Your peace?

LITTLE BEAR.   Inside myself. Oh, it don't mean I understand about dyin'. I don't. But you do go on living. The next day. The next year. So if you love your Grandpa like I loved my Papa . . .

TISH.   Oh, I do.

TISH.   How?

LITTLE BEAR.   Tell him goodbye . . . by giving your most to the living. I'm wanting to do something . . . something big . . . just for Papa.

BEAR.   *(Off)* All is ready!

TISH.   Please, dance with him. He needs you.

LITTLE BEAR.   Well, I like to help folks.

TISH.   You said, "Give to the living."

LITTLE BEAR.   And I do like the dance!

TISH.   *(Excited with a new idea)* This is the big thing you can do for your Papa.

LITTLE BEAR.   For Papa?

TISH.   *(Points with her hand as she visualizes it)* Your name will be in lights. You will be the NEW World's Greatest Dancing Bear!

BEAR.   *(Bear and Mime enter, Bear wearing his Russian Cossack hat)* Let the flags fly! Let the band play!

(To Little Bear)

We will start with a simple waltz. My mother's famous skating waltz. One, two, three; one, two, three . . .

(He dances, continuing during the next speeches)

LITTLE BEAR.   *(Tries to do the step, then stops)* No. I'm just a country bear, with no schoolin'.

TISH.   You will be the famous . . . "Arkansas Bear!"

(Urges him on)

LITTLE BEAR.   Arkansas. I ain't right sure how to spell Arkansas.

(He moves in one spot to the beat of the music, wanting to dance, but afraid)

TISH.   Like it sounds. A — R — — K — A — N — — — —

LITTLE BEAR.   *(Shouts, eager to dance)* S — A — W!

(With a burst of energy he follows Bear and dances with joy, counting loudly and happily.)

One! Two! Three! One! Two! Three! I'm doing it!

(The first chime of midnight is heard, loud and distinct. The other chimes follow slowly. Mime runs to Bear, motions for him to listen.)

TISH.   What is it?

BEAR.   The chimes are striking twelve.

LITTLE BEAR.   It's the end of the day. Midnight.

BEAR.   No! No! Not yet! I have not taught you my dances. Stop the clock!

TISH.   Run! Hide! Before he comes back!

BEAR.   Where?

LITTLE BEAR.   In the caves! In the hills!

TISH.   Hurry!

(Tish and Little Bear help Bear. Mime carries box. All start toward back. Soft calliope music is heard. Ringmaster enters R.)

RINGMASTER.   Twelve.

(They stop)

Your day is ended. Your time is up. I will take you to the Great Center Ring.

BEAR.   No. No!

TISH.   Is he here?

BEAR.   Yes, he has come for me.

(Comes down stage. Backs off towards L.)

Stop him.

RINGMASTER.   There is no way to stop death.

TISH. I know a way.

(Grabs Mime and points up toward star)

You! Make a wish on the first star you see. Say,

(Shouts)

Star light, star bright,
First star I see tonight . . .

(Mime quickly points and looks up, rapidly miming the words of the rhyme)

STAR BRIGHT. *(Off)* Louder, please.

RINGMASTER. Come.

(Holds out his hand and slowly crosses toward Bear at far L)

TISH. *(Mime pantomimes, repeating with larger gestures, while Tish says the words)*

I wish I may, I wish I might,
Have the wish I wish tonight.

STAR BRIGHT. *(Quickly descends into view)* Wish quickly chanted. Wish quickly granted.

TISH. *(Mime pantomimes her words)* Stop death!

(With a sound effect of a roll on a cymbal, Star Bright points at Ringmaster, who has advanced almost to Bear. Ringmaster stops in a walking position.)

Make him go away!

(A roll on a cymbal is heard, as Star Bright makes a circle with his hand. Ringmaster slowly turns around.)

LOCK HIM UP IN THE TREE!

(Another roll on the cymbal)

STAR BRIGHT. Walk to the tree.

(Ringmaster slowly walks to a tree.)

Your home it will be . . . for a time.

(Ringmaster stops. Star Bright points to tree again. There is a roll on a cymbal as the trunk slowly opens.)

It is open wide . . . to welcome you. Step inside.

(Ringmaster faces tree and slowly steps inside the tree trunk, and turns and faces audience.)

Let it enfold and hold you . . . for a time.

(Waves his hand. There is a last roll on a cymbal. The tree trunk slowly closes shut.)

Locked, blocked, and enclosed!

(He laughs)

BEAR. *(To Tish)* You did it! You stopped death!

TISH. *(She and Bear shout together, while Mime jumps with joy and blows whistle.)* We did it!

BEAR. We did it!

STAR BRIGHT. *(Claps his hands)* Remember . . . soon will come the morning sun, and then . . . Remember that is when . . . all wishes become . . . undone.

(Star music and light begin as he ascends out of sight, and then stop)

BEAR. *(Their joy changes to concern)* It is true! Time is short! Quick. I must teach the little one —

(Looks about. Little Bear has, unnoticed, slipped away when Ringmaster appeared.)

Where is he?

TISH. Little Bear!

(Pause. There is no answer.)

BEAR. Little Bear, come back!

TISH. *(She and Mime run looking for him)* Little Bear?

BEAR. He was frightened . . .

(Looks at tree)

of death. He is gone. And with him all my hopes are gone.

(He slumps, wearily)

TISH. *(Concerned, rushes to him)* You must rest, like Grandpa.

BEAR. Your Grandfather has you.

(Amused)

A chip off the old block, eh?

(She nods)

You gave him happiness in life . . . peace in death.

TISH.   Are you all right?

BEAR.   I am old, and weary and tired. And I am going to die.

TISH.   No. We stopped death.

BEAR.   But only for a brief time. Death, they say is a clock. Every minute our lives are ticking away. Now . . . soon . . . my clock will stop.

TISH.   No.

BEAR.   When I was young like you, I wondered, "Where did I come from?" And now when I am old, I wonder, "Where am I going?"

(Mime looks and listens off R, then runs to them and excitedly mimes that Little Bear is coming.)

What is it?

(Mime pantomimes more)

Who? Where?

(Mime points to R. All watch as Little Bear enters)

You have come back.

LITTLE BEAR.   I left my fishing pole.

BEAR.   Have no fear. Death is locked in the tree.

(Little Bear reacts with fright at tree)

TISH.   You have come back to help.

LITTLE BEAR.   I come back to learn all your fancy dancin'.

TISH.   *(Runs to Little Bear and hugs him)* Oh, you are the best, the sweetest, the most wonderful little bear in the world!

(Little Bear is embarrassed)

BEAR.   Yes! Quick! We must begin the lesson. There is so little time and so much to learn.

(Looks frightened off R. To Mime)

Stand watch. Yes, watch for the first rays of the sun!

(Mime stands at R, anxiously looking off. Tish sits on box. Bear motions to Little Bear.)

Come! Come! Attention! I will teach you all I know.

(Takes position)

First, you smile to the right.

(Bear does the action with the words. Little Bear watches and tries to do the action.)

You smile to the left. You bow to the center. And then . . . begin . . . to dance. We will start with my father's famous Russian dance. Master this and all else will be easy.

(To Mime)

How many more minutes?

(Mime holds up ten fingers)

Ten! Position. Position!

(Little Bear imitates him)

Listen to the beat . . . the beat . . .

(Taps foot)

LITTLE BEAR.   Beat what?

BEAR.   Your feet! Your feet! The beat . . . the beat . . .

(Taps foot. Little Bear slowly and timidly taps beat)

Too slow. Too slow.
(Little Bear pivots in a circle, weight on one foot while tapping fast with the other foot.)

Too fast. Too fast.

(Little Bear does it right)

Ah! Ah! Ah! Good! Good!

LITTLE BEAR.   I'm doing it right!

BEAR.   *(Shows him next Russian step)* The first step. Hop, hop, hop, switch, hop.

(Little Bear tries, awkward at first, then better)

Hop, hop, hop, switch, hop. Yes, hop, hop, hop, switch, hop. Yes! Yes!

(Shows him next step)

Deep knee, hop.

(Little Bear shakes his head)

Try. Try.

(Little Bear tries deep knee bends with a hop)

Deep knee, hop. Lower. Lower.

(Little Bear puts hands on floor in front of him and does a step. He smiles at the audience at the easiness of it.)

No, no, no! No hands!

(Lifts Little Bear up. Little Bear continues to kick his feet.)

The next step. The finale.

(Shows step)

Turn, two, up, two. Turn, two, up, two.

LITTLE BEAR. Oh, my!

BEAR. Turn, two, up, two.

(Little Bear tries)

Turn, two, up, two. Faster. Faster.

LITTLE BEAR. *(Falls)* I can't do it. I can't do it.

BEAR. You will. You must do it. I must leave my dances with you.

TISH. Try, please, Please, try.

LITTLE BEAR. Well . . .

(Gets up)

BEAR. Again. Again. Ready. Turn, two, up, two.

(Bear keeps repeating the count, and Little Bear does the step better and better, until he is perfect — and happy.)

He did it! He did it!

TISH. He did it!

LITTLE BEAR. I did it!

BEAR. *(To Mime)* How many minutes are left?

(Mime holds up eight fingers)

Eight minutes. Time is running out. Quick. The polka. The dance of the people. Music!

(Mime motions. Music is heard. Bear dances a few steps. Little Bear quickly follows him and masters them. Music stops. Bear breathes heavily.)

How many more minutes?

(Mime holds up seven fingers)

Only seven minutes left! Hurry. My famous tarentella.

(Mime motions and music is heard. Bear does a few steps. Little Bear again quickly does them and they dance together. Music stops. Bear pants for breath. Mime runs to him and holds up six fingers.)

Six minutes. And at the end take your bow. The first bow.

(Bear bows, short of breath)

The second bow.

(Bear bows, pauses, then with trembling voice he speaks with emotion, knowing it is his last bow.)

And the last and final bow.

TISH.   More, more! Encore! Encore!

(Bear slumps to the floor. She rushes to him.)

He's fallen.

(She and Mime cradle Bear on either side)

Are you all right?

BEAR.   *(Stirs, weakly)* How . . . many more minutes . . . do I have left?

(Mime holds up five fingers)

My little one, you will do my dances, you will carry on for me?

LITTLE BEAR.   Yes. Yes.

BEAR.   Take my father's hat . . . and it was HIS father's hat . . .

LITTLE BEAR.   No, you must wear it.

BEAR.   I will not need it where I am going. I have taken my last bow.

TISH.   No.

(Buries her head on his shoulder)

BEAR.   Ah, tears can be beautiful. But there is no need to cry. I am content. I was a part of what went before and I will be a part of what is yet to come. That is the answer to the riddle of life.

(Weakly)

How many more minutes?

(Mime holds up two fingers)

Two. Bring me my traveling hat. I will wear it on my last journey.

(Little Bear gets traveling hat from box, as Mime and Tish help Bear to stand)

I must look my best when I enter the Great Center Ring.

(Mime puts hat on Bear, who smiles at Tish)

Does it look stylish?

TISH. Yes.

BEAR. Is it becoming?

(She nods)

Then I am ready.

(Gently pushes Tish and Mime away)

No. This journey I must go alone.

(Extends hand to Mime)

Goodbye, good friend. Thank you for everything. And sometimes when the band plays . . . think of an old bear.

(Mime motions for Bear to wait. Mime quickly gets a pink balloon on a string from the side and holds it out to Bear)

Yes, I remember when once we said, "Life is like a bright balloon." Hold it tight. Hold it tight. Because . . . once you let it go . . . it floats away forever.

(Breathless)

How many more minutes?

(Mime holds up one finger. Bear turns to Tish.)

I have one last request. When the end comes . . . when I enter the Great Center Ring . . . I want music. I want you to whistle the tune your Grandfather taught you.

TISH. "O Susannah."

BEAR. *(Nods and smiles)* You will find that when you whistle you cannot cry at the same time.

(A rooster is heard crowing)

Listen.

LITTLE BEAR. It's a rooster crowin'. It's almost mornin'.

TISH.   The sun is up. The stars are fading away.

STAR BRIGHT.   (*Star music is heard as Star Bright descends into view. He speaks softly.*) Announcing: the first ray of sun is peeping out. Warning: all wishes end as the sun begins. The new day is starting, the old departing. That is the great pattern . . . The circle of life. Tomorrow is today.

(*He points at the tree, and claps his hands. The tree trunk opens.*)

And the night and the stars fade away . . . fade away.

(*There is star music as Star Bright disappears. Soft calliope music is heard which continues during the scene.*)

RINGMASTER.   (*Steps out from tree trunk. He speaks with authority.*)

There is no more time. The book is closed.

BEAR.   Poets tell us death is but a sleep, but who can tell me what I will dream?

RINGMASTER.   (*Walks slowly to Bear*) Take my hand.

BEAR.   Tell me, tell me what is death?

RINGMASTER.   When there is no answer, you do not ask the question. Come.

BEAR.   Yes, I am ready.

(*To Little Bear*)

My little one . . . I give you my feather . . . and you . . . give joy . . . to the world.

(*Gives turkey feather to Little Bear. He whispers.*)

Let the balloon go.

(*Ringmaster holds out his hand, which Bear takes. Together they walk off L slowly. Mime lets the balloon go. He, Tish and Little Bear watch as it floats up and out of sight. At the same time the calliope music builds in volume. There is a second of silence. Then the Announcer's voice is heard, loud and distinctly.*)

ANNOUNCER'S VOICE.   Ladies and gentlemen: presenting for your pleasure and entertainment, the new dancing bear, the world's famous, the world's favorite, the world's greatest — The Arkansaw Bear!

(*During the announcement, Mime points to Little Bear. Little Bear looks frightened, amazed and pleased. Mime holds up mirror and Little Bear puts feather in his hat. Mime motions for Little Bear*) *to step forward, then motions a circle of light on the floor. Spotlight comes on and Little Bear steps into the light.)*

BEAR'S VOICE. *(Over the loud speaker, Bear's voice is heard. He speaks softly and with emotion. Little Bear follows his instructions.)* You smile to the right . . . smile to the left . . . bow to the center . . . and then begin to dance!

(Music begins, lively "Turkey in the Straw." Little Bear begins his dance.)

My dances . . . your dances . . . and make the world spin round and round with joy.

(Little Bear dances with fun, excitement, and joy, a wonderful short dance. During this Tish exits, and Mime exits with box. At the end of the dance, Little Bear bows as the audience applauds, and exits at L, peeks out and waves again. Spotlight goes out. Fantasy music is heard and a soft night light illuminates the tree. Tish is leaning against it. She looks up, sighs, picks up the flowers, and slowly circles back to the downstage area of the first scene, which becomes light as the tree area dims out. Fantasy music also fades out. Mother's and Aunt Ellen's voices are heard, and Tish answers as if they were standing on each side of her downstage.)

MOTHER'S VOICE. *(Worried)* Tish? Tish, is that you?

TISH. Yes, mother.

MOTHER'S VOICE. ·Where have you been?

TISH. I went up the hill to my tree. I want to see Grandpa.

AUNT ELLEN'S VOICE. He's dead . . . dead.

(Cries)

TISH. *(Trying to be brave)* Dead. Tears can be beautiful, Aunt Ellen. But you have to give him up. Let the balloon go.

AUNT ELLEN'S VOICE. What?

TISH. *(Trying to keep back her tears)* I know everyone . . . everything has a time to die . . . and it's sad. But Grandpa knew the answer to the riddle.

AUNT ELLEN'S VOICE. The riddle?

TISH. He left his footprint. He left a chip off the old block.

MOTHER'S VOICE. What, dear? What did he leave?

TISH. Me! And I want to do something . . . something big for Grandpa. Because that's the best way to say goodbye.

677

(Softly)

Let me give him his flowers . . . the pink ones.

MOTHER'S VOICE. *(Positive, and with a mother's love and authority)* All right, dear. Come along. We'll go together and see Grandpa.

(Tish starts L, and begins to whistle)

What are you doing?

TISH. Whistling . . . for the bear . . . and for Grandpa. Because it helps . . . when you are afraid and in the dark. And . . . when you whistle, you can't cry.

(Whispers)

Goodbye, Grandpa, I . . . I love you.

(Tish exits L, bravely trying to control her crying. At the same time, lights slowly come up so the full stage is seen. The light on Tish's area dims out. The stage is bright with soft beautiful colors. The lone whistling of "O Susannah," the same as at the beginning of the play, is heard. There is a moment of a final picture — the living tree standing, as it has through the years, against a beautiful endless sky. The whistling continues as the curtains close.)

APPENDIX A

A Chronological Guide to Selected Plays
Published Prior to 1940

1880–1899

1889   *Little Lord Fauntleroy* by Frances H. Burnett (French)

1890   *The Seven Old Ladies of Lavender Town* (operetta) by Henry Bunner (Gillet)

1891   *The Magician and the Ring* by Florence D. Adams (Dramatic)

1891   *The Toy Shop* by Frederick S. Isham (French)

1891   *Princess Marguerite's Choice* by Florence D. Adams (Dramatic)

1898   *Alice in Wonderland* by Constance C. Harrison (Dramatic)

1900–1909

1902   *The House that Jack Built* by Alice C. Riley (C. F. Summy)

1902   *Maid of Plymouth* by Stanley Schell (Werner)

1903   *The Toy-Shop: An Operetta for Children* by Mary Packer (Schirmer)

1904   *A Masque of Beauty and the Beast* by Alice M. Buckton (C. F. Hodgson)

1905   *Eager Heart, A Christmas Mystery Play* by Alice M. Buckton (Chappell)

1906   *The Fairy Ring* by Marjorie B. Cooke (Dramatic)

1907   *The Lost Prince* by John J. Chapman (Piester)

1908   *A Rose o' Plymouth-town* by Beulah M. Dix and Evelyn Sutherland (Dramatic)

1909   *The Piper* by Josephine Peabody (Houghton Mifflin)

1909   *The Blue Bird* by Maurice Maeterlinck. Translated by A. Teixeira de Mattos (Dodd, Mead)

1909   *Nimble-wit and Fingerkin* by C. D. Mackay (French)

1909   *The Enchanted Garden* by C. D. Mackay (French)

1909   *The Elf Child* by C. D. Mackay (French)

1909   *The Christmas Guest* by C. D. Mackay (French)

1910–1919

1910   *The Twig of Thorn: An Irish Fairy Play in Two Acts* by Marie Warren (Baker)

1911   *The Little Princess* by Frances H. Burnett (French)

1911   *Miles Standish* by Edith Ashby (E. Mathews)

1913   *Snow White and the Seven Dwarfs* by Jessie Braham White (French)

1914   *Master Skylark* by Anna M. Luetkenhaus (Century)

1914   *Yotcheka: An Indian Play in One Act* by Helen P. Kane (French)

1914   *The Pied Piper* by E. Elliot Stock (Dutton)

1914   *The Magic Chest* by E. Elliot Stock (Dutton)

1914   *The Little King* by Witter Bynner (Kennerly)

1915   *Treasure Island* by Jules Eckert Goodman (French)

1915   *Hansel and Gretel* by Jane M. Mclaren and Edith Harvey (Stokes)

1915   *Why the Chimes Rang* by Elizabeth McFadden (French)

1915   *Alice in Wonderland* by Alice Gerstenberg (McClurg)

1916   *Master Will of Stratford* by Mrs. Louise A. Garnett (Macmillan)

1916   *The Steadfast Princess* by Cornelia Meigs (Macmillan)

1916   *The Fairy Bride* by Norreys J. O'Connor (Lane)

1916   *Master Skylark: or Will Shakespeare's Ward* by Edgar White Burril (Century)

1917   *Six Who Pass While the Lentils Boil* by Stuart Walker (Stewart Kidd)

1917   *The Peddler of Hearts* by Gertrude Knevels (Baker)

1918   *The Travelling Man* by Lady Augusta Gregory (Putnam's)

1919   *The Birthday of the Infanta* by Stuart Walker (Stewart Kidd)

1919   *Abraham Lincoln* by John Drinkwater (Houghton Mifflin)

1919   *Snickerty Nick and the Giant* by Julia E. Ford (Dramatists)

1920–1929

1920   *The House that Jack Built* (operetta) by Alice C. D. Riley (Summy)

1920   *The Dragon* by Lady Augusta Gregory (Putnam's)

1921   *The Forest Ring* by William C. DeMille and Charles Barnard (French)

1921   *Little John and the Miller Join Robin Hood's Band* by Perry Corneau (Old Tower)

1922   *The Treasure Chest* by Josephine Thorp (Old Tower)

1923   *Crossings: A Fairy Play* by Walter De La Mare (Knopf)

1923   *Robin Hood* by Owen Davis (French)

1923   *The Little Shakeresses* by Carla F. Rosenthal (Old Tower)

1924   *Kinfolk of Robin Hood* by Percy Mackaye (French)

1925   *Sweet Times and the Blue Policeman* by Stark Young (Holt)

1925   *The Moon Maid* by James Haynes (Old Tower)

1925   *Make Believe* by A. A. Milne (French)

1925   *The Evil Kettle* by Lord Dunsany (Putnam's)

1926   *The Boy Who Discovered Easter* by Elizabeth McFadden (French)

1926   *Rackety Packety House* by Frances H. Burnett (French)

1928   *Heidi* by Ethel H. Freeman (French)

1928   *Little Black Sambo* by Hazel S. Kaufman (French)

1928   *Mr. Scrooge* by Ashley Miller (Dodd Mead)

1928   *The Wizard of Oz* by Elizabeth Fuller Chapman (French)

1929   *Helga and the White Peacock* by Cornelia Meigs (Macmillan)

1929   *Toad of Toad Hall* by A. A. Milne (Scribner's)

1930–1939

1930   *The Princess and the Swine Herd* by Gwendolen Seiler (Macmillan)
1930   *The Scotch Twins* by Eleanor Perkins (French)
1930   *The Patchwork Girl of Oz* by Mrs. James Waller Marshall (French)
1932   *Mr. Dooley Jr.* by Rose Franken and Jane Lewen (French)
1932   *The Emperor's New Clothes* by Charlotte B. Chorpenning (French)
1932   *Alice in Wonderland* by Eva Le Gallienne and Florida Freibus (French)
1934   *Cinderella* by Frances Homer (Dramatic)
1934   *The Princess and Mr. Parker* by Gwendolen Seiler (French)
1935   *The Christmas Nightingale* by Phyllis Newman Groff (Children's Theatre Press)
1935   *The Sleeping Beauty* by Frances Homer (Dramatic)
1935   *Rip Van Winkle* by Grace D. Ruthenburg (Children's Theatre Press)
1935   *The Reluctant Dragon* by Emma Sterne (French)
1935   *Ozma of Oz* by Mary Buchanan (French)
1935   *Jack in the Beanstalk* by Charlotte B. Chorpenning (Children's Theatre Press)
1936   *Heidi* by Lucille Miller (Children's Theatre Press)
1936   *Jack in the Beanstalk* by Nora Nixon (French)
1937   *The Indian Captive* by Charlotte B. Chorpenning (Children's Theatre Press)
1937   *Hans Brinker: or, The Silver Skates* by Tom Taggart (French)
1937   *Tom Sawyer's Treasure Hunt* by Charlotte B. Chorpenning (French)
1938   *Oliver Twist* by Muriel Brown (Children's Theatre Press)
1938   *Seven Little Rebels* by Rosemary Musil (Children's Theatre Press)
1939   *Treasure Island* by Dorothy Drew (Children's Theatre Press)

APPENDIX B

Publication Information of Plays Discussed in Text

Aiken, George L. *Uncle Tom's Cabin*. In *Dramas From the American Theatre 1762–1909*. Ed. Richard Moody. Cleveland: World, 1966.

Atkin, Flora. *Golliwhoppers*. Rowayton, Ct.: New Plays, 1973.

Barrie, James M. *Peter Pan* (musical version). New York: Samuel French, 1928.

Bronson, Bernice. *In the Beginning*. Rowayton, Ct.: New Plays, 1971.

——————. *Most Powerful Jujus*. Rowayton, Ct.: New Plays, 1974.

Broadhurst, Alan. *The Great Cross Country Race*. Anchorage Press, New Orleans, La.

Burnett, Frances H. *Little Lord Fauntleroy*. New York: S. French, 1889.

——————. *The Little Princess*. New York: Samuel French, 1911.

——————. *Rackety Packety House*. New York: S. French, 1927.

Chorpenning, Charlotte B. *The Emperor's New Clothes*. New York: Samuel French, 1932.

——————. *Hansel and Gretel*. Chicago; Coach House Press, 1956.

——————. *Jack and the Beanstalk*. Anchorage Press, New Orleans, La, 1935.

——————. *Radio Rescue*. New York: Dramatists, 1938. Chicago: Coach House, 1956.

——————. *Rumpelstiltskin*. Anchorage Press, New Orleans, La., 1944.

——————. *The Sleeping Beauty*. Anchorage Press, New Orleans, La., 1947.

Cullen, Alan. *The Beeple*. Anchorage Press, New Orleans, La., 1968.

Everndon, Margery. *King Arthur's Sword*. Chicago: Coach House Press, 1959.

Falls, Greg and Kurt Beattie. *The Odyssey*. New Orleans: Anchorage Press, 1980.

Fauquez, Arthur. *Don Quixote of La Mancha*. Translated by Margaret Leona. New Orleans: Anchorage Press, 1967.

——————. *The Man Who Killed Time*. Translated by Margaret Leona and Marie-Louis Roelants. New Orleans: Anchorage Press, 1964.

——————. *Reynard the Fox*. Anchorage Press, New Orleans, La., 1962.

Gagliano, Frank. *The Hide and Seek Odyssey of Madeline Gimple*. New York: Dramatists, 1970.

Gerstenberg, Alice. *Alice in Wonderland*. Chicago: A. C. McClurg, 1915.

Goldberg, Moses, *Aladdin*. New Orleans: Anchorage Press, 1977.

——————. *Hansel and Gretel*. Rowayton, Ct.: New Plays, 1972.

——————. *The Men's Cottage*. New Orleans: Anchorage Press, 1980.

Goodman, Jules Eckert. *Treasure Island*. New York: S. French, 1915.

Gray, Nicholas Stuart. *Beauty and the Beast*. New York: S. French, 1951.

——————. *The Princess and the Swineherd*. New York: S. French, 1952.

Graczyk, Ed. *Aesop's Falables*. New Orleans: Anchorage Press, 1969.

Grielson, Frank. *The Wizard of Oz* (musical). New York: Tams-Witmark, 1938.

Harder, Eleanor and Ray Harder. *The Near Sighted Knight and the Far Sighted Dragon*. New Orleans: Anchorage Press, 1977.

Harris, Aurand. *Androcles and the Lion*. New Orleans, La.: Anchorage Press, 1964.

——————. *The Arkansaw Bear*. New Orleans, La.: Anchorage Press, 1980.

——————. *The Brave Little Tailor*. New Orleans, La.: Anchorage Press, 1961.

——————. *Just So Stories*. New Orleans, La.: Anchorage Press, 1971.

——————. *Once Upon a Clothesline*. New York: Row Peterson, 1945.

——————. *The Plain Princess*. New Orleans, La.: Anchorage Press, 1955.

——————. *Steal Away Home*. New Orleans, La.: Anchorage Press, 1972.

——————. *Yankee Doodle*. New Orleans, La.: Anchorage Press, 1975.

Jefferson, Joseph. *Rip Van Winkle*. New York: Dodd, Mead and Co., 1903.

Kesselman, Wendy. "Maggie Magalita." Unpublished. Lucy Kroll Agency. 390 West End Ave., New York, N.Y.

King, Martha Bennett. *Peter Peter Pumpkin Eater*. New Orleans, La.: Anchorage Press, 1945.

——————. *The Snow Queen and the Goblin*. Chicago: Coach House Press, 1956.

Kral, Brian. *Special Class*. New Orleans: Anchorage Press, 1981.

Kraus, Joanna H. *Circus Home*. Rowayton, Ct.: New Plays, 1979.

——————. *The Ice Wolf*. Rowayton, Ct.: New Plays, 1963.

——————. *Mean to be Free*. Rowayton, Ct.: New Plays, 1967.

——————. *Two Plays from the Far East*. Rowayton, Ct.: New Plays, 1967.

——————. *Vasalisa*. Rowayton, Ct.: New Plays, 1973.

Levitt, Saul. *Jim Thorpe, All-American*. New Orleans: Anchorage Press, 1980.

Levy, Jonathan. *The Marvelous Adventures of Tyl*. Rowayton, Ct.: New Plays, 1973.

MacAlvay, Nora T. and Charlotte B. Chorpenning. *The Elves and the Shoemaker*. New Orleans, La.: Anchorage Press, 1946.

Maeterlinck, Maurice. *The Blue Bird*. Translated by Alexander Teixeira de Mattos. New York: Dodd, Mead and Co., 1909.

Melwood, Mary. *Five Minutes to Morning*. Rowayton, Ct.: New Plays, 1966.

———. *The Tingalary Bird*. Rowayton, Ct.: New Plays, 1969.

Miller, Madge. *The Emperor's Nightingale*. New Orleans, La.: Anchorage Press, 1961.

———. *Hansel and Gretel*. New Orleans, La.: Anchorage Press, 1951.

———. *The Land of the Dragon*. New Orleans, La.: Anchorage Press, 1946.

———. *The Princess and the Swineherd*. Chicago: Dramatic Publishing Co., 1946.

———. *Robinson Crusoe*. New Orleans, La.: Anchorage Press, 1954.

Milne, A. A. *Make Believe*. New York: S. French, 1925.

———. *Toad of Toad Hall*. New York: S. French, 1932.

Musil, Rosemary. *Five Little Peppers*. New Orleans, La.: Anchorage Press, 1940.

———. *The Ghost of Mr. Penny*. New Orleans, La.: Anchorage Press, 1939.

———. *Mystery at the Old Fort*. New Orleans, La.: Anchorage Press, 1944.

———. *Seven Little Rebels*. New Orleans, La.: Anchorage Press, 1938.

Norris, James. *Aladdin and the Wonderful Lamp*. New Orleans, La.: Anchorage Press, 1940.

Seale, Nancy. *The Little Princess, Sara Crewe*. New Orleans, La.: Anchorage Press, 1982.

Sergel, Kirstin. *Winnie the Pooh*. Chicago: Dramatic, 1957.

Siks, Geraldine B. *Marco Polo*. New Orleans, La.: Anchorage Press, 1941.

Sills, Paul. *Story Theatre*. New York: S. French, 1971.

Walker, Stuart. *The Birthday of the Infanta*. In *Portmanteau Adaptations*. Cincinnati: Stewart Kidd, 1919.

———. *Jonathan Makes a Wish*. In *More Portmanteau Plays*. Cincinnati: Stewart Kidd, 1919.

———. *Six Who Pass While the Lentils Boil*. In *Portmanteau Plays*. Cincinnati: Stewart Kidd, 1917.

Way, Brian. *The Mirrorman*. Boston: Baker's Plays, 1977.

———. *On Trial*. Boston: Baker's Plays, 1977.

White, Jessie Braham. *Snow White and the Seven Dwarfs*. New York: Dodd, Mead and Co., 1913.

Zeder, Suzan. *Ozma of Oz*. New Orleans: Anchorage Press, 1981.

———. *Step on a Crack*. New Orleans: Anchorage Press, 1976.

———. *Wiley and the Hairy Man*. New Orleans: Anchorage Press, 1978.

Bibliography

APPENDIX C
Anthologies of Plays for Children

Arkwright, Ruth. *Brownikins and Other Fancies.* New York: F. A. Stokes, 1911.

Barbee, Lindsey. *Fanciful Plays for Children.* Chicago: Denison, 1917.

Bell, Florence E. E. *Fairy Tale Plays and How to Act Them.* New York: Longmans, Green, 1899.

Bird, Grace E. and Starling, Maud. *Historical Plays for Children.* New York: Macmillan, 1912.

Birner, William B. *Twenty Plays for Young People.* New Orleans: Anchorage Press, 1967.

Barbee, Lindsay. *Cinderella and Five Other Fairy Plays.* Chicago: Denison, 1922.

Bunner, Henry C. *Three Operettas.* New York: Harper, 1897.

Chapman, John Jay. *Four Plays for Children.* New York: Moffat, Yard, 1908.

——————. *Neptune's Isle and Other Plays for Children.* New York: Moffat, Yard, 1911.

Comer, Virginia, and MacAlvay, Nora T., eds. *First Performance.* New York: Harcourt, Brace, 1952.

DeMille, William C. *Christmas Spirit, Vote for Fairies; Two Plays for Children.* New York: John Martins, 1913.

Dix, Beulah M. *A Legend of St. Nicholas and Other Plays.* New York: Samuel French, 1927.

Donahue, John Clark. *The Cookie Jar and Other Plays.* Edited by Linda Walsh Jenkins. Minneapolis: University of Minnesota, 1975.

Donahue, John Clark, and Jenkins, Linda Walsh, eds. *Five Plays from The Children's Theatre Company of Minneapolis.* Minneapolis: University of Minnesota, 1975.

Dugan, Caro A. *The King's Jester and Other Short Plays for School Stages.* New York: Houghton, Mifflin, 1899.

Farrar, John C. *The Magic Sea Shell and Other Plays for Children.* New York: Doran, 1923.

Frank, Florence K. *Three Plays for a Children's Theatre.* New York: Vinal, 1926.

Frank, Maude M. *Short Plays About Famous Authors.* New York: Holt, 1915.

Fyleman, Rose. *Eight Little Plays for Children.* New York: Doran, 1925.

Harris, Aurand. *Six Plays for Children.* Edited by Coleman A. Jennings. Austin: University of Texas, 1977.

Jagendorf, Moritz A. *One-Act Plays for Young Folks.* New York: Brentano's, 1924.

——————, ed. *Nine Short Plays for Children.* New York: Macmillan, 1928.

Jennings, Coleman A. and Harris, Aurand, eds. *Plays Children Love: A Treasury of Contemporary and Classic Plays for Children.* New York: Doubleday, 1981.

Lifton, Betty Jean, ed. *Contemporary Children's Theatre.* New York: Avon, 1974.

Lütkenhaus, Anna M., ed. *New Plays for School Children.* New York: Century, 1915.

Mackay, Constance D'Arcy. *Forest Princess and Other Masques.* New York: Holt, 1916.

——————. *The House of the Heart and Other Plays for Children.* New York: Holt, 1909.

——————. *Patriotic Plays and Pageants for Young People.* New York: Holt, 1912.

——————. *The Silver Thread and Other Folk Plays for Young People.* New York: Holt, 1910.

——————. *Youth's Highway and Other Plays for Young People.* New York: Holt, 1929.

Major, Clare Tree. *Playing Theatre: Six Plays for Children.* New York: Oxford Univ., 1930.

Merington, Marguerite. *Fairy Tale Plays.* New York: Duffield, 1916.

——————. *More Fairy Tale Plays.* New York: Duffield, 1916.

Miller, Madge. *Miniature Plays.* Anchorage, Ky.: Children's Theatre Press, 1954.

Moe, Christian, and Payne, Darwin Reid, eds. *Six New Plays for Children.* Carbondale: Southern Illinois University, 1971.

Morton, Miriam, ed. and trans. *Russian Plays for Young Audiences.* Rowayton, Ct.: New Plays, 1977.

Moses, Montrose, ed. *Another Treasury of Plays for Children.* Boston: Little, Brown, 1926.

——————. *Ring Up the Curtain.* Boston: Little, Brown, 1932.

——————. *A Treasury of Plays for Children.* Boston: Little, Brown, 1922.

Riley, Alice C. D. *Let's Pretend; Four Half Hour Plays for Young People.* Boston: Baker, 1934.

——————. *Ten Minutes by the Clock and Three Other Plays for Outdoor and Indoor Production.* New York: Doran, 1923.

St. Nicholas Book of Plays and Operettas. New York: Century Co., 1900.

St. Nicholas Book of Plays and Operettas. Second Series. New York: Century Co., 1916.

Sidgwick, Ethel. *Four Plays for Children.* Boston: Small, Maynard, 1914.

——————. *Three Golden Hairs (More Plays for Children).* Boston: Small, Maynard, 1922.

Skinner, Eleanor L. *Tales and Plays of Robin Hood.* New York: American Book, 1915.

Skinner, Eleanor L. and Skinner, Ada M. *Children's Plays.* New York:

D. Appleton-Century, 1918.

Sterne, Emma. *Far Town Road; Plays to be Acted and Read.* New York: Dodd, Mead, 1935.

Swortzell, Lowell. *All the World's a Stage.* New York: Delacorte Press, 1972.

Syrett, Netta. *The Fairy Doll and Other Plays for Children.* New York: Dodd, Mead, 1922.

——————. *Robin Goodfellow and Other Fairy Plays for Children.* New York: Lane, 1918.

——————. *Six Fairy Plays.* New York: Lane, 1904.

Thomas, C. S., ed. *Atlantic Book of Junior Plays.* Boston: Atlantic Monthly, 1924.

Walker, Stuart. *More Portmanteau Plays.* Edited by Edward H. Bierstadt. Cincinnati: Stewart Kidd, 1919.

——————. *Portmanteau Adaptations.* Edited by Edward H. Bierstadt. Cincinnati: Stewart Kidd, 1921.

——————. *Portmanteau Plays.* Edited by Edward H. Bierstadt. Cincinnati: Stewart Kidd, 1917.

Webber, J. P., and Webster, H. H., eds. *Short Plays for Young Children.* New York: Houghton Mifflin, 1925.

Zipes, Jack, ed. and trans. *Political Plays for Children.* St. Louis: Telos Press, 1976.

APPENDIX D

BREAKING OUT OF THE EGG: CHILDREN'S LITERATURE IN AMERICA, 1880–1980

by Douglas Street

In 1880, children's dramatic literature was still in its embryonic form, far behind the other areas of children's literature then growing quickly toward their first great "golden age." The ultimate recognition of the child as suitable for literature bent more on entertainment than education reached its peak in the offerings of the 1880s and 1890s, and enabled its audiences to select from a variety of first-class fiction. While, as in the drama, the influence of foreign writers was still far-reaching, this period nevertheless produced as never before, a brigade of accomplished American artists who wrote for American children from a distinctly American vantage point. At last the U.S. had quality indigenous tales for the young. To better realize the importance and richness of this first era — 1880 to 1920 — and its affinity with the concurrently produced drama of childhood, one must examine the foundations.

The thrust of this literary movement emerged after 1865. The Civil War had ended and the ensuing period of reconstruction brought with it a reexamination of the role and needs of the child within the newly reorganized society. The change came abruptly — with the 1865 publication of Lewis Carroll's *Alice's Adventures in Wonderland* the English-speaking child audience was provided with the first tool for cracking the heretofore invincible shell traditionally "protecting" the juvenile reader. With the advent of *Alice*, the boundaries of "propriety" in juvenile fiction stretched and buckled. Authors on both sides of the Atlantic, with Carroll in the lead, began an enthusiastic onslaught on the old concepts and new latitude.

Louisia May Alcott was one of this nation's first juvenile authors to distinguish herself and her country internationally in this crusade. Her 1868 publication, *Little Women*, was an influential model in the family story genre. From her debut through her 1886 *Jo's Boys*, the trials and tribulations of the March family firmly held the child readership at home and abroad. Her great success is evidenced in the several Alcott imitations, in the countless stage dramatizations, and in the attraction of her works for 20th century film and television audiences. While the invincible Louisa was giving the U.S. a note of respectability in the family market, native practitioners of the adventure genre were similarly captivating their European readers with tales of a distinctly American heritage. The 1870's, in preface to the golden years, presented its book buyers substantial adventure, from Thomas Aldritch's *Story of a Bad Boy* through Mark Twain's *Adventures of Tom Sawyer*.

In a different vein, fantasy of the early years, though still largely anglophilic, was yet blessed by at least one indigenous virtuoso. *The Floating Prince, The Queen's Museum,* and *The Griffin and the Minor Canon* (recently transformed into the musical *Good Grief A Griffin!* by Eleanor & Ray Harder), represents Frank Stockton as a pioneer among American fantasists.

To better appreciate the diversity of the period from 1880 to 1920, which was developed upon this literary foundation, we need to view it in terms of its generic offerings. The waning years of the last century were prolific for the juvenile writers, and among the more popular of these were the creators of adventure. Youth was tantalized by Noah Brooks' tales of *Boy Emigrants* and *Boy Settlers,* and by James Otis Kaler and his big-top adventures of *Toby Tyler.* Though "boy books" dominated, Kate Douglas Wiggin made a successful contribution to the genre with her 1903 classic, *Rebecca of Sunnybrook Farm.* The landmark of the genre and of the era came from Mark Twain. In his *Adventures of Huckleberry Finn* (1884), he produced an international champion for American literary respectability. Today literati find Twain a diamond among lesser gems; in his time, to the child reader, he was but one among a handful of treasured writers.

While Twain gave readers an insider's view of life along the Mississippi, he like other creators was equally drawn to past times and different cultures — a strong appeal for a populace perched uncertainly on the brink of the twentieth century. Historical fiction included solid works, among them Twain's own *Prince and the Pauper.* Knighthood flowered again through Americans Sidney Lanier and Howard Pyle. Lanier recreated *The Boy's King Arthur* and other sagas, while Pyle retold and illustrated *The Merry Adventures of Robin Hood* and tales of *Otto of the Silver Hand* and *Men of Iron.* While Twain held sway in realistic fiction circles at home and abroad, Pyle garnered the accolades as the premier historical writer and artist-storyteller. In like fashion, the creations of Robert Louis Stevenson, of the Highlands and the High Seas, competed successfully with the best of both continents.

As this first great era derived an impetus abroad from Alcott's family novels, so, too, did the time retain several of her proponents. Susan Coolidge with *What Katy Did,* began a string of episodes through the decades which kept her heroine on equal footing with her New England predecessor. 1880 saw the publication of Lucretia P. Hale's *Peterkin Papers,* an American family story linked clearly with the Dickensian Pickwicks. Margaret Sydney's *The Five Little Peppers and How They Grew,* published the next year, is still a successful competitor for bookshelf popularity. After Alcott, the great practitioner of the genre, and one of the foremost of the period, was Frances Hodgson Burnett. Her style and content adapted to, influenced, and transcended the age. Burnett's three most important works, offered over a twenty-five year span, *Little Lord Fauntleroy* (1886), *Sara Crewe* (1888 and republished in 1905 as *A Little Princess* after a successful Broadway stage run under that title), and *The Secret Garden* (1911), retain immense popularity as continuous theatrical, film and television adaptations of each clearly attest.

The worlds of fantasy were created mainly by foreigners until the 1880's. But Americans were not idle. Typically American (sometimes regionally inspired) offerings appeared as early as 1881 in the form of Joel Chandler Harris's *Uncle Remus: His Songs and Sayings* — the heritage of Harris's Georgia begat the antics of Brer Rabbit, Brer Fox and others. Howard Pyle, solidifying his popularity further, produced three fairy tale fantasies in *Pepper and Salt* (1886), *The Wonder Clock* (1888), and *Garden Behind the Moon* (1895). As strong as the *Alice* influence was on fantasy, it was not surprising that one of the age's best native works blatantly paid tribute to the Carrollian masterwork — Charles Carryl not only mastered the Britisher's form, but in giving the reader *Davy and the Goblin* (1886) he did so while incorporating recognizably American mindsets and characters. While Carryl's Goblin was taking his readers on "a believing voyage," Palmer Cox was leading his Brownies on a romp through the issues of *St. Nicholas Magazine* and into *The Brownies: Their Book*, by 1887. So popular were these sprites that they engendered several more volumes and a highly successful Broadway operetta. Even in the creation of fantasy, American writers seemed resolutely nationalistic. *The Brownies* and such regionally inspired yarns as Albert Bigelow Paine's Southern folk fantasy of *The Arkansaw Bear* (1898) epitomized this tendency. As the new century began, *The Wonderful Wizard of Oz* was published, and became this country's greatest indigenous fairy tale. L. Frank Baum's first of fourteen "Oz" books did for the fantasy genre in early-twentieth-century U.S.A. what Carroll's "Alice" books had done in Victorian England. The breaks in the protective egg of nineteenth-century childhood propriety were now irreparable; one more blow remained to make the emergence complete. It came with reinforcement from abroad.

The European writers had always found a wide readership in the United States. American children welcomed Grimm tales in the 1850's, Andersen's tales at about the same time, and the Norse tales of Asbjornsen and Moe in the 1860's. 1884 proved eventful for youth in the U.S. as they learned of the wonders of Switzerland and of a little girl named *Heidi*. *Pinocchio*, from Carlo Collodi, appeared in the same decade. The adventures of this Italian marionette were wholly unlike anything else encountered by child readers of the time.

The bulk of the imports came from Great Britain, and, over a forty year span, the American audience shared great literary wealth with its English cousins. Oscar Wilde created such tales as "The Happy Prince," "The Selfish Giant," and "The Birthday of the Infanta" (which was to provide excellent theatrical material for Stuart Walker). Rudyard Kipling told of India in his captivating *Kim* (1901) and *The Just So Stories* (1902). *Peter Rabbit* bounded onto the scene in Beatrix Potter's 1902 picture book. The Kenneth Grahame chronicle of *The Wind in the Willows* (1908) garnered a permanent place on the bookshelves and in the hearts of young and old. Yet childhood's crowning achievement came in theatrical not literary shape. From the London and Broadway stages emerged Peter Pan, and with his 1904 debut and his subsequent transformation into print — first as *Peter Pan in Kensington Gardens* (1906) and next as *Peter Pan and Wendy* (1911) — America gained a childhood identity and a rallying cry long in forming. With a world war rearing its head on the horizon, the twentieth-century child cried defiantly with Peter: "I'm youth, I'm joy, I'm a little bird that has broken out of the egg." The shell had finally broken, yet it would take decades more for the child to find solid footing.

The United States emerged unscathed and victorious from the First World War, bringing with it new technology. The 1920's found the fledgling children's book industry developing into a sophisticated, commercial business. The realization that the nation's youth were becoming a major market for booksellers led to marketing and commercialization spawning experimentation in content and format which, while producing few well remembered titles, did lay groundwork for much of the noteworthy publication of the thirties. Increased immigration and the rigors of a foreign war forced Americans into an international awareness. The early years supplied significant literary offerings indicative of such concern. The most delightful children's writer from the decade was Hugh Lofting; playing on the aspects of the well-established nonsense mode, and the growing intrigue in foreign exploration and scientific experimentation, he presented the fantastic *Story of Doctor Dolittle* to the young people of 1920. So popular was this that Lofting continued in *The Voyages of Doctor Dolittle*, for which, in 1923, he received the second of the newly inaugurated "John Newbery Medal for the Most Distinguished Contribution to American Literature for Children." The Newbery Award was to signify both excellence in the field and a new commitment to the quality of reading matter for the child audience.

The end of the decade welcomed the first and finest of Wanda Gág's successful picture storybooks, *Millions of Cats*, a work heralding this nation's entrance into the heretofore European dominated market. While throughout the decade the old reliable folk and fairy tales remained popular, on the page and in the theater, new editions of Grimm, Andersen, and the rest were now enriched by a modern breed of storyteller exemplified by the Irish-American Padraic Colum. His 1921 *Golden Fleece and Heroes Who Lived Before Achilles* and his 1925 *Voyagers* set in motion a prolific career spanning five decades.

694

APPENDIX

In these and other works he gave renewed wonders to the worlds of the ancient Greeks, Norse, and Celts.

Of the writers from abroad, only England's A. A. Milne created a lasting impact. *Winnie-The-Pooh* reached our shores in 1926. The magnetic *House At Pooh Corner* arrived with full fanfare two years later. Sandwiched between these was the author's imaginative poetry, *Now We Are Six* and *When We Were Very Young*. While his poetry and fiction gained continuous acclaim, the children could satiate themselves by adding to this repertoire his lyrical play adaptation of Grahame's novel, *Toad of Toad Hall*, premiering in 1929. The 1920's in the U.S. cast a decidedly British aura, what with the Anglo-American offerings of Lofting and the ever-so-English antics of Milne's Christopher Robin. Add the long-awaited publication of the James Barrie *Peter Pan* playscript, and these years seem "jolly good" for Mother England.

Soon prosperity and optimism were dashed by the Great Depression. The eyes of the nation turned inward. The tenor of the literature then produced became almost self-consciously nationalistic. The thirties saw the popularization of juvenile biography — accounts of the men and women who made America were intended to instill pride in our past and a steadfastness for our future. Typical of these offerings, was the Newberry Award-winning Alcott biography by Cornelia Meigs, *Invincible Louisa* (1932). Interest in the heroes and legends was likewise reinforced by fictional retellings of the lives and exploits of *Davy Crockett* (Constance Rourke, 1934), *Pecos Bill* (James C. Bowman, 1937), and *Daniel Boone* (James Daugherty, 1939). And while the lives of these historical figures commanded their share of the reading hour, several literary offspring emerged with similarly attractive sagas. Most astute at bridging the forms was Laura Ingalls Wilder. Her "Little House" adventures established a historical family of identity and impact rivalled only by the Marches of *Little Women* for believability and importance to the child reader.

For Wilder and other writers it was a simple transition from biography to historical fiction. Yet, unlike the regional/historical romances of past generations, the kings and queens were now largely relegated to the fantastic in favor of the settlers and trailblazers (male and female) who pioneered the new land. And while the majority of noteworthy biographies immortalized masculine figures, the fictional trend was decidedly in the woman's favor. As Wilder in the thirties explored convincingly the heritage of her pioneer upbringing, several female authors found their voice and identity within the historical fictional form. Rachel Field, already a noted writer, began the decade with her *Calico Bush*; Carol Brink topped her with *Caddie Woodlawn* (the 1936 Newbery choice). In reading of Caddie Woodlawn, Laura Ingalls, the invincible Louisa Alcott, one realizes that the changes from the early century and before have brought about better developed, staunchly independent juvenile protagonists — figures who lead, take chances, and affect situations. Echoing Roger Bedard on the drama of the age, novelists (like Burnett and Wiggin), "operating under the guise of contemporary realism, pictured children as doll-like characters with little identity and less individuality." Though in the fiction these counterparts were not so meek, they were, unlike Alice, pawns who seldom became queens. By 1940, writers had brought the literature a step away from that view by presenting (as Bedard notes) children as more recognizably real people. Compare *Rebecca of Sunnybrook Farm* to *Caddie Woodlawn*, novel to novel and girl to girl, and one sees clearly the evolution that has transpired in a short time.

Fantasy in forms other than the tall tale was but for one significant exception still decidedly British. The two great works of the period, both among the century's best though in quite distinct ways, were P. L. Travers' zany adventures of *Mary Poppins* (1934) and the complex, Middle-Earth saga of Bilbo Baggins, *The Hobbit* (1937). Well-received, these both largely remained for future generations to better appreciate. The lone U.S. entrant in the 1930's fantasy hiearchy was the Edward Lear-inspired Theodore Geisel. With Geisel's *And To Think That I Saw It On Mulberry Street* (1937), and his *Five Hundred Hats of Bartholomew Cubbins* (1938), "Dr. Seuss" was born, as was a delightful era of American nonsense picturebooks that would see their creator through five crazy decades.

With few notable exceptions, the 1940's are best remembered in the childhood genre for the continuation of trends and ideas that gained acceptance in the thirties, and for spawning trends and literary concepts which would reach maturity in the following decade. With the world in turmoil the fiction appeared to foster escapism. While some, like Lois Lenski in her myriad of regionally based plots, continued in the steps of Wiggin or Wilder (Wilder's last "Little House" book appeared in 1943), the consensus seemed to favor the style of the light fantasy. Esther Forbes' provocative retelling of *Johnny Tremain* (a boy caught in revolution not far removed from that which other "Johnnies" found themselves in the forties) won a best book award in 1943; yet the other highlights of these war years remained the ethereal Thurber tale "Many Moons," and Robert Lawson's imaginative romp on *Rabbit Hill*. The American who best typified these years in concerns and content in his fiction, as witnessed within the fantastic or improbable, was no doubt Robert McCloskey. In 1943 he created *Homer Price*, and a more representative child of the day was not to be found. Though rather formulaic, McCloskey's Homer, in his many escapades, emerged as the boy wonder of the burgeoning Atomic Age.

The post-War forties accelerated emphasis on the ethnic history and diversity of the nation. From 1946 through 1950 a major push for black culture awareness began with significant creations like Harold Courlander's 1947 *Cow-Tail Switch and Other West African Stories,* Arna Bontemps' 1949 *Story of the Negro,* and Elizabeth Yates's *Amos Fortune Free Man.* On an adjacent front, the success of author-illustrator Leo Politi's stories brought children's eyes into the world of Mexican-America. Authors found promise in portraying the many cultures of their country, and they gained support from playwright like Madge Miller who, with her oriental *Land of the Dragon,* was exploring similar themes in the theatre.

More than anything else, the literature from the thirty year span between 1920 to 1950, gave the child new freedom from the embryonic shell of the past century's protectiveness. Also, this period witnessed a breaking of the barriers heretofore holding America in isolation both from its true self and from its international neighbors. By 1950, the child was poised for the second golden age of children's literature. During this most recent period there was an emergence from world war into the space age, complete with all its trappings. New boundaries were to be tested, new worlds to be conquered. As the space race epitomized this era, the fifties were a time of experimentation and cautious preparation for the shoot-for-the-moon eruptions of the following decade. Celestial heights were achieved in 1969 (man on the moon), and science and literature turned their sights to supplementary goals. The age of the computer commenced in 1970 with its new problems and pandemonium. But, because the process found form in the fifties, it is there one must commence.

Though television began exerting a sway over juvenile reading habits, as it would continue to do throughout the decades, the children's book industry churned out a record number of titles. For every award-winning novel published, several more worthy, widely read works were its companions. If the egg had broken by 1920, firm footing established by 1940, then in this decade of the fifties, all began to take wing. The literary fare showed a natural division between realism, and animal and faerie fantasy; a healthy number of foreign writers supplemented both.

In realistic fiction the emphasis was on character in a number of locales and situations. Like Politi and his "Pedro" books, several writers focused on the Hispanic in and out of the native culture. One of the best in this regard was Ann Nolan Clark in her 1952, prize-winning portrayal of a young boy living in isolation in *Secret of the Andes.* Equalling Clark's work was Joseph Krumgold. His classic *. . . And Now Miguel* chronicles a Mexican boy in New Mexico's desolate Sangre de Cristo Mountains. In the mold of the Clark novels, Krumgold too captures fascinating, multi-leveled character portraits. Two other titles need mention to show the genre as representative: Fred Gipson's 1956 Texas family saga, *Old Yeller,* and the haunting

Jean C. George novel, *My Side of the Mountain* (1959). Each exhibits an emotional quality and a familial honesty typifying the mood of the genre in this decade.

As realism brought forth memorable animal characters like the Blue Canyon Horse and Old Yeller, fantasy outstripped it in animal portrayal. Top medals went to E. B. White who bettered his acclaimed *Stuart Little* (1945) with his 1952 barnyard adventure, *Charlotte's Web*. With the advent of *Charlotte* the American child possessed an animal fantasy of the stature of Britain's *Wind in the Willows*. Another popular character, who in 1957 began a lengthy love affair with the American public, was Dr. Seuss's nicely nonsensical *Cat in the Hat*.

Two fine flights of fancy, more in the British style so popular at this time, appeared during the decade. The delightful *Wonderful Flight to the Mushroom Planet*, Eleanor Cameron's initial tale portending the virtuosity of style to be her trademark in later creations, reached readers in 1954. Carol Kendall in the 1959 *Gammadge Cup,* a humorous jaunt with undersized adventures and their full-sized cohorts, seemed to pay a debt to the British "Borrowers" who invaded our shores in their own 1952 adventures.

The British fantasists did invade, in greater numbers than at any time after World War I; they brought with them a potpourri of marvelous lands and creations to enrapt the waiting public. Mary Norton's *The Borrowers* had arrived in 1952, and so popular were these characters that they spawned several sequels. The sequel seemed popular; bookstores clamored for the more notable — one of the finest being the "Chronicles of Narnia" by C. S. Lewis. The decade's loving tribute to fantastic animal characters ended in similar fashion with Margery Sharp's rodent *Rescuers*, and Michael Bond's *Bear Called Paddington*. The English did not totally dominate the import market place. Sweden's Astrid Lindgren was a strong contender with her frolicking *Pippi Longstocking* adventures. In Pippi, one sees America's children poised for the independence of the sixties generation of juvenilia.

The turbulance of the 1960's, the crusade for racial equality, "Flower Power," free speech, Vietnam, and the open questioning and criticism of both governmental and cultural policies, spawned within the publishing world a vigorous experimentation to redefine the boundaries of the "children's book," and challenged long implicit subject-matter taboos. Carrying concerns and triumphs of the earlier decade, the writers of this most innovative decade since the 1880's developed and expanded them to points previously considered unpublishable. Death, family crises, child identity crises, divorce, racism and religious persecution all were dealt with in frank yet artistic stories geared to and welcomed by the young audience. Even in the historical fiction and in a large sampling of the fantasy, many of these same issues came sharply into focus.

The realism of the time mirrored the society around it — problems broached in the earlier years were now confronted head-on. The decade started with major works of historical themes yet in Karana's narrative from the *Island of the Blue Dolphins* (Scott O'Dell, 1960), author Maia Wojciechowska's story of a boy's rites of passage in the 1964 *Shadow of the Bull*, and Irene Hunt's Civil War chronicle *Across Five Aprils* (1964), child readers digested frank — at times stark — portrayals as the path toward adulthood was shown to be precarious and rocky. Paula Fox shared her colleagues' straightforwardness. With her unrelenting portraits in *How Many Miles To Babylon?*, *Stone-Faced Boy*, and *Blowfish Live in the Sea*, she was quick to raise the ire of the adult community. Not all the writers were so direct; contemporary fiction offered examples where humor was available to make the relevance palatable. Louise Fitzhugh mastered the technique in *Harriet The Spy* and E. L. Konigsburg did likewise in *From the Mixed-Up Files of Mrs. Basil E. Frankweiler*. Both focused on the problematic side of childhood in manners allowing readers alternate responses of knowing nod and happy chuckle. The animal adventure too did not escape the decade's new consciousness; in fine form W. H. Armstrong's *Sounder* (1969) elevated feelings and themes, only partially inherent in Gipson's *Old Yeller*, to a new level of awareness.

The sixties fantasy veered along three general paths: nonsense, heroic adventure, and science fiction. The nonsense, heavily dosed with the Carrollian spirit, was epitomized by the Norton Juster allegorical extravaganza of Milo's journey through *The Phantom Tollbooth* (1961). Though fantastic, the grains of truth soon become evident as this boy takes a trip through the Kingdom of Wisdom in search of Rhyme and Reason. Journeying was popular, as characters in the age's heroic Narnian heir, Lloyd Alexander's "Chronicles of Prydain," (five volumes spanning the decade) forged into new mishaps in new realms. Science fiction's most respected practitioner, *A Wrinkle in Time*'s Madeleine L'Engle, made marked use of other worldly voyages to explore and develop self-concepts in childhood. The writer making the most far-reaching statements of the preoccupations and thematic concerns of the times in picturebook form was the gifted Maurice Sendak. In his *Sign on Rosie's Door* from 1960 (eventually becoming the play *Really Rosie*), his classic *Where the Wild Things Are* (1963) and *In The Night Kitchen* (1970), he sums up visually the character shifts and story sophistication that occurred in the craft at the Sputnik launch and the U.S. moonwalk.

The inquiries and issues of the sixties carried the day into the seventies where new boundaries and priorities were tested. In the 1970's, realism came in several guises. Among the family/juvenile problem novels of the age many works received recognition. Perhaps the more controversial belong to Judy Blume. From her 1970 appearance with *Are You There God? It's Me Margaret*, it appeared that the last taboos of the children's writer were crumbling; parents were outraged, children ecstatic, publishers cautiously optimistic. Through *It's Not the End of the World* (1972), *Blubber* (1974) and more recent exposes, Blume consistently calls matters as she sees them, regardless of adult antagonism. In these novels, and those from Katherine Paterson, Betsy Byers and others, the images and concerns of the dramatists like Suzan Zeder and Aurand Harris find kinship. Byers developed accepted studies of the mentally retarded for her *Summer of the Swans*, and the extreme introvert in her *The T.V. Kid*. Such subject matter bolstered the dramatists' vision of the same world allowing the stage to receive bold experiments like Brian Kral's *Special Class*. Paterson's well-honed child protagonists, both in *Bridges to Terabithia* (a richly wrought piece joined to Harris's *Arkansaw Bear* in its treatment of death) and her *Great Gily Hopkins* (developing illegitimacy, rebellion and their toll on the child), show depth and compassion highlighting the technical development of the genre.

Racial consciousness produced fine pieces by knowledgeable writers: Virginia Hamilton, *The Planet of Junior Brown* and *M. C. Higgins The Great*; Alice Childress, the playwright-turned novelist for *Hero Ain't Nothing But A Sandwich*; and Mildred Taylor, whose *Roll of Thunder, Hear My Cry* captured the 1977 Newbery honors. These and other authors brought Black awareness into homes never before so forcefully and intimately touched. Scott O'Dell, with *Sing Down The Moon* and *Child of Fire*, in a manner equal to his earlier triumphs, explored the problems of Hispanic youth in the Anglo world. The milieu of the Asian-Americans was at last thrust before us powerfully; — one must read Yoshiko Uchida's *Journey to Topaz*, a story of the U.S., World War II Japanese internment camps, and Laurence Yep's poignant chronicles of Chinese in America *(Dragonwings, Child of the Owl*, and others) for a rarely seen glimpse into a country within our country.

Fantasy from America and Europe followed a similarly richly textured tapestry. While wholly original novels tantalized the young, great fantasies like *Mrs. Frisby and the Rats of NIMH* from Robert C. O'Brien, *The Court of the Stone Children* from Eleanor Cameron, *Tuck Everlasting* from Natalie Babbitt, or even the fantastically real *Julie of the Wolves* (Jean George's work exhibiting marked kinship to Joanna Kraus's play *The Ice Wolf*), the prevailing trend seemed toward "Tolkienesque" heroic saga based on traditional lore. Consequently, much of the memorable adventures leaves readers with recollections of Arthur, Gawain, or a Middle-Earth. Ursula LeGuin's *Wizard of Earthsea* trilogy, Susan Cooper's arthurian tales of *The Dark is Rising*, and Mollie Hunter's Celtic *Bodach* and *A Stranger Comes Ashore* were devoured. Patricia Wrightson led U.S. voyagers into Australian mythology through *An Older Kind of Magic, The Nargun and the Stars*, and *The Ice Is Coming*. New editions of the Grimm's tales (1973) and Andersen (1974) affirmed the abiding delight of the traditional in the decade of the ultra-contemporary.

The century, 1880 to 1980, began with a flourish — fantasy, family stories, retelling of the traditional lore, and a sincere commitment to quality, meaning, and entertainment within the realm of fiction for the young. Such values and concerns remain today — some are unchanged, others transformed with the temper of the time. In child awareness and subject matter the worlds of fiction and drama have developed markedly since Alice first tumbled after the White Rabbit, or Peter Pan vanquished Hook in Never-Neverland; yet in other ways they have remained constant. The joys of youth are still with us, though now they seem enhanced by an acute recognition of the not-so-joyous. But Pan will remain, as will Alice, Jo March, and others of influence; they will stand assuredly beside the likes of Pippi Long-stocking, M. C. Higgins, and the Great Gilly Hopkins. Echoing C. S. Lewis, "The good ones last." And bolstered by new and glorious offerings for all, from the page and the stage, one at times drawing life from the other, they give wings to the fancies of the computer generation, letting them soar like Peter and Wendy to their own neverlands, to pause long enough to give notice to the world: "We are youth, we are joy, we are the little birds that have been broken out of their eggs — watch us fly!"

—Douglas Street

SELECTED BIBLIOGRAPHY

The American Library Association. *Notable Children's Books, 1940–1970.* Chicago: American Library Association, 1977.

Andrews, Siri, ed. *The Hewins Lectures, 1947–1962.* Boston: Horn Book, 1963.

Kirkpatrick, D. L., ed. *Twentieth-Century Children's Writers.* New York: St. Martin's Press, 1978.

Meigs, Cornelia, et. al. *A Critical History of Children's Literature,* Revised Edition. New York: Macmillan, 1969.

Moses, Montrose J. *Children's Books and Reading.* rpt. Detroit: Gale, 1975.

DOUGLAS STREET has taught English and Theatre at Texas A&M University. He holds a doctorate in English as a Children's Literature specialist and a M.F.A. in Directing and Children's Drama. Before moving to Texas, a seven year stay at the University of Nebraska-Lincoln allowed him opportunity to institute course offerings both in the history of children's literature and in dramatic literature for children, the latter in tandem with his team-taught course in children's theatre. Dr. Street is on the Board of Directors for the international Children's Literature Association, and a regular columnist on children's drama for the *Children's Literature Quarterly.* He has published widely in children's literature, theatre, and film, and is the editor of *The Classic Children's Novel and the Movies* for Frederick Ungar Publishers.

SELECTED BIBLIOGRAPHY

Addams, Jane. *The Second Twenty Years at Hull House.* New York: Macmillan, 1930.

——————. *The Spirit of Youth in the City Streets.* New York: Macmillan, 1909.

——————. *Twenty Years at Hull House.* New York: The Macmillan Co., 1910.

Chorpenning, Charlotte B. *Twenty One Years with Children's Theatre.* Anchorage, Ky.: Children's Theatre Press, 1954.

Ciaccio, Mary Eleanor. *Prologue to Production.* New York: Association of Junior Leagues of America, 1951.

Davis, Jed. H., and Mary Jane Evans. *Theatre, Children and Youth.* New Orleans: Anchorage Press, 1982.

Davis, Jed. H., and Mary Jane Larson Watkins. *Children's Theatre: Play Production for the Child Audience.* New York: Harper and Row, 1960.

Fisher, Caroline and Hazel Robertson. *Children and the Theatre.* Rev. ed. Stanford, California: Stanford Univ. Press, 1950.

Fordyce, Rachel. *Children's Theatre and Creative Dramatics: An Annotated Bibliography of Critical Works.* Boston: G. K. Hall & Co., 1975.

Forkert, O. M., ed. *Children's Theatre that Captures its Audience.* Chicago: Coach House Press, 1962.

Fry, Emma Sheridan. *Educational Dramatics.* New York: Moffat, Yard and Co., 1913.

Goldberg, Moses. *Children's Theatre: A Philosophy and a Method.* Englewood Cliffs, N.J.: Prentice-Hall, 1974.

Hale, Pat, ed. *Participation Theatre for Young Audiences.* New York: New Plays, 1972.

Hazeltine, Alice, ed. *Plays for Children: An Annotated Index.* New York: American Library Assoc., 1921.

Herts, Alice Minnie. *The Children's Educational Theatre.* New York: Harper, 1911.

——————. *The Kingdom of the Child.* New York: Dutton, 1918.

Hilliard, Evelyne, Theodora McCormick, Kate Oglebay. *Amateur and Educational Dramatics.* New York: Macmillan, 1917.

Horton, Louis, ed. *Handbook for Children's Theatre Directors.* Cincinnati: National Thespian Society, 1949.

Hyatt, Aeola L., compiler. *Index to Children's Plays,* third ed. Chicago: American Library Assoc., 1931.

Kase, C. Robert. *Children's Theatre Comes of Age.* New York: Samuel French, 1956.

Kennedy, Carol Jean. *Child Drama: A Selected and Annotated Bibliography, 1974–1979.* Washington, D.C.: Children's Theatre Association of America, 1981.

MacGowan, Kenneth. *Footlights Across America*. New York: Harcourt Brace, 1929.

Mackay, Constance D'Arcy, *Children's Theatre and Plays*. New York: Appleton, 1927.

——————. *How to Produce Children's Plays*. New York: Holt, 1915.

——————. *Patriotic Drama in Your Town*. New York: Holt, 1918.

Mackaye, Percy. *The Civic Theatre*. New York: Mitchell, Kennerly, 1912.

——————. *Community Drama*. New York: Houghton, Mifflin, 1917.

Mathews, Jane Dehart. *The Federal Theatre 1935–1939. Plays, Relief, and Politics*. Princeton: Princeton Univ. Press, 1967.

McCaslin, Nellie. *Theatre for Children in the United States: A History*. Norman, OK: Univ. of Oklahoma Press, 1971.

Oglebay, Kate. *Plays for Children. A Selected List*. New York: H. W. Wilson, 1920.

Patten, Cora Mel, Comp. *Plays for Children*. Chicago: Drama League of America, 1923.

Plays and Pageants, A List of. Prepared by the Committee on Pageantry and Drama, War Work Council, Young Women's Christian Association, 1919,

Siks, Geraldine Brain, and Hazel Brain Dunnington, eds. *Children's Theatre and Creative Dramatics*. Seattle: Univ. of Washington Press, 1961.

Van Tassel, Wesley, ed. *Children's Theatre Bibliography*. Washington, D.C.: American Theatre Association, 1975.

Wald, Lillian. *The House on Henry Street*. New York: Holt, 1915.

Ward, Winifred. *Theatre for Children*. New York: D. Appleton, Century, 1939.

ROGER L. BEDARD, Editor of *Dramatic Literature for Children: A Century in Review*, began his career in educational theatre as a scene designer, and teacher, at Illinois Central College. At Boise State he served in the same position, but teaching assignments led him into the child drama field and caused him to return to school for more specialized study in theatre for children. In 1978, as a doctoral student at the University of Kansas, he was named the first Winifred Ward Scholar by the Children's Theatre Association of America.

After completing his Ph.D. in 1979, he returned to Boise State to develop the child drama program. A short time later he was appointed Coordinator of the MFA program in Child Drama at Virginia Polytechnic Institute and State University — a position he currently holds.

Active in children's theatre activities in the region and nation, Dr. Bedard is currently Vice President for Education and Theatre Development for tthe Children's Theatre Association of America. He is an Associate editor for *The Children's Theatre Review*, and is involved in a variety of CTAA programs and projects. He is a co-author of *Theatre Arts for the Handicapped*, a project of the Virginia State Department of Education.

Dr. Bedard received his B.A. from the University of Northern Iowa (1968) and an M.F.A. in Scene Design from the University of Oregon (1971). He lives in Blacksburg, Virginia, with his wife, Jo and their daughter, Sarah.